Parallel Algorithms
for VLSI Computer-Aided Design

Prithviraj Banerjee

University of Illinois

PTR Prentice Hall
Englewood Cliffs, New Jersey 07632

Library of Congress Cataloging-in-Publication Data

Banerjee, Prithviraj

Parallel algorithms for VLSI computer-aided design applications /
by Prithviraj Banerjee

p. cm.

Includes index.

ISBN 0-13-015835-6

1. Integrated circuits--Very large scale integration--Design and
construction--Data processing.   2. Computer-aided design.
3. Computer algorithms   4. Parallel processing (Electronic
computers)   I. Title.

TK7874.75.B36   1994

621.39'5--dc20   94-10079

                                                            CIP

Editorial/production supervision: *Camille Trentacoste*
Manufacturing manager: *Alexis Heydt*
Acquisitions editor: *Karen Gettman*
Cover design: *Aren Graphics*

© 1994 by PTR Prentice Hall
Prentice-Hall, Inc.
A Paramount Communications Company
Englewood Cliffs, New Jersey 07632

The publisher offers discounts on this book when ordered in bulk quantities.

For more information, contact:

Corporate Sales Department
PTR Prentice Hall
113 Sylvan Avenue
Englewood Cliffs, NJ 07632

Phone: 201-592-2863
FAX: 201-592-2249

All product names mentioned herein are the trademarks of their respective owners.

Printed in the United States of America
10 9 8 7 6 5 4 3 2 1

ISBN 0-13-015835-6

Prentice-Hall International (UK) Limited, *London*
Prentice-Hall of Australia Pty. Limited, *Sydney*
Prentice-Hall Canada Inc., *Toronto*
Prentice-Hall Hispanoamericana, S.A., *Mexico*
Prentice-Hall of India Private Limited, *New Delhi*
Prentice-Hall of Japan, Inc., *Tokyo*
Simon & Schuster Asia Pte. Ltd., *Singapore*
Editora Prentice-Hall do Brasil, Ltda., *Rio de Janeiro*

Dedication

This book is dedicated to my late parents, Sunil and Anima, and to my wife Swati.

About The Author

Prithviraj Banerjee received his B.Tech. degree in Electronics and Electrical Engineering from the Indian Institute of Technology, Kharagpur, India, in August 1981, and the M.S. and Ph.D degrees in Electrical Engineering from the University of Illinois at Urbana-Champaign in December 1982 and December 1984, respectively.

He is currently Professor of Electrical and Computer Engineering and the Coordinated Science Laboratory at the University of Illinois at Urbana-Champaign. His research interests are in parallel algorithms for VLSI design automation, and distributed memory parallel architectures, is the author of over 140 papers in these areas. and has supervised 10 Ph.D. theses so far. He has been working on parallel algorithms for numerous VLSI design automation applications for the last 10 years.

Dr. Banerjee was the recipient of the President of India Gold Medal from the Indian Institute of Technology, Kharagpur, in 1981, the IBM Young Faculty Development Award in 1986, the National Science Foundation's Presidential Young Investigators' Award in 1987, the IEEE Senior Membership in 1990, the Senior Xerox Research Award in 1992, and the University Scholar award from the University of Illinois in 1993.

Dr. Banerjee has served on the program and organizing committees of the 1988, 1989, and 1993 Fault Tolerant Computing Symposia, the 1992, 1994, and 1995 International Parallel Processing Symposium, the 1991, 1992, and 1994 International Symposia on Computer Architecture, and the 1990, 1993, and 1994 International Symposium on VLSI Design. In addition he has also served as General Chairman of the International Workshop on Hardware Fault Tolerance in Multiprocessors, 1989. He is an associate editor of the *IEEE Transactions on VLSI Systems*, the *Journal of Parallel and Distributed Computing*, the *Journal of Circuits, Systems and Computers*, and was the editor of the *Electronic Newsletter on Fault Tolerant Computing*, 1990-1992. He is also a consultant to AT&T, Westinghouse Corporation, Jet Propulsion Laboratory, General Electric, the Research Triangle Institute, and United Nations Development Program.

Contents

PREFACE

Parallel computing is becoming an increasing cost-effective and affordable means for providing enormous computing power. Workstations are currently using parallel processing technology and will use it even more in the future. A large number of medium-priced multiprocessors are commercially available today. Numerous vendors of workstations are currently marketing multiprocessor-based workstations as well. More such powerful workstations will be available in the future. It should be noted that while it is relatively easy to build parallel machines whose peak performance will be thousands of MFLOPS and MIPS (adequate for future VLSI CAD requirements), it is extremely difficult to harness the computational power effectively to actually have the machines deliver all those MFLOPS and MIPS to the VLSI CAD user. Therein lies the challenge: design of good, efficient, parallel algorithms that can use the hardware resources to get the maximum performance.

This book will discuss the use of parallel processing for solving problems in a growing application area whose computational requirements are enormous: VLSI CAD applications. While numerous books exist on general parallel algorithms for regular matrix problems or graph theory problems, they are mostly theoretical in nature. This book will discuss *practical* parallel algorithms for shared memory MIMD, message passing MIMD, and SIMD parallel machines. The first two chapters provide a detailed introduction to the field of parallel computing: architectures, algorithms, and programming and forms the groundwork for writing parallel programs for parallel machines. The Chapters 3 through 9 deal with different CAD applications, and Chapter 10 provides a summary and a look at the future.

The area of parallelizing compilers (that take sequential programs and produce parallel programs automatically) is in its infancy. We can only parallelize relatively simple sequential code dealing with structured applications, for example, FORTRAN programs dealing with arrays. Most applications in VLSI CAD written in C are unstructured, with lots of dynamically allocated memory and pointer-based data structures, and are therefore very difficult to parallelize automatically. Hence, the design of parallel algorithms for VLSI CAD is a growing area of research. Unless good, efficient parallel algorithms for VLSI CAD applications are developed, the multiprocessors and multiprocessor workstations will not be able to deliver the computational power to the VLSI designers.

In view of the increasing complexity of VLSI circuits, there is a need for sophisticated computer-aided design (CAD) tools to automate the synthesis and verification steps in the design of VLSI systems. Many tasks in VLSI CAD, from synthesis, to simulation, to verification, take large amounts of computation time, sometimes days or weeks to run one application for large VLSI chip designs. To reduce the time-to-market for future chip designs, it is imperative to look at ways to reduce the runtime for each CAD application. Even though the computing platforms (workstations) for VLSI designers are getting faster and faster, the chips that the designers are attempting to design are growing at a much faster rate. Special-purpose hardware accelerators have been proposed in the past to speed up various tasks in VLSI CAD. However, this approach is not always cost effective because of the tremendous time and resources required to implement such machines, which soon become outdated owing to changing technologies.

General-purpose parallel processing can offer the large speed improvements that are needed in the computing platforms of VLSI designers of the future. A point in favor of general-purpose multiprocessors over special-purpose hardware accelerators is that the former can offer tremendous speed improvements and are at the same time extremely cost effective; since they are general purpose, they can be reprogrammed as newer sequential algorithms and objective functions are discovered in various VLSI CAD applications.

This book will discuss the latest, current approaches to the use of parallel processing for numerous CAD applications, such as placement and routing, layout verification, circuit extraction, logic and circuit simulation, test generation and fault simulation, and logic synthesis and verification. The advantages and disadvantages of choosing each of these approaches will be discussed with results of case studies given for specific applications. The book will provide an in-depth discussion of parallel implementations for numerous VLSI CAD tools on various types of multiprocessors.

We will discuss practical parallel algorithms for most of the time consuming VLSI CAD applications at the logic, circuit, and physical level of VLSI design. The domain of behavioral synthesis at the functional level is still in its infancy, even for serial algorithms: hence not much work has been done on parallel algorithms yet.

The book is organized as follows. Chapter 1 provides a brief overview of the VLSI CAD area. It discusses the basic VLSI CAD tools required in an automated design environment. It also motivates why parallel CAD is important and lists all the available options of parallel processing for CAD. Finally, it provides an introduction to the basic concepts of parallel processing.

Chapter 2 provides a brief introduction to parallel architectures and parallel programming. It describes the different general-purpose parallel processing platforms available today, specifically, shared memory MIMD multiprocessors, message passing distributed memory MIMD multiprocessors, SIMD multiprocessors, and distributed networks of computers. For each of these architectures, the chapter presents an example hardware architecture, a programming model, and some example parallel programming library functions and gives an example parallel application program.

The rest of the chapters are devoted to parallel algorithms for various VLSI CAD tasks. Chapters 3 through 5 deal with physical level synthesis, analysis, and verification. Specifically, Chapter 3 describes placement and floorplanning. Chapter 4 deals with global and detailed routing. Chapter 5 addresses layout verification and analysis problems such as design rule checking and circuit extraction. Chapter 6 deals with circuit simulation. Chapters 7 through 9 deal with logic level synthesis, analysis, and verification. Specifically, Chapter 7 describes logic simulation, Chapter 8 deals with test generation and fault simulation, Chapter 9 addresses logic synthesis and verification.

Chapter 3 deals with the placement and floorplanning problems in automated physical design synthesis. Since there has been a large number of sequential heuristic approaches to solve the placement and floorplanning problems, parallel algorithms for these problems are typically based on one or more of these sequential heuristics. Hence, there has been a lot of work reported in the area of parallel placement and floorplanning algorithms. This chapter classifies the various parallel algorithms by different heuristic approaches such as pairwise exchange, simulated annealing, genetic algorithms, simulated evolution, and hierarchical decompositions. For each approach, we discuss both shared memory and distributed memory parallel algorithms and specific implementations where appropriate.

Chapter 4 deals with the global and detailed routing problems in physical design synthesis. It classifies various types of routing problems into detailed general-purpose routing, detailed restricted routing, and global routing. For each of these routing problems, numerous parallel algorithms have been proposed over the years based on different sequential heuristics: graph search, iterative improvement, simulated annealing, hierarchical decompositions, and so on. Again, since the routing problem is NP complete, no one algorithm produces the best result or the fastest result. Hence the chapter classifies the parallel algorithms by the sequential heuristics on which they are based, and discusses parallel algorithms for shared memory and distributed memory MIMD multiprocessors based on each of the approaches.

Chapter 5 deals with design rule checking and circuits extraction problems in physical design analysis and verification. Contrary to placement and routing, this problem is more tractable in that the amount of computation required is polynomially bounded by the size of the problem, for example, the number of rectangles. However, since in typical mask layouts, we deal with huge data sizes (tens of millions of rectangles), it is important to look at efficient parallel algorithms. Various parallel algorithms for design rule checking and circuit extraction are discussed based on data decomposition, functional decomposition, and hierarchical decomposition. Again, suitable parallel algorithms are discussed for both shared memory and distributed memory multiprocessors.

Chapter 6 deals with circuit-level simulation. This application is perhaps one of the most time-consuming parts in any VLSI design cycle. There are three basic approaches to solve circuit simulation: direct methods, nonlinear relaxation methods, and waveform relaxation methods. The chapter discusses parallel algorithms based on each approach, and describes the parallelism at various levels and for different programming models, shared memory and distributed memory MIMD multiprocessors.

Chapter 7 deals with logic- and switch-level simulation. The chapter classifies parallel logic simulation algorithms according to data parallelism, functional parallelism, and circuit parallelism. Within circuit parallelism, the chapter classifies logic simulation algorithms according to whether they are synchronous or asynchronous, compiled or event driven, with optimistic or conservative lookahead in the algorithms. For each parallel approach, parallel algorithms are described for shared memory and distributed memory multiprocessors.

Chapter 8 deals with test generation and fault simulation for both combinational and sequential logic circuits. The chapter characterizes the different parallelism approaches within test generation as fault parallelism, heuristic parallelism, and branch-and-bound search parallelism. The chapter also classifies parallelism within fault simulation as data parallelism, fault parallelism, and circuit parallelism. Again, specific parallel algorithms are discussed for both shared memory and distributed memory MIMD multiprocessors.

Chapter 9 deals with logic synthesis and verification for both two-level and multilevel combinational circuits. The chapter discusses a parallel algorithm for two-level logic synthesis based on the ESPRESSO algorithm. It also describes parallel algorithms for multilevel logic synthesis based on the MIS algorithm and the transduction method. Finally, the chapter also discusses parallel algorithms for logic verification based on implicit enumeration and tautology checking.

Chapter 10 summarizes the current status of parallel CAD and points out some future directions in the field.

For each CAD application, when there are more than one approach to solve the problem, we first discuss the sequential algorithm for each approach and then the corresponding parallel algorithm. Where applicable, the book discusses specific parallel algorithms for shared memory and distributed memory MIMD multiprocessors and finally SIMD multiprocessors. Also, a brief review is provided of the hardware accelerators in those areas. Each chapter ends with a complete bibliography to guide the reader for further reading.

This book will be useful in a graduate-level course in electrical engineering and computer science. It bridges the gap between parallel processing and one application area that can benefit from it, VLSI CAD. It will also be of tremendous value to professionals in the VLSI CAD field if they wish to efficiently use the technology of parallel processing to solve the problems of the future.

Some examples of potential users of this book are listed below.

1. An engineer in a VLSI CAD company, who wishes to learn how to use parallel processing technology for his or her application.

2. An engineer in parallel computer company trying to develop useful software for marketing parallel machines or to benchmark machines or redesign parallel machines.

3. Professors and graduate students in electrical engineering and computer science who are knowledgeable in VLSI CAD area, but wish to learn about parallel processing to accelerate their own applications or to look at potential research areas since a detailed bibliography is provided for each chapter.

4. Professors and graduate students in electrical engineering and computer science who are knowledgeable about the parallel processing area, but who currently solve toy problems, but wish to learn about an exciting new application area that is related to the person's field.

5. Professors and graduate students who are experts on theoretical parallel algorithms, who converse fluently in PRAM models of computation and $O(n)$ notations of computational complexity, and are interested in seeing if any of these theoretical parallel algorithms will actually result in speedups on real machines. Readers can find out about *practical parallel machines* and *practical parallel algorithms* on real-world problems. They can read about experimental results of load balancing, scheduling, speedups, and the like to extract speedups on real machines and real problems.

Graduate-level courses on this book's topic could be offered at many universities. A set of lecture transparencies has been developed to teach the material from this book. They may be obtained by contacting the author.

Acknowledgements

This book was started three years ago in January 1991 when I was on sabbatical from the University of Illinois. I am grateful to my university administrators, notably Tim Trick, Head of the Electrical and Computer Engineering department, and Bill Schowalter, Dean of the College of engineering, for encouraging me in this project. I would also like to thank all my colleagues at the Center for Reliable and High Performance Computing (CRHC) in the Coordinated Science Laboratory, Kent Fuchs, Wen-Mei Hwu, Ravi Iyer, Janak Patel, Dan Saab, and Ben Wah, for the excellent collaborative environment that was crucial for executing this creative endeavor. I am grateful to all the students in CRHC over the years for their constant support and to my students in particular.

This book is the result of nearly ten years of work in the area of parallel algorithms for VLSI computer-aided design performed by me and my graduate students at the University of Illinois. I would like to thank my graduate students who have helped me form the foundations of many of the chapters. I would like to thank Mark Jones, Jeff Sargeant Randall Brouwer, Sungho Kim, and John Chandy, for some of the sections in Chapter 3 dealing with parallel algorithms for placement. Thanks are due to Randall Brouwer again for some of the sections on parallel routing discussed in Chapter 4. I would like to thank Krishna Prasad Belkhale and Balkrishna Ramkumar for some sections on parallel circuit extraction described in Chapter 5. I am grateful to Srinivas Patil, Balkrishna Ramkumar and Steven Parkes for portions of Chapter 8 dealing with parallel test generation and fault simulation. Thanks are due to Chieng Fai Lim, Kaushik De and John Chandy for sections on parallel logic synthesis included in Chapter 9. Finally, I would like to thank Balkrishna Ramkumar and Steven Parkes for their work in the ProperCAD project which has been described in Chapter 10. Many of the figures in the various chapters have been extracted from the papers, reports and theses written by the above graduate students.

I would like to thank the authors of numerous research articles in the area of parallel algorithms for VLSI CAD whose work I have tried to summarize in this book. Often I have used many of their illustrations and examples in trying to explain the algorithms. I have tried to give appropriate credit to the sources that I have used. I offer my apologies for any omissions in citing sources that I may have made. I have tried to include most of the work on parallel CAD in this book but may have made some omissions. Any omission that I have made is unintentional and I take full blame for it. I also realize that many more important parallel algorithms are being developed even today since this is a rapidly developing field. Some of the very recent research results may have been omitted for that reason.

I am extremely grateful to my research sponsors who have funded this work on parallel algorithms for VLSI CAD at Illinois over the last ten years. Special thanks go to the National Science Foundation for giving me the Presidential Young Investigator award which helped me to start on a new research topic without having to worry about trying to secure the initial research funding in this area. NSF has been extremely good with continued support with other grants in related topics as well. I am indebted to the Semiconductor Research Corporation for supporting the work on parallel CAD algorithms even at a time when it was not quite mature, and more recently with the ProperCAD project described in Chapter 10. Thanks are also due to NASA and the Office of Naval Research for some of their initial support of this and related work. Finally, I would like to thank many of the companies who have funded my research in this general area, notably IBM, General Electric and Intel. Without the generous support of these sponsors, I could not have carried out work in this area over such a long time.

I would like to thank the referees of the manuscript, Tom Dillinger from IBM, Pinaki Mazumder from University of Michigan, and Balkrishna Ramkumar from University of Iowa, for their thorough and in-depth reviews which have greatly helped to improve the quality of the manuscript. I have tried to incorporate most of their comments and suggestions.

Special thanks go to my administrative assistant Carolin Rouse who helped me draw many of the figures in the book. She put in numerous hours in editing the manuscript for corrections marked by the copy editor. She was also instrumental in obtaining numerous copyright permissions. I could not have finished the book on time without her terrific support.

When I had agreed to do a camera-ready manuscript, I had no idea what I was getting into. I thought naively that since I had done numerous camera-ready versions of conference papers, this was going to be trivial. Without the help of our local LATEX expert Steven Parkes, I could not have generated any of the fancy fonts and styles that Prentice Hall wanted me to use. Steven Parkes must have put in at least 50-100 hours on various aspects of styles and fonts for this book. It is too bad I am not writing a second book! I could have used the same styles.

I would like to thank the team of editors from Prentice Hall who is publishing the book. I had heard all kinds of horror stories about publishers. I must say I have been extremely fortunate with the persons I have worked with. I would like to thank my senior editor Karen Gettman, for encouraging me to start this project, and for managing the project throughout the term. My production editor Camille Trentacoste deserves a special round of thanks for her promptness in managing the proof editing and copy editing. I would also like to thank the art production editor Gail Cocker-Bogusz for the numerous ideas of style and layout of the chapters in the book.

Above all, I am especially indebted to my wife Swati and my 4-year old son Siraj for their continued support during this 3 year project, which included many hours of neglect. I have promised to spend more time with them after my book project is complete!

CHAPTER 1

Introduction

1.1 BACKGROUND

Parallel computing is becoming an increasingly cost-effective and affordable means for providing enormous computing power and represents a challenge to costly conventional supercomputers. Parallel computers are built by connecting several (tens or hundreds or thousands) low-cost processors and memories together through some interconnection network. A parallel computer is termed a massively parallel processor (MPP) if it has 1000 or more processors. MPP machines are being introduced by many computer vendors. Examples of MPP machines include the Intel Paragon™, the Kendall Squares KSR-1™, the Thinking Machines CM-5™, the Cray T3D™, and others. A large number of medium-priced moderately parallel (using 10 to 100 processors) multiprocessors are also commercially available today. Examples of moderately parallel machines include the Sequent Symmetry™, Encore Multimax™, and IBM SP-1™. Numerous vendors of workstations are currently marketing multiprocessor-based workstations as well. Examples of multiprocessor workstations include the DEC Firefly™, the Solbourne™ workstations, the SUN SPARCcenter 2000™, and the Silicon Graphics IRIS Challenger™ workstations. Finally, networks of workstations are common in all computing environments and can be thought of as parallel computers.

Although it is relatively easy to build parallel machines whose peak performance will be thousands of MFLOPS (millions of floating point operations per second) and MIPS (millions of instructions per second), it is extremely difficult to harness the computational power effectively to actually have the machines deliver all those MFLOPS and MIPS to the user. Therein lies the challenge: design of good, efficient, parallel algorithms that can use the hardware resources to get the maximum performance. This book will discuss the use of parallel processing for solving problems in a growing application area whose computational requirements are enormous: very large scale integrated (VLSI) circuit computer-aided design (CAD) applications.

The study of parallel algorithms for VLSI CAD applications is important for two reasons:

1. The application area of VLSI CAD desperately needs increases in the computing power to solve the problems of the future. In view of the increasing complexity of VLSI circuits, there is a growing need for sophisticated CAD tools to automate the synthesis, analysis, and verification steps in the design of VLSI systems. Future CAD tools have to enable designs that are too large or complex to undertake otherwise, shorten design time, improve product quality, and reduce product costs. Parallel processing offers an effective solution to handle the large complexity of VLSI designs of the future.

2. VLSI CAD applications represent a rich class of important, nonnumerical, unstructured, applications that are generally difficult to parallelize effectively. Researchers and users of parallel computers are typically exposed to parallel algorithms for structured numerical problems, such as matrix multiplication and fast Fourier transform, and often fail to appreciate the intricacies of solving a large nonnumerical, unstructured problem in parallel.

In this chapter, we will first provide an overview of various VLSI CAD applications and then motivate how they may benefit from the use of parallel processing. We will subsequently provide a brief introduction to parallel computing and parallel algorithm design and conclude with a look at the various options for the use of parallel processing for VLSI CAD applications.

1.2 OVERVIEW OF VLSI CAD

The VLSI design process can be viewed as a sequence of transformations on behavioral, structural, and physical design representations. Behavioral representations describe a circuit's outputs as a function of its inputs. Procedural and Boolean descriptions are behavioral representations. Structural representations describe the composition of circuits in terms of components and interconnections among them.

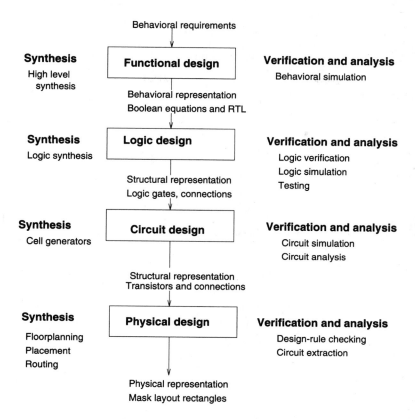

Figure 1.1 Phases of VLSI design

Physical representations are characterized by information used in the manufacture and fabrication of physical systems, such as geometric layout or topological constraints. Excellent introductions to the VLSI systems design methodology can be found in [19, 20, 32]. For more detailed overviews of the VLSI CAD domain, the reader is referred to [10, 24, 26, 31].

A top-down design methodology of electronic systems divides the design process into phases. As shown in the Figure 1.1, the phases are functional design, logic design, circuit design, and physical design. Each phase in the design consists of two steps, synthesis, and verification and analysis.

Figure 1.2 shows an example of the representation used during each phase of VLSI design. The design specification phase considers the application, performance requirement, interfaces, costs, and the like. This is usually done manually and is used as an input to the next stage, namely functional design. During functional design, a functional behavior is synthesized to meet the specifications. High-level synthesis

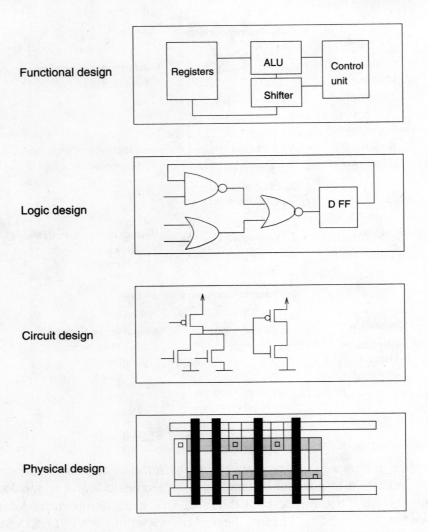

Figure 1.2 Example representations at each phase of VLSI design

tools such as silicon compilers take a design specification as input and output a behavioral description. Behavioral simulation is the analysis method at this level. The output of this design stage is a behavioral representation of the logic in the forms of register-transfer-level (RTL) statements and Boolean equations.

During logic design, a logic structure is developed that implements the functional design. Logic synthesis tools typically take a behavioral representation and output a structural representation in the form of a netlist of logic gates and connections. The logic design is validated by comparing the results of logic simulation with behavioral simulation. Test generation and fault simulation tools are run at this level to check if manufacturing defects, modeled at the logic level, can be detected by logic patterns applied to the inputs of the circuit.

The circuit design phase governs the detailed circuit design of the basic circuit elements: transistors, resistors, capacitors, and inductors. Automatic synthesis tools produce a transistor-level interconnection with appropriate sizing information to meet signal delay requirements. Specifically, cell generators are used to produce transistor level designs for the best performance. Analysis is performed via circuit and timing simulations. Timing verification tools are used to determine if signal specifications are met.

The physical design phase transforms the structural representation of a circuit into geometric shapes representating actual fabrication mask layouts. Synthesis tools perform placement of cells and routing of the wires to connect the cells. Analysis tools include design rule checking, and verification tools include circuit extraction and netlist comparison.

1.3 MOTIVATION FOR PARALLEL CAD

Almost all the VLSI CAD applications in synthesis, analysis, and verification tasks at various levels in the VLSI design hierarchy (functional, logical, circuit, and physical levels) take large runtimes on existing sequential computers. The use of parallel processing for VLSI CAD applications is essential for the following reasons.

1.3.1 Faster Runtimes

A large subset of problems in VLSI CAD is computationally intensive, and future CAD tools will require even more accuracy and computational capabilities from these tools. Table 1.1 shows some example CAD tools and their runtimes on a SUN/4 SPARC™ workstation, rated to operate at about 20 MIPS.

The circuit sizes in each of the problems are quite moderate, about 1000 to 10,000 gates. It is clear that for circuits that are a hundred times larger, 100,000 to 1 million gates, the runtime requirements will increase 100 times. CAD tools that take hours to run on current designs may take weeks or months to run on future designs. In fact, some of the industrial CAD tools running on the leading edge ASIC (application-specific integrated circuits) gate-array chips containing 500,000 gates take weeks to run tasks such as placement, routing, and layout verification.

Let us now take a look at the increasing problem complexity of VLSI designs. Figure 1.3 shows the increase in the number of transistors per chip (roughly correlated with the number of gates) with the years and the projected size in the year 2000. It is clear from the figure that the number of gates on a chip will be more than a million by the year 2000.

TABLE 1.1 Example runtimes of VLSI CAD tools on a SUN/4™ workstation

Application	CAD tool	Circuit Size	Runtime
Extraction	HPEX3.0	1,000,000 rectangles	1 hour
Placement	Timberwolf6.0	2,907 cells	1 hour
Logic synthesis	MIS2.2	7,657 gates	2 hours
Test generation	HITEC2.0	17,793 gates	5 hours
Circuit simulation	RELAX2.0	40,000 elements	1 month

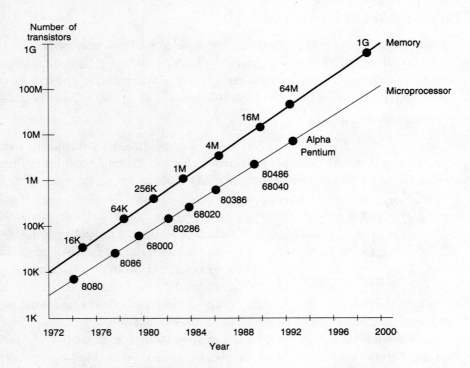

Figure 1.3 Increase in circuit complexity with years

Given such increased complexity of CAD tools of the future, the only way to address the complexity of the problem is to apply parallel processing to speed up the CAD tasks. Many problems are suitable for parallelization, hence parallel processing can offer faster runtime performance for most CAD applications. We will discuss numerous parallel algorithms for speeding up different VLSI CAD applications in Chapters 3 through 8.

1.3.2 Larger Problem Sizes

Very often a particular CAD tool cannot handle a large problem because of its unaffordable runtime requirements or memory limitations. Given the same amount of design turnaround time from a designer, parallel processing allows us to address larger problems since they are solved faster. Also, since parallel machines come with larger memories, we can solve larger problem sizes than we could solve earlier on conventional machines. It has been observed that circuit extractors that cannot extract large circuits containing millions of rectangles on a workstation due to memory limitations can be extracted on a parallel processor by suitably partitioning the rectangles of the chip area among the processors.

1.3.3 Better Quality of Results

Since many VLSI CAD problems can be formulated as optimization problems that are NP complete, heuristics are often used to solve the problems, which always give nonoptimal solutions. By using parallel search techniques, it has been observed that we can frequently obtain better quality results. For example, it has been observed that a parallel implementation of an automatic test pattern generator obtains higher fault coverage than the corresponding serial implementation.

1.3.4 Affordable and Available Technology

Parallel processing has become affordable and available recently owing to the availability of low-cost, high-performance microprocessors and memories. Medium-priced moderately parallel multiprocessors are available for several hundred thousand dollars. Multiprocessor workstations are now available for tens of thousands of dollars.

1.3.5 Efficient Parallel Algorithm Design

It is often claimed that, rather than investigating parallel algorithms, it is perhaps better to investigate sophisticated techniques to automatically parallelize programs as is done by parallelizing compilers [23, 33]. However, the status of existing parallelizing compilers is such that they can only work on FORTRAN programs with large numbers of independent DO LOOPS working on array data structures. While these techniques are appropriate for structured numerical applications involving dense matrices, they will not be able to extract sufficient parallelism from VLSI CAD applications. By nature, algorithms for VLSI CAD applications are highly unstructured (for example, they do not have well-structured DO LOOPS and array data structures). Hence, to speed up VLSI CAD applications, it is necessary to investigate parallel algorithms for them.

1.3.6 Commercial Parallel CAD Products

Numerous CAD vendors have already announced products that exploit parallel machines. For example, Mentor Graphics has a product called PARADE, which performs cell placement in parallel. Mentor Graphics also has a parallel implementation of design rule checking and extraction called CHECKMATE™. Cadence Design Systems has a product called VERIFAULT™ that runs fault simulation in parallel on a network of workstations. Crosscheck Technology has a parallel test generator called the AIDA-II™ for combinational circuits. Silvaco markets a product for lithography simulation called VIRTUAL WAFER FAB™ and, for 3D device simulation, one called THUNDER™ on massively parallel MasPar MP-1™ systems. In the future, numerous other parallel implementations of VLSI CAD tools will become available.

1.4 PARALLEL ARCHITECTURE BASICS

We will now provide a brief overview of parallel architectures. More details on this topic will be provided in Chapter 2. A large variety of general-purpose parallel processors exist, which can be characterized by different parameters. Excellent introductions to the organizations of parallel computers can be found in [2, 14, 15, 16, 30].

1.4.1 Moderately Parallel versus Massively Parallel

Although parallel processing has been around for a long time, computer users and designers have used the term massively parallel and moderate parallel in a somewhat ad hoc manner. An accepted term for *massively parallel* processing is an architecture that uses more than 1000 processors. An architecture using 10 to a 100 processors is termed *moderately parallel*. The Connection Machine CM-2™, the CM-5™, and the Kendall Squares KSR-1™, and the Intel Paragon™ machines are massively parallel, while the Sequent Symmetry™ and the Intel iPSC™ hypercubes are moderately parallel machines.

1.4.2 SIMD versus MIMD Architectures

General-purpose parallel processors are broadly classified as single-instruction, multiple-data (SIMD) parallel processors or multiple-instruction, multiple-data (MIMD) multiprocessors. In an *SIMD* parallel processor, a central controller broadcasts the same instruction to different processors. Each processor then executes the instruction on its data. It is possible to mask some processors from executing the instruction by appropriately setting some mask registers at each processor. In an *MIMD* multiprocessor, the processors execute different instructions on different data. In other words, there are multiple instruction streams, as opposed to a single instruction stream in the case of SIMD multiprocessors. The Thinking Machines CM-2™, and the MasPar MP-1™ machines are SIMD machines, while the Intel iPSC™, the Thinking Machines CM-5™, the IBM SP-1™ and the BBN Butterfly™ machines are MIMD machines.

1.4.3 Shared Memory versus Distributed Memory

General-purpose MIMD multiprocessors are further classified as shared memory multiprocessors and distributed memory multiprocessors (more accurately termed multicomputers). In a shared memory MIMD multiprocessor, all processors can access all memory locations.

In a distributed memory MIMD multicomputer, each processor has its own local memory which it can access. This is illustrated in Figure 1.4.

Even though shared memory MIMD multiprocessors provide a logical view of a uniform shared single address space, the processors and memories are physically organized in one of two ways, centralized or distributed. The latter organization (logically shared, physically distributed) resembles the distributed memory MIMD multicomputers. More details on this topic will be provided in Chapter 2.

The Sequent Symmetry™, the Encore Multimax™, the Kendall Squares KSR-1™, and the CRAY T3D™ are are shared memory MIMD multiprocessors. The Intel iPSC™ hypercube, the Intel Paragon™, the Thinking Machines CM-5™, and the IBM SP-1™ are distributed memory MIMD multicomputers.

1.4.4 Topology of Interconnect

In the case of both shared memory multiprocessors and distributed memory multicomputers, the different processors are connected through an interconnection network. Typical interconnection networks include the bus, the crossbar, multistage networks, rings, meshes, trees, and hypercubes.

The Sequent Symmetry™, the Encore Multimax™, and the SUN SPARCcenter 2000™ use buses as the interconnection. The Alliant FX/8™ multiprocessors use a crossbar. The BBN Butterfly™ and TC2000™ multiprocessors use multistage interconnection networks. The Intel iPSC™ uses a hypercube connection. The Intel Paragon™ and the MasPar MP-1™ use a 2-dimensional mesh topology. The Thinking Machines CM-5™ uses a fat-tree topology. The Kendall Squares KSR-1™ machine uses a hierarchical ring-of-rings topology.

1.4.5 Fine Grain versus Coarse Grain

The term grain size refers to the number of instructions executed in a processor before synchronizing with or communicating some data with another processor. *Fine-grain*

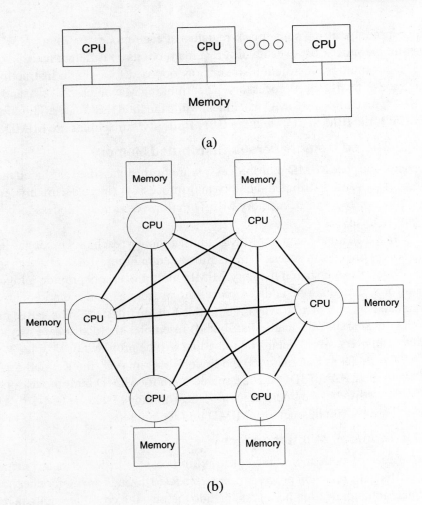

Figure 1.4 Shared and distributed memory multiprocessors. (a) Shared memory organization. (b) Distributed memory organization.

parallel processing involves synchronizing the processors after every few instructions. *Coarse-grain* parallel processing involves synchronizing the processors after tens of thousands of instructions. More recently, the term *medium-grain* parallel processing has been used to characterize a grain size somewhere in the middle, for example, several hundred instructions between synchronizations. The Thinking Machines CM-2™ synchronizes all the processors after every clock cycle, and is a fine grained parallel processor. The Intel iPSC™ hypercube and the Sequent Symmetry™ synchronize after several hundred to thousand clock cycles and are medium-grain parallel processors. A distributed network of workstations synchronizes after several hundreds of thousands of clock cycles and can be classified as a coarse-grain parallel processor.

1.5 PARALLEL PROGRAMMING BASICS

We will now outline the basic methods used in programming parallel computers. More details on this topic will be provided in Chapter 2. We will distinguish between data and functional parallelism, between fine-grain and coarse-grain parallelism, between single-instruction, multiple-data (SIMD) and multiple-instruction, multiple-data (MIMD) programming, and between shared memory and message-passing parallel programming. We will show examples of each approach. We will explain the problem of data dependence, classify different forms of data dependence, and explain how that affects parallelism. Excellent introductions to parallel computing from a programmer's perspective can be found in [4, 6, 12].

1.5.1 Data versus Functional Parallelism

There are two common forms of exploiting parallelism in an application, using different forms of partitioning of the problem. *Data parallelism* involves creating multiple, identical processes and assigning a portion of the data to each process. Data parallelism is appropriate for applications that perform the same operations repeatedly on large collections of data. In programming terms, data parallelism is appropriate for applications requiring loops to perform calculations on arrays or matrices: data partitioning is done by executing the loop iterations in parallel.

Functional parallelism (also called *task parallelism* or *control parallelism*) involves creating multiple processes and having them perform different operations on a shared data set. In programming terms, functional parallelism is appropriate for applications that include many unique subroutines or functions.

Figure 1.5 shows examples of data and function parallelism. In part (a) we show the same procedure A being applied to various data elements; hence procedure A is parallelized by putting each data element or group of data elements on a different processor, and the same procedure A is executed on each processor on different data elements. In part (b) we show four different procedures, A, B, C, and D, that are independent of each other and are therefore mapped onto different processors such that they are independently executed.

While both programming methods can be effective, the data parallelism method fits more applications and has the advantages of providing more uniform load balance across processors, minimal programming effort, and the scalability of the parallelization with larger number of processors.

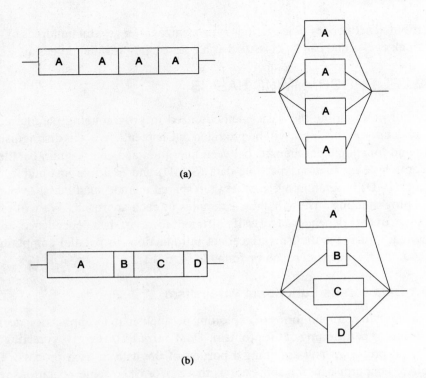

(a)

(b)

Figure 1.5 Examples of data and functional parallelism. (a) Data parallelism. (b) Functional parallelism

1.5.2 Fine-grain versus Coarse-grain Parallelism

The other important classification of parallel computation is the grain size of parallelism. The granularity determines the distribution of the *compute work* performed over independent subtasks executed in parallel. Grain size can be categorized into *fine grain* and *coarse grain*. Fine-grain distributions spread the total work to be done by the parallelized algorithm over many small subtasks, each representing a few instructions of execution. Coarse-grain distributions have fewer subtasks, each doing more work representing several thousand instructions of execution. The distinction between the two is relative, not absolute. Intermediate grain sizes (say few hundreds of instructions) are often termed *medium-grain parallelism.*

The two parallel computing models, data versus functional parallelism and fine-grain versus coarse-grain parallelism, are orthogonal to each other; hence we can actually have four possible combinations of the classifications.

1.5.3 Parallelization and Data Dependence

Consider the following loop of a C program.

```
for (i=0; i < 100; i++)
    a[i] = b[i] + c[i];
```

If we unfold the loops, the statements would be executed as follows:

```
a[0] = b[0] + c[0];
a[1] = b[1] + c[1];
a[2] = b[2] + c[2];
a[3] = b[3] + c[3];
. . . . .
. . . . .
a[99] = b[99] + c[99];
```

Since each statement for each iteration of the loop performs computations of different elements of a, b, and c, each iteration can be executed in parallel. This is the basis of data parallelism.

However, not all loops can be parallelized, the reason being data dependence. For example, consider the following loop:

```
for (i=1; i < 100; i++)
    a[i] = a[i-1] + b[i];
```

If we unfold the loops, the statements would be executed as follows:

```
S1:    a[1] = a[0] + b[1];
S2:    a[2] = a[1] + b[2];
S3:    a[3] = a[2] + b[3];
       . . . . .
       . . . . .
S99: a[99] = a[98] + b[99];
```

Note that the two statements $S1$ and $S2$ cannot be executed in parallel since there is a data dependence between $S1$ and $S2$, called a *true data dependence*, where the value of $a[1]$ produced by statement $S1$ is used in statement $S2$. Similarly, statements $S2$ and $S3$ cannot be executed in parallel due to the data dependence of $a[2]$.

As an example of another form of dependence, consider the following sequence of statements:

```
for (i=1; i < 100; i++)
    a[i] = a[i+1] + b[i];
```

If one unfolds the loops, the statements would be executed as follows:

```
S1:    a[1] = a[2] + b[1];
S2:    a[2] = a[3] + b[2];
S3:    a[3] = a[4] + b[3];
       .....
       .....
S99: a[99] = a[100] + b[99];
```

Note that the two statements $S1$ and $S2$ again cannot be executed in parallel since there is a data dependence between $S1$ and $S2$, called an *data anti-dependence*, where the value of $a[2]$ in statement $S1$ has to be read before it is written in statement $S2$. Similarly, statements $S2$ and $S3$ cannot be executed in parallel due to the data anti-dependence on $a[3]$.

As an example of a third form of dependence, consider the following sequence of statements:

```
for (i=1; i < 100; i++)
    sum = a[i] + b[i];
```

If we unfold the loops, the statements would be executed as follows:

```
S1:    sum = a[1] + b[1];
```

```
S2:      sum = a[2] + b[2];
S3:      sum = a[3] + b[3];
         . . . . .

         . . . . .
S99:     sum = a[99] + b[99];
```

Note that the two statements $S1$ and $S2$ again cannot be executed in parallel since there is a data dependence between $S1$ and $S2$, called an *output data dependence*, where the value of *sum* in statement *S1* has to be written in *S1* before it is rewritten in statement *S2* so that, after both the statements are executed, the resultant value of *sum* is that produced by $S2$.

For a given program, we must analyze its data dependence to determine which loops can be parallelized. If the array indexes have the form $a[i + constant]$, then the analysis is trivial and can be performed by automatic parallelizing compilers [23, 33]. However, if the indexes have more general forms, for example, $a[i + k]$, then the analysis becomes difficult. If $k = 0$, then the loop becomes parallel; if $k \neq 0$, the loop cannot be parallelized. Often, the value of k is not known at compile time, and hence a compiler cannot make any decisions about parallelization. At other times, the indexes are of the form of subscripted subscripts, for example, $a[b[i]]$, and compilers cannot resolve these data dependencies at all.

1.5.4 Examples of Different Parallel Computing Models

It was remarked earlier that the two parallel computing models, data versus functional parallelism and fine-grain versus coarse-grain parallelism, are orthogonal to each other; hence one can actually have four possible combinations of classifications.

Examples of *fine-grain data parallelism* are C program loops where each iteration of a loop is independent and represents a simple statement free of function calls. Each loop iteration is executed on a different processor.

```
for (i=0; i < 1000; i++)
    a[i] = b[i] + c[i];
```

Examples of *coarse-grain data parallelism* are C program loops where each iteration of a loop is independent but represents a complex set of statements containing function calls. A group of loop iterations is executed on a different processor.

```
for (i=0; i < 1000; i++) {
  a[i] = b[i] + c[i] * work(d[i]);
}
```

Examples of *fine-grain functional parallelism* are multiple C program loops which cannot be parallelized individually, but the different code blocks are independent. Each code block represents a small amount of work without function calls. Each block is executed on a different processor.

```
for (i=0; i < 3; i++)   /* block 1 */
  b[i-1] = b[i] + c[i];

  . . .

for (j=0; j < 5; i++)    /* block n */
  a[j-1] = a[j] + d[j];
```

Examples of *coarse-grain functional parallelism* are multiple C program loops that cannot be parallelized individually, but the different code blocks are independent. Each code block represents a large amount of work with function calls. Each block is executed on a different processor.

```
for (i=0; i < 1000; i++)         /* block 1 */
  b[i-1] = b[i] + c[i] * work(e[i]);

  . . .

for (j=0; j < 5000; i++)          /* block n */
  a[j-1] = a[j] + d[j] * otherwork(f[j]);
```

To select a programming method, we use the following procedure. First, use a profiling procedure to identify the subprogram where the program spends most of its time. Then the subprogram's call graph is examined for all its ancestors until the outermost ancestor is identified that contains a loop. Starting from this ancestor, examine each ancestor in calling sequence until an independent loop is identified. The data partitioning method can be used on this loop. If no such loop is found, functional partitioning can be applied, or loop dependencies can be removed by program transformations to exploit data partitioning.

1.5.5 SIMD versus MIMD Programming Model

General-purpose parallel computers are broadly classified as single-instruction, multiple-data (SIMD) or multiple-instruction, multiple-data (MIMD) multiprocessors.

In an SIMD parallel processor, all the processors executes a particular instruction in parallel on different data elements stored in each processor. SIMD parallel processors are programmed using array constructs such as those in Fortran 90 or C* (discussed in more detail in Chapter 2) using a fine-grain, data-parallel model of computation. In such a programming model, we assume that we have an unlimited set of virtual processors, whose number depends on the problem size. Each element of a distinct data structure, such as an array, gets mapped to a unique processor. All processors are programmed to execute the same instruction at a time. For example, the following parallel loop of a C program,

```
for (i=0; i < 100; i++)
   a[i] = b[i] + c[i];
```

would be expressed in the SIMD data-parallel model as follows (more details on the program syntax will be provided in Chapter 2):

```
shape [100] s;
float: s a,b,c;

a = b + c;
```

In an MIMD multiprocessor, the processors execute different instructions on different data. In other words, there are multiple instruction streams, as opposed to a single instruction stream in the case of SIMD parallel processors. MIMD parallel processors are programmed using either loop-level parallelism or task-level parallelism. An example of loop-level parallelism for the preceding loop containing 100 iterations over 20 processors is as follows:

```
/* create 20 processes with different process id */
id = m_fork(20);

/* assign 100/20 = 5 iterations per process */
for (i = id * 5; i < (id+1) * 5; i++);
```

```
        a[i] = b[i] * c[i];
}
```

In this example, process 0 gets loop iterations 0, 1, ..., 4, process 1 gets loop iterations 5, 6, ..., 9, process 19 gets loop iterations 95, 96, ..., 99.

In addition to loop level parallelism, MIMD multiprocessors support task level parallelism. In divide and conquer applications, we can think of tasks getting created as an algorithm proceeds. These tasks get queued in some centralized or distributed work queues and are executed by different processors in parallel. An example of task parallelism is as follows.

```
/* creates 3 processes to work in parallel */
id = m_fork(3);

while (task_queue_not_empty) {
  task = get_task();
  execute(task,id);
}
```

1.5.6 Shared Memory versus Message Passing

Within MIMD multiprocessors, we have the distinction between shared memory multiprocessors and distributed memory message passing multiprocessors (more accurately, called multicomputers).

The shared memory programming model assumes that all processors share a common logical address space. All the variables are necessary to be shared by all processors may be read and written by all processors. The distributed memory message passing programming model assumes that each processor has its own separate address space. A processor can only read and write variables from its own local memory. Any synchronization and data access of nonlocal data have to be performed using explicit message passing between processors.

The MasPar MP-1™ and the Thinking Machines CM-2™ provide an SIMD parallel programming model. The Sequent Symmetry™, the Encore Multimax™, the SUN SPARCcenter 2000™, the BBN TC2000™, and the Kendall Squares KSR-1™ machines provide a shared memory MIMD programming model. The Intel iPSC™ hypercube, the Intel Paragon™, the Thinking Machines CM-5™, and the IBM SP-1™ provide a message passing distributed memory MIMD programming model.

1.6 PARALLEL ALGORITHM BASICS

In this section, we will provide a framework for the design of efficient parallel algorithms. Given a problem, a serial algorithm provides a precise step by step description
of the computational steps that need to be performed sequentially to solve it. A parallel
algorithm provides a precise description of how the given problem is to be decomposed into smaller subproblems, how each of these subproblems is to be solved, how
these subproblems interact among each other, and how these subproblem solutions
can be merged back to solve the original problem. The purpose of parallel algorithm
design is to come up with techniques to solve the given problem *faster* than the original sequential algorithm. The ratio of the execution times of the sequential algorithm
and the parallel algorithm is referred to as the *speedup* of the parallel algorithm. An
excellent introduction to the theory of parallel algorithm design and analysis can be
found in [17, 18, 25].

We will now provide some simple analysis of the speedups achievable through
parallel algorithms and subsequently give the general guidelines to how one can design
efficient parallel algorithms.

Let us denote:

T = time for the best serial algorithm

T_p = time for a parallel algorithm using p processors

Speedup $S_p = \frac{T}{T_p}$

Efficiency or utilization $E_p = \frac{S_p}{p}$

If the parallel algorithm for a problem is 100% efficient, then we observe *linear*
speedups, where $S_p = p$. However, in the real world, the efficiency is never 100%
owing to two main reasons: (1) cost of synchronization, scheduling, or communication
across parallel processors; (2) suboptimal load balance among parallel processors.
Figure 1.6 illustrates the effects of these two factors on the speedup.

Figure 1.6(a) shows the total time required in the serial algorithm to be 100 time
units. Suppose the application is parallelized and executed on four processors. Each
processor in the ideal case would get an equal amount of work evenly distributed,
such that each performs about 25 units of computation, as shown in Figure 1.6(b). In
this case we assume that the processors spend no time in synchronization; hence the
speedup is 100/25 = 4 on four processors.

Now, let us consider the case where there is a need for synchronization among
the parallel tasks. Let us assume that the synchronization takes 10 time units, as
shown in Figure 1.6(c). The total parallel algorithm execution time = 25 + 10 = 35.
The speedup is then 100/35 = 2.85 on four processors.

Next, let us consider the case of no synchronization costs, but a suboptimal

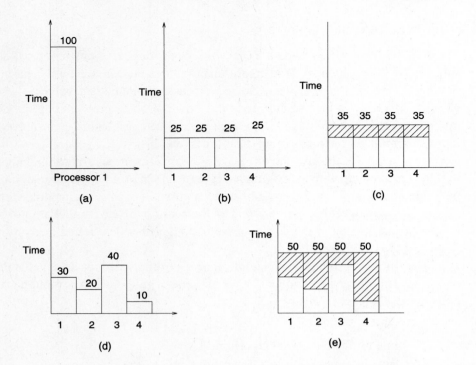

Figure 1.6 Time charts of serial and parallel algorithms. (a) Serial case. (b) Four processor, ideal case. (c) Ideal load balance, synchronization/communication cost = 10. (d) No synchronization cost, poor load balance. (e) Poor load balance, synchronization/communication cost = 10.

workload distribution as shown in Figure 1.6(d). We assume that due to the load imbalance, processor 3 gets the largest amount of computation = 40 time units, whereas the other processors get 20, 30 and 10 time units. The overall completion time of the algorithm is the time for the most loaded processor to completion = 40. The speedup of this algorithm is 100/40 = 2.5 on four processors.

In the worst case (which happens in practice), the two bad effects are combined: there is load imbalance and there is a synchonization cost as shown in Figure 1.6(e). We then get the time for completion of the algorithm as 40 + 10 = 50. The speedup of this algorithm is 100/50 = 2 on four processors with an efficiency of 50%.

Unfortunately, the two factors (synchronization/communication versus load balance) are opposing forces. Consider a scheme that runs everything on one processor even though p processors are available. Such a scheme will have poor load balance (all the load is on one processor, the others are idle), whereas there will be no communication/synchronization cost.

On the other hand, if we decompose the given problem into the finest grain of computations, such a scheme will have the best load balance, yet the scheme will also have a high cost of communication/synchronization among the threads of computation.

1.6.1 Amdahl's Law

Let us now look at a fundamental limitation that commonly limits the maximum speedup that can be achievable for a problem, commonly termed Amdahl's law [13]. The law simply states that the performance improvement that can be gained by a parallel implementation is limited by the fraction of time the parallel mode can be used in an application.

Consider an application that takes T time units when executed in a serial mode on a single processor. When the application is parallelized, we assume that a parameter, α, constitutes the serial fraction of the algorithm that cannot be parallelized. Assuming p processors in a parallel implementation, the time for execution on p processors is given by the following expression, assuming perfect speedups in the portion of the application that can be parallelized.

$$T_p = \alpha + (1 - \alpha)\frac{T}{p}$$

Then the speedup that is achievable on p processors is:

$$S_p = \frac{T_s}{T_p} = \frac{p}{1 + (p - 1)\alpha} = \frac{1}{\alpha + (1 - \alpha)/p}$$

If we assume that the serial fraction is fixed, then the speedup for infinite processors is limited by $1/\alpha$. For example, if $\alpha = 10\%$, then the maximum speedup is 10, even if we use an infinite number of processors. Looking at Equation (1.2), we might think that there is no hope for parallel processing. However, there is some hope in the following observation.

The Amdahl's fraction α in practice depends on the problem size n and the number of processors p. An effective parallel algorithm has

$$\alpha(n, p) \to 0 \quad \text{as} \quad n \to \infty$$

For such a case, even if one fixes p, the number of processors, we can get linear speedups by choosing a suitably large problem size.

$$S_p = \frac{T_s}{T_p} = \frac{p}{1 + (p - 1)\alpha(n, p)} \to p \quad \text{as} \quad n \to \infty$$

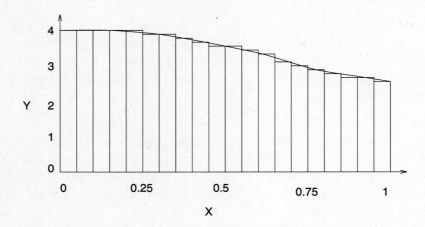

Figure 1.7 Computation of π through numerical integration

Hence, theoretically, to extract large speedups for a fixed number of processors, we have to increase the problem size. Practically, the problem size that we can run for a particular problem is limited by the memory of the parallel computer. Hence, indirectly, the speedup of a parallel implementation is dictated by the number of processors *and* the amount of memory available on the parallel machine.

1.6.2 Example Parallel Algorithm and Analysis

As an example of the design and analysis of a parallel algorithm, let us consider a parallel algorithm for computing the value of π through numerical integration. The detailed parallel algorithm and its parallel implementation on shared memory and distributed memory MIMD multiprocessors will be discussed in Chapter 2.

$$\pi = \int_0^1 \frac{4}{1 + x^2}$$

This integration can be evaluated by computing the area under the curve for $f(x) = \frac{4}{1 + x^2}$ from 0 to 1. With numerical integration using the rectangle rule decomposition, we divide the region x from 0 to 1 into n points. The value of the function $f(x) = \frac{4}{1 + x^2}$ is evaluated at the midpoint of each interval. The values are summed up and multiplied by the width of one chunk. The computation of π is illustrated in Figure 1.7.

An approximate program listing for a sequential program is given next.

```
computepi()

{
```

```
h = 1.0 / n;
sum = 0.0;
for (i=0; i < n; i++) {
   x = h * (i - 0.5);
   sum = sum + 4.0 / (1 + x * x);
}
pi = h * sum;
}
```

We now present a parallel algorithm of the π computation. We assume that each procesor will perform a local computation of the numerical integration for a subrange of x. This step can be performed in parallel. The algorithm uses a static interleaved scheduling of the i index loop as shown in Figure 1.8. Static interleaved scheduling will be discused in next section. Each processor computes on a set of about n/p points which are allocated to each processor in a cyclic manner. Finally, we assume that the local values of π are accumulated among the p processors under synchronization.

```
computepi()

{

   id = my_processor_id();
   nprocs = number_of_processors();

   h = 1.0 / n;
   sum = 0.0;

   /* each processor computes bounds of pi */
   /* using static interleaved scheduling */

   for (i=id; i < n; i = i + nprocs) {
      x = h * (i - 0.5);
      sum = sum + 4.0 / (1 + x * x);
   }

   localpi = sum * h;
```

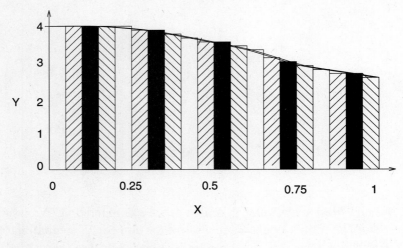

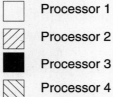

Processor 1

Processor 2

Processor 3

Processor 4

Figure 1.8 Parallel computation of π

```
/* perform accumulation of pi using  */
/* tree-based combining under synchronization */

use_tree_based_combining_for_critical_section();
   pi = pi + localpi;
end_critical_section();


}
```

We now perform an analysis of the speedup of this parallel algorithm. We assume that the computation of π is performed over n points.

The sequential algorithm performs six operations (two multiplications, one division, three addition) per point on the X axis. Hence, for n points, the number of operations executed in the sequential algorithm is:

$$T_s = 6n$$

The parallel algorithm uses p processors with static interleaved scheduling. Each processor computes on a set of m points which are allocated to each processor in a cyclic manner. The expression for m is given by $m \leq \frac{n}{p} + 1$, if p does not exactly divide n. The runtime for the parallel algorithm for the parallel computation of the local values of π is

$$T_p = 6m = 6\frac{n}{p} + 6$$

The accumulation of the local values of π using a tree-based combining can be optimally performed in $\log_2(p)$ steps. The total runtime for the parallel algorithm for the computation of π including the parallel computation and the combining is

$$T_p = 6\frac{n}{p} + 6 + \log(p)$$

The speedup of the parallel algorithm is:

$$S_p = \frac{T_s}{T_p} = \frac{6n}{6\frac{n}{p} + 6 + \log(p)}$$

The Amdahl's fraction for this parallel algorithm can be determined by rewriting the previous equation as:

$$S_p = \frac{p}{1 + \frac{p}{n} + \frac{p\log(p)}{6n}}$$

which should be set equal to

$$S_p = \frac{p}{1 + (p - 1)\alpha(n, p)}$$

Hence, the Amdahl's fraction $\alpha(n, p)$ is:

$$\alpha(n, p) = \frac{p}{(p - 1)n} + \frac{p\log(p)}{6n(p - 1)}$$

We finally note that

$$\alpha(n, p) \rightarrow 0 \quad \text{as} \quad n \rightarrow \infty \quad \text{for fixed } p$$

Hence, the preceding parallel algorithm for computation of π can give linear speedups for large problem sizes and is therefore effective.

1.6.3 Load Balancing and Scheduling

The key to efficient parallel algorithm design is to devise a method to distribute the workload as uniformly as possible among various processors, to keep the synchronization overhead as low as possible, and to keep the serial fraction as low as possible.

In this section we will address the basic concepts in achieving uniform load balance. Consider the example parallel loop that we looked at earlier. Each iteration of the *for* loop computes a particular value of the array element $a[i]$.

```
for (i=0; i < 14; i++) {
  a[i] = b[i] * c[i];
}
```

Since the elements of array $a[i]$ can be computed independently, the iterations can be executed in parallel and constitute parallel tasks. The problem of assigning specific tasks to processors is called task scheduling. The parallel tasks can be scheduled among processes using three types of algorithms: (1) prescheduling (2) static scheduling (3) dynamic scheduling.

In *prescheduling*, the task division is explicitly determined by the programmer before the program is compiled. Such a method cannot be varied for different sizes of data and number of processors, hence this approach is good for function partitioning, that is, assigning specific tasks to specific processors.

In *static scheduling*, the tasks are scheduled by the processes at runtime, but are divided in some predetermined way. For a loop having N iterations using P processors (the number being determined at runtime), processor 1 will be assigned iterations $1..N/P$, processor 2 to $N/P + 1..2N/P$, and so on. Such a scheme of assigning continuous blocks of iterations is called *static-blocked scheduling*.

Often we have a case where successive iterations of a loop have to perform monotonically increasing or decreasing work per iteration. In that case, the previous static block scheduling will overload the processor performing the contiguous blocks of most work. An alternative method of static scheduling for better load distribution is one where we can assign iterations in a round-robin cyclic manner in a scheme callel *static-interleaved scheduling*.

In *dynamic scheduling*, each process schedules its task at runtime by checking a centralized task queue from which the next available tasks are removed, and new tasks are entered.

The advantage of dynamic scheduling is better load balancing, however, there is an overhead for searching through centralized task queues in the presence of con-

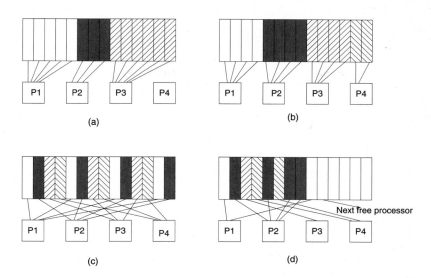

Figure 1.9 Example of four scheduling algorithms. (a) Prescheduled code for three processors. Note that processor 4 is idle. (b) Static blocked scheduling. (c) Static interleaved scheduling. (d) Dynamic scheduling.

tention. Static and prescheduled scheduling produces the least overhead, however, it can produce load imbalances.

Let us apply the four types of scheduling algorithms on the example parallel *for* loop described previously. Figure 1.9 shows the four scheduling algorithms for scheduling the 14 loop iterations on four processors.

Figure 1.9(a) shows an example of prescheduling, where at compile time the programmer decides that the work will be distributed on three processors with the exact allocation specified. At run time, even though four processors are available, only three do useful work, while the fourth is idle. This is the most inefficient scheme, but is appropriate for use in functional parallelism.

Figure 1.9(b) shows the case of static blocked scheduling where at runtime the program checks the number of processors available and allocates continuous blocks of iterations to each processor. This method is very simple to implement and has no runtime overhead.

Figure 1.9(c) shows the case of static interleaved scheduling where at runtime, the program checks the number of processors available and allocates iterations in a cyclic manner to each processor. Note that the allocation is still static. This method is a little more complex to implement, but has no runtime overhead.

Finally, in some cases there is no way to predict how much work each iteration will take. In such cases, the iterations are distributed dynamically to each processor when they become free. This is shown in Figure 1.9(d). This method gives the best load balance, but has a high cost of runtime overhead for searching for the next available piece of work among the processors, especially since this has to be performed such that there are no races between multiple free processors picking the same next available iteration.

Often, a compromise of static and dynamic scheduling is used, where each time a processor is free it gets a small chunk of iterations (for example, 10 iterations) so that the cost of synchronization is not paid for each iteration, but each chunk of iteration. If the chunk size is set to the number of iterations divided by the number of processors, it reverts to the simple static blocked scheduling.

In summary, a variety of methods exists for load balancing and scheduling, and an efficient parallel algorithm has to pick one for an application that evenly distributes the workload the best for the smallest cost at compile time or runtime and balances the ease of implementation.

1.7 PARALLEL CAD OPTIONS

Having taken a brief look at the parallel processing technology, we are ready to look at how we can apply parallel processing to speed up VLSI CAD applications. Developers of applications for parallel processing must choose between implementing their ideas in special-purpose or general-purpose hardware. The primary trade-off is performance gain versus flexibility in implementing applications. Special hardware usually yields higher performance for specific applications whereas general-purpose hardware can be programmed for a variety of applications. Both approaches have been pursued in the past by researchers in the VLSI design automation community.

1.7.1 Special-purpose Parallel Processing for CAD

In spite of the trade-offs and difficulties, many different special purpose CAD engines have been proposed [5]. Special-purpose hardware accelerators achieve significant performance improvements, and the speedup techniques they use fall into similar categories:

- Removing extemporaneous software processes

- Using a faster processor

- Customizing a processor for a specific task

- Matching intra processor communication with the algorithm

- Partitioning the problem data into separate processors

• Matching inter processor communication to the problem data

Logic simulation has been implemented on special parallel processors with limited instruction sets tailored for simulation. The IBM Yorktown Simulation Engine YSE™ used a cross-point switch to communicate between processors [22]. The NEC Hardware Logic Simulator™ used a multi-stage network to support communication between processors [28]. The ZYCAD Logic Evaluator LE-series™ machines used a common bus and a control processor to monitor communication between processors [8]. A number of special purpose machines have been proposed for routing. The Distributed Array Processor DAP™ had an array of 64×64 one-bit processing elements connected in an orthogonal mesh [11]. The IBM Wire Routing Machine™ had an 8×8 MIMD array of processors used for global routing [21]. Several special-purpose machines have been proposed for performing design-rule checks on mask layout. The Cytocomputer originally developed for image processing has been used for the design-rule checking and routing problems using Boolean transformations between layers [27].

Similar special purpose parallel machines have been proposed for a variety of VLSI CAD applications. More recently, the MARS™ hardware accelerator has been proposed for a wide range of VLSI CAD applications[1]. We will discuss the details of some of those architectures for specific applications in Chapters 3 through 9.

1.7.2 General-purpose Parallel Processing for CAD

Even though a special-purpose hardware engine can give a large performance improvement, its usefulness is limited in that it is not very cost effective. If we have to propose a new architecture for every new algorithm or application, it is quite conceivable that the problem definition will be changed by the time an appropriate engine is fully implemented. Recently, researchers have therefore started to investigate parallel algorithms for various CAD applications on commercially available general-purpose multiprocessors [3, 9].

Parallel processing has become affordable and available recently owing to the availability of low-cost, high-performance microprocessors and memories. With respect to VLSI CAD applications, the parallel processing options that exist are as follows:

1. *Use of network of workstations.* Almost every CAD organization has some form of networked environment of workstations, not all of which are completely used all the time. This is perhaps the least costly approach to the use of parallel processing.

2. *Use of shared memory MIMD multiprocessors.* A number of medium-priced bus-based shared memory multiprocessors are available commercially today. The programming of these machines can be easily done by parallelizing sequential programs

either manually or by parallelizing compilers. Shared memory multiprocessor-based workstations have been introduced as well.

3. *Use of distributed memory MIMD multiprocessors.* A number of medium-priced distributed memory multiprocessors are commercially available today based on the hypercube and mesh topology. The advantage of these architectures is that they are more scalable to large number of processors than shared memory multiprocessors. However, the programming of these distributed memory machines using a message-passing style is quite difficult.

4. *Use of SIMD parallel processors.* Finally, a number of massively parallel SIMD processors are commercially available today.

It is clear from this list that there are a lot of choices with respect to the use of parallel processing for VLSI CAD applications. The remaining chapters of the book will describe the different approaches for various CAD applications.

1.8 SUMMARY

Many tasks in VLSI CAD from synthesis, to simulation, to verification, take large amounts of computation time, sometimes days or weeks to run one application for large VLSI chip designs. To reduce the time-to-market for future chip designs, it is imperative to look at ways to reduce the runtime for each CAD application. Even though the computing platforms (workstations) for VLSI designers are getting faster and faster, the chips that the designers are attempting to design are growing at a much faster rate. Special-purpose hardware accelerators have been proposed in the past to speed up various tasks in VLSI CAD. However, this approach is not always cost effective because of the tremendous time and resources required to implement such machines which soon become outdated owing to changing technologies.

General-purpose parallel processing can offer the large speed improvements that are needed in the computing platforms of VLSI designers of the future. A point in favor of general-purpose multiprocessors over special purpose hardware accelerators is that the former can offer tremendous speed improvements and are at the same time extremely cost effective; since they are general purpose, they can be reprogrammed as newer sequential algorithms and objective functions are discovered in various VLSI CAD applications.

In the remainder of the book, we will discuss parallel algorithms for VLSI CAD applications at the logic, circuit and physical level of VLSI design. The domain of behavioral synthesis at the functional level is still in its infancy even for serial algorithms, hence not much work has been done on parallel algorithms yet. We will therefore not describe any parallel CAD algorithms at the functional level in this book.

For each CAD application, often there is more than one approach to solve the problem. For each approach, we will first discuss the sequential algorithm, and then the corresponding parallel algorithm. Where applicable, we will discuss specific parallel algorithms for shared memory and distributed memory MIMD multiprocessors, and finally SIMD multiprocessors. Also we will briefly review the hardware accelerators, if any, in each of those areas.

1.9 PROBLEMS

1.1   Distinguish between data and functional parallelism. Give examples of each on a simple program.

1.2   Distinguish between fine-grain and coarse-grain parallelism. Give examples of each on a simple program.

1.3   Distinguish between shared memory and message passing parallel programming. Give examples of commercial parallel machines that support each type of programming model.

1.4   Write a parallel algorithm for multiplying two $n \times n$ matrices on p processors, $C = A \cdot B$ on a distributed memory message passing multiprocessor. Assume n/p rows of matrix A and all rows of matrix B are distributed among all processors. Analyze the algorithm, determine the speedup expression in terms of n and p, and compute the input/output times.

1.5   What are the different levels of design in a VLSI design hierarchy? What is the input and output at each level?

1.6   Give some examples of CAD applications at each level in a VLSI design.

1.7   Assuming that the runtime of a cell placement program grows linearly with the size of a circuit, estimate the runtime of the Timberwolf cell placement program [29] on a circuit with 100,000 cells on a SUN/4 workstation. Refer to Table 1.1. How many processors would be needed to run the same problem in 4 hours, assuming a parallelization efficiency of 40%? Assume each processor of parallel processor to be the same speed as a SUN/4.

1.8   Assuming that the runtime of a logic synthesis program grows with the square of the size of a circuit, estimate the runtime of the MIS synthesis program program [7] on a circuit with 50,000 literals on a SUN/4 workstation. Refer to Table 1.1. How many processors would be needed to run the same problem in 3 hours, assuming an Amdahl's fraction of parallelization of 10%? Assume each processor of the parallel processor to be the same speed as a SUN/4.

1.9   You are given a problem with takes 1000 seconds to run serially. You develop a parallel version of the program to run on 10 processors. The times for running each of the 10 parts are 90, 100, 110, 45, 60, 220, 75, 50, 100, and 150 seconds, respectively. Assume that the synchronization overhead in the parallelization is 5 seconds. What is the expected speedup? Assume that the synchronization cost becomes 50 seconds. What is the speedup?

1.10 REFERENCES

[1]   P. Agrawal, W. J. Dally, W. C. Fischer, H. V. Jagdish, A. S. Krishnakumar, and R. Tutundjian. MARS: A Multiprocessor-based Programmable Accelerator. *IEEE Design Test Computers*, 4(5):28–36, Oct. 1987.

[2]   G. Almasi and A. Gottlieb. *Highly Parallel Computing*. Benjamin Cummings Press, Redwood City, CA, 1989.

[3]   P. Banerjee. The Use of Parallel Processing for VLSI CAD Applications: A Tutorial. Technical Report UILU-ENG-89-2215, CSG-104, University of Illinois Coordinated Science Lab, Urbana, IL, May 1989.

[4]   B. E. Bauer. *Practical Parallel Programming*. Academic Press, San Diego, CA, 1992.

[5]   T. Blank. A Survey of Hardware Accelerators Used in Computer-aided Design. *IEEE Design Test Computers*, 1(3):21–39, Aug. 1984.

[6]   S. Brawer. *Introduction to Parallel Programming*. Academic Press, San Diego, CA, 1989.

[7]   R. Brayton, R. Rudell, A. Sangiovanni-Vincentelli, and A. Wang. MIS: A Multiple-level Logic Optimization System. *IEEE Trans. Computer-aided Design Integrated Circuits Systems*, CAD-6(6):1062–1081, Nov. 1987.

[8]   ZYCAD Co. Zycad Logic Evaluator LE-1000 series –Product Description. Technical report, St. Paul, MN, 1987.

[9]   F. Darema and G. F. Pfister. Multipurpose Parallelism for VLSI CAD on the RP3. *IEEE Design Test Computers*, 4(5):19–27, Oct. 1987.

[10]   W. Fichtner and M. Morf. *VLSI CAD Tools and Applications*. Kluwer Academic Publishers, Norwell, MA, 1987.

[11]   P. M. Flanders, D. J. Hunt, and S. F. Reddaway. *High-speed Computer and Algorithm Organization*. Academic Press, New York, NY, 1977.

[12]   G. C. Fox, M. A. Johnson, G. A. Lyzenga, S. W. Otto, and J. K. Salmon. *Solving Problems on Concurrent Processors*. Prentice Hall, Englewood Cliffs, NJ, 1989.

[13]   G.M.Amdahl. Validity of the Single Processor Approach to Achieving Large Scale Computing Capabilities. *Proc. AFIPS Spring Joint Comp. Conf.*, 30:483–485, Apr. 1967.

[14]   J. L. Hennessy and D. A. Patterson. *Computer Architecture: A Quantitative Approach*. Morgan Kaufman Publishers, San Mateo, CA, 1990.

[15]   R. W. Hockney and C. R. Jesshope. *Parallel Computers*. Adam Hilger Ltd., Bristol, England, 1981.

[16]   K. Hwang and F. Briggs. *Computer Architecture and Parallel Processing*. McGraw-Hill Book Co., New York, NY, 1984.

[17]   J. Jaja. *An Introduction to Parallel Algorithms*. Addison-Wesley, Reading, MA, 1992.

[18]   F. T. Leighton. *Introduction to Parallel Algorithms and Architectures: Arrays, Trees, Hypercubes*. Morgan Kaufman Publishers, San Mateo, CA, 1992.

[19]   C. Mead and L. Conway. *Introduction to VLSI Systems*. Addison-Wesley, Reading, MA, 1980.

[20]   A. Mukherjee. *An Introduction to nMOS and CMOS VLSI Systems Design*. Prentice Hall, Englewoods Cliffs, NJ, 1986.

[21]   R. Nair, S. J. Hong, S. Liles, and R. Villani. Global Wiring on a Wire Routing Machine. *Proc. 19th Design Automation Conf.*, pages 224–231, June 1982.

[22]   G. Pfister. The Yorktown Simulation Engine: Introduction. *Proc. 19th Design Automation Conf.*, pages 51–54, June 1982.

[23]   C. D. Polychronopoulos. *Parallel Programming and Compilers*. Kluwer Academic Publishers, Norwell, MA, 1988.

[24]   B. Preas and M. Lorenzetti. *Physical Design Automation of VLSI Systems*. Benjamin-Cummings Publishing Co., Menlo Park, CA, 1988.

[25]   J. Reif, editor. *Synthesis of Parallel Algorithms*. Morgan Kaufmann Publishers, San Mateo, CA, 1993.

[26]   S. M. Rubin. *Computer Aids for VLSI Design*. Addison-Wesley, Reading, MA, 1987.

[27]   R. A. Rutenbar, T. N. Mudge, and D. E. Atkins. A Class of Cellular Architectures to Support Physical Design Automation. *IEEE Trans. Computer-aided Design Integrated Circuits Systems of Circuits and Systems*, CAD-3(4):264–278, Oct. 1984.

[28]   T. Sasaki. HAL: A Block Level Hardware Logic Simulator. *Proc. 20th Design Automation Conf.*, pages 150–156, June 1983.

[29]   C. Sechen and A. Sangiovanni-Vincentelli. The TimberWolf Placement and Routing Package. *J. Solid-State Circuits*, 20(2):510–522, 1985.

[30]   H. S. Stone. *High-Performance Computer Architecture*. Addison-Wesley, Reading, MA, 1990.

[31]   J. D. Ullman. *Computational Aspects of VLSI*. Computer Science Press, Rockville, MD, 1984.

[32]   N. Weste and K. Eshraghian. *Principles of CMOS VLSI Design: A Systems Perspective*. Addison-Wesley, Reading, MA, 1985.

[33]   M. J. Wolfe. Optimizing Compilers for Supercomputers. Technical Report CSRD-82-329, Center for Supercomputing Research and Development, University of Illinois, Urbana, IL, Oct. 1982.

CHAPTER 2

Parallel Architectures and Programming

2.1 INTRODUCTION

In Chapter 1, we provided an introduction to parallel computing and motivated how we may use it for solving VLSI CAD problems. In this chapter, we will go into more detail on parallel architectures and parallel programming. This detailed treatment will enable the reader to understand and implement the various parallel algorithms for VLSI CAD that will be described in the remaining chapters.

Parallel processing machines have been categorized [27] into two basic types: single-instruction stream, multiple-data stream (SIMD) machines and multiple-instruction stream, multiple-data stream (MIMD) machines. This is to be contrasted with the conventional sequential computers which are single-instruction stream, single-data stream (SISD) machines.

In an SIMD machine, multiple identical function units operate on different data elements in parallel, but they execute the *same* instruction at a given time. Instructions are executed in a synchronous manner on each functional unit at each instruction cycle.

In an MIMD machine, there are multiple computational units (CPUs), each of which can execute a different instruction on a different data item in parallel. Instructions need not be synchronized at each instruction cycle. Within MIMD machines, there are two subclasses, called shared memory MIMD multiprocessors and distributed memory MIMD multicomputers, depending on whether the processors in such MIMD systems see a logically shared address space or distinct address spaces.

In the following, we will discuss some of the general-purpose parallel machines of the

35

MIMD and SIMD class. Excellent introductions to all three forms of parallel computers can be found in [31, 32, 35]. In special-purpose machines such as image processors, signal processors, and systolic processors, the algorithms are coded into the hardware or in microcode.

In this chapter, we wish to consider only general-purpose parallel machines and look at the programming interface for high-level programs in the C programming language. We will briefly review the architectures and programming of all three types of general purpose parallel machines, the shared memory MIMD multiprocessors, the distributed memory MIMD multicomputers, and the SIMD parallel processors. All three types of parallel machines have been used by researchers in the parallel CAD area. Section 2.2 distinguishes parallel computers from vector computers, which have been used until recently as the traditional architecture of supercomputers. Section 2.3 provides an overview of shared memory MIMD parallel architectures and outlines the architectures of various commercial machines of this class. Section 2.4 discusses parallel programming using the shared memory MIMD paradigm. Distributed memory MIMD parallel architectures are discussed in Section 2.5, along with a brief discussion of various commercial offerings of this type. Section 2.6 introduces message-passing parallel programming for distributed memory MIMD machines. Section 2.7 provides an overview of SIMD parallel architectures and discusses some commercial machines of this type. Data parallel SIMD programming is described in Section 2.8. Section 2.9 shows three example applications, programmed in each of the three forms of parallel programming. Finally, Section 2.10 concludes with some general remarks about parallel architectures and programming.

2.2 PARALLEL AND VECTOR COMPUTERS

Supercomputers are defined to be the fastest and most powerful (in terms of processing and memory) computers available at any specific time. Conventionally, supercomputers such as the Cray machines have been based on *vector architectures*. In this section, we will review the basic concepts in such vector architectures and distinguish them from parallel computers. Excellent discussions on vector processors and their relation to parallel processors appear in [31, 34].

A *vector* is a set of scalar data items, all of the same type, stored in memory. Usually, the vector elements are stored in main memory in an ordered manner so as to have a fixed addressing increment between successive elements, called a *stride*. A vector processor is a collection of hardware resources that includes vector registers, functional pipelines, processing elements, and register counters for performing vector operations. Vector processing happens when arithmetic or logical operations are performed on vectors. Figure 2.1 shows a typical vector architecture.

We can define various types of vector instructions as follows. In a vector-vector instruction, one or two vector operands are fetched from the respective vector registers, enter a functional pipeline such as a floating point adder, and produce results for another vector register. In a vector-memory instruction, such as a vector load/store, elements of a vector are loaded/stored element by element from/to a memory to/from a vector register. In general, vector operations are faster than scalar operations. This is accomplished by matching the vector element access times with the execution times in each stage of a pipelined functional unit.

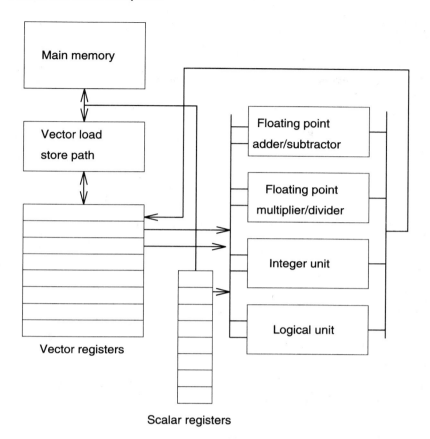

Figure 2.1 Organization of a vector supercomputer (Adapted from Hennessy and Patterson, *Computer Architecture: A Quantitative Approach*, 1990, Morgan Kaufmann Publishers, Inc)

Supercomputers deliver fast performance by making the clock frequency very high and the clock cycle very low; for example, the clock cycle in the Cray YMP™ is 4.2 nanoseconds (ns). This is achieved by using very aggressive circuit technology, such as bipolar devices, and advanced architectural designs such as deep pipelining and multiple functional units. Such high performance is achieved at the cost of very high power requirements, and such systems typically require massive air-conditioning systems to support them. Using such technology, supercomputers provide very high performance, for example, 1 GFLOPS on the Cray Y/MP.

Another way to achieve high performance is to connect a large number of relatively low cost microprocessors and memories, with relatively slow clocks, for example, 20 MHz, corresponding to 50-ns clock cycles. Such a processor would have a performance of 10 MFLOPS, assuming a floating point operation takes two cycles. By connecting 100 such processors together, it is possible to achieve the same computational power (1 GFLOPS) as a supercomputer. Let us assume that a conventional workstation using such a processor is equipped with 4 Mbytes of RAM memory. The cost of such a processor-memory board would be around $2000. The cost of 100 such boards consisting of off-the shelf microprocessors and memories would be $200,000, which is much less than that of a supercomputer costing several million dollars.

There are clearly some fallacies in our argument. First, the vector processor can provide a high throughput for even nonvector code; hence vector supercomputers can provide very high performance for all applications. It is not clear that all problems can be effectively parallelized to provide 100 times the speed of a single processor. Second, the cost of the network and system integration for the parallel processor has not be considered in the previous calculation. Often, these costs can be rather large. Finally, the cost of a system should include the hardware and software components. Parallel software (for example, operating systems, compilers, debuggers) is very expensive to develop. Despite these caveats, we can make a case for parallel processing as being a cost-effective alternative for supercomputing.

We can make another argument in favor of parallel processing. If we look at the trends in microprocessor design, it is clear that microprocessors are achieving scalar performance comparable to traditional supercomputers. The clock frequency of some of the modern RISC microprocessors is close to 150 to 200 MHz, for example, the DEC Alpha™ and the Intel Pentium™ chip. These microprocessors use multiple functional units and deep pipelining to generate performances close to supercomputers, for example, 150 to 200 MFLOPS on a single processor. In the past, the clock cycles of the supercomputers had been 100 times smaller that those of microprocessors, but that trend is disappearing. The clock cycles are becoming comparable in both microprocessors and vector processors. Given that trend, if we assume that the best performance we can achieve with today's technology using either superscalar RISC microprocessors or vector processors is 1 GFLOPS, the only way to achieve 1000 GFLOPS of performance is through parallel processing.

Recently, many computers have tried to combine the best of both worlds by providing parallel processing using vector processors. Examples of these products include the Alliant FX/80™ [14], the Cray C-90™ [37], and the Fujitsu VPP500™ [17]. These architectures will be discussed later.

2.3 SHARED MEMORY MIMD ARCHITECTURES

A shared memory MIMD machine shown in Figure 2.2 has a single global memory accessible to all processors. Each processor may have some local memory such as registers or cache, but the operating system presents the user with the image of totally shared memory. A key feature of a shared memory system is that the access time to a piece of data is independent of the processor making the request.

2.3.1 Physical Organization

Even though shared memory multiprocessors provide a logical view of a uniform shared single address space, the processors and memories are physically implemented in one of two ways, centralized or distributed. The two organizations are shown in Figure 2.3. An excellent survey of shared memory MIMD multiprocessors is given in [9].

In the centralized memory organization, the memory is centralized in a pool. The

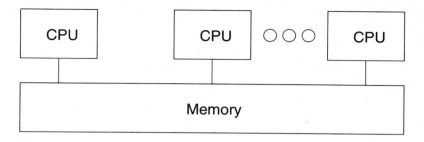

Figure 2.2 Logical organization of a shared memory system

processors are on one side of the switch or interconnection network, and the memory modules are on the other side. The interconnection network is typically a bus (for example, the Sequent Symmetry™ [40], the Encore Multimax™ [16], and the SUN SPARCcenter 2000™ [43]), or a crossbar (for example, Alliant FX/80™ [14], the Fujitsu VPP500™ [17], the Cray C-90™ [37]), or a multistage network (for example, the University of Illinois CEDAR machine [30]).

In the physically distributed memory organization, the processors and memories are physically located together at one node, and multiple nodes are connected together by a switch or interconnection network. Switches constitute a bottleneck on the overall performance and limit system size for every computer, thus the switch is the determinant of the computer's scalability. The BBN Butterfly™ and the TC2000™ [36] and the IBM RP3™ [49] machine uses a multistage network. A two-dimensional mesh is used in the Stanford University DASH multiprocessor [46]. A three-dimensional mesh is used in the CRAY T3D™ [38]. The Kendall Squares KSR-1™ machines use a hierarchical ring-of-rings topology [39]. The networks such as the two-dimensional or three-dimensional meshes allow an arbitrarily large number of computers to be connected together; such multiprocessors are called scalable shared memory multiprocessors.

Some example topologies of interconnections in centralized shared memory MIMD multiprocessor systems are shown in Figure 2.4.

2.3.2 Cache Memory Organizations

The memory systems on shared memory multiprocessors are hierarchically organized. If every read or write request from any processor of a shared memory system has to go through an interconnection network to read or write a memory location, the performance of such a system would be extremely slow. Hence all shared memory systems use caches (faster memories) associated with each processor. Caches are used to keep a copy of a recently referenced block from main memory. In single processor systems, caches can effectively reduce the access time of memory references that are reused. The principle of cache operation is based on the observation that, due to the high temporal and spatial locality of program behavior of real programs, a data value that is referenced at some point in time is highly likely to be referenced again in the near future. Cache memories provide a processor with an access time nearly equal to that of the cache (which typically can support a memory request in one processor cycle, as opposed to main memory that can take about 10 cycles).

However, in multiprocessor systems, we have a problem with consistency among multi-

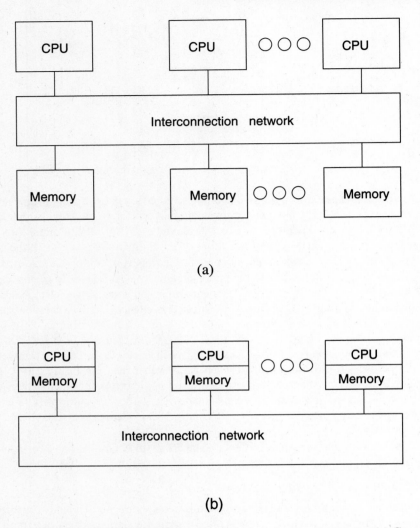

(a)

(b)

Figure 2.3 Physical organizations of a shared memory system. (a) Central-ized. (b) Distributed.

ple copies of a data element among different caches of different processors. A program running on multiple processors will often want to have copies of the same data in several caches. For example, Figure 2.5 shows three processors making read/write references in different time steps to a shared variable X. Assuming that the variable X in main memory stored the value $X = 10$, the first read request from $CPU1$ will read that value into its own cache. If no other processors were accessing X, then the next read request from $CPU1$ would return the value of X stored in its cache and hence reduce the memory reference request time. Since $CPU2$ has asserted a write request, storing the value 15, the next read request from $CPU1$ should

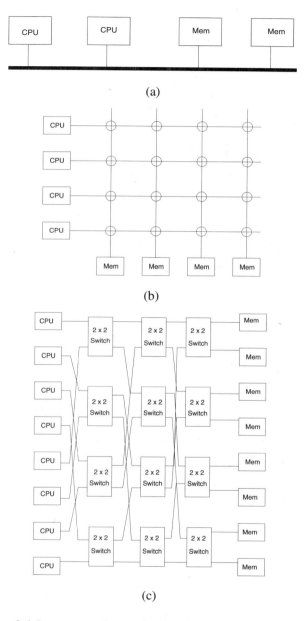

Figure 2.4 Some example topologies of interconnect in centralized shared memory MIMD systems. (a) Bus. (b) Crossbar. (c) Multistage network

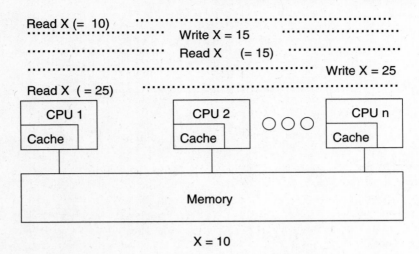

Figure 2.5 Problem of cache coherence

read this new value of $X = 15$ and not use the old stored value of X. Subsequently, $CPUn$ makes another write request, which sets $X = 25$; hence the new value of X that is read by $CPU1$ will be 25.

The protocols to maintain coherency for multiple processors are called cache-consistency protocols. The cache-consistency protocols distinguish different shared memory multiprocessors. There are two classes of protocols for maintaining cache consistency: (1) snooping bus protocols and (2) directory-based protocols. An excellent discussion of cache consistency protocols appears in [31].

In *snooping-bus-based schemes*, every cache that has a copy of the data from a block of physical memory also has a copy of the information about it. These caches are used on a shared memory bus, and all cache controllers monitor or snoop on the bus to determine whether or not they have a copy of the shared block.

The sequence of operations under a read request is as follows. When a processor makes a *read* request for a variable X, the cache controller checks the cache if the block containing that memory location is present in its cache and if it is valid (that is, its value is the latest copy in the system; no other writes have taken place in the copy in main memory by other processors). If it is present and valid, it constitutes a *hit*, and the variable is returned to the processor in one cycle. If the variable is not present or if the block is invalid or dirty (to be described later), it constitutes a *miss*. The cache controller has to read the variable from main memory, give it to the processor, and store it in the cache for future reuse. In the process, one block (for example, the least recently used block) will be replaced by the controller. For example, in Figure 2.5, after $CPU1$ performs the first read, the value of X is cached. However, when $CPU2$ subsequently writes a new value of X, the $CPU1$'s value of X is invalidated. Subsequently, when $CPU1$ performs a read on X, it finds that the entry of X in the cache is invalid; hence it reads X from main memory, which is the latest current value of X.

The protocols for a *write* reference are as follows. Several schemes are available. In a *write-through scheme*, when a processor writes to variable X, it is written to the cache and simultaneously also written to main memory. Such a scheme is good for cache consistency since the copy in main memory is the most recent copy of a write in any processor. Any processor trying to read the variable X can simply get the latest copy from main memory. However, since such a scheme only caches the reads and not the writes, it clearly reduces the main memory traffic only for the reads.

In a *write-back scheme*, a processor only writes to its cache and will write back to main memory when that cache gets replaced in the future. This scheme reduces memory traffic on the bus for both reads and writes, and is therefore commonly used. Now the problem is that multiple processors may be writing into the same variable X. In some schemes, only one processor is allowed to own a cache block; all others can keep a copy of it for a read. Under such a scheme, when a different processor requests a read of the cache block and finds that its local copy is invalid, it signals a read miss. Then all cache controllers snoop on the bus to check if they have a copy of the requested block and then supply the data to the cache that missed. Similarly, on a write, all caches check to see if they have a copy and then act accordingly, perhaps invalidating their copy or changing their copy to the new value. Such schemes are easy to implement in bus-based snooping systems, since each cache controller can monitor memory transactions on the bus and invalidate a local copy if it sees a write on the same block address. Such schemes require each cache block to be in several states: present-absent, valid-invalid, or owned-shared. Writeback schemes are of two types depending on what happens during a write: (1) write invalidate or (2) write broadcast or write update.

In a *write-invalidate scheme*, before the writing processor writes on that block, it invalidates all other copies of the block in other caches. The writing processor is now free to update it many times until another processor asks for it.

Another type of write-back protocol is called *write broadcast*. In such a scheme, rather than invalidate every block that is shared, the writing processor broadcasts the new data over the bus; all copies are then updated with the new value. This scheme continuously broadcasts writes to the shared data, while write invalidate deletes all other copies so that there is only one local copy for subsequent writes.

Since bus-based systems are not scalable to large numbers of processors, snooping protocols cannot be used in systems with more complex interconnection networks such as multistage networks or mesh networks, since cache controllers sitting on the processor end of the network cannot talk to each other directly. In *directory-based protocols*, there is logically a single directory that keeps the state of every block in main memory. Information in the directory can include which caches have copies of the block, whether it is dirty or not, and so on. Of course, directory entries can be distributed so that different requests can go to different memories, thereby reducing contention. However, they retain the characteristic that the status of a block is always in a single known location.

The Sequent Symmetry and the Encore Multimax use a write-invalidate based writeback snooping bus protocol [40], while the Stanford DASH multiprocessor and the Kendall Squares KSR-1™ machine use a directory based protocol [46].

2.3.3 Architecture of Commercial Machines

A number of shared memory multiprocessors are available today. Examples of research prototypes include the IBM RP3™ [49], the CEDAR machine at Illinois [30], and the Stanford DASH multiprocessor [46]. Examples of commercial machines include the Sequent Symmetry™ [40], the Encore Multimax™ [16], the Alliant FX/80™ [14], the BBN TC2000™ [36], the Kendall Squares KSR-1™ [39], the Cray C-90™ [37], and the Cray T3D™ [38]. Examples of shared memory multiprocessor-based workstations include the DEC Firefly™ [15], the Solbourne™ [42], the Xerox Dragon™ [22], the Silicon Graphics IRIS Challenger™ stations [41], and the SUN SPARCcenter 2000™ [43]. In this section we will provide brief discussions of some commercially available shared memory multiprocessors.

Sequent Symmetry The Sequent Symmetry™ Series is a bus-based shared memory multiprocessor system [40]. It can contain from two to thirty 32-bit microprocessors with a total performance of 100 MIPS. Each processor subsystem contains an Intel 80386/80387™ microprocessor/floating point unit, an optional Weitek 1167™ floating point accelerator, and a 64-Kbyte private cache. The system features a 53 Mbytes/sec bus, upto 240 Mbytes of main memory, and a diagnostic and console processor. Figure 2.6 shows the architecture of the Sequent Symmetry system.

The memory system on the Sequent Symmetry is hierarchically organized. The complete system has up to six memory controllers. Each memory controller interleaves memories as two memory banks so that each memory bank of 32 bits can be used to transfer data over a wide 64-bit bus. Each processor has a large 64-Kbyte cache, which stores the most frequently used data. The large cache size serves to increase the hit rates of the cache and thereby reduce the bus traffic on the shared system bus. The bus-based snooping cache coherency keeps consistency among the contents in main memory and copies of the data on cache. A write-back cache consistency protocol based on write-invalidate methods is used.

Encore Multimax The Encore Multimax 320™ system is a bus-based shared memory multiprocessor connecting up to 20 processors [16]. Each processor contains a National NS32332™ microprocessor, with the National NS32081™ floating point coprocessor. Each processor card contains two CPUs. The system has a maximum of ten processors cards. The peak performance of the machine is 40 MIPS (since each processor is rated at 2 MIPS). The shared memory cards are each 16 Mbytes. The system can have a maximum of eight memory cards (total 128 Mbytes), which are eight way interleaved. The bus connecting the processors and memories has a peak bandwidth of 60 Mbytes/s. A bus-based snooping cache coherency keeps consistency among the contents in main memory and copies of the data on cache.

Alliant FX/80 The Alliant FX/80™ is a crossbar-based shared memory vector multiprocessor consisting of a maximum of eight processors [14]. Each processor is a custom vector processor called an Advanced Computational Element (ACE), which supports the Motorola 68020™ instruction set with special vector and parallel instructions. Each ACE also contains a Weitek 1064/1065™ floating point accelerator. In addition, the system has 12 interactive processors. The system can have a maximum of 256 Mbytes of memory organized as eight memory modules of 32 Mbytes each. The system has a 512 Kbyte shared cache, shared among all the processors, and hence does not suffer from a cache consistency problem.

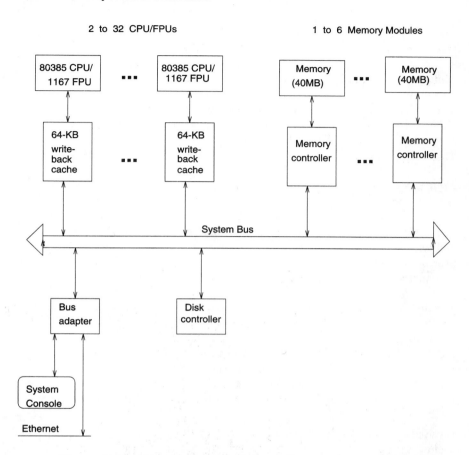

Figure 2.6 Architecture of the Sequent Symmetry system (Courtesy of Sequent Computer Systems, Inc.)

BBN TC2000 The BBN TC2000™ is a shared memory multiprocessor connecting 504 computing processors and eight I/O processors through a multistage network [36]. Each processor is a Motorola 88000™ RISC CPU, rated at 17 MIPS, and 20 MFLOPS. Each processor board has 16 Mbytes of memory, and 16 Kbytes of data cache, and 16 Kbytes of instruction cache. The network is a 512×512 multistage network built out of 8×8 crossbar switches.

Cray C-90 The Cray C-90™ is a crossbar-based shared memory vector multiprocessor containing 16 processors [37]. Each processor is a Cray Y/MP vector processor. In each cycle, two vector pipes and two functional units can operate in parallel. The 64-way parallelism (16 processors, each four-way) coupled with a 4.2-ns clock cycle, leads to a peak performance of 16 GFLOPS. The system has 2 Gbytes of shared memory. The interconnection network for the system is a 16×16 crossbar, with a bandwidth of 13.6 Gbytes/s. Up to four such Cray C-90 systems can be used in a clustered configuration to form a 64-GFLOPS system.

Cray T3D The Cray T3D™ is Cray Corporation's first entry into the massively parallel processing market [38]. It connects up to 2048 Digital Alpha™ RISC processors (each rated at 150 MFLOPS), for a total system performance of 300 GFLOPS. The memory system is configured as a physically distributed, logically shared address space. Each processor can potentially address any memory location in the entire system, although references to local memory are considerably cheaper than remote references. The interconnection network is a three-dimensional toroidal mesh that operates at a 150 MHz clock matching the DEC Alpha chips. Latency hiding is provided by data prefetching, fast synchronization, and parallel I/O. The system uses a Mach-based microkernel operating system on each node.

Fujitsu VPP500 The VPP500™ is a parallel vector multiprocessor announced by Fujitsu Corporation [17]. The architecture can scale up to 222 processing elements, where each processing element is a vector processor rated at 1.6 GFLOPS. The peak system performance is 335 GFLOPS. The system uses a 224×224 crossbar switch to connect 222 processors and two control processors, and provides a 800 Mbytes/s bandwidth per processor. Each processing element has up to 256 Mbytes of memory, but can address any memory in the system logically. The entire system has 55 Gbytes of memory.

Kendall Squares KSR-1 The Kendall Squares KSR-1™ machine is a massively parallel machine connecting up to 1088 processors in a hierarchical ring-of-rings topology [39]. Each processor is a 64-bit superscalar processor, built out of a set of four custom chips. Each processor has 32 Mbytes of cache, and cache transfers are performed in terms of 128-byte subpages. The machine is configured in two levels, each of which is a ring. At the lowest level, 32 processors are connected together as a ring. Up to 34 such rings are connected together in a ring at the next level. Figure 2.7 shows the architecture of the KSR-1 Machine.

  The memory is physically distributed, but is logically shared. The memory organization is called an ALLCACHE™ architecture, which means that the entire shared memory appears cached in different processors of the system. A single 40-bit virtual address space exists across the entire machine. Cache consistency is maintained by a directory-based cache invalidation protocol. The directory maintains the status of each subpage in the system. When a processor makes a request to a data item, it gets a unique copy of writeable data and gets a copy of read-only data. An extremely fast search engine finds and copies the subpages using a slotted packetized rotating pipeline in the ring of rings network, whose bandwidth is 1 Gbyte/s.

2.4 SHARED MEMORY MIMD PROGRAMMING

Most shared memory MIMD multiprocessors supports two basic kinds of parallel programming: multiprogramming and multitasking. *Multiprogramming* allows the execution of multiple unrelated programs concurrently. *Multitasking* allows a single application to consist of multiple processes executing concurrently. An excellent introduction to shared memory parallel programming can be found in [8, 11]. Most users are familiar with multiprogramming since it is used in sequential computers as well.

  We will now describe multitasking. There are two basic methods to perform multitasking: data partitioning and function or task partitioning, as discussed in Chapter 1.

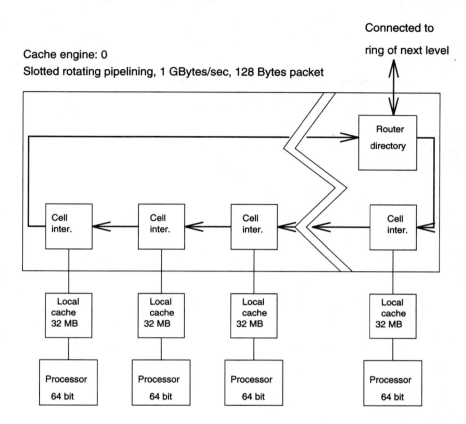

Cache engine: 0
Slotted rotating pipelining, 1 GBytes/sec, 128 Bytes packet

Figure 2.7 Architecture of the KSR-1 machine (Courtesy of Kendall Squares Research)

2.4.1 Example Shared Memory Parallel Programming Library

In the following we list the DYNIX parallel programming library on the Sequent multi-processor to illustrate a concrete example of how one would program a shared memory multiprocessor. Other shared memory multiprocessors provide similar parallel programming support.

m_fork:	Execute a subprogram in parallel
m_kill_procs():	Terminate child processes
m_set_procs():	Set number of child processes
m_get_myid():	Return process identification number
m_lock():	Lock a lock
m_unlock():	Unlock a lock
m_sync():	Check in at barrier
m_next():	Increment shared global counter

In a later section we will show how these calls can be used to write some parallel applications for shared memory multiprocessors. We will now explain some of the calls through their uses.

2.4.2 Process Creation and Termination

In the DYNIX™ operating system on the Sequent Symmetry multiprocessor, a new process is usually created using a system call named an *m_fork*. The new child process is a duplicate copy of the old parent process, with the same data, register contents, program counter, file ownership, and access rights to shared memory. A process identification number (process ID) is returned to each new process created. A forking operation is expensive (takes several milliseconds); hence a parallel application forks as many processes as it is likely to need at the beginning of the program and does not terminate any process until the program is complete. Processes are terminated by the *m-kill-procs()* primitive.

2.4.3 Shared and Private Data

Multitasking programs use both shared and private data. Shared data is accessible by both parent and child processes, private data is accessible only by the current process creating the private data. Program variables need to be explicitly tagged as shared or private. Again dynamic memory that is allocated can be shared or private.

Consider the following program declaration. The variables a and b will be shared, whereas c will be local to each process.

```
shared float a[100], b[100];
float c[100];
```

2.4.4 Synchronization

When two or more processes read and write the same data structure, it constitutes a data dependency since the results of the program depend on when a given process references the data structure.

Let us look at an example code that is being executed by two processors in parallel where *count* is a shared variable.

PROCESSOR 1	PROCESSOR 2
count = count + 1;	count = count - 1;

This statement will be compiled into the following pseudo machine code on the two processors.

PROCESSOR 1	PROCESSOR 2
LOAD R1, count	LOAD R2, count
ADD R1, 1	SUB R2, 1
STORE R1, count	STORE R2, count

If these sets of three machine instructions are executed in any order on two processors, the result of count can be either 6, 7, or 8 assuming that the value of *count* was 7 to begin with, and depending on when the different processors actually read the value of *count* into their registers. For example, the sequence P1-LOAD, P1-ADD, P1-STORE, P2-LOAD, P2-SUB, P2-STORE results in the variable *count* getting the value 7. On the other hand, the sequence P1-LOAD, P2-LOAD, P1-ADD, P1-SUB, P1-STORE, P2-STORE results in the variable *count* getting the value 6.

Code sections that contain dependencies are called *critical regions*. When it is necessary to ensure that processes execute the dependent critical sections one at a time or in a specific order, the communications are set up by *semaphores* and *locks*. A semaphore is a shared data structure used to synchronize the actions of multiple cooperating processes. The simplest form of a semaphore is a *lock*.

A *lock* ensures that only one process can access a shared data structure. A lock has two values: locked and unlocked. Before attempting to access a shared data structure, a process waits until the lock associated with the data structure is unlocked, indicating that no other process is accessing the data structure.

Suppose we have a lock variable called L; then each processor would update the shared variable *count* as follows.

```
PROCESSOR 1                    PROCESSOR 2
    m_lock(L);                     m_lock(L);
        count = count + 1;             count = count - 1;
    m_unlock(L);                   m_unlock(L);
```

The *m_lock( )* and *m_unlock( )* routines are defined as follows. The lock variable L is initially in state 0. The *m_lock( )* function will atomically in one operation try to read the value of L, and if the value is 0, acquire it, increment it to 1, and write the value back, *all in one indivisible operation under hardware support*. If the value of the lock variable is already 1 when it is being read, the process that called the *m_lock( )* function will block until the lock variable is reset to 0. The *m_unlock( )* function is defined as *an indivisible operation* that resets the value of the lock variable to 0. In this example, either PROCESSOR 1 or PROCESSOR 2 can acquire the lock at one time, getting exclusive access to the critical section where the value of count is changed, and then the lock is released.

We can think of this technique being used to access a shared data structure, not a simple variable such as *count*. Under the general model, a process locks the lock, accesses the data structure, and unlocks the lock. While a process is waiting for a lock to be unlocked, it spins in a tight loop - such a condition is called spinlock, or busy waiting. Figure 2.8 shows the example of a lock for guarding critical sections. The time spent in waiting for a lock accounts for the synchronization overhead mentioned in Section 1.6.

Other types of semaphores exist. Ordering semaphores ensure that order-dependent code segments are executed in the proper order. Counting semaphores are used in queue or buffer management by assigning a lock to the process that has waited longest for it.

An event is something that must happen before a process can proceed. Examples of events are completion of a task, arrival of needed data, and the like. Events have two values,

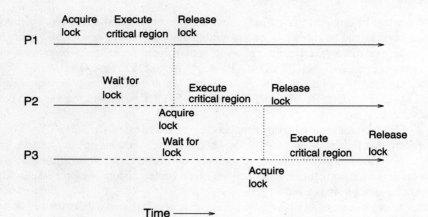

Figure 2.8 The use of a lock to guard critical sections

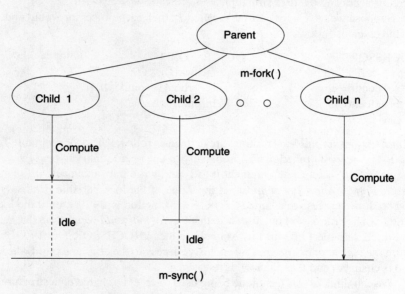

Figure 2.9 Forking and barrier synchronization

posted and cleared. One or more processes wait for an event until another process posts the event. The waiting processes then proceed.

A barrier is a synchronization point used to make sure that all processes executing a barrier call, arrive and wait at the synchronization point before proceeding. Figure 2.9 shows the illustration of forking and barrier synchronization.

Different shared memory multiprocessors provide a variety of synchronization mechanisms that are similar to those described previously.

2.4.5 Scheduling Algorithms

In the following example, each iteration of the *for* loop computes a particular value of the array element $a[i]$:

```
for (i=0; i < 100; i++) {
  a[i] = b[i] * c[i];
}
```

Since the elements of a[i] can be computed independently as discussed in Chapter 1, the iterations can be executed in parallel and constitute parallel tasks. As discussed earlier, the problem of assigning specific tasks to processors is called task scheduling. Recall that the parallel tasks can be scheduled among processes using four types of algorithms: (1) prescheduling, (2) static blocked scheduling, (3) static interleaved scheduling, and (4) dynamic scheduling. Let us apply the four types of scheduling algorithms on the example parallel *for* loop described here.

Prescheduling In prescheduled task scheduling, the task division is explicitly determined by the programmer before the program is compiled. Such a method cannot be varied for different sizes of data and numbers of processors; hence this approach is good for functional partitioning, that is, assigning specific tasks to specific processors. In this scheduling method, we assume that there will be a fixed number of processors (for example, three), and the tasks are allocated as follows. Let us now look at an actual code that will accomplish prescheduling. We assume that iterations 0 to 29 of our loop should be executed on processor 0, iterations 30 to 69 should be executed on processor 1, and iterations 70 to 99 should be executed on processor 2. Note that if, during runtime, we have actually more than three processors, those extra processors would remain idle in this code.

```
id = m_fork(3);
if (id == 0) {
  for (i=0; i < 30; i++) {
      a[i] = b[i] * c[i];
  }
}
if (id == 1) {
  for (i=30; i < 70; i++) {
      a[i] = b[i] * c[i];
  }
}
if (id == 2) {
  for (i=70; i < 100; i++) {
      a[i] = b[i] * c[i];
  }
```

```
}
```

Static blocked scheduling In static scheduling, the tasks are scheduled by the processors at runtime, but are divided in some predetermined way. For a loop having N iterations, using P processors, processor 1 will be assigned iterations $1..N/P$, processor 2 to $N/P+1..2N/P$, and so on. Such a scheme is called *static blocked scheduling* since contiguous blocks of iterations are allocated to each processor. In static scheduling, we would determine the number of processors at the runtime, and then perform a task scheduling statically. Our loop would be scheduled in the following manner. Assuming that there are 10 processors available at runtime, iterations 0 to 9 will be executed on processor 0, iterations 10 to 19 on processor 1, and so on.

```
nprocs = get_num_procs();
id = m_fork(nprocs);
lb = id * 100 / nprocs;
ub = (id +1) * 100 / nprocs;
for (i = lb; i < ub; i++)
    a[i] = b[i] * c[i];
```

Static interleaved scheduling In many cases, the work that is performed in each iteration of the loop varies (in some uniform way, either increasing or decreasing). In such cases it is often better to interleave the iterations statically among the processors for better load balancing. Specifically, assuming 10 processors, processor 0 executes the iterations 0, 10, 20, 30, ..., processor 1 executes iterations 1, 11, 21, 31, ..., and processor 9 executes iterations 9, 19, 29, 39, ... Such a scheme is called *static interleaved scheduling*. The actual code for our example loop using static interleaved scheduling would be as follows:

```
nprocs = get_num_procs();
id = m_fork(nprocs);
for (i = id; i < 100; i= i+nprocs);
    a[i] = b[i] * c[i];
}
```

Dynamic scheduling Finally, in many cases it may be difficult to predict the amount of execution time for each iteration. For these situations, we resort to *dynamic scheduling*. In dynamic scheduling, each process schedules its task at runtime by checking a shared task queue from which the next available tasks are removed and new tasks are entered. For our example loop, we assume that there is a shared variable $global\_i$, representing the iteration of the loop (task) that needs to be executed next. The value of $global\_i$ is accessed under mutual exclusion using locks, and the value is read, incremented, and then unlocked. The actual code for the above example using dynamic scheduling would look like this:

```
nprocs = get_num_procs();
id = m_fork(nprocs);
/* shared counter representing next iteration */
global_i = 0;

while (i < 100) {
   m_lock();
   i = global_i;
   global_i = global_i + 1;
   m_unlock();
   if (i <= 100)
      a[i] = b[i] * c[i];
}
```

We have given a brief description of how simple loop-level parallelism is exploited in shared memory MIMD multiprocessors. Other ways of exploiting parallelism that we will use in some parallel CAD algorithms will involve the creation of a shared task queue from which processors will remove and add tasks using locks as the synchronization primitive.

2.5 DISTRIBUTED MEMORY MIMD ARCHITECTURES

Contrasted with a shared memory MIMD multiprocessor system, in which we have a single globally addressable memory that is shared and accessible to all processors, a distributed memory message-passing MIMD multicomputer system is configured so that each processor has its own local memory and address space. The only way for a parallel application to share data among processors is for the programmer to explicitly program commands to move data from one node (processor-memory pair) to another using message passing [45]. An excellent introduction to message-passing multicomputers can be found in [4, 50, 51].

The time it takes for a processor to access data depends on its distance from the processor that currently has the data in its local memory. Figure 2.10 shows a fully interconnected distributed memory message-passing multicomputer in which each processor has a direct connection to every other processor.

2.5.1 Distributed Memory Organizations

A fully connected scheme for distributed memory multicomputers as shown in Figure 2.10 is clearly impractical since we need to have $N(N - 1)$ connections for an N processor system, and each processor needs to have $N - 1$ ports to connect to other processors. Therefore, designers are forced to choose less dense wirings.

Figure 2.11 shows some example topologies of interconnect for distributed memory systems. They consist of the linear array, the ring, the two-dimensional and three-dimensional meshes, the two- and three-dimensional tori, the hypercube, the tree, and others.

The simplest approach is to connect the processors in a ring, as shown in Figure 2.11(c), with each processor connected to its two nearest neighbors. In such a machine, if there are

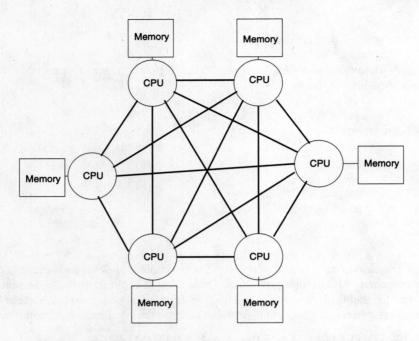

Figure 2.10 Architecture of a distributed memory fully interconnected system

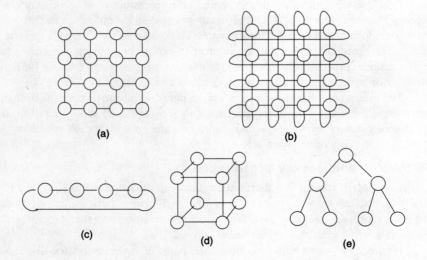

Figure 2.11 Example topologies of interconnect in distributed memory systems. (a) Two-dimensional mesh. (b) Two-dimensional torus. (c) Ring. (d) Three-dimensional hypercube. (e) Binary Tree.

N processors, it takes worst-case time proportional to N to send data from one processor to another.

An interconnection with a denser wiring is a mesh in which the processors are connected as a two-dimensional grid, as shown in Figure 2.11(a), Each processor is connected to its north, south, east and west neighbors. If there are N processors in the machine, it takes time proportional to $2\sqrt{N}$ to send data between any two processors.

A torus is similar to a mesh topology except that it has wraparound connections across the boundary processors, so each processor looks homogeneous, that is, connected to four neighbors, as shown in Figure 2.11(b). The advantage is that the maximum distance between any two processors for an N processor system becomes $\sqrt{N}$ for the torus instead of $2\sqrt{N}$ for the mesh.

We may generalize the above discussion of two-dimensional meshes to meshes of higher dimension. For example, a three-dimensional mesh will have each processor connected to its north, south, east, west, top, and bottom neighbors. We can then visualize a three-dimensional toroidal mesh, where the boundary processors have wrap-around connections.

An even denser wiring is provided by the hypercube topology, shown in Figure 2.11(d). Each processor is assigned an address $0 \leq N \leq 2^d - 1$, where d is called the dimension of the hypercube. Two processors are connected through a port if their addresses differ only in the corresponding bit in the address. The advantage of this configuration is that the largest distance between processors is proportional to $\log(N)$.

Another popular connection network is that of a binary tree where each processor is connected to one parent and two children, as shown in Figure 2.11(e). In this architecture, for N processors, the maximum distance between any two processors is proportional to $2\log(N)$.

Recently, the Fat-tree network has been used in the Connection Machine CM-5™, which is a variant of the tree network. All the processing nodes of a parallel machine are kept at the leaves of a binary tree. The intermediate nodes of the tree are used as switches. The interesting point of this design is that the channel bandwidth of the Fat tree increases as we ascend from leaves to the root.

The particular choice of network has a significant influence in the algorithms to be run on the machine. An algorithm designed for one machine with a certain topology can perform badly on a machine with a different topology.

2.5.2 Architecture of Commercial Machines

A number of distributed memory multicomputers are available today. Research prototypes include the MARK-I/II/III series of hypercubes built at the Jet Propulsion Laboratory [48] and the WARP system built at Carnegie-Mellon University [3]. Commercial products include the Intel iPSC™ hypercube [12, 13], the Intel Paragon™ [24], the NCUBE™ hypercube [19], the Ametek Symult 2010™ [25], the Thinking Machines CM-5™ [21], and the INMOS™ transputers [47]. We will discuss some commercial distributed memory multiprocessors in this section.

Intel iPSC/860 hypercube The Intel iPSC/860™ is a distributed memory multicomputer consisting of 16 to 128 processors connected in a hypercube topology [13]. Each hypercube node contains a 40 MHz Intel i860™ CPU (rated at 40 MFLOPS), with 8 to 64 Mbytes of memory. The total peak computing capacity of the machine with 128 processors is 5.1 GFLOPS.

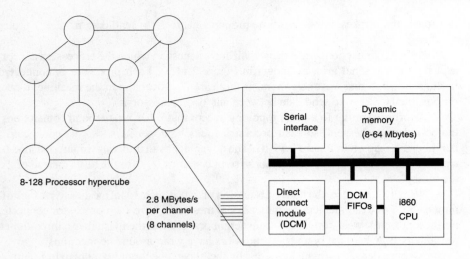

Figure 2.12 Architecture of the Intel iPSC/860 system (Courtesy of Intel Corporation)

Message routing is managed via a direct-connect module, which supports a form of circuit switched message routing in hardware at a rate of 2.8 Mbytes/s on all of 8 channels. When a node sends a message to another node, it goes directly to the receiving node without disturbing intermediate nodes. This provides to the user a view of an ensemble of fully connected nodes with almost uniform message latencies. It is possible to add a vector coprocessor to each node. Also, the system comes with an optional concurrent I/O and file system support. The hypercube system is managed by a host system, which is also an Intel i860-based processor. Figure 2.12 shows the architecture of the Intel iPSC/860 system.

NCUBE/10 The NCUBE/10™ is a 1024 processor hypercube based multicomputer [19]. Each processor is a custom processor with the routing hardware built into the chip. Each node in the machine runs the VERTEX™ microkernel. The nodes are controlled by a host computer that runs UNIX™. The network is a 10-dimensional hypercube, where each link in the hypercube is a bit-serial link.

Intel Paragon The Intel Paragon™ is a distributed memory message-passing MIMD multi-computer, which consists of 1024 processors connected as a two-dimensional toroidal mesh [24]. Each node in the mesh has up to four application processors and one message processor. Each processor is a 50 MHz Intel i860 XP™ processor, rated at 75 MFLOPS. The total system performance is rated at 300 GFLOPS of 64-bit floating point computations. Each processor has between 16 and 128 Mbytes of memory, but sees a separate virtual address space and runs the OSF/1 operating system. The total system memory is 128 Gbytes. Different processors communicate via message passing using the same iPSC send and receive calls as the Intel iPSC hypercubes. The network is a two-dimensional toroidal mesh with a total bandwidth of 500 Gbytes/s, and uses a fast mesh routing chip (MRC) at each node of the mesh to accomplish the routing. Figure 2.13 shows the architecture of the Intel Paragon system.

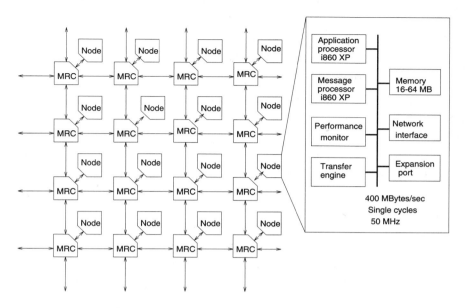

Figure 2.13 Architecture of the Intel Paragon system (Courtesy of Intel Corporation)

Thinking Machines CM-5   The CM-5™ multicomputer from Thinking Machines Corporation is a distributed memory message-passing multicomputer connecting 1024 processors in the form of a Fat tree [21]. Each processor node is a SUN SPARC™ RISC CPU, rated at 22 MIPS, and has four custom vector processors and 32 Mbytes of memory. Each vector unit has 32 MFLOPS of peak floating point performance and 32 MOPS of integer performance. The 32 Mbytes of memory is interleaved into four banks of 8 Mbytes each. Each vector units has a dedicated 72-bit path to its associated memory bank, and provides a peak memory bandwidth of 128 Mbytes/s per vector unit. The vector units execute vector instructions issued to them by the RISC microprocessor, which takes care of housekeeping computations such as address calculation and loop control. Together, the vector units provide 512-Mbytes/s bandwidth and 128 MFLOPS performance per node of the machines. Together, the 1024 nodes in the CM5 can deliver a peak performance of 128 GFLOPS. Figure 2.14 shows the architecture of the Thinking Machines CM5 system.

There is a separate data and control network in the system, both organized as Fat trees. The data network is used for passing messages, and the control network is used for synchronization. The interesting part of this machine design is that the machine can be operated in an SIMD mode or in a distributed memory MIMD mode. In the SIMD mode, instructions are broadcast from a host computer through the control network to all the processors in lock step, which perform operations in SIMD mode on its data elements. The MIMD mode is the more traditional message-passing form of operation.

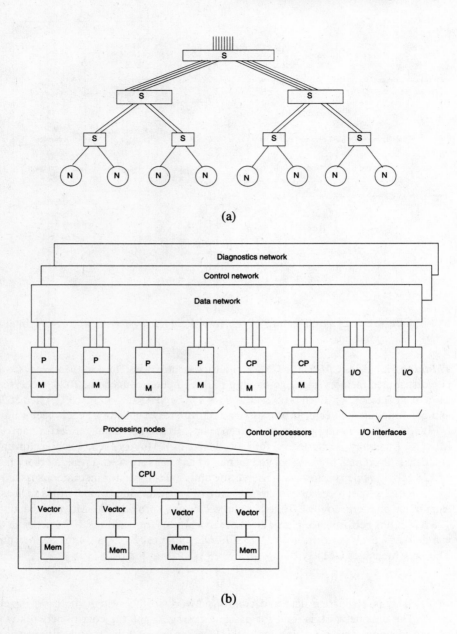

(a)

(b)

Figure 2.14 Architecture of the Thinking Machines CM5 system. (a) Fat tree topology. (b) Overall architecture. (Courtesy of Thinking Machines Corporation)

IBM SP-1 The IBM PowerParallel SP-1™ is a distributed memory message-passing multicomputer which connects up to 64 processors in the form of a multistage network [18]. Each processor is an IBM RS/6000™ RISC CPU rated at 128 MFLOPS, with 256 Mbytes of memory. The total system performance is rated at 8 GFLOPS, and the total system memory is 16 Gbytes. The system is configured out of four physical frames, each frame housing 16 processors. A high-performance multistage network consisting of three stages of 4 × 4 crossbar switches connects the 64 processors. Each processor has 256 Mbytes of physical memory but has virtual memory on each node. However, each node has a separate address space. The AIX™ operating system runs on each node. Different processors communicate via message passing.

2.6 DISTRIBUTED MEMORY MIMD PROGRAMMING

Distributed memory MIMD multicomputers consist of a set of processors each with its own local memory and address space and are programmed via message passing. A parallel program for a distributed memory multiprocessor consists of a separate host program and a separate node program. The host loads the node programs onto the nodes and distributes the data. The nodes execute applications in parallel and perform message passing for synchronization. The host collects the result data at the end. It is possible for multiple users to share a hypercube system by allocating different sized subcubes.

Programming distributed memory MIMD multiprocessors such as the Intel iPSC hypercube is more complicated than shared memory MIMD multiprocessors. There is no notion of shared variables. Shared variables have to be explicitly replicated on all the computing nodes. Processes running on these nodes execute their own node programs and communicate asynchronously via message passing.

Distributed memory multiprocessors also support multiprogramming and multitasking. Multiprogramming involves multiple users sharing various subcubes. Multitasking involves multiple processes on a subcube running an application in parallel. There are again two methods for multitasking: data partitioning and function partitioning.

Data partitioning involves distributing the data set of the problem among various processors in the system, each process loading the same program. Each processor executes the same program, using possibly different control paths within the program, and on its own data. The programs synchronize via message sends and receives. Such a programming style is termed single-program, multiple-data (SPMD) [45].

Function partitioning involves partitioning different functions of a given program among various processors, each processor getting a different function or set of functions. on the same set of data in a pipelined fashion. In this case, we can have different program parts mapped to different processors. Such a programming style is also called multiple-program, multiple-data (MPMD) [45].

Most message passing parallel programs are written using the SPMD style of programming.

2.6.1 Example Distributed Memory Parallel Programming Library

In the following, we will discuss the Intel iPSC/860™ parallel programming library as a concrete example of how we would program a distributed memory MIMD multicomputer

[12]. The programming support of the other distributed memory machines is similar. On the Intel iPSC hypercube system, the host operating system is System V UNIX™, which handles the compilation, loading, I/O and execution of programs. The node operating system is a node resident propriety system called NX™ that manages process scheduling, and message handling. The nodes do not support virtual memory. The application programs for the hypercube system can be written in Fortran, C, and CLISP with message-passing library routines. Here are some example interfaces to C programs.

csend():	Send a message and wait for completion
isend():	Send a message, do not wait for completion
crecv():	Receive message, wait for completion
irecv():	Receive message, do not wait
mynode():	Obtain node id of calling process
mypid():	Obtain process id of calling process
numnodes():	Obtain number of nodes assigned to program

In a later section we will show how these calls can be used to write some parallel applications for distributed memory multiprocessors. Excellent treatments of parallel algorithms an distributed memory MIMD multicomputers appear in [28, 29, 50].

2.6.2 Message Communication

Multiple processes in a distributed memory system communicate through explicit message passing. There is no notion of any shared resources. If there is a single variable that every processor needs to read, the programmer has to explicitly make a copy of that variable for every process. Again it is the programmer's responsibility to maintain consistency of the data through explicit message passing.

There is no notion of semaphores, locks, barriers, or shared variables. When processes communicate messages, the sender process executes a *send* call, and at the same time the receiver process on a different processor executes a *receive* call. There are two types of sends and receives, *synchronous* or *blocking* and *asynchronous* or *nonblocking*.

In synchronous calls, the calling process blocks until the send or receive procedure is completed. An example of a synchronous message sending call is

```
csend(TYPE, BUF, LEN, NODE, PID)
```

In this call, the various parameters denote the following:

TYPE is an integer that specifies the *type* of message we are is sending. Any nonnegative number is valid. This provides a mechanism for a sender and receiver of a particular message to communicate in an environment where messages can arrive in any arbitrary order due to unpredictable message delays through an interconnection network.

BUF is the buffer that contains the message to be sent. Any legal data type is allowed.

LEN is an integer that specifies the length of the message (in bytes) we wish to send.

NODE is an integer specifying the destination node.

PID is an integer specifying the destination process id.

The corresponding synchronous message receive call is

```
crecv(TYPE, BUF, LEN)
```

In this call, the various parameters mean the following:

TYPE is an integer that specifies the *type* of message we are waiting for. Any non-negative number is valid. Note that this has to match the type of the message sent by the *csend* call described earlier.

BUF is the buffer one specifies to store the message once it is received. Any legal data type is allowed.

LEN is an integer that specifies the length of the message (in bytes) we wish to receive.

In asynchronous sends and receives, the calling process does not block. The calls are similar in format but are called *isend()* and *irecv()*.

In the following we show a simple node program that sends some data (contents of the array *a* to array *b*) from processor 0 to processor 1 in a distributed memory multicomputer.

```
#define DATA 10
float a[100];
float b[100];

main()

{
   for(i=0; i < 100; i++) {
      b[i] = 0;
      a[i] = i;
   }

   if (mynode() == 0)
     csend(DATA, &a, 100, 1, 0);
   else if (mynode() == 1)
     crecv(DATA, &b, 100);

   /* here proc 1 has values of b equal to a */
}
```

2.6.3 Global versus Local Indexes

An important concept that we must learn about distributed memory programming is the difference between *global indexes* and *local indexes* in single-program, multiple-data (SPMD) programs on distributed memory MIMD multicomputers [45]. Distributed memory machines are programmed by explicitly *distributing the data* when created so that each processor only operates on its local data. For example, consider the following sequential program containing a simple loop defined over 100 iterations, on data elements that are each 100 elements long.

```
/* sequential program */

int a[100] b[100] c[100];

main()
{
   for(i=0; i < 100; i++)
     a[i] = b[i] * c[i];
}
```

If this were to be programmed on a distributed memory machine with four processors, each processor would have array elements of size 25, and they would each perform 25 iterations. The program would then look like the following. Note the sizes of the local array distributions.

```
/* dist. memory program on dist. data */

int a[25] b[25] c[25];

main()
{
   for(i=0; i < 25; i++)
     a[i] = b[i] * c[i];
}
```

Now, suppose the sequential program is slightly different, that is, the statement inside the loop accesses the element $b[i + 1]$ as well as $b[i]$.

```
/* modified sequential program */

int a[100] b[100] c[100];

main()
{
   for(i=0; i < 100; i++)
     a[i] = b[i+1] + b[i] * c[i];
}
```

The distributed memory program would then be written as follows. We assume that the processors are arranged as a linear array, 0, 1, 2, and 3. Then, by distributing the arrays a, b, and c among the four processors, each processor has all the values of a, b, and c except the value of b needed in the 24th iteration. For each processor p, the array element $b[25]$ that is required for the iteration number 24 needs to be obtained from the processor $p + 1$ (the next processor in the linear array). Hence note that the array declaration of b is extended by 1 to $b[26]$ instead of $b[25]$.

```
/* dist memory modified program on dist data */

int a[25] b[26] c[25];

main()
{
    id = mynode();
    csend(BTYPE,&b[0],4,id+1,0);
    crecv(BTYPE,&b[25],4);
    for(i=0; i < 25; i++)
        a[i] = b[i+1] + b[i] * c[i];
}
```

2.6.4 Scheduling Algorithms

In this section we will describe how we can schedule tasks for exploiting loop-level parallelism in message-passing parallel programs. In the example described next (which we had looked at earlier), each iteration of the loop computes a particular value of the array element $a[i]$.

```
for (i=0; i < 100; i++) {
    a[i] = b[i] * c[i];
}
```

Since the elements of $a[i]$ can be computed independently, the iterations can be executed in parallel and constitute parallel tasks. Again, the parallel tasks can be scheduled among processes using four types of algorithms: (1) prescheduling, (2) static blocked scheduling, (3) static interleaved scheduling, and (4) dynamic scheduling. Let us apply the four types of scheduling algorithms on the example loop just described.

It should be noted that in the actual parallel code generation for the our example sequential program, we assume that the data for the array variables $a[i]$, $b[i]$, $c[i]$ are initially present in processor 0, which acts as a central repository of data in the program, and the result of the loop execution will be stored again in processor 0.

Prescheduling In prescheduled task scheduling, we assume that there will be a fixed number of processors (for example, three), and the tasks are allocated as follows. Iterations 0 to 29 are executed on processor 0, iterations 30 to 69 are executed on processor 1, and iterations 70 to 100 are executed on processor 2. The important point to note here is that one of the processors (processor 0 in this case) is designated as the master processor which originally holds the data in the arrays a, b, c. It has to distribute the computations to the other server processors and has to send those processors, the necessary data. When those server processors are done with their computations, they will return the data computed back to the master processor. For example, when iterations 30 to 69 are assigned to processor 1, processor 0 has to send the data for array elements $b[30 - 69]$ and array elements $c[30 - 69]$ to processor 1, and will receive the array elements $a[30 - 69]$ from processor 1 after the latter processor is finished with the computations. Finally, note that the global to local index transformation is performed by the statement $btmp[j - 30] = b[i]$, which is executed before sending those data elements of the b array to processor 1.

```
id = mynode();
if (id == 0) {

   /* compute iterations 0
        to 29 itself */
   for (i=0; i < 30; i++) {
      a[i] = b[i] * c[i];
   }

   /* send data for iterations 30
        to 69 to node 1 */
   for (i=30; i < 70; i++) {
      btmp[j-30] = b[i];
      ctmp[j-30] = c[i];
   }
   csend(BTYPE, &btmp, 40*sizeof(int), 1, 0);
   csend(CTYPE, &ctmp, 40*sizeof(int), 1, 0);


   /* send data for iterations 30
        to 69 to node 1 */
   for (i=70; i < 100; i++) {
      btmp[i-70] = b[i];
      ctmp[i-70] = c[i];
   }
   csend(BTYPE, &btmp, 30*sizeof(int), 1, 0);
   csend(CTYPE, &ctmp, 30*sizeof(int), 1, 0);

   /* receives result for iterations 30
        to 69 from node 1 */
   crecv(ATYPEFROM1, &atmp1, 40*sizeof(int));
   for(i=30; i < 70; i++)
```

```
         a[i] = atmp1[i-30];

   /* receive result for iterations 70
           to 99 from node 2 */

   crecv(ATYPEFROM2, &atmp2, 30*sizeof(int));
   for(i=70; i < 100; i++)
      a[i] = atmp2[i-70];
   }


   if (id == 1) {
   /* node 1 receives data for iterations
           30-69 from node 0 */
      crecv(BTYPE, &b, 40 * sizeof(int));
      crecv(CTYPE, &c, 40 * sizeof(int));
      for(i=0;i <40; i++) {
         a[i] = b[i] * c[i];
      }
   /* node 1 sends result for iterations
           30-69 to node 0 */
      csend(ATYPEFROM1, &a, 40 * sizeof(int), 0, 0);
   }


   if (id == 2) {
   /* node 2 receives data for iterations
           70-99 from node 0 */
      crecv(BTYPE, &b, 30 * sizeof(int));
      crecv(CTYPE, &c, 30 * sizeof(int));
      for(i=0;i <30; i++) {
         a[i] = b[i] * c[i];
      }
   /* node 2 sends results for iterations
           70-99 to node 0 */
      csend(ATYPEFROM2, &a, 30 * sizeof(int), 0, 0);
   }
}
```

Static blocked scheduling We will now describe the parallelization of the same example loop using *static blocked scheduling*, where contiguous blocks of iterations are allocated to each processor.

```
for (i=0; i < 100; i++) {
  a[i] = b[i] * c[i];
}
```

In static blocked scheduling, we determine the number of processors at the runtime and then perform the task scheduling statically.

It should be noted again that in the actual parallel code generation for our example sequential program, we assume that the data for the array variables $a[i]$, $b[i]$, $c[i]$ are initially present in processor 0, which acts as a central repository of data in the program, and the result of the loop execution will be stored again in processor 0.

Our loop would be scheduled in the following manner. Assuming that there are 10 processors available at runtime, iterations 0 to 9 will be executed on processor 0, iterations 10 to 19 on processor 1, and so on. The important point to note again here is that one of the processors (processor 0 in this case) is designated as the master processor which originally holds the data in the arrays a, b, and c. It has to distribute the computations to the other server processors and has to send those processors the necessary data. When those server processors are done with their computations, they will return the data computed back to the master processor. For example, when iterations 10 to 19 are assigned to processor 1, processor 0 has to send the data for array elements $b[10 - 19]$ and array elements $c[10 - 19]$ to processor 1 and will receive the array elements $a[10 - 19]$ from processor 1 after the latter processor is finished with the computations.

```
id = mynode();
nprocs = numnodes();

if (id == 0) {

  /* compute iterations 0 to
        (100/nprocs) itself */
  for (i=0; 100/nprocs; i++) {
    a[i] = b[i] * c[i];
  }

  for (p=1; p <= nprocs; p++) {
  /* send iterations lb to ub
        to to node p */
    lb = p * 100 / nprocs;
    ub = (p +1) * 100 / nprocs;

    for (i=lb; i < ub; i++) {
        /* copy with global to local
            index transform */
        btmp[i-lb] = b[i];
```

```
            ctmp[i-lb] = c[i];
        }
        csend(BTYPE, &btmp,
            100/nprocs*sizeof(int), p, 0);
        csend(CTYPE, &ctmp,
            100/nprocs*sizeof(int), p, 0);
    }

    for (p=1; p <= nprocs; p++) {
     /* encode the sending processor's
            address in receive type */
        crecv(ATYPE+p, &atmp,
            100/nprocs*sizeof(int));

        /* compute lower and upper bounds
            of iterations */
        lb = p * 100 / nprocs;
        ub = (p+1) * 100 / nprocs;

        for(i=lb; i < ub; i++);
            a[i+lb] = atmp[i];
    }

    else {
        /* (id != 0) */

        crecv(BTYPE, &b,
            100/nprocs * sizeof(int));
        crecv(CTYPE, &c,
            100/nprocs * sizeof(int));
        for(i=0;i <100/nprocs; i++) {
            a[i] = b[i] * c[i];
        }

     /* encode the sending processor's
            address in send type */
        csend(ATYPE+id, &a,
            100/nprocs * sizeof(int), 0, 0);
    }
}
```

In the preceding code, note that the receiver processor addresses are used as part of the type of the message to explicitly specify a source-destination pair during the last phase of computation, that is, the collection of data from the result vector $c[]$ into processor 0. Specifically, the calls $csend(ATYPE+id,...)$ and $crecv(ATYPE+p,...)$ are synchronized with processor addresses in the code.

Static interleaved scheduling The preceding subsection illustrated the use of static blocked scheduling. In many cases, the work that is performed in each iteration of the loop varies (in some uniform way, either increasing or decreasing). In such cases it is often better to interleave the iterations statically among the processors for better load balancing. We will now describe the parallelization of the same example code using *static interleaved scheduling*, where iterations are allocated to each processor in an interleaved manner.

```
for (i=0; i < 100; i++) {
   a[i] = b[i] * c[i];
}
```

Specifically, assuming 10 processors, processor 0 executes the iterations 0, 10, 20, 30, ..., processor 1 executes iterations 1, 11, 21, 31, ..., and processor 9 executes iterations 9, 19, 29, 39, ... An example of static interleaved scheduling would be as follows.

It should be noted again that in the actual parallel code generation for our example sequential program we assume that the data for the array variables $a[i], b[i], c[i]$ are initially present in processor 0, which acts as a central repository of data in the program, and the result of the loop execution will be stored again in processor 0. Processor 0 has to distribute the computations to the other server processors and has to send those processors the necessary data. When those server processors are done with their computations, they will return the data computed back to the master processor. For example, when iterations 1, 11, 21, 31, ... are assigned to processor 1, processor 0 has to send the data for array elements $b[1], b[11], b[21]$, and $b[31]$ and array elements $c[1], c[11], c[21]$, and $c[31]$ to processor 1 and will receive the array elements $a[1], a[11], a[21]$, and $a[31]$ from processor 1 after the latter processor is finished with the computations.

```
id = mynode();
nprocs = numnodes();

if (id == 0) {

  /* compute iterations
       0,p,2p,... itself */

  for (i=0; i < 100; i=i+nprocs) {
     a[i] = b[i] * c[i];
  }
```

```
for (p=1; p <= nprocs; p++) {
 /* send iterations lb to ub
      to to node p */

   for (i=p; i < 100; i=i+nprocs) {
      /* perform global to local
          index transform */
      btmp[i / nprocs] = b[i];
      ctmp[i / nprocs] = c[i];
    }
    csend(BTYPE, &btmp,
        100/nprocs*sizeof(int), p, 0);
    csend(CTYPE, &ctmp,
        100/nprocs*sizeof(int), p, 0);
}

for (p=1; p <= nprocs; p++) {
   /* encode sending processor
      address in receive message type */
   crecv(ATYPE+p, &atmp,
       100/nprocs*sizeof(int));

   for(i=0; i < 100/nprocs; i++);
       /* perform local to global
           index transform */
       a[i*nprocs +p] = atmp[i];
}

else {
   /* (id != 0) */

   crecv(BTYPE, &b,
        100/nprocs * sizeof(int));
   crecv(CTYPE, &c,
        100/nprocs * sizeof(int));
   for(i=0;i <100/nprocs; i++) {
      a[i] = b[i] * c[i];
   }
   /* encode the sending processor address
       in sending message type */
   csend(ATYPE+id, &a,
        100/nprocs * sizeof(int), 0, 0);
}
}
```

Dynamic Scheduling Finally, in many cases it may be difficult to predict the amount of execution time for each iteration. For these situations, we resort to dynamic scheduling. We assume that there is a scheduler processor 0 that distributes work in multiples of *chunk* number of iterations to the other processors. It also controls the termination of the entire program, by informing other processors if there is work remaining in the system by sending a logical variable *thereiswork* to all processors.

It should be noted again that in the actual parallel code generation for our example sequential program we assume that the data for the array variables $a[i]$, $b[i]$, $c[i]$ are initially present in processor 0, which acts as a central repository of data in the program, and the result of the loop execution will be stored again in processor 0. Processor 0 has to distribute the computations to the other server processors and has to send those processors the necessary data. When those server processors are done with their computations they will return the data computed back to the master processor.

```
id = mynode();
nprocs = numnodes();

/* chunk number of iterations given
   to each processor each time a
   processor asks for work */

chunk = 10;

if (id == 0) {
  thereiswork = TRUE;
  global_i = 0;
  while (global_i < 100) {
      for (p=1; p <= nprocs; p++) {
      /* send iterations lb to ub
          to to node p */
        if (global_i > 100) {
          thereiswork = FALSE;
          for (p=1; p <= nprocs; p++)
             csend(TERMTYPE,&thereiswork,1,p,0);
          break;
        }

        /* node p requests for work */
        crecv(WREQ+p,&requestwork,1);

        lb = global_i;
        ub = global_i + chunk;
```

```
            global_i = global_i + chunk;
            for (i=lb; i < ub; i++) {
            /* perform global to local index transform */
                btmp[i-lb] = b[i];
                ctmp[i-lb] = c[i];
            }
            /* send work to processor p */
            csend(BTYPE, &btmp,
                chunk*sizeof(int), p, 0);
            csend(CTYPE, &ctmp,
                chunk * sizeof(int), p, 0);

            /* get result back from processor p */
            crecv(ATYPE+p, &atmp, chunk * sizeof(int));
            for(i=lb; i < ub; i++);
            /* perform local to global index transform */
                a[i+lb] = atmp[i];
        }
    }
}
else {
    /* (id != 0) */
    thereiswork = TRUE;
    while (thereiswork) {

        /* find from node 0 if
            there is work left */
        crecv(TERMTYPE,&thereiswork,1);

        if (thereiswork)
          /* receive work, perform work,
              and send result */
          crecv(BTYPE, &b,
              chunk * sizeof(int));
          crecv(CTYPE, &c,
              chunk * sizeof(int));
          for(i=0;i < chunk; i++) {
             a[i] = b[i] * c[i];
          csend(ATYPE+id, &a,
              chunk * sizeof(int), 0, 0);
          }
        else break;
    }
}
```

}

Discussion As can be seen, task scheduling in message-passing distributed memory MIMD multicomputers is quite complicated owing to the fact that each processor has a separate address space, and any data that are shared among processors have to be explicitly sent via messages among the processors.

We should note that in the preceding example, we assumed that the data for the array variables $a[i]$, $b[i]$, and $c[i]$ were present in processor 0, which acted as a central repository of data in the program. This was one of the main reasons for the complexity of the above code.

Distributed memory MIMD multicomputers are programmed, however, by explicitly *distributing the data* when created so that each processor only operates on its local data. For example, consider the following sequential program containing a simple loop defined over 100 iterations, on data elements that are each 100 elements long.

```
/* sequential program */

int a[100] b[100] c[100];

main()
{
    for(i=0; i < 100; i++)
      a[i] = b[i] * c[i];
}
```

If this were to be programmed on a distributed memory MIMD multicomputer with four processors, each processor would have array elements of size 25, and they would each perform 25 iterations that are statically allocated. The program would then look like the following, which does not look that complex.

```
/* distributed memory program on distributed data */

int a[25] b[25] c[25];

main()
{
    for(i=0; i < 25; i++)
      a[i] = b[i] * c[i];
}
```

In summary, programming distributed memory MIMD multiprocessors is more complex than for shared memory MIMD multiprocessors since we must worry about not only the parallel algorithm, but also how to distribute the code and how to explicitly distribute the data across processors in separate address spaces.

We finally note that even though it is possible to implement all four forms of scheduling of loop level parallelism, that is, (1) prescheduled, (2) static blocked, (3) static interleaved, and (4) dynamic scheduling, the cost of dynamic scheduling is rather expensive in distributed memory MIMD machines, hence good static scheduling methods are usually used.

2.7 SIMD PARALLEL ARCHITECTURES

Contrasted with MIMD parallel architectures, in the SIMD (single-instruction, multiple-data) model, all processors execute the same instruction at a given instant. Each processor operates on a different data element. Processors may *sit out* a sequence of instructions if the instruction sent to them does not apply to the data elements that they own.

In SIMD parallel architectures, a single control unit (CU) fetches and decodes instructions. Then the instruction is executed either in the CU itself (for example, a jump instruction) or it is broadcast to a collection of processing elements (PEs). These PEs operate synchronously, but their local memories have different contents. PEs communicate with their neighbors through a network. SIMD processors are typically organized as arrays of processing elements and are suited for problems involving vector processing and for grid problems. Figure 2.15 shows an example typical organization of an SIMD array processor. An excellent survey of SIMD machine architectures, hardware, software, and applications appears in [33].

2.7.1 Architecture of Commercial Machines

Research prototypes of SIMD processors include the ILLIAC-IV built at the University of Illinois [5], the STARAN™ [6], the Goodyear MPP™ [7], and the DAP system™ [26]. A number of SIMD array processors are available today. Commercial products include the Thinking Machines CM-2™ [20], the MasPar MP-1™ [23], and the Active Memory Technology DAP™ system. We will discuss some example SIMD multiprocessors in this section.

Thinking Machines CM-2 The CM-2™ Connection Machine from Thinking Machines Corporation is a massively parallel SIMD computing system consisting of 64K, 32K, or 16K data processors [20] (where K stands for 1024). Each data processor has 64 Kbits (8 Kbytes) of bit-addressable local memory, a bit-serial ALU that can operate on variable length operands, four 1-bit flag registers, a router interface, a NEWS grid interface, and an I/O interface. Each data processor can access memory at the rate of 5 Mbits/s. A fully configured CM-2 thus has 512 Mbytes of memory that can be read or written at the rate of 300 Gbits/s. When 64K data processors are operating in parallel, each performing a 32-bit addition, the CM-2 parallel processing unit operates at about 2500 MIPS. In addition to the standard ALU, the CM-2 unit allows for optional floating point accelerator chips that are shared among every group of 32 data processors, so the aggregate peak floating point performance of the CM-2 is 3500 MFLOPS.

The CM-2 system provides two forms of communication within the parallel processing unit. The more general mechanism is known as the router, which allows any processor to communicate with any other processor. We may think of the router as allowing every processor to send a message to any other processor, with all messages being sent and delivered at the same time. Alternatively, we may think of the router as allowing every processor to access

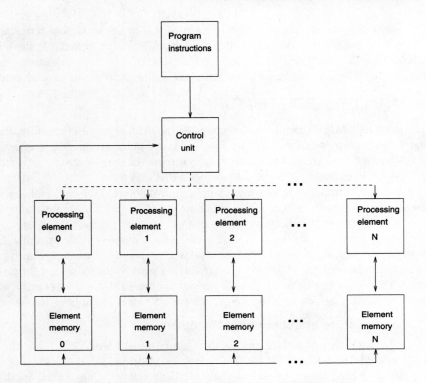

Figure 2.15 Typical organization of an SIMD parallel processor

any memory location within the parallel processing unit, with all processors making memory accesses at the same time.

The CM-2 system has a more structured somewhat faster communication mechanism called the NEWS grid that allows the communication to take place among processors configured into any size multidimensional grid. Possible grid configurations include 256×256, 1024×64, $64 \times 32 \times 32$, and $8 \times 8 \times 4 \times 8 \times 8 \times 8 \times 4$. The NEWS grid allows processors to pass data according to a regular rectangular pattern. For example, in a two dimensional grid, each processor can receive a data item from its neighbor to the east, thereby shifting the data items one position to the left.

The CM-2 system is designed to operate under the programmed control of a front end computer which may be a SUN/4™ workstation, a Symbolics 3600™ LISP machine, or a DEC VAX 8000™ series computer. The front end machines provide the program development and execution environment. All Connection Machine programs execute in the front end; during the course of the execution the front end issues instructions to the CM-2 parallel processing unit. The set of instructions that the front end may issue to the parallel processing unit is called Paris™.

The data processors do not execute Paris instructions directly. Instead, Paris instructions from the front end are processed by a sequencer in the parallel processing unit. The task of the

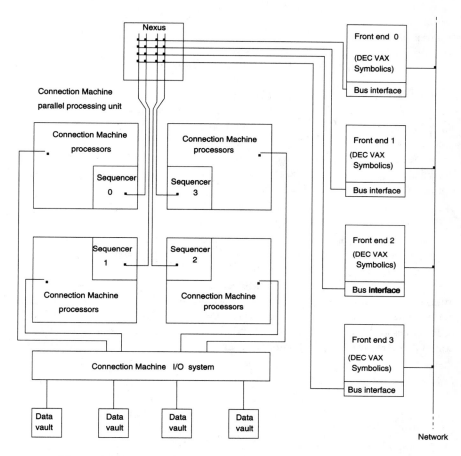

Figure 2.16 Architecture of the CM-2 Connection Machine (Courtesy of Thinking Machines Corporation)

sequencer is to break down each Paris instruction into a sequence of low-level data processor and memory operations. The sequencer broadcasts these low-level instructions to the data processors, which execute them at a rate of several million a second.

Figure 2.16 shows the architecture of the CM-2 Connection Machine.

MasPar MP-1 The MasPar MP-1 system from MasPar Computer Corporation is an SIMD parallel processor connecting from 1024 to 16,384 custom processors arranged as a two-dimensional array [23]. The array processor elements (PE) are controlled by an array control unit (ACU). which broadcasts all processing element (PE) instructions. A front end to the system is a UNIX-based subsystem. The communication mechanism within the PE array is provided by the X-router, which provides nearest-neighbor communication that is very efficient, and takes place in a few cycles. A separate network forms the global router that permits random processor-to-processor communication. Global routing is more complex and requires several tens of cycles. The instructions are broadcast to the processor elements by the array control unit through a common bus.

2.8 SIMD PARALLEL PROGRAMMING

The programming model for SIMD parallel processors uses fine-grain data parallelism. Conceptually, a processor is associated with each data element in a parallel program. At one time, the same instruction is executed by all active processors on different data processors' local data. SIMD parallel processors are programmed using array constructs such as those in Fortran 90 or C* to be described later.

In such a programming model, we assume that we have an unlimited set of virtual processors, whose number depends on the problem size. Each element of a distinct data structure, such as an array, gets mapped to a unique processor. All processors are programmed to execute the same instruction at one time. To program interesting applications, it is possible to mask some data processors to be active conditionally depending on a condition evaluated locally on a previous instruction. For example, suppose we plan to write a simple program to compute an element-by-element reciprocal of a large matrix. We would distribute the matrix, one element per processor. Then one instruction will check if the element within each processor is equal to zero or not and set a condition flag. A subsequent instruction will compute the reciprocal of only those elements that are nonzero. Hence, only those processors that are holding nonzero elements will be activated and executed this instruction. Other parallel applications are programmed in a similar manner.

Different SIMD parallel processors provide different extensions of conventional programming languages. For example, the Connection Machine CM-2 provides programming capability in LISP, C*™, CM-Fortran™, and Paris™The Fortran-90™ programming language allows users to specify array constructs, and SIMD-style data parallelism.

The C* programming on the Connection Machine is an extension of the C programming language, designed to support programming in a data parallel style. A programmer writes code as if a processor were associated with each data element. C* features a new data type and a synchronous execution model and relies on existing C operators applied to parallel data to express such notions as broadcasting, reduction, and interprocessor communication in both regular and irregular patterns.

C* assumes a synchronous model of computation in which all instructions are issued from a single source, a distinguished processor called the front end. All the other processors are data processors. At any time, the data processors are executing the instruction stream sent out from the front end are called the *active set*. The local memory of an idle processor does not change unless another processor writes it. The layout of the memory within each data processor is conventional. Except for the fact that no code is stored in the memory of the data processor, memory is laid out as for a C program in a conventional computer. One end holds statically allocated variables and the other end is the stack area. Processor memory layout can be described by a record structure.

2.8.1 Example SIMD Parallel Programming Library

In the following, we will discuss the CM-2 parallel programming library for the C* language to illustrate how we would program an SIMD parallel processor. The parallel programming support of other SIMD parallel machines is similar.

shape:	A way of logically configuring parallel data structure
with:	Statement to select a current shape
where:	Statement to select active processors
pcoord():	Function to provide regular communication in a grid
reduce():	Global function to perform reduction operation on parallel data
spread():	Spreads result of an operation into parallel variable

We will now explain the use of some of these statements for simple SIMD parallel programming.

2.8.2 Structuring Parallel Data

A set of statements of the following form creates three parallel arrays, a, b, c of size 100×100 floating point numbers each residing in a data processor. There are 10,000 data processors created, each storing one element of the matrices $a[\,]$, $b[\,]$ and $c[\,]$.

```
shape [100][100] s;
float:s a,b,c;
```

2.8.3 Parallel Functions

The statement

```
c = a + b;
```

means that each array element of c gets the sum of the corresponding elements of a and b on a data processor described above.

The statement

```
a = b + 2. * c
```

means that the scalar, 2, gets broadcast to each data processor, and each processor performs the element-wise computation of $a = b + 2 * c$.

A selection statement activates all instances of a specified domain and then executes a statement.

The statement

```
if (expression) statement1 else statement2
```

means that *statement1* is executed by those instances that were active whose test values were nonzero, and the *statement2* was executed by those instances whose test values were zero.

The *with* statement selects a current shape. In general, parallel variables must be of the current shape before parallel operations can take place in parallel. An example code is as follows:

```
shape [16384] t;
int t: p1, p2, p3;

with (t)
    p3 = p2 + p1;
```

The *where* statement restricts the sets of positions on which operations are to take place, called active.

```
with (t)
  where (p1 != 0)
    p3 = p2 / p1;
```

2.8.4 Parallel Communication

C* provides two methods of parallel communication: regular and irregular. In regular communication, C* uses an intrinsic function *pcoord* to provide a self index for a parallel variable along a specific axis of its shape. For example, the statement

```
p1 = pcoord(0);
```

will assign the value 0 to p1[0], the value 1 to p1[1] and so on.

The *pcoord*() function is used to provide regular communication. For example, the following code sends the values of the *source* to the the elements of *dest* that are one coordinate higher along axis 0.

```
[pcoord(0) + 1] dest = source;
```

For a two-dimensional shape, we could describe a transfer as follows, moving an element one position to the east and two positions to the south.

```
[pcoord(0) + 1] [pcoord(1) - 2] dest = source;
```

Irregular communication is achieved by a left indexing facility.

```
dest = [index] source
```

In this example, the different instances of the parallel variable *dest* get the values from different instances of *source*; the values of *index* specify which element of *source* is to go to which element of *dest*.

2.8.5 Parallel Operations

The *reduce* function is used to put the result of an operation into a single parallel variable element. The syntax of the call is as follows:

```
reduce(destp, source, axis, combiner, to_coord);
```

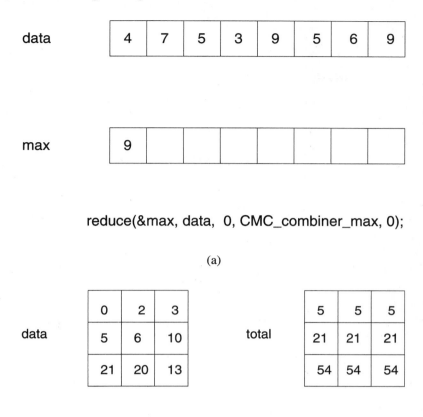

reduce(&max, data, 0, CMC_combiner_max, 0);

(a)

total = spread(data, 1, CMC_combiner_add);

(b)

Figure 2.17 Examples of parallel operations in an SIMD program. (a) Reduce operation. (b) Spread operation.

where *destp* is a scalar pointer to a parallel variable, *source* is a parallel variable whose values are to be used in the operation, *axis* specifies the axis along which the new scan class will be created, *combiner* specifies the operation that *reduce* is to carry out, and *to_coord* specifies the coordinate of the layout of the parallel variable pointed to by *destp* that is to receive the result of the operation. Examples of parallel operations are *CMC_combiner_max, CMC_combiner_min, CMC_combiner_add, CMC_combiner_add*, and *CMC_combiner_logicor*. An example of the reduce call is illustrated in Figure 2.17(a).

The *spread* function is used to place the result of an operation into all the elements of a specified parallel variable. The spread function call has the following syntax:

```
spread(source,axis,combiner);
```

where *source* is a parallel variable whose values are to be used in the operation, *axis* specifies the axis along which the scan class is to be created, and *combiner* refers to the type of operation to be performed, similar to the operations described above. An example of the spread call is illustrated in Figure 2.17(b).

2.9 EXAMPLE PARALLEL PROGRAMMING

In this section we will discuss three example applications: the computation of π, matrix-vector multiplication, and matrix-matrix multiplication. For each application, we will first show a sequential program in C, and then present a shared memory MIMD parallel implementation, a distributed memory message-passing MIMD parallel implementation, and an SIMD massively parallel implementation. The message passing implementations will be based on the single-program, multiple-data (SPMD) style of programming [45]. More details about different parallel algorithms can be found in [10, 28]. Other examples of parallel programming can be found in [8, 11, 44].

2.9.1 Example Application 1: Computation of Pi

In this subsection we will discuss one simple application: computing the value of π through numerical integration that was introduced in Chapter 1.

$$\pi = \int_0^1 \frac{4}{1 + x^2} \tag{2.1}$$

As described earlier, this integration can be evaluated by computing the area under the curve for $f(x) = \frac{4}{1 + x^2}$ from 0 to 1. With numerical integration using the rectangle rule for decomposition, one divides the region x from 0 to 1 into n points. The value of the function $f(x) = \frac{4}{1 + x^2}$ is evaluated at the midpoint of each interval, as shown in Figure 2.18. The values are summed up and multiplied by the width of one interval. The computation of π is illustrated in Figure 2.18.

The program listing for a sequential program is given next.

```
/*  serial pi program  */

float h,sum,x,pi;
int i,n;

main()

{
    printf("Enter the number of intervals\n");
    scanf("%d",&n);
   /* call procedure to compute pi */
    computepi(n);
```

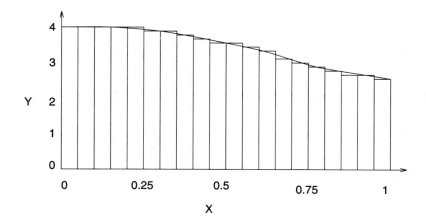

Figure 2.18 Computation of π through numerical integration

```
    printf("Value of pi is %f\n",pi);
}

computepi()

{

    h = 1.0 / n;
    sum = 0.0;
    for (i=0; i < n; i++) {
      x = h * (i - 0.5);
      sum = sum + 4.0 / (1 + x * x);
    }
    pi = h * sum;
}
```

Shared memory MIMD parallel implementation We now present a shared memory MIMD
parallel implementation of the pi computation. The algorithm uses a dynamic scheduling of
the i index loop to get the next value of i stored in the *global_i* variable, which is incremented
under locks. Each processor performs a local computation of π and stores it in the *localpi*
variable. Finally, the individual values of *localpi* are added up to the global value of π, named
the *pi* variable under locks.

```
/*  parallel pi program  */
```

```c
#include <stdio.h>
#include <parallel/microtask.h>
#include <parallel/parallel.h>

shared int n, global_i;
shared float h, pi;

main()

{
    int nprocs;
    void computepi();

    printf("Enter the number of intervals\n");
    scanf("%d",&n);
    printf("Enter the number of processors\n");
    scanf("%d",&nprocs);
    /* initialize global index, pi, h */
    global_i = 0;
    pi = 0;
    h = 1.0 / n;
    /* create nprocs parallel threads */
    m_set_procs(nprocs);

    /* compute pi in parallel */
    m_fork(computepi);

    /* wait for all threads to complete */
    m_sync();

    printf("Value of pi is %f\n",pi);
}

void computepi()

{
    int i;
    float sum, localpi, x;

    sum = 0.0;

    while (i < n) {

        m_lock();
```

```
        i = global_i;
        global_i = global_i + 1;
    m_unlock();

    x = h * (i - 0.5);
    sum = sum + 4.0 / (1 + x * x);
    }

    localpi = h * sum;
    m_lock();
        pi = pi + localpi;
    m_unlock();
}
```

Distributed memory MIMD parallel implementation We now present a distributed memory parallel implementation of the π computation. The algorithm uses a static blocked scheduling of the i index loop. Processor 0 is the control processor that reads the value of n, and informs all other processors through sending messages. Each processor then gets a contiguous block of n/p iterations and computes the value of *localpi* using numerical integration. Finally, each processor sends the local value of π, called *localpi*, to processor 0, which accumulates it in the variable *pi* and prints the value.

```
#include "header.h"
/*  parallel pi program  */

int n, i;
float h, localpi, pi;

main()

{
    int id,nnodes;
    void readn(),computepi(),addpi();

    nnodes = numnodes();
    id = mynode();

    /* read value of intervals */
    readn();

    /* compute pi in parallel */
    computepi();
```

```
      /* accumulate the local values of pi */
      addpi();

      if (id == 0)
        printf("Value of pi is %f\n",pi);
}

void readn()

{
      int id;

      id = mynode();
      if (id == 0) {

          /* input n */

          printf("Enter number of intervals\n");
          scanf("%d",&n);

          /* send value of n to all nodes */

          csend(NTYPE, &n, 4, -1, 0);
      }
      else {

          /* receive values of n from processor 0 */

          crecv(NTYPE, &n, 4);
      }

}

void computepi()

{
      int i,id,lb,ub,nnodes;
      float sum, x;

      id = mynode();
      nnodes = numnodes();

      h = 1.0 / n;
```

```
      sum = 0.0;


      /* each processor computes bounds
         of pi computations using
         static block scheduling */

      lb = id * n / nnodes;
      ub = (id + 1) * n / nnodes;

      for (i=lb; i < ub; i ++) {
        x = h * (i - 0.5);
        sum = sum + 4.0 / (1 + x * x);
      }

      localpi = sum * h;
}


void addpi()

{
      int id,nnodes,p;
      float tmp;

      id = mynode();
      nnodes = numnodes();


      if (id != 0) {

          /* send local pi to processor 0 */
          csend(PITYPE,&localpi,4,0,0);

      }
      else {

          /* processor 0 receives local
             pi data from each processor
             and adds them */

          pi = localpi;
          for (p = 1; p < nnodes; p++) {
             crecv(PITYPE,&tmp,4);
```

```
                  pi = pi + tmp;
            }
        }
    }
```

SIMD parallel implementation In this section we will show the implementation of the computation of PI on an SIMD machine. Note that a parallel variable type *s* is created as an array of 8K (8192) entries. Hence, 8192 data processors are created. Each data processor computes the value of the function $f(x)$ at the midpoint of the interval denoted by its element in the parallel variable. Finally, the *reduce* operation is called which accumulates the individual values of *height* into the variable *hsum* that is used to compute the value of *pi*.

```
#include <stdio.h>
#include <cscomm.h>
#define n 8192

#define ADD CMC_combiner_add

double pi;

/* set up a linear array of size 8192 */
shape [n] s;

double:s height, h, x, hsum;
int:s mpoint;

main()

{
    /* compute interval size */
    h = 1.0 / n;

  /* an intrinsic function providing
      the  self address of each processor */
    mpoint = pcoord(0);

    x = h * (mpoint - 0.5);
    height = 4.0 / (1.0 + x * x);

    /* syntax:
    reduce(dest, src, dim, combine, dest_index) */
```

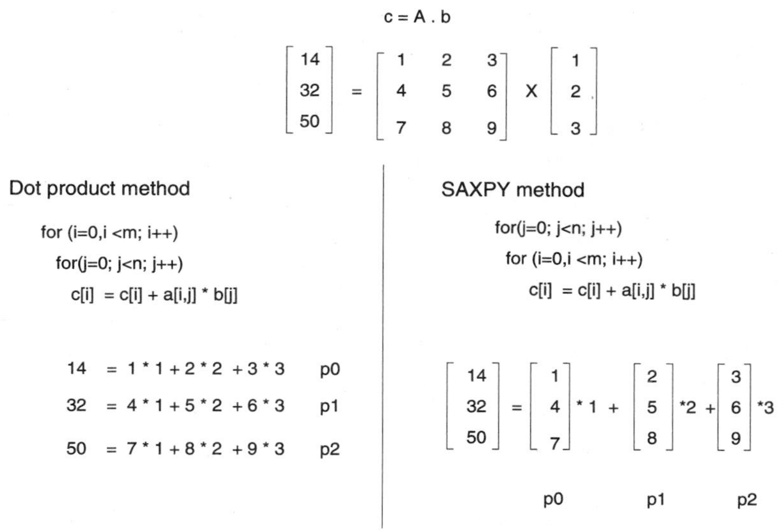

$$c = A \cdot b$$

$$
\begin{bmatrix} 14 \\ 32 \\ 50 \end{bmatrix} =
\begin{bmatrix} 1 & 2 & 3 \\ 4 & 5 & 6 \\ 7 & 8 & 9 \end{bmatrix} \times
\begin{bmatrix} 1 \\ 2 \\ 3 \end{bmatrix}
$$

Dot product method

    for (i=0,i <m; i++)
      for(j=0; j<n; j++)
        c[i] = c[i] + a[i,j] * b[j]

    14 = 1 * 1 + 2 * 2 + 3 * 3   p0
    32 = 4 * 1 + 5 * 2 + 6 * 3   p1
    50 = 7 * 1 + 8 * 2 + 9 * 3   p2

SAXPY method

    for(j=0; j<n; j++)
      for (i=0,i <m; i++)
        c[i] = c[i] + a[i,j] * b[j]

$$
\begin{bmatrix} 14 \\ 32 \\ 50 \end{bmatrix} =
\begin{bmatrix} 1 \\ 4 \\ 7 \end{bmatrix} * 1 +
\begin{bmatrix} 2 \\ 5 \\ 8 \end{bmatrix} * 2 +
\begin{bmatrix} 3 \\ 6 \\ 9 \end{bmatrix} * 3
$$

              p0   p1   p2

Figure 2.19 Two methods of matrix-vector multiply

```
reduce(&hsum, height, 0, ADD, 0);

pi = [0]h * [0]hsum;

printf("%f\n",pi);
}
```

2.9.2 Example Application 2: Matrix Vector Multiplication

The second application that we will consider is that of matrix-vector multiplication. Specifically, we will develop a parallel application for multiplying a matrix of m rows and n columns times a vector of n elements to produce a vector of m elements.

Note that the multiplication can be performed many ways; we will describe two ways as shown in Figure 2.19. In both methods, we first need to initialize the elements of the resultant vector to zero. The subsequent steps of the two methods are different, called the (i, j) loop versus the (j, i) loop respectively.

The first way [called the *DOTPRODUCT or (i,j) method*] is to compute each element of the result output vector as a inner product of a row vector of the input matrix a to the vector b.

The second method [called the *SAXPY or (j,i) method*] proceeds as follows. The algorithm proceeds by computing the scalar product of each element of the b vector with a column vector of the a matrix and summing up the intermediate result vectors to form the output vector. We will use the second method for our parallel implementation.

We first give a program listing in C of the SAXPY method of a matrix vector multiplication program on a serial computer. The program first queries the user for the number of rows and columns of the matrix and then reads in the matrix and vector elements. Finally, it calls a procedure called *matvec* to multiply the matrix with the vector and prints out the result vector.

```c
/* serial matrix vector multiplication program */

#define max 100

float a[max][max], b[max], c[max];
int i,j,m,n;

main()

{
    /* input m and n */

    printf("Enter number of rows and columns\n");
    scanf("%d %d",&m,&n);

    /* read data */
    readdata();

    /* perform matrix vector multiplication */
    matvec();

    /* print output */
    printdata();

}

readdata()

{

    FILE *fpa,*fpb;
    int i,j;

    /* read matrix a   */

    fpa = fopen("a","r");
    for (i=0; i < m; i++)
      for (j=0; j < n; j++)
          fscanf(fpa,"%f", &a[i][j]);
    fclose(fpa);
```

```
    /* read vector b */
    /* read vector b */

    fpb = fopen("b","r");
    for (j=0; j < n; j++)
        fscanf(fpb,"%f",&b[j]);
    fclose(fpb);


    /* initialize vector c */

    for (i=0; i < m; i++) {
        c[i] = 0;
    }
}

printdata(c)

{
    int i;
    FILE *fpc;

    /* print out results */

    fpc = fopen("c","w");
    for (i=0; i < m; i++)
        fprintf(fpc,"%f\n",c[i]);
    fclose(fpc);
}

matvec()

{
    int i,j;

    for (j=0; j < n; j++) {
        for (i=0; i < m; i++) {
            c[i] = c[i] + a[i][j] * b[j];
        }
    }
}
```

Shared memory MIMD parallel implementation We now describe a parallel version of the preceding program suitable for execution on a shared memory MIMD multiprocessor. We will partition the problem by allowing each processor to perform the multiplication of a set of columns of the input matrix times the corresponding sets of elements of the input vector to produce an intermediate result vector. The computations of each intermediate vector will be performed in parallel among all the processors. These intermediate vectors are going to be accumulated among the processors in a sequential step. We will use a static interleaved scheduling algorithm for distributing the j index iterations of the matrix vector multiplication loop. A processor i picks the iterations $i, i + p, i + 2p$, and so on, where p is the number of processors, determined at runtime.

The program listing of the parallel version of matrix-vector multiplication is as follows:

```c
/* parallel matrix vector multiplication program */

#include <stdio.h>
#include <parallel/microtask.h>
#include <parallel/parallel.h>

#define max 100

shared float a[max][max], b[max], c[max];
shared int m,n;

main()

{
    int i,j,nproc;
    void readdata(),matvec(),printdata();

    /* input m and n */

    printf("Enter number of rows and columns\n");
    scanf("%d %d",&m,&n);
    printf("Enter number of processors\n");
    scanf("%d",&nproc);
    /* read data */
    readdata();

    /* create nprocs parallel threads */
    m_set_procs(nproc);

    /* perform parallel multiplication */
    m_fork(matvec);
```

```
        /* wait for all threads to complete */
        m_sync();

        /* print output */
        printdata();

}

void readdata()

{
    FILE *fpa,*fpb;
    int i,j;

    /* read matrix a  */

    fpa = fopen("a","r");
    for (i=0; i < m; i++)
      for (j=0; j < n; j++)
          fscanf(fpa,"%f", &a[i][j]);
    fclose(fpa);


    /* read vector b */

    /* printf("Enter vector b elements\n");*/

    fpb = fopen("b","r");
    for (j=0; j < n; j++)
        fscanf(fpb,"%f",&b[j]);
    fclose(fpb);


    /* initialize vector c */

    for (i=0; i < m; i++)
        c[i] = 0;
}

void printdata()

{
    int i;
```

```
        FILE *fpc;

        /* print out results */

        fpc = fopen("c","w");
        for (i=0; i < m; i++)
            fprintf(fpc,"%f\n",c[i]);
        fclose(fpc);
}

void matvec()

{

    int i,j,nprocs,myid;
    float tmp[max];

    nprocs = m_get_numprocs();
    myid = m_get_myid();

    for (j = myid; j < n; j = j + nprocs) {
        for (i=0; i < m; i++)
            tmp[i] = tmp[i] + a[i][j] * b[j];
        m_lock();
        for (i=0; i < m; i++)
            c[i] = c[i] + tmp[i];
        m_unlock();
    }
}
```

Distributed memory MIMD parallel implementation We will now describe a distributed memory, message-passing, MIMD version of the parallel matrix-vector multiplication example. We will partition the problem by allowing each processor to perform the multiplication of one column of the input matrix times one element of the input vector to produce one intermediate result vector. These intermediate vectors are going to be accumulated. We will use a static interleaved scheduling algorithm for distributing the j index iterations of the matrix vector multiplication loop. A processor i picks the iterations $i, i + p, i + 2p$, and so on.

Processor 0 acts as the master processor; it reads the values of the sizes of the matrix and vector, and sends the information to all other nodes in the procedure *readmn()*. Next, processor 0 reads the matrix and vector values in the procedure *readdata()* and distributes the data to other processors in the procedure *distributedata()*. The submatrices that are sent to a processor i are the columns $i, i + p, i + 2p, ...$ of the original matrix. Next, the entire vector is sent to all the processors. Subsequently, the main computation step is performed by each processor on its own submatrix times the input vector to produce the local value of the result vector. The individual processors send the local values of the result vector to processor 0, which accumulates the values and computes the result vector in the procedure *addvector()*. The result vector is printed out by processor 0.

      The program listing of the parallel version of matrix-vector multiplication is as follows:

```
/* parallel matrix vector multiplication program */
#include <cube.h>
#include <stdio.h>

#define max 100
#define MTYPE 1000
#define NTYPE 2000
#define MATTYPE 3000
#define VECTTYPE 4000

float a[max][max], b[max], c[max];
int m,n;

main()

{
    int id;
    void readmn(),readdata(),distributedata();
    void matvec(),addvector(),printdata();

    id = mynode();
    /* read values of m and n */
    readmn();

     /* read data */
    if (id == 0) {
       readdata();
    }
   /* node 0 distributes data to all */
    distributedata();

   /* perform parallel multiplication */
    matvec();

    addvector();
    if (id == 0)
      printdata();
}
```

```
void readmn()

{
   int id;

   id = mynode();
   if (id == 0) {

      /* input m and n */

       printf("Enter number of rows and columns\n");
       scanf("%d %d",&m,&n);

      /* send value of m and n to all nodes */

       csend(MTYPE, &m, 4, -1, 0);
       csend(NTYPE, &n, 4, -1, 0);
   }
    else
    {
     /* receive m and n from processor 0 */

      crecv(MTYPE, &m, 4);
      crecv(NTYPE, &n, 4);
    }
}

void readdata()

{
   int i,j;
   FILE *fpa,*fpb;

   /* read matrix a  */

   fpa = fopen("a","r");
   for (i=0; i < m; i++)
     for (j=0; j < n; j++)
         fscanf(fpa,"%f", &a[i][j]);

   /* read vector b */
```

```
    fpb = fopen("b","r");
    for (j=0; j < n; j++)
        fscanf(fpb,"%f",&b[j]);
    fclose(fpb);

}

void printdata()

{
    int i;
    FILE *fpc;

    /* print out results */

    fpc = fopen("c","w");
    for (i=0; i < m; i++)
        fprintf(fpc,"%f\n",c[i]);
    fclose(fpc);

}

void distributedata()

{
    int id,i,j,p,nnodes,mesgsize,jlocal;
    float tmp[max];

    nnodes = numnodes();
    mesgsize = 4 * n / nnodes;
    id = mynode();

    if (id == 0) {

      /* send different submatrix of a, and
           vector b to each processor */

      for (p = 1; p < nnodes; p++) {

          /* copy portion of a to be sent to
             processor p into buffer tmp */

          for (i=0; i < m; i++) {
             for (j=p,jlocal=0;j<n;j+=nnodes,jlocal++)
```

```
                    /* determine j iterations for static
                            interleaved scheduling */
                    tmp[jlocal] = a[i][j];

              /* send the data from buffer tmp */
              csend(MATTYPE+i,tmp,mesgsize,p,0);
              }

              /* send the vector b */

          for(j=p,jlocal=0;j<n;j+=nnodes,jlocal++)
              tmp[jlocal] = b[j];
          csend(VECTTYPE,tmp,mesgsize,p,0);
        }

        /* change own indices from global to local */
        for (i=0; i < m; i++)
            for (j=0,jlocal=0;j<n;j+=nnodes,jlocal++)
                a[i][jlocal] = a[i][j];
            for (j=0,jlocal=0;j<n;j+=nnodes,jlocal++)
        b[jlocal] = b[j];
      }
      else
      {
        /* each processor receives own submatrix
            of a and vector b */

        for(i=0; i <m; i++)
          crecv(MATTYPE+i,a[i],mesgsize);

        crecv(VECTTYPE,b,mesgsize);
      }
}


void matvec()

{
    int i,j,nnodes;

    /* initialize vector c */

    nnodes = numnodes();
```

```
    for (i=0;  i < m;  i++)
        c[i] = 0;

    /* multiply owned submatrix a with vector b */

    for (j = 0;  j < n/nnodes;  j++)
        for (i=0;  i < m;  i++)
            c[i] = c[i] + a[i][j] * b[j];
}

void addvector()

{
    int id,i,vectsize,p,nnodes;
    float ctmp[max];

    id = mynode();
    nnodes = numnodes();
    vectsize = 4 * m;

    if (id != 0)

        /* send data to processor 0 */
         csend(VECTTYPE,c,vectsize,0,0);

    else{
        for (p = 1;  p < nnodes;  p++) {

            /* receive data from p */
            crecv(VECTTYPE,ctmp,vectsize);

            for (i=0;  i < m;  i++)
                c[i] = c[i] + ctmp[i];
        }
    }
}
```

SIMD parallel implementation An example of SIMD programming of the matrix-vector multiplication algorithm is given next. In the following code, we note that matrices a, b, c, and t are defined as the same shape n by m where $n = 256$ and $m = 64$. This specifies a 256 by 64 array, which creates 16K data processors. One data processor is created per element of the array.

The matrix-vector product $a \times v = c$ can be computed by adding m vectors each of shape $n \times 1$. These m vectors of shape $n \times 1$ can be computed by a single array multiplication of two matrices of shape $n \times m$. These two matrices can be formed by taking the original matrix a and replicating the vector v in the second dimension. along different dimensions as shown in Figure 2.20. The replication of a matrix can be achieved by the *copy_spread()* library call in C*, which transforms the one-dimensional vector v into a two-dimensional form, t; this is shown in the program. Subsequently, an element by element multiplication of the matrices is performed on each data processor and the results are stored in t. The *reduce()* library call performs a summation of the matrix elements of the second dimension of the matrix t. Subsequently, the reduced vector is copied to the c vector.

The complete SIMD parallel program is as follows:

```
#include <stdio.h>
#include <cscomm.h>
#define ADD CMC_combiner_add

#define n 256
#define m 64

/* define a shape of n by m array */
shape [n][m] s;

/* temporary  matrix */
float:s t;

/* n x m matrix */
float:s a;

/* vectors stored on edge of nxm matrix */
float:s v,c;

main()
{
   with (s)
   {

/*
   Either read matrix a and vector v in parallel
      readmatrix(a);
      readvector(v);

   Or initialize matrix and
   vector by self addresses
```

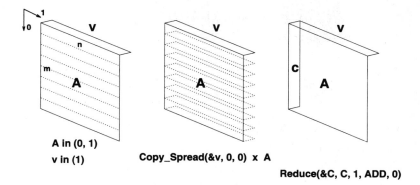

Figure 2.20 Matrix-vector multiply on an SIMD machine

```
*/
      a = pcoord(0);
      [0][.]v = pcoord(1);

      /* copy to temporary */
      [0][pcoord(1)]t = [0][pcoord(1)]v;

      /* spread and multiply */
      t = copy_spread(&t, 0, 0) * a;

      /* sum to result */
      reduce(&t, t, 1, ADD, 0);

      /* copy result */
      [pcoord(0)][0]c = [pcoord(0)][0]t;

      /* prints values of c in parallel */
      printmatrix(c);
   }
}
```

2.9.3 Example Application 3: Matrix-Matrix Multiplication

We finally look at a third application: matrix-matrix multiplication. There are many ways of performing matrix multiplication. We show one way in the following program, which multiplies matrices a and b of sizes $n \times n$ and produces a result matrix c. Each result matrix element is obtained as an inner product of a row of the a matrix (containing n elements) times a column of the b matrix (containing n elements). The program first reads the value of the size of the matrices, then reads the data for the two matrices, an then performs the matrix computation and prints out the results.

The complete program is as follows:

```c
/* serial matrix matrix multiplication */

#define max 100

float a[max][max], b[max][max], c[max][max];
int n;

main()
{
   /* input n the size of matrices */

    printf("Enter n, the size of matrices\n");
    scanf("%d",&n);
    /* reads matrix a and b */
    readdata();
    /* call procedure to multiply matrices */
    matmul();
    /* prints matrix c */
    printdata();
}

void readdata()

{

    int i,j;
    FILE *fpa,*fpb;

    /* read matrix a   */

    fpa = fopen("a","r");
    for (i=0; i < n; i++)
      for (j=0; j < n; j++)
          fscanf(fpa,"%f", &a[i][j]);
    fclose(fpa);

    /* read matrix b   */

    fpb = fopen("b","r");
    for (i=0; i < n; i++)
      for (j=0; j < n; j++)
```

```
            fscanf(fpb,"%f", &b[i][j]);
     fclose(fpb);
}

void printdata()

{
    int i,j;
    FILE *fpc;

    /* print out results */

    fpc = fopen("c","w");
    for (i=0; i < n; i++)
       for (j = 0; j < n; j++)
          fprintf(fpc,"%f\n",c[i][j]);
    fclose(fpc);


matmul()

{
  int i, j, k;


  for (i = 0; i < n; i++) {
     for (j = 0; j < n;  j++) {
        c[i][j] = 0.0;
        for (k = 0 ; k < n; k++) {
           c[i][j] = c[i][j] + a[i][k] * b [k][j];
        }
     }
  }

}
```

Shared memory MIMD parallel implementation The preceding application is parallelized
on a shared memory MIMD multiprocessor using static block-wise scheduling; however, the
blocking is done in *both dimensions of the matrix.* Given two $n \times n$ matrices, a and b, the
parallel program has to generate a result matrix c. For a P processor system, the processors
are logically arranged as a $\sqrt{P} \times \sqrt{P}$ array on which the result c matrix is logically mapped.
Each processor is assigned the computations of a rectangular subblock of the c matrix. The
computation of each subblock of the c matrix involves accessing a row subblock of the a

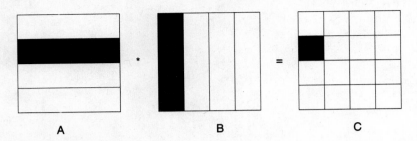

NOTE: Shaded regions show computation of one processor (2,1)

Figure 2.21 Matrix multiplication on a 16-processor multiprocessor

matrix and a column subblock of the b matrix. Figure 2.21 illustrates the matrix multiplication on a 16-processor multiprocessor, logically arranged as a 4×4 array of processors where the computation of processor on the second row and first column of the array is highlighted.

The details of the program are as follows. The main process reads the sizes of the matrices and the matrix data themselves. It then calls the matrix multiplication routine in parallel by calling $P - 1$ child processes. Note the computation of the lower and upper bounds of the i and j loops among the P processes arranges as a square array. Finally, the main process prints out the result matrix.

The complete parallel program for a shared memory multiprocessor with static block wise scheduling would then look like this.

```
#include <math.h>
#include <stdio.h>
#include <parallel/microtask.h>
#include <parallel/parallel.h>

#define max 100

shared float a[max][max], b[max][max], c[max][max];
shared int n;

main()

{
    int nprocs;
    void readdata(),matmul(),printdata();

    /* input n the size of matrices */
```

```
      printf("Enter the size of matrices\n");
      scanf("%d",&n);
      printf("Enter the number of processors\n");
      scanf("%d",&nprocs);

      /* reads matrix a and b */
      readdata();

    /* set number of processes */
    m_set_procs(nprocs);

    /* execute parallel loop */
    m_fork(matmul);

     /* kill child processes */
     m_kill_procs();

    /* prints matrix c */
     printdata();
}

void readdata()

{

    int i,j;
    FILE *fpa,*fpb;

    /* read matrix a   */

    fpa = fopen("a","r");
    for (i=0; i < n; i++)
      for (j=0; j < n; j++)
          fscanf(fpa,"%f", &a[i][j]);
    fclose(fpa);

    /* read matrix b */

    fpb = fopen("b","r");
    for (i=0; i < n; i++)
      for (j=0; j < n; j++)
          fscanf(fpb,"%f", &b[i][j]);
    fclose(fpb);
}
```

```
    void printdata()

    {
       int i,j;
       FILE *fpc;

       /* print out results */

       fpc = fopen("c","w");
       for (i=0; i < n; i++)
          for (j = 0; j < n; j++)
             fprintf(fpc,"%f\n",c[i][j]);
       fclose(fpc);
    }



    void matmul()

    {
      int i, j, k;
      int nprocs, iprocs, jprocs;
      int my_id, i_id,j_id,ilb,iub,jlb,jub;

     /* number of processors */
      nprocs = m_get_numprocs();

      /* number of processors in i direction */
      iprocs = (int) sqrt((double) nprocs);

      /* number of processors in j direction */
      jprocs = nprocs / iprocs;

      my_id = m_get_myid();
      /* get processor ID in i and j dimensions */
      i_id = my_id % iprocs;
      j_id = my_id % jprocs;
      /* find lower and upper bounds of i loop */
      ilb = i_id * n / iprocs;
      iub = (i_id + 1) * (n / iprocs);

      /* find lower and upper bounds of j loop */
      jlb = j_id * n / jprocs;
```

```
jub = (j_id + 1) * (n / jprocs);

for (i = ilb; i < iub; i++)
   for (j = jlb; j < jub;  j++) {
      c[i][j] = 0.0;
      for (k = 0 ; k < n; k++)
         c[i][j] = c[i][j] + a[i][k] * b [k][j];
   }
}
```

Distributed memory MIMD parallel implementation We will now describe a parallel program for a distributed memory MIMD multiprocessor with static block-wise scheduling. The computation of the matrix c is blocked in *both the dimensions of i and j*. We distribute the matrix a by contiguous blocks of rows, and we distribute matrix b by contiguous blocks of columns. The processors as arranged as a $\sqrt{P} \times \sqrt{P}$ grid of processors, as shown in Figure 2.21. Each processor performs a blocked matrix multiplication and produces a contiguous block of matrix c, and then returns the results to the processor 0.

Processor 0 acts as the master processor; it reads the values of the sizes of the two matrices and then sends the information to all other nodes in the procedure *readmn()*. Next, processor 0 reads the matrix values in the procedure *readdata()* and distributes the data to other processors in the procedure *distributedata()*. The matrix a is distributed by contiguous blocks of rows, and the matrix b is distributed by contiguous blocks of columns. These submatrices are sent to the appropriate processors by processor 0. Note that the processors are arranged as a $\sqrt{P} \times \sqrt{P}$ grid of processors. The b submatrices that are sent to a processor i are the contiguous blocks of columns $i \cdot n/\sqrt{P}$ to $(i+1) \cdot n/\sqrt{P}$ of the original b matrix residing in processor 0. Subsequently, the main computation step is performed by each processor. Each element of the subblock of the c matrix owned by the processor is computed as an inner product of the appropriate row and column of the owned submatrices of a and b. Each processor therefore computes the value of a subblock of the c matrix. The individual processors send the local values of the result matrix c to processor 0. Processor 0 composes the result matrix by performing the required local to global index transformations in the procedure *composematrix()*. The result matrix is printed out by processor 0.

The complete program looks like this.

```
/* parallel matrix matrix multiplication */
/* a[n][n] X b[n][n] = c[n][n]   */

#include <cube.h>
#include <stdio.h>
#include <math.h>
```

```
#define max 100
#define MAX 10000
#define NTYPE 1000
#define ATYPE 2000
#define BTYPE 3000
#define CTYPE 4000

float a[max][max], b[max][max], c[max][max];
int n;

main()
{
    int id;
    void readn(),readdata(),distributedata();
    void matmul(),composematrix(),printdata();

    id = mynode();
    /* read value of n */
    readn();

     /* read data */
    if (id == 0)
       readdata();

    /* node 0 distributes data to all */
    distributedata();

   /* perform parallel matrix multiplication */
    matmul();

   /* node 0 collects submatrices of c from all */
    composematrix();

    /* node 0 prints matrix */
    if (id == 0)
      printdata();

}

void readn()

{
    int id;
```

```
    id = mynode();

    if (id == 0) {

        /* input size of n by n matrix */

        printf("Enter number of rows/columns\n");
        scanf("%d",&n);

        /* send value of n to all nodes */

        csend(NTYPE, &n, 4, -1, 0);
    }
    else {

        /* receive values of n from processor 0 */

        crecv(NTYPE, &n, 4);
    }

}


void readdata()

{

    int i,j;
    FILE *fpa,*fpb;

    /* read matrix a   */

    fpa = fopen("a","r");
    for (i=0; i < n; i++)
      for (j=0; j < n; j++)
          fscanf(fpa,"%f", &a[i][j]);
    fclose(fpa);

    /* read matrix b */

    fpb = fopen("b","r");
    for (i=0; i < n; i++)
      for (j=0; j < n; j++)
          fscanf(fpb,"%f", &b[i][j]);
```

```
        fclose(fpb);
}


void distributedata()

{
    int p,nnodes,lb,ub,blocksize;
    int i, j, k;
    int nprocs, ijprocs,proc;
    int size;
    int id, ijlb,ijub;
    float tmp[max];

    nprocs = numnodes();

    /* number of processors in i and j directions */
    ijprocs = (int) sqrt((double) nprocs);

    size = n*sizeof(float);

    id = mynode();

    if (id == 0) {

    /* send different submatrix of
       a and b to each processor */

      for (p = 0; p < ijprocs; p++) {

          /* copy portion of a to be sent to
             processor p into buffer tmp */

        /* find lower and upper bounds of i,j loops */
          ijlb = p * n / ijprocs;
          ijub = (p + 1) * (n / ijprocs);

          for (i = ijlb; i < ijub; i++) {
             for (k=0; k < n; k++)
             /* determine i iterations for static
                 blocked scheduling */
               tmp[k] = a[i][k];

          /* send the data from buffer tmp */
          for(proc=p*ijprocs;proc<(p+1)*ijprocs;proc++)
```

```
                        csend(ATYPE+i-ijlb,tmp,size,proc,0);
              }

          /* copy portion of b to be sent to processor p
              into buffer tmp */

              for (j=ijlb; j < ijub; j++) {
                for (k = 0; k < n; k++)
                /* determine j iterations for static
                     blocked scheduling */
                  tmp[k] = b[k][j];

                /* send the data from buffer tmp */
                for(proc=p;proc<p+ijprocs*ijprocs;proc+=ijprocs)
                    csend(BTYPE+j-ijlb,tmp,size,proc,0);
            }
        }
      }

    else (if id != 0) {

       /* each processor receives own submatrix
              of a and submatrix of b */

       for(i=0;i<n/ijprocs;i++)
          crecv(ATYPE+i,a[i],size);
       for(j=0;j<n/ijprocs;j++)
          crecv(BTYPE+j,b[j],size);
       }
}


void composematrix()

{
    int p,i,j,k;
    int nprocs,ijprocs;
    int size;
    int id, i_id,j_id,ilb,iub,jlb,jub;
    float tmp[MAX];


    /* find number of processors in i,j direction */
    nprocs = numnodes();
    ijprocs = (int) sqrt((double)nprocs);
```

```
        size = n*n*sizeof(float)/nprocs;

    id = mynode();
    if (id == 0) {
      for (p = 1; p < nprocs; p++) {
        /* encode sending address of processor */
         crecv(CTYPE+p,tmp,size);
         /* get processor ID in i and j dimensions */
         i_id = p / ijprocs;
         j_id = p % ijprocs;

        /* determine lower bounds of i and j loop */
        ilb = i_id * n / ijprocs;

        jlb = j_id * n / ijprocs;

           for (i = 0; i < n/ijprocs; i++)
              for (j=0; j < n/ijprocs; j++)

                 /* transform local to global indices */
                  c[i+ilb][j+jlb] = tmp[i*n/ijprocs+j];
        }
    }
    else {
         /* compose a buffer to send out with
            the id tagged at end */

         for (i = 0; i < n/ijprocs; i++)
            for (j=0; j < n/ijprocs; j++)
               tmp[i*n/ijprocs+j] = c[i][j];

         /* encode id of processor with message type */
          csend(CTYPE+id,tmp,size,0,0);


    }
}

void printdata()

{
    int i,j;
    FILE *fpc;
```

```
     /* print out results */

     fpc = fopen("c","w");
     for (i=0; i < n; i++)
        for (j = 0; j < n; j++)
           fprintf(fpc,"%f\n",c[i][j]);
     fclose(fpc);

}


void matmul()

{
   int i, j, k;

   int nprocs, ijprocs;
   int ijub;

   /* find number of processors in i,j direction */
   nprocs = numnodes();
   ijprocs = (int) sqrt((double) nprocs);

   /* find upper bound of i and j loops */
   ijub = n / ijprocs;

   /*  Each processor multiplies a[n/ijprocs][n] */
   /*  with b[n][n/ijprocs] to produce */
   /*  c[n/ijprocs][n/ijprocs] */

   for (i = 0; i < ijub; i++)
      for (j = 0; j < ijub;  j++) {
         c[i][j] = 0.0;
         for (k = 0 ; k < n; k++)
            c[i][j] = c[i][j] + a[i][k] * b [j][k];
      }
}
```

SIMD parallel implementation The SIMD programming of the matrix-matrix multiplication algorithm will now be described. In the following code, we note that matrices a, b, c, and t are defined as having the same shape n by n by n, where n is set to 32. This creates 32K data processors, one for each element of the 32 by 32 by 32 array.

The matrix multiplication $c = a \times b$ can be computed by adding n matrices each of

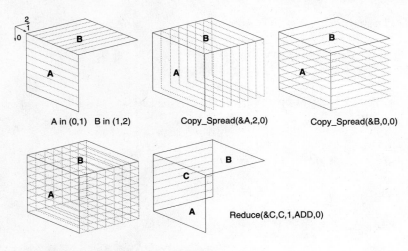

A in (0,1) B in (1,2)   Copy_Spread(&A,2,0)   Copy_Spread(&B,0,0)

Reduce(&C,C,1,ADD,0)

Copy_Spread(&A,2,0) X Copy_Spread(&B,0,0)

Figure 2.22 Matrix-matrix multiply on an SIMD machine

shape $n \times n$. These n matrices of shape $n \times n$ can be computed by a single array multiplication of two matrices of shape $n \times n \times n$. These two matrices can be formed by replicating a and b along different dimensions, as shown in Figure 2.22. The $n \times n$ matrix a is read into the 0-1 plane of a $n \times n \times n$ matrix ta. The $n \times n$ matrix b is read into the 1-2 plane of a $n \times n \times n$ matrix tb.

The spreading of a matrix can be achieved by the *copy_spread* library call in C*. The *copy_spread* (&ta,2,0) call spreads the values of the A matrix along the planes of ta in axis 2. The *copy_spread* (&tb,0,0) call spreads the values of the B matrix along the planes of tb in axis 0. These operations are illustrated in Figure 2.22. Subsequently, an element by element multiplication of the spreaded matrices ta and tb of shape n by n by n is performed on each data processor and the result is stored in t.

The *reduce* (& t,T,1,ADD,0) library call performs a summation of the matrix elements in the dimension 1 of the matrix t and stores the result in the data processors corresponding to the 0-2 plane of the t matrix. The results are copied to the c matrix and printed out.

The complete SIMD program is as follows:

```
#include <stdio.h>
#include <cscomm.h>
#define ADD CMC_combiner_add

#define N 128

/* define a shape of n x n x n  array */
shape [N][N][N] s;
```

```
/* temporary matrices */
float:s t,ta,tb;
/* A X B = C (each stored in [.][.][0] */
float:s a,b,c;

main()
{
   with (s)
   {
/*
   Either read matrices a and b in parallel

       readmatrix(a);
       readmatrix(b);

   Or initialize matrices by self addresses
*/
       [.][.][0]a = pcoord(0);
       [.][.][0]b = pcoord(0)+pcoord(1);

       /* place in working matrix */

       [pcoord(0)][pcoord(1)][0]ta =
            [pcoord(0)][pcoord(1)][0]a;
       [0][pcoord(1)][pcoord(2)]tb =
            [pcoord(1)][pcoord(2)][0]b;

       /* spread mult */
       t = copy_spread(&ta,2,0)*copy_spread(&tb,0,0);

       /* sum to result */
       reduce(&t, t, 1, ADD, 0);

       /* copy result */
       [pcoord(0)][pcoord(1)][0]c =
            [pcoord(0)][0][pcoord(1)]t;

       /* print matrix c elements in parallel */
       printmatrix(c);
   }
}
```

2.10 SUMMARY

In this chapter we have discussed various forms of general-purpose parallel processors, which were classified into MIMD and SIMD forms. MIMD machines were subclassified into shared memory multiprocessors or distributed memory multicomputers. All the approaches to parallel processing are being vigorously pursued by the parallel computing community. Ongoing research is underway to simulate one type of MIMD machine on another. The virtual parallel machine that the user sees can be either message-passing or shared memory type. The underlying physical machine can be anything.

Some of the salient characteristics of shared memory MIMD multiprocessors are the ease of programmability and the existence of automated parallelizing compilers to parallelize sequential programs. Bus-based shared memory systems are easy and inexpensive to build, and several such commercial products are available, but such architectures are not scalable to large numbers of processors. Typically, the maximum number of processors that can be connected to a bus is about 20 to 30. Larger shared memory systems consisting of hundreds or thousands of processors are physically organized as distributed memory machines connected by an interconnection network with a logically uniform address space. Examples of such architectures are the BBN TC2000™, and the Kendall Squares Research KSR-1™machines. While the programmer sees a uniform memory space, the operating system and hardware of these machines perform the appropriate movement of data and code among the memories.

The programming of distributed memory multicomputers is more complex than that of shared memory multiprocessors since we must worry about not only the parallel algorithm, but also how to distribute the code and how to explicitly distribute and communicate the data across processors in separate address spaces. Since this is a newer technology, there is not much support for automated parallelization of sequential programs for such machines. It is relatively inexpensive to build very large systems using either the mesh or hypercube topology, and several such commercial machines having hundred to a thousand processors exist. For example, the Intel iPSC/860™hypercube has up to 128 processors connected as a hypercube, and the Intel Paragon™has 1024 processors connected as a mesh. Once a program is developed on such a machine, we can obtain truly scalable parallel performance from these machines since the data and code are placed under user control. Contrast this with the *ease* of programming shared memory machines, where the same data and code movement has to happen as well, but the code and data movement is performed by the hardware and operating system. Such indiscriminate use of data movements may result in large cache misses in shared memory systems, which may result in poor parallel performance in these machines. Recently, there has been some research directed on compiling shared memory programs on cache-coherent shared memory multiprocessors to exploit the data locality and to minimize the data transfers [1, 2].

The SIMD processors are easier to program than message-passing MIMD processors for data parallel algorithms. Such programs make extensive use of high-level structured library calls for distributing data, hence such SIMD programs look very compact. However, the SIMD programs have limited applicability since not all problems can be effectively decomposed into data-parallel form using thousands of processors.

2.11 PROBLEMS

2.1   Distinguish between centralized and distributed organizations of logically shared memory architectures. What are the advantages and disadvantages of such architectures. Give examples of each type of architecture.

2.2   Show how a snooping bus write-back cache coherence protocol with write-invalidate will avoid the cache coherence problem for the example in Figure 2.5. Repeat steps for the write-broadcast scheme. Assume that the interconnection network is not a bus, but a multistage network. Show how a directory scheme will handle the situation.

2.3   Identify the advantages and disadvantages of prescheduled, static blocked, static interleaved, and dynamic scheduling.

2.4   For the shared memory implementation of the computation of π described in the chapter, we have used dynamic scheduling. Write a parallel program assuming static blocked scheduling and static interleaved scheduling using the Sequent Symmetry™parallel library.

2.5   For the distributed memory implementation of the computation of π described in the chapter, we have used static blocked scheduling. Write a parallel program assuming dynamic scheduling, assuming a chunk size of 5 iterations at a time for dynamic scheduling using the Intel iPSC™library.

2.6   For the shared memory implementation of the matrix-vector multiplication described in the chapter, we have used static interleaved scheduling. Write parallel versions of the program assuming static blocked scheduling, and dynamic scheduling using the Sequent Symmetry™parallel library.

2.7   For the distributed memory implementation of the matrix-matrix multiplication described in the chapter, we have used static blocked scheduling. Write a parallel program assuming dynamic scheduling using the Intel iPSC™library.

2.8   Write an SIMD parallel program using the Connection Machine CM-2™library for (1) adding two arrays of floating point numbers, (2) determining their maximum element, and (3) dividing each element of the resultant array by the maximum element. Assume array sizes of 2000 elements.

2.12 REFERENCES

[1]   S. G. Abraham and D. E. Hudak. Compile-time Partitioning of Iterative Parallel Loops to Reduce Cache Coherence Traffic. *IEEE Trans. Parallel Distributed Systems*, 2(3):318–328, July 1991.

[2]   A. Agarwal, D. Krantz, and V. Natarajan. Automatic Partitioning of Parallel Loops for Cahce-Coherent Multiprocessors. *Proc. Int. Conf. Parallel Processing*, pages I:2–11, Aug. 1993.

[3]   M. Annaratone, E. Arnould, T. Gross, H. T. Kung, M. S. Lam, O. Menzilcioglu, K. Sarocky, and J. A. Webb. Warp Architecture and Implementation. *Proc. 13th Int. Symp. Computer Architecture*, pages 346–356, June 1986.

[4]   W. C. Athas and C. L. Seitz. Multicomputers: Message-passing Concurrent Computers. *IEEE Computer*, 21(8):9–24, Aug. 1988.

[5]   G. H. Barnes, R. M. Brown, M. Kato, D. J. Kuck, D. J. Slotnick, and R. A. Stokes. The ILLIAC IV Computer. *IEEE Trans. Computers*, C-17(8):746–757, Aug. 1968.

[6]   K. E. Batcher. STARAN Parallel Processor System Hardware. *Proc. AFIPS National Computer Conf.*, pages 405–410, 1974.

[7]   K. E. Batcher. Design of a Massively Parallel Processor. *IEEE Trans. Computers*, C-29(9):836–840, Sept. 1980.

[8]   B. E. Bauer. *Practical Parallel Programming*. Academic Press, San Diego, CA, 1992.

[9]   G. Bell. Ultracomputers: A Teraflop before Its Time. *Comm. ACM*, 35(8):27–47, Aug. 1992.

[10]   D. Berktekas and J. Tsitiklis. *Parallel and Distributed Computation: Numerical Methods*. Prentice Hall, Englewoods Cliffs, NJ, 1989.

[11]   S. Brawer. *Introduction to Parallel Programming*. Academic Press, San Diego, CA, 1989.

[12]   Intel Scientific Computers. iPSC: The First Family of Concurrent Supercomputers. Technical report, Beaverton, OR, 1985.

[13]   Intel Scientific Computers. The iPSC/860 Family of Concurrent Supercomputers. Technical report, Beaverton, OR, 1989.

[14]   Alliant Computer Systems Corp. Alliant FX/Series Product Summary. Technical report, Littleton, MA, Oct. 1986.

[15]   Digital Equipment Corp. DEC Firefly Multiprocessing Workstations: Product Overview. Technical report, Marlborough, MA, 1988.

[16]   Encore Computer Corp. The Multimax Family of Computer Systems. Technical report, Marlborough, MA, 1988.

[17]   Fujitsu Corp. VPP500 Vector Parallel Processor. Technical report, San Jose, CA, 1992.

[18]   IBM Corp. The IBM Scalable POWER/Parallel Systems - 9076 SP-1. Technical report, Kingston, NY, 1992.

[19]   NCUBE Corp. The NCUBE/10 System. Technical report, Beaverton, OR, 1986.

[20]   Thinking Machine Corp. The Connection Machine CM-2 Technical Summary. Technical report, Cambridge, MA, 1987.

[21]   Thinking Machine Corp. The Connection Machine CM-5 Technical Summary. Technical report, Cambridge, MA, 1991.

[22]   Xerox Corp. Xerox Dragon Multiprocessing Workstations: Product Overview. Technical report, Palo Alto, CA, 1988.

[23]   Maspar Computer Corporation. The MasPar Family of Data-Parallel Computers. Technical report, Sunnyvale, CA, 1991.

[24]   Intel Supercomputing Systems Division. Paragon XP/S Product Overview. Technical report, Beaverton, OR, 1991.

[25]   C. L. Seitz et al. The Architecture and Programming of the Ametek Series 2010 Multicomputer. *Proc. 3rd Conf. Hypercube Concurrent Computers and Applications*, pages 33–36, Jan. 1988.

[26]   P. M. Flanders, D. J. Hunt, and S. F. Reddaway. *High-speed Computer and Algorithm Organization*. Academic Press, New York, NY, 1977.

[27]   M. J. Flynn. Very High Speed Computing Systems. *Proc. IEEE*, 54:1901–1909, 1966.

[28]   G. C. Fox, M. A. Johnson, G. A. Lyzenga, S. W. Otto, and J. K. Salmon. *Solving Problems on Concurrent Processors*. Prentice Hall, Englewood Cliffs, NJ, 1989.

[29]   G. C. Fox and S. W. Otto. Algorithms for Concurrent Processors. *Physics Today*, 37(5):50–59, May 1984.

[30]   D. Gajski, D. J. Kuck, D. Lawrie, and A. Sameh. CEDAR - A Large Scale Multiprocessor. *Proc. Int. Conf. Parallel Processing*, pages 524–529, Aug. 1983.

[31]   J. L. Hennessy and D. A. Patterson. *Computer Architecture: A Quantitative Approach*. Morgan Kaufman Publishers, San Mateo, CA, 1990.

[32]   R. W. Hockney and C. R. Jesshope. *Parallel Computers*. Adam Hilger Ltd., Bristol, England, 1981.

[33]   R. M. Hord. *Parallel Supercomputing in SIMD Architectures*. CRC Press, Boca Raton, FL, 1990.

[34]   K. Hwang. *Advanced Computer Architecture: Parallelism, Scalability, Programmability*. McGraw Hill Book Co., New York, NY, 1993.

[35]   K. Hwang and F. Briggs. *Computer Architecture and Parallel Processing*. McGraw-Hill Book Co., New York, NY, 1984.

[36]   BBN Advanced Computers Inc. TC2000 Technical Product Summary. Technical report, Cambridge, MA, 1989.

[37]   Cray Research Inc. The Cray Y/MP C-90 Supercomputer System. Technical report, Eagan, MN, 1991.

[38]   Cray Research Inc. The Cray T3D Massively Parallel Processing Supercomputer System. Technical report, Eagan, MN, 1993.

[39]   Kendall Squares Research Inc. KSR-1 Overview. Technical report, Waltham, MA, 1991.

[40]   Sequent Computer Systems Inc. The Sequent Symmetry Multiprocessor System. Technical report, Beaverton, OR, 1986.

[41]   Silicon Graphics Inc. SGI IRIS Challenger Multiprocessing Workstations: Product Overview. Technical report, San Jose, CA, 1993.

[42]   Solbourne Computer Inc. The Solbourne Series 500/600 Multiprocessing Workstations: Product Overview. Technical report, Longmont, CO, 1990.

[43]   SUN Microsystems Inc. SPARCCenter 2000 Multiprocessing Workstations: Product Overview. Technical report, Sunnyvale, CA, 1993.

[44]   M. Kallstrom and S. S. Thakkar. Programming Three Parallel Computers. *IEEE Software*, pages 11–22, Jan. 1988.

[45]   A. H. Karp. Programming for Parallelism. *IEEE Computer*, pages 43–57, May 1987.

[46]   D. Lenoski, J. Laudon, K. Gharachorloo, W. D. Weber, A. Gupta, J. Hennessy, M. Horowitz, and M. Lam. The Stanford DASH Multiprocessor. *IEEE Computer*, Mar. 1992.

[47]   INMOS Ltd. INMOS Transputer Product Description. Technical report, Bristol, England, 1988.

[48]   J. C. Peterson, J. Tuazon, D. Lieberman, and M. Pniel. The Mark III Hypercube-Ensemble Concurrent Computer. *Proc. Int. Conf. Parallel Processing*, pages 71–73, Aug. 1985.

[49]   G. F. Pfister, W. C. Brantley, D. A. George, S. L. Harvey, W. J. Kleinfelder, K. P. McAuliffe, E. A. Melton, V. A. Norton, and J. Weiss. The IBM Research Parallel Processor Prototype (RP3): Introduction and Architecture. *Proc. Int. Conf. Parallel Processing*, pages 764–771, 1985.

[50]   J. Rattner. Concurrent Processing: A New Direction in Scientific Computing. *Proc. AFIPS Spring Joint Comp. Conf.*, 54:159–166, 1985.

[51]   C. L. Seitz. The Cosmic Cube. *Comm. of the ACM*, 28:22–33, Jan. 1985.

CHAPTER 3

Placement and Floorplanning

3.1 INTRODUCTION

The VLSI cell placement problem involves placing a set of cells on a VLSI layout, given a netlist that provides the connectivity between each cell and a library containing layout information for each type of cell. The primary goal of cell placement is to determine the best location of each cell so as to optimize one or more objectives, such as minimization of the total area of the layout or minimization of the delays on interconnect lines. The floorplan design problem can be viewed as a generalized version of placement of building blocks, where the building blocks during a floorplanning stage may have several possible orientations.

The cell placement and floorplanning problems are known to be NP complete. A large number of heuristic approaches exist in the literature to solve the problems, which vary in their runtime requirements and layout quality produced. Unfortunately, approaches that produce extremely good quality of layout often take large amounts of computation time. Hence, in recent years, researchers have turned to parallel processing as a viable approach to achieve the tremendous performance improvements that will be needed to design future generations of VLSI chips.

Since there has been a large number of sequential heuristic approaches to solve the placement and floorplanning problems, parallel algorithms for these problems are typically based on one or more of these sequential heuristics. Hence, there has been a lot of work reported in the area of parallel placement and floorplanning algorithms, all of which is difficult to cover in detail in a single chapter. Therefore this chapter should be viewed as an introduction to the field; the reader is encouraged to read the references for more detail.

The chapter is organized as follows. Section 3.2 will provide a description of various layout styles and will also formulate the placement problem. Sections 3.3 through 3.9 will review various approaches to parallel placement algorithms. Six different classes of parallel algorithms for placement are discussed based on the following methods: (1) pairwise interchange, (2) force-directed moves, (3) simulated annealing, (4) simulated evolution, (5) genetic algorithms, and (6) hierarchical decomposition techniques. Section 3.9 discusses some parallel placement algorithms that combine a variety of these approaches. For each approach, both shared memory MIMD and distributed memory MIMD parallel algorithms will be described. Where appropriate, SIMD parallel algorithms will be discussed as well. Section 3.10 will describe the floorplanning problem and outline some of the sequential algorithms. Sections 3.11 through 3.13 will discuss different classes of parallel algorithms for floorplanning. Three classes of parallel floorplanning algorithms will be discussed for both shared memory and distributed memory multiprocessors: (1) simulated annealing, (2) genetic algorithms, and (3) branch and bound techniques. Section 3.14 discusses the use of hardware accelerators for placement. Section 3.15 concludes with some general observations on the need for future research in this field.

3.2 PLACEMENT PROBLEM

3.2.1 Review of Automated Layout Styles

To understand the placement and floorplanning problems, we must be familiar with the various automated layout design styles that exist. They include *standard cell, gate array, sea-of-gates,* and *macro cell* or *building block* design styles. Different placement algorithms have been proposed for each of these layout styles. We will first review some of the design styles and then discuss the important placement algorithms.

In the *standard cell* design style, cells corresponding to frequently used logic modules are predesigned and stored in libraries. These cells have fixed height, but varying widths, depending on the module functionality and driving capabilities. These cells are laid out in rows, with routing channels reserved between rows of cells for the interconnects. Power and ground lines run horizontally through the cells, and the logical inputs and outputs of the cells are brought out at terminals along the top or bottom edge of the cell or both. Connections between the terminals of cells are made by running interconnects through the routing channels. Connections from one row to another are made by using feedthrough cells, which are standard-height cells with a few vertical interconnects. A typical standard cell layout is shown in Figure 3.1.

Figure 3.2 shows what a typical *gate array* layout would look like. The circuit again consists of predefined libraries of modules, except that most of the mask layers are prefabricated on the wafer. Specifically, the layout is comprised of a two-dimensional array of *basic cells,* all of equal size, laid out in rows that are separated by routing areas called channels. Basic cells contain isolated transistors and must be "programmed" with connections in different layers of metal. By programming and connecting one or more basic cells together, all the basic logic gates (AND, NOR, NOT, ...) and flip-flops can be created. To reduce the fabrication time and cost per new design, wafers of gate array chips are fabricated in large amounts until the point

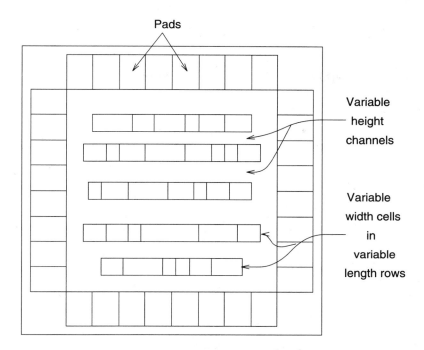

Figure 3.1 Example of a standard cell design

of programming and connecting the basic cells is reached. This means that the locations of the basic cells and the height of the channels are fixed. Each new design will then require only a few fabrication steps on the prefabricated wafers and can be completed in much less time. Although the fabrication time is much less, there are some drawbacks to gate array layout. There is an absolute upper bound on the number of basic cells available and so the number of possible gates is limited. Also, the fixed size of the channels can either restrict the routing of nets or cause much wasted chip area. Often, basic cell utilization is much less than 100%.

Sea-of-gates designs are very similar to gate arrays. The primary difference is that there are no predefined areas for routing. Instead, it is assumed that an extra layer of metal can be used for over-the-cell connections. The number of basic cells is much higher than that of the gate array, but the fabrication is more costly since more metal layers are necessary and the layout is more difficult.

In *macro block* or *building block* design, macro cells and corresponding to larger pre-designed functional units such as memory arrays, decoder, and ALUs are placed on a VLSI chip. The macro cells can be of irregular shapes and sizes and do not necessarily fit together in regular rows or columns. Space is left around the modules for wiring. Figure 3.3 shows an example of a macro-block placement layout.

Automated layout consists of two primary functions: (1) determining the positions of the modules (standard cells, gates, and macro cells) on the VLSI chip, called *placement,* and (2) interconnecting the modules with wiring, called *routing.* Although placement and routing are

Pads

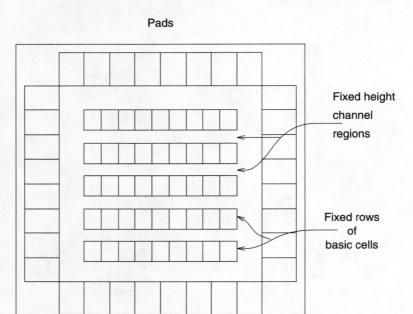

Figure 3.2 Example of a gate array design

intimately related and interdependent, they have been traditionally separately solved because of their computational complexities. Hence placement algorithms use some crude measures to estimate the routing complexities of various placement, which are refined during the actual routing steps.

3.2.2 Placement Problem

The VLSI cell placement problem involves placing a set of cells on a VLSI layout, given a netlist that provides the connectivity between each cell and a library containing layout information for each type of cell. This layout information includes the width and height of the cell, the location of each pin, the presence of equivalent (internally connected) pins, and the possible presence of feedthrough paths within the cell. The primary goal of cell placement is to determine the best location of each cell so as to minimize the total area of the layout and the length of the nets connecting the cells together. We need to minimize the chip area in order to fit more functionality in a chip. Another objective is to minimize the wirelength in order to reduce capacitive delays associated with longer nets and to speed up the operation of the chip. The goals are related since the area of a chip layout is the area of the modules plus the area of the interconnect, hence if the wirelength is reduced, the area of the layout is minimized as well.

3.2.3 Placement Algorithms

Placement methods can be divided into two classes [18, 20, 44]: *constructive* and *iterative*. Constructive methods produce a complete placement (all cells have assigned positions) based

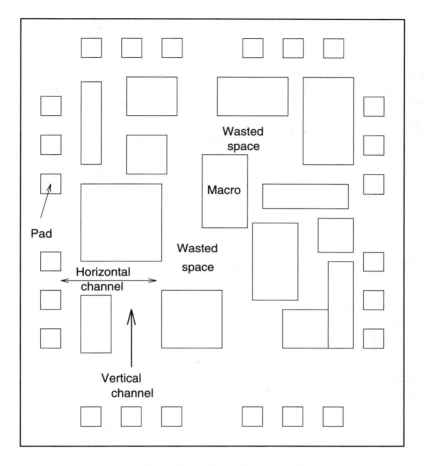

Figure 3.3 Macro block layout style

on a partial placement (some or all cells do not have assigned positions). Constructive algorithms are typically divided into the following classes: (1) cluster growth [17], (2) partitioning-based placement [5, 14, 28], (3) global techniques such as quadratic assignment and convex function optimization [18], and (4) branch-and-bound techniques.

Iterative methods attempt to improve a complete placement by performing heuristic optimizations. Constructive placement algorithms are normally used for initial placement and are usually followed by iterative algorithms. Within one iteration, certain cells are selected and moved to alternative locations. If the resulting configuration is better than the old one, the new configuration is retained; otherwise, the previous configuration is restored. Some of the conventional iterative improvement techniques include pairwise interchange [50], force-directed interchange, force-directed relaxation [19], and successive overrelaxation methods [9, 56].

Most of these iterative techniques accept trial placements only if the objective function does not increase. This characteristic may cause an algorithm to get stuck in a local minimum rather than finding the global optimum. The simulated annealing technique proposed by Kirkpatrick et al. [30] is a general combinatorial optimization technique that uses a probabilistic hill-climbing method to get around this problem. However, this algorithm has several drawbacks, mainly its large CPU time requirements and the need for an efficient annealing schedule [23]. Simulated annealing has been proved to converge to a globally optimal result given an arbitrary amount of computation time. If less CPU time is provided, it will produce near-optimal solutions. The simulated annealing technique has been successfully used in the standard cell placement problem in the TimberWolf placement and routing package [51]. Other implementations of simulated annealing applied to standard cell placement have been reported as well [16].

Simulated evolution is another heuristic for standard cell placement that combines the features of iterative improvement and constructive placement with the ability to avoid getting stuck at local minima using a stochastic approach. The heuristic is based on an analogy between the natural selection process in biological environments and the method of solving engineering problems by iterative improvements. Descriptions of implementations of the evolution-based algorithm can be found in [31, 33, 32].

Recently, another placement algorithm called genetic placement has been proposed, which uses the concepts of maintaining a set of solutions (population) and performing crossover and mutation operations on those populations to produce better populations [12, 53].

For more details on various sequential placement algorithms, the reader is referred to excellent surveys in [22, 43, 44, 52].

3.2.4 Placement Cost Functions

Each of the preceding placement methods depends on the cost function employed in order to measure the acceptability of a current placement. Since the two fold goal of cell placement is to minimize the placement area while ensuring the routability of the layout, cost functions have examined various criteria such as estimated wire length and cell congestion. One simple method for estimating the wire length is to measure the half-perimeter of a box that bounds the pins of a given net. Figure 3.4 graphically shows how the bounding box measure would be calculated. A more computationally intensive measure is to calculate the wire length of the minimal Steiner tree connecting all the terminals.

One way to measure cell congestion is to calculate the number of nets that connect separate partitions of the set of cells. The goal is then to minimize the number of nets cut by a line separating the partitions. Figure 3.5 shows a high- and low-cost configuration for a small example circuit. Some placement algorithms try to minimize the total wire length, or the congestion, or some combination of both.

A simplified model of placement used by some sequential and parallel placement algorithms is as follows. Given a set of modules of equal size and a connection matrix describing their interconnections, the placement problem can be viewed simply as assigning the modules in rows and columns in an array of positions on a chip image. This assumes that multiterminal nets have been decomposed into a collection of two-terminal nets; hence a multiterminal netlist of connections can be represented as a set of two-terminal connections specified as a connection matrix $C = [c_{ij}]$ that gives the number of connections between module i and

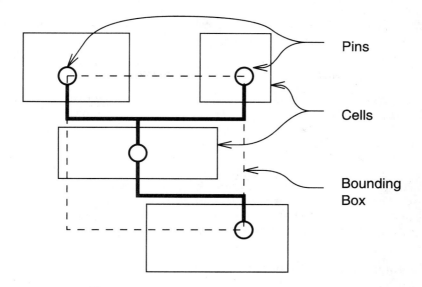

Figure 3.4 Wire length estimation by bounding box

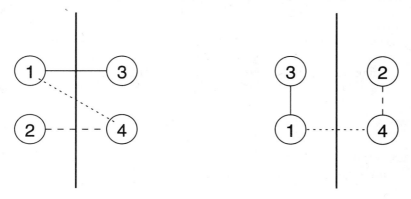

Figure 3.5 Cell congestion estimation by net cut count

module j. Assuming fixed-sized modules to be placed in fixed locations in the chip layout, a distance matrix $D = d_{ij}]$ can be defined that measures the Euclidean distance between the modules i and j. The objective function that is minimized is

$$\mathcal{F} = \sum_{i,j} c_{ij} \cdot d_{ij}$$

Another placement cost function, used in the Timberwolf algorithm for for standard cell placement using simulated annealing, [51] consists of three parts:

1. Estimate of the wire length of all nets as the half perimeter of the bounding box which is the smallest aligned rectangle which contains all terminals in a net (W)

2. Overshoot or undershoot of each row length over the desired row length (R)
3. Area overlap between cells in the same row (O)

$$\mathcal{F} = \alpha \cdot W + \beta \cdot R + \gamma O$$

A third cost function, used in an IBM cell placement program using simulated annealing, [13] assumes a uniform two dimensional placement grid of equal sized cells.

$$\mathcal{F} = W + \alpha \cdot C$$

where W is the total wire length as measured by the half-perimeter of the bounding box of nets and C is the congestion, as measured by counting the number of nets above a certain threshold that crosses each row or column. The evaluation of the congestion is done with the help of a histogram that stores the wire count for every row and column.

From this discussion, is clear that a variety of cost functions have been used by researchers to develop different placement algorithms.

3.2.5 Timing-driven Placement

Recently, as the need for performance- based designs continually increases, it has become important to deal with timing issues during placement. The primary goal of a timing-driven placement algorithm is the minimization of the longest signal delay through the system, or minimization of the total wire length, provided the longest path delay does not exceed a prespecified value. In synchronous digital systems, the performance is determined by its cycle time, which is affected by the longest path delay in the circuit. The signal propagation delay for a net is estimated by taking the product of the output resistance R_{out} of the driving module, and the capacitance of the wiring on the net, C_{out}. Hence for net i, the delay expression becomes

$$d_i = R_{out}^i C_H(|x_i^{max} - x_i^{min}|) + C_V(|y_i^{max} - y_i^{min}|)$$

where C_H and C_V are the horizontal and vertical capacitances per unit length of the horizontal and vertical wires.

Let us consider a circuit described by its logic diagram consisting of modules that are connected to each other. Each connection has an associated delay consisting of a fixed module delay D_i and a delay of a net driven by the module d_i. The timing-driven placement problem is to determine the positions of the modules (which in turn determine the net delays) such that all the delays in all the paths $P_{k,h}$ from primary inputs/storage elements to the primary outputs/storage elements do not exceed prespecified values.

$$\forall k, h \forall P_{k,h} \sum_{i \in P_{k,h}} (D_i + d_i) \leq H_k$$

where $1 < k < $ K, is the number of primary outputs/storage elements, and H_k is the required arrival time for the primary output O_k.

The above timing constraints are handled in different ways by timing-driven placement algorithms. One way is to translate the timing constraints into the net-length bounds prior to execution of the placement program. The net-length bounds remain constant during the placement. In such a case, the placement algorithm will try to minimize the total wirelength of all nets subject to keeping the wirelength of each net within the bound.

Another way to handle timing driven placement is to map the timing constraints into a set of weights which are updated during the execution of the placement program. This is obtained for example by computing a term called the slack $S(i)$ for each net i as the difference between the required arrival time and the actual arrival time of the signal at net i. A slack tells us the most that the delay of a node can be increased without violating the long path contraints. However, delay increases in one node may influence the delay increases of other nodes. Slacks are used in placement programs to determine how much freedom there is in adjusting the positions of modules. One method of assigning weights to nets is to compute the ratio of the current expression of the delay to the slack for each net.

These weights w_i of nets are used to minimize the cost function below that tries to shorten the nets having higher criticality.

$$\mathcal{F} = \sum_N \sum_{i \in N} w_i (|x_i^{max} - x_i^{min}| + |y_i^{max} - y_i^{min}|)$$

3.2.6 Overview of Parallel Placement

Having given a brief overview of the placement problem and various algorithms we will now describe some parallel algorithms that have been proposed for these algorithms. We will classify them into the following classes and describe the detailed algorithms for them in subsequent sections:

- Approach using pairwise cell interchange

- Approach using force-directed cell movement

- Approach using simulated annealing

- Approach using simulated evolution

- Approach using genetic algorithms

- Approach using hierarchical decomposition

- Approach using a combination of some of these techniques

For each of the above classes of algorithms, we will discuss first the sequential algorithms on which they are based and then describe the parallel algorithms. Even though the parallel placement algorithms may be explicitly dealing with the wirelength minimization objective, it is relatively straightforward to extend the algorithms to handle timing-driven constraints as well as shown in the previous subsection. The parallel algorithms will be discussed for shared memory MIMD multiprocessors, distributed memory MIMD message-passing multiprocessors, and SIMD processors.

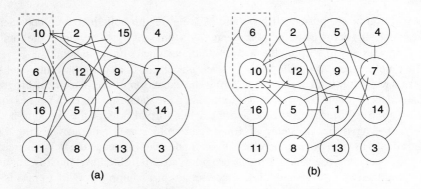

Figure 3.6 Example of placement improvement by iterative improvement (a) before exchange and (b) after exchange (Courtesy of Ueda et al., *IEEE Trans. Computer-Aided Design,* ©IEEE 1983)

3.3 PLACEMENT USING PAIRWISE INTERCHANGE

3.3.1 Overview

We will now describe a parallel algorithm for placement using an adjacent pair-wise exchange approach based on the work of two groups of researchers, Chyan and Breuer [10], and Ueda, Komatsubara, and Hosaka [58].

The adjacent pairwise exchange method of placement improvement uses the simplified model of placing cells of fixed size whose connections are specified by a connection matrix representing connections using two terminal nets. The objective function to be minimized is the total wirelength using the sum of the Euclidean distances between cells weighted by the number of connections between cells, as described in the Section 3.2.4.

The iterative algorithm proceeds as follows. First, select a single pair of neighboring cells in a given sequential order and calculate the sum of the wire length associated with each cell in the pair. If the total wirelength associated with the pair can be decreased by the exchange, these two cells are actually exchanged. Otherwise, they are not exchanged. These steps are repeated until no more improvement is obtained. This procedure is illustrated in Figure 3.6 for a 4 × 4 array of cells. The cell pairs that are chosen for exchange considerations are only immediate neighbors. Figure 3.7 and 3.8 show example ordering of cell pairings for cases N even and odd respectively, which will be executed in sequence from 1 to 24 for $N = 4$ and 1 to 40 for $N = 5$. Such an ordering guarantees that after a set of iterations involving repeated executions of pairwise swaps of categories (a), (b), (c) and (d) any cell can move to any other location in the chip layout using a set of adjacent moves.

3.3.2 Massively Parallel SIMD Algorithm

We will now describe a massively parallel SIMD algorithm for the preceding adjacent pairwise exchange placement algorithm. The algorithm proceeds by assigning a location of the chip area, along with the currently occupying cell, to each processor. For an $N \times N$ array of cells to be placed, one would need using N^2 processors, the processors are arranged as an $N \times N$ array of processors. The cells are initially placed through random assignment or some

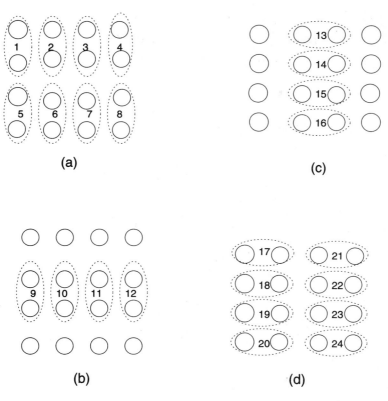

Figure 3.7 Cell pair combination categories in adjacent pair exchange algorithm for N even (Courtesy of Ueda et al., *IEEE Trans. Computer-Aided Design,* ©IEEE 1983)

simple clustering algorithm. The parallel iterative improvement algorithm involves forming independent pairs of cells to be exchanged in parallel among the various processors. All pairs of cell exchanges that are shown in ellipses in Figures 3.7 and 3.8 for categories (a), (b), (c) and (d) can be performed in parallel. This is because the processors are accessing cells that are guaranteed to be independent by the spatial data distribution. During one such iteration, pairs of processors make local decisions regarding whether or not to actually swap the pair of corresponding cells. After one such iteration, the state of the cell placement needs to be informed to all the processors, hence a global update of all cell locations is performed through broadcasting. This enables the processors in a subsequent iteration to properly calculate the wirelength costs of all the cells.

An outline of the massively parallel SIMD placement algorithm entitled *SIMD-PARALLEL-ITERATIVE-PLACEMENT* (for SIMD parallel algorithm for placement using iterative exchange) is given below.

Procedure *SIMD-PARALLEL-ITERATIVE-PLACEMENT;*

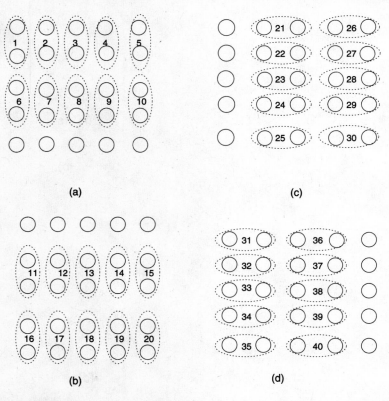

Figure 3.8 Cell pair combination categories in adjacent pair exchange algorithm for N odd (Courtesy of Ueda et al., *IEEE Trans. Computer-Aided Design,* ©IEEE 1983)

Initially allocate one layout location and one cell to each
processor with an initial random placement;

FOR I Iterations in sequence DO
  FOR Cycles (a), (b), (c) , (d) in sequence DO
    FORALL processors in PARALLEL DO

      1. For category (a) .. (d), identify the pair of cells
         to form independent pair to be exchanged;
         Since the pair of cells exist on different processors,
         identify neighboring processor to be the mates for
         category (a) .. (d) to form independent pair, and
         select cells to be considered for exchange;

Identify one processor to be Master, other to be slave for each pair;

2. Each processor calculates amount of addition or reduction of wirelength associated with cell when cell is exchanged with cell of present mate processor;
Master processor receives resultant data;
Data calculated and added to value from Slave
Master determines whether to exchange cells;
IF there is reduction in wirelength
THEN an actual cell exchange is marked;

3. Each processor broadcasts information about new cell locations to affected processors related to the exchanged cells;

END FORALL
ENDFOR
ENDFOR

End Procedure

In the previous discussion it was assumed that all the selected pairs of cells are totally independent from each other in the parallel placement improvement process. By investigating the parallel improvement process in more detail. Ueda et al. have identified [58] the cases where some cell pairs become dependent on the other pairs under certain conditions. There are two cases to consider. (1) connections between cells in different pairs of rows and (2) connections between cells in same pairs of rows.

Case 1. Connections between different pairs of rows. Let us consider the examples of Figure 3.9(a). In this case, pair A judges that the sum of its wire-lengths will increase by 2 if cell 1 and cell 2 are exchanged. Therefore, the cells are not actually exchanged. This judgment is obviously correct independent of whether their related cells 5 and 6 in pairs C and E are exchanged. It can be shown that, for more general cases, if the connections are between cells in different pairs of rows, the exchange judgments are always correct for these cases.

Case 2. Connections in the same pair row. When a given pair of nodes to be exchanged has connectivity with nodes within the same pair row, errors in judgment may occur. Let us consider the general case of Figure 3.10, which shows various cases of node pairs (XY) being considered for exchange while having connections to nodes in the same regions R1 or R2. In Figure 3.10(a), the node X has a connection to node T in region R2. When node pair XY is exchanged, if node T is not exchanged as well, the expected amount of wire-length reduction is obtained. If node T is exchanged in addition, an extra amount of reduction is obtained. Hence this case does not produce an incorrect judgment. Next consider case Figure 3.10(b),

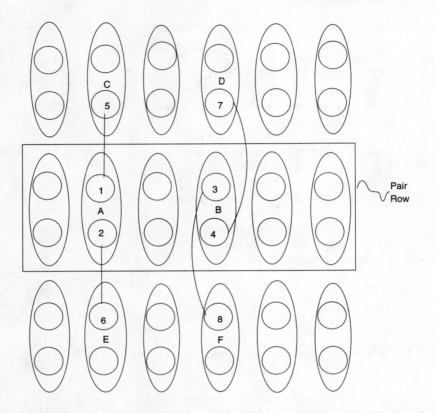

Figure 3.9 Analysis of dependencies of cell exchanges for independent pairs, where connections exist between different pairs of rows (Courtesy of Ueda et al., *IEEE Trans. Computer-Aided Design,* ©IEEE 1983)

where node X has a connection to node U in region R1. In this case under exchange of XY, a wire-length reduction of 1 is expected. If node U moves as well, the reduction becomes zero. If there are two or more connections to nodes in region R1, as shown in Figure 3.10(c), then there is an incorrect judgment. Similarly, Figure 3.10(d) has a possibility of incorrect judgment.

Analysis We now evaluate the parallelism theoretically exploited by this algorithm. With the sequential algorithm, only a single pair of cells is selected and processed at a time, while with the parallel processing algorithm executing on N^2 processors, on the average, $N(N-1)/2$ pairs of cells are processed concurrently.

With a sequential algorithm, only a single pair of cells can be selected and processed at a time, while with the parallel algorithm, $N(N-1)/2$ pairs of nodes are selected and processed concurrently.

The number of iteration cycles that is consumed for obtaining a final placement with the sequential algorithm increases proportional to N^2 as determined through simulation results

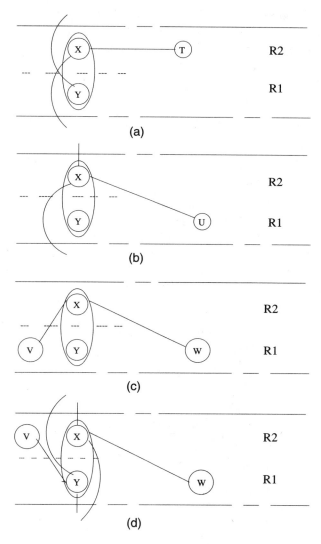

Figure 3.10 Analysis of dependencies where connections exist at same pair row (Courtesy of Ueda et al.,*IEEE Trans. Computer-Aided Design,* ©IEEE 1983)

on some benchmark circuits. Since numerous cells are processed concurrently in the parallel algorithm, it leads to the reduction of the number of iteration cycles consumed to obtain the final placement compared to the sequential algorithm; hence a cycle reduction rate of $N(N-1)/2$ is obtained. From simulation results, the theoretical cycle reduction rate of $N(N-1)/2$ has been verified for a set of benchmark circuits.

However, this reduction rate value does not necessarily correspond to processing time reduction because the period of the parallel processing cycle is generally different from the sequential processing cycle. This is because the cell location update phase in a parallel processor can be an expensive synchronization overhead resulting in less than expected speedups.

Implementation None of the parallel algorithms have been actually implemented on real parallel machines. Ueda et al [58] have reported simulation results on some randomly generated circuits of on a 4×4 array, 6×6 array, and others The data obtained by the simulation programs showed that through parallel processing they have been able to achieve final placement quality as good as the corresponding sequential algorithms.

3.3.3 Distributed Memory MIMD Parallel Algorithm

We now describe an adaptation of the preceding parallel algorithm for the adjacent pairwise interchange for distributed memory MIMD multiprocessors. The parallel exchange placement algorithm proceeds by distributing regions of the layout and the corresponding cells to different processors. For an $N \times N$ array of cells to be placed using P processors, the processors are arranged as a $\sqrt{P} \times \sqrt{P}$ array of processors. Each processor gets assigned a square subregion of chip corresponding to the subarray $\frac{N}{\sqrt{P}} \times \frac{N}{\sqrt{P}}$ of cells. The cells are initially placed through random assignment or some simple clustering algorithm.

The parallel iterative improvement algorithm involves forming independent pairs of cells to be exchanged in parallel among the various processors. All pairs of cell exchanges that are shown in ellipses in Figures 3.7 and 3.8 for categories (a), (b), (c), and (d) can be performed in parallel. This is because the processors are accessing cells that are guaranteed to be independent by the spatial data distribution. During one such iteration, individual processors or pairs of processors make local decisions regarding whether to actually swap the pair of corresponding cells. After one such iteration, the state of the cell placement needs to be passed on to all the processors, hence a global update of all cell locations is performed through broadcasting. This enables the processors in a subsequent iteration to properly calculate the wire-length costs of all the cells.

An outline of the parallel placement algorithm entitled *DM-PARALLEL-ITERATIVE-PLACEMENT* (for distributed memory parallel algorithm using iterative exchange) is given next.

Procedure *DM-PARALLEL-ITERATIVE-PLACEMENT;*

Initially allocate layout regions and groups of cells to each
    processor with an initial random placement;

FOR I Iterations in sequence DO
    FOR Cycles (a), (b), (c) , (d) in sequence DO

FORALL processors in PARALLEL DO

1. For category (a) .. (d), identify the pair of cells
   to form independent pair to be exchanged;
   If both the cells are within the same processor,
   calculate the amount of addition or reduction in
   wire-length associated with the cell exchange locally;
2. If the pair of cells exists on different processors,
   identify neighboring processor to be the mates for
   category (a) .. (d) to form independent pair, and
   select cells to be considered for exchange
   Identify one processor to be Master, other to be
   slave for each pair;
3. Each processor calculates amount of addition or
   reduction of wire-length associated with cell
   when cell is exchanged with cell of
   present mate processor;
   IF processor = Slave THEN
       Send result to Master;
   IF processor = Master THEN
       Receive partial result from Slave;
       Add result to own value;
       IF there is reduction THEN
           Decide to exchange cells;
4. Each processor broadcasts information about
   new cell locations to affected processors
   related to the exchanged cells;

   END FORALL
   ENDFOR
ENDFOR

End Procedure

The same analysis of move dependencies exists in this parallel algorithm as for the SIMD parallel algorithm regarding possibilities of incorrect judgment. There have been no reported implementations of this algorithm on a distributed memory MIMD machine.

3.4 PLACEMENT USING FORCE-DIRECTED MOVES

3.4.1 Overview

In this section we will describe a parallel algorithm for cell placement using a force-directed technique based on work reported by Horvath [21]. Force-directed techniques seeks to move cells with greater connectivity closer together.

The sequential algorithm for force-directed/ placement proceeds as follows. Initially, cells are randomly assigned to positions in the layout so that no cell overlaps with any other. Since the cells' positions are known, it is possible to define a displacement that will move connected cells toward one another. A given cell is displaced by no more than $2*$ *displacement_value* at any iteration. The *displacement_value*, denoted as $delta$, is the total distance in either the x or y direction that a cell is allowed to move in one iteration. The magnitude of attraction of cell i to cell j is determined by $\delta_{ij} = \frac{c_{ij}}{\sum_{k=1}^{n} c_{ik}}\delta$. The total displacement of cell i in the x and y direction can be determined by $\delta x_i = \sum_{j=1}^{n} \delta x_{ij}$ and $\delta y_i = \sum_{j=1}^{n} \delta y_{ij}$, where the δ_{ij} values are defined as follows: If $x_j > x_i$, then $\delta x_{ij} = \delta_{ij}$; otherwise, $\delta x_{ij} = -\delta_{ij}$. The values of δy_{ij} are similarly defined. All modules are then moved as follows. $x_i = x_i + \delta x_i$, and $y_i = y_i + \delta y_i$.

In such a scheme, cells would eventually overlap and cluster. To avoid this condition, when adjacent cells overlap by more than a given percentage of the average height or width of the modules (say 5%), the cells are exchanged.

The iterative procedure is repeated many times, and the best configuration found throughout the search process is output. Some cleanup is performed to remove any remaining overlap.

3.4.2 Massively Parallel SIMD Algorithm

We will now describe a massively parallel SIMD algorithm for cell placement using the force-directed sequential algorithm based on work reported by Horvath [21].

In the parallel algorithm, the processors are assumed to be logically organized as a two-dimensional array. Each processor is assigned a cell and a location on the 2D layout of the chip. The cells are assigned to the processor array so that they are placed on the same relative positions in the processor array as they are on the 2D layout.

The host controller of the SIMD machine passes the *displacement_value*, the percentage of overlap allowed, the current x and y coordinates, the previous x and y coordinates, and the height and width of the cells, to the data processors. The computation of the displacements, overlaps, and exchanges is performed in parallel among the processors. These computation and interchange steps are performed in a checkerboarding pattern as shown in Figure 3.11 so that multiple interchanges are not made at the same time to the same cell.

An outline of the parallel placement algorithm entitled *SIMD-PARALLEL-FORCE-DIRECTED-PLACEMENT* (for massively parallel SIMD placement algorithm using force-directed techniques) is given next.

Procedure *SIMD-PARALLEL-FORCE-DIRECTED-PLACEMENT;*

Initially allocate a layout region and one cell to each
    processor with an initial random placement;

FOR I Iterations in sequence DO
    FORALL processors in PARALLEL DO

        For owned cell i
        Compute displacement of cell i in x direction;

Processor address (ixproc, iyproc)

White ((ixproc + iyproc) mod 2 == 0)

Gray ((ixproc + iyproc) mod 2 == 1)

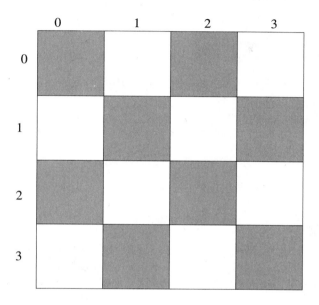

Figure 3.11 Checkerboarding pattern (Courtesy of Horvath, Florida Atlantic Univ. Tech. Report, 1992)

Compute displacement of cell i in y direction;
Compute overlap of cell i in x direction;
Compute overlap of cell i in y direction;

```
/* Select a checkerboard pattern */
/* For processor addressed (ixproc, iyproc) */
IF (ixproc mod 2 == 0)
    THEN IF (overlapx > allowed overlap)
        Exchange cells in east and west direction;
IF (ixproc mod 2 == 1)
    THEN IF (overlapx > allowed overlap)
        Exchange cells in east and west direction;
IF (iyproc mod 2 == 0)
    THEN IF (overlapy > allowed overlap)
        Exchange cells in north and south direction;
IF (ixproc mod 2 == 1)
    THEN IF (overlapy > allowed overlap)
```

TABLE 3.1 Runtimes (seconds) and Wire-length of Serial Timberwolf3.2 Program and SIMD Parallel Program PIREN on the MasPar MP-2™

Circuit	Cells	Serial (VAX 6320)			SIMD (MasPar MP2.2)		
		Wire-Length	Runtime	Speedup	Wire-Length	Runtime	Speedup
regfile	160	144,700	1,258	1.0	1,365,540	49	25.7
decin	138	3,370,560	784	1.0	2,772,755	104	7.5
primary1	833	12,871,425	33,333	1.0	11,289,645	205	162.6

Exchange cells in north and south direction;

Broadcast new cell locations to all processors;
END FORALL
END FOR

End Procedure

Implementation The preceding parallel algorithm for cell placement has been implemented in the PIREN2.0 program on a MasPar MP2.2™ SIMD parallel processor. Results of the wire-length and runtimes of the PIREN algorithm running on a sequential VAX 6320™ computer have been comparable to that of Timberwolf version 3.2. Table 3.1 shows some example results on three benchmark circuits of the runtimes (in seconds), the speedups, and the quality of placements (in terms of total weighted wire-length). As can be observed, orders of magnitude speedups were obtained over sequential execution.

3.5 PLACEMENT USING SIMULATED ANNEALING

3.5.1 Overview

Simulated annealing is a powerful technique that has been used to solve combinatorial optimization problems using a probabilistic hill-climbing algorithm, with the added ability to escape from local minima in the search space [30]. The technique has been successfully applied to the cell placement application, giving excellent quality of results at large computational costs.

A general simulated annealing algorithm for cell placement proceeds as follows.

Procedure *SIMULATED-ANNEALING-PLACEMENT*;

Start with an initial placement solution (state) S;
Set $T = T_0$ (initial temperature);

REPEAT /* outer loop */

```
moves_attempted = 0;
REPEAT /* inner loop */

    Generate a move;
        Select move (cell exchange or cell displacement type);
        IF displacement THEN
            Select random cell;
            Move cell to random location;
        IF exchange THEN
            Select two random cells;
            Exchange cell locations;
    Move perturbs S to generate a new state, Sn;
    Evaluate cost change ΔE = E(Sn) - E(S);
    Decide to accept or reject move;
    IF (ΔE < 0 ) THEN
        Accept move;
    ELSE IF random(0,1) < e^(-ΔE/T) THEN
        Accept move;
    ELSE Reject move;
    Update state if accept, i.e., replace S with Sn;
    Increment moves_attempted;

UNTIL moves_attempted = max_moves; /* inner loop */
Update T (control temperature);
UNTIL termination condition; /* end outer loop */
```

End Procedure

In any simulated annealing algorithm, four important criteria are the choice of the initial temperature, the equilibrium detection condition at a particular temperature, the rate of decrease of the temperature, and the frozen or termination condition. The set of these criteria is referred to as the *annealing schedule*. Most implementations of simulated annealing use a fixed sequence of temperatures derived empirically [30, 51]. Huang et al. have proposed an adaptive cooling schedule based on the characteristics of the cost distribution and the annealing curve itself (average cost versus logarithm of the temperature) [23].

Theoretical studies have shown that a global optimum can be reached with unit probability provided a set of conditions on the annealing schedule is satisfied, which might take infinite time. In practice, since the computations have to be carried out in finite time, simulated annealing converges to near-optimal solutions. The real disadvantage of the simulated annealing approach is the massive computing times required to converge to a near-optimal solution. Various approaches have therefore been proposed to speed up the simulated annealing process in the sequential algorithm, such as changing the annealing schedules and investigating better move sets.

The simulated annealing technique has been successfully applied to the standard cell placement problem in a program called TimberWolf [51]. The cost function used in the original version of the Timberwolf algorithm (version 3.2) for standard cell placement [51] consists of three parts, as described earlier in Section 3.2.4.

1. Estimate of the wire length of all nets as the half-perimeter of the bounding box that contains all terminals in a net
2. Overshoot or undershoot of each row length over the desired row length
3. Area overlap between cells in the same row

Two types of moves are used to generate new configurations. Either a cell is chosen randomly and displaced to a random location on the chip, or two cells are selected randomly and exchanged. The ratios of displacement to exchange moves is set to about 5:1. A temperature-dependent range limiter is used to limit the distance over which a cell can move. Initially, the span of the range limiter is set such that a cell can move anywhere on the chip. Subsequently, the span decreases logarithmically with temperature. The annealing schedule is a fixed one. At each temperature, a fixed number of moves per cell is attempted. The initial temperature is set to a very high fixed temperature, and the final temperature is a very low fixed temperature. The cooling schedule is represented by $T_{i+1} = \alpha(T) \cdot T_i$, where α varies between 0.8 to 0.95.

Other implementations of simulated annealing algorithms for cell placement have been reported. For example, in a future version of Timberwolf (version 4.2), several improvements have been made to improve the runtime performance. The cost function is the same as the earlier version. However, the move generation and cost computation have been changed. Each row is divided into nonoverlapping bins, with the use of these the computation of the row overlap and row overshoot functions become very efficient. The following procedure is adopted for move generation. A cell is selected randomly, and a random location is selected as a destination. If the destination is vacant, a displacement is performed, otherwise an exchange is performed. The temperature profile is again a set of fixed temperatures but over a smaller range. More recent versions of Timberwolf (version 6.0) use the notion of early rejection of bad moves. The basic idea is that, before initiating the costly evaluation of the wire-length portion of the cost function, the row and cell overlaps are determined, and on the basis of those costs, if it is determined that the move is clearly not going to be accepted, the wire-length evaluation is bypassed.

In the next section we will investigate techniques for speeding up simulated annealing algorithms for cell placement by running them on parallel processor systems. For the purpose of this discussion, we will use the Timberwolf (version 3.2) approach discussed previously. The ideas of the more recent versions of sequential simulated annealing algorithms can be easily incorporated into the parallel algorithms as well.

3.5.2 Overview of Parallel Approaches

There are various ways to apply parallelism in simulated annealing.

A. Use parallel evaluation within each move. In this approach, each individual move is evaluated faster by breaking up the task of evaluating a move into subtasks and allocating various subtasks to different processors. This approach is also called move decomposition and is an instance of functional partitioning described in Chapter 1.

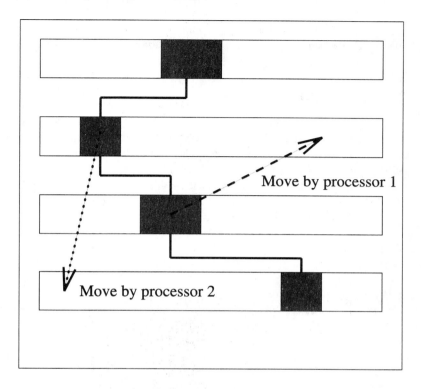

Figure 3.12 Parallel move interaction

B. Use parallel evaluation of multiple moves. In this approach, each processor evaluates a different move (cell displacement or cell exchange) in parallel. Unfortunately, there is a problem with using parallelism to propose and evaluate several moves simultaneously since global information about the state is required in order to evaluate the cost function. The cost function calculations may be incorrect due to interacting moves, as shown in Figure 3.12. If two processors are simultaneously considering moves involving different cells, one processor may move a cell after the second processor reads the state of the layout. The second processor now has inaccurate information about the positions of the cells and will use this out-of-date information to compute the cost of the proposed move. The resulting evaluation will be wrong and may lead to a wrong decision in accepting or rejecting a move. There are two subapproaches for handling move interactions in parallel moves.

B.1. Use parallel evaluation of multiple moves and acceptance of moves that do not interact. In this approach, a set of moves can be identified either statically or dynamically such that they do not interact and apply parallelism to those moves. The convergence characteristics of the parallel algorithm are identical to the serial algorithm. However, since many possibly good moves are left unused, a majority of computations are wasted. Hence the effective useful parallelism is limited.

B.2.Use parallel evaluation and acceptance of multiple interacting moves. In this case, multiple moves are evaluated for acceptance based on inaccurate information, that is, some errors in computations of cost functions are allowed. Here there can be problems with move interactions, affecting the convergence characteristics of the parallel algorithm. However, this approach has the scope for maximum parallelism. In such schemes, a large number of parallel moves are evaluated and accepted on the basis of the past state information. The new cell positions are updated after every set of parallel moves. The reason that such an approach may succeed is that the sequential algorithm is probabilistic to begin with, where some bad moves are accepted at random. If the errors in the parallel algorithm are limited to small values, then the results of the parallel algorithm should be similar to the serial algorithm.

We will now look at each of the proposed algorithm in more detail.

3.5.3 Parallel Evaluation within Moves

In this approach, parallelism is used to generate a move faster. The work of a move consists of selecting a feasible move, evaluating the cost changes, deciding to accept or reject a move, and perhaps updating the global database. Kravitz and Rutenbar [37] have proposed two different approaches to move decomposition. In one approach, called *object decomposition*, the responsibility of moving a set of objects is delegated to a particular processor. For example, we can divide the cells and nets into groups and assign each group to a processor. All operations with respect to moving, accepting, evaluating, and updating that set of cells are done by that processor. Another approach, called *functional decomposition*, delegates the individual portions of work such as wire-length evaluation and updating to different processors.

The object and functional decomposition can be further divided into *static* and *dynamic* cases. If the distribution of objects to processors occurs at initialization and never changes, the strategy is *static object decomposition*. If the objects can be reassigned during execution, the scheme is characterized as *dynamic object decomposition*. Similarly, within functional decomposition, we can have static and dynamic cases. In the *static functional decomposition* method, the operations involved in the move evaluation and acceptance are statically allocated to different processors and the allocation remains unchanged. In the *dynamic functional decomposition* method, the operations involved in the move evaluation and acceptance are divided into a number of subtasks, which are dynamically scheduled on to different processors.

It should be noted that such approaches to parallelization are limited to shared memory algorithms only and have limited scope for parallelism.

Shared Memory MIMD Parallel Algorithm We now describe a shared memory MIMD parallel algorithm for accelerating each move evaluation based on work reported by Kravitz and Rutenbar [37].

In the parallel algorithm, a master process forks several slave processes equal to the number of physical processors, and itself performs all the serial parts of the computation, while the parallel slave processes perform the computation-intensive annealing tasks.

The dynamic functional move decomposition partitions each move into subtasks and distributes the jobs to processors. Figure 3.13 shows the details of the dynamic functional move evaluation. Each move is dynamically divided into several jobs that are inserted into a shared task queue data structure. Each processor removes tasks from the shared task queue

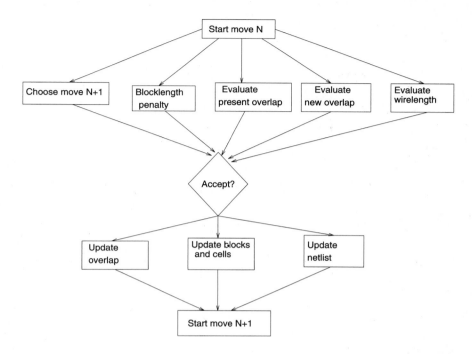

Figure 3.13 Dynamic functional move decomposition (Courtesy of Kravitz
and Rutenbar, *IEEE Trans. Computer-Aided Design,* ©IEEE 1987)

structure using locks, executes each task, generates new tasks, and again inserts them in the
shared task queue structure using locks.

An outline of the algorithm entitled *SM-PARALLEL-SA-DYNAMIC-FUNC-DECOMP*
(for shared memory parallel algorithm using simulated annealing with dynamic functional
move decomposition) is given next.

Procedure *SM-PARALLEL-SA-DYNAMIC-FUNC-DECOMP*;

Initialize shared task queue with first move subtask;

FORALL processors in PARALLEL DO
   WHILE there are tasks in shared task queue DO
      Lock shared queue;
         Remove tasks;
      Unlock shared queue;
      Check task type;
      Execute task of particular type
         (one box in Figure 3.13)
      Generate new tasks;

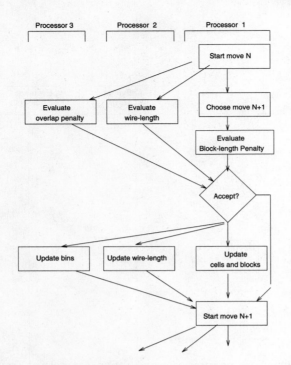

Figure 3.14 Static functional move decomposition (Courtesy of Kravitz and Rutenbar, *IEEE Trans. Computer-Aided Design,* ©IEEE 1987)

```
        Lock shared task queue;
            Insert new tasks on task queue;
        Unlock shared task queue;
      ENDWHILE
   END FORALL
```

End Procedure

The static functional decomposition implementation eliminates the need for synchronization of the subtasks of the dynamic scheme by statically dividing the work into three parts. Figure 3.14 shows the division of labor in the static functional decomposition implementation.

An outline of the algorithm entitled *SM-PARALLEL-SA-STATIC-FUNC-DECOMP*, (for shared memory parallel algorithm using simulated annealing with static functional move decomposition) is given next.

Procedure *SM-PARALLEL-SA-STATIC-FUNC-DECOMP*;

Initialize task queues;

```
FORALL processors in PARALLEL DO
    WHILE there are moves to be evaluated
        IF (processor = 1) THEN
            Start Move N;
            Insert tasks in processor 2 and 3 queue;

        IF (processor = 2) THEN
            Pick up current move;
            Evaluate Wire-Length;
        IF (processor = 3) THEN
            Pick up current move;
            Evaluate Overlap Penalty;

        IF (processor = 1) THEN
            Pick up current move;
            Evaluate Block-Length Penalty;
            Decide on Accept/Reject;

        IF (accept AND processor = 1) THEN
            Update cells;
        IF (accept AND processor = 2) THEN
            Update wire-length;
        IF (accept AND processor = 3) THEN
            Update Bins;
    END WHILE
END FORALL
```

End Procedure

Implementation   Kravitz and Rutenbar have implemented the preceding parallel algorithms for accelerating each move evaluation on a shared memory multiprocessor, a four processor VAX cluster™ [37]. In the parallel implementation, a master process forks several slave processes equal to the number of physical processors (= 4 in their implementation) and itself performs all the serial parts of the computation, while the parallel slave processes perform the computation-intensive annealing tasks.

From the experimental results it was determined that the dynamic functional decomposition was not successful because scheduling the numerous subtasks added too much overhead and created a bottleneck at the task queue. The static functional decomposition used fewer subtasks, was more successful, and gave a speedup of 2 on three processors.

Note that such approaches to parallelization are limited to shared memory multiprocessors only and have limited scope for parallelism (speedups of about 3 to 4).

3.5.4 Noninteracting Parallel Moves

In this approach, one processor is applied to each move so that moves can be generated and evaluated simultaneously. One of the earliest implementations of the strategy of parallel evaluation and acceptance of noninteracting moves was proposed by Rutenbar and Kravitz [37]. They proposed the use of parallel evaluation of moves, but accepting only *a serializable set of moves*. Suppose a set S of moves is evaluated in parallel. Let a subset S^n be a subset of noninteracting moves in S. By concurrently applying all the moves to the same initial configuration, we reach the same final configuration by applying the moves in any order. Such a set of moves is said to be serializable. To gain the maximum parallelism, we must determine a maximum set of serializable moves. However, the determination of the largest set of serializable moves is itself a hard problem. Hence, we resort to heuristics to approximate this strategy.

There are several alternatives to choose from. One such heuristic is that only one of the "acceptable" moves is really accepted. This approach has the penalty of sacrificing some potential parallelism. A second strategy is for each processor to choose moves independently from the entire set of available moves. A third strategy is to bias each processor's move choices using a spatial decomposition where each processor is assigned to perform moves within a region. We will briefly review some of the parallel algorithms that have been reported on shared memory and distributed memory multiprocessors to address these issues.

Shared Memory MIMD Parallel Algorithm A very simple strategy for parallel move evaluation and acceptance of noninteracting moves on shared memory multiprocessors is to accept only one of the *acceptable* moves even though multiple moves are evaluated in parallel. This approach has the penalty of sacrificing some potential parallelism. Under such an approach, the parallel moves are evaluated asynchronously. All the moves need not start and finish at the same time. If all moves are rejected, parallel evaluation can proceed with no further synchronization. There is a synchronization after the first acceptable move is found. A process can prevent other processes from starting the evaluation of a move by setting a lock. Once a process has begun evaluating a move, it can terminate in one of three ways: reject a move, accept a move, or abort a move. An outline of the algorithm entitled *SM-PARALLEL-SA-NONINTER-LOCKSTATE* (for shared memory parallel algorithm using simulated annealing with parallel noninteractive moves using locking of entire state) is given next.

Procedure *SM-PARALLEL-SA-NONINTER-LOCKSTATE*;

Start with an initial placement solution (state) S
Set $T = T_0$ (initial temperature)

REPEAT /* outer loop */
   moves_attempted = 0;
   REPEAT /* inner loop */
      FORALL processors asynchronously in PARALLEL DO
         Generate a move to perturb S to new state, S_n;
         Evaluate cost change $\Delta E = E(S_n) - E(S)$;
         Decide to accept or reject move;

IF decision = Accept THEN
  Attempt to lock state;
IF Lock successful THEN
  Update state, replace S with S_n;
  Synchronize other processors;
ELSE Abort Move;
 Increment moves_attempted;
 END FORALL
UNTIL moves_attempted = max_moves; /* inner loop */
Update T (control temperature);
UNTIL termination condition; /* end outer loop */

End Procedure

  Darema et al. have reported a different parallel algorithm for simulated annealing on a shared memory multiprocessor [13]. Since multiple processors attempt to perturb the configuration, it is important to ensure that no more than one processor attempts to move any cell at any instant of time. A lock is therefore associated with each cell. A processor attempts a move by selecting two cells at random. The pair of cells and also the cells connected to the pair of cells are locked to ensure that another processor will not attempt to move them simultaneously. Before a processor proposes a move, it first checks to see if the lock associated with the cell or other cells connected to the nets belonging to the cells are free. If so, it sets the locks in those cells and proceeds further. If the lock is not free, then the processor tries at random to find another cell whose corresponding locks are free. The effect of a move proposed by a processor is evaluated by it under the assumption that no other perturbations of the configuration are being accepted at the same time by any other processor. If the move is accepted, the processor updates the global copy of the circuit. The cycle of propose-in-parallel, evaluate-in-parallel, accept-in-parallel is repeated until the inner loop criterion is satisfied.

  An outline of the algorithm entitled *SM-PARAL-LEL-SA-NONINTER-LOCKCELL* (for shared memory parallel algorithm using simulated annealing with parallel noninteractive moves using a lock on cells approach) is given next.

Procedure *SM-PARALLEL-SA-NONINTER-LOCKCELL*;

Start with an initial placement solution (state) S;
Set $T = T_0$ (initial temperature)

REPEAT /* outer loop */
 moves_attempted = 0;
 REPEAT /* inner loop */
  FORALL processors asynchronously in PARALLEL DO
   Generate a move;
    Select move (cell exchange or cell displacement type);
    IF displacement THEN

```
                    Select random unlocked cell;
                    Lock cell and its neighbors;
                    Move cell to random location;
                IF exchange THEN
                    Select two random unlocked cells;
                    Lock cells and its neighbors;
                    Exchange cell locations;
                Evaluate cost change ΔE = E(Sₙ) - E(S);
                Decide to accept or reject move;
                IF (ΔE < 0 )
                   THEN Accept move;
                   ELSE IF random(0,1) < e^(-ΔE/T)
                   THEN Accept move;
                   ELSE Reject move;
                Update state if accept, i.e., replace S with Sₙ;
                Unlock cells;
                Increment moves_attempted;
            END FORALL
        UNTIL moves_attempted = max_moves; /* inner loop */
        Update T (control temperature);
    UNTIL termination condition; /* end outer loop */
```

End Procedure

Implementation Kravitz and Rutenbar implemented the first parallel algorithm described, *SM-PARALLEL-SA-NONINTER-LOCKSTATE*, on a four processor VAX cluster™ multiprocessor [37], and showed a speedup of about 2 to 2.5 times faster than their own version of simulated annealing based on TimberWolf3.2 that allowed only two types of moves, cell displacement and exchanges. No results were reported on the quality of placements produced by their parallel algorithm.

Darema et al [13] implemented the second parallel algorithm described, *SM-PARALLEL-SA-NONINTER-LOCKCELL*, on an experimental simulated multiprocessor. The authors experimented with both the runtimes and the quality of the results of the parallel algorithm for a small 81-cell example on a 9×9 grid for which the optimal solution was known. They investigated the variations of the average energy versus the temperature. The parallel algorithm showed results similar to the serial algorithm because it was trying to follow the uniprocessor algorithm. On a simulated 16-processor multiprocessor, the method gave a speedup of about 7.

Distributed Memory MIMD Parallel Algorithm We now describe a distributed memory MIMD parallel algorithm for supporting parallel noninteractive move evaluation and acceptance using a combination of spatial decomposition and cell decomposition based on work reported by Banerjee et al. [3, 49].

The parallel algorithm is suitable for execution on a hypercube-based distributed memory

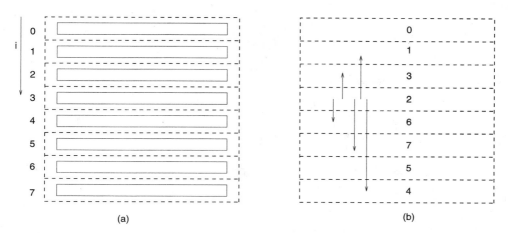

Figure 3.15 Row partitioning of an eight row circuit to an eight-processor hypercube. (a) Row partitioning. (b) Region assignment to processors

multiprocessor. Given the problem of placing a set of standard cells on a hypercube of 2^d processors, the basic idea used in this algorithm is to assign a row or set of rows of the VLSI chip image, including all cells currently placed in that row, to each processor in the hypercube and to have parallel movements of cells within rows and between rows. The rows are mapped to the processors of the hypercube using a binary reflected gray code mapping [48]. For example, for a standard circuit with eight rows of cells, each processor in an eight-processor hypercube will be assigned an entire row, as shown in Figure 3.15.

Cells are assigned an initial position, but are free to migrate between processors as they move around the chip area. Using a distributed data structure, this algorithm is able to support parallel moves. Processors pair up to evaluate a single move type - either a displacement or an exchange of cells. We can therefore guarantee that the cells that will be selected for parallel moves by different processors are different. For a 2^d processor hypercube, up to $2^d - 1$ parallel moves (cell exchanges or displacements) are evaluated and accepted or rejected at a time. After one set of parallel moves, all the new cell locations are broadcast to all the processors.

The advantage of the row partitioning scheme is that each processor has all the relevant neighborhood cell placement information and therefore has exact knowledge of the two penalty cost components (the row overlap and the cell overlap). Hence, under parallel move evaluation and acceptance, the only error that can accumulate due to parallel moves is error in total wire length.

Since cells are owned by processors that are assigned to specific regions, two processors cannot move a single cell simultaneously, hence there is no need for locks on cells in this algorithm. However, some errors can still develop due to simultaneous movement of a cell and its neighbor, since each move evaluation assumes that the neighbor cells are fixed.

An efficient circuit preprocessing algorithm called *heuristic cell coloring* is used that completely eliminates the error in the wire-length computation as well. This is achieved

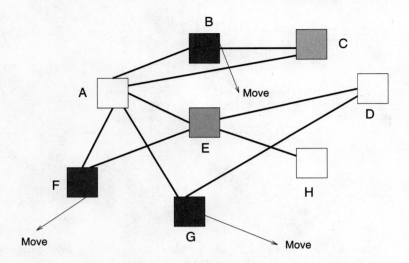

Cells A,D,H of same color can be moved simultaneously

Cells B,F,G of same color can be moved simultaneously

Cells C and E of same color can be moved simultaneously

Figure 3.16 Cell coloring to determine parallel noninteracting moves. Cells A,D,H of same color can be moved simultaneously. Cells B,F,G of same color can be moved simultaneously. Cells C and E of same color can be moved simultaneously.

by identifyings sets of noninteracting cells, that is, cells that do not have any common nets statically through analysis of the net connectivity of the cells. Figure 3.16 illustrates an example circuit containing eight cells. On the basis of the cell connectivity, cells A, D, H are white, cells C, E are lightly shaded, and cells B, F, G are dark shaded. Noninteracting cells can be moved repeatedly and in parallel without any accumulation of cell position misinformation in the distributed database. For example, cells A, D, H can be moved simultaneously without any error in the wire length.

Finding sets of unconnected nodes in an arbitrary graph is analogous to graph coloring. By viewing the circuit description of a standard-cell circuit as a graph where cells correspond to nodes and nets correspond to edges, the graph is colored so that no two connected nodes are the same color. All nodes (cells) of the same color are noninteracting, and can be moved repeatedly between updates without any error accumulation. Although optimal graph-coloring for arbitrary graphs is NP complete, fast heuristic graph-coloring methods are available for graphs that are not *pathological cases* [4, 57].

An outline of the algorithm entitled *DM-PARALLEL-SA-NONINT-OWNCELL-COLOR* (for distributed memory parallel algorithm using simulated annealing with parallel noninteractive moves using cell ownership and coloring) is given next.

Procedure *DM-PARALLEL-SA-NONINT-OWNCELL-COLOR*;

Start with an initial placement solution (state) S;
Partition chip area by rows, assign row/rows to each processor;
Ownership of cells by processors owning chip subregions;
Set $T = T_0$ (initial temperature);

REPEAT /* outer loop */
   moves_attempted = 0;
   REPEAT /* inner loop */
      FORALL processors in PARALLEL DO
         Identify processor pairs for various
            dimensions of hypercube;
         Each processor-pair generates a move cooperatively;

         FOR each color of move in sequence DO
            Select move (cell exchange or cell displacement type);
            IF displacement THEN
               Select random cell of specific color within processor;
               Move to random location within processor pairs region;
            IF exchange THEN
               Select two random cells of specific color within processor pair;
               Exchange cell locations;
            Each processor pair accepts/rejects move on own cost;
            Broadcast updated cell locations;
         END FOR
      END FORALL
      Increment moves_attempted;
   UNTIL moves_attempted = max_moves; /* inner loop */
   Update T (control temperature);
UNTIL termination condition; /* end outer loop */

End Procedure

Implementation   Banerjee and Sargent have reported on the results of an implementation of the above algorithm on a eight processor Intel iPSC/2™ hypercube. Table 3.2 shows some example results for three benchmark circuits of the runtimes (in seconds), the speedups, and the quality of placements (in terms of total weighted wire-length).
Speedups of about 3 to 4 on eight processors were reported. However, the quality of the results was actually inferior (about 10%) to the serial simulated annealing algorithm.
     This loss of quality can be attributed to the following reasons. While in the serial algorithm cells can be selected randomly and can be moved to random locations in the chip, the preceding parallel algorithm constrained the randomization in the search process in two

TABLE 3.2 Runtimes (seconds) and Wire-length of Parallel Algorithm on the Intel iPSC/2™ Hypercube

Circuit	Cells	1 processor		8 processor	
		Wire-Length	Runtime (speedup)	Wire-Length	Runtime (speedup)
1	32	6,803	420 (1.0)	6,663	1,682 (4.0)
2	64	25,098	2,280 (1.0)	22,320	760 (3.0)
3	183	102,191	32,520 (1.0)	119,648	7,680 (4.2)

ways. First, only cells of a particular color were chosen for displacement or exchange at a time. Second, the cells were only allowed to move from the geographically assigned region of one processor to the region of another processor with which the processor was communicating at the time. These two restrictions actually affected the full effectiveness of the simulated annealing search procedure. Of the two reasons, we believe that the cell coloring is more restrictive and damaging to the convergence process, since other spatial decomposition techniques have been proposed to be discussed later and have been observed not to affect the convergence of the solution significantly.

3.5.5 Parallel Interacting Moves

It was noted earlier that independently evaluated parallel moves may interact and hence give erroneous accept/reject decisions. While the previous approaches to parallel move evaluation in annealing either restricted the number of accepted moves to unity or accepted multiple moves if they were noninteracting, a variety of schemes has been proposed for allowing multiple interacting moves to be accepted but somehow trying to bound the errors in the move evaluation. We will discuss several such approaches next, both for shared memory MIMD multiprocessors and for distributed memory MIMD multicomputers.

Shared Memory MIMD Parallel Algorithm We will now describe a parallel algorithm for cell placement of equal sized cells and multiterminal nets with parallel move evaluation and acceptance on a shared memory MIMD multiprocessor. The algorithm is based on work reported by Darema et al. [13]. Let us consider a simplified problem of placing a number of equal-sized cells connected by multiterminal nets on a chip represented as a rectangular array. The entire grid area is divided into vertical and horizontal channels around the cell locations representing the wiring areas. The cost function used in this algorithm is the third cost function described in Section 3.2.4, $F = L + wC$, where L is the total wire-length as measured by the half-perimeter of the bounding box of nets and C is the congestion, as measured by counting the number of nets above a certain threshold that crosses each row or column. The evaluation of the congestion can be done with the help of a histogram that stores the wire count for every row and column.

In the parallel implementation, each processor has a local copy of the histograms. A global copy is kept in shared memory as well. Since multiple processors attempt to perturb the configuration, it is important to ensure that no more than one processor attempts to move a cell at any instant of time. A lock is therefore associated with each cell. A processor attempts a move by selecting two cells at random. The pair of cells are locked to ensure that another processor will not attempt to move them simultaneously. Note that this algorithm differs from the algorithm described in the previous section where the pair of cells *and* its neighbors are locked. In this algorithm the neighbors of the pair of cells are not locked. The algorithm also uses the local copy of the histograms to compute the change in the cost function. This method guarantees that the global histogram will be correct once all the processors have finished. It also guarantees that the wire-length calculations will be correct.

Before a processor proposes a move, it first checks to see if the lock associated with the cell is free. If so, it sets the lock in that cell and proceeds further. If the lock is not free, then the processor tries at random to find another cell whose corresponding lock is free. The effect of a move proposed by a processor is evaluated by it under the assumption that no other perturbations of the configuration are being accepted at the same time by any other processor. If the move is accepted, the processor updates the global copy of the histogram by adding or subtracting 1 from the correct rows and columns. The cycle of propose-in-parallel, evaluate-in-parallel, accept-in-parallel is repeated until the inner loop criterion is satisfied. An outline of the algorithm entitled *SM-PARALLEL-SA-INTER-LOCKCELL* (for shared memory parallel algorithm using simulated annealing with parallel interactive moves using a lock on cells approach and local histograms) is given next.

Procedure *SM-PARALLEL-SA-INTER-LOCKCELL*;

Start with an initial placement solution (state) S;
Set $T = T_0$ (initial temperature)

REPEAT /* outer loop */
  moves_attempted = 0;
  REPEAT /* inner loop */
    FORALL processors asynchronously in PARALLEL DO
      Generate a move;
        Select move (cell exchange or cell displacement type);
        IF displacement THEN
          Select random unlocked cell;
          Lock cell;
          Move cell to random location;
        IF exchange THEN
          Select two random unlocked cells;
          Lock cells;
          Exchange cell locations;
      Evaluate cost change $\Delta E = E(S_n) - E(S)$;
      Decide to accept or reject move;
      IF ($\Delta E < 0$)
        THEN Accept move;

ELSE IF random$(0,1) < e^{-\Delta E/T}$
    THEN Accept move;
    ELSE Reject move;
Update circuit and histogram if accept, i.e., replace S with S_n;
Unlock cells;
Increment moves_attempted;
  END FORALL
  UNTIL moves_attempted = max_moves; /* inner loop */
  Update T (control temperature);
UNTIL termination condition; /* end outer loop */

End Procedure

The algorithm is similar to the one discussed earlier for noninteracting move acceptances, except that, instead of locking all the cells connected on the nets associated with the pair of cells being considered for a move, only the pair of cells considered for the move is locked.

We now describe a a different parallel simulated annealing algorithm on a shared memory MIMD multiprocessor using a decomposition approach based on the work reported by Natarajan and Kirkpatrick [40]. In this algorithm, the layout area is divided into many subareas, and placement within each subarea is improved by a separate processor. The partitioning into subareas is varied during the run of the algorithm to ensure unrestricted movement of the circuit cells across the entire chip area.

An outline of the algorithm entitled *SM-PARALLEL-SA-DOMAIN* (for shared memory parallel algorithm using simulated annealing with domain partitioning) is given next.

Procedure *SM-PARALLEL-SA-DOMAIN*;

Start with an initial solution (state) S in the search space;
Partition the chip area into p domains $A_1, .., A_p$;
Set $T = T_0$ (initial temperature);

REPEAT /* outer loop */
  moves_attempted = 0;
  REPEAT /* inner loop */
    Assign Domain A_i to processor P_i;
    FOR each domain type DO
      FORALL processors in PARALLEL DO
        Each processor P_i works in own domain A_i;
        Generate a move in own domain, A_i;
        Select move (cell exchange or cell displacement type);
        IF displacement THEN
          Select random cell within domain, A_i;
          Move to random location within domain, A_i;

        IF exchange THEN
           Select two random cells within domain, A_i;
           Exchange cell locations;
        Move perturbs S to generate a new state, S_n;
        Evaluate cost change $\Delta E = E(S_n) - E(S)$;
        Decide to accept or reject move on basis of own costs;
        IF $(\Delta E < 0)$
           THEN ACCEPT-IN-PARALLEL move;
           ELSE IF random(0,1) $< e^{-\Delta E/T}$
              THEN ACCEPT-IN-PARALLEL move;
              ELSE Reject move;
      END FORALL
      Update GLOBAL STATE;
      Increment moves_attempted
      Modify domain partitioning;
    END FOR
  UNTIL moves_attempted = max_moves /* inner loop */
  Update T;
UNTIL termination condition /* end outer loop */

End Procedure

    Computation in the inner loop is shared among multiple processors as follows. Each processor proposes a move in parallel with other processors. Processor P_i is allowed to choose cells within its own domain A_i. The effect of a move proposed by a processor is evaluated under the assumption that no other perturbations of the configuration are being accepted simultaneously by another processor. If a move is accepted by a processor, it performs an ACCEPT-IN-PARALLEL step. This step consists of modifying the globally shared values of the histogram values of channels, and the cost function. This is performed using locks on the shared values by each processor before performing the updates. Even though this allows for correct update of the shared data stucture after a sequence of moves, there can still be errors in the computation of the cost function by each processor since each processor assumes that the rest of the placement remains unchanged, when in fact they are not.

    The choice of a partitioning strategy is discussed next when a parallel algorithm is run with K processors. For each K, this approach uses a predetermined set $D_1, D_2, ...D_{m_k}$, consisting of m_k different K-way partitions of the chip. These are illustrated in Figure 3.17 for four different three-way decompositions of the chip area. For each iteration of the inner loop, the processors use a fixed partition. The cycle of partitions is repeated so that a cell can go potentially from any location to any other location of the chip. The set of partitions is not unique. Some possible choices include dividing the chip into rectilinear regions that are modified at runtime to ensure unrestricted movement of cells. Experiments run by the authors did not show any one way of partitioning to be consistently better than the rest. Therefore, this is left to the user.

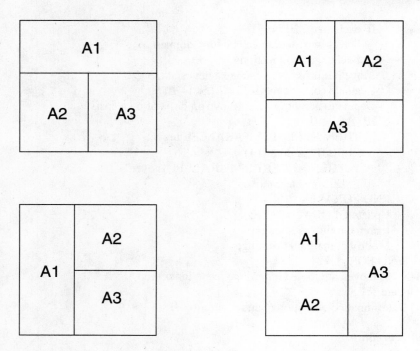

Figure 3.17 Four different three-way decompositions of chip area (Courtesy of Natarajan and Kirkpatrick, IBM Technical Report, 1989)

We now describe a third parallel algorithm for simulated annealing based on cell partitioning across processors. The algorithm was proposed by Casotto et al. for the macrocell placement problem [7], but we will adapt the algorithm for the cell placement problem. The basic approach in parallelizing this algorithm is to partition the set of cells among the processors in such a way as to minimize the interaction among parallel cell movements and hence reduce the error. The initial partitioning is random, but it is successively updated according to a criterion to be described later. A single copy of the current state of the chip is kept in global memory. The cells are distributed evenly among the processors. Each processor asynchronously attempts to move a cell assigned to it either by displacing the cell or by exchanging it with another cell. Displacements do not require any synchronization. If a processor attempts to exchange a cell with another cell belonging to a different processor, it stops the other processor before completing the move. Since the ratio of displacements to exchanges is 10:1 the synchronization overheads are relatively low.

An outline of the algorithm entitled *SM-PARALLEL-SA-INTER-OWNCELL* (for shared memory parallel algorithm using simulated annealing with parallel interactive moves with cell ownership) is given next.

Procedure *SM-PARALLEL-SA-INTER-OWNCELL*;

Start with an initial solution (state) S in the search space;

Partition the set of cells into P partitions, $C_1, C_2, .., C_P$;
Set $T = T_0$ (initial temperature);

REPEAT /* outer loop */
  moves_attempted = 0;
  REPEAT /* inner loop */
    Assign Partition of cells C_i to processor P_i;
    FORALL processors in PARALLEL DO
      Each processor P_i works in own partition C_i of cells;
      Generate a move in own partition, C_i;
      Select a random cell within partition, C_i;
      Select move (displacement exchange);
      IF displacement THEN
        Move cell to random location anywhere in chip;
      IF exchange THEN
        Select a second random cell anywhere;
        (NOTE: The second cell need be in partition C_i)
        Ask processor of second cell to lock second cell;
        Exchange cell locations;
      Move perturbs S to generate a new state, S_n;
      Evaluate cost change $\Delta E = E(S_n) - E(S)$;
      Decide to accept or reject move;
      IF ($\Delta E < 0$)
        THEN ACCEPT-IN-PARALLEL move;
        ELSE IF random(0,1) $< e^{-\Delta E/T}$;
          THEN ACCEPT-IN-PARALLEL move;
          ELSE Reject move;
    END FORALL
    Lock state;
      Update GLOBAL STATE;
      Modify cell partitioning among processors if necessary;
    Unlock state;
    Increment moves_attempted
  UNTIL moves_attempted = max_moves; /* inner loop */
UNTIL termination condition; /* end outer loop */

End Procedure

    Some details of the implementation of the parallel algorithm involve the minimization of the error in computing the cost function by assigning the cells to processors such that they rarely interact. The cost functions consists of a total estimated wire-length, the overlap area among cells, and the total area of the chip as measured by the area of the enclosing rectangle. Errors in computing the cost function occur because the total wire-length is not

TABLE 3.3 Runtimes (seconds) and Wire-Length of Parallel Algorithm on the Sequent Balance™ Multiprocessor

Circuit	Cells	Processors	Wire-Length	Runtime	Speedup
1	30	1	38,286	12,900	1.0
		4	38,223	3,360	3.3
		8	38,334	2,016	6.4

computed accurately, or because the cell overlap estimates were incorrect. The error in overlap computations and area computations can be minimized by assigning cells that are physically adjacent in the chip area to the same processor. Since cell locations dynamically change during the placement algorithm, Casotto et al. [7] have proposed the use of another simulated-annealing-based algorithm for assigning the cells to the processors that performs the cell assignment to processors using this clustering concept. This algorithm runs concurrently with the placement algorithm and periodically is used to rearrange the cell ownerships among processors.

Implementation   Darema et al. [13] have implemented the first algorithm described, *SM-PARALLEL-SA-INTER-LOCKCELL* on a 16-processor simulated multiprocessor. They have performed some experiments on a sample 81-cell placement example. The results of the layout quality were always inferior to that produced by a sequential algorithm due to the acceptance of interacting moves, but the speedups measured were much higher; speedups of about 11 on 16 processors were obtained, compared to the speedups of about 7 using the full locking schemes. Casotto et al. reported results of the second algorithm described above, *SM-PARALLEL-SA-INTER-OWNCELL*, for various macro-cell circuits on an eight processor Sequent Balance 8000™ multiprocessor [7]. Table 3.3 shows some example results on one benchmark circuit of the runtimes (in seconds), the speedups, and the quality of placements (in terms of total wire-length).

The quality of results produced by the parallel algorithm was similar to that produced by a serial algorithm. Also, the speedups were about 6.4 on eight processors.

Distributed Memory MIMD Parallel Algorithm In this section we will describe parallel simulated annealing algorithms for cell placement that are suitable for execution on distributed memory MIMD multicomputers.

We first describe a parallel algorithm for cell placement based on geographic chip area partitioning that is suitable for execution on hypercube-based distributed memory multicomputers. The algorithm is based on work reported by Banerjee, Jones, and Sargent [2, 3, 26, 49].

Given the problem of placing a set of standard cells on a hypercube of 2^d processors, the basic idea used in this algorithm is to assign a subarea of the VLSI chip image including all cells currently located in that subarea to each processor of the hypercube, and to have parallel movements of cells between subareas. The subareas are mapped using either a grid-wise or row-wise partitioning scheme. Cells are assigned an initial position, but are free to migrate between processors as they move around the chip area. Using a distributed data structure, this algorithm is able to support parallel moves. Processors pair up to evaluate a single move type - either a displacement or an exchange of cells. Only processors that are connected by direct hypercube links are paired up to evaluate a parallel move in the grid-wise partitioned algorithm. We can therefore guarantee that the cells that will be selected for parallel moves by different processors are different. For a 2^d processor hypercube, up to $2^d - 1$ parallel moves (cell exchanges or displacements) are to be evaluated and accepted/rejected by assuming that there is no interaction among the moves. After one set of parallel moves, all the new cell locations are broadcast to all the processors. In practice, there will be some interaction between the individual moves, hence there are some errors in the evaluation of the cost functions. However, the errors are temporary and do not accumulate since we synchronize after one set of 2^{d-1} moves using our global broadcast mechanism. The number of moves attempted by each processor per temperature, is the total number of moves attempted in the sequential algorithm divided by 2^{d-1}. An outline of the algorithm entitled *DM-PARALLEL-SA-INTER-DOMAIN* (for distributed memory parallel algorithm using simulated annealing with parallel interactive moves using domain partitioning among processors) is given next.

Procedure *DM-PARALLEL-SA-INTER-DOMAIN*;

Start with an initial placement solution (state) S;
Partition chip area by grid or row mapping;
Assign chip subregions to processors;
Ownership of cells by processors owning chip subregions;
Set $T = T_0$ (initial temperature);

REPEAT /* outer loop */
  moves_attempted = 0;
  REPEAT /* inner loop */
    FORALL processors in PARALLEL DO
      Identify processor pairs for various dimensions of hypercube;
      Each processor pair generates a move cooperatively;
        Select move (cell exchange or cell displacement type);
        IF displacement THEN
          Select a random cell;
          Move cell to random location;
          within processor pairs region;
        IF exchange THEN
          Select two random cells;
          Exchange cell locations;
        Each processor pair accepts/rejects move on own cost;
      Broadcast updated cell locations;
    END FORALL
    Increment moves_attempted;
  UNTIL moves_attempted = max_moves; /* inner loop */

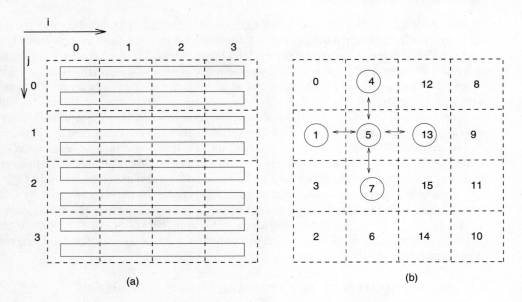

Figure 3.18 Grid partitioning for eight row circuit on 16-processor hypercube. (a) Grid partitioning (b) Region assignment to processors

    Update T (control temperature);
UNTIL termination condition; /* end outer loop */

End Procedure

    The parallel algorithm divides the circuit into a number of parts equal to the number of processors in the hypercube = 2^d. Two forms of partitioning have been proposed. In the grid partitioning scheme, the circuit is divided into rectangular regions by forming 2^k strips in the i dimension and $2^d - k$ strips in the j dimension as shown in Figure 3.18(a) for $d = 4$, and $k = 2$. The region assignment to different processors in the hypercube is performed in the following manner. The region $A(i, j)$ is assigned to the processor $G(i, j)$ using the binary reflected gray code mapping [48]. The assignment of regions in the partition in Figure 3.18(a) to processors of the hypercube is shown in Figure 3.18(b). The advantage of this region assignment is that processors that are assigned physically adjacent regions, $G(i, j)$ and $G(i + 1, j)$ [similarly, processors $G(i, j)$ and $G(i, j + 1)$], are physically adjacent, that is, connected by direct links in the hypercube. This region assignment results in processors communicating with each other in the parallel algorithm to also be physically near each other. Since a lot of communication occurs between processors that are assigned regions that are physically near each other, this partitioning will result in more localized messages and hence improved performance. Note that in this assignment each virtual grid corresponds to a horizontal portion of a number of rows. For example, for a standard cell circuit with eight rows of cells, each processor in a 16-processor hypercube will be assigned one-fourth the horizontal length of two of the rows, as shown in Figure 3.18(a).

A second partitioning scheme has been proposed in which each processor of the hypercube is assigned an entire row or set of rows of the standard cell layout. The rows are mapped, using a binary reflected gray code mapping [48], to the processors of the hypercube, as shown in Figure 3.15. Row partitioning cannot achieve as fine a data granularity as grid partitioning, because the subarea corresponding to a row of cells can be allocated to only one processor. The primary benefit of row partitioning is that the entire cost of any move type can be computed solely on the basis of local information, along with its partner node as will be discussed later.

The cost function used in this algorithm is identical to that used in TimberWolf3.2 [51] and consists of three subcosts: (1) estimated wire length using bounding boxes, (2) nonideal row length penalty, and (3) overlapping cell area penalty.

Since there is no concept of a shared database on a distributed memory machine, a distributed data structure is used to support the parallel annealing algorithm. In the grid wise partitioning, each processor contains the following information to aid in the computation of the cost function in parallel among processors in the distributed memory machine: (1) A list of cells currently assigned to this processor along with the following information for each cell: (2) The width of the cell; (3) The (x, y) coordinate location at which the center of the cell is currently placed; (4) A list of nets to which this cell is connected; (5) For each net listed in (4), a list of other cells to which the net is connected, along with the (x, y) pin location(s) within these cells; and (6) A list of (x, y) locations and widths of all cells that are assigned to processors that are adjacent in the two dimensions of the hypercube corresponding to the east-west nearest neighbors in the physical area map. This allows the calculation of the cell overlap and row length penalty in the cost function.

In row-wise partitioning, each processor maintains a list of cells currently assigned to this processor along with netlist information necessary to compute the bounding box portion of the cost function. Note that the data structure need not contain any information about the cells in the east and west neighbor processors for every processor.

Pairs of processors cooperate to perform two kinds of cell moves: cell displacements and pairwise move exchanges. The ratio of displacements to exchanges is maintained at approximately 5:1 as used by TimberWolf3.2. One processor assumes the role of master, the other of Slave. The relative master/slave relationship between any two processors alternates in time to avoid load imbalance in cell complements. The master determines the type of move that will be made and informs the slave. Hence, this approach also uses parallelism. This is where we apply parallelism within a move evaluation (strategy A characterized in the introduction to parallel annealing approaches). Theoretically, two cooperating processors can perform a cell move in half the time of a single processor; however, the precedence of computational steps in resolving a move does not always allow master and slave to operate concurrently. There are two subclasses of moves for both displacements and exchanges, or four move types in total:

(1) intraprocessor cell displacement; (2) intraprocessor cell exchange; (3) interprocessor cell displacement; and (4) interprocessor cell exchange.

During an intraprocessor cell displacement, the master displaces a single cell to another location within its allocated chip area. The candidate location is chosen randomly from within a range-limiting rectangle centered around the cell's current location. During an intraprocessor cell exchange move, the master selects two candidate cells and exchanges their position. The change in cost is calculated entirely by the master, as is the decision to accept the move. If the bounding box created by the two candidate cells exceeds the range-limiting window in either dimension the exchange is rejected. During an interprocessor cell displacement, the master selects the candidate cell, computes the effect of its loss, and sends a copy of the cell to the slave. The slave picks a new location from the area created by the intersection of the slave's subarea and the range-limiting box centered around the cell's previous location. Accounting for the master's loss, the slave computes the total cost of accepting the move and decides accordingly. During an interprocessor cell exchange move, master and slave both select random cells, and both compute partial exchange costs. The slave informs the master of its partial cost-change calculations and the master then makes the decision to accept the move. As in intraprocessor exchanges, the move is rejected outright if the two cells are too far apart.

Processors pair up to perform one of the four types of cell moves described earlier. In grid-wise partitioning, the processors with which each processor pairs up are determined by the direct links of the hypercube. For example, Figure 3.18(b) shows the neighbors of processor 5. The row-wise mapping using the binary reflected gray codes [48] satisfies the property of processor proximity, while providing a more geographically uniform move selection. A mapping corresponding to a binary reflected gray-code sequence has the additional property that two processors with node numbers P_i and $P_{i \pm 2j}$ will be separated by at most two linkhops for $0 < j < P/2$ [48]. An example of this mapping, and the pairwise communication that is possible with such a mapping are shown in Figure 3.15(b) for processor 2 in an eight-processor hypercube. Arrows originating in the row allocated to processor $n = 2$ indicate pairwise move resolution with other processors $n \pm 2j$, $0 < j < 2$. This provides geographic uniformity for hypercubes of any size.

We now describe a second parallel algorithm for distributed memory multiprocessors that is independent of the machine topology (not specific to a hypercube) based on the work reported by Kim, Ramkumar, and Banerjee [29]. The programming model for the parallel algorithm assumes a concurrent object-oriented model of computation such as the ones provide by the CHARM [15, 27] and PROPERCAD2 systems [42] described in Chapter 10. Conceptually, the PROPERCAD2 and CHARM systems maintain a pool of objects representing work that are created by the application program. Information is exchanged between these objects via messages. The objects in the work pool are distributed and periodically balanced across the available processors by the runtime system.

In this algorithm, before the annealing procedure starts, the *entire circuit is replicated* on each processor, and the *ownership of specific cells* to processors is determined for each row. We give each processor the ownership of consecutive standard cell rows, shown as shaded regions in Figure 3.19. This enables the cost function calculation involving cells inside the region to be more accurate. Because an entire row, not a subpart, is owned by a processor, there

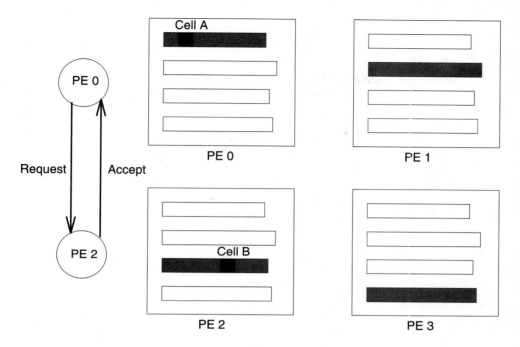

Figure 3.19 Circuit replication and row ownership among processors

cannot be an error in the calculation of cell overlaps and row lengths during the simultaneous evaluation of multiple moves. Note that this approach assumes that the number of rows is greater than or equal to the number of processors. If not, the rows can be split into a number of subrows in a manner similar to the grid partitioning algorithm described earlier. However, for such an approach, some row overlap penalties may be calculated erroneously. We will assume row ownership in the remainder of the discussion.

After the ownership is determined for each row, one *annealing* process is created per processor and the sequential simulated annealing is performed by each processor (*annealing* process) independently.

Each processor is responsible for moving cells that it owns. If a cell moves to a region owned by another processor, the ownership of the cell goes to the new processor. As mentioned before, to evaluate the cost function accurately, each processor has complete cell location information in its local database. Therefore, after a processor accepts a move, it has to pass on the accepted move to other processors so that each processor maintains more or less the same information about the cell locations.

This task of keeping coherent the state of the current placement is the responsibility of the *placement* process created on each processor. The coherence is maintained by keeping track of the changes to its state with respect to each of the other *placement* processes and notifying the other processes of its change periodically. It will also receive notification of changes in other *placement* processes and will update its own state appropriately. A user-defined threshold L is used to limit the number of moves that may be performed in succession before updating the new cell locations at all processors.

An outline of the algorithm entitled *DM-PARALLEL-SA-INTER-REPLICATED* (for distributed memory parallel algorithm using simulated annealing with parallel interactive moves using circuit replication and row-wise cell ownership among processors) is given next.

Procedure *DM-PARALLEL-SA-INTER-REPLICATED*;

Start with an initial placement solution (state) S;
Replicate placement solution and netlist connectivity
   on all processors;

Partition chip area by rows;
Assign row ownership to processors;
Ownership of cells by processors owning
   rows currently containing cell;
Set $T = T_0$ (initial temperature);

REPEAT /* outer loop */
   moves_attempted = 0;
   REPEAT /* inner loop */
      FORALL processors in PARALLEL DO
         Select move;
         IF displacement THEN
            Select a random cell A;
            Move cell to random location (x,y);
            IF (x,y) within current processor's region
               THEN movetype = M1;
               ELSE movetype = M3;
         IF exchange THEN
            Select a random cell A;
            Select a random cell B within range limiter of A;
            IF (cell B owned by current processor)
               THEN movetype = M2;
               ELSE movetype = M4;
                   in cooperation within cell B owner processor;

         Evaluate move (M1,M2,M3,M4) on own copy of circuit;

         IF (accept(move)) THEN
            IF (movetype = M4) THEN
               Freeze(A,B);
               Send AskPermission Message to owner of B;
            ELSE

                    Accept the move M1,M2,M3;
                    Update local database;
                    SendUpdate(move);
                    /* Inform other processors of acceptance of move */
                ELSE Reject the move;
        END FORALL
        Increment moves_attempted;
      UNTIL moves_attempted = max_moves; /* inner loop */
      Update T (control temperature);
  UNTIL termination condition; /* end outer loop */

End Procedure

There are four types of moves in the parallel algorithm:

1. **(M1) Intraprocessor cell displacement:** when cell A moves to a new location owned by the same processor

2. **(M2) Intraprocessor cell exchange:** when two cells A and B owned by the same processor exchange their locations

3. **(M3) Interprocessor cell displacement:** when cell A moves to a new location owned by a different processor

4. **(M4) Interprocessor cell exchange:** when two cells A and B owned by different processors are exchanged

An example of each type of move is shown in Figure 3.20. Notice that the first three types of moves (M1, M2, M3) can be done alone by PE0, the owner of cell A. To execute move M4, however, PE0 needs permission from PE2, which owns cell B. This is because it is possible that cell B may have been moved to another location or is being considered for some other move proposed by another processor, and this information may have not reached processor PE0 yet. Because the information about cell B may be out of date in the database of PE0, PE0 locks cell A and cell B and sends a request message to PE2. Upon receiving the request message, PE2 examines the state of cell B and determines whether to allow the exchange. Upon making a decision, PE2 sends it to PE0 by returning an $answer\_request$ message to PE0. PE0 then unlocks cells A and B and makes the move if the request is permitted. These messages corresponding to M4 are sent and received by the $placement$ process in each processor.

Once one of these four moves is selected randomly, the change in cost function, $\Delta cost = cost_{new} - cost_{old}$ is calculated, and a decision is made to accept or reject the move. If the move is accepted, the $SendUpdate()$ function is called and adds the move to a buffer called $update$. When the $update$ buffer becomes full, the $placement$ process sends the $update$ buffer contents to other processors. This $update$ message is received by the $placement$ process of other processors by invoking a $ReceiveUpdate()$ function.

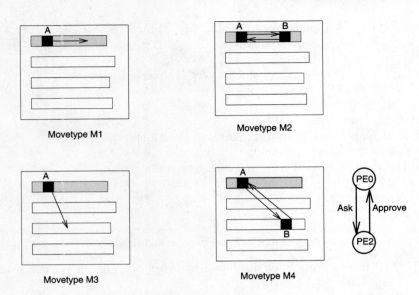

Figure 3.20 Four types of moves in parallel placement algorithm

If the move selected by a processor p is of type M4, the cells involved in the interprocessor exchange (cells A and B) are temporarily locked, and an $ask\_permission$ message is sent by processor p to the processor q that owns cell B. The locked cells remain in their current locations until the $move\_permission$ message, which is sent by processor q, is received. The locked cells cannot be involved in any further operation unless they are first unlocked. Upon receiving a $move\_permission$ message, processor p finishes the move, unlocks the locked cells, and broadcasts its change in location to other processors if necessary.

It is important to note that there is no global synchronization in this algorithm; hence we call this an asynchronous parallel algorithm. After sending an $ask\_permission$ message, processor p does not remain idle until a $move\_permission$ message is received, but goes ahead with the annealing process with unlocked cells.

The success of this parallel simulated annealing algorithm depends on the effectiveness of the interprocessor communication scheme. If the change in cell location is passed on to other processors too infrequently, the placement cost function calculation may have too many errors, resulting in wrong moves. As a result, the placement solution may be worse than that of a uniprocessor algorithm. On the other hand, if the update of cell location changes is done too often, the communication overhead may become too large and this would prevent good speedups. To balance this need for good solution quality and for obtaining good speedups, the following message passing schemes can be used.

We now describe the use of priorities to help reduce the database inconsistencies and therefore to obtain a better placement solution. In the parallel simulated annealing algorithm, the majority of messages passed among processes are one of the following: (1) update, (2) continue-annealing, (3) ask-permission, (4) and move-permission. We give the highest priority to $ask\_permission$. This reduces the probability that cell B owned by processor

q is moved to another location before an $ask\_permission$ message is received. Messages $update$ and $move\_permission$ are given the next highest priority. Finally, the message $continue\_annealing$ is given the lowest priority. By giving a higher priority to message $update$, the most up-to-date information is used at the beginning of each block of L operations that is initiated by $continue\_annealing$. In small circuits, sometimes, a large percentage of cells is locked and does not participate in the annealing process. If such a phenomenon is observed, the priority of $move\_permission$ can be increased to unlock the cells faster.

We now discuss the use of dynamic message sizing of the update message buffer used during updates of states. To reduce the communication overhead, a processor broadcasts an $update$ message to other processors periodically after accumulating a number of accepted moves, not after each move. Now the problem is to determine the frequency of this update message or, equivalently, the number of accepted moves between updates. We define the message size as the number of moves in an $update$ message. If the message size is too large, accepted moves by a processor do not appear on another processor's database on time. Consequently, the error E in the cost function calculation increases and results in degradation of the solution quality. On the contrary, if the message size is too small, the number of messages sent is increased and results in large communication overheads.

A naive approach in determining the message size is to use a static method in which the message size is predetermined and fixed. The problem with this static approach is that there is no good way to determine this message size a priori. In a dynamic approach, the message size is determined dynamically during the annealing process by monitoring the size of the error in the cost function present in the system. If the size of the error during the annealing process becomes too large, the message size automatically becomes smaller to reduce the error at the cost of an increased number of messages. On the other hand, if the size of the error becomes very small, the message size increases to reduce the number of messages. As long as the size of error is bounded, this dynamic approach will produce a good quality solution (equivalent to the serial algorithm) with good speedup.

We now discuss an error control mechanism that can be integrated into the annealing schedule for the parallel implementation to minimize the degradation in quality of solutions generated by the parallel interacting moves. In the parallel algorithm proposed by Kim, Ramkumar and Banerjee [29], the error in the cost function is defined to be the difference between the *real* change in cost from the initial to final configurations and the estimated change in cost equal to the sum of locally perceived changes in cost at each processor. If C_i is the exact initial cost, ΔC_j is the change in cost computed locally at processor P_j, and C_f is the exact cost of the new configuration after a series of moves, then

$$C_i + \sum_{j=1}^{n} \Delta C_j = C_f + \text{error}$$

Since the processors in the asynchronous parallel algorithm do not synchonize to exchange cell position information, C_f is available only at the end of the annealing, process at which time each processor has an identical copy of the entire circuit. Consequently, the error cannot be obtained during the placement process.

In an asynchronous approach, one can only guess (or estimate) what the error will be

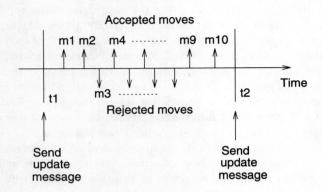

M = 10

Accepted moves

m1 m2   m4 ·········   m9 m10

t1

m3 ·········

Rejected moves

Time

t2

Send
update
message

Send
update
message

Figure 3.21 Moves between update messages with $M = 10$

during the placement process. In the proposed parallel algorithm, instead of estimating the error, we estimate, E, the error that each processor contributes by moving its own cells. The advantage of obtaining the error this way is that it can be calculated by each processor independently without any synchronization.

In Figure 3.21, PE0 makes a sequence of M moves ($m1$, $m2$,..., $m10$). While these M ($= 10$) moves are proposed, evaluated, and accepted, no update message is sent to the other processors. This may cause error in the cost function calculations in the other processors if the accepted moves in M have some nets connected to some cells in the other processors (remote cells). In addition, earlier moves have a higher chance of causing such an error than later ones. For example, $m1$, if accepted, is more likely to cause an error than $m10$ because a larger number of remote cells will be moved during the time between $m1$ and t_2 than between $m10$ and t_2.

In the parallel algorithm, each processor calculates the error that it is contributing to the other processors by

$$E_{\text{estimate}} = \frac{\sum_{i \in A} e(i) \cdot p(i)}{N}$$

In this equation, A is a set of N accepted moves within a time interval $[t_1, t_2]$. $e(i)$ is the upper bound on the amount of error for move i, which is the amount of cell displacement. $p(i)$ is the probability that some nets connected to cell i will be moved by other processors during the time between accepting move i and sending the next *update* message:

$$p(i) = 1 - \prod_{j \,=\, \text{all remote gates sharing a net with i}} (1 - P(j)),$$

where $P(j)$ is the probability that gate j is moved during the time between accepting move i and sending the next *update* message:

$$P(j) = \alpha(j)\frac{M - m(j)}{n(j)}$$

where $\alpha(j)$ is the acceptance rate on the processor that is the owner of j, M is the number of move attempts between *update* messages, $m(j)$ is the number of move attempts since sending the last *update* message by the owner of j, and $n(j)$ is the number of cells owned by the owner of j.

Figure 3.22 shows an example of error estimation on a single displacement move. In the figure are three standard cell rows, which are owned by processor 1, processor 2, and processor 3, respectively. Suppose that gate i moves to a new location by the distance of 10, as shown by an arrow in the figure. Since the cells A, B, C, and E, which are connected to cell i through a net, may be moved before PE2 sends the next update message, there may be an error in calculating the cost function by PE1 and PE3. Let us assume that each processor owns 100 cells and that the current acceptance rate of simulated annealing is 0.5 for PE1 and 0.2 for PE3. Also, assume that PE2 has attempted 50 moves since broadcasting the update message. Then $P(A) = P(B) = P(C) = 0.5 \cdot \frac{50}{100} = 0.25$. $P(E) = 0.2 \cdot \frac{50}{100} = 0.1$. Therefore, $p(i)$ = 1 - (1 - 0.25) (1 - 0.25)(1 - 0.25)(1 - 0.1) = 0.62 and $E_{estimate}(i) = 0.62 \cdot e(i)$ where $e(i)$ is the amount of displacement of cell i, an upper bound on the error. Because $e(i) = 10$ in this example, $E_{estimate}(i) = 6.2$.

This error accumulated over M moves is used to control the *message_size* of each processor. In the parallel algorithm, we put a bound on the error in the cost function as originally reported in [3]. In the simulated annealing algorithm, the probability of accepting a move is

$$P = e^{-\Delta C/T} \cdot \text{Prob}(\Delta C > 0) + \text{Prob}(\Delta C < 0)$$

In the presence of error, the composite acceptance rate changes slightly; however, the probability of generating good or bad moves is invariant with respect to error:

$$P_E = e^{-(\Delta C + -E)/T} \cdot \text{Prob}(\Delta C > 0) + \text{Prob}(\Delta C < 0)$$

To bound the acceptance rate with error P_E to within 5% of normal P, that is,

$$\frac{P - P_E}{P} \le 0.05$$

Hence, we find a bound on the magnitude of error:

$$E <= -T / \ln(1 - 0.05) \approx T/21$$

An empirical rule for decreasing the message size is to reduce the *current_size* to *current_size*/$2(1 - e^{-\frac{E}{k}})$, where $k = 0.0687 \cdot T$, whenever the computed error E is higher than $T/21$. If the error is very low, then the message size is increased similarly.

Because the time to evaluate each move differs, some processors perform annealing much faster than others. Also, the number of cells owned by each processor may vary

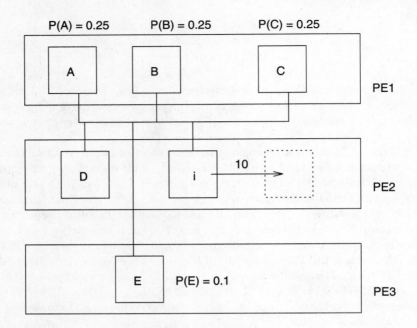

Figure 3.22 An example of error estimation

considerably because cells are allowed to move to other processors. To maintain approximately the same number of cells on each processor, we need to rebalance the cells among processors. In the parallel algorithm, load balance can be achieved by varying the type of moves proposed and accepted depending on the number of cells. For example, when the number of cells falls below two-thirds of the original assignment, we can reduce the number of interprocessor moves. Because this reduces the probability that a cell moves out of this processor, the number of cells moving into this processor's region becomes greater than the number moving away. Therefore, the balance is maintained by this simple technique. Similarly, if a processor owns many more cells than the average, more interprocessor moves are proposed to increase the probability of cells moving out. This change in move types does not affect the placement solution.

Rose et al. [47] have reported a different parallel algorithm for placement which involves a combination of two different algorithms suitable for execution on distributed memory message-passing multiprocessors. Two different approaches are presented, one to replace the high-temperature portion of annealing, and the other to speed up the low-temperature region. The first step of the approach is to divide up the search space. A mincut- based algorithm is used to recursively subdivide a placement while minimizing the number of wires crossing a division line. A constructive initial partitioning step is introduced to aid the iterative improvement for mincut-based placement.

The second part of the algorithm uses simulated annealing for the lower-temperature region, which begins with an interim placement. This placement is divided up geographically into subareas. The subareas and the cells contained in those areas are assigned to separate processors. The subareas are kept are square as possible. Each processor then generates moves, in parallel, for the cells that it is assigned and tests those moves for acceptance. If a move is accepted, then the accepting processor transmits the move to other processors so that they can maintain a consistent view of the cell positions. Some details about the parallel algorithm are given next.

As processors generate moves in parallel, there are two choices for synchronization. Each processor can either stop after every move and wait for the others to finish (the synchronous case) or continuously generate moves without regard to the state of other processors; hence the asynchronous case allows the processors to run faster. The authors used the asynchronous case in their algorithm.

The database containing the cell locations in a distributed memory multiprocessor can be kept separately or in a central location. A central database makes it easier to update and maintain consistency; however, it becomes a bottleneck. The authors therefore implemented a version of separate databases in their parallel algorithm. Given that each processor maintains its own separate database, the issue is what happens if a processor accepts a move. In a *full-broadcast mode*, as soon as a processor accepts a move, it broadcasts the move to all other processors. Such a strategy generates a lot of messages, and a lot of time is wasted in updating the database. Instead the researchers proposed a *need-to-know based broadcast* in which a processor only receives an update message if it contains a cell connected to a moved cell, or it contains at least one cell that is less than a certain distance away from the boundary to calculate the overlap penalties, or it contains a row whose total width has changed due to a move (to calculate the row overlap penalties).

The types of moves used in this implementation were (1) single-cell displacements within and across processor boundaries and (2) two-cell exchanges within a processor boundary. From experimental measurements, it has been noted that not allowing the cell exchanges across processor boundaries did not hamper the convergence of the algorithm.

Implementation   Banerjee et al. have reported results of the parallel algorithm *DM-PARALLEL-SA-INTER-DOMAIN* on an Intel iPSC/2™ hypercube-based distributed memory multiprocessor using both row and grid partitioning on a variety of benchmark circuits [3]. They have reported speedups of about 12 on 16 processors with comparable quality of placement results with respect to the serial algorithms.

Kim, Ramkumar, and Banerjee have reported an implementation of the algorithm *DM-PARALLEL-SA-INTER-REPLICATED* on an Intel iPSC/860™ hypercube. Table 3.4 shows some example results on five benchmark circuits of the runtimes (in seconds), the speedups, and the quality of placements (in terms of total weighted wire-length).

Speedups of about 4 on eight processors were reported. The qualities of the results were comparable to the the the best available serial simulated annealing algorithm, Timberwolf version 6.0.

The parallel algorithm developed by Rose et al. has been implemented on a five processor experimental message passing multiprocessor and speedups of about 4 on five processors have been reported [47].

TABLE 3.4 Runtimes (seconds) and Wire-length of Parallel Algorithm on the Intel iPSC/860™ Hypercube

Circuit	Cells	1 proc		8 proc	
		Wire-Length	Runtime (speedup)	Wire-Length	Runtime (speedup)
s298	133	32528	190 (1.0)	33312	43 (4.4)
s420	185	38052	288 (1.0)	39740	71 (4.0)
fract	125	22189	537 (1.0)	23139	132 (4.1)
primary1	752	2718819	2342 (1.0)	288589	606 (3.9)
primary2	2907	6148143	9341 (1.0)	6518083	2050 (4.6)

Massively Parallel SIMD Algorithm In this section we will discuss a massively parallel SIMD algorithm for cell placement using simulated annealing that is based on the algorithms reported by two groups of researchers on the Thinking Machines CM-2™ Connection Machine [8, 60]. The parallel algorithm is based on the Timberwolf sequential algorithm for standard cell placement [51]. A single global description of the state is maintained across all the processors comprised of two data structures, one for nets and the other for cells.

Viewing the connection as an array of processors, the data structure for each cell is stored on a sequence of adjacent processors in this array. The head processor in the sequence contains general information about the cell, while the second, third, and fourth processors contain the x coordinate, y coordinate, and width information of the cell. After the fourth processor comes a processor for each terminal on the cell, which contains the position of the terminal with respect to the center of the cell. A sequence of terminals is used to represent each net. The head processor contains general information about the net, while the processors that follow contain the absolute position of each terminal on the net, one terminal per processor.

The algorithm begins by selecting approximately half the head cells' processors. These processors consider moving their cells to a new location by either an exchange or a displacement. Next, all processors simultaneously compute the change in the cost function associated with the current move, each move assuming that the other cells are fixed (which actually, they are not, hence there are some temporary errors in the cost calculation).

The algorithm computes the absolute position of each terminal from the current absolute position of the cell and the relative position of the terminal. It then stores that position information in the processor associated with the same terminal in the net data structure. It uses the net data structure to compute the coordinates of the bounding box to approximate the wire length. Each cell structure uses the results of these calculations to decide whether to accept or reject the move and update its absolute position if necessary.

Since the algorithm stores a single description of the state across the machine, it ensures that after each iteration the state description is correct. During each iteration, however, the simultaneous movements of cells introduces an error.

An outline of the algorithm entitled *SIMD-PARALLEL-SA-INTER* (for SIMD parallel algorithm using simulated annealing with parallel interactive moves) is given next.

Procedure *SIMD-PARALLEL-SA-INTER*;

Start with an initial placement solution (state) S;
Create a single global description of the state that is maintained
across all the processors
View machine as array of processors;
Global state comprises two data structures,
one for nets and the other for cells;
Set $T = T_0$ (initial temperature);

REPEAT /* outer loop */
  moves_attempted = 0;
  REPEAT /* inner loop */
    FORALL processors in PARALLEL DO
      Select half head-cell processors randomly;
      Head-cell processor chooses move of cell;
      IF displacement THEN
        Move cell to random location (x,y);
      IF exchange THEN
        Exchange cell with cell in location (x,y);
        Cooperate with head cell processor of location (x,y);

      Processors evaluate each move independently;
      Processors accept/reject each move independently;

      Update global data structure of new cell positions;

    END FORALL
    Increment moves_attempted;
  UNTIL moves_attempted = max_moves; /* inner loop */
  Update T (control temperature);
UNTIL termination condition; /* end outer loop */

End Procedure

Implementation   Two groups of researchers [8, 60] have reported implementations of the massively parallel algorithms on the 16,000-processor Thinking Machines CM-2™ system and the implementations have been tested on a set of real benchmark cases. Typically, in such massively parallel algorithms about 500 to 900 moves are attempted simultaneously on 16,000-processors. Despite the errors due to simultaneous moves, the algorithms converged and obtained results within 2% of the serial simulated annealing results.

3.6 PLACEMENT USING SIMULATED EVOLUTION

3.6.1 Overview

Simulated evolution is a novel optimization method that is based on an analogy of the optimization process to the natural selection process in biological environments. The biological solution to the adaptation process is the *evolution* from one generation to the next one by eliminating ill-suited constituents and keeping near-optimal ones. Every constituent of each generation must constantly prove its functionality under the current conditions in order to remain unaltered. The purpose of this process is to gradually create stable structures that are finally perfectly adapted to the given constraints. The simulated evolution heuristic has been applied to many VLSI optimization problems such as placement, routing, and partitioning.

The simulated evolution algorithm for placement basically consists of a main loop in which three procedures are executed sequentially [33]. Each iteration of the loop completes one generation. Related to the placement problem, the three steps consist of *evaluation, selection,* and *allocation.* First, each cell in the population is subjected to *evaluation,* a phase that determines its normalized goodness, a figure of merit that reflects how well a cell is placed in its current position. Next, the *selection* procedure selects cells for replacement. For each cell separately, a trial is performed in which the cell's goodness determines its probability of survival in its current location. Cells with high goodness values are therefore less likely to be selected than ones with low goodnesses. Finally, the *allocation* procedure removes all selected cells from the placement. For each cell individually, a search is performed to find an improved location in the vicinity of its old position. A number of trial placements are evaluated and then a choice is made based on the amount of wire length reduction. When all selected cells have been replaced, the current iteration is complete and a new generation (= placement) has been formed. The simulated evolution method is stochastic in nature and provides means of escaping local minima of the objective function on its path to the global optimum, thus following the biological model. A brief outline of the simulated evolution algorithm is given next.

Procedure *SIMULATED-EVOLUTION*;

Start with an initial placement of cells;

REPEAT
    FOR each cell in the chip DO
        Evaluate goodness of cell in current cell
           position using cost function;
    FOR each cell in the chip DO
        IF random(0,1) > goodness of cell
           THEN select cell, place in queue for new allocation;
    FOR each cell in allocation queue DO
        Allocate cell in empty locations;
    UNTIL (termination condition);

End Procedure

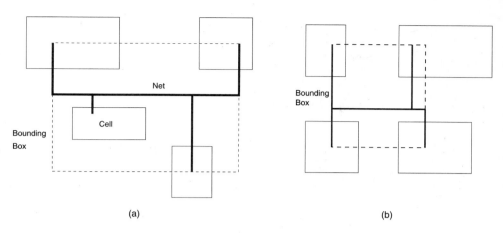

(a)   (b)

Figure 3.23 Computation of goodness values in simulated evolution algorithm. (a) Evaluation (b) Precomputation

In the following, we give a more detailed description of the basic steps in the simulated evolution algorithm. The first step of the iterative loop is the evaluation of the goodness of the current placement, which is obtained by evaluating the goodness value of every cell. The goodness of a cell cannot be computed directly. Instead, we have to compute goodness values for all nets first. The evaluation procedure, which is done for every net separately, is illustrated in Figure 3.23. The wire length of the *current net* is calculated by computing half the perimeter of its bounding box, which is the smallest rectangle enclosing all pins belonging to a net. As a first approximation of an optimal relative placement, all cells of the *current net* are assumed to be placed next to each other without horizontal space in between. Row spacing is considered and included in the computation. The half-perimeter of the enclosing rectangle serves as the lower bound on the wire length of the *current net*. The ratio of its precomputed optimal wiring cost over its current wire length is determined to be the goodness measure for the net. These steps are repeated for each net in the design. Subsequently, the goodness of each cell can be computed by taking the average of the goodness values of its set of nets. The result is then normalized in the range (0,1). Averaging over the goodness values of all cells, a global goodness of the current layout is also computed. Finally, the total wire length of the current placement is calculated. It should be noted that other goodness measures can be suitably defined.

The next step is called the selection phase which determines whether a cell will retain its current position in the next generation or if it will be scheduled for new allocation. This is done by comparing its placement value to a random number generated for each cell in the range (0, 1). If the goodness of the cell is larger than the random number, it will survive in its present position. Otherwise, it is placed in a queue for new allocation. By using this selection process, each cell's chance of survival at its current location is exactly equal to its placement value.

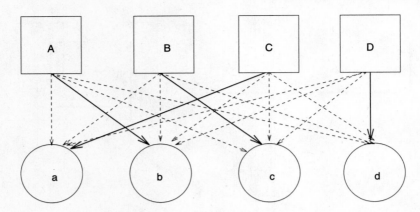

Figure 3.24 Weighted bipartite matching allocation

The primary operations of the allocation routine are the replacement of the selected cells into the layout, and a final realignment step to remove empty spaces and overlaps. Several allocation procedure have been proposed. One method is based on a *weighted bipartite matching algorithm*. The basic principle of this method is shown in Figure 3.24. Before the actual replacement starts, the goodness of each cell in the queue is evaluated in every target location. This yields a table of size s^2. The matching algorithm now tries to assign each cell to a location, such that the overall wire length is minimized. This can be done optimally in $O(s^3)$ time complexity. The computation can be only as accurate as the preceding evaluation. Therefore, wires connecting unplaced cells are not considered. Since the cell that is to be placed and the empty slot are generally of different widths, special consideration has to be given to the problem of possible overlaps and unused spaces. This is important because the subsequent realignment of the cells can cause the expected improvement in the total wire length to be diminished or even negated. It has been found that realignment after each allocation phase does not seriously disturb the convergence of the algorithm. Removing the overlaps and unused spaces between cells simplifies the program and yields legal placements at any stage of the iteration.

3.6.2 Distributed Memory MIMD Parallel Algorithm

In this section we will describe a a distributed memory parallel algorithm for placement using simulated evolution that has been reported by Kling and Banerjee [35].

The basic approach to parallelizing the algorithm involved assigning a subset of the physical placement grid to each processor. The partitioning is done row-wise because this greatly simplifies the adaptation of the algorithm to the parallel environment and avoids adverse effects created by unequal cell lengths. A set of rows is mapped to each processor; it is assumed that the number of rows is much greater than the number of processors, at least three to four times greater. Two different partitioning patterns are sufficient to ensure correct operation of the algorithm on any (small) number of processors. The pattern for each processor alternates every iteration to ensure that each cell can move to any position on the grid in at most two steps, as long as the number of rows per processor is sufficiently large. The

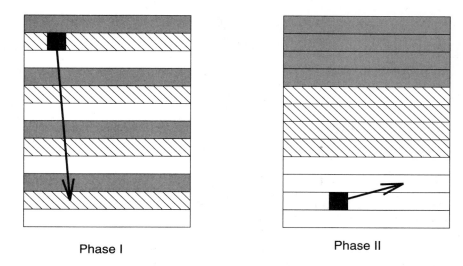

Phase I   Phase II

Figure 3.25 Workload partitioning in distributed simulated evolution

left pattern (I) shows the distribution for odd-numbered iterations and the right one (II) the partitioning for even-numbered cycles. A partitioning example for three processors is shown in Figure 3.25, along with a two step move of a cell from one region to another. The different shadings represent the assignment of rows to the different processors.

Each processor performs a complete iteration of the evolution-based algorithm on the subset of cells assigned to it and on its assigned regions on the chip. During a subsequent communication phase, the processors update their placement information by combining all individual results to the new common placement. Then, the whole process repeats itself, starting with the assignment of new partitions. An outline of the algorithm entitled *DM-PARALLEL-SE-DOMAIN* (for distributed memory parallel algorithm using simulated evolution with domain partitioning) is given next.

Procedure *DM-PARALLEL-SE-DOMAIN*;

Start with an initial placement of cells;
Partition the chip area among processors by rows;
Ownership of cells by processors owning chip subregions;

REPEAT
    FORALL processors in PARALLEL DO
        Broadcast current cell positions to all processors;

        Start partitioning pattern 1
        FOR each cell in the chip DO
            Evaluate goodness of cell using cost function;
        FOR each cell in the chip DO

    IF random(0,1) > goodness of cell;
        THEN select cell, place in queue for new allocation;
  FOR each cell in allocation queue DO
    Allocate cell in empty locations among own regions;
  Broadcast current cell positions to all processors;

  Start partitioning pattern 2
  FOR each cell in the chip DO
    Evaluate goodness of cell using cost function;
  FOR each cell in the chip DO
    IF random(0,1) > goodness of cell
        THEN select cell, place in queue for new allocation;
  FOR each cell in allocation queue DO
    Allocate cell in empty locations among own regions;
 END FORALL
UNTIL (termination condition);

End Procedure

It should be noted that the preceding parallel algorithm is effective for cases where the number of processors is much less than the number of rows. When the number of processors is equal or greater than the number of rows, a different parallel algorithm needs to be designed. In such a case, the basic strategy is to partition the cells and associated nets among the processors. A copy of the entire chip layout is replicated on each processor. A processor is responsible for evaluation, selection, and allocation of the cells that are owned by it. After a single iteration of evaluation, selection and allocation of cells, the processors update the global state information of the layout and resolve any inconsistencies through realignment of the cells in the various rows. The global synchronization is performed during the realignment phase by as many processors as there are rows, with each processor responsible for one row. After that, each processor will broadcast the latest correct state of its row to all the processors. The cycle of evaluation, selection, allocation, and update will be iterated. Naturally, conflicts will again arise during allocation of cells to the same empty slots in the layout. These conflicts are resolved by the realignment stage.

Implementation Kling and Banerjee [32, 36] have reported an implementation of the preceding parallel algorithm on a network of workstations connected by a local area network. From measurements generated by placing actual circuits on a network of one to four workstations, the following results were obtained. For sufficiently large examples, that is, 250 to 300 cells per processor, they achieved linear speedup. In this case, the processing time is at least one magnitude larger than the communication cost. In addition, the final placement quality of the distributed method was reported to be comparable to the uniprocessor case. This proved the effectiveness of this workload partitioning scheme.

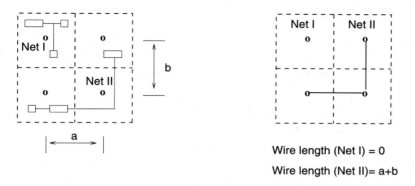

Wire length (Net I) = 0

Wire length (Net II)= a+b

Figure 3.26 Bin partitioning in a hierarchical simulated evolution algorithm

3.6.3 Shared Memory MIMD Parallel Algorithm

In this section we will describe a parallel algorithm for cell placement using simulated evolution that is based on an extension to the basic simulated evolution algorithm using the concepts of windowing and hierarchy [32, 36].

The basic simulated evolution algorithm has been extended to use a hierarchical concept that is based on the partitioning of the physical layout area containing standard cells into bins. The center coordinates of each bin represent the point to which all nets of any cell inside the bin are attached. Furthermore, each bin has a capacity according to the physical area it encloses. An attempt to allocate more cells into a bin than its capacity allows incurs an overlap penalty. A sample bin layout is shown in Figure 3.26.

Initially, a random placement of cells is generated, and the cells are partitioned into four bins. Each cell retains its individuality with respect to its net connections, size, and the like. However, since all nets of a bin connect to the common center point, the length of any net entirely within a bin is set to zero. Nets connecting cells that are located in different bins are assigned wire lengths according to the physical distance between the bins. This scheme allows the *global* structure of the circuit to be optimized without interference by *local* constraints. There are no fixed positions for the cells within each bin, only the overlap penalty is enforced.

Next, the simulated evolution algorithm is executed using the bin configuration to iteratively improve the total wire-length measured as described previously. The method is similar to the conventional flat simulated evolution optimization procedure. The evaluation procedure determines the goodness of each cell with regard to the new wire-length metric. Cells that lead to suboptimal wire-lengths are penalized by low goodness values while cells with optimal nets are rewarded. The selection procedure selects a number of cells based on their current goodness values. The allocation procedure tries to replace the selected cells in improved positions by first attempting to conditionally place them in several = 2 or 3) window C of the passing parent is chosen randomly, different bins and then choosing an improved configuration based on the overall gain. This gain is determined by the difference in wire-length between the old and the new placement and the difference in overhead penalty.

The algorithm iterates until no significant improvement can be achieved. At this point, the bins are split alternatively in either the x or y dimensions as shown in Figure 3.27.

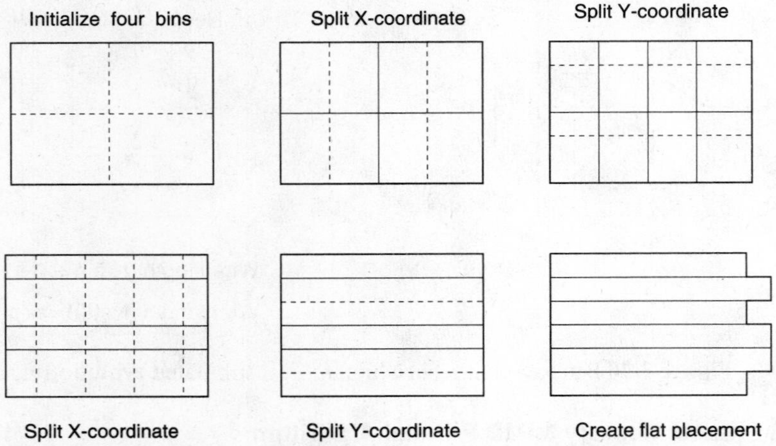

Initialize four bins   Split X-coordinate   Split Y-coordinate

Split X-coordinate   Split Y-coordinate   Create flat placement

Figure 3.27 Bin splitting used in hierarchical simulated evolution

The partitioning routine splits one bin at a time, trying to make a reasonable decision about which cells to place into each half. The splitting of bins is a single-pass, noniterative procedure. After all bins have been processed, their center coordinates and overlap penalties are recalculated. Subsequently, the iterative simulated evolution algorithm is restarted on the new bin configuration.

The entire process is repeated until the bins are too small to be split in either direction. At this point, a regular placement is reconstructed by placing each cell within the outline of its respective bin. Finally, a standard simulated evolution optimization process is started on the flat placement. An outline of the sequential hierarchical simulated evolution algorithm is given next.

Procedure *HIERARCHICAL-SIMULATED-EVOLUTION*;

Start with an initial placement of cells;
Partition chip into four 2×2 bins;

WHILE bins not flattened DO
    Partition current bin into 2×2 bins;
    REPEAT
        FOR each cell in the chip DO,
            Evaluate goodness of cell using cost function
                at current bin level;
        FOR each cell in the chip DO
            IF random$(0, 1) >$ goodness of cell
                THEN select cell, place in queue for new allocation;
        FOR each cell in allocation queue DO
            Allocate cell in empty locations

at current bin level;
UNTIL (termination condition);

END WHILE

End Procedure

To reduce computation time, only neighboring bins are considered for replacing each cell during the allocation procedure. Instead of the allocation procedure proposed in the earlier version of evolution, a new allocation procedure was devised using windowing. A 3×3 active window is formed centered around the previous bin position of each cell selected for replacement. The cell is tentatively placed in each of the nine locations and the goodness values evaluated. From those tentative placements, a final solution is chosen using a probabilistic normalization allocation function that biases the choice of making the final allocation in favor of placement locations that have high goodness values. The active window usually contains nine or fewer bins, thereby limiting the computation to a constant value independent of the total number of bins.

The windowing scheme eliminates unnecessary computations on the assumption that long range moves will occur only very rarely. In fact, the very nature of the hierarchical concept supports this paradigm since such moves should have been resolved at a previous hierarchical level. Hierarchical techniques using larger window sizes show only insignificant performance gains at best. However, the required computation time increases drastically due to the increased search space during allocation.

The main reason for the success of the hierarchical method is its inherent top-down approach to circuit partitioning. It should be noted that no predefined clustering scheme is employed, that could potentially severely limit convergence by imposing an inflexible framework. The method instead relies on the fact that the nets which are the longest in the circuit will be placed first without being constrained by the requirements of shorter nets. This effectively reduces the number of local minima encountered by the optimization procedure, thereby reducing its likelihood of getting trapped and avoiding the overhead associated with escaping local minima.

With each splitting of the bins, the granularity of the optimization algorithm is refined and ever shorter nets are considered, thereby slowly progressing from global to local optimization. When the final flat optimization stage is reached, the remaining amount of disturbance that requires improvement is usually minimal.

We now describe a shared memory parallel algorithm based on the hierarchical simulated evolution algorithm. The entire hierarchical algorithm is executed as a set of phases in each level in the hierarchy, which are synchronized by barriers across processors.

The evaluation procedure is parallelized as follows. A single global copy of the state of the layout, that is, the locations of the cells in the appropriate level in the hierarchy, is kept in a shared memory. The total number of cells is distributed equally among all the processors statically. It is possible to achieve good load balancing since all cells are subjected to the evaluation and selection phases at every step in the algorithm. The cost of evaluating a cell depends on the number of nets it is connected to and, for each net, the number of cells on the net. A good static load balancing strategy is to sort the cells by the number of connections and assign the cells in a cyclic manner to the processors. That is, the cells $1, N+1, 2N+1, 3N+1, \ldots$ are assigned to the first processor, the cells $2, N+2, 2N+2, 3N+2, \ldots$ to the second processor, and so on.

The selection procedure is a simple random number generator call followed by a decision to select or not select the cell and is therefore easy to load balance. A barrier synchronization is performed at the end of the selection phase.

At the end of the selection phase, all the selected cells owned by each processor are removed from their current cell locations and placed on each processor's allocation queue. Processors take each cell from their own queues and apply the allocation function on each cell's window of 3×3 cells and use a stochastic procedure to accept a particular allocation. If there is a single queue of cells to be replaced, there will be conflicts for access from the shared single queue; hence, it is desirable to have multiple queues, one per processor.

When all the cells from the queue(s) have been placed, a barrier synchronization is performed, and cell realignment is performed on each row of the layout in parallel by different processors. This procedure is repeated many times at a particular hierarchical level until no improvement occurs. At that point, the bins are split again and the parallel simulated evolution algorithm is performed at the next level in the hierarchy.

An outline of the parallel algorithm entitled *SM-PARALLEL-SE-HIERARCHICAL-OWNCELL* (for shared memory parallel algorithm using simulated evolution using hierarchical decomposition and cell ownership) is given next.

Procedure *SM-PARALLEL-SE-HIERARCHICAL-OWNCELL*;

Start with an initial placement of cells;
Partition cells among processors by sorting cells;
   by number of net connections, and assigning cyclically;
Partition chip into one bin;

WHILE bins not flattened DO
   Partition current bin into 2 by 2 bins;
     REPEAT iterative step
      · FORALL processors in PARALLEL DO
        FOR each cell owned by processor DO
          Evaluate goodness of cell using cost function
            at current bin level;
        FOR each cell owned by processor DO
          IF random(0,1) > goodness of cell
            THEN select cell, place in separate
            queue for new allocation, one per processor;
      END FORALL
      Synchronize all processors
      FORALL processors in PARALLEL DO

WHILE there are cells in own allocation queue DO
Allocate cell in 3 × 3 window around cell
at current bin level;
END FORALL
Realign cells in each row;
Synchronize all processors;
UNTIL (termination condition);

END WHILE

End Procedure

No actual data on the speedups of real circuits on a real multiprocessor have been reported. The following points should be noted about the parallel simulated evolution algorithm. The problems faced by parallel simulated annealing algorithms about errors in evaluating parallel moves are not experienced by this parallel algorithm because the simulated evolution algorithm is naturally parallel. The sequential algorithm for allocation ignores the placement information of the cells that are on the replacement queue. Hence the parallel algorithm also makes the same inaccuracies in the judgment as the sequential algorithm, and the result of the solution does not deteriorate with increasing number of processors. As an aside, it has been shown through a theoretical Markov chain analysis [36] that the simulated evolution algorithm with the new allocation scheme will converge to the optimal solution given infinite time. This result is similar to an analogous convergence theory for simulated annealing. Some experimental results on benchmark circuits have shown that the quality of placements produced by a hierarchical simulated evolution algorithm is similar to those produced by the best simulated annealing algorithms for comparable times [36].

3.7 PLACEMENT USING GENETIC ALGORITHMS

3.7.1 Overview

Genetic algorithms have been proposed as another probabilistic optimization technique that has been applied successfully to several optimization problems. Recently, researchers have applied genetic algorithms to solve problems in VLSI CAD such as placement and floorplanning.

Genetic algorithms represent and transform solutions from a problem's state space in a way that represents the mechanics of natural evolution. The subspace of solutions currently being looked at is called a population. Solutions are represented as strings of symbols. The solution strings are ranked by a function that assigns a score to the string, which is a quality measure of the string. During each iteration of a genetic algorithm, a certain fraction of the population is selected to be parents by a choice function. New solutions called offsprings are created by combining pairs of parents in such a way that each parent contributes to the information carried by its associated offspring string. This operation is referred to as crossover. From the combined set of the original population and offsprings, a set of strings equal in size to the original population is probabilistically selected to survive to the next iteration or generation. In addition to crossover, another operation called mutation periodically performs some random changes within each surviving strings. Over many generations, better scoring strings representing solutions of better quality survive, and weaker solutions become extinct.

In this section we will describe a cell placement algorithm that is based on the general genetic algorithm described previously. Two implementations of genetic algorithms for placement have been reported [12, 53] and have been found to produce results comparable to a basic simulated annealing algorithm in about the same runtimes.

The string representation in a genetic placement algorithm is as follows. The ith element within a string corresponds to the placement of the ith cell in row major order among all possible placement locations in all the rows of the standard cell layout. The scoring function is the sum of the half-perimeter bounding box for each net (an estimate of the total wire-length) and a component that penalizes the usage of channels whose usage is one standard deviation more than the average (an estimate of congestion). The initial population is constructed using a combination of random placements and constructive placements using seed-clustering-based ideas, where after some seed cells are placed, other cells on nets connected to the placed cells are assigned to locations in the immediate vicinity in row major order. The choice function chooses parents to be the solutions whose quality is better than the average quality of the population. The crossover operator selects two parent strings and exchanges substrings between parent strings to create offsprings. The selection operator probabilistically favors solutions with better qualities to survive. The mutation operator selects two cells from one string and exchanges their locations.

Numerous crossover operators have been proposed by researchers. One such crossover operator will be described next. One parent is selected randomly to be the basis of the offspring, and is called the target parent. The other parent is called the passing parent. A $k \times k$ (where $k = 2$ or 3) window C of the passing parent is chosen randomly and is copied into the corresponding window D in the target parent. In this cut-and-paste method, an illegal solution is obtained since some of the cells are repeated and other cells have no assigned locations. This solution is corrected by moving cells that are in window D but not in C to the positions of cells in window C but not in D. This operation is illustrated in Figure 3.28.

Other crossover operators have been proposed. For example, the order crossover operator randomly chooses a cut point in the string representation, and copies the cells from one parent to the offspring to the left of the cut point. The remaining portion of the offspring are copied from the other parent by selecting cells that were left out in the order of appearance in the second parent. In a cycle crossover, illustrated in Figure 3.29, in the offspring each cell is in the same location of either one of the parents. Start with a cell in location 1 of parent 1, and copy the cell to location 1 of the offspring. The cell in location 1 of parent 2 cannot appear in location 1 of the offspring; hence, search for the location x in parent 1 where that cell is located, and copy that cell to location x of offspring. Now, the cell in location x in parent 2 cannot be copied to location x in offspring. Hence a similar search is repeated until a cycle is completed where we reach a cell that has already been passed. The same procedure is started again from a cell from the second parent and is repeated until all the cells are assigned positions.

A typical genetic algorithm for placement would appear as follows:

Procedure *GENETIC-PLACEMENT*;

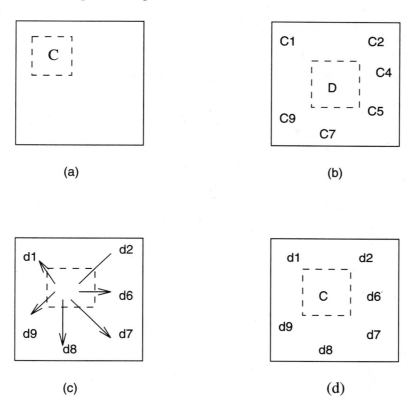

Figure 3.28 Cut-and-paste crossover operator in genetic placement (Courtesy of Cohoon and Paris, *IEEE Trans. Computer-Aided Design,* ©IEEE 1987)

Read net list and create initial populations
    of placement configurations;
Evaluate all placement configurations in the population;

FOR G Generations DO
    /* Run Genetic Algorithm */
        WHILE number of offsprings created $< n \times C$ DO
            Select two solutions;
            Crossover the two solutions to create an offspring;
        END WHILE
        Add all offsprings to subpopulation;
        Select a population of n elements;
        Generate $n \times M$ random mutations;
        Find Average fitness;

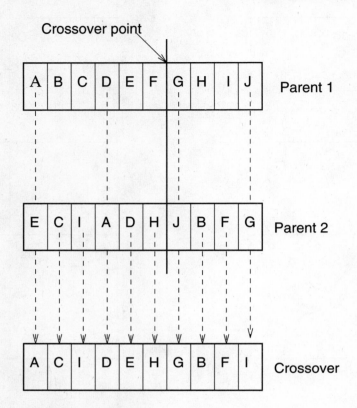

Figure 3.29 Cycle crossover in genetic placement (Courtesy of Shahookar and Mazumder, *IEEE Trans. Computer-Aided Design,* ©IEEE 1990)

Select configurations for next generation
    with fitter individuals getting higher
    probability of selection;
END FOR
End Procedure

Shahookar and Mazumder have proposed [53] another variation of the basic genetic placement algorithm. A genetic algorithm is characterized by the number of offsprings to be generated (crossover rate, $0 < C < 1$) and the fraction of populations to be mutated (mutation rate, $0 < M < 1$). Optimal values for these parameters, C and M, are obtained automatically by running another meta-genetic algorithm for optimization of those parameters.

3.7.2 Distributed Memory MIMD Parallel Algorithm

We now describe a parallel algorithm for cell placement using genetic algorithms that is suitable for execution on distributed memory multicomputers based on implementations reported in

[11, 39],

The distributed placement procedure runs a basic genetic algorithm on each processor in the multiprocessor and introduces a new genetic operator, called migration, which transfers placement information (some placement solutions) from one processor to another across a network once every few generations. An outline of the parallel algorithm entitled *DM-PARALLEL-GENETIC-PLACEMENT-POPULATION* (for distributed memory parallel algorithm using genetic placement with population decomposition) is given next.

Procedure *DM-PARALLEL-GENETIC-PLACEMENT-POPULATION*;

Read net list and create initial populations
 of placement configurations;
Partition populations among processors;

FORALL processors in PARALLEL DO
 Evaluate all placement configurations in processor;
 FOR E iterations DO
  FOR G Generations DO
   /* Run Genetic Algorithm */
   WHILE number of offsprings created $< n \times C$ DO
    Select two solutions;
    Crossover the two solutions to create an offspring;
   END WHILE
   Add all offsprings to subpopulation;
   Select a population of n elements;
   Generate $n \times M$ random mutations;
   Find Average fitness;
   Select configurations for next generation
    with fitter individuals getting higher
    probability of selection;
  END FOR

  /* Perform Migration */
  FOR each neighbor j of current processor i DO
   Send/Receive a set of solutions S_{ij}
    from processor i to processor j;
  END FOR
  Select n element configurations for next generation
   with fitter individuals getting higher
   probability of selection;
 END FOR (E iterations)
END FORALL

End Procedure

TABLE 3.5 Normalized Runtimes and Quality (Wire-length) of Parallel Genetic Algorithm on a Network of Workstations

Circuit	Cells	1 processor		8 processor	
		Wire-Length	Runtime (speedup)	Wire-Length	Runtime (speedup)
A	100	1.0	1.0	1.06	0.14 (7.0)
B	183	1.0	1.0	1.10	0.15 (6.5)
C	469	1.0	1.0	1.07	0.15 (6.5)
E	800	1.0	1.0	1.08	0.14 (7.0)
G	2,907	1.0	1.0	1.05	0.15 (6.5)

An epoch length E is defined as the number of generations between two successive migrations. The effectiveness of the migration mechanisms depends on several factors, such as the number of individuals transferred in each migration, the selection of the individuals for migration, and the epoch length. Too much migration can force the populations on different processors to become identical, making the parallel algorithm inefficient, where as too little migration may not effectively combine the subpopulations. The speedup of the parallel algorithm depends on the migration process. The communication time increases with the migration rate.

Implementation   The preceding algorithm has been implemented in a network of workstations. A master processor determines the communication pattern and also acts as a routing controller among the various processors. It controls the slave processors to execute the basic genetic algorithm on each of them for various populations. Mohan and Mazumder have reported experimental results on the quality of results produced by the algorithm and the speedups [39]. The total population size was kept constant for the uniprocessor and multiple processor runs. For example, the size was 48 for the uniprocessor and 6 per processor for an eight-processor case. It was found in most of the cases that the results of the multiprocessor quality were within 10% of the quality produced by a uniprocessor run. The speedups measured were almost linear. Table 3.5 shows the results of speedups and wire-length quality of the parallel algorithm on a network of workstations.

It should be noted that the preceding algorithm is not scalable for very large number of processors, because typically the optimal population size in such applications has been found to be less than 25; hence, through parallel processing, if we split the population up to less than 10, the genetic nature of the algorithm would be affected and the quality of the solution would be degraded.

3.7.3 Shared Memory MIMD Parallel Algorithm

The preceding parallel algorithm can be easily modified to execute on a shared memory MIMD multiprocessor. Essentially, the entire set of solutions can be kept in global memory.

However, the populations will be partitioned into subpopulations allocated to individual processors. Processors acquire two solutions from within their population subspace, stored in a separate queue, and perform the crossover and mutation operators on them to generate offsprings. Next the processors perform the choice function on the subpopulations in order to select the surviving populations. The migration operation will be performed by selecting a set of solutions from queues of each processor and copying them into the solution regions (queues) of other processors. This copying needs to be performed by locking the appropriate population queues corresponding to regions that will perform the exchange of their solutions. No actual implementations of a shared memory algorithm has been reported, but we should expect similar linear speedups as the distributed memory implementations.

3.8 PLACEMENT USING HIERARCHY

3.8.1 Overview

In this section we will discuss two parallel algorithms for placement, one for shared memory MIMD multiprocessors, and one for distributed memory MIMD message-passing multicomputers. Both the algorithms have the common theme of hierarchically dividing the problem and solving each subproblem in parallel among various processors. The actual decomposition approaches are different in the two algorithms.

Placement methods that are based on a partitioning strategy usually have a goal of minimizing the number of nets crossing over the partition boundaries. The bisection (or mincut) method [14] partitions the layout (the circuit cells) into two groups, performing cell swaps or displacements between the groups, until the number of nets crossing the single boundary is minimized while maintaining a balance in the cell area of both halves. In the quadrisection method of Suaris and Kedem [54, 55], the layout is partitioned into four groups (a two-by-two array of bins) instead of two groups, and cell movements occur among any of the four groups. An extension of the bisection heuristic for the selection of the cells is applied, which minimizes the net cuts over all four boundary segments of the two-by-two bin array through the movement of the selected cells. By approaching the layout problem in two dimensions instead of one, the authors have demonstrated results much better than those attained with the use of bisection placement. At each level of the quadrisection decomposition, a portion of the layout is selected and divided into four quadrants. At level k in the decomposition, the entire layout is divided up into a $2^k \times 2^k$ array of quadrisection regions. Figure 3.30(a) shows the quadrisection approach on a chip layout.

If a net connection from the area outside the layout portion must enter into one of the quadrants, a *pseudo pin* is fixed in that quadrant for the net. These pseudo pins are the result of previous placement evaluations, which have determined that certain nets cross into the layout portion through specific segments of the quadrisection outer boundary. The quadrant associated with the boundary segment receives the pseudo pin. According to [54], each net can be associated with a cost thatis calculated as a function of the net's routing configuration for this set of quadrants. The cost function shown in Figure 3.30(b) assumes that the shortest path is always available for connecting the pins in the quadrants. The horizontal (hw) and vertical (vw) weights are used to account for the costs for routing in the horizontal and vertical directions.

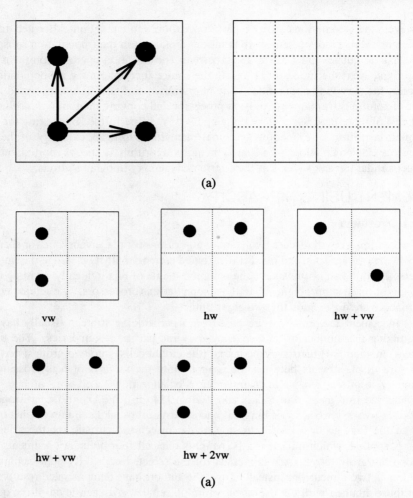

Figure 3.30 Quadrisection approach to cell placement. (a) Placement steps.
(b) Cost function.

If a given cell c in quadrant q were to be moved to quadrant r, the nets associated with c may have to be rerouted to make the connections to the new pin in r. Furthermore, if c were the only connection for a net n in q, the connections to q for n may be removed also. These changes or reroutings of the nets cause changes in the calculated cost of the net. To account for the change in cost, a set of *gain tables* is used that reflects the change (gain) in the cost of the nets with respect to movements of cells from one quadrant to another. Since the goal is to minimize the net length and cost, a cell is selected for movement from a gain table when it has the best (smallest) cost gain.

In addition to the determination of the minimum gain cell, another important criterion in the selection of cells is the determination of whether the movement of the cell would cause an imbalance in the total area of the cells occupied by each quadrant. The sequence of selecting and moving cells is repeated until no cells can be selected for movement or when a sequence of selections of cells with gains > 0 has taken place.

3.8.2 Shared Memory MIMD Parallel Algorithm

We will now describe a shared memory MIMD parallel algorithm for placement using hierarchical decomposition techniques based on work reported by Brouwer and Banerjee [6]. The parallel algorithm consists of a number of operations that are executed in a certain sequence at each level of the hierarchical decomposition. The operations are (1) the placement of the current set of cells, based on the quadrisection algorithm, (2) the restricted global X bisection of cells, and (3) the restricted global Y bisection of cells. Each operation intimately depends on the results of the other operations.

1. *Quadrisection operation.* The algorithm uses a quadrisection-based placement algorithm to place cells into four quadrants at a particular level in the hierarchy.

2. *Restricted global X bisection.* The initial placement of cells in the partitioning for quadrisection is performed using a method called restricted global bisection. The bisection is performed separately in the X dimension and the Y dimension. The X dimension bisection consists of the set of cells between the coordinates x_{lo} and x_{hi} and the top and bottom borders of the layout. The values for x_{lo} and x_{hi} are determined by the quadrisections at the previous level in the hierarchical decomposition. The vertical lines separating the quadrisection regions and the vertical lines that cut down the middle of a column of quadrisection regions are used as the domain of the values of x_{lo} and x_{hi}, thus giving 2^k separate X dimension bisection regions, where k is the current hierarchy level. Given x_{lo} and x_{hi} for a bisection, the set of cells is then partitioned into two groups, separated by a line (x_{mid}) halfway between x_{lo} and x_{hi}. The bisection region is further divided up vertically, with the number of partitions $PRT_{bsect} = 2^k$. Throughout the bisection algorithm, the cells are restricted to horizontal movements only. Thus every cell stays in the same vertical partition and each cell's Y coordinate remains untouched.

3. *Restricted global Y bisection.* Alternately, the Y dimension restricted global bisection algorithm partitions the layout into horizontal strips the width of the layout area. By applying the cost function horizontally, we reduce the demand of the nets for a high number of feedthroughs and route each net in as few channels as possible.

An example showing the operations at level 2 in the decomposition of one region of the layout is shown in Figure 3.31. In Figure 3.31(a), the region under consideration is the square outlined in bold. The dashed lines denote the boundaries of the bisection region for level 2. The dotted lines represent the internal axis lines of the bisections and quadrisections for level 2. At level 3 the dotted lines would represent the bisection and quadrisection borders. Figures 3.31(b) and (c) show the Y direction horizontal and X direction vertical bisections, respectively. The cells being displaced must remain between the pairs of bold dotted lines. Figure 3.31(d) shows the quadrisection placement performed on that region. The steps are repeated for finer and finer decompositions of each region.

Since the X and Y bisection algorithms exclusively alter the x and y coordinates of

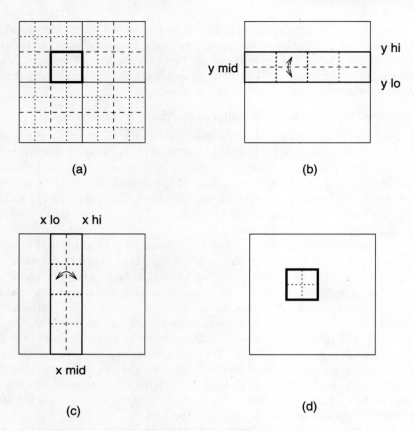

Figure 3.31 Parallel decomposition example. (a) Region under consideration. (b) Y bisection placement. (c) X bisection placement. (d) Quadrisection placement.

the cells (respectively), they are independent of each other, and the two dimensions can be
evaluated simultaneously. Following both evaluations, the cells have been preplaced in one
of the quadrants of the quadrisection to be involved in the current level of the decomposition.

The overall flow of the parallel algorithm using all three placement steps discussed
is illustrated in Figure 3.32. In this figure, each operation performed at each level of the
hierarchical decomposition is denoted by a set of circles between a pair of horizontal dashed
lines intersecting the appropriate column. The circles represent instances of the operations to
be performed on a portion of the layout. For example, in the quadrisection placement column,
one circle at hierarchy level 0 represents a quadrisection covering the entire layout. Four
circles at level 1 represent the four quadrisections, each covering one-fourth of the layout.

We now describe the implementation of a shared memory MIMD parallel algorithm
based on this hierarchical decomposition of the placement problem. Processors execute tasks
from a globally shared task queue. Since there are different types of tasks (for example,

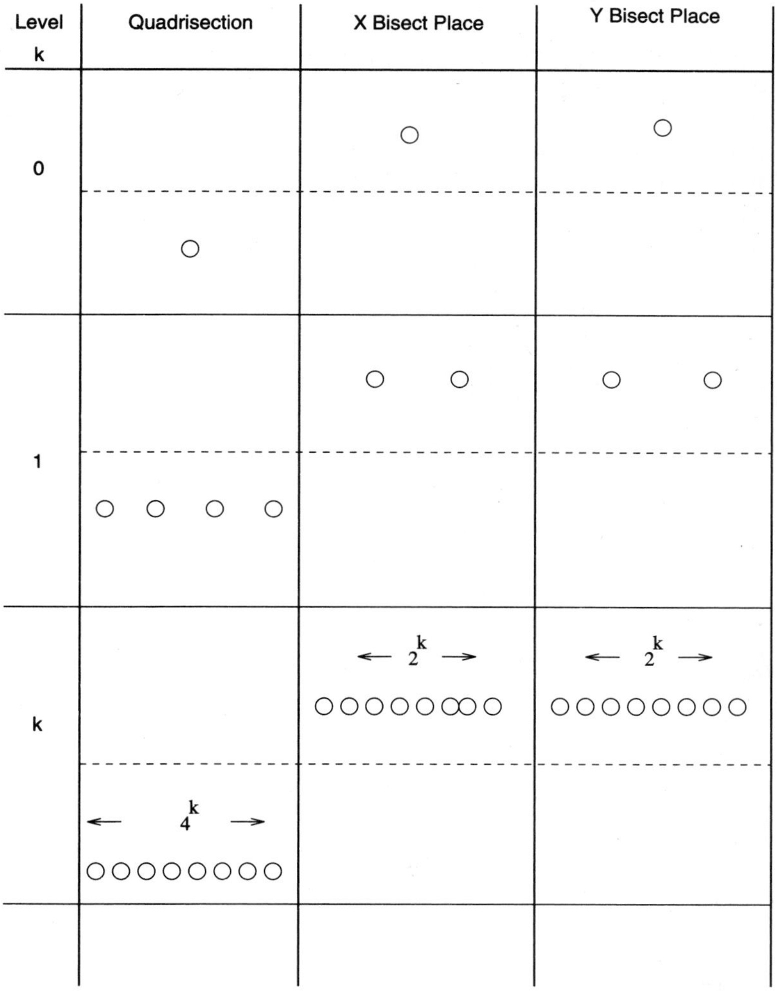

Figure 3.32 Parallel quadrisection and bisection task decomposition (a) Region under consideration. (b) Y bisection placement. (c) X bisection placement. (d) Quadrisection placement.

quadrisection, X dimension bisection) each type of task is maintained in a separate task queue. As tasks are created, they are placed on the end of the proper task queue and await execution by any of the processors that become available. Since there are dependencies from one operation to the next, it is necessary to synchronize after every operation to guarantee the correctness of the solution. For example, the quadrisection placement of a particular level k depends on the preceding bisection placement in order to perform an initial placement of cells and nets crossing their boundaries. After synchronization, the next operation task queue is enabled, and waiting processes are allowed to take tasks from the new operation's task queue.

An outline of the parallel algorithm entitled *SM-PARALLEL-HIERARCHICAL-PLACE* (for shared memory parallel algorithm using hierarchical decomposition) is given next.

Procedure *SM-PARALLEL-HIERARCHICAL-PLACE*;

Read in circuit and initialize;
Set level k = 0;
Create one X-bisection task on whole region;
Create one Y-bisection task on whole region;

FORALL processors in PARALLEL DO
   WHILE (not DONE) DO
     WHILE (there X Bisection tasks at level k) DO
       Gettask(X-bisection,level k);
       Execute X-bisection task;
     ENDWHILE ;

     WHILE (there Y Bisection tasks at level k) DO
       Gettask(Y-bisection,level k);
       Execute Y-bisection task;
     ENDWHILE ;

     Barrier Synchronize();
     Enable Quadrisection tasks of level k;

     WHILE (there Quadrisection tasks at level k) DO
       Gettask(Quadrisection,level k);
       Execute Quadrisection task;
     ENDWHILE ;

     Barrier Synchronize();

     Increment k = k +1;
     Create 2^k X-dimension bisections tasks
       on restricted subregions;
     Create 2^k Y-dimension bisections tasks

TABLE 3.6 Runtimes (seconds) and Wire-length of Parallel Algorithm on the Encore Multimax™ Multiprocessor

		1 processor		4 processor	
Circuit	Cells	Wire-Length	Runtime (speedup)	Wire-Length	Runtime (speedup)
1	469	518	124 (1.0)	518	47 (2.6)
2	1691	17,272	1,648 (1.0)	17,272	721 (2.2)
3	2776	7,934	3,062 (1.0)	7,934	1,318 (2.3)
primary1	752	1,918	270 (1.0)	1,918	109 (2.5)
primary2	2,907	16,080	3,988 (1.0)	16,080	1,555 (2.6)

on restricted subregions;
Create 4^k quadrisections tasks
on restricted subregions;

ENDWHILE
END FORALL

End Procedure

Implementation The parallel algorithm for placement has been implemented on an Encore Multimax™ shared memory multiprocessor by Brouwer and Banerjee [6]. The authors have reported on the results of the placement qualities and speedups on various benchmark circuits on a four-processor multiprocessor. Table 3.6 shows some example results on five benchmark circuits of the runtimes (in seconds), the speedups, and the quality of placements (in terms of total weighted wire-length).

The qualities of the circuits produced were equivalent to those obtained by the sequential quadrisection algorithm of Suaris and Kedem [55]. A point to note is that the quality of the circuits produced by the parallel algorithm was identical for different number of processors. This should be contrasted with the varying qualities of results produced in parallel algorithms for placement based on iterative improvement.

3.8.3 Distributed Memory MIMD Parallel Algorithm

A different parallel algorithm for cell placement using a divide and conquer approach has been proposed by Ravikumar and Sastry [45]. It is based on the simple placement model of placing a set of equal-sized cells on a two-dimensional array of slots. The connections between the cells are specified in terms of a connectivity matrix C, where the element $c_{ij} = c_{ji}$ = the number of connections between cells i and j, assuming only two terminal nets. Assuming fixed-sized modules to be placed in fixed locations in the chip layout, a distance matrix $D = [d_{ij}]$ can be defined that measures the Euclidean distance between the modules i and j. The

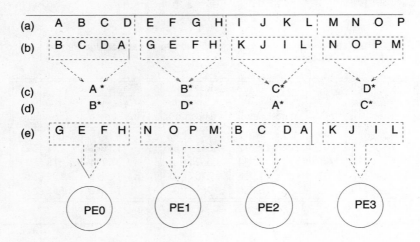

Figure 3.33 Example application of divide and conquer placement. (a) Four-way partitioning of 16 modules. (b) Local placement phase. (c) Shrinking the C matrix. (d) Cluster placement. (e) Final placement. (Courtesy of Ravikumar and Sastry, *Proc. Int. Conf. Parallel Processing*, Pennsylvania State University Press, 1989)

objective function that is minimized is

$$\mathcal{F} = \sum_{i,j} c_{ij} \cdot d_{ij}$$

which is the first cost function discussed in Section 3.2.4.

The basic approach of the parallel algorithm involves divide and conquer. The placement proceeds by breaking up the connectivity matrix C into smaller pieces. Each submatrix corresponds to a cluster of cells. A cluster represents a placement problem of size small enough to be placed optimally using exhaustive or branch and bound techniques. Following the local placement phase, the clusters are shrunk into hypothetical cells, obtaining a placement problem whose size is the same as the number of clusters, m. If m is small enough, the clusters are placed optimally. Otherwise, the divide and conquer procedure is recursively applied. Figure 3.33 illustrates the divide and conquer procedure for $N = 16$ and $m = 4$.

This basic concept is used to develop a parallel placement algorithm for a hypercube-based distributed memory multiprocessor. An outline of the parallel algorithm entitled *DM-PARALLEL-DIVIDE-CONQUER* (for distributed memory parallel algorithm for placement using divide and conquer techniques) is given next.

Procedure *DM-PARALLEL-DIVIDE-CONQUER*;

Partition N cells into $\frac{N}{m}$ clusters;
Cluster distributed equally among processors;

REPEAT
    FORALL processors in PARALLEL DO
        Each processor works on $\frac{N}{m.P}$ local placements of size m;
        Local placement done by semi-enumerative techniques;
        At end of placement, each processor i computes cost
            of the local placement, L_i;
        Each processor i computes the collapsed connectivity
            by collapsing the clusters into hypothetical cells;
        Place $\frac{N}{m}$ hypothetical cells among P processors
            by a distributed placement algorithm minimizing
            intercluster cost by parallel iterative improvement;

        The global cost GC is calculated by summing up the
            local costs L_i and the Intercluster costs;

        A master processor decides to accept or reject
            current placement based on the value of the global cost
            by comparing the value of the GC for the previous placement;
        A greedy criterion or Metropolis criterion may be used
            to accept/reject the move;

        Perform placement perturbation of two types;
        The first is an intracluster perturbation, where cells
        within a cluster are subjected to a random change;
        The second form of perturbation is among cells belonging
        to different clusters;
        This is done by partitioning the hypercube into two half-
        cubes, and letting clusters that exist across directly
        connected processors in the two half cubes to interact;
    END FORALL
UNTIL a certain number of iterations completed (user parameter);
End Procedure

    This parallel algorithm has not been implemented, hence there are no experimental results on speedups, or the quality of the placements produced by this algorithm. The performance of the parallel divide and conquer algorithm has been analyzed theoretically. The speedup S on P processors for N cells has been determined to be $S = \frac{1}{1/P + \log(P)/N}$, which converges to P for large values of N.

3.9 PLACEMENT USING A COMBINATION OF TECHNIQUES

It is often a common practice in sequential implementations of good placement algorithms to combine a variety of approaches. For example, constructive approaches such as mincut-based placement are often followed by iterative-improvement-based placement algorithms.

Until now we have discussed parallel algorithms for placement by parallelizing the placement algorithm in one particular way. Many researchers have actually proposed parallel placement implementations that combine a set of approaches to get the best results.

The first such work was reported by Kravitz and Rutenbar [37], who combined two forms of parallel annealing approaches to exploit the best feature of each scheme at different temperatures. (1) move decomposition at high temperatures and (2) parallel moves at low temperatures. At low temperatures, since a relatively small fraction of moves get accepted, the parallel moves strategy with acceptance of only a single move gives a lot of parallelism. At high temperatures, a large number of potential good moves are not accepted, so it gives poor speedups. The move decomposition strategy gives good speedups at high temperatures. Determination of the optimum crossover temperature at which to switch strategies is a hard problem. One approach is to estimate the speedup of the static function move acceleration as a function of temperature and compare it to the speedup obtained through the parallel moves strategy. The strategies are switched at the point that the speedup of the parallel moves strategy is higher than the move acceleration strategy.

Rose et al. [47], have reported another parallel implementation for placement that involves a combination of two different algorithms: one to replace the high temperature portion of annealing, and the other to speed up the low-temperature region. In the regular simulated annealing algorithm at high temperatures, the general search space being investigated changes rapidly due to the high acceptance ratio and the large scale of moves. The result of the high-temperature phase is a coarse placement that assigns each cell to a general area. An alternative to sequentially searching a number of coarse placements is to generate and investigate different coarse placements in parallel. This is the basic idea of what the authors have termed heuristic spanning.

Essentially a heuristic algorithm is used to generate a number of grossly different but plausible placements at the same time on different processors. These are evaluated by another heuristic procedure to produce an interim goodness measure. The best of the interim placements is chosen to be annealed further. A key point is that the heuristic algorithm runs much faster than simulated annealing. The first step of the Heuristic Spanning approach is to divide up the search space. A mincut-based algorithm is used to recursively subdivide a placement while minimizing the number of wires crossing a division line. A constructive initial partitioning step is introduced to aid the iterative improvement for mincut-based placement. Experience has shown that using different seeds has a marked effect on the quality of the final placement. The idea of heuristic spanning is to let multiple processors start from different seeds that are as far apart from each other as possible. The second is of the heuristic spanning approach is to choose one of the interim placements to be annealed further at low temperatures. The authors have found experimentally that choosing the interim placement with the lowest interim cost function generates the lowest final cost function at the end of annealing as well.

The final step is the low temperature annealing. The choice of the starting temperature of the annealing process is difficult. The following method has been recommended by the authors. The cost of the interim placement is determined. In a regular simulated annealing run, a table of cost function versus temperature is obtained. From that table, the temperature of the simulated annealing run that has the closest cost function to the interim cost function is determined. That temperature is chosen as the starting temperature. A problem with this strategy is that we need to perform a simulated annealing run for the circuit to determine the table of cost versus temperature, which defeats the purpose of parallelizing the annealing algorithm for better performance. However, the resulting temperature was empirically found to be constant over the circuit sizes tried; for instance, it corresponded to the twelfth temperature in a 27-temperature fixed temperature schedule of the simulated annealing approach that was tried out by the authors.

Another approach developed by researchers to determine the starting temperature of annealing has been reported recently. The temperature of a given placement can be estimated by making use of the equilibrium characteristics of simulated annealing [46]. The approach involves starting at any temperature, generating several hundred moves, and evaluating the total net cost change of accepted moves at that temperature. If the net change is negative, the temperature should be higher and if positive, the temperature should be lower. Using this approach, a binary search can be performed to quickly converge to the correct starting temperature.

The final part of the parallel placement algorithm uses Section Annealing for the lower-temperature region that begins with an interim placement. This placement is divided up geographically into subareas. The subareas and the cells contained in those areas are assigned to separate processors. The subareas were kept are square as possible. Each processor then generates moves, in parallel, for the cells that it is assigned and tests those moves for acceptance. If a move is accepted, then the accepting processor transmits the move to other processors so that they can maintain a consistent view of the cell positions.

Natarajan and Kirkpatrick have proposed a different strategy for combining heuristics [41]. Using an implementation of a parallel simulated annealing algorithm based on the parallel algorithm of Darema et al. [13] discussed earlier, which allowed acceptance of multiple moves that interact, they performed several experiments on an eight-processor shared memory multiprocessor. The authors performed a set of experiments on four placement problem instances having different connectivity characteristics and for whom the optimal solutions were known. This allowed the authors to compare the quality of the results produced by various heuristic approaches. Each instance was run a large number of times to study the statistical variation in the results. Some general conclusions were as follows. In all instances of the placement problem, the quality of the placement solution deteriorated with increasing number of processors in a parallel simulated annealing run. In particular the average and standard deviation of the cost of the final solution tended to increase with the addition of processors. In all instances of the problem, the total computational effort measured by adding the amount of CPU seconds spent over all the participating processors per run of the algorithm showed a tendency to increase with increased number of processors. Since a decline in the quality of solution and increase in total work done per iteration are both undesirable characteristics of any parallel implementations of the simulated annealing algorithm, an interesting extension of the algorithm was studied.

The parallel algorithm involved the use of multiple independent simulated annealing runs until the best solution is obtained that meets a specified confidence level. The general conclusion of that study was the following. Given a P processor system, the best approach is to divide the P processors into k groups each containing m processors, where $k * m = P$. Run k independent and simultaneous runs of a simulated annealing algorithm and in each of these runs use m processors in parallel. Choose the best of the placements obtained in the k independent runs. An optimal value $m*$ for the parameter m can be obtained experimentally. The authors studied an implementation on an eight-processor shared memory multiprocessor and reported that the optimal number for $m*$ is around 3. The best strategy is to have three groups of processors $(1, 2, 3)$ $(4, 5, 6)$ and $(7, 8)$ performing 3 independent parallel simulated annealing runs, where each run is performed on two to three processors.

3.10 FLOORPLANNING PROBLEM

The floorplan design problem can be viewed as a generalized version of the placement of building blocks. The building blocks during a floorplanning stage may have several possible orientations. An example is a register file consisting of 16 registers in a CPU, which can be organized as a 1×16, 2×8, 4×4, 8×2, or 16×1 array of memory elements, as shown in Figure 3.34(a). Given the floorplan of the chip, we wish to take advantage of the many possible implementations of the building block and search for those implementations yielding the minimum area layout. The floorplan design problem is to arrange a given set of cells of fixed area but variable aspect ratios in a plane to minimize the weighted sum of the area within the bounding rectangle of the arranged cells and the wire-length measures between cells that must be connected in the circuit, as shown in Figure 3.34(b). In this way, floorplan design can be seen as an optimization problem. Researchers have applied a variety of approaches to solve this problem, which can be viewed as a generalized cell placement problem. Most algorithm for floorplanning use the following formulation.

There is a set of m cells, denoted M_i for $i = 1, 2, ..., m$. The cells are restricted to be rectangular, and each cell is characterized by a triple (A_i, l_i, u_i), where A_i is the area of the cell, and l_i and u_i are the lower and upper bounds of the aspect ratio, that is, the ratio of the height h_i to width w_i of the cell. Hence $w_i h_i = A_i$, and $l_i \leq \frac{h_i}{w_i} \leq u_i$. A floorplan for the given m cells consists of a bounding rectangle, R, partitioned by horizontal and vertical line segments into m nonoverlapping rectangle regions denoted r_i, each having width x_i and height y_i. Each floorplan is evaluated by an objective function having a total area component and a total wire-length component as follows.

$$\text{score} = \sum_{i=1}^{m} x_i y_i + \sum_{i,j=1}^{m} c_{ij} d_{ij}$$

where d_{ij} corresponds to the Manhattan distance between the centers of cells i and j, and c_{ij} corresponds to the connectivity between the cells.

There are constructive and iterative approaches to solve the problem. Examples of constructive approaches include the cluster based techniques [43], branch-and bound methods [59], and partitioning and slicing using a modified mincut approach [38]. Examples of iterative floorplanning include simulated annealing [61], and genetic algorithms [11].

In the following we will discuss some of the approaches proposed for parallel floorplanning. We will classify them into the following classes using the corresponding classification of the sequential placement algorithms:

- Approach using simulated annealing

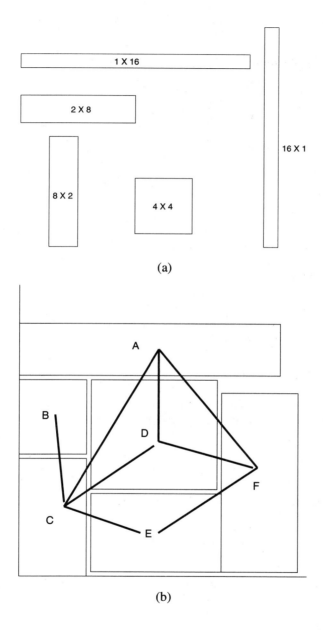

(a)

(b)

Figure 3.34 Floorplanning problem. (a) Various shapes of a module. (b) An Example floorplan.

- Approach using genetic algorithms

- Approach using branch and bound

For each of these classes we will discuss parallel algorithms suitable for execution on both shared memory multiprocessors and distributed memory multiprocessors.

3.11 FLOORPLANNING USING SIMULATED ANNEALING

3.11.1 Overview

We will now describe an algorithm for floorplanning based on simulated annealing that proposed by Jayaraman and Rutenbar [25]. Modules are represented as rectangles which are allowed to move freely around the surface of the chip. Individual moves can relocate cells by translation, pair swap, rotation, or resize them from a set of alternative sizes to explore alternative floorplans. Module overlaps are allowed during moves, but are penalized to remove all overlaps in the final floorplan. The cost function consists of the weighted sum of the estimated wire-length, cell overlap, and total floorplan area. A serial floorplanner has been implemented using simulated annealing style moves [25]. The solutions produced by the floorplanner were better than those using a slicing-tree-based constructive scheme [38].

3.11.2 Distributed Memory MIMD Parallel Algorithm

We will now describe a parallel floorplanning algorithm suitable for execution on a hypercube based distributed memory multiprocessor based on work reported in [25]. The parallel algorithm uses a combination of move decomposition and parallel move evaluation which were described earlier for parallel algorithms for cell placement [37]. Processors in a hypercube are organized as clusters of processors (for example, clusters of four-processor subcubes). The set of cells is partitioned among the different clusters. The partitioning of the cells is done by ownership to different clusters and not by their geographical location.

Clusters of cooperating processors are used to propose, evaluate, and accept or reject moves using the notion of move decomposition. Because of this cooperation, the frequency of message traffic between processors in a cluster is high; hence, the topological arrangement of the processors within a cluster becomes important. Figure 3.35(a) shows such a clustering in a eight-processor hypercube.

An outline of the parallel algorithm entitled *DM-PARALLEL-FP-SA-MOVEDECOM-INTERACTIVE* (for distributed memory parallel algorithm for floorplanning using simulated annealing with move decomposition and parallel interactive moves) is given next.

Procedure *DM-PARALLEL-FP-SA-MOVEDECOM-INTERACTIVE*;

Start with an initial floorplan solution (state) S;
Partition processors into clusters;
Partition cells among clusters of processors;
Set $T = T_0$ (initial temperature);

REPEAT /* outer loop */
   moves_attempted = 0;

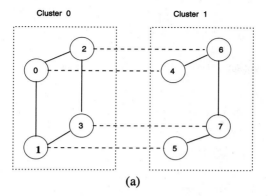

(a)

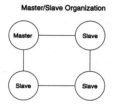

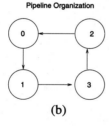

(b)

Figure 3.35 Clustering and various forms of move decomposition techniques in parallel floorplanning. (a) Clustering. (b) Two forms of move decomposition. (Courtesy of Jayaraman and Rutenbar, *Proc. Int. Conf. Computer-Aided Design,* ©IEEE 1987)

REPEAT /* inner loop */
   FORALL clusters of processors in PARALLEL DO
     Identify processors within a cluster;
     Select move (translation, rotation, exchange, resize);
     Partition function among processors of cluster;

       IF translation THEN
         Select a random cell;

Move to random location anywhere on chip;
IF rotation THEN
    Select a random cell;
    Rotate randomly in 90 degree steps;
IF resizing THEN
    Select a random cell;
    Resize to random size among size choices;
IF exchange THEN
    Select two random cells;
    Exchange cell locations;

Each cluster accepts/rejects move on own cost;
Update cell locations using Global or Partial method;
Increment moves_attempted
UNTIL moves_attempted = max_moves; /* inner loop */
Update T (control temperature);
UNTIL termination condition; /* end outer loop */

End Procedure

In addition to move decomposition, the strategy of parallel evaluation and acceptance of multiple moves is applied across the clusters that perform moves in parallel independently. Moves are not restricted to subregions of the chip, but occur on the entire chip area. To avoid contention such as two clusters attempting to move the same cell, the right to move a specific cell is given to its owning cluster. Since the assignment limits the set of feasible moves, the ownership rights are periodically randomized during the annealing process.

Since the moves are evaluated and accepted independently, errors due to interacting moves occur as in the parallel cell placement algorithms described earlier. Hence the global states need to be updated frequently to limit the errors. Two approaches of state updates have been investigated.

In the *global state updating method*, all the clusters get a consistent view of the state of the system. Since such a synchronization is rather expensive, each local cluster performs a stream of moves before performing the global update operation. In a global update, all the local views of the global layout are collected and integrated to obtain a correct view that is distributed to each of the clusters. To reduce the serial bottleneck of this scheme, a scheme of *partial updates* has been proposed. During a partial update, each cluster distributes its local state information to a select subset of the other clusters. By careful design of the topological arrangement of the clusters, it is possible to guarantee that all the clusters will eventually receive this update information, although it may be delayed.

Two parallel versions of move decomposition can be used. They are illustrated in Figure 3.35(b). The first employs a master-slave structure for each cluster. The master proposes a move, and evaluation is shared by the master and the slaves. After each cluster performs a variable length stream of moves, a centralized global update is done. Each cluster sends its local view to a predefined synchronizing node that integrates all these local views into a single correct global state, which is broadcast to all the clusters using a spanning-tree-based broadcasting mechanism on the hypercube.

The second version of move decomposition uses a more complex move decomposition and state update mechanism. Each cluster is mapped onto a subcube of the hypercube. Within a cluster, move computations are pipelined; the first processor proposes a move and the subsequent processors perform various parts of the cost evaluation and acceptance decision. Such a scheme is attractive for long streams of move evaluation. A lazy scheme of partial state updating is used by connecting the clusters in the form of a ring in the hypercube such that the overall arrangement is a connection of a ring of rings. Hence each cluster only sends its result to one adjacent cluster, but other schemes of partial updates are possible.

Implementation The preceding parallel algorithm has been implemented by Jayaraman and Rutenbar [25] on an Intel iPSC™ hypercube of 16 processors in the PASHA floorplanner. The authors reported experimental studies on a 20-cell floorplan example and demonstrated speedups of 4.5 for PASA-P1 to 7.5 for PASHA-P2 for identical serial and parallel annealing schedules. The move stream length was set to six moves. They reported that the results of the quality of the floorplan were always comparable to the serial algorithms for floorplanning.

3.11.3 Shared Memory MIMD Parallel Algorithm

The preceding parallel algorithm can be implemented easily on shared memory multiprocessors. The notion of move decomposition can be implemented by static allocation of the functions of move evaluation to three or four processors, similar to the approach discussed in the corresponding scheme for cell placement [37]

The notion of parallel move evalution and acceptance can be implemented as follows, similarly to the parallel algorithm for macro cell placement of Casotto et al. [7].

Each cluster of processors can be assigned a set of cells. The owning cluster is responsible for performing simulated annealing style moves on the owned cells anywhere within the chip layout. A global copy of the chip layout information is kept in shared memory, but each processor cluster keeps a local copy of the layout information on which it performs the move decisions. After a set of parallel moves, the local copies are updated from the global copy. Again, parallel move interactions can occur in this algorithm, but the convergence will not be affected if the updates from the global copies are made frequently. Periodically the cell ownerships can be randomized among the processor clusters.

No actual implementations of this shared memory algorithm have been reported.

3.12 FLOORPLANNING USING GENETIC ALGORITHM

3.12.1 Overview

The genetic algorithm paradigm described in the cell placement has been applied to the floorplanning application by Cohoon et al. [11]. In a genetic algorithm, a population of solutions to the problem at hand is maintained and allowed to evolve through successive generations. A suitable encoding of each solution in the population is used to represent legal solutions. In the context of floorplanning, the representation is that of Polish expressions [61].

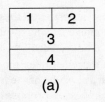

(a)

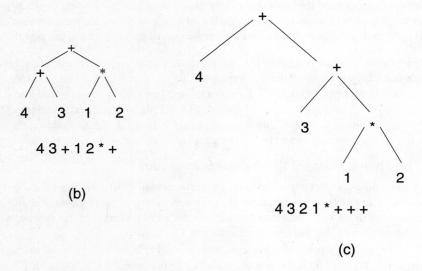

(b)

(c)

Figure 3.36 Slicing representation of floorplanning (Courtesy of Cohoon et al., *IEEE Trans. Computer-Aided Design,* ©IEEE 1991)

By restricting the partitions to recursive subdivisions, we obtain a slicing structure, an example of which is shown in Figure 3.36. Let the operations of a horizontal cut and a vertical cut be denoted by the operators + and *, respectively. Then the slicing structures comprising the m operands can be represented by slicing trees or Polish expressions. The Polish expression associated with a slicing tree is the postorder traversal of the tree as shown in Figure 3.36 Even though there can be more than one slicing tree representation of a given slicing structure, one can uniquely represent a particular tree as the normalized polish expression in which two operators of the same type do not appear adjacent to each other. A normalized Polish expression therefore uniquely identifies a floorplan structure. The string encoding used in the genetic algorithm is this unique Polish expression.

The solutions of various floorplans in the genetic algorithm are evaluated by a fitness measure, which is the weighted sum of the estimated wire-length and the area of the bounding rectangle of all the cells. This cost function is used to compute the fitness, that is, the solution's competence. To create a new generation, new solutions are formed by either merging two random solutions from the parent population via a crossover operation or modifying an existing solution using a mutation operation.

In the context of floorplanning, several crossover operators have been proposed that take two parent strings of Polish expressions and creates an offspring Polish expression by borrowing some characteristics from both parents. We will now describe the crossover and mutation operators in the context of floorplanning. Cohoon et al. [11] have proposed four types of crossover operators in terms of determining the offspring of two parent solutions that are represented by the strings of operands and operators in the Polish expression representation of a floorplan. The first operator copies the operands from the first parent into the corresponding positions in the offspring. Then it copies the operators from the second parent into the free slots. The second operator starts out by copying the operators from the first parent into the offspring and then copies the operands from the second parent into the free slots of the offspring. The remaining two operators function in terms of subtrees such that the overall slicing structure is maintained, and a particular subexpression is altered, or two subexpressions are exchanged. Examples of the crossover operators are shown in Figure 3.37.

The solutions to be included in the next generation are probabilistically selected according to the fitness values from the set comprising the newly formed solution ande the current generation. Typically, a constant number of solutions are selected so as to maintain population of a fixed size. After an arbitrary number of generations the process is terminated and the best remaining solution or the best seen solution is reported. The basic genetic algorithm has been extended with the theory of punctuated equilibria, which states that after an equilibrium is reached in the environment a powerful method of generating a new species is to thrust an old species into a new environment.

3.12.2 Distributed Memory MIMD Parallel Algorithm

We will now describe a distributed memory MIMD parallel algorithm for floorplanning using the theory of punctuated equilibria for genetic algorithms based on work by Cohoon et al. [11]. A set of n solutions is assigned to each of N processors for a total population size of $n \times N$. The set assigned to each processor is its subpopulation. The processors are connected by a connection network such as a hypercube or a mesh that offers sufficient connectivity and small diameter to ensure adequate mixing of populations as time progresses. An outline of the parallel algorithm entitled *DM-PARALLEL-FP-GA-POPULATION* (for distributed memory parallel algorithm for floorplanning using genetic algorithms and population decomposition) is given next.

Procedure *DM-PARALLEL-FP-GA-POPULATION*;
Read net list and create initial populations
    of floorplan configurations;
Partition populations among processors;

FORALL processors in PARALLEL DO
    Evaluate all floorplan configurations
        in population owned by processor;
    FOR E iterations DO
        FOR G Generations DO
            Run Genetic Algorithm

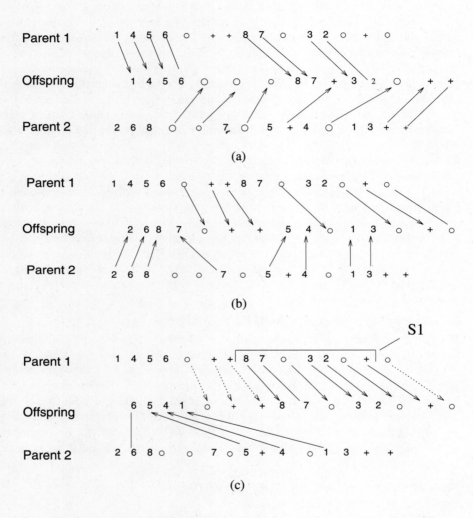

Figure 3.37 Example crossover operators in floorplanning.(a) First crossover operator. (b) Second crossover operator. (c) Third crossover operator. (Courtesy of Cohoon et al., *IEEE Trans. Computer-Aided Design,* ©IEEE 1991)

> WHILE number of offsprings created $< n \times C$ DO
>   Select two solutions;
>   Crossover the two solutions to create an offspring;
> END WHILE
> Add all offsprings to subpopulation;
> Select a population of n elements;
> Generate $n \times M$ random mutations;
> Find Average fitness;
> Select configurations for next generation
>   with fitter individuals getting higher
>   probability of selection;
> END FOR
> FOR each neighbor of current processor DO
>   Send/Receive a set of solutions S_{ij}
>   from processor i to processor j
> END FOR
> Select n element configurations for next generation
>   with fitter individuals getting higher
>   probability of selection;
> END FOR (E iterations)
> END FORALL
> **End Procedure**

The E major iterations are called epochs. During each epoch, each processor disjointly and in parallel executes a genetic algorithm on its subpopulations. After this phase, each processor sends randomly selected subsets of subpopulations of size s to each of its neighbors. Finally, each processor probabilistically selects a set of n solutions to survive using a fitness measure.

The crossover rate, $0 \leq C \leq 1$, determines how many offsprings are created during each generation. The mutation rate, $0 \leq M \leq 1$, determines how many mutations are performed each generation.

Implementation Cohoon et al. [11] have implemented the preceding parallel algorithm in a program called GAPE and have evaluated the performance of the algorithm on simulated configurations on hypercubes and meshes. The authors have obtained near-linear speedups with increasing processors since there is relatively little communication overhead in the algorithm. They have mainly reported on the quality of the floorplans obtained from their algorithm on two example problems of 16 and 20 cells and have compared their quality to an implementation based on simulated annealing. The results of their genetic algorithm were found to be always better in quality than simulated annealing for an equal amount of search work performed. No speedup results have been reported.

3.12.3 Shared Memory MIMD Parallel Algorithm

The preceding parallel algorithm can be easily adapted to a shared memory MIMD multiprocessor. In the parallel algorithm, the entire set of solutions is kept in global memory. However, the populations will be partitioned into subpopulations allocated to individual processors, each of which is on a separate queue, with each processor having exclusive control over reading and writing to that subpopulation queue. Each processor acquires two solutions from within its own population subspace and performs the crossover and mutation operators on them to generate offsprings. Next each processor performs the choice function on the subpopulations in order to select the surviving populations. The migration operation is performed by selecting a set of solutions from each processor and copying them into the solution regions of other processors. This copying needs to be performed by locking the pair of subpopulation region queues corresponding to the pair of processors that will perform the exchange of their solutions. No actual implementations of a shared memory algorithm has been reported but we should expect similar linear speedups as for the distributed memory implementations.

3.13 FLOORPLANNING USING BRANCH AND BOUND

3.13.1 Overview

One way of performing floorplanning is to execute it in two stages. The first stage which determines the relative placements of the rectangular blocks is executed using some estimate of wire-length or congestion minimization and is usually based on a mincut-based partitioning method. In the second stage, optimization of the total area is performed to determine which of several possible implementations of the cells to use given a relative placement of the cells. Wimer et al. have proposed a solution to the floorplanning problem using a branch and bound algorithm [59].

In this formulation, a floorplan is represented as a pair of dual polar graphs called the G-graph and the H graph. Each vertex in the G graph corresponds to a vertical line segment in the floorplan. There exists an arc from one vertex to another if there is a cell in the floorplan whose left and right edges lie on the vertical segments corresponding to those vertices. The vertical segments correspond to those vertices. The H graph is similarly defined for the horizontal line segments. Figure 3.38(a) shows an example floorplan. The corresponding G graph (representing the relationships among the vertical segments) and the H graph representing the relationships among the horizontal segments are shown in Figure 3.38(b). Each block has a fixed area but is allowed to have several possible implementations with varying widths and heights. For example, block $B1$ has area of 4 units and is allowed to take two possible shapes, 2 X 2, and 1 X 4. Block $B2$ has area of 16 units, and is allowed to take two possible shapes, 2X8, and 8X2. Block $B3$ has area of 4 units, and is allowed to take two possible shapes, 4X1, and 2X2. Given an implementation of each block, the width and height are assigned to the arcs in the G and H graphs. Then the overall area of the floorplan is simply the product of the longest paths in G and H. It is therefore necessary to select an implementation for each block such that the overall area of the floorplan is minimized.

The sequential algorithm for this problem consists of enumerating the state space as a tree whose nodes corresponds to partial layouts. The successors of a node correspond to the implementation of the block to be considered next. A path from the root to a leaf represents

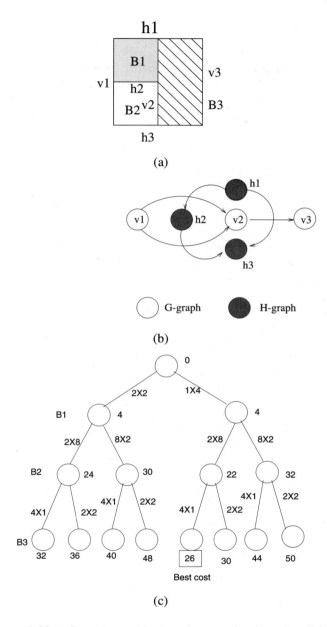

Figure 3.38 A floorplan and its search tree using branch and bound algorithm. (a) Example floorplan. (b) G graph and H graph representation. (c) Search tree. (Courtesy of Wimer et al., *Proc. 25th Design Automation Conf.*, ©IEEE 1988)

a complete layout. The algorithm uses a form of branch and bound to eliminate searching in regions of the search space whose area of the layout is provably greater than an existing solution already found [59]. The search tree for the three cell layout of the example in Figure 3.38(a) is shown in Figure 3.38(c). The nodes in the search tree represent the choices of the aspect ratios for each of the cells, B1, B2, and B3 at the different levels of the tree. Associated with the nodes, are the partial cost values of the floorplan, using which the branch-and-bound search is performed. The best solution of 26 square units is shown in the figure. This corresponds to the choice of 1 X 4 configuration for B1, 2 X 8 for B2, and 4 X 1 for B3.

3.13.2 Shared Memory MIMD Parallel Algorithm

We will now describe a parallel algorithm for floorplanning proposed by Arvindam et al. [1] that is based on applying parallel depth first search strategies in this search tree. The spaces searched by individual processors are disjoint. Each processor executes a sequential branch-and-bound algorithm on the search space allocated to it with a local value of the bounding function. Idle processors request work from other processors. Each transfer involves only two processors. When all processors run out of work, the search terminates. This approach is guaranteed to find the optimal solution, but would be more efficient on pruning the search space, that is, would work with a tight lower bound, if the processors frequently update their local values of the bounding function to the current best value of the area found so far globally.

On a shared memory machine, the current best value of A_{min} can be globally maintained and can be atomically updated every time a processor generates a better solution. Request for work can be made using a centralized scheme for which a global variable TARGET is maintained to point to the next donor processor. An idle processor requests the processor whose identity is TARGET for work. It also atomically increments TARGET by 1 modulo the number of processors. If the work is not available from the chosen processor, the requesting processor repeats these steps. A global variable ACTIVE is maintained to count the number of active processors. The search terminates when the value of this variable is zero.

An outline of the parallel algorithm entitled *SM-PARALLEL-FP-BBSEARCH* (for shared memory parallel algorithm for floorplanning using branch and bound search methods) is given next.

Procedure *SM-PARALLEL-FP-BBSEARCH*;

Read and store circuit in shared memory;
Create G graph and H graphs in shared memory;
Set shared flag ACTIVE = number of processors;
Set shared flag TARGET = 1;

FORALL processors in PARALLEL DO
   WHILE in Branch and Bound Search loop DO
      Check shared flag ACTIVE;
      IF ACTIVE = 0 THEN
         Terminate search and Exit;
      ELSE
      Perform one iteration of branch and bound search;

        Find new state S;
        IF S < best and Cost(S) < Amin THEN
            Amin = cost(S);
            best = S;
        IF search space on current processor exhausted THEN
            Search for work from another processor;
            WHILE target processor not found DO
                TARGET = TARGET + 1 mod P;
                IF TARGET processor has work THEN
                    Split workspace of TARGET processor
                    and take half work;
            ENDWHILE
    ENDWHILE
END FORALL

End Procedure

3.13.3 Distributed Memory MIMD Parallel Algorithm

On a distributed memory machine, the preceding scheme can be implemented as follows. The variable TARGET is stored in a specially designated processor. The atomic read-and-increment is simulated by exchanging messages from the requesting processors to this special processor. In another workload distribution scheme, a random polling can be used to identify busy processors, by which processor randomly selects a processor to request work from. A third scheme is to send a request to neighbors of the distributed memory machine.

Implementation   Arvindam et al. [1] have reported an implementation of the parallel algorithm on a 128-processor Ametek Symult S2010™ message-passing, mesh-based multiprocessor. The authors ran the algorithm for numerous problem instances with the number of blocks ranging from 20 to 30. They have demonstrated that the speedups become close to linear for larger problem sizes and have observed speedups of about 100 on 128 processors for some large circuits.

3.14 HARDWARE ACCELERATORS

In this section we will briefly review some of the hardware accelerators that have been proposed for the placement problem.

        A parallel implementation of the adjacent-pair exchange based iterative improvement algorithm has been reported independently by Chyan and Breuer [10], and by Ueda et al. [58]. Both approaches involve a two-dimensional array of processors controlled by a central host, as shown in Figure 3.39. In this design, it is assumed that the number of cells required to be placed is equal to the number of processors in the array. The control processor is necessary for performing initial placement of data into every node processor. The data exchange between adjacent node processors is done via the direct paths. Each node processor pairs up with another processor in different cycles and independently evaluates whether the corresponding cells in

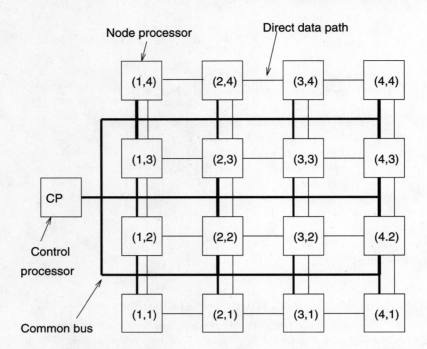

Figure 3.39 Parallel placement on array processor (Courtesy of Ueda et al., *IEEE Trans. Computer-Aided Design,* ©IEEE 1983)

those processors should be exchanged by calculating the amount of addition or reduction of its wire-length associated with all the related nodes. After the decision to exchange the cells is taken, the relevant global state information is broadcast to all the processors.

Iosupovici, King, and Breuer have proposed a special-purpose hardware architecture using a pipelined processor [24] to rapidly evaluate alternative configurations of placements through placement interchanges among cells. The different steps involved in the computation of a cost increment of a new placement were implemented in four pipeline stages. An actual implementation of the hardware showed about 10 times performance improvement over a software implementation of the placement interchange step.

Kling and Banerjee have reported on another hardware accelerator for placement as a coprocessor to a commercial microprocessor [34]. The coprocessor supports instructions such as evaluating lengths of a particular net, or evaluating lengths of all nets connected to a cell. It uses an address unit, two ALUs, and a cache to store recently used cell data. A CMOS VLSI chip implementation of this coprocessor was fabricated and tested using this concept; it performed wire-length computations 40 times faster than corresponding software implementations.

3.15 SUMMARY

In this chapter we have reviewed some parallel algorithms for placement and floorplanning. Since these problems are NP complete to begin with, heuristic approaches are used to solve such problems. Newer heuristics are being continually developed. We have discussed some approaches to develop parallel algorithms for some of the better known heuristics for these applications for shared and distributed memory multiprocessors. We now summarize the basic features and advantages of each parallel algorithm.

The parallel algorithm based on *iterative pairwise exchange* exchanges $N/2$ pairs of adjacent cells simultaneously and is suitable for execution on SIMD and MIMD parallel machines. The advantage of this algorithm is that it has a large degree of parallelism. The main disadvantage is that the quality of the solutions produced by this algorithm is quite poor. A second disadvantage is that due to interaction among parallel moves, there is a chance of oscillation around the placement solution.

The parallel algorithm based on *force-directed placement* is suitable for SIMD parallel machines. The advantage of this algorithm is that there is a large degree of parallelism, and the solution quality obtained from the algorithm is fairly good, better than the pair-wise exchange algorithm, but inferior to simulated annealing.

We discussed several parallel algorithms based on *simulated annealing*. The advantage of this algorithm is that it gives the best quality of the solution among all sequential algorithms for the placement problem. The parallel algorithms based on move decomposition breaks up the task involved in simulated annealing into a set of subtasks and allocates each task to a different processor. This approach is only suitable for shared memory MIMD machines and typically gives only small speedups of about 2 to 3. The parallel algorithms based on parallel move evaluation give large speedups, and are suitable for both SIMD and MIMD machines, but we have to be careful about interactive parallel moves. Parallel algorithms based on parallel evaluation and acceptance of noninteracting moves give low speedups. Parallel algorithms based on parallel interactive moves can give good speedups, but can give rise to about 5% degradation in quality of the solution with an increasing number of processors. One point to note about parallel algorithms using simulated annealing is that the sequential algorithm takes a long time to execute, so even though we get good speedups, the resultant runtimes on parallel processors are still quite high.

We have also discussed parallel algorithms for placement based on *simulated evolution* in which a processor is allocated a region of the chip area and its set of cells and runs the simulated evolution algorithm procedures of evaluation, selection, and allocation on its cells. The parallel algorithm is suitable for both shared memory and distributed memory MIMD machines and gives good speedups. However, the quality of the solution is not as good as simulated annealing.

The parallel algorithms for placement based on *genetic algorithms* allocate a subset of population of cells to each processor, and each processor runs a genetic algorthm on its own population, and periodically exchanges subsets of populations with other processors. The algorithm gives reasonably good quality of solution and large speedups. The disadvantage of this algorithm is its large memory requirements, which need to store several hundred different placement solutions simultaneously.

The parallel algorithms for placement based on *hierarchical decomposition* use a divide and conquer method of solution by recursively decomposing the placement solution on the entire chip into subproblems of the placement of cells on smaller chip regions. The advantage of the parallel algorithm is that the solution quality does not degrade with an increasing number of processors. However, the disadvantage is that the speedups are not scalable with a large number of processors, since the topmost nodes in the task graph that execute on a few processors take the longest time to execute, and it takes a long time for all the processors to become busy doing useful work.

We also described several parallel algorithms for floorplanning. The algorithm using *simulated annealing* is suitable for both shared memory and distributed memory MIMD machines, gives the best solution quality, and also gives good speedups. However, the sequential algorithm takes a long time to execute, so even though we get good speedups, the resultant runtimes on parallel processors are still quite high.

The parallel algorithm for floorplanning using a genetic algorithm is suitable for both shared memory and distributed memory MIMD machines, gives excellent speedups, and generates solutions of good quality. The disadvantage is the large memory requirements in maintaining several hundred floorplan solutions. However, since the floorplanning problem typically has about 100 cells to deal with, the memory problem is not as severe as the placement problem which deals typically with tens of thousands of cells.

The parallel floorplanning algorithm using branch and bound search is suitable for both shared memory and distributed memory MIMD machines and gives good speedups. However, the quality of the solutions is not as good as with simulated annealing.

We end this chapter making the following observations. While there are numerous heuristics for solving the placement and floorplanning problem, each heuristic has its own advantages. Methods based on constructive techniques such as mincut and quadrisection are very fast, but they give poor quality of results. Methods based on probabilistic search techniques such as simulated annealing, simulated evolution or genetic approaches give very good quality of results, but take extremely long times. If the goal of the CAD designer is to produce layouts of the best quality, we have to use these extremely time consuming methods. That is exactly where parallel processing can help: to provide the best quality of results in the shortest runtimes.

A problem that is commonly faced in the design of efficient parallel algorithms for placement is that every year better and better sequential heuristics are being discovered, which improve on previous methods in terms of quality of layouts produced, better objective functions, and runtimes. Newer sequential placement algorithms handle better and improved objective functions, that is, performance driven layout. Unless the parallel algorithms can be designed such that these newer efficient techniques can be rapidly incorporated into the parallel implementations, the latter will become rapidly obsolete in terms of practical use. We will address these problems in Chapter 10.

3.16 PROBLEMS

3.1   In the parallel pairwise interchange placement algorithm, we can have oscillations when multiple pairs of cells are simultaneously moved, that is, each cell assumes that by exchanging positions it will improve the cost, and both cells in a pair of connected cells get exchanged.

Figure 3.10 shows some examples of incorrect judgment. Design an algorithm to avoid these incorrect judgments and the oscillations.

3.2   Develop and implement the parallel force-directed placement algorithm for a distributed memory multicomputer. Use the Intel iPSC™ library calls discussed in Chapter 2.

3.3   Design and implement an asynchronous parallel placement algorithm using simulated annealing for a distributed memory multiprocessor that uses parallel evaluation and acceptance of interacting moves, using geographic partitioning of the chip area and its cells, but letting each cell be moved anywhere in the chip. The algorithm should be a combination of the algorithms *DM-PARALLEL-SA-INTER-DOMAIN* and *DM-PARALLEL-SA-INTER-REPLICATED*.

3.4   Implement the algorithm for error estimation to control the amount of error in parallel moves in a parallel annealing placement algorithm. The scheme described in the chapter uses a rough estimate of the error. Develop a more accurate error estimation scheme for synchronous and asynchronous parallel algorithms.

3.5   Analyze the speedup characteristics of the different parallel simulated annealing algorithms described in the chapter. Assume a relative computation cost of evaluating a move to the communication cost of updating the state to be α. Derive an expression for the speedup on a hypercube multiprocessor of P processors and N cells, and assume that each cell is connected to an average of d other cells. Assume that there are T temperatures in the annealing and M moves per temperature.

3.6   Design and implement a shared memory parallel algorithm for simulated-evolution -based nonhierachical placement using geographic partitioning of the chip area and the cells, similar to the parallel placement algorithms using simulated annealing. Consider various load balancing strategies, static blocked, static interleaved, and dynamic. Compare its performance with the distributed memory parallel algorithm *DM-PARALLEL-SE-DOMAIN* described in the chapter.

3.7   Design and implement a shared memory parallel algorithm for genetic placement based on the corresponding distributed memory algorithm. *DM-PARALLEL-GENETIC-PLACEMENT-POPULATION*. How would you provide better load balance than the distributed memory algorithm.

3.8   Analyze the performance of the parallel hierarchical placement algorithm *SM-PARALLEL-HIERARCHICAL-PLACE*. Assume that the computation cost of each task (quadrisection or bisection placement) to be proportional to the number of cells involved in the task. Determine the expected speedups on a P processor shared memory multiprocessor.

3.9   Design and implement a shared memory parallel algorithm for floorplanning using geographic partitioning and module partitioning. Analyze the performance of the algorithm assuming P processors and M modules.

3.10   Design and implement a distributed memory parallel floorplanning algorithm based on branch and bound search techniques similar to the *SM-PARALLEL-FP-BBSEARCH* algorithm. Analyze the performance of the algorithm.

3.17 REFERENCES

[1]   S. Arvindam, V. Kumar, and V. Nageshwara Rao. Floorplan Optimization on Multiprocessors. *Proc. Int. Conf. Computer Design (ICCD-89)*, Oct. 1989.

[2]   P. Banerjee and M. Jones. A Parallel Simulated Annealing for Standard Cell Placement on a Hypercube Computer. *Proc. Int. Conf. Computer-aided Design*, pages 34–37, Nov. 1986.

[3]   P. Banerjee, M. H. Jones, and J. S. Sargent. Parallel Simulated Annealing Algorithms for Standard Cell Placement on Hypercube Multiprocessors. *IEEE Trans. Parallel Distributed Systems*, 1(1):91–106, Jan. 1990.

[4]   D. Brelaz. New Methods to Color the Vertices of a Graph. *Comm. of ACM*, 22:251–256, 1979.

[5]   M. A. Breuer. Min-cut Placement. *J. Design Automation Fault Tolerant Computing*, 1:343–382, Oct. 1977.

[6]   R. J. Brouwer and P. Banerjee. PARAGRAPH: A Parallel Algorithm for Simultaneous Placement and Routing Using Hierarchy. *Proc. European Design Automation Conf. (EDAC-92)*, Mar. 1992.

[7]   A. Casotto, F. Romeo, and A. Sangiovanni-Vincentelli. A Parallel Simulated Annealing Algorithm for the Placement of Macro-Cells. *IEEE Trans. Computer-aided Design Integrated Circuits Systems*, pages 838–847, Sept. 1987.

[8]   A. Casotto and A. Sangiovanni-Vincentelli. Placement of Standard Cells Using Simulated Annealing on the Connection Machine. *Proc. Int. Conf. Computer-aided Design*, pages 350–353, Nov. 1987.

[9]   C. Cheng and E. Kuh. Module Placement Based on Resistive NetWork Optimization. *IEEE Trans. Computer-aided Design Integrated Circuits Systems*, 3(7):218–225, July 1984.

[10]   D. J. Chyan and M. A. Breuer. A Placement Algorithm for Array Processors. *Proc. 20th Design Automation Conf.*, pages 182–188, June 1983.

[11]   J. P. Cohoon, S. U. Hegde, W. N. Martin, and D. Richards. Distributed Genetic Algorithms for the Floorplan Design Problem. *IEEE Trans. Computer-aided Design Integrated Circuits Systems*, 10(4):483–492, Apr. 1991.

[12]   J. P. Cohoon and W. D. Paris. Genetic Placement. *IEEE Trans. Computer-aided Design Integrated Circuits Systems*, pages 956–964, Nov. 1987.

[13]   F. Darema, S. Kirkpatrick, and V. A. Norton. Parallel Algorithms for Chip Placement by Simulated Annealing. *IBM J. Research Dev.*, May 1987.

[14]   A. E. Dunlop and B. W. Kernighan. A Procedure for Placement of Standard-Cell VLSI Circuits. *IEEE Trans. Computer-aided Design Integrated Circuits Systems of Circuits and Systems*, CAD-4(1):92–98, Jan. 1985.

[15]   W. Fenton, B. Ramkumar, V. A. Saletore, A. B. Sinha, and L. V. Kale. Supporting Machine Independent Programming on Diverse Parallel Architecture. *Proc. Int. Conf. Parallel Processing*, Aug. 1991.

[16]   L. K. Grover. Standard Cell Placement Using Simulated Sintering. *Proc. 24th Design Automation Conf.*, pages 60–66, June 1987.

[17]   M. Hanan and J. M. Kurtzberg. Placement Techniques. In M. A. Breuer, editor, *Design Automation of Digital Systems: Theory and Techniques*, pages 213–282. Prentice Hall, 1972.

[18]   M. Hanan and J. M. Kurtzberg. A Review of the Placement and the Quadratic Assignment Problem, Apr. 1972.

[19]   M. Hanan and P. K. Wolff. Survey of placement techniques. *J. Design Automation and Fault Tolerant Computing*, pages 28–61, Oct. 1976.

[20]   M. R. Hartoog. Analysis of Placement Procedures for VLSI Standard Cell Layout. *Proc. 23rd Design Automation Conf.*, pages 314–319, June 1986.

[21]   E. I. Horvath. A Parallel Force Directed Standard Cell Placement Algorithm. Technical report, Dept. Computer Science, Florida Atlantic University, Boca Raton, FL, 1992.

[22]   T. C. Hu and E. S. Kuh. *VLSI Circuit Layout*. IEEE Press, New York, NY, 1985.

[23]   M. D. Huang, F. Romeo, and A. Sangiovanni-Vincentelli. An Efficient General Cooling Schedule for Simulated Annealing. *Proc. Int. Conf. Computer-aided Design*, pages 381–384, Nov. 1986.

[24]   A. Iosupovici, C. King, and M. A. Breuer. A Module Interchange Placement Machine. *Proc. 20th Design Automation Conf.*, pages 171–174, June 1983.

[25]   R. Jayaraman and R. Rutenbar. Floorplanning by Annealing on a Hypercube Multiprocessor. *Proc. Int. Conf. Computer-aided Design*, pages 346–349, Nov. 1987.

[26]   M. Jones and P. Banerjee. Performance of a Parallel Algorithm for Standard Cell Placement on the Intel Hypercube. *Proc. 24th Design Automation Conf.*, pages 807–813, June 1987.

[27]   L. V. Kale. The Chare Kernel Parallel Programming System. *Proc. Int. Conf. Parallel Processing*, Aug. 1990.

[28]   B. W. Kernighan and S. Lin. An Efficient Heuristic for Partitioning Graphs. *Bell Syst. Tech. J.*, 49:291–307, Feb. 1970.

[29]   S. Kim, B. Ramkumar, J. Chandy, S. Parkes, and P. Banerjee. ProperPLACE: A Portable Parallel Algorithm for Standard Cell Placement. *Proc. 8th Int. Parallel Processing Symp. (IPPS-94)*, Apr. 1994.

[30]   S. Kirkpatrick, C. D. Gelatt, and M. P. Vecchi. Optimization by Simulated Annealing. *Science*, 220:671–680, May 1983.

[31]   R. M. Kling and P. Banerjee. ESP: A New Standard Cell Placement Package Using Simulated Evolution. *Proc. 24th Design Automation Conf.*, pages 60–66, June 1987.

[32]   R. M. Kling and P. Banerjee. Optimization by Simulated Evolution with Application to Standard Cell Placement. *27th Design Automation Conf.*, pages 20–25, June 1990.

[33]   R. M. Kling and P. Banerjee. ESP: Placement by Simulated Evolution. *IEEE Trans. Computer-aided Design Integrated Circuits Systems*, 8(3):245–256, Mar. 1989.

[34]   R. M. Kling and P. Banerjee. A Special Purpose Coprocessor for Cell Placement and Floorplanning. *Proc. Custom Integrated Circuits Conf.*, May 1989.

[35]   R. M. Kling and P. Banerjee. Concurrent ESP: A Placement Algorithm for Execution on Distributed Processors. *Proc. Int. Conf. on Computer-aided Design*, pages 354–357, Nov. 1987.

[36]   R. M. Kling and P. Banerjee. Empirical and Theoretical Studies of the Simulated Evolution Method Applied to Standard Cell Placement. *IEEE Trans. Computer-aided Design Integrated Circuits Systems*, 10(10):1303–1315, Oct. 1991.

[37]   S. A. Kravitz and R. A. Rutenbar. Placement by Simulated Annealing on a Multiprocessor. *IEEE Trans. Computer-aided Design Integrated Circuits Systems*, CAD-6(4):534–549, June 1987.

[38]   D. P. Lapotin and S. W. Director. Mason: A Global Floorplanning Tool. *Proc. Int. Conf. Computer-aided Design (ICCAD-85)*, pages 143–145, Nov. 1985.

[39]   S. Mohan and P. Mazumder. Wolverines: Standard Cell Placement on a Network of Workstations. *IEEE Trans. Computer-aided Design Integrated Circuits Systems*, 12(9):1312–1326, Sept. 1993.

[40]   K. Natarajan and S. Kirkpatrick. Evaluation of Parallel Placement by Simulated Annealing: Part I - The Decomposition Approach. Technical Report RC 15246 IBM, IBM Technical Report, Nov. 1989.

[41]   K. Natarajan and S. Kirkpatrick. Evaluation of Parallel Placement by Simulated Annealing : Part II - The Flat Approach. Technical Report RC 15247 IBM, IBM Technical Report, Nov. 1989.

[42]   S. Parkes, J. Chandy, and P. Banerjee. ProperCAD II: A Run-time Library for Portable, Parallel, Object-Oriented Programming with Applications to VLSI CAD. Technical Report CRHC-93-22/UILU-ENG-93-2250, University of Illinois, Coordinated Science Lab, Urbana, IL, Dec. 1993.

[43]   B. Preas and M. Lorenzetti. *Physical Design Automation of VLSI Systems*. Benjamin-Cummings Publishing Co., Menlo Park, CA, 1988.

[44]   B. T. Preas and P. G. Karger. Automatic Placement: A Review of Current Techniques. *Proc. 23rd Design Automation Conf.*, pages 622–629, June 1986.

[45]   C. P. Ravikumar and S. Sastry. Parallel Placement on Hypercube Architectures. *Proc. Int. Conf. Parallel Processing (ICPP89)*, pages III:97–III:100, Aug. 1989.

[46]   J. Rose, W. Klebsch, and J. Wolf. Temperature measurement and equilibrium dynamics of simulated annealing placements. *IEEE Trans. Computer-aided Design Integrated Circuits Systems*, 9(10):253–259, Oct. 1990.

[47]   J. S. Rose, W. M. Snelgrove, and Z. G. Vranesic. Parallel Standard Cell Placement Algorithms with Quality Equivalent to Simulated Annealing. *IEEE Trans. Computer-aided Design Integrated Circuits Systems*, pages 387–396, Mar. 1988.

[48]   Y. Saad and M. H. Schultz. Topological Properties of Hypercubes. *IEEE Trans. Computers*, 37, No. 7:867–872, July 1988.

[49]   J. Sargent and P. Banerjee. A Parallel Row-Based Algorithm for Standard Cell Placement with Integrated Error Control. *Proc. 26th Design Automation Conf.*, pages 590–594, June 1989.

[50]   D. G. Schweikert. A 2-dimensional Placement Algorithm for the Layout of Electrical Circuits. *Proc. 13th Design Automation Conf.*, pages 408–416, June 1976.

[51]   C. Sechen and A. Sangiovanni-Vincentelli. The TimberWolf Placement and Routing Package. *J. Solid-State Circuits*, 20(2):510–522, 1985.

[52]   K. Shahookar and P. Mazumder. VLSI Placement Techniques. *ACM Computing Surveys*, 23(2):143–220, June 1991.

[53]   K. Shahookar and P. Mazumder. A Genetic Approach to Standard Cell Placement Using Meta-Genetic Parameter Optimization. *IEEE Trans. Computer-aided Design Integrated Circuits Systems*, 9(5):500–511, May 1990.

[54]   P. Suaris and G. Kedem. An Algorithm for Quadrisection and Its Application to Standard Cell Placement. *IEEE Trans. Circuits and Systems*, 35(3):294–303, Mar. 1988.

[55]   P. Suaris and G. Kedem. A Quadrisection-Based Combined Place and Route Scheme for Standard Cells. *IEEE Trans. Computer-aided Design Integrated Circuits Systems*, 8(3):234–244, Mar. 1989.

[56]   R. Tsay, E. Kuh, and C. Hsu. Module Placement for Large Chips Based on Sparse Linear Equations. *Int. J. Circuit Theory Appl.*, 16:411–423, 1988.

[57]   J. S. Turner. Almost All k-coloring Graphs are Easy to Color. *J. Algorithms*, pages 63–82, Mar. 1988.

[58]   K. Ueda, T. Komatsubara, and T. Hosaka. A Parallel Module Placement Approach for Logic Module Placement. *IEEE Trans. Computer-aided Design Integrated Circuits Systems of Integrated Circuits and Systems*, CAD-2(1):39–47, Jan. 1983.

[59]   S. Wimer, I. Koren, and I. Cederbaum. Optimal Aspect Ratios of Building Blocks in VLSI. *Proc. 25th Design Automation Conf. (DAC-88)*, pages 66–72, June 1988.

[60]   C. P. Wong and R. D. Fiebrich. Simulated Annealing-Based Circuit Placement on the Connection Machine System. *Proc. Int. Conf. Computer Design*, pages 78–82, Oct. 1987.

[61]   D. F. Wong and C. L. Liu. A New Algorithm for Floorplan Design. *Proc. 23rd Design Automation Conf.*, pages 101–107, June 1986.

CHAPTER 4

Detailed and Global Routing

4.1 INTRODUCTION

Automated layout consists of two primary functions: (1) determining the positions of the modules (standard cells, gates, macro cells) on the VLSI chip, called *placement*, and (2) interconnecting the modules with wiring, called *routing*. Although placement and routing are intimately related and interdependent, they have been traditionally separately solved because of their computational complexities. Hence placement algorithms use some crude measures to estimate the routing complexities of various placements. The routing algorithms subsequently take a given placement and perform the exact wiring of the nets. Both placement and routing problems are NP complete; hence a large number of heuristics exist for solving the problems, which vary in their runtime requirements and qualities of layout produced. Unfortunately, routing algorithms that produce high quality layouts often take large amounts of computation time. Recently, researchers have therefore turned to parallel processing to solve complex routing problems quickly and with high-quality. In this chapter we will describe various parallel algorithms for routing.

To understand the parallel algorithms for routing, we must be familiar with the different routing styles. We will therefore first provide a brief introduction to the field of routing.

After modules or cells are placed on a chip area, their pins have to be connected together using a number of wiring layers. Figure 4.1 shows an example of a routing problem for a standard cell layout. The figure shows a set of standard cells labeled C arranged in different rows by a placement algorithm, surrounded by pads labeled P. The connections among the

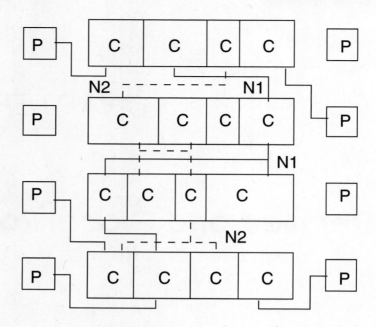

Figure 4.1 Example routing problem for standard cell layout

cells and pads are made by routing the nets in the different routing channels.The solid and dashed lines represent two different nets $N1$ and $N2$ that are routed as shown. In general, many sets of points must be electrically connected. The routing problem is to connect all the points in each set and ensure that the wiring paths of the different sets do not intersect on any layer. In addition, there are several routing aspects need to be optimized. Long wire lengths cause propagation delays, hence wire lengths have to be minimized. Available routing space is often a variant, and hence overall area has to be minimized. Nets carrying critical signals are often minimized at the expense of others.

With the increasing complexity of the routing problems in ICs dealing with several thousands of nets, the large problems are decomposed into small subproblems using a divide and conquer approach. Routing algorithms are used as part of a two step process. A *global router* performs coarse routing; it performs assignment of nets to a subset of routing areas. The exact routing of the nets is done by a *detailed router*.

To aid in the discussion of the chapter, we will provide a routing taxonomy as described in [20]. Routers can be classified as *global* or *detailed routers* in the first level of hierarchy. Within global routers, we have routers based on graph search methods, Steiner tree approaches, and iterative improvement. Within detailed routers, there are two classes, *general purpose* and *restricted*.

Detailed general-purpose routers work on the entire design in a serial fashion and are appropriate for small to medium designs. Figure 4.2 shows an example of a detailed general purpose routing problem. In the figure, the terminals $T1, T2$, and $T3$ need to be connected by a net. Commonly, two terminals are initially picked, for example, $T1$ and $T2$, and an optimal

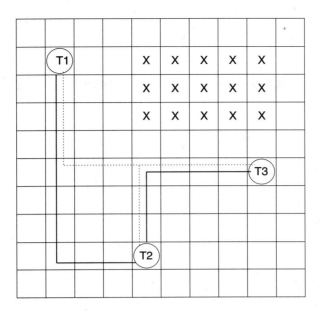

Figure 4.2 Example detailed general-purpose routing problem (Courtesy of
Watanabe et al., *IEEE Trans. Computer-Aided Design,* ©IEEE 1987)

shortest path route is determined between $T1$ and $T2$. Subsequently, a shortest path between
$T3$ to either $T1$ or $T2$ or any intermediate point in the net between $T1$ and $T2$ is determined.
Detailed general-purpose routers include maze routers and line expansion routers.

Detailed restricted routers require some constraints on the routing problem, such as
empty rectangular areas with all the pins at the periphery. Because of the limited scope, these
routers do a better job of modeling the contention of nets for the routing resources. The
restricted routers include channel routers and switchbox routers. Figure 4.3 shows an example
of a detailed restricted channel routing problem. Channel routers assume that horizontal wire
segments are laid in one wiring layer, and vertical wire segments are laid in another wiring
layer. Two different nets cannot use the same horizontal track or vertical column, since they
will form a connection. Horizontal and vertical wires can cross over without any electrical
connection. If a connection is desired, a *via* or contact is placed at the intersection. In the
figure, net 1 needs to connect to terminals 2 and 5 at the top boundary of the channel, and net
5 needs to be connected between terminals 3 and 5 at the bottom of channel, and terminal 4
at the top of the channel. An example channel route is shown in the figure. Channel routers
typically try to minimize the number of horizontal tracks used to route a given number of nets
in a channel and also try to minimize the number of via connections.

Almost all forms of routing are NP complete hence a number of sequential heuristics
have been proposed to solve the problems. Techniques that produce extremely good quality
of routing always take large amounts of computation time. Hence, in recent years, researchers
have been investigating parallel algorithms for them.

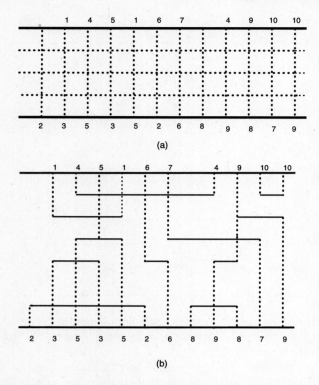

Figure 4.3 Example of a restricted detailed channel routing problem. (a) Terminal assignment. (b) Possible routing.

This chapter is organized as follows. Section 4.2 will describe the detailed routing problem. Section 4.3 will present parallel algorithms for detailed general-purpose routing using the maze routing and line routing approaches. Section 4.4 will describe the detailed restricted routing problem, that is, channel and switchbox routings. Sections 4.5 through 4.8 will describe parallel algorithms for detailed restricted channel routing using several approaches: (1) greedy channel routing, (2) hierarchical decomposition, (3) simulated annealing, and (4) iterative Improvement. For each approach, we will first describe the sequential algorithm for the problem and then discuss both shared memory and distributed memory MIMD parallel algorithms where appropriate. Section 4.9 will describe the global routing problem. Sections 4.10 through 4.12 will describe parallel algorithms for global routing using a variety of approaches: (1) graph search, (2) iterative improvement, and (3) hierarchical decomposition. Again, for each of the approaches, we will first describe the sequential algorithm for the problem and then discuss both shared memory and distributed memory MIMD parallel algorithms where appropriate. Section 4.13 will present a summary of hardware accelerators for routing. Finally, Section 4.14 will conclude with some observations about the future of parallel algorithms for routing.

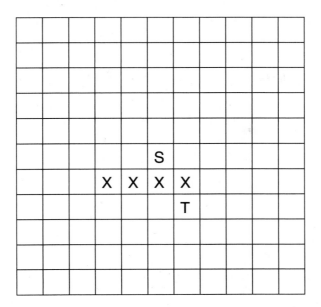

Figure 4.4 Detailed routing problem

4.2 DETAILED ROUTING PROBLEM

A detailed general-purpose router reads the information regarding the exact geometrical coordinates of the points that have to be connected and produces wire segments and vias to realize the required connections. There are no constraints about the absence of obstacles in the routing regions or about the shape of the region. Figure 4.4 shows an example of a routing grid of a general-purpose detailed routing problem, where a net needs to be connected between the cells S and T in the presence of obstacles X. The obstacles may be the result of previous nets that have been routed. General-purpose routers work on the entire design in a serial fashion by determining wiring paths for a single connection at a time.

One of the most popular detailed general- purpose routing algorithms is the maze router, variants of that have been used in many routing algorithms. The term *maze router* refers to a set of general-purpose routing algorithms that operate on a gridded model and route a single connection at a time within that model. In a gridded model, the entire routing surface is represented as a rectangular array of cells. The size of the cells is defined such that wires can be routed through adjacent cells without violating the width and spacing rules for the wires. In this model, two points are connected by finding a set of adjacent cells between the cells containing the two points. Cells that are unusable because they already contain some wiring or some other obstruction are marked as blocked.

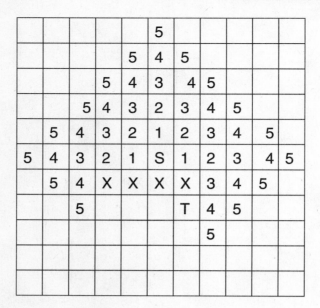

Figure 4.5 Maze Routing Phases

4.3 DETAILED ROUTING USING MAZE ROUTING

4.3.1 Overview

The Lee-Moore maze routing algorithm is the most widely used technique for detailed general-purpose wire routing [13, 17]. For the single layer case, the wiring surface is represented as a grid as shown in Figure 4.4. There are two special cells for the source S and target T, and blocked cells are shown as X. A wire begins at S and passes through available cells and finally reaches T. The algorithm consists of three phases: front wave expansion, path recovery, and sweeping. In the front wave expansion phase, a breadth-first search beginning at S is performed. Cells that are one unit from S are labeled as 1, then those that are two units away are labeled as 2, and so on. This labeling continues until the target cell T is reached. Blocked cells are not labeled. After the front wave expansion reaches the target cell T, the path recovery phase traces back the path from T to S, thereby identifying the wire path. The sweeping phase clears all the labels and marks the cells on the wired path as blocked. The basic procedure is illustrated in Figure 4.5.

The maze routing algorithm is important because it guarantees shortest paths. However, since it routes one net at a time, it has no provision for ensuring that an early connection will not prevent the routing of a connection not yet processed. Also, it can handle only two point nets, whereas most nets have multiple points. The multiple-point net problem is usually solved by decomposing the problem into two-point subproblems that are solved sequentially. Figure 4.2 shows an example of a general purpose detailed router with three terminals, $T1, T2$, and $T3$. Commonly, two terminals are initially picked, for example $T1$ and $T2$, and an optimal shortest path route is determined between $T1$ and $T2$. Subsequently, a shortest path between $T3$ to either $T1$ or $T2$ or any intermediate point in the net between $T1$ and $T2$ is determined. The quality of the maze routing solution depends on the order in which the nets are routed. Other disadvantages include the large memory requirements and long search times proportional to the square of the length of connections.

The basic maze routing algorithm has been extended to handle multiple-point nets by starting at a source pin and expanding until another pin is reached. A path traceback determines a partial tree connection. Next, multiple expansions are performed from each of the grid points on the subtree until another pin is reached, and the new paths are retraced. This procedure is repeated until all the pins are connected as shown in Figure 4.2.

To reduce the runtimes of the maze routing algorithms, line expansion routers were proposed by Mikami and Tabuchi [16] and Hightower [12]. These routers do not store the entire routing surface in memory in the form of a grid; instead they model the routing surface as lists of lines. The basic idea of these routers is to project line probes from a point until there is no obstruction. The algorithm starts by determining the two points to be connected. From each point, potential wiring segments are projected as far as possible in both the horizontal and vertical directions. If the probes intersect, the routing is complete. If the probes are stopped by some obstruction, the algorithm must choose a new escape point along the current probes from which additional probes are sent out. Figure 4.6 shows the sequence of probes generated to connect the source S and target T. Solid lines represent actual wire segments and dashed lines are the line-probes generated. Points denoted as E are the escape points.

Organization of the data to allow efficient search for obstructions to a probe is a key consideration. A typical organization is two lists for each layer: one for horizontal lines and one for vertical lines. Two lists are required because vertical probes are only limited by horizontal lines and horizontal probes are only limited by vertical lines. Separate lists allow lines parallel to the direction of the probe to be ignored without slowing down the search time. The horizontal list is sorted by y coordinates and the vertical list by x coordinates.

The process of choosing escape points is the difference between the two original line-probe algorithms. In Mikami and Tabuchi's algorithm, additional perpendicular lines at each grid intersection for each existing line segment at a given level, is essentially a complete bread-first search and guarantees a solution if it exists. Hightower's algorithm tries to add only a single escape point to each line probe. While the number of escape points in the Hightower algorithm is significantly less than that of the Mikami and Tabuchi algorithm, it may not produce a successful connection even if it exists. When compared to the grid based models used in maze routers, line probe routers have a major advantage in use of memory.

Watanabe et al. [28] have proposed another detailed routing algorithm that is based on a variant of the maze routing algorithm to handle multiple-point nets and to control the quality of the routing. The authors have proposed a controllable path quality algorithm that has combined the conventional Lee-Moore maze routing algorithm and line expansion based algorithms by introducing the concept of an expansion distance D_{ex}. This algorithm differs from the original maze routing in that the expansion distance is not limited to unity but can take any value for each step. When D_{ex} is set to unity, it becomes the Lee-Moore algorithm, when it is set to infinity, it becomes a parallel line search or line expansion algorithm. Figure 4.8 shows an example of the routing algorithm.

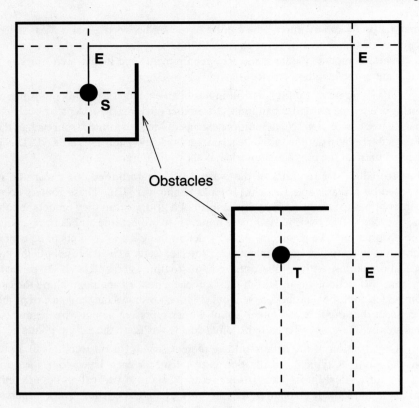

Figure 4.6 Line expansion routing

4.3.2 Distributed Memory MIMD Parallel Algorithm

We will now discuss a parallel algorithm for detailed routing based on the Lee-Moore maze routing algorithm for two-point nets on a distributed memory hypercube multiprocessor. The algorithm is based on work reported by Won and Sahni [29]. The basic idea is to partition the routing grid among the processors and have each processor participate in the different phases of the conventional maze routing algorithm, that is, front wave expansion, path traceback and sweeping. An outline of the parallel routing algorithm entitled *DM-PARALLEL-MAZE-ROUTING* (for distributed memory parallel maze routing algorithm) is given next.

Procedure *DM-PARALLEL-MAZE-ROUTING*;

Grid Partitioning and Mapping

Partition the $n \times n$ routing grid into P parts;
Assign one partition to each of P processors;

Front Wave Expansion

REPEAT
    FORALL processors in PARALLEL DO
        Each processor maintains a queue of front wave cells
        that are in its grid partition;
        Each grid cell on the current wave is expanded
        (cells to its north, south, east, west are examined);
        Some of these expanded cells are in the processor's grid partition
        while others are in the grid partition of other processors;
        Expansion may require communication with other processors;
        All communication requests are saved;

Interprocessor communication.

        Each processor sends its communication packets
        to the appropriate destination processor;

Process communication packets.

        Each processor examines the packets its receives
        and labels the front wave contained in these packets;
    END FORALL
UNTIL either the target cell is reached or
    the new front wave has no cells in it;

Path Trace Back and Sweeping.

Set label number initially to the search number
    of the front wave expansion;
REPEAT with reduced label numbers

Reverse wave expansion

    FORALL processors in PARALLEL DO

        Starting from the target cell begin expanding
        in all four directions;
        Identify cell of label one lower than present;
        Store that pair of cells as a path segment;

Inter processor communication

        Each processor sends its communication packets of
        path segments when it crosses processor grid boundaries;

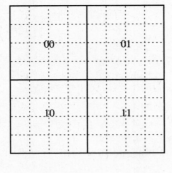

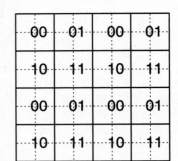

(a)   (b)

Figure 4.7 Grid partitioning and mapping to a 4 processor hypercube (Courtesy of Won and Sahni, *Proc. Int. Conf. Parallel Processing*, Pennsylvania State University Press, 1987)

For each cell in path segment, label cells as
blocked for future nets;
END FORALL

UNTIL start cell is reached;

End Procedure

We now describe several strategies for mapping the routing grid on a hypercube multiprocessor. Assume that an $n \times n$ routing grid (where n is a power of 2, $n = 2^d$) has to be mapped on to 2^d processors of a hypercube. An embedded mesh mapping of the processors of the hypercube can be employed using the binary reflected gray code mapping [25]. Two examples of mapping an 8×8 routing grid on four processors are shown in Figure 4.7

The first partitioning strategy, called a two-dimensional blocked distribution and shown in Figure 4.7(a), uses a covering of the $2^p \times 2^p$ routing grid with rectangles of size $2^{p-d/2} \times 2^{p-d/2}$. Each rectangle of the cover defines a continuous partition of the grid. A second partitioning strategy, called a two-dimensional cyclic distribution and shown in Figure 4.7(b), uses a covering of the $2^p \times 2^p$ routing grid by rectangles of size $h \times w$, where both h and w are less than $2^d/2$. ($h = w = 2$ in the figure.)

The advantage of the first partitioning strategy is that interprocessor communication is reduced. A grid cell is said to be on a partition boundary if at least one of its neighbor cells is in a different partition. Since boundary cells require interprocessor communication, it is clear that the first partitioning strategy will generate fewer communications than the second. For Figure 4.7, the number of boundary cells is 28 for the first scheme and 60 for the second scheme. The advantage of the second partitioning strategy is that the load balance is improved. Suppose the start cell S is located at the top-left corner of the routing grid, and the target cell T is located in the bottom-right corner. Then in the first partitioning scheme, the first several cycles, only processor 00 will be busy, and the other processors will be idle. In the second partitioning scheme, processors 01 and 10 will become active as soon as the expansion phase crosses into these processor boundaries. Hence the idle times of processors are reduced. There is a trade-off between processor utilization and inter-processor communication. Experimentally, the authors reported results on a 16-processor NCUBE/1™ hypercube running a 256×256 routing problem, and the best values of w and h were determined to be 4. The optimal values of w and h clearly depend on the ratio of computation costs to communication cost of the particular parallel architecture.

We now present several strategies for synchronization. A front wave expansion cycle consists of one execution of the REPEAT loop of the algorithm. When all the processors have completed the nth cycle, the front wave consists of cells that are distance n away from the source S. One way to guarantee that the multiprocessor algorithm finds the shortest path is to synchronize all the processors after every cycle using a global synchronization. Another synchronization strategy is a δ synchronization approach. This approach is based on noting the fact that, given that the Manhattan distance between the source and target $= M$, the processors can perform M cycles of forward expansion without synchronization. At that point, if the target cell is not reached, then the processors proceed for another δ cycles. If δ is 1, then the shortest paths are determined, but the algorithm synchronizes every cycle; hence the overhead goes up. If δ is a large number, say N, then in the worst case the path lengths can be greater than the shortest paths by $N - 1$. The value of δ has been empirically determined to be between $0.2M$ and $0.3M$ to trade off the runtime performance of the algorithm for the quality of the results.

We now describe a variant of the preceding parallel detailed routing algorithm that is based on a variant of the maze routing algorithm to handle multiple point nets and to control the quality of the routing. The algorithm is based on the work of Watanabe et al. [28], in which the authors have proposed a controllable path quality algorithm that has combined the conventional Lee-Moore maze routing algorithm and line expansion-based algorithms by introducing the concept of an expansion distance D_{ex}. This algorithm differs from the original maze routing in that the expansion distance is not limited to unity but can take any value for each step. When D_{ex} is set to unity, it becomes the Lee-Moore algorithm; when it is set to infinity, it becomes a parallel line search or line expansion algorithm. Figure 4.8 shows an example of the routing algorithm.

An outline of the parallel routing algorithm entitled *DM-PARALLEL-LINE-ROUTING* (for distributed memory parallel algorithm using line expansion routing) is given next..

Procedure *DM-PARALLEL-LINE-ROUTING*;

Initially partition the $n \times n$ routing grid among
into P regions;
Assign each routing subregion
to each one of P processors;

Path Search Phase.

FORALL processors in PARALLEL DO
   REPEAT
        First clear all the cells in each processor's region;
        Set obstruction cells, start cell, and target cells;
        Set start cell as expanding cells;
        Set label number or search number to unity;

        Expand zones from current expanding cells
        vertically and horizontally to the distance D_{ex}
        unless expansion is obstructed;
        Set current search label on expanded zone;

        Each processor does the expansion on the cells
        within its own routing region;
        IF expanded cells are within the processor's routing grid
           THEN they are placed into the processor's local
           routing queues;
        ELSE expanded cells that are in other processor's
           routing regions are placed in the appropriate
           processor's send queues;

        All communication requests are saved and combined
        into one communication per pair of processors;

        IF one of expanded zones hits the target cell
           THEN enter trace back phase;

        Increment search label by unity;
        Set expanded zone and starting cell to expanding zone;
   UNTIL target cell reached or current cell cannot be expanded;
END FORALL

Synchronize Processors;

Trace Back Phase.

FORALL processors DO
   REPEAT
        Set label number to the search number of the
        path search phase;

        Starting from the target cell, begin expanding horizontally
        and vertically in parallel, until one of the expanded lines

hits a cell of label one lower than present;
Store the line segment as the path;

UNTIL start cell reached;
END FORALL

End Procedure

We now describe an extension of the preceding algorithm for solving the multipin net problem. Routing for a three-point net is explained with Figure 4.2. For a multipin net, start from any arbitrary pin as a start cell $T1$ and expand forward until one of the multiple target cells is reached. This finds a set of possible shortest paths between cells $T1$ and $T2$, which can be found by expanding backward from the target cell with decrementing labels. The restricted routing region identifies all the possible shortest paths between $T1$ and $T2$. The choice of the specific path depends on the location of the next pin. Hence another double wave expansion is made from the periphery of the restricted area and the next target cell to determine another restricted area for routing. The intersection of the two restricted areas gives a branch point and helps then to determine the minimum Steiner tree for the multipin net. For the routing area restriction phase, the parallel line maze routing algorithm described preceding is used with a distance of unity. For the actual path determination, the parallel line maze routing algorithm is used with an expansion distance D_{ex} equal to the length of the routing areas. Figure 4.9 shows an example of the modified routing algorithm for multiple-point nets. The issues regarding the parallel implementation are similar to the earlier algorithm since essentially the original algorithm is being called repeatedly.

The preceding algorithm can be implemented on a distributed memory multiprocessor such as a hypercube by assigning equal parts of the chip layout grid to each processor, and having the expansions and tracebacks performed by various processors on their assigned regions. The issues and solutions of partitioning and synchronization are similar to those discussed earlier for the simple parallel maze routing algorithm on a distributed memory multiprocessor.

Implementation Won and Sahni have implemented the preceding parallel algorithm *DM-PARALLEL-MAZE-ROUTING* on a 64 processor NCUBE/1™ hypercube system [29]. Table 4.1 shows some example results on three benchmark routing grids of the runtimes (in seconds) using the global and δ synchronization approaches. The results show the δ synchronization method outperforms the other synchronization methods.

Recently, Yen et al. [30] have extended the preceding parallel algorithm for different partitioning methods through simulations. No actual implementations have been reported.

Watanabe et al. [28] have implemented the parallel algorithm *DM-PARALLEL-LINE-ROUTING* on the AAP-1 array processor hardware [28]. We will discuss the hardware architecture in Section 4.13.

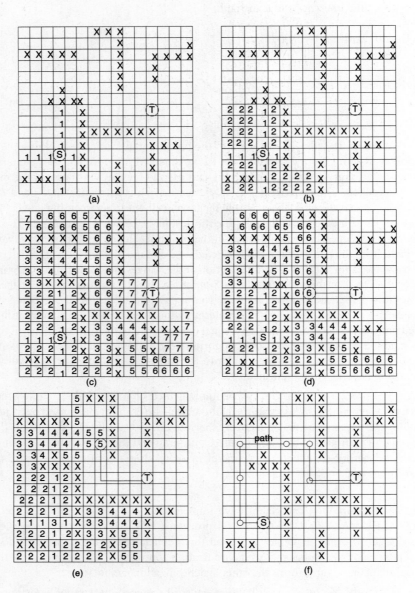

Figure 4.8 Example of the parallel line-maze routing algorithm (Courtesy of Watanabe et al, *IEEE Trans. Computer-Aided Design*, ©IEEE 1987)

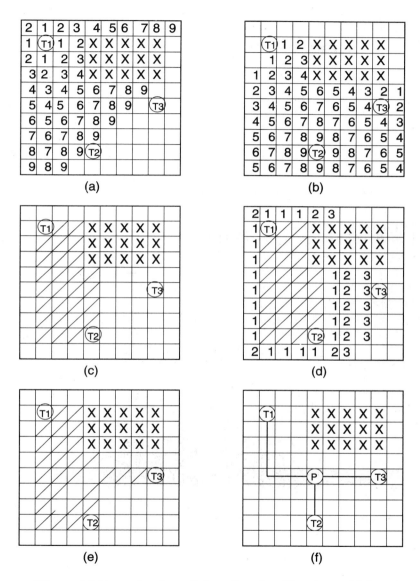

Figure 4.9 Example of parallel routing algorithm for multiple-point nets (Courtesy of Watanabe et al., *IEEE Trans. Computer-Aided Design,* ©IEEE 1987)

TABLE 4.1 Runtimes (seconds) of Parallel Maze Routing Algorithm on the NCUBE/1™ Hypercube

Circuit	Grid	Global Sync		Delta Sync	
		16 Processors	64 Processors	16 Processors	64 Processors
1	64×64	8.5	10.6	2.3	2.4
2	256×256	30.5	36.1	15.6	11.2
3	512×512	110.9	100.2	65.2	30.1

4.3.3 Shared Memory MIMD Parallel Algorithm

We will now describe the modification of the preceding parallel maze routing algorithms for execution on a shared memory MIMD multiprocessor. The front wave expansion of the simplest maze routing algorithm for two terminal nets can be parallelized as follows.

The status of routing of the entire region is kept in global memory. The $n \times n$ routing grid is geographically partitioned into P square subregions (assuming P processors), and a task queue is assigned to each subregion that is associated with each processor. The partitioning can be performed using either of the schemes illustrated in Figure 4.7. A processor takes routing tasks off its own task queue, but can insert routing tasks into other processors' task queues. To prevent multiple processors accessing a task queue, locks are associated with the task queues. A routing task involves a grid cell on the current wavefront. A processor takes a task off its task queue and expands the wavefront. If the expanded cell is within the processors own subregion and the cell has not been labeled yet, it places the routing task for the cell on its own task queue. If the expanded cell belongs to another processor's region, it inserts the cell on the other processor's task queue. Insertion of the routing task on another processor's task queue is done by locking and unlocking the appropriate task queue. Initially, only the source cell of the net will have a routing task, so the corresponding processor that owns the source region will have work to perform. After a set of cycles, the front wave will encompass a large number of cells and there will be routing tasks in each processor's region. At the end of each expansion, the routing grid is updated in global shared memory by the different processors again by using locks on the shared array.

An outline of the parallel routing algorithm entitled *SM-PARALLEL-MAZE-ROUTING* (for shared memory parallel routing algorithm using maze routing) is given next..

Procedure *SM-PARALLEL-MAZE-ROUTING*;

Grid Partitioning and Mapping

Partition the $n \times n$ routing grid into P parts;
Assign one routing subregion to each of the processors;
Create a shared routing array shared among all processors;
Create one task queue of cells on each processor representing a subregion;

Initialize task queue on appropriate processor with start cell;

Front Wave Expansion

FORALL processors in PARALLEL DO
   REPEAT
      Remove routing task from task queue involving
      a grid cell on current wavefront;
      The grid cell is expanded
      (cells to its north, south, east, west are examined);
      IF expanded cell in processor's owned region
         THEN place new routing task (for expanded cell) on
         own task queue;
         ELSE place routing task on appropriate processor queue;
   UNTIL either the target cell is reached or
      the new front wave has no cells in it;
END FORALL

Path Trace Back and Sweeping.

FORALL processors in PARALLEL DO
   Set label number initially to the search number
   of the front wave expansion;
   REPEAT with reduced label numbers
      Starting from the target cell begin expanding
      in all four directions;
      Remove routing task from own queue;
      Identify cell of label one lower than present;
      Store that pair of cells as a path segment;

      Each processor marks path segments when it
      crosses processor grid boundaries;

      For each cell in path segment, label cells as
      blocked for future nets;
   UNTIL start cell is reached;
END FORALL

End Procedure

     The other variants of the maze routing algorithm with the line expansion options can also be parallelized in a similar manner by using the notion of routing tasks on geographically partitioned regions.

No actual implementations of this algorithm on a shared memory multiprocessor have been reported.

4.4 CHANNEL AND SWITCHBOX ROUTING PROBLEM

A majority of modern IC routers are based on channel routers. These systems use a divide and conquer approach in which the layout surface is divided into several channel or switchbox routing problems that can be solved independently. Decomposition of the entire routing problem into several independent channel routing problems is done by the channel decomposition and global routing steps to be discussed later.

The problem of channel routing deals with a rectangular wiring area called a channel, with pins on the top and bottom edges of the channel, and a collection of nets that are sets of pins that must be interconnected. Nets are routed with horizontal wire segments on one layer and vertical wire segments on another. Connections between the two layers are made through *via* holes. The objective of a channel router is to interconnect all the nets so as to minimize various criteria, such as the area of the channel and the number of vias used. Figure 4.3 shows an example channel routing problem and solution.

A variant to the channel routing problem is the switchbox routing problem. A switchbox defines a routing problem on a rectangular region where there are terminals on all four sides as shown in Figure 4.15.

Several algorithms for the channel and switchbox routing problems exist in the literature that apply various heuristics. Channel routers impose restrictions on net topology; this allows them to consider connections in parallel and thereby avoid the inherent problems of serial approaches such as maze and line expansion routing. Most channel routers assume that there are two layers available for routing. There are two basic approaches to solving the channel routing problem: constructive and iterative. The three constructive approaches are the left-edge trackwise algorithm, the greedy columnwise router, and the hierarchical router.

The first constructive approach to channel routing is the left-edge algorithm [11] and its variants, which perform the channel routing by proceeding one track at a time. The algorithm starts at the left-edge of the channel, and places unplaced segments into various tracks. To fill the track as much as possible, the algorithm scans for the segments that will fit in the track, until the end of the track is reached. After completing the assignment of the horizontal layer, the vertical branches can be easily added. A second constructive approach to the channel routing algorithm uses a greedy strategy [21]. By moving across the channel left to right, segments are placed at a given column completely before proceeding to the next column. In each column, a set of greedy heuristics is used to place the nets on the columns. A third constructive approach to channel routing uses a hierarchical algorithm by solving routing on two-by-N regions recursively [8].

Among the iterative improvement algorithms, some are based on simulated annealing. In the algorithm proposed by Leong, Wong, and Liu [14], the basic idea is to start with a set of two terminal nets and form a vertical constraint graph that represents the constraints regarding which horizontal segments of a net have to be above or next. other horizontal segments. By partitioning the nets into sets such that no two nets have a horizontal constraint, a valid channel routing solution is obtained. A simulated-annealing based iterative improvement technique is used to move nets between tracks representing partitions such that the resultant graph does not have cycles. Brouwer and Banerjee have proposed a different formulation of simulated-annealing-based channel routing [5]. The basic idea of the algorithm is to start with the number of tracks equal to the channel density, initially assigning nets to tracks randomly or by some simple initial heuristics, while allowing for both horizontal and vertical overlaps. An iterative algorithm then selects certain nets from their present tracks and tries to place them in different tracks.

The simplest and most obvious way to develop a parallel approach to detailed restricted routing is to route individual channels independently on different processors. In a typical layout problem of standard cells or gate arrays, enough channel routing problems are required to be solved, that using parallel processors is trivial.

If we are interested in parallelizing a particular channel routing problem, then the following algorithms are useful. We will now describe parallel algorithms for detailed restricted routing using several approaches:

- Approach using constructive, greedy routing

- Approach using hierarchical decomposition

- Approach using simulated annealing

For each approach shared memory and distributed memory parallel algorithms will be presented where appropriate.

4.5 CHANNEL ROUTING USING CONSTRUCTIVE APPROACH

4.5.1 Overview

A constructive approach to the channel routing algorithm uses a greedy strategy and works column by column [21]. By moving across the channel left to right, segments are placed in tracks of a given column completely before proceeding to the next column. In each column, a set of greedy heuristics is used to place the nets on the tracks.

4.5.2 Shared Memory MIMD Parallel Algorithm

We will now describe a parallel algorithm for channel routing using a constructive approach based on the algorithm proposed by Zargham [31]. The basic approach in the parallel algorithm is based on the notion of dividing the channel region columnwise into subregions and performing the routing of individual subregions on a different processor. A key concept is in determining how to partition the channel into subregions. The first phase of the algorithm begins by dividing the routing region into several regions by selecting certain columns among all the columns in the routing area. The selection of the columns separating the regions is made such that the selected columns have a density as close to the channel density as possible and equalize the size of the regions for good load balance. The selection of a column with a large number of nets will limit the number of choices for assigning a track to its nets. Then for every selected column it finds a suitable track and layer assignment to the segments that are passing through that column.

The second phase of the algorithm performs a suitable track assignment to the nets of the selected columns. The assignment of segments to tracks is done by first finding a preferred

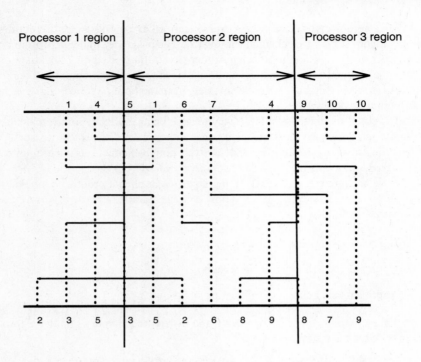

Figure 4.10 Column-wise channel decomposition in parallel algorithm

horizontal layer for each segment, then determining a preliminary partial ordering between the segments, subsequently obtaining a final ordering between the segments, and finally assigning layers and tracks to the segments, based on a partial ordering using the vertical constraint graphs.

Having performed this track assignment to the leftmost and rightmost columns of each region, the third phase of the algorithm tries to route each region on each processor independently using a conventional channel routing algorithm. It should be noted that it is possible that the individual channel routing solutions on separate regions will give rise to conflicting track assignments on the border columns.

An iterative improvement method subsequently moves segments to other tracks and layers. Sometimes, segments are exchanged across tracks using 45-degree crossovers when other techniques fail. The fact that each processor can independently route its own region is allowed by the crucial assumption that 45-degree crossovers are allowed. Some technologies may not allow such 45-degree routes, in which case such a parallel algorithm may not be feasible.

The preceding algorithm for channel routing is suitable for implementation in a shared memory multiprocessor. Figure 4.10 shows the division of a channel region into three processors by selecting certain columns (4 and 9) as the channel separators and the resultant solution.

An outline of the parallel routing algorithm entitled *SM-PARALLEL-CHANNEL-ROUT-ING-COLUMNWISE* (for shared memory parallel algorithm for channel routing using column-wise partitioning) is given next..

Procedure *SM-PARALLEL-CHANNEL-ROUTING-COLUMNWISE;*
    Read in channel description;
    Select certain columns to partition channel;
    Choose columns with maximum density, and equalize load balance;
    Perform preliminary track and layer assignment to columns;
    Partition channel region by columns into subregions;
    Assign each subregion to a processor;

    FORALL processors in PARALLEL DO
        Perform track assignment of nets in columns
            owned by processor;
        Find preferred horizontal layer for each segment;
        Obtain a partial ordering between segments;
        Find a total ordering between segments;
        Perform track assignments;

        Initiate solution merge across processors;
        Each processor looks at tracks of segments assigned
        in own region and in adjoining region;
        Perform iterative movement of nets to tracks to align
        tracks on boundaries;

        IF tracks not aligned for each segment
            THEN use 45 degree crossover to match segments

    END FORALL

End Procedure

Implementation Zargham [31] has reported an implementation of the preceding parallel algorithm on a Sequent Balance 8000 shared memory multiprocessor with speedups of about 2 on three processors on some example circuits.

4.6 CHANNEL ROUTING USING HIERARCHY

4.6.1 Overview

A different constructive approach to channel routing uses a hierarchical algorithm [8]. Consider the general routing problem for M by N routing channel with terminal connections specified on the top and bottom boundaries, where M is the number of horizontal tracks of the channel and N is the length of the channel. The given M-by-N routing channel is partitioned into two parts, $M/2$-by-N subgrids. Consider vertical strips of these subgrids as single supercells. We then end up with two horizontal strips, each a two-by-N routing grid. Vertical boundary capacities (corresponding to the maximum number of wires that can be routed through a particular grid point) of this new routing grid will be the sums of the corresponding boundary capacities of the original grid. The horizontal capacities of the new routing grid will be the same as the original grid. This is illustrated in Figure 4.11.

Using a two-by-N routing algorithm, each of the connections (nets) is allocated to one of the two regions. The two-by-N algorithm routes each net serially using a minimum Steiner tree determination algorithm. It performs random rerouting of connections after all connections are routed, that helps to smooth out the congestion.

The algorithm is illustrated on an example channel routing problem for five nets, 1,2,3,5, and 10 in Figure 4.11(a) for a 6×14 routing grid. Parts (b) and (c) of Figure 4.11 show the first level of the hierarchical decomposition where the routing grid is considered as a 2×14 grid. The routing of net 1 at the first level of the hierarchy is shown in Figure 4.11(b); the routing of the nets 2, 3, 5, and 10 in the first level of the hierarchy is shown in Figure 4.11(c). Assuming that the routing within this 2×14 grid is obtained, we now partition each of the horizontal strips of the grid into two parts, thus generating two 2×14 subproblems in the second level of the hierarchy.

The global routes from the previous level define terminal positions for wiring the new 2×14 subproblems. Parts (d) and (e) of Figure 4.11 show the second level of the hierarchical decomposition. The routing of net 1 at the second level of the hierarchy is shown in Figure 4.11(d), and the routing of the nets 2, 3, 5, and 10 in the second level of the hierarchy is shown in Figure 4.11(e).

The process of splitting the routing region is repeated in a hierarchical fashion until each channel section requires one track. If the two-by-N router fails to obtain a legal routing, then all vertical capacities of boundaries in the same horizontal strip are increased by 1, which is equivalent to addition of a new horizontal track to the original problem.

4.6.2 Shared Memory MIMD Parallel Algorithm

We now describe a parallel algorithm for channel routing using a hierarchical approach based on the parallel algorithms proposed by Brouwer and Banerjee in [7]. The hierarchical routing algorithm described previously is very amenable to parallel processing, since each two-by-N routing task can be assigned to a processor. On a shared memory multiprocessor, tasks are maintained on a shared task queue. Processors remove tasks from the task queue, perform the routing, and insert new routing tasks on the queue. The removal and insertion of tasks on the task queue is performed using locks.

At the topmost level of the hierarchy, only one processor will be active, but the number of active processors rapidly increases with increasing level in the hierarchy, keeping all processors active. Figure 4.12 shows such a decomposition of routing tasks in which each node represents a two-by-N routing task.

An outline of the parallel algorithm entitled *SM-PARALLEL-ROUTING-HIERARCHY* (for shared memory parallel routing algorithm using hierarchical decomposition) is given next.

Procedure *SM-PARALLEL-ROUTING-HIERARCHY*;

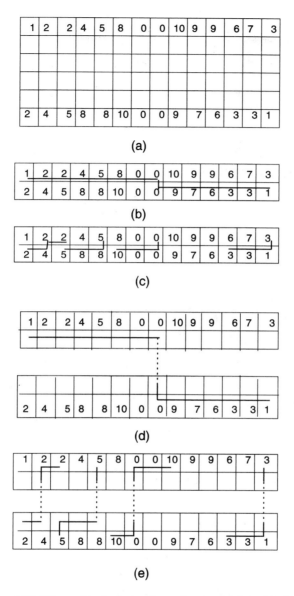

Figure 4.11 Hierarchical channel routing example. (a) Original routing problem. (b) Routing of net 1 in the first level of the hierarchy. (c) Routing of nets 2, 3, 5, and 10 in the first level of the hierarchy. (d) Routing of net 1 in the second level of the hierarchy. (e) Routing of nets 2, 3, 5, and 10 in the first level of the hierarchy. (Courtesy of Burstein and Pelavin, *Proc. Design Automation Conf.,* ©IEEE 1983)

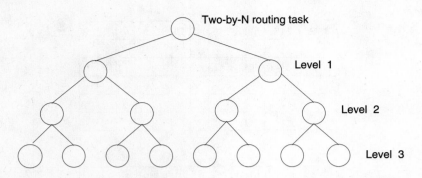

Figure 4.12 Hierarchical-tree-based decomposition of tasks

Read in circuit and initialize;
Create top level two-by-N routing task;
Set Level = 0;

FORALL processors in PARALLEL DO
   WHILE (not DONE) DO
      WHILE (GetRoutingTask()) DO
         Solve two-by-N Routing Task(Level);
         Create two two-by-N routing subtasks (Level+1);
      END WHILE;

      Level = Level + 1;

      Check if DONE;
   END WHILE;
END FORALL

End Procedure

No actual implementation of this parallel algorithm has been reported on real machines, but parallel algorithms using such hierarchical decompositions have been theoretically reported and analyzed in [6].

4.7 CHANNEL ROUTING USING SIMULATED ANNEALING

4.7.1 Overview

Recently, some iterative improvement algorithms for channel routing, based on simulated annealing have been reported. In the algorithm proposed by Leong, Wong, and Liu [14], the basic idea is to start with a set of two terminal nets and form a vertical constraint graph that represents the constraints regarding which horizontal segments of a net has to be above or

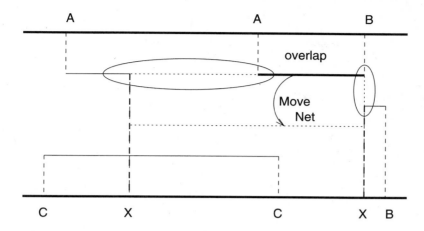

Figure 4.13 Channel routing example with movement of nets

next. other horizontal segments. By partitioning the nets into sets such that no two nets have a horizontal constraint, a valid channel routing solution is obtained. A simulated annealing based iterative improvement technique is used to move nets between tracks representing partitions such that the resultant graph does not have cycles.

Banerjee and Brouwer have proposed a different formulation of channel routing using simulated annealing [5]. The basic idea of the algorithm is to start with the number of tracks equal to the channel density, initially assigning nets to tracks randomly or by some simple initial heuristics, while allowing for both horizontal and vertical overlaps. An iterative algorithm then selects certain nets from their present tracks and tries to place them in different tracks. Hence the *move set* in this simulated annealing algorithm consists of moving nets among tracks. Such an approach is illustrated in Figure 4.13.

The *objective function* to be minimized is the total horizontal and vertical overlap. Once the function reaches zero, the optimum solution is obtained. Note that we keep the total number of tracks equal to the channel density throughout the algorithm. The acceptance of a particular move follows the probabilistic function similar to the conventional annealing algorithms. The algorithm proposed is also very versatile as it can easily be extended to handle switch-box routing and obstacle avoidance.

4.7.2 Distributed Memory MIMD Parallel Algorithm

On the basis of the preceding simple simulated annealing algorithm, Banerjee and Brouwer have developed a parallel algorithm for channel routing suitable for execution on a hypercube based distributed memory multiprocessor [5]. The algorithm assigns sets of adjacent tracks to processors arranged in a linear array using the binary reflected gray code mapping [25] as shown in Figure 4.14 for an 8 processor hypercube. Processors pair up among themselves and selectively move nets in parallel between tracks that are assigned to the processors, and broadcast the information to other processors to update their data structures. The net movement process is repeated until a proper final *channel state* is achieved. Although nets overlapping in the final *channel state* are forbidden, a certain amount of overlap is allowed during the

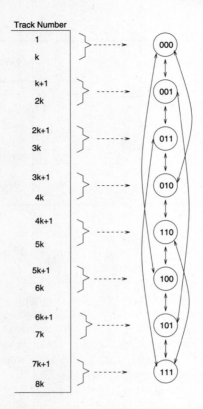

Figure 4.14 Mapping of tracks to processors in channel routing and communication among processors

annealing process, subject to the cost constraints and the overall objective of minimizing such overlap.

An outline of the parallel routing algorithm entitled *DM-PARALLEL-CHANNEL-ROUTING-SA* (for distributed memory parallel algorithm for channel routing using simulated annealing) is given next.

Procedure *DM-PARALLEL-CHANNEL-ROUTING-SA*;

Start with an initial routing solution (state) S;
Partition channel area by tracks and perform row mapping;
Assign channel subregions to processors;
Ownership of nets by processors owning channel subregions;
Set $T = T_0$ (initial temperature);

REPEAT /* outer loop */
  REPEAT /* inner loop */

FORALL processors in PARALLEL DO
        Identify processor pairs for various dimensions of hypercube;
        Each processor-pair generates a move cooperatively;
            Select move (net exchange or net displacement type);
            IF intra-processor displacement THEN
                Select a random net;
                Move to random track
                within processor region;
            IF inter-processor displacement THEN
                Select a random net;
                Move to random track
                within processor pairs region;
            IF intra-processor exchange THEN
                Select two random nets within processor;
                Exchange net tracks;
            IF inter-processor exchange THEN
                Select two random nets within processor pair;
                Exchange net tracks;
            Each processor pair accepts/rejects move on own cost;
        Broadcast updated net locations;
    END FOR
    Increment moves_attempted;
  UNTIL moves_attempted = max_moves; /* inner loop */
  Update T (control temperature);
UNTIL termination condition; /* end outer loop */
Perform cleanup phase to remove any final overlaps;

End Procedure

We now describe the strategy for mapping the channel region (set of tracks) onto the processors of the hypercube arranged as a linear array. Since the number of tracks in the channel is fixed throughout the annealing process, the initial distribution of tracks to the linear array of processors is maintained until the annealing is completed. Each processor only stores information about the horizontal space used by each subnet in the tracks assigned to it because it is unnecessary for each processor to know what sections of its neighbor's tracks are occupied. However, a copy of the entire column data array is maintained in each processor for faster accessing and to reduce the amount of updating required for the vertical segment data.

The processors of a hypercube are mapped onto a linear array of processors using a binary reflected gray code mapping [25]. In the parallel algorithm, independent pairs of processors P_i and $P_{i\pm 2^j}$ for all values of $j = 0, 1, ..., d-1$ cooperate to perform the desired transformation. The gray code mapping guarantees that the pairs of processors that need to communicate at each stage are at most two hops away on the hypercube, hence this mapping gives rise to a large locality of communication. Figure 4.14 shows this mapping for an 8 processor hypercube along with the assignment of tracks to the processors, and the communication stages for $j = 0$, $j = 1$, and $j = 2$. During the evaluation of a move, one processor of the pair acts as a master, and the other a slave. The following moves are used:

MOVE 1: Intraprocessor-Displacement: Each processor of a pair performs a displacement move within its own set of subnets and tracks.

MOVE 2: Interprocessor-Displacement: The master processor displaces a subnet from its track domain to a track within the domain of the slave processor.

MOVE 3: Intraprocessor-Exchange: Each processor of a pair performs an exchange move within its own set of subnets and tracks.

MOVE 4: Interprocessor-Exchange: The master and slave processors each select a subnet to exchange between each other.

By applying the inter-processor moves, it is possible to utilize the connections between processors not adjacent on the linear array to move a subnet a large distance up or down the channel in a single move. The selection of processors as master and slave is done alternately so that displacement of subnets from one to the other is balanced.

The selection of the move for a pair of processors is performed at the beginning of an iteration stage by the master processor. The ratio of intra-processor to inter-processor moves is $1 : 1$. Intra-processor moves improve the performance and speedup, but inter-processor moves are equally necessary to be able to move the subnets throughout the channel. The ratio of displacement moves to exchange moves is $15 : 1$.

Since overlaps are allowed during the annealing process, the algorithm can be easily extended to include obstacle avoidance. Obstacle avoidance is important to consider if some sections of the routing area could be used for power or ground routing or any other element of the chip that must be pre-placed there. By applying a very high cost to any subnet occupying those areas it is possible to retain the necessary freedom for the subnets at high temperatures to be placed almost anywhere and then as the temperature is reduced, those overlaps can gradually be eliminated. Switchbox routing is similar to channel routing, except that nets are given terminals on all sides of the rectangle instead of just two sides. Although this problem is much more difficult than the channel routing problem, it is not as difficult to extend the algorithm to handle switchboxes. Since there are many more constraints on the placement of subnets, it is even more important to allow the subnets to overlap during high temperature annealing.

Implementation Brouwer and Banerjee have reported on the implementation of the parallel algorithm on an Intel iPSC/2™ hypercube multiprocessor [5]. On several benchmark channel routing examples, speedups of about 14 on 16 processors were reported. Table 4.2 shows some example results on four benchmark circuits of the runtimes (in seconds), the speedups, and the quality of routing (in terms of horizontal tracks required). The parallel algorithm produced solutions equal to the channel density in most of the cases. However, on some examples, the simulated annealing algorithm did not give a valid final solution, i.e. the solutions had some vertical overlaps. Those overlaps were removed by a clean-up phase using detour routing. Sometimes, the parallel algorithm gave superlinear speedups, due to the fact that the parallel algorithm actually converged faster than the serial algorithm.

TABLE 4.2 Runtimes (seconds) and Routing Quality of Parallel Algorithm on the Intel iPSC/2™ Hypercube

Circuit	Nets	1 proc		8 proc	
		Tracks	Runtime (Speedup)	Tracks	Runtime (Speedup)
1	39	12	22.8 (1.0)	12	4.32 (5.3)
2	73	15	243 (1.0)	15	41.1 (5.9)
3	131	17	798 (1.0)	17	95.7 (8.3)
4	229	19	1952 (1.0)	19	190 (10.3)

4.8 SWITCHBOX ROUTING USING ITERATIVE IMPROVEMENT

4.8.1 Overview

We will now describe an algorithm for switchbox routing. A switchbox defines a routing problem on a rectangular region where there are terminals on all four sides, as shown in Figure 4.15. Several switchbox routing algorithms have been proposed. The hierarchical channel routing algorithm described in a previous section can be used to solve the switchbox routing problem by recursively decomposing the region into two-by-N routing regions. The simulated-annealing channel routing algorithm described earlier can also be used to solve the switchbox routing problem. We will now describe an algorithm based on iterative improvement by ripping up and rerouting nets.

The representation scheme of a routed net is shown by two types of segments: horizontal wire and vertical wire. A segment is represented by five tuples: a net identifier, whether it is a horizontal or vertical segment, the row (column) index for the horizontal (vertical) segment, and two column (row) indices of the low end and high end of the segment. For managing the segments and easily determining conflicts, they are stored in three data structures.

A net-segment tree (NST) stores information of the vertical and horizontal segments of a net in a tree. These segments are found by a rectilinear Steiner tree finding algorithm. A horizontal segment tree (HST) stores information on all the horizontal segments of all nets sorted by the nonincreasing order of the left end. Similarly, a vertical segment tree (VST) stores information of all the vertical segments on all nets sorted by the nonincreasing order of the left end.

There are three types of conflicts among segments in a row or column. A grid-conflict exists if two or more horizontal or vertical segments belonging to different nets meet in a grid unit. A segment-conflict exists between two grid conflicts if a segment is involved in both grid conflicts. A via-conflict exists if two grid conflicts or segment conflicts share a via. A conflict group is constructed with a set of segments involved in the conflicts when an HST or VST is constructed from the NST.

The algorithm for routing is as follows. Given a switchbox terminal assignment each net is independently routed using the cheapest rectilinear Steiner tree routing algorithm. The

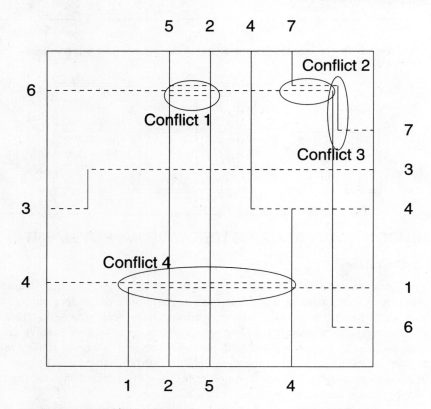

Figure 4.15 Conflicts in switchbox after initial routing (Courtesy of Cho et al, *IEEE Trans. Computer-Aided Design*, ©IEEE 1994)

resultant net segment graphs of each net is used to build the horizontal and vertical segment trees. At this point, all the conflicts are identified. The conflicts for an example switchbox route are shown after the initial Steiner Tree routes for each net in Figure 4.15. The conflicts are next resolved through ripup and reroute of the net segments using a branch and bound search method, which is implemented by searching through all possibilities using search lists.

A search list maintains an order of segments that is used to search for paths for a conflict group. If there are n segments in a conflict group, n search lists are constructed. Each search list is used to find a local solution to the conflict area (by ripup and reroute), by keeping the first segment unchanged, while changing the paths of the other segments, one by one, according to the order in the search list. The first search list is identical to the order of the conflicts. The second search list can be constructed by placing the last segment of the first search list at the first place of the second search list. The remaining $n - 2$ search lists are constructed similarly.

4.8.2 Shared Memory MIMD Parallel Algorithm

We will now describe a parallel algorithm for switchbox routing that is suitable for execution on shared memory MIMD multiprocessors based on the work reported by Cho, et al. [10].

The basic idea of the algorithm is to create as many parallel processes as nets, which enables the use of maximal parallelism. Each process is responsible for routing the assigned net. Routing conflicts are handled by the conflict group data structures described previously.

Each process finds a rectilinear Steiner tree for its own net. The rectilinear Steiner tree is converted into a horizontal segment tree and vertical segment tree, and a net segment tree. Conflict groups are built from the HST and VST. Using the NST and conflict groups, partial solutions are found by each process. The partial solutions are merged into a globally optimum solution using a parallel branch and bound search technique.

An outline of the parallel routing algorithm entitled *SM-PARALLEL-SWITCHBOX-ROUTING-ITER* (for shared memory parallel algorithm for switchbox routing using iterative improvement) is given next.

Procedure *SM-PARALLEL-SWITCHBOX-ROUTING-ITER;*
Read net information;
Create as many processes as number of nets;
Assign one net to each process;

FORALL processes in PARALLEL DO
    Determine Rectilinear Steiner Tree for net n;
    Build HST and VST;
    Construct Net Segment Graph;
    Construct conflict groups;
    Create search lists from conflict groups;
    IF own net is part of conflict group THEN
        Solve ripup-and-reroute using parallel branch and bound;
    Merge solutions;
END FORALL

End Procedure

Implementation Cho et al. [10] have implemented the preceding parallel algorithm on a Sequent Symmetry™ shared memory multiprocessor. Table 4.3 shows some example results on three benchmark circuits of the runtimes (in seconds), the speedups, and the quality of routing (in terms of wirelength) on 26 processors. It should be noted that the parallel algorithm gave no degradation of quality with the increased number of processors and gave reasonaby good speedups.

4.9 GLOBAL ROUTING PROBLEM

Global routing deals with the phase of wiring in which wires are allocated to channels in a chip without specifically assigning tracks within the channels. The task of global routing is to take a netlist, a list of pin positions, and a description of the available routing resources and determine the connections and macro paths for each net. Figure 4.1 shows a simple global routing problem for a chip with pads and standard cells in rows connected by nets. A global

TABLE 4.3 Runtimes (seconds) and Routing Quality of Parallel Routing Algorithm on the Sequent Symmetry™ Multiprocessor

Circuit	Nets	1 Processor		26 Processor	
		Wirelength	Runtime (Speedup)	Wirelength	Runtime (Speedup)
1	8	70	4.9 (1.0)	70	1.1 (4.8)
2	20	508	17.8 (1.0)	508	1.9 (9.2)
3	26	539	86.4 (1.0)	539	25.2 (3.4)

router must make choices between alternative paths for a net. In Figure 4.1, one such choice is between routing the given net using the paths $N1$ or $N2$. Furthermore, global routers must determine how to connect wires from one row to another. Some criteria used to evaluate the quality of the routing include total net length, total chip area, the number of tracks required (row-based routing), the number of feedthroughs used, and the number of vias required. For row-based layout, the output of the global router is normally used to set up the channels to be routed by a channel router.

This step is applied to a gate array design style as follows. In a gate array design, components are placed in well-defined slots and the interconnection space is fixed and limited. In such a case the global routing algorithm takes as input the dimensions of the rectangular array of slots and an estimate of the available channel capacity in each of the four directions for each component placed in the slots. Built-in feedthroughs are available in each row through which vertical connections across rows of gates can be made. The list of interconnections to be made is provided as a set of sets, for which each net is represented as a set of coordinate points that are to be made electrically common. Often a global routing algorithm will fail on a given placement of gates, since either the channel capacity or feedthrough capacity is violated.

In a standard cell design environment, a global router has some flexibility of adding extra feedthrough cells or increasing the channel height to accommodate more wires in the vertical or horizontal direction in some region of the chip.

Since global routing is also an NP complete problem, a variety of heuristics has been proposed to solve the problem. Specifically, we have global routers based on graph search methods, Steiner tree approaches, iterative improvement, and hierarchical decomposition techniques. In the following sections we will describe parallel algorithms for global routing using a variety of approaches:

- Graph search

- Iterative improvement

- Hierarchical decompositions

For each approach, both shared memory MIMD and distributed memory MIMD parallel algorithms will be presented where appropriate.

4.10 GLOBAL ROUTING USING GRAPH SEARCH

4.10.1 Overview

We will now describe an algorithm for global wiring based on graph search techniques using the Lee-Moore algorithm for detailed routing [13, 17]. Although the Lee-Moore algorithm is known to perform well for connecting two points, the success of wiring of nets depends on the choice of specific paths among all shortest paths, or even the choice of a path that is not the shortest. A variant of the algorithm has been developed by Akers for global routing [2], that assigns costs of traversal to each of the boundaries of the cell. Hence the algorithm for routing should find the cheapest path and not the shortest path.

In this cheapest path routing algorithm, each cell is given a score that represents the sum of the costs of all the cell boundaries traversed by the cheapest path from the source to that cell. At any given step, a list of cells will be processed at that step. For each cell, the directional score is computed for each of its four directions as the score of the neighbor of that direction plus the cost of crossing that boundary. If the minimum of the four directional scores is less that the score currently assigned to that cell, the score is updated to the minimum value and the four neighboring cells are put in the list of cells to be processed at the next step. The list of cells initially contains the neighbors of the source cell, whose score is initially zero. The algorithm terminates when the list is empty or when all the updated scores at the end of some step are equal to or higher than the score assigned to one of the target cells. The backtrace procedure identifies the path through which a target cell was reached from the source using the pointer information.

Figure 4.16 shows the steps in the algorithm. In Figure 4.16(a), we show a routing grid with two terminals, A and B that need to be connected together. The costs of crossing the boundaries of each routing cell are marked. Figure 4.16(b) shows the scores of each cell after two iterations of executing the cheapest path routing algorithm. The scores show the cheapest path found so far from the source cell A to the current cell. Figure 4.16(c) shows the final cheapest cost route from A to B. It is clear that the cheapest cost route is not the same as the shortest path route from A to B.

For multiterminal nets, the source cell, the destination cell with the least score, and all the cells that are on the backtrace path become additional source cells for the next forward propagation iteration.

Nair, et al. have proposed an improved global routing algorithm based on the preceding algorithm that tries to alleviate the problems associated with the ordering of nets in the graph search approach. [18]. The effectiveness of the algorithm depends on the accuracy of the cost estimates at the various boundaries. Some sophisticated cost computation methods are used in this algorithm, which consist of three components: (1) the demand measure which characterizes the requirement of all nets that are yet to be wired, (2) the supply measure which estimates the remaining number of tracks left after a certain number of nets have been routed, (3) the cost of traversal which takes into account the physical complexity of the cell and (4) the cost of placing vias on adjacent intersections.

The demand-based measure is based on the observation that most nets will be routed on minimum length and with at most two bends; hence, by enumerating all possible routes of wires between pairs of points on a rectangular grid, we can estimate the congestion distribution

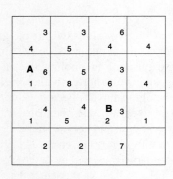

(a)

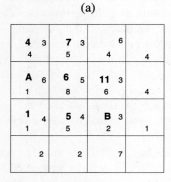

(b)

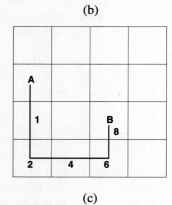

(c)

Figure 4.16 Cheapest path global routing algorithm. (a) Grid with boundary costs and terminals A and B. (b) Grid with scores of cells after two iterations. (c) Grid with cheapest cost path from A to B.

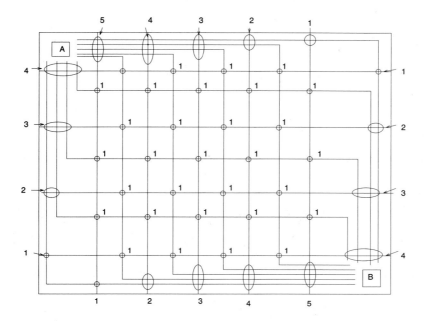

Figure 4.17 All possible paths with two or fewer bends (Courtesy of Nair et al, *Proc. Design Automation Conf.,* ©IEEE 1982)

on points on the rectangular grid. Figure 4.17 shows all possible paths with two or fewer bends in the minimum rectangle of a two point net. An empirical cost estimate that has been found to work well is that cells at the source and target of a net get a cost of $\alpha = 8$, the cells that are distance one away in the same row or column get a cost of $\alpha - 1$, cells at distance 2 in the same row or column get a cost of $\alpha - 2$, and so on until it reaches unity.

Nair et al. have also looked at the issue of paths with detours, ones whose length of the cheapest cost path L_c between the source and destination is more than the length of the shortest path, $L_{\min}$. They have proposed search strategies to limit the detour to some finite quantity, for example 3 or 4.

4.10.2 Shared Memory MIMD Parallel Algorithm

We will now describe a parallel algorithm for global routing that is suitable for execution on a shared memory multiprocessor that is based on the parallel algorithm proposed by Nair et al on an array processor hardware [18].

Consider an $n \times n$ array of cells that has to be routed. Each cell contains information about the wiring capacity in the horizontal and vertical direction. The global routing phase allocates wires to the channels in the chip without specifically assigning tracks within the channel. The latter assignment is accomplished subsequently by an exact embedding algorithm.

The information regarding wiring capacity about each cell and the actual state of wiring of each cell in the horizontal and vertical direction can be kept in global shared memory in a shared memory multiprocessor. The tasks related to the routing for each cell are associated with each processor through two different cell assignment approaches.

Assuming unlimited processors, we can conceive of n^2 processors configured as an $n \times n$ array, in which each cell gets assigned to a processor. Since the number of processors P is typically less than n^2, two ways of mapping the $n \times n$ array of cells on the processors can be used. Assume that we have a 9×9 array of cells to be routed on 9 processors, which we will configure as a 3×3 array of processors. In one method illustrated in Figure 4.18(a), we simply partition the array of cells into continuous 3×3 blocks of cell, and assign each block to a processor. Cell (i, j) gets mapped to processor $(i \text{ div } \sqrt{P}, j \text{ div } \sqrt{P})$. This corresponds to a two-dimensional blocked distribution of the routing grid to the processors. The advantage of this approach is that during the forward propagation phase, when a cell wishes to send updates to its four neighbors, most of the time, the neighbors are within the processor itself. All updates among sets of cells shared between a pair of processors can be performed together, thereby reducing the synchronization overhead compared to the computation times. The disadvantage of this partititioning algorithm is that only the processor that owns the regions of cells over which a net will be routed will perform useful work, while the other processors will remain idle. Also, during forward propagation, a large number of computation steps have to be executed before the computation wavefront crosses the boundary of the source processor's assigned region. Subsequently, the neighbors of the processors become active, and so on. This gives rise to a severe load imbalance problem.

In the second method, the $n \times n$ array of cells is folded onto a reduced array of processors. Basically, the P processors are organized as a $\sqrt{P} \times \sqrt{P}$ mesh, and each processor gets cells of the $n \times n$ array using a cyclic assignment. That is the cell (i, j) gets mapped on to processor $(i \bmod \sqrt{P}, j \bmod \sqrt{P})$. This corresponds to a two-dimensional cyclic distribution of the routing grid to the processors. Figure 4.18(b) shows the assignment of a 9×9 array of cells on a 3×3 array of processors. Using such a cell assignment, the wave expansion from the start cell will in the next step make four cells and their corresponding processors active, and in the next step will make other neighbors of the previous four cells, and their corresponding processors active. Hence very soon, all the processors will be performing useful work that is very well load balanced. The problem with this approach is that a synchronization cost is incurred by all the processors after every computation step.

The parallel algorithm for global routing using either one of the preceding cell distribution approaches is as follows. Before starting global wiring, each processor computes the total number of wiring tracks available in each of the four directions for the cells it has been assigned. It is also provided with a list of nets that have a terminal in the assigned cells.

An outline of the parallel routing algorithm entitled *SM-PARALLEL-GLOBAL-ROUTING-GRAPH-SEARCH* (for shared memory parallel algorithm for global routing using graph search) is given next.

Procedure *SM-PARALLEL-GLOBAL-ROUTING-GRAPH-SEARCH;*

Partition chip region ownership (array of cells) among processors
using one of two techniques (blocked or cyclic);

FORALL processors in PARALLEL DO

1	1	1	2	2	2	3	3	3
1	1	1	2	2	2	3	3	3
1	1	1	2	2	2	3	3	3
4	4	4	5	5	5	6	6	6
4	4	4	5	5	5	6	6	6
4	4	4	5	5	5	6	6	6
7	7	7	8	8	8	9	9	9
7	7	7	8	8	8	9	9	9
7	7	7	8	8	8	9	9	9

(a)

1	2	3	1	2	3	1	2	3
4	5	6	4	5	6	4	5	6
7	8	9	7	8	9	7	8	9
1	2	3	1	2	3	1	2	3
4	5	6	4	5	6	4	5	6
7	8	9	7	8	9	7	8	9
1	2	3	1	2	3	1	2	3
4	5	6	4	5	6	4	5	6
7	8	9	7	8	9	7	8	9

(b)

Figure 4.18 Two different mappings of a 9×9 array of cells on a 3×3 array of processors. (a) Two-dimensional blocked distribution. (b) Two-dimensional cyclic distribution.

```
    FOR each net n_i DO
        FOR each cell c_j owned by processor DO
            For net n_i to be wired, whether it has a terminal
                in cell c_j or not;
            Compute the likelihood of cell being a member
                of some connection in net in each direction;
            Add an appropriate cost to the congestion estimate
                in that direction ( a decreasing function of
                the distance of the cell from a terminal cell
                of the net);
        END FOR
    END FOR
END FORALL


FORALL processors in parallel DO
    FOR each net n_i DO
        FOR each cell c_j owned by processor DO
            For net n_i, cell c_j subtracts its own contribution
                to the congestion estimate for net n_i from the total
                remaining congestion estimate for each of the four
                directions of the cell c_j;
            Based on the number of unused tracks and the updated
                congestion estimate at each port,
                cell c_j computes the port costs for each of the four directions
                which is a measure of the penalty for occupying a track
                in that direction;
        END FOR
    END FOR
END FORALL


Synchronize all processors;
```

Forward propagation phase

```
FORALL processors in parallel DO
    FOR each net n_i DO
        FOR each cell c_j owned by processor DO
            One of the terminals of net n_i is called source
                all the others are sinks;
            IF cell is source cell THEN
                In all the four directions,
                Update the port cost of
                the neighbor cell in that direction;
                IF the neighbor cell is within the same processor
```

THEN operation is performed within the processor;
ELSE operation performed on neighbor processor;
ELSE /* if cell is not source cell /*
Update the port cost of neighbor
by arbitrarily large value;

At each subsequent time step, each cell
determines the minimum of values coming from ports;
A pointer is set to the direction
from which this minimum came from;
For each of its ports, the cell adds the port cost
to the minimum value and sends the modified value
to the neighbors;

IF sink cell gets a meaningful value (less than
the arbitrarily large value)
THEN its notifies all other cells to
stop the forward propagation process
and enter backtrace phase;
END FOR cell
END FOR net
END FORALL processors

Synchronize all processors;

Backtrace phase

FORALL processors in parallel DO
FOR each net n_i DO
FOR each cell c_j owned by processor DO
IF cell c_j is sink cell
THEN it prompts the neighbor cell in the direction
of its stored pointer;

REPEAT
IF cell c_j has just been prompted by its neighbor
THEN it prompts another cell in the direction
stored by it during the forward propagation phase;
Any prompted cell decrements the available channel
capacity in the appropriate ports,
and records the entry and exit points against that net;
UNTIL the source cell is reached;

All cells that have recorded entry/exit points for the current

net become sources for the next forward propagation;
All net terminals remaining to be connected act as sinks;
The process for a net terminates when no sinks remain for a net;

END FOR each cell
END FOR each net
END FORALL processors

End Procedure

On a limited processor algorithm the maximum speedup can be achieved by the cyclic cell assignment to processors. Since at every expansion step, the neighbors of the expanded cells are guaranteed to be on different processors, when all processors are busy, P cells can be visited in parallel for P processors.

Implementation Nair et al. have reported on results of global wiring of some example circuits on a 32×32 array of processors and have shown almost linear speedups [18]. No implementations have been reported on any general-purpose shared memory multiprocessor.

4.10.3 Distributed Memory MIMD Parallel Algorithm

We will now describe a parallel algorithm for global routing that is based on using maze routing on two different grids in two phases, a coarse grid during an initial global routing phase and a fine grid during the the detailed wiring phase. The algorithm using wave expansion has been proposed by Olukotun and Mudge [19] and is suitable for execution on a hypercube-based distributed memory multiprocessor.

The routing region is partitioned using a two-dimensional blocked distribution among the various processors of a hypercube as shown in Figure4.7(a). At the edges of each partition, crossings connect each partition to other partitions. Each edge has a fixed capacity of crossings in which nets can be routed. The global routing phase assigns nets to partitions of the routing region. This step assumes there are two terminal nets and that all nets can be wired within the minimum bounding box. Figure 4.19 shows the coarse routing grid on the detailed routing grid for a two terminal net.

Given N processors of a hypercube, the chip region is partitioned into N regions that are mapped to a logical two-dimensional array of processors using the binary reflected gray code [25]. If the grid has A square units of area, each partition contains $\frac{A}{N}$ grid points. Each processor keeps track of the number of crossings available at the eastern and southern boundaries of the partition assigned to it. The global expansion phase begins with the processor responsible for the partition containing the source of a net sending a message to its neighboring processor contained within the bounding rectangle of the net. On the reception of this expansion message, a processor checks if it is a target processor for the message. If not, it forwards the message to its neighbors within the bounding rectangle. A processor waits for messages from both the x and y neighbors before advancing the least-cost message with an updated cost representing the edge costs of its partition. Once the target processor is reached, a backtrace phase is entered in which a path of least-cost expansion is retraced by sending

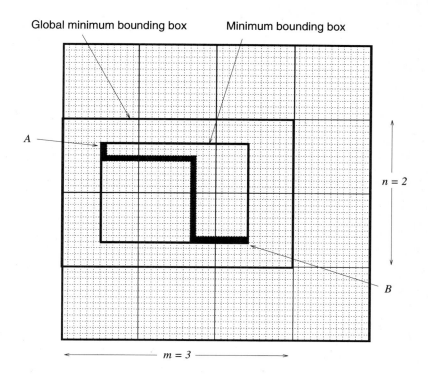

Figure 4.19 Coarse and detailed routing grid showing grid boundaries (Courtesy of Olukotun and Mudge, *Proc. Design Automation Conf.,* ©ACM 1987)

messages in the reverse direction. Overall, if the bounding rectangle for a two-terminal net occupies an area that is $n \times m$ partitions, then the global routing algorithm generates $2(mn-1)$ messages. Computation can be overlapped with the communication so this represents the time taken for this phase of the algorithm.

In this global routing phase, each processor is responsible for nets whose source points are contained within its partition. All processors simultaneously initiate global routing of all the nets in its region. Hence the messages that are sent carry information about which net is being routed, the source and the target processor, and so on. Although significant speedup can be observed with this approach, it is possible that during the parallel backtrace phase, a backtrace message may arrive at a processor to find that all the available crossings have been claimed by other nets. If this situation happens, a new global routing step has to be performed for that failed net.

Once the global routing is performed, in order to decompose the routing problem into a set of independent routing problems that can be solved in parallel, it is necessary for a processor and its four neighbors to decide on the placement of nets that cross their common boundaries. A crossing placement algorithm is executed in parallel.

Initially, all crossings have an undefined value. The crossing placement algorithm uses an iterative improvement method, in which each processor computes the position of a crossing on either its southern or eastern borders, based on a weighted average of the current position of the crossing, if it is defined, and the positions of the crossings as projected on the crossing border of strands to which a crossing is connected. The closer a crossing is to the one being placed the more weight it is given. Crossings on borders opposite to the crossing are given more weight and source and target are given even more weight. Each iteration of the algorithm consists of two steps. The first step starts from the processors on the western border and proceeds toward the east for the eastern boundaries on each processor; the second step starts at the processors on the northern border and proceeds to the south. In practice, convergence is achieved quickly. Each iteration generates $3(m + n - 2)$ messages.

Finally, the parallel routing algorithm involves a detailed maze routing in parallel on each processor on its independent partition.

An outline of the parallel global routing algorithm entitled *DM-PARALLEL-GLOBAL-ROUTING-GRAPHSEARCH* (for distributed memory parallel algorithm for global routing using graph search) is given next.

Procedure *DM-PARALLEL-GLOBAL-ROUTING-GRAPHSEARCH;*

Grid Partitioning and Mapping

Partition the routing grid into N parts;
Assign one partition to each of the N processors;
Each processor keeps track of number of crossings available
in eastern and southern boundary;

Front Wave Expansion

FORALL processors in PARALLEL DO
   FOR each net simultaneously DO
      IF processor owns source of a net (for all nets)
         THEN send message to x and y neighbor processors
            within bounding rectangle of net (for all nets);
      IF processor receives expansion message from x and y neighbor
      THEN IF processor is target cell of net (for all nets)
         THEN begin backtrace process for net;
           ELSE send message with least x-y cost to its x and y neighbor
            processors within bounding rectangle of net (for all nets);
   END FOR net
END FORALL processors

Backtrace process

FORALL Processors DO

```
       FOR each net simultaneously DO
          IF processor owns target cell of net THEN
             Identify least cost in x or y direction;
             Identify paths in x or y direction of least cost;
             Store that pair of cells as a path segment;
             Mark crossing as used, i.e. update availability at boundary;
          END FOR nets
       END FORALL
```

Crossing placement of nets Phase

```
FORALL processors in parallel DO
   FOR phase = westeast, northsouth DO
       Compute crossings of nets in south and east border;
       Use weighted costs;
   END FOR
END FORALL
```

Detailed routing Phase

```
FORALL processors in parallel DO
   FOR all nets in processor region
       Perform detailed routing of net using maze routing;
   END FOR
END FORALL
```

End Procedure

Implementation Olukotun and Mudge have reported an implementation of the preceding algorithm on a 64-processor NCUBE/1™ hypercube [19]. Table 4.4 shows some example runtimes (seconds) on a printed circuit board routing benchmark consisting of a routing grid of 512×512 consisting of about 200 nets on various numbers on processors.

The runtime of the algorithm on 64 processors was determined to be faster than the 16-processor version. No uniprocessor results were reported due to memory limitations on one processor of the hypercube.

4.11 GLOBAL ROUTING USING ITERATIVE IMPROVEMENT

4.11.1 Overview

We will now describe a global routing algorithm for standard cell design using an iterative improvement approach [22, 23]. In a standard cell design, the global routing determines the following for each wire in the circuit.

1. *Segment decomposition.* Each multipoint net is divided into a set of two-point segments using a minimum spanning tree algorithm.

TABLE 4.4 Runtimes (seconds) of the Parallel Algorithm on the NCUBE/1™ Hypercube

Circuit	Grid	Nets	Processors	Runtime
1	512×512	200	16	49.9
			64	12.4
			256	12.7

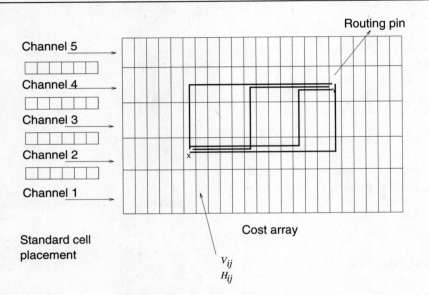

Figure 4.20 Global routing cost model (Courtesy of Rose, *IEEE Trans. Computer-Aided Design,* ©IEEE 1990)

2. *Route generation and evaluation.* A low-cost path is found for each permutation by evaluating a subset of two-bend routes between each pin pair.

3. *Reconstruct and record.* This step joins all the segments back together and records the presence of the newly routed wire so that later wires can take it into account.

The algorithm uses an iterative technique to route wires. After all the wires are sequentially routed, each is ripped up and then rerouted. This procedure is repeated about 5 to 10 times. The cost model for the algorithm is illustrated in Figure 4.20. The cost array has a vertical dimension equal to the number of rows plus 1, and a horizontal dimension of the width of the placement in routing grids, that is, the routing position in a channel. Each element of the cost array, H_{ij}, contains the number of wire routes that pass horizontally through the channel i in routing grid j. These values change as wires are routed. The cost of a path P if given by $\text{cost}(P) = \sum_P H_{ij} + v \times C$, where C is the number of cell rows that are crossed in the path and v is the assigned cost of a row crossing.

For each set of two pins that is to be routed, a set of two bend routes (L shaped and Z-shaped) is evaluated, and the one with the lowest cost is chosen. Instead of searching all possible two bend routes, the set of routes that is evaluated is prioritized such that the space of routes is evenly spanned.

4.11.2 Shared Memory MIMD Parallel Algorithm

We now describe a a parallel algorithm for global routing based on the preceding algorithm [22, 23] that is suitable for execution on a shared memory multiprocessor. Parallelism can be applied at several levels in this algorithm, each of which is orthogonal:

1. *Wire-by-wire level parallelism.* Each processor is given a wire to route in parallel.
2. *Segment-based parallelism.* Each two-point segment produced by a minimum spanning tree decomposition is routed in parallel.

In the wire-by-wire parallel approach, each processor routes a different wire at the same time, such that the cost array is shared across all the processors. The master processor initializes the cost array and sets up each individual wire as a task on one central queue. All processors then remove wire tasks from the queue and execute the routing algorithm reading the shared cost array and updating the cost array with the best route so found. Figure 4.21 illustrates the wire-by-wire parallel approach. The wire-by-wire approach does not produce the same route as the serial algorithm. In the sequential algorithm, a data dependency which dictates that wires be routed sequentially. After the wire is routed, its presence is recorded in the cost array so that subsequent wires can take this into account. In the wire-by-wire parallel approach, there is a chaotic parallelism for which data dependencies are relaxed under the assumption that the quality of the results will be marginally different, since the cost array does not reflect the cost of wires being simultaneously routed by other processors.

This degradation is reduced by a geographic wire assignment approach. In the ideal case, each processor is assigned wires that reside in a specific area of the chip such that a processor will change the area of the cost array that only it reads. A simple version of this strategy is one in which the chip is divided into distinct geographic areas, one for each processor. Each area has its own task queue associated with it. A wire is assigned to a queue if the position of its leftmost point falls within the assigned area of the task queue. This does not generate totally independent tasks, because wires from different task queues or processors can still overlap in space and time, but it does reduce the amount of overlap. This approach creates an imbalance of workload among the processors because each queue may not represent the same amount of work. To prevent loss of work when a processor associated with a queue becomes empty, it searches for a nonempty queue and routes wires from that queue.

An important problem that limits speedup in this algorithm is how to perform synchronization. In the wire-by-wire parallel approach, several processors may be updating the cost array at the same time, incrementing the cost array when a best route is found, and decrementing the array during the rip-up for future iterations. The cost array must be locked to provide exclusive access to the data to adhere to strict parallel programming. However, such a scheme involves too much overhead. Hence, instead of performing the locks, we can rely on the geographic wire assignment to create semiindependent tasks. There is a trade-off of increased performance with degradation in the quality of the results.

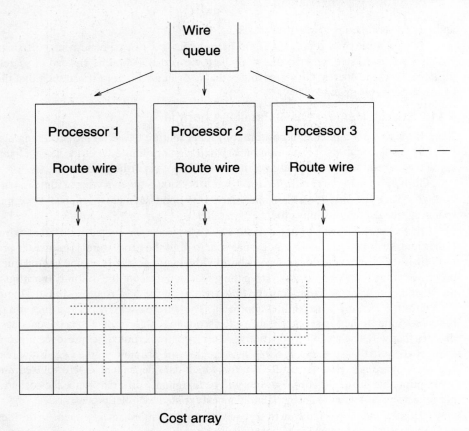

Cost array

Figure 4.21 Wire-by-wire parallel approach (Courtesy of Rose, *IEEE Trans. Computer-Aided Design,* ©IEEE 1990)

An outline of the parallel routing algorithm entitled *SM-PARALLEL-ROUTING-ITER-ATIVE-WIREBASED* (for shared memory parallel routing algorithm using iterative improvement and wire-by wire parallelism) is given next.

Procedure *SM-PARALLEL-ROUTING-ITERATIVE-WIREBASED;*

Read in circuit description and wires;
Create shared cost array;
Partition chip into regions;
Assign regions to processors;
Assign wires to processors by geographic assignment
    depending on location of leftmost point of wire;
Assign wires to task queues of processors using assignment;

TABLE 4.5 Runtimes (seconds) and routing quality of parallel algorithm on the Encore Multimax™ Multiprocessor

Circuit	Nets	1 proc		8 proc	
		Tracks	Runtime (Speedup)	Tracks	Runtime (Speedup)
BNRE	420	129	78 (1.0)	135	13 (5.8)
BNRD	774	181	156 (1.0)	185	22 (7.0)
Primary1	904	262	321 (1.0)	264	47 (6.8)
BNRA	1634	300	878 (1.0)	311	124 (7.1)
Primary2	3029	560	4334 (1.0)	584	574 (7.6)

REPEAT rip-up-reroute cycle
  FORALL processors in PARALLEL DO
    WHILE NOT DONE DO
      WHILE current task queue not empty DO
        Pick up next wire from task queue;
        Route wire;
        Update shared cost array;
      END WHILE
      IF own task queue empty
      THEN pick up next wire from another
        processors queue;
    END WHILE
  END FORALL
  Rip up some wires;
  Place wires on task queues of processors;
    by geographic assignment;
UNTIL convergence of rip-up-reroute

End Procedure

Implementation Rose has reported an actual implementation of the wire-by-wire parallel algorithm on an Encore Multimax™ shared memory multiprocessor [22, 23]. Table 4.5 shows some example results od five benchmark circuits on the the quality of routing (in terms of horizontal tracks required), the runtimes (in seconds), and the speedups on eight processors using wire-based parallelism.

Experimentally, it was observed that the minor incorrect updates of the cost array did not produce significantly poorer quality results. Specifically, for some example circuits running the algorithm on 15 processors, the number of tracks increased by at most two by removing the locks, but decreased the runtimes by about 40%. The wire-based parallel approach exhibited a speedup of about 10 to 13 on 15 processors using a geographic wire assignment, with an overall degradation in wiring quality of no more than 3% to 5% for a large number of circuits. The quality of the routing deteriorated with increasing number of processors. However, the use of geographic wire assignment helped to control the degradation in the quality of the routing. For an example circuit, the number of tracks went up from 560 using one processor to 590 using 16 processors without using geographic assignment and up to 575 on 16 processors using the geographic wire assignment.

In the segment-based parallelism, each two-point segment of a multipoint net is routed in parallel. There is a severe problem of load imbalance with this approach. The time taken to route a two-point segment is proportional to the Manhattan distance between the points. For a multipoint net, if the distances between different pairs of points are widely different, each processor will take widely different times. Hence the overall effective speedup has been measured to be about 1.1 on two processors. Hence such an approach has been used in combination with a wire-based parallelism on a large number of processors where one extra processor may be used to route an extra segment of one of the wires.

4.11.3 Distributed Memory MIMD Parallel Algorithm

We will now describe a distributed memory MIMD parallel version of the preceding algorithm based on work reported by Martonosi and Gupta [15].

In the shared memory parallel algorithm, the entire cost array is shared by all the processors, which read and perform updates on the array; hence a single consistent copy is kept. In a distributed memory implementation, the cost array has to be distributed among the processors. One simple approach is to divide the array into equal regions and assign one subarray to a processor. Each processor performs routing on its own region. If a routing extends to another region, the routing task is passed to another processor owning that region. Such an approach has load balancing problems if many wires lie in a single processor's region. Also, since many routes are explored for each wire, this method could generate a large amount of message traffic.

A second approach to designing a distributed memory version of the parallel routing algorithm involves the division of the cost array into sections such that each processor is the owner of one section. However, each processor has a view of the whole cost array. Figure 4.22 shows a 4-processor example with the owned regions highlighted. A new data structure called the delta array is added that has the same dimensions as the cost array and keeps track of the changes made to the cost array between updates. This delta array is used to notify other processors of changes that have been made.

In a shared memory MIMD parallel programming paradigm, wires can be either assigned dynamically or statically using locality and load balancing heuristics. In a distributed memory MIMD parallel programming approach, dynamic wire allocation requires message transactions on the network which can be quite expensive, hence a static allocation is chosen. Because the cost array is divided into owned regions, the wires are assigned for routing to the processor that owns the region where the leftmost pin of the wire resides. This corresponds to the geographic wire assignment algorithm of Rose in the shared memory implementation [22, 23].

The preceding strategy gives poor load balancing; hence it is modified as follows. A cost measure is computed for each wire based on length. Any wire with cost less than a threshold

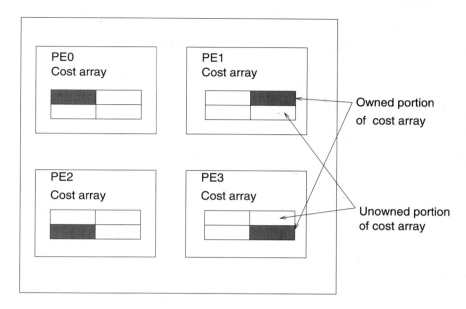

Figure 4.22 Division of cost array among processors in distributed memory multiprocessors (Courtesy of Martonosi and Gupta, *Proc. Int. Conf. Parallel Processing,* Pennsylvania State University Press, 1989)

parameter is assigned to the owner processor of the leftmost pin. All longer wires whose costs are greater than the threshold are held until a final step in the static wire assignment step where they are assigned to balance the load ignoring locality.

In most circuits, wires assigned to one processor will extend into regions owned by other processors. Hence different methods of updating the cost array have been studied, as illustrated in Figure 4.23. Updates can be initiated by the sender or the receiver, and each can be of type absolute or delta, depending on whether the actual cost information or the change in cost is sent.

A sender-initiated update is used to inform other processors of the owner processor's view of the owned region and to inform an owner processor of changes that another processor has made to the owner processor's owned region. A receiver-initiated update is used when a processor wants to update its view of a remotely owned region of the cost array. For each wire a processor determines which regions contain the wire, and since the wire assignment is static, the processor knows in advance which regions to get updates from. If such receives are nonblocking, we can overlap computation with communication, and get the data just before they are needed.

An outline of the parallel routing algorithm entitled *DM-PARALLEL-ROUTING-ITER-ATIVE-WIREBASED* (for distributed memory parallel routing algorithm using iterative improvement and wire-by-wire parallelism) follows.

Procedure *DM-PARALLEL-ROUTING-ITERATIVE-WIREBASED;*

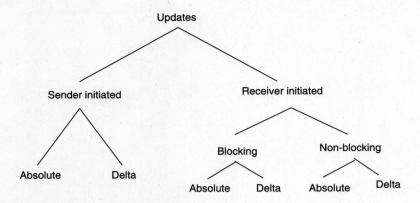

Figure 4.23 Classification of update strategies (Courtesy of Martonosi and Gupta,*Proc. Int. Conf. Parallel Processing,* Pennsylvania State University Press, 1989)

Read in circuit description and wires;
Create cost array;
Partition chip and cost array into regions;
Assign regions and cost array sections to processors;
Each processor owns subarray but copy of whole array;
Assign wires to processors by geographic assignment
    depending on location of leftmost point of wire
    if cost of wire less than a threshold, otherwise
    use dynamic wire balancing
Assign wires to task queues of processors;

REPEAT rip-up-reroute cycle
    FORALL processors in PARALLEL DO
        WHILE NOT DONE DO
            WHILE current task queue not empty DO
                Pick up next wire from task queue;
                Route wire;
                Compute delta cost array;
                Send/Receive update messages to other
                    processors of delta costs using
                    sender/receiver initiated methods;
                Update cost array
            END WHILE
            IF own task queue empty THEN
                Pick next wire from central wire queue;
        END WHILE

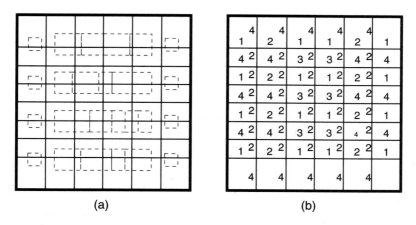

4	4	4	4	4
1	2	1	1	2	1

Figure 4.24 Routing cell model. (a) Layout block setup. (b) Capacity determination.

END FORALL
Rip up some wires
Place wires on task queues of processors by geographic assignment
UNTIL convergence of rip-up-reroute

End Procedure

Implementation Martonosi and Gupta have reported an implementation of the preceding algorithm on an Intel iPSC™ hypercube [15]. The authors ran some experiments to determine experimentally the quality of the solutions produced and the runtimes of the algorithms using different forms of updates. The overall result was that the sender initiated update strategies give the best results in terms of circuit quality; however, the network traffic is about 10 times higher than for receiver-initiated strategies and thus the runtimes were very high.

4.12 GLOBAL ROUTING USING HIERARCHY

4.12.1 Overview

We will now describe a hierarchical approach to global routing of standard cell layouts based on work reported by Burstein and Pelavin [9], and Brouwer and Banerjee [7]. The entire layout area (including pads) is divided into a two-dimensional array of *routing cells*. Each routing cell is assigned routing capacity information for each of its four boundaries based on the physical dimensions of the routing cell and the underlying layout. Figure 4.24 demonstrates how the routing cell array in (b) is derived from a given layout in (a). The dimensions of the routing cell array are determined from the number of cell rows in the layout. The numbers along the grid lines in Figure 4.24(b) represent the wiring capacity along either the vertical or horizontal edges of the routing cell. The values given are based on the channel width, the number of built-in feedthroughs, and the actual size of the routing cell.

At each level of the hierarchical decomposition, the current set of routing cells is divided into four regions or supercells, forming a two-by-two supercell array as shown in Figure 4.24. During each stage of the decomposition, these supercells are further divided into smaller regions until a supercell only contains one routing cell.

Each net in the given problem is cast into one of 15 net types based on the presence of pins in each of the four supercells. The 11 net types consisting of two or more pins are shown in Figure 4.26, along with all the possible routings for each net type, respectively. The remaining four net types are for nets with all pins in the same quadrant. It is unnecessary to include these in the routing evaluation. Each possible routing can be assigned a unique variable number to be used in solving a linear program. Such a formulation was proposed by Burstein and Pelavin [9].

A linear (integer) programming formulation of the problem (LP) then is defined such that

For all x, MAX(px)

subject to $Ax \leq a$ and $Bx = b$,

where x represents the variable space, p represents the objective function, A and a represent the inequality constraints, and B and b represent any equality constraints. In our problem, the set of variables, $x_i, 0 \leq i \leq 27$, represents each of the 28 possible net routings from Figure 4.25 and the set of 15 constraints is based on the available routing capacities and the types of nets being routed. Four of the constraints limit the number of nets crossing between adjacent supercells. The remaining 11 constraints limit the variable values for each of the 11 net types. The objective function is designed to minimize interconnection lengths of the nets by weighing the shorter-length variables more than the longer ones. For example, in Figure 4.25, x_0 would have a higher weight than x_1 and x_4 would have a high weight than x_5. The values of the variables x_i resulting from the solution of the linear program represent the number of nets routed in the particular pattern which the variable represents. After a solution to the LP is found, the nets are then assigned to the appropriate configuration using some greedy heuristics.

In the routing capacity model, it is sufficient for each routing cell to maintain capacity information for only two of its four shared edges (for example the top and right edges). Denote the vertical capacity for a routing cell in row r and column c as $v_{r,c}$ (across the top edge), and the horizontal capacity as $h_{r,c}$ (across the right edge). Let L, R, T, and B be the left, right, top, and bottom edges (rows and columns) of the region to be solved. Let X and Y be the locations of the vertical (Y) and horizontal (X) axes respectively of the two-by-two supercell array. Let $\text{CAP}_i, i \in \{A, B, C, D\}$ represent the capacities of the four axis segments in clockwise order around the two-by-two supercell array, as shown in Figure 4.26(a).

Then

$$\text{CAP}_A = \sum_{i=Y}^{T} \min(h_{i,X-1}, h_{i,X}, h_{i,X+1})$$

$$\text{CAP}_B = \sum_{i=X}^{R} \min(v_{Y-1,i}, v_{Y,i}, v_{Y+1,i})$$

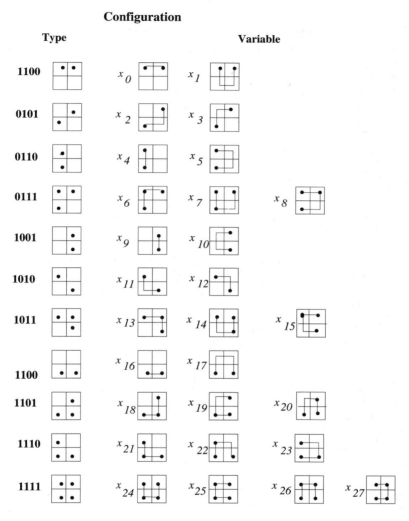

Figure 4.25 Net types and possible routings. Nets are categorized by the number of pins they are connected to in four quadrants. For example, net 0111 is connected to three quadrants. For each net type, there can be several possible routings. For example, for net 0111, one can route by either options $x6$, $x7$, or $x8$, each of which is represented by a variable in the linear programming formulation

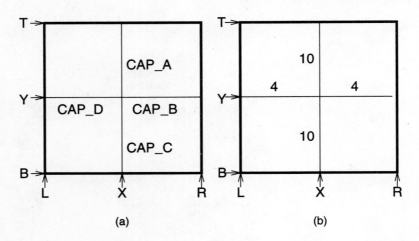

Figure 4.26 Axes capacities. (a)Axis capacities of 2×2 supercell. (b) Example.

$$CAP_C = \sum_{i=B}^{Y} \min(h_{i,X-1}, h_{i,X}, h_{i,X+1})$$

$$CAP_D = \sum_{i=L}^{X} \min(v_{Y-1,i}, v_{Y,i}, v_{Y+1,i})$$

This scheme quickly estimates the capacity of the axes with little chance of over estimating by concentrating on the regions closest to the axis. Cases in which the cell capacities are nonuniform near an axis are handled as well. Figure 4.26(b) illustrates the capacity estimation for the example in Figure 4.24.

In a row-based layout, feedthroughs must be inserted into the rows to make connections when no built-in feedthroughs or equivalent pins are available when connections must be made from row_i to row_{i+2}. The algorithm handles the problem through the simplex computations. After the problem has been set up, if sufficient routing facilities are available a solution will be found, else the simplex algorithm will terminate with an infeasible initial problem. By analyzing the simplex state and the given routing problem, adjustments to certain capacities will provide a feasible initial problem for the simplex algorithm. Under certain simplex state conditions, these adjustments immediately generate a feasible initial problem. Otherwise, selected capacities are increased until a feasible problem is achieved. Adjustments to CAP_A and CAP_C are equivalent to increasing the channel width. Adjustments to CAP_B and CAP_D are equivalent to inserting feedthroughs in the row along the X axis.

4.12.2 Shared Memory MIMD Parallel Algorithm

We will now describe a parallel algorithm for global routing that is suitable for execution on a shared memory multiprocessor based on the work reported by Brouwer and Banerjee [7].

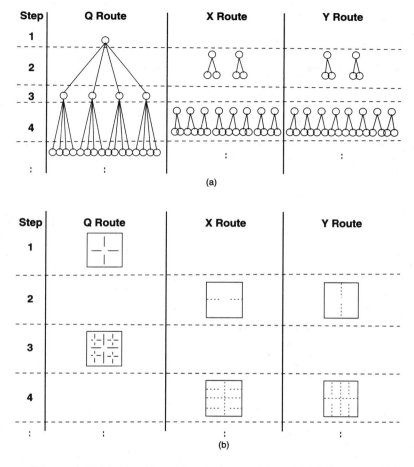

Figure 4.27 Maximal boundary decomposition. (a) Task graph. (b) Example.

The parallel algorithm applies two-dimensional hierarchical decomposition methods to the global routing problem. At each stage of the hierarchy we divide a larger problem into four smaller subproblems (divide and conquer). Deciding how to partition the subproblems so that they are independent of each other is very important. One primary decision has to do with how net-crossing locations along the boundaries between the subproblems are determined and locked in place. We will describe two approaches in the following.

The first strategy completely determines the net crossing locations by recursively decomposing along the axes of interest down to the routing cell level. This strategy is computationally quite costly, but the advantage is that the boundary interface is determined hierarchically as well. Figure 4.27(a) shows the first steps in the decomposition for this strategy. The nodes of the graph represent a complete solution of a two-by-two routing problem, consisting of net analysis, linear program setup, linear program solution, and assignment of nets to particular route types. The arcs of the graph represent dependencies from the parent nodes (above) to the children nodes (next). The odd-numbered steps represent single two-by-two supercell routings. These are shown as solid line segments inside the squares of the example in Figure 4.27(b). The even-numbered steps represent two-by-two routings of each axis from the previous step and are shown as dotted lines in Figure 4.27(b). In steps 1 and 2, the topmost two-by-two solution is followed first by the recursive two-by-two subdivision and solution of the X axis, down to the level of individual routing cells, and second by the recursive two-by-two subdivision and solution of the Y axis. After completing these steps, the net crossings have been completely determined and locked into place along both axes of the two-by-two supercell problem, and the four subproblems for step 3 are completely independent of each other. This sequence of steps is then recursively repeated until the size of the supercell equals the size of the routing cell and the net crossings through all routing cell edges have been determined. This strategy utilizes the maximum number of two-by-two routing solutions.

A second strategy for hierarchical decomposition of tasks is less computation intensive. Figure 4.28(a) shows the first steps in the hierarchical decomposition for this second strategy. The top-most two-by-two problem is solved (step 1), followed by quick heuristic approximations of the crossings of nets instead of applying a two-by-two routing of each axis. The four subproblems are then completely independent in step 2. These steps are repeated recursively until the routing cell level (supercell = routing cell) is reached. This strategy utilizes the fewest two-by-two routing solutions for a hierarchical routing.

The strategy of the minimal determination of the boundary lines is by far the fastest since the number of nodes in the graph (or solutions of two-by-two routing instances) is much less than for the maximal boundary determination strategy; however, there is a trade off in the expected quality of the solution for computation speed. The routing difficulty occurs because without a costly complete analysis, it is extremely hard to determine exactly at what point along the boundaries each net should cross. Some approximations based on the pin locations of each net are used to estimate the crossing, but if the boundaries are not well predicted, the quality of the routing will be severely degraded starting from the topmost two-by-two solution (step 1). The maximal strategy takes the extra effort to completely analyze the routing constraints along the subproblem boundaries in a hierarchical fashion.

Since the ratio of execution time to synchronization or communication time for the nodes of the execution graph is very large, these tasks are considered to be coarse grained. The parallel execution of a tree-based computation structure is a well-known paradigm, and as, we discussed in previous sections, the hierarchical routing execution in the global routing algorithm takes the form of a tree in which the nodes of the tree represent the LP setup, the LP solution, and the net assignments for a single two-by-two routing problem. Furthermore, each node of the tree that is currently being evaluated is completely independent of all other active nodes. The local information for the current subproblem is derived from its parent node's data structures and global pin location information, which is strictly read-only. The solution of the routing subproblem causes the executing process to write the results to a global (shared) output data structure. Furthermore, since the tasks are spatially independent, there is no need for critical sections of code to lock out other processes as a process writes out its results. After writing the results, the process creates two or four child routing subtasks depending on the

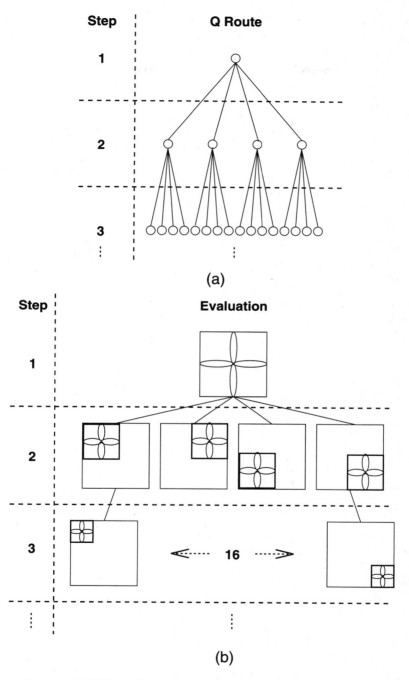

Figure 4.28 Minimal boundary decomposition. (a) Task graph. (b) Example.

number of immediate descendants of the node. Each child subproblem is assigned to an idle and waiting process. The number of processes created and initially available for task solution is set equal to the number of processors available to the user.

Three specific subtasks can be executed in parallel at a fine-grained level. First, during the LP setup, the type for each net of the current two-by-two problem is determined. Since each net is independent, the nets may be divided between available processes and evaluated in parallel. Second, the exchange operations required to solve the linear or integer program may also be divided between available processes for parallel execution. Finally, the assignment of nets could also be done in parallel, based on specific net types. Each of these areas of parallelism is orthogonal to the other.

However, since the amount of parallelism available at the task level is so great, the exploitation of parallelism at the fine-grain level would not provide significant improvement. Only during the startup phase of the execution tree will specific processes be idle. From experimental studies, the authors reported that the part of the execution in large problems for which fine-grain parallelism can be useful is extremely small. Furthermore, parallelism of the simplex solution would not be effective since the average number of pivoting operations for solution is less than 6. Therefore, it is unnecessary to implement these tasks at such a fine-grain level.

An outline of the parallel algorithm entitled *SM-PARALLEL-ROUTING-HIERARCHY* (for shared memory parallel routing algorithm using hierarchical decomposition) follows:

Procedure *SM-PARALLEL-ROUTING-HIERARCHY;*

Read in circuit and initialize;
Set Top level of decomposition, k = 0;
Create top level Quadrisection routing task;

FORALL processors in PARALLEL DO
   WHILE (not DONE) DO
      TYPE = Quadrisection Routing (QR);
      WHILE (GetTask(QR)) DO
         Evaluate(QR, level k);
         Perform net analysis;
         Setup and solve linear program;
         Assign nets to particular route types;
      END WHILE;

      Create 2^k X-Bisection-Route Tasks;
      Create 2^k Y-Bisection-Route Tasks;

      Barrier Synchronize (Type = X-Bisection Route (XBR));

      WHILE (GetTask(XBR)) DO
         Evaluate(XBR, level k);

Perform net analysis;
Setup and solve linear program;
Assign nets to particular route types;
END WHILE

Barrier Synchronize (Type = Y-Bisection Route (YBR));

WHILE (GetTask(YBR)) DO
Evaluate(YBR, level k);
Perform net analysis;
Setup and solve linear program;
Assign nets to particular route types;
END WHILE
Check if DONE, i.e. if routing area has been
decomposed to the level of individual routing cells;

IF not DONE THEN
Create 4^k Quadrisection Routing tasks;

Level k = k + 1;

END WHILE;

END FORALL

End Procedure

Implementation Brouwer and Banerjee have reported on the implementation of the preceding parallel global routing algorithm on an eight processor Encore Multimax™ shared memory multiprocessor [7]. Table 4.6 shows some example results on four benchmark circuits of the quality of routing (in terms of horizontal tracks required), the runtimes (in seconds), and the speedups on eight processors using wire-based parallelism.

The routing quality of the parallel algorithm compares favorably with the routing results of very good global routers. Furthermore, there is no degradation in routing quality when we go from a single-processor implementation to one using multiple processors. In addition, very good speedups are achieved (for example, >6 for eight processors). Since the hierarchical decomposition creates a large number of tasks after the first few steps, this algorithm is scalable to a large numbers of processors.

4.13 HARDWARE ACCELERATORS

Numerous attempts have been made to speed up the routing problem using hardware accelerators, many of them are based on variants of the Lee-Moore routing algorithm [13, 17]. Some are based on array processors, and others are based on pipelined processors.

TABLE 4.6 Runtimes (seconds) and Routing Quality of Parallel Algorithm on the Encore Multimax™ Multiprocessor

		1 processor		8 processors	
			Runtime		Runtime
Circuit	Nets	Tracks	(speedup)	Tracks	(speedup)
Primary1	1185	177	66 (1.0)	177	14 (4.7)
X1	1979	416	202 (1.0)	416	36 (5.6)
Primary2	3710	404	257 (1.0)	404	42 (6.1)
X2	3013	515	284 (1.0)	515	44 (6.5)

Adshead has discussed the implementation of the Lee-Moore routing algorithm on the ICL Distributed Array processor which is composed of a 64×64 one-bit processing elements connected as a rectangular mesh [1]. Blank et al. have developed the Virtual Bit Mapped Processor, which is a hardware implementation of a three-dimensional array of a binary 1-bit data structure [3] on which the same routing algorithm was implemented. Watanabe et al. have proposed the AAP-1 processor architecture which is a 256×256 array of 1-bit processors connected as an octagonal mesh [28]. Venkateswaran and Mazumder have proposed a hexagonal array of processors to perform multilayer routing [27].

Sahni and Won have proposed an architecture consisting of three processors in a pipeline [26]. Shamsa and Breuer have proposed another pipelined hardware architecture for such a router [4]. Finally, Rutenbar et al. have proposed the use of a 10-processor pipelined processor, originally designed for image-processing tasks, to perform routing [24].

4.14 SUMMARY

In this chapter we have discussed several parallel algorithms for global and detailed routing. Since these problems are NP complete to begin with, heuristic approaches are used to solve such problems. Newer heuristics are being continually developed. We have discussed some approaches to develop parallel algorithms for some of the better known heuristics for these applications for shared memory MIMD multiprocessors and distributed memory MIMD multicomputers.

We described parallel algorithms for detailed maze routing and detailed line routing using different grid partitioning strategies. The algorithms are suitable for both shared memory and distributed memory MIMD machines. The advantage of the maze routing algorithm is that it is guaranteed to determine the shortest path for a given two-terminal net. Excellent speedups can be obtained on this algorithm since it naturally scales with the number of processors. The main disadvantage of this algorithm is its enormous memory requirement since we need to store the state of every grid point of the routing grid, which for large chips can be an extremely large number. The other disadvantages of this algorithm are (1) the order of routing the nets is very important to the solution quality and (2) multiple terminal nets are not easy to handle. The line routing algorithm minimizes memory and computation requirements at the cost of giving up on the routing quality.

We described several parallel algorithms for channel routing. The advantage of these algorithms is that they handle the problem of net routing simultaneously. The algorithm based on simulated annealing gives good quality of the routing solution and excellent speedups; however, the sequential algorithm takes a very large amount of runtime. Hence even after running the algorithm on multiple processors, its runtime is slower compared to the best serial algorithms.

The parallel channel routing algorithm based on the greedy track assignment by columns basically partitions the channel region by column separators and routes each region independently. The choice of the columns for separating the regions is determined at the points of maximum channel density. This might give rise to load imbalances in the parallel algorithm. Also, by solving the channel routing problem independently, there is no guarantee that the nets will be assigned to the same tracks on the boundaries. When such a solution cannot be found, the algorithm uses the assumption of 45-degree bends at the boundaries to change tracks. Such a technology may not be allowed.

The parallel channel routing algorithm based on hierarchical decomposition creates two-by-N routing tasks recursively and solves each task on a processor. The algorithm has the advantage of giving good routing solutions, and the quality of the solution does not degrade with increasing number of processors. However, the disadvantage is that the task graph is a binary tree and, in the beginning, many processors remain idle since not enough tasks exist. Hence, the speedup using this algorithm is not very high.

We described a parallel algorithm for switchbox routing based on conflict resolution and iterative improvement. The algorithm assigned each net to a different processor and routed each net independently. Conflicts in the routing were resolved and corrected by an iterative improvement phase. The parallel algorithm gave no degradation of quality with the increased number of processors and gave reasonably good speedups.

We discussed several parallel algorithms for global routing. The parallel algorithms using graph search use a wave expansion algorithm similar to maze routing on a coarse routing grid to determine approximate routing assignments. The routing grid is partitioned among the processors using different methods. The advantage of the algorithm is that it gives very good routing quality and excellent speedups. The disadvantage of the algorithm is that the sequential algorithm takes a large computing time; hence, the runtimes on parallel processors are still quite large.

The parallel algorithm for global routing using iterative improvement considers a subset of possibilities for routing nets (L-shaped and a few Z-shaped layouts) and routes multiple wires simultaneously. The advantages are that the runtimes are quite low and excellent speedups are obtained. However, the routing quality is not as good, and the routing quality degrades slightly with increasing number of processors.

The parallel algorithm for global routing using hierarchical decomposition essentially divides the global routing problem on a grid into 2×2 subregions and solves the routing tasks recursively in a top-down manner. The advantages of the algorithm are that the runtimes are quite low and the routing quality is reasonably good. There is no degradation in routing quality with increasing number of processors. The speedups are reasonably good since, even though the task graph is in the form of a tree and at the top of the task graph there are not many tasks to keep the processors busy, the task graph expands very quickly and creates enough work for the later stages of the algorithm to effectively use all processors.

We end this chapter making the following observations. The problems with parallel algorithms for routing are similar to the problems with parallel placement algorithms discussed in Chapter 3. Many parallel algorithms produce inferior quality results with increasing number of processors. This is often not acceptable. Continuing research in the area will investigate the use of parallel processing such that the quality of the solutions is at least equal to if not better than the quality of uniprocessor solutions.

Second, every year better and better sequential heuristics are being discovered for routing, which improve on previous methods in terms of quality of routes produced and runtimes. Unless the parallel algorithms can be designed such that these newer efficient techniques can be rapidly incorporated into the parallel implementations, the latter will become rapidly obsolete in terms of practical use.

It is perhaps important to investigate frameworks for parallel routing algorithms that will allow researchers and developers to rapidly incorporate the best sequential routing heuristics and cost functions into the parallel algorithms. Hence the research in parallel routing algorithms should probably be directed to investigating good decomposition strategies for partitioning large routing problems into smaller independent or dependent routing subproblems, each of which may be solved in parallel by the best sequential routing algorithms.

4.15 PROBLEMS

4.1   Construct a routing grid of 20×20 points. Assume that the points on the two-dimensional grid addressed as (i, j), where $0 < i, j < 21$. Consider the following net connections. Net 1 connects $(5, 1)$ to $(8, 10)$. Net 2 connects $(2, 6)$ to $(12, 4)$. Net 3 connects $(1, 2)$ to $(15, 6)$ and $(4, 17)$. Net 4 connects $(2, 4)$ to $(5, 9)$. Apply the parallel maze routing algorithm to perform routing of the grid assuming one layer of routing on 16 processors, where each processor gets a block of 5×5 array of points.

4.2   In Figure 4.7 we discussed two different grid mapping strategies for the parallel maze routing algorithm. Analyze the performance of the parallel algorithm and determine optimal values of parameters w and h of the two dimensional cyclic distribution. Assume some distribution of the terminals of nets and a ratio α of computation to communication cost for the parallel architecture.

4.3   Design and implement the shared memory parallel maze routing algorithm *SM-PARALLEL-MAZE-ROUTING* on a shared memory multiprocessor. Use the Sequent runtime library described in Chapter 2. Consider various forms of load balancing and scheduling of routing tasks, static blocked, static interleaved, and dynamic grid.

4.4   Analyze the performance of the shared memory parallel hierarchical channel routing algorithm *SM-PARALLEL-ROUTING-HIERARCHY*. Assume that each node in the hierarchical task graph takes time proportional to the number of nets in that partition. Assume you have N nets and P processors.

4.5   Design and implement a shared memory parallel algorithm for channel routing using simulated annealing based on the algorithm *DM-PARALLEL-CHANNEL-ROUTING-SA*. Assume that each processor owns some rows and its nets, but can move the nets to any other row in the channel during a move. Investigate static and dynamic mapping of nets and rows to processors.

4.6   Design a distributed memory version of the parallel global routing algorithm for global routing using the graph search approach, *SM-PARALLEL-GLOBAL-ROUTING-GRAPHSEARCH*. Implement this algorithm on a distributed memory message-passing multicomputer such as an Intel iPSC hypercube. Use the Intel iPSC message-passing library discussed in Chapter 2.

4.7   Analyze the performance of the parallel global routing algorithm using iterative improvement, *SM-PARALLEL-ROUTING-ITERATIVE-WIREBASED*. Assume you have N wires, each of which has T terminals on the average, and P processors. Assume some uniform distribution of the positions of terminals on the chip area. Analyze the cases for wire-based and segment-based parallelism.

4.8   Implement the distributed memory parallel algorithm for global routing using an iterative improvement approach and exploiting the wire-based parallelism, *DM-PARALLEL-ROUTING-ITERATIVE-WIREBASED*. Use the Intel iPSC message-passing library described in Chapter 2.

4.9   Compare the performances of the two variants of the parallel hierarchical global routing algorithm, *SM-PARALLEL-ROUTING-HIERARCHICAL*, that use minimal and maximal decompositions respectively, Assume N nets and P processors and that the computation task corresponding to a node in the hierarchical task graph is proportional to the number of nets.

4.10 Consider the distributed memory parallel algorithm for global routing using iterative improvement and wire based parallelism, *DM-PARALLEL-ROUTING-ITERATIVE-WIREBASED*. A key component of this parallel algorithm is the decision regarding how to update the cost array. Analyze the performance of the sender initiated and receiver initiated updates. Assume you have N wires, each of which has T terminals on the average, and P processors. Assume some uniform distribution of the positions of terminals on the chip area. Assume some ratio of computation to communication in the parallel machine.

4.16 REFERENCES

[1]   H. G. Adshead. Employing a Distributed Array Processor in a Dedicated Gate Array Layout System. *IEEE Int. Conf. Circuits Computers*, pages 411–414, Sept. 1982.

[2]   S. Akers. Routing. In M. A. Breuer, editor, *Design Automation of Digital Systems: Theory and Techniques*, volume 1, pages 283–333. Prentice Hall, Englewood Cliffs, NJ, 1972.

[3]   T. Blank, M. Stefik, and W. vanCleemput. A Parallel Bit Map Architecture for DA Algorithms. *Proc. 18th Design Automation Conf.*, pages 837–845, June 1981.

[4]   M. A. Breuer and K. Shamsa. A Hardware Router. *J. Digital Systems*, 4(4):393–408, 1980.

[5]   R. Brouwer and P. Banerjee. A Parallel Simulated Annealing Algorithm for Channel Routing on a Hypercube Multiprocessor. *Proc. Int. Conf. Computer Design (ICCD-88)*, pages 4–7, Oct. 1988.

[6]   R. J. Brouwer. Parallel Algorithms for Placement and Routing in VLSI Design. Technical Report Ph.D. Thesis, CRHC-91-2, Coordinated Science Lab, University of Illinois, Urbana, IL, Feb. 1991.

[7]   R. J. Brouwer and P. Banerjee. PHIGURE:A Parallel Hierarchical Global Router. *Proc. 27th Design Automation Conf.*, pages 360–364, June 1990.

[8]   M. Burstein and R. Pelavin. Hierarchical Channel Router. *Proc. 20th Design Automation Conf.*, pages 591–597, June 1983.

[9]   M. Burstein and R. Pelavin. Hierarchical wire routing. *IEEE Trans. Computer-aided Design Integrated Circuits Systems*, CAD-2, no. 4:223–234, Oct. 1983.

[10]   T. W. Cho, S. S. Pyo, and J. R. Heath. PARALLEX: A Parallel Approach to Switchbox Routing. *IEEE Trans. Computer-aided Design Integrated Circuits Systems*, 1994 (to appear).

[11]   A. Hashimoto and J. Stevens. Wire Routing by Optimizing Channel Assignment. *Proc. 8th Design Automation Conf.*, pages 214–224, June 1971.

[12]   D. W. Hightower. A Solution to the Line Routing Problem on a Continuous Plane. *Proc. 6th Design Automation Workshop*, pages 1–24, June 1969.

[13]   C. Lee. An Algorithm for Path Connections and its Applications. *IRE Trans. Electronic Computers*, VEC-10:346–365, Sept. 1961.

[14]   H. W. Leong, D. F. Wong, and C. L. Liu. A Simulated Annealing Channel Router. *Proc. 22nd Design Automation Conf.*, pages 226–228, June 1985.

[15]   M. Martonosi and A. Gupta. Tradeoffs in Message Passing and Shared Memory Implementations of a Standard Cell Router. *Proc. Int. Conf. Parallel Processing (ICPP89)*, III:88–96, Aug. 1989.

[16]   K. Mikami and K. Tabuchi. A Computer Program for Optimal Routing of Printed Circuit Board Connections. *IFIPS Proc.*, H47:1475–1478, 1968.

[17]   E. F. Moore. The Shortest Path through a Maze. *Annals of the Computation Laboratory of Harvard University*, 30:285–292, 1959.

[18]   R. Nair, S. J. Hong, S. Liles, and R. Villani. Global Wiring on a Wire Routing Machine. *Proc. 19th Design Automation Conf.*, pages 224–231, June 1982.

[19]   O. A. Olukotun and T. N. Mudge. A Preliminary Investigation into Parallel Routing on a Hypercube. *Proc. Design Automation Conf.*, pages 814–820, June 1987.

[20]   B. Preas and M. Lorenzetti. *Physical Design Automation of VLSI Systems*. Benjamin-Cummings Publishing Co., Menlo Park, CA, 1988.

[21]   R. L. Rivest and C. M. Fidducia. A Greedy Channel Router. *Proc. 19th Design Automation Conf.*, pages 418–424, June 1982.

[22]   J. Rose. Locusroute: A Parallel Global Router for Standard Cells. *Proc. Design Automation Conf.*, pages 189–195, June 1988.

[23]   J. Rose. Parallel Global Routing for Standard Cells. *IEEE Trans. Computer-aided Design Integrated Circuits Systems*, pages 1085–1095, Oct. 1990.

[24]   R. A. Rutenbar, T. N. Mudge, and D. E. Atkins. A Class of Cellular Architectures to Support Physical Design Automation. *IEEE Trans. Computer-aided Design Integrated Circuits Systems of Circuits and Systems*, CAD-3(4):264–278, Oct. 1984.

[25]   Y. Saad and M. H. Schultz. Topological Properties of Hypercubes. *IEEE Trans. Computers*, 37, No. 7:867–872, July 1988.

[26]   S. Sahni and Y. Won. A Hardware Accelerator for Maze Routing. *Proc. Design Automation Conf.*, pages 800–806, June 1987.

[27]   R. Venkateswaran and P. Mazumder. A Hexagonal Array Machine for Multi-Layer Wire Routing. *IEEE Trans. Computer-aided Design Integrated Circuits Systems*, CAD-9(10):1096–1112, Oct. 1990.

[28]   T. Watanabe, H. Kitazawa, and Y. Sugiyama. A Parallel Adaptable Routing Algorithm and its Implementation on a Two Dimensional Array Processor. *IEEE Trans. Computer-aided Design Integrated Circuits Systems*, CAD-6(2):241–250, Mar. 1987.

[29]   Y. Won and S. Sahni. Maze Routing on a Hypercube Multiprocessor Computer. *Proc. Int. Conf. Parallel Processing*, pages 630–637, Aug. 1987.

[30]   I. L. Yen, R. M. Dubash, and F. B. Bastani. Strategies for Mapping Lee's Maze Routing Algorithm onto Parallel Architectures. Technical report, Michigan State University, East Lansing, MI, 1993.

[31]   M. R. Zargham. Parallel Channel Routing. *Proc. Design Automation Conf.*, pages 128–133, June 1988.

CHAPTER 5

Layout Verification and Analysis

5.1 INTRODUCTION

Integrated circuit artwork depicts a layout as a collection of polygons of various shades or colors corresponding to different mask levels in the fabrication process. Figure 5.1 shows the layout of an inverter in CMOS technology. Layout verification determines whether the polygons that represent different mask layers in the chip conform to the technology specifications. Layout analysis obtains circuit information about the actual circuit implemented by the chip layout. Both layout verification and analysis perform large amounts of computation on the polygons representing the mask layers.

In this chapter, we will discuss parallel algorithms for applications dealing with layout verification and analysis. Three kinds of layout verification and analysis tools will be discussed: design rule checking, netlist extraction, and parameter extraction.

Design rule checkers detect violations of rules that govern the technology in which the chip is to be fabricated. A circuit extractor determines the circuit implemented by the chip layout and estimates various electrical parameters, such as the resistances of lines, capacitances of nodes, and dimensions of devices. There are two phases in circuit extraction. The first phase is the identification of devices, the determination of electrically connected regions (called nets). This phase is called *netlist extraction*. The second phase involves the estimation of the electrical parameters of nets and devices. This phase is called *parameter extraction*. The output of an extractor can be fed into a circuit, switch or logic level simulator.

The chapter is organized as follows. Sections 5.2 through 5.6 deal with design rule

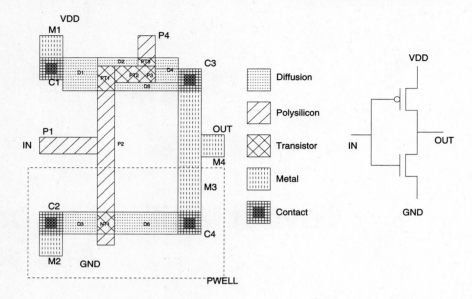

Figure 5.1 Example layout of inverter in CMOS technology

checking, Sections 5.7 through 5.9 with netlist extraction, Sections 5.10 through 5.12 with parameter extraction. For each problem we open the discussion with a description of the problem and outline the different parallel algorithmic approaches. Within each approach, there is a brief description of the sequential algorithm, followed by descriptions of parallel algorithms for shared or distributed memory MIMD machines or SIMD machines. Section 5.13 describes hardware accelerators that have been proposed for the layout verification and analysis problems. Finally, Section 5.14 concludes with remarks about promising parallel algorithms for layout verification and analysis problems.

5.2 DESIGN RULE CHECKING PROBLEM

The goal of design rule checking is to detect possible inconsistencies between the layout of the integrated circuit and the design rules that have been specified for a particular process. Typical rules specify minimum spacing between lines, minimum separation between lines, and maximum extension of one layer over another to form an active element [39] as shown in Figure 5.2. Design rule checkers perform simple Boolean operations, (AND, OR, XOR) on a set of geometrical shapes which are in most cases rectangles, tagged with an identifier of the corresponding mask layer. The logic operations are based on the elementary operation of detecting the intersection between sets of rectangles. The computational complexity of DRC programs is not due to the intrinsic complexity of each operation but to large number of parts in the layout. Assuming an average number of 10 pieces of geometry for any active component, that is a transistor, a chip with 1 million transistors will have about 10 million rectangles. A naive DRC algorithm checking for all possible interaction of all the N^2 pairs of rectangles would execute 10^{14} pairwise comparisons. The efficiency of a DRC program

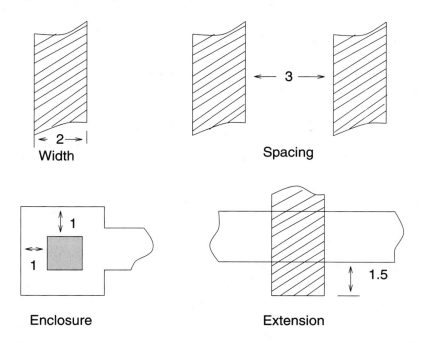

Figure 5.2 Typical design rules in VLSI layouts (Courtesy of Szymanski and Van Wyk, *Layout Analysis and Verification*, chapter in *Physical Design Automation of VLSI Systems*, Preas and Lorenzetti: Editors, Benjamin Cummings, 1988)

depends on the algorithm on which it is based and on how the layout is represented.

The first way to describe a layout is to explicitly specify all the rectangles in the circuit at all the mask layers; this is called the flattened representation. The second type uses a hierarchical representation approach by which in addition to the ability to specify elemental geometries, a set of geometries can be grouped into a symbol, often representing a logic function like a memory cell. Symbol calls can be nested in higher-level definitions of symbols providing a tool for structured design.

In the following subsections, we will describe parallel algorithms for design rule checking using several approaches.

- Area decomposition approach on flattened circuits

- Hierarchical decomposition approach on hierarchical circuits

- Functional decomposition approach on flattened and hierarchical circuits

- Edge decomposition approach on flattened circuits

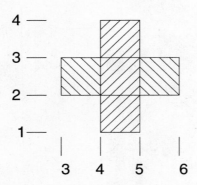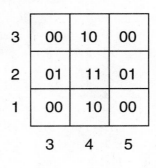

Figure 5.3 A two layer layout represented by a pixelmap (Courtesy of Szymanski and Van Wyk, *Layout Analysis and Verification*, chapter in *Physical Design Automation of VLSI Systems*, Preas and Lorenzetti: Editors, Benjamin Cummings, 1988)

5.3 AREA PARTITIONED DESIGN RULE CHECKING

5.3.1 Overview

In this section we will describe a parallel algorithm for design rule checking on flattened circuits using an area decomposition approach that is suitable for execution on distributed memory and shared memory MIMD parallel machines.

We will now describe some sequential algorithms for performing DRC on flattened layouts for which the entire chip layout is specified in terms of rectangles (can be generalized to polygons) at mask layouts. There are three commonly used geometric representations of mask layout data. The first is the polygon representation in which every polygon of every mask layer is represented as a list of vertices with their x, y coordinates. This representation takes $O(N)$ memory space where N is the number of vertices. Despite the advantages of this representation, computations on these polygons are expensive. To determine any design rule violation such as a spacing check, for each polygon edge we have to search all other polygon edges for proximity, an operation that takes $O(N^2)$ time.

The second mask representation is the pixelmap (also called bitmap or raster) representation which is used to define regions in terms of integer x and y coordinates in a lambda grid (where lambda is a technology independent scalable minimum feature size). Position *(x,y)* in the pixelmap corresponds to a unit cell or pixel $[x, x + 1] \times [y, y + 1]$ in the plane. Each pixel contains several bits, each of which corresponds to a mask layer. The value of a bit is 1 if the corresponding pixel is covered by a region in the corresponding mask layer or 0 if it is not. Figure 5.3 shows an example two mask layer layout and its corresponding pixelmap representation [39]. Baker developed a raster-scan-based algorithm [2] for design rule checking on this lambda grid by noting that all design rule checks are local in nature and can be performed on a $(k + 1) \times (k + 1)$ window for which the maximum design rule magnitude is k. (For example, if the maximum design rule is 3λ for a CMOS design, a 4×4 window is sufficient). This window scans the bitmap such that each pixel appears in every position of the window. To discover width and spacing violations of width λ, a 3×3 window is sufficient. Each pattern of 1s and 0s in the 3×3 window can be characterized as legal or erroneous. Figure 5.4 shows some example patterns of legal and illegal designs on the bitmap. The patterns are classified by a parameter called the alternation number A, which equals the number of transitions from 0 to 1, and from 1 to 0 in the bit sequence in the perimeter. Thus if the perimeter contains 01011011, then $A = 6$. With a 1 in the center, this indicates a wire of insufficient width passing through the region (assuming that wires have to be at least 2λ wide); hence it constitutes an error. For the pattern $A = 2$, it corresponds to wires of width 1 poking into the region, which is not a violation; hence it is a legal pattern.

The design rule checking algorithm is table driven. The disadvantage of this algorithm is that it reports false errors since it does not have knowledge of the electrical connectivity of the component parts. It is therefore necessary to combine circuit extraction and analysis with design rule checking. A simpler method, which eliminates most of the false reportings, is to use a larger 10×10 window for connectivity in the neighborhood of any 4×4 window that checked an error in the first place. Another major disadvantage of this algorithm is the tremendous memory requirements, which grow as $0(k^2)$ for a $k \times k$ grid representation of a circuit.

The third representation of mask layouts is in the form of an edge-based representation that uses a list of edges of the polygons. However, the edges are not stored around the boundary of each polygon but are rearranged and tagged with useful information. We will describe a scheme for Manhattan rectangles (where edges of rectangles are parallel to the X and Y axes), but the scheme can be extended for arbitrary polygons. The masks of a Manhattan geometry can be represented by horizontal edges only because the vertical edges can be reconstructed if we store whether the regions above and below each edge represent opaque or transparent parts of the relevant mask. The scan line data structure only requires $(O\sqrt{N})$ space, where N is the number of edges and most operations can be performed in $O(\log(\sqrt{N}))$ time.

We will now describe a sequential algorithm for performing design rule checking based on the scan line algorithm [26, 40]. We first sort the rectangles (represented by the edges) in the circuit along the minimum x coordinate. The basic idea of a scan line algorithm is to sweep a virtual vertical line across the individual edges comprising a mask. Only those edges that encounter the scanline need to be considered at a time. At any scan line stop (a term used to refer to a particular scan line location), the rectangles whose left end points touch the scan line are taken from the sorted list and added to the scanline data structure. This is illustrated in Figure 5.5. For each rectangle R added, the rectangles in the scan line data structure that overlap or abut it are determined. This is used to perform the different Boolean mask operations. In the figure, at the current position of the scan line, the rectangles C, E, D, B, and G are present in the scan line data structure; hence, we need only check for overlap, width, and separation violations among these rectangles. If an abutting or overlapping rectangle P is in a layer that electrically connects to R's layer, then R and P are determined to be in the same net. It is possible to also check for width, spacing or extension violations by checking distance violations in the vertical direction within each scan line and the horizontal direction across scan lines. Within a scan line, for each edge we can simply check the distance to the first edge below it, and then the second edge below it, and so on, until we search up to the prescribed design rule distance. For horizontal distance violations, for each edge on some source scan

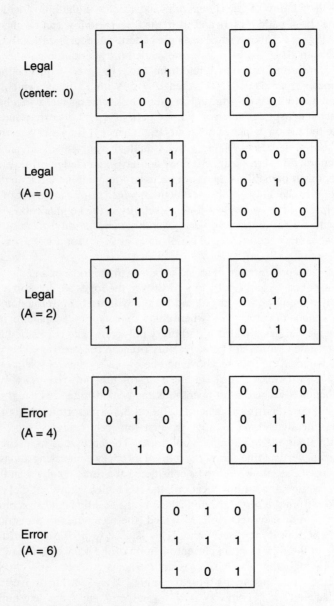

Figure 5.4 Typical 3×3 windows in DRC algorithm (Courtesy of Mukherjee, *Introduction to nMOS and CMOS VLSI Systems Design*, Prentice Hall., 1986)

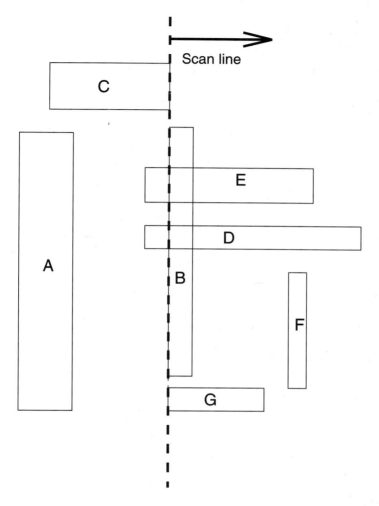

Figure 5.5 A scan line moving left to right

line we can check against nearby edges in a different target scan line. Each source scan line first checks its eastward neighbor, then its eastward neighbor two scan lines away, and so on, up to the relevant design rule distance.

5.3.2 Distributed Memory MIMD Parallel Algorithm

We will now describe a parallel algorithm for design rule checking proposed by Bier and Pleszkun [13] which works on the flattened representation of mask layouts and uses an area decomposition strategy; that is, the rectangles (polygons) of a particular area of the chip are distributed to various processors of a parallel processor, and each processor performs a complete set of design rule checks on its own allocated set of rectangles (polygons). The algorithm is independent of the internal geometric representation of the sequential algorithm and can work on either the polygon, the pixelmap, or the edge-based representations.

In any set of design rules, there is a maximum design rule interaction distance (DRID) that is equal to the size of the largest constraint placed on the layout. If a design rule error exists between any two coordinates, it must be less than or equal to this value. If we partition a fully expanded design by drawing a vertical line through it and then check each half separately, many errors will be introduced and missed because of this cut as shown in Figure 5.6. However, all errors reported one DRID from the cut in either half are still correct because the missing geometry across the cut is too far away to interact. Thus the problem with the simple cut is discovering real errors within one DRID on either side of the cut. A solution is to introduce an overlap while cutting. This overlap must be equal to or greater than one DRID on either side of the midpoint. Checking is performed on each half plus the overlap of one DRID. Again errors will be missed or introduced by the cut. To take care of this, an extra step is performed after checking, which assumes that all errors introduced inside the overlap are not real errors and removes them. The completed error file contains only the errors for its half of the design, exclusive of the errors in the overlap region, as shown in Figure 5.6.

The extension of this technique to parallel processors is to partition a layout file into as many vertical slices as desired. Each slice is overlapped with its neighboring slice within one DRID distance. Each slice is checked independently on a separate processor without any need for communication among the slices. The postprocessing of removing extraneous errors can be done as soon as each individual processor returns its error file.

An outline of the parallel routing algorithm entitled *DM-PARALLEL-DRC-AREA* (for distributed memory parallel design rule checking using area decomposition) follows.

Procedure *DM-PARALLEL-DRC-AREA;*

    Read flattened mask layout;
    Partition mask layout description by vertical slices
       using an overlap of DRID on each partition;
    FORALL processors in PARALLEL DO
       Perform design rule checking on own partition
          Use polygon, or pixelmap or scan line edge-based method;
       Report errors for partition;
    END FORALL
    Perform postprocessing to remove errors in overlap regions;

End Procedure

Implementation The preceding parallel algorithm has been implemented by Bier and Pleszkun [13] on the CRYSTAL™ multiprocessor, an experimental distributed memory multiprocessor developed at the University of Wisconsin. The underlying design rule checking programs were based on CAESAR™ and LYRA™. A CUTTER program performed the creation of the partitions with the overlaps equal to the DRID distance. The speedups observed by the authors

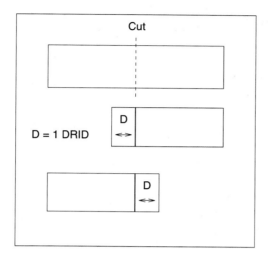

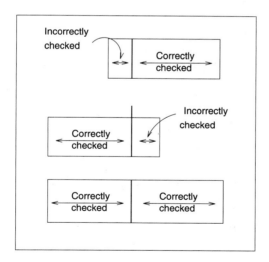

Figure 5.6 Concept of DRID and removing error reports from overlap regions (Courtesy of Bier and Pleszkun, *Proc. Design Automation Conf.,* ©IEEE 1985)

were about 8 on a 14 processor multiprocessor for various chip layouts. The speedups were not linear due to load imbalance problems across the vertical slices; that is, different slices of equal area had varying numbers of rectangles due to the variation of the device density across the layout.

5.3.3 Shared Memory MIMD Parallel Algorithm

The preceding algorithm can be easily extended to a shared memory multiprocessor environment, where the given layout is stored in a shared memory. The given layout can be partitioned into a larger number of vertical slices than the number of processors for more efficient load balance. The tasks corresponding to each vertical slice can be kept in a shared memory task queue, from where the next idle processors can fetch the tasks and copy the vertical slices to the processor's local memory (cache). At the end of the DRC tasks on each slice, the postprocessing tasks are started for each of the $N - 1$ intermediate boundaries of the N slices. Again these tasks can be kept in a shared workspace.

An outline of the parallel routing algorithm entitled *SM-PARALLEL-DRC-DATA* (for shared memory parallel design rule checking using data decomposition) is given next.

Procedure *SM-PARALLEL-DRC-DATA;*

> Read flattened mask layout;
> Partition mask layout description by N vertical slices
>> using an overlap of DRID on each partition;
> Partition into more partitions than number of processors;
> Create a task queue of mask partitions;
> FORALL processors in PARALLEL DO
>> WHILE there are tasks in the task queue DO
>>> Pick a DRC task from task queue under lock;
>>> Perform design rule checking on own partition
>>>> Use polygon, or pixelmap or scan line edge-based method;
>>> Report errors for partition;
>> END WHILE
> END FORALL
> Create postprocessing tasks for N-1 intermediate slices;
> WHILE there are postprocessing tasks in queue DO
>> Perform postprocessing task;
> END WHILE;

End Procedure

No implementations of this shared memory algorithm have been reported in the literature.

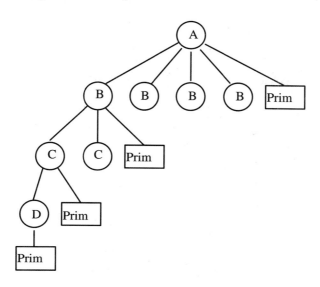

Figure 5.7 Use of hierarchy to represent layout

5.4 HIERARCHICAL DESIGN RULE CHECKING

5.4.1 Overview

In this section we will describe a parallel algorithm for design rule checking using a hierarchical decomposition approach.

The efficiency of a DRC program depends on the algorithm on which it is based and on how the layout is represented. The first way to describe a layout is to explicitly specify all the rectangles in the circuit at all the mask layers; this is called the flattened representation. The second type uses a hierarchical representation approach in which in addition to the ability to specify elemental geometries, a set of geometries can be grouped into a symbol, often representing a logic function like a memory cell. Symbol calls can be nested in higher-level definitions of symbols, providing a tool for structured design. Figure 5.7 shows an example of a hierarchically specified layout.

Design rule checking (DRC) programs that operate on the flattened description require large amounts of memory. Besides, hiding the regularity of a layout often leads to unnecessary repetition of the DRC operations and also to a meaningless amount of repeated reporting of errors when an error occurs in an elementary component of a regular structure. DRC programs operating on a hierarchical representation reduce the complexity of such steps.

We now describe a sequential algorithm for design rule checking that works on a hierarchical description of the circuit. Bentley and Ottman have shown that the problem of detecting intersections in a hierarchically described set of rectangles is NP complete in the general case [12]. However, for IC layouts two restrictions apply that make the problem more tractable. First, the overlapping between instances of called symbols is generally low, and second, the nesting of a symbol call is in general limited to a maximum of seven to eight levels.

5.4.2 Shared Memory MIMD Parallel Algorithm

We now describe a shared memory MIMD parallel algorithm for hierarchical design rule checking based on the work of Gregoretti and Segall [22]. The algorithm uses a parallel bottom-up approach to the problem of finding all intersections in a hierarchical described layout. A hierarchical description of a layout comprises a set of tokens, and each token may be one of the following items: (1) the specification of a primitive rectangular element defined by the coordinates of its lower-left and upper-right corners edges are parallel to the X and Y axes (Manhattan rectangles), or (2) call to a symbol that has already been defined. Transformations like translation, mirroring, or rotation of multiples of 90 degrees may be applied to the symbol at calling time.

The parallel algorithm for hierarchical design rule checking (DRC) creates the following DRC tasks which are executed in parallel among various processors.

1. A *check symbol task, CHS(A),* checks the intersection between all tokens of a given symbol A. When it finds an intersection, if it is between two boxes, it reports it; when it is between two called symbols B and C, it queues a compare symbols $COS(B, C)$ request; if it is between a box b and a called symbol B, it queues a compare symbol with box, $CSB(b, B)$ request.

2. A *compare symbol task, COS(A,B),* expands each symbol, A and B, into its tokens and checks for the intersection between any token of the first symbol A and any token of the second one, B. When it finds an intersection, if it is between two boxes, it reports it; when it is between two called symbols C and D, it queues a compare symbols, $COS(C, D)$, request; if it is between a box b and a called symbol B, it queues a compare symbol with box, $CSB(b, B)$, request.

3. A *compare symbol to box task, CSB(b,B)* expands the symbol B into its tokens and checks for intersections between the box b and the tokens of the symbol B; when it finds an intersection, if it is between two boxes, it reports it; if it is between a box c and a called symbol C, it queues a compare symbol with box, $CSB(c, C)$, request.

Each processor fetches a request for the execution of one of three types of tasks from a common task queue. At the beginning, this queue is initialized with check symbol requests for all the symbols in the layout. During the analysis of a request a processor will, in general, produce other tasks requests, which are put in the common queue and executed by different processors. The parallel hierarchical algorithm is shown in Figure 5.8, where an 8-bit adder unit is checked hierarchically by checking the interactions among the two 4-bit adder subcomponents, and each 4-bit adder is checked at the interface of the two 2-bit adders, and so on, until finally, each 1-bit adder is checked in a flattened mode.

An outline of the parallel design rule checking algorithm entitled *SM-PARALLEL-DRC- HIERARCHY* (for shared memory parallel design rule checking using hierarchical decomposition) follows.

Procedure *SM-PARALLEL-DRC-HIERARCHY;*

    Read hierarchical mask design;
    FOR each unique cell A in hierarchical design DO
      Create a CheckSymbol(A) task;

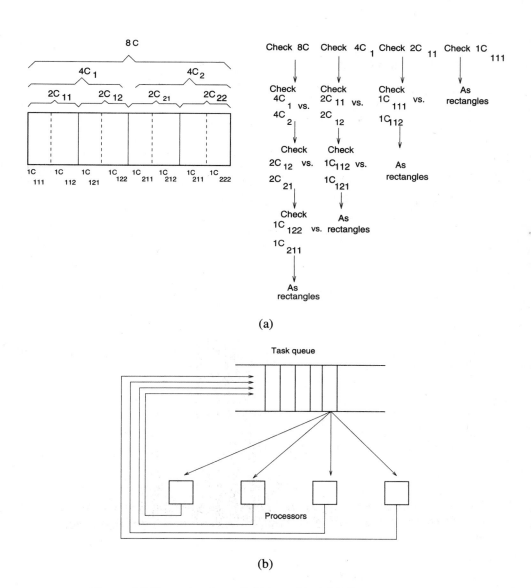

(a)

(b)

Figure 5.8 Example of parallel hierarchical DRC. (a) An example of hierarchical DRC on an 8-bit adder. (b) Task scheduling in parallel hierarchical DRC. (Courtesy of Gregoretti and Segall, *Proc. Int. Conf. Parallel Processing,* ©IEEE 1984)

```
        Insert task into task queue;
    END FOR;

    FORALL processors in PARALLEL DO
        WHILE there are tasks in the task queue DO
            Pick a DRC task from task queue under lock;
            IF TaskType = CheckSymbol(A) THEN
                Perform DRC on boxes and symbols within symbol A;
                IF both tokens are boxes
                    THEN perform regular DRC and report errors;
                IF symbol A has other symbols defined within
                THEN FOR each symbol B defined within A DO
                    Create CheckSymbol(B) task;
                    Insert task in task queue;
                    FOR each box inside A DO
                        Create CompareSymbolBox(B,box) task;
                        Insert task in task queue;
                    END FOR
                ENDIF
            ENDIF;
            IF TaskType = CompareSymbol(B,C) THEN
                Perform DRC between all tokens of B and C;
                Create other tasks if some tokens are symbols;
            ENDIF
            IF TaskType = CompareSymbolBox(A,box) THEN
                Perform DRC between box and tokens within A;
                Create other tasks if some tokens with A are symbols;
            ENDIF
        END WHILE
    END FORALL
```

End Procedure

Implementation Gregoretti and Segall [22] have reported an implementation of the preceding parallel algorithm on a 15-processor CM*™ shared memory multiprocessor, which was an experimental multiprocessor built at Carnegie Mellon University. Table 5.1 shows some example results on five benchmark circuits of the runtimes (in seconds) and the speedups on different numbers of processors.

5.5 FUNCTION PARTITIONED DESIGN RULE CHECKING

5.5.1 Overview

We will now describe an algorithm for design rule checking for flattened circuit descriptions using a different way of decomposing the problem,, that of functional decomposition of the

TABLE 5.1 Runtimes (seconds) and Speedups of Parallel Algorithm on the CM*™
Multiprocessor

Circuit	1 proc		15 proc	
	Runtime	Speedup	Runtime	Speedup
pads	12	1.0	2	6.0
slice	30	1.0	5	6.0
test	140	1.0	20	7.0
cherry	260	1.0	20	13.0
fifo	310	1.0	24	13.0

rules that need to be checked for among various processors. The algorithm that will be described next is applicable to any of the forms of geometric representations discussed earlier, namely the explicit polygon representation, the pixelmap representation, and the edge-based representation using scan lines.

5.5.2 Distributed Memory MIMD Parallel Algorithm

We will now describe a parallel algorithm for design rule checking that is based on functional task decomposition on flattened mask layouts and is suitable for execution on distributed memory MIMD multicomputers. The algorithm is based on work reported by Marantz [28]. The crucial observation made in this approach is that a design rule check does not entail the execution of a single algorithm but instead the sequential execution of many computationally independent algorithms, each corresponding to checking for a different design rule. Conceptually, there is no data dependency between the rules. Therefore each rule can be checked independently by a separate processor. This is not very efficient, because there are often intermediate computations that contribute to the checking of a rule, and the results of these computations are often used in the checking of more than one rule. We would like to perform these computations only once and share the results among all the processors that need them.

These intermediate computations are explicitly listed in the rules file of a DRC program such as DRACULA™ [43] that is used to control each DRC run. The rules are written in a language whose statements imply performing operations on various layers of the chip such as polysilicon and diffusion to create another layer. Some statements do logical operations such as pixel-wise AND and OR of two layers, producing new layers. Other statements check the spacing or width checks on a given layer at a given tolerance limit.

Each statement in the rules file can be mapped directly onto a sequence of operating system commands that causes the statement to be executed. By comparing the inputs and outputs of statements, we can determine the data dependency between the execution of the statements and hence build a data dependency graph. The data dependency graph has a set of roots or nodes whose input files are part of the input to the whole task, rather than outputs of another node. The computation begins at the roots and proceeds to other nodes, depending on the scheduling policy.

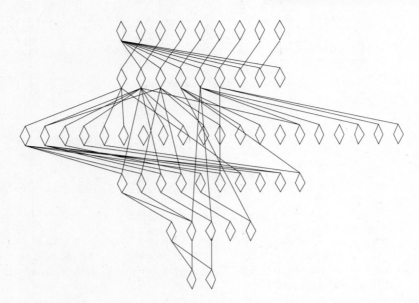

Figure 5.9 Data dependency graph of a DRC program for the MOSIS CMOS design rules (Courtesy of Marantz, *Proc. Int. Conf. Computer Design,* ©IEEE 1986)

The first step in such a functional decomposition approach is to divide the data dependence graph into levels or levels, as shown in Figure 5.9 for the MOSIS CMOS design rules. Each level contains all the nodes in the graph that have a given distance from the roots of the graph. The approach proceeds by executing nodes of a given level one at a time. Every node in the current level has to be completed before any node in the next level can start. This guarantees that data dependencies will not be violated. A drawback of this method is that if we have a set of inhomogeneous processors, at the end of execution of each level, the faster processors remain idle, while the slower processors finish up the tasks. Also, if a processor becomes overloaded after a task is assigned to it in a multiuser multiprogrammed environment, the entire DRC execution can become blocked.

The parallel algorithm can be implemented by having one master processor controlling the remaining slave processors. The master maintains a set of slaves to which it assigns tasks. Each slave can execute only one task at a time and can be in one of two states, busy or idle. Tasks are placed on the ready queue of a slave processor if all its predecessors have been computed. With a list of free slaves and a ready task queue, the master can control the computation by assigning ready tasks to free slaves until all the tasks are completed.

An outline of the parallel design rule checking algorithm entitled *DM-PARALLEL-DRC-FUNCTIONAL* (for distributed memory parallel design rule checking using functional decomposition) follows.

Procedure *DM-PARALLEL-DRC-FUNCTIONAL;*

Read mask description;
Assign one processor as Master and P-1 as Slaves;

FORALL processors in PARALLEL DO
IF Master processor THEN
    Read design rules;
    WHILE there are design rules left to be checked DO
        Pick design rule that is not dependent on any
            other design rule that has not yet been checked;
        Create a DRC task on entire mask;
        Send DRC task to task queue of particular
            Slave processor using static scheduling heuristics;
        IF any DRC tasks completed by any Slave
            THEN inform its dependent DRC tasks;
        END WHILE
    ENDFOR;
ENDIF (Master)

IF Slave processor THEN
WHILE NOT DONE DO
    WHILE there are tasks in the task queue DO
        Pick a DRC task from task queue if data dependencies met;
        Read flattened mask layout;
        Perform design rule checking on entire mask for that rule;
        Report errors;
        Inform Master that this DRC task is complete;
    END WHILE
END WHILE
END FORALL

End Procedure

Different static scheduling algorithms can be used for assigning the tasks onto processors to minimize the total execution time given the dependency graph. Even though the optimal task scheduling is an NP-complete problem, some heuristics have been proposed for solving it. The basic idea is to assign a priority to the ready tasks based on either the height or the size of the task. Both heuristics try to estimate the criticality of the task. The *height* measure estimates the minimum execution time for completion of the task assuming infinite processors. The *size* measure tries to include information about how many other tasks are waiting for the present task's completion. Figure 5.10 shows an example data dependency graph containing 12 nodes representing DRC operations and its scheduling on 4-processors (called A,B,C,D) using the height and size heuristics. It is shown in the figure that the *height* heuristic gives a completion time of five steps, whereas the *size* heuristic gives a completion time of six steps.

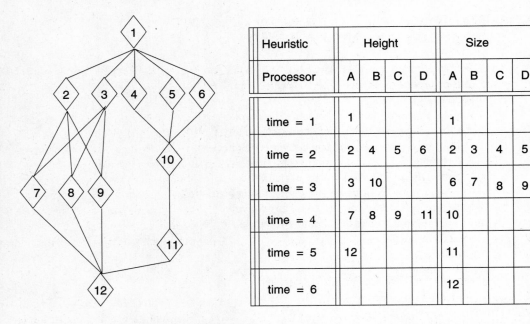

Heuristic	Height				Size			
Processor	A	B	C	D	A	B	C	D
time = 1	1				1			
time = 2	2	4	5	6	2	3	4	5
time = 3	3	10			6	7	8	9
time = 4	7	8	9	11	10			
time = 5	12				11			
time = 6					12			

Figure 5.10 DRC data dependency graph and its mapping on four processors (Courtesy of Marantz, *Proc. Int. Conf. Computer Design,* ©IEEE 1986)

Implementation Marantz developed the EPIC system which automatically generated parallel calls to the DRC programs in two parallel environments, a VAX cluster™ and distributed network of workstations [28]. The system that was developed provided a general method of controlling the execution of any program that can be divided into a finite set of tasks, which is defined as a unit of computation that can be executed using a sequence of standard operating system commands. Each task has a known finite set of inputs and outputs, each of which is a disk file. The strategy used for parallel DRC involves distributing the design rules to the various processors. Each processor applies its subset of rules to the whole chip. The extent of parallelism is limited by the data dependencies within the task list and by the relative time spent between input/output and computation of the DRC rules.

Both the heuristics were implemented on a three processor VAX cluster™ and a six processor network of computers; speedups of about 2.6 were observed on a the three processor VAX cluster, and speedups of 4.1 were observed on six processors of a network while performing DRC using the MOSIS CMOS design rules on some example circuits.

A major limitation of this approach is in the limited parallelism achievable through functional decomposition. To get larger speedups it is essential to perform data decomposition, that is, perform DRC on portions of the chip layout. Another drawback of this approach is that the static scheduling algorithm assumes that each task takes the same amount of time. This is an unrealistic assumption since different DRC rules take different amounts of time on various chip layout distributions.

5.6 EDGE PARTITIONED DESIGN RULE CHECKING

5.6.1 Overview

In this section we will describe a parallel algorithm for design rule checking using an edge-based decomposition approach that is suitable for execution on SIMD massively parallel machines.

We will first discuss a sequential algorithm for performing design rule checking on flattened mask representations based on the scan line algorithm [26, 40]. The basic idea of a scan line algorithm is to sweep a virtual vertical line across the individual edges comprising a mask. Only those edges that encounter the scan line need to be considered. By maintaining appropriate state information between successive scan line locations, most of the actual checking operations simply involve stepping through the active edges on the scan line in the appropriate order. The original scan line algorithm is inherently sequential, since one scan line must be completely checked before its successor can be started because both the location of the next scan line stop and the set of edges intercepted by this next stop are determined by computations done in the previous scan line.

5.6.2 Massively Parallel SIMD Algorithm

We will now describe a massively parallel SIMD algorithm for the preceding sequential scan-line-based algorithm for design rule checking on flattened representations. The algorithm is based on work reported by Carlson and Rutenbar [15, 17]. The parallel algorithm involves the determination of *all* scan line stops in parallel at the start of the checking and then processing all the scan lines in parallel. This approach increases the amount of work required to be done by making more edges to handle, but exposes more parallelism. The phases in the parallel algorithm are as follows.

The first phase is to generate *complete edge intersections*. A set of edges is said to be completely intersected if all edge intersections occur at edge end points. This form is attractive because it eliminates the need to check for edge intersections as possible locations where the scan line must stop to examine edges. The edges that cross a scan line stop are also split at the point of intersection, generating twice as many edges. Figure 5.11 shows the complete intersections of mask layers for a layout of a CMOS inverter. This is accomplished in parallel by assigning an edge to a processor. The edges are sorted in order of the minimum X coordinate and are mapped onto consecutively numbered processors. Next, each processor examines its own X coordinate and the X coordinate of its higher numbered neighbor. All edges with a common minimum X coordinate are determined to be scan line stops in parallel. The next step is to split all the edges that cross one of these unique scan line stops. Each edge in each scan line can determine in parallel if it crosses its neighboring scan line, and those edges that do are split at the X value and the newly created edge is sent to a new processor. These steps are repeated until no scan line holds an edge that can possibly intersect the X location of any other scan line.

The second phase is performing the Boolean operations such as unions, intersections, and complements for mask layers to generate new mask layers. This can be done in parallel on each scan line. This is shown in Figure 5.12. Also, all edges within each scan line can be processed simultaneously. The basic idea for processing each scan line is to assign to each

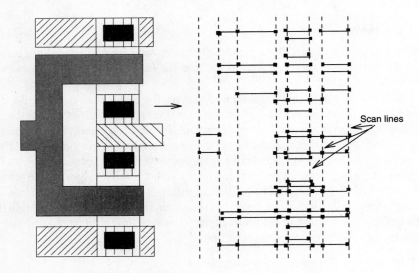

Figure 5.11 Complete intersections of mask layers (Courtesy of Carlson and Rutenbar, *Proc. Design Automation Conf.*, ©IEEE 1988)

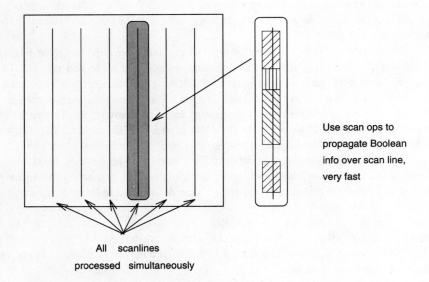

Figure 5.12 Parallel Boolean mask operations (Courtesy of Carlson and Rutenbar, *Proc. Design Automation Conf.*, ©IEEE 1988)

edge on each layer a direction that can be used to determine the opaque and transparent regions between edges on a scan line using counters for edges [26]. Boolean operations on regions are transformed into Boolean operations on counter values on edges. These Boolean operations on edges can be performed in parallel as well.

The third phase is to perform region numbering to assign electrical net numbers to each electrically connected region. Again, these operations require a set of sorting operations and Boolean operations, each of which can be performed in parallel.

The final phase of the algorithm is to perform the actual design rule checking for width, spacing and extension violations. This is accomplished by checking distance violations in the vertical direction within each scan line and the horizontal direction across scan lines. Within a scan line, each edge can in parallel simply check the distance to the first edge below it, and then the second edge below it, and so on, until we search up to the prescribed design rule distance. For horizontal distance violations, each edge on some source scan line checks itself against nearby edges in a different target scan line. Each source scan line first checks its eastward neighbor, then its eastward neighbor two scan lines away, and so on, until the relevant design rule distance.

An outline of the parallel design rule checking algorithm entitled *SIMD-PARALLEL-DRC-EDGE* (for massively parallel SIMD design rule checking using edge-based data decomposition) is given next.

Procedure *SIMD-PARALLEL-DRC-EDGE;*

Generate complete edge intersections Phase

    Read flattened mask layout;
    Create edge representations;
    Assign one edge per processor;
    FORALL processors in PARALLEL DO
        Each processor examines X coordinate of own edge
            and that of higher neighbor;
        Determine common minimum X coordinate as scan line stop;
        Determine if own edge crosses scan line stop;
        IF edge crosses scan line stop THEN
            Split edge into two edges;
            Keep one edge on own processor;
            Assign other edge to new processor;
    END FORALL

Generate mask layers Phase

FORALL processors in PARALLEL DO
    FOR each scan line DO
        FOR each edge DO
            Perform Boolean operation to generate mask layers;

```
        END FOR
      END FOR
    END FORALL
```

Region numbering Phase

```
FORALL processors in PARALLEL DO
    Perform region numbering to assign electrical net numbers
        Use various parallel sorting operations;
END FORALL
```

Perform actual DRC Phase

```
FORALL processors in PARALLEL DO
    FOR each scan line DO
        IF edge owned by processor on scan line THEN
            For vertical violations, perform Boolean
            operations to check width, spacing, overlap rules
            to the first edge below it,
            and then to second edge below it, etc.
            upto prescribed design rule distance;

            For horizontal violations, perform Boolean
            operations to check width, spacing, overlap rules
            to the first edge to left of it,
            and then to second edge to left of it, etc.
            upto prescribed design rule distance;
        END FOR
    END FOR
END FORALL
```

End Procedure

Implementation The preceding parallel algorithm for design rule checking has been implemented on the Thinking Machines CM-2™ system by Carlson and Rutenbar [15, 17]. The runtime performance of the above parallel DRC algorithm running on a 16K processor CM-2™ was compared to an equivalent algorithm running on a VAX-11/785™, and speedups of about 100 times were reported [17]. In a separate study, the speed of a different parallel implementation JIGSAW™ running on a 32K CM-2™ processor was compared to the industrial standard DRACULA™ program on an Apollo DN4000™ workstation, and a speedup of about 20 to 50 times was reported for three industrial benchmark circuits [15].

5.7 NETLIST EXTRACTION PROBLEM

A VLSI layout is described as a set of polygons in different mask levels. A netlist extractor determines the electrical circuit the layout represents by identifying the devices and electrically connected regions (called nets). The output of a netlist extractor can be fed into a switch or logic-level simulator.

A number of circuit extractors of varying accuracy and speed exist [20, 23, 24, 29, 36, 38, 40, 43]. Some extractors work on the flattened representation of a circuit. Other extractors use the hierarchical information available in the circuit. Hierarchical extractors exploit the repetition information in this representation by extracting a cell that is used many times only once and appropriately modifying it wherever it is used [24, 36, 38, 41]. The difference in analysis time obtained by using hierarchical methods can vary from gaining a factor of several hundred on highly regular designs to losing a factor of 5 on designs that do not involve much repetition. The main problem in hierarchical extraction, which is responsible for the overhead, is that the properties of a cell will change if it overlaps another cell, or some base level geometry. Some hierarchical extractors such as [41] forbid any overlapping of cells. However, this is inconvenient and unnecessarily restrictive. Other extractors like [30, 38] transform the circuit with overlapping cells to a circuit in which there are no overlapping cells. The transformation usually involves instantiating a subcell, that overlaps another subcell or base level geometry, at the higher level. This process is repeated until all the subcells of a cell do not overlap each other or the base level geometry. In the worst case, the whole circuit might be converted into a single cell.

In the following subsections, we will describe parallel algorithms for netlist extraction using two approaches.

- Area decomposition approach on flattened circuit descriptions

- Hierarchical decomposition approach on hierarchical descriptions

5.8 AREA PARTITIONED NETLIST EXTRACTION

5.8.1 Overview

Despite the existence of good hierarchical extractors, often an actual chip design is subjected to a complete flattened extraction and netlist comparison before sending for fabrication. Thus there is a need for speeding up flat extraction. In this section we will describe a parallel algorithm for netlist extraction that uses an area partitioned approach on flattened circuits.

Many approaches are known for flat netlist extraction. A very efficient approach to netlist extraction, used by many extractors, uses the scan line paradigm. The basic idea in the scan line approach is to sweep an imaginary line in the plane from one end to the other. At any time, the only geometries of interest are those that intersect the scan line. At each stop of the scan line, some problem dependent processing is performed and the scan line is advanced. The important aspect of a scan-line algorithm is the data structure for storing the geometry intersecting the scan line.

In applying this method to netlist extraction, the rectangles in a circuit are first sorted along one dimension, say the X dimension, without any loss of generality. The imaginary scan line is then assumed to move from left to right, as shown in Figure 5.5 earlier. At any stop, the rectangles whose left end points touch the scan line are taken from the sorted list and added to the scan-line data structure. For each rectangle R added, the rectangles in the scan-line data structure that overlap or abut it are determined. This is used to perform the different Boolean mask operations. If an abutting or overlapping rectangle P is in a layer that electrically connects to R's layer, then R and P are determined to be in the same net. Similarly, if R and P together form a device, then the rectangle corresponding to the device is constructed. Connecting device rectangles are grouped into devices in a manner similar to the method used for obtaining nets. When a scan line is advanced, all those rectangles whose right end points have been past by the scan line are deleted from the scan line data structure. For example, in Figure 5.5, the rectangles B and G are added to the scan line data structure. The rectangles E, C, and D are already in the scan-line data structure. When B is added, it will be found to be connected to rectangles E and D. Thus B, D, and E will be grouped together in the same net. When the scan line is advanced, the rectangle C will be removed from the scan-line data structure. The scan-line data structure can be organized as a link list, tree, or a collection of bins, the latter being the most efficient in practice.

The output of the netlist extraction phase for a circuit is a list of devices and a list of nets. A device is described as a collection of device rectangles. For each device, the output contains information about the nets connecting to the different terminals of the device. A net is described as a collection of rectangles. For each net, the output contains information about the devices that connect to the net.

5.8.2 Distributed Memory MIMD Parallel Algorithm

A parallel circuit extractor basically divides the circuit into smaller parts and performs various tasks in circuit extraction on each in parallel, the results of which are combined to complete the extraction of the whole circuit. The issues in parallel circuit extraction, therefore, are to design efficient algorithms that can be used in the partitioning and combining steps. In this section, we discuss parallel algorithms for circuit extraction that operate on a flattened description of a Manhattan VLSI layout. The parallel algorithms are suitable for execution on hypercube-based distributed memory multiprocessors and are based on algorithms reported by Belkhale and Banerjee [7, 8, 9].

Area Partitioning Step The first step in the parallel algorithm is the area decomposition strategy. Four partitioning strategies are implemented in the *PACE* algorithm as illustrated in Figure 5.13. These are classified as equal-area-based and equal-point-based methods. We discuss these strategies assuming there are $P = 2^d$ processors. In the equal-area-based methods, partitioning is done based on the area of each partition. Two strategies are possible. The first strategy is called slice partitioning, or one-dimensional blocked partitioning. The second strategy is called rectangular partitioning, or two-dimensional blocked partitioning. In the first case, the circuit is divided into slices of equal area along one dimension. In the second case, the circuit is divided into 2^k slices in the x dimension and 2^{d-k} slices in the y dimension. Thus the circuit is divided into rectangular regions. In the point-based methods, we represent a rectangle by a point in two dimensions, for example, the center of the rectangle. The objective then is to divide the domain into regions so that each region has approximately the same number of points. Two partitioning strategies are possible slice and rectangular

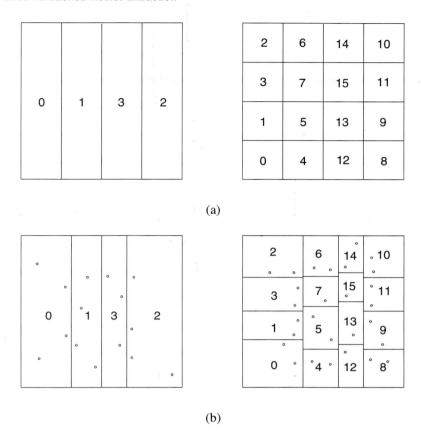

(a)

(b)

Figure 5.13 Area- and Point-based decomposition. (a) Equal area based partitioning, slice and rectangular. (b) Equal points based partitioning, slice and rectangular. Labels of regions correspond to binary reflected Gray code labeling on hypercube multiprocessor.

partitioning. In the first case, the domain is divided into slices in one dimension such that each slice has nearly the same number of points. Again, the direction of division is chosen as before to be along the longer dimension. In the second case, the domain is first divided in the x direction into 2^k slices containing nearly the same number of points, and each slice is in turn divided in the y direction into 2^{d-k} regions each carrying nearly the same number of points.

Each processor p gets all those rectangles that touch or overlap the region assigned to the processor $R\ (p)$. Before starting the net list extraction, these rectangles are cut so that the processor retains only the portion within $R\prime(p)$ [the expanded version of $R(p)$ by the amount equal to the maximum interaction distance among all mask layers]. It should be noted that the regions $R/(p)$ for different processors p overlap. Hence, the processors will have some overlapping information on the circuit at the borders of its region. Assuming a rectangular partition on a hypercube-based distributed memory multiprocessor, the region $A(i, j)$ is assigned to the processor $G(i, j) = B(i) * 2^{d-k} + B(j)$ where $B(i)$ is the binary reflected gray code for i, which gives locality of communication in subsequent stages of the parallel algorithm [35]. The region assignment is illustrated in Figure 5.13.

Implementing the area-based methods is relatively easy. The host computer controlling the distributed memory machine reads the input and sends rectangles in batches to processor $G(0, 0)$. These rectangles are then distributed to the processors using a tree with processor $G(0, 0)$ as the root. A processor retains all those rectangles that intersect or abut its assigned region. The implementation of the point-based methods is an interesting problem. The partitioning can be done by the host or by a node processor after the whole circuit has been read. However, there are two problems with this approach. The first problem is that the processor may take a lot of time in doing the partitioning. The second problem is that there may not be enough memory at a processor to read in the whole circuit. This problem is solved by storing the points as a distributed data structure, based on the partitioning strategy. The host reads the circuit in batches of K rectangles and issues an add instruction to the distributed data structure for every batch. Addition or deletion of points from the data structure involves restructuring the partitions so that the resulting regions have the same number of points. Belkhale and Banerjee have obtained an efficient algorithm for this problem for the case of a general recursive partition [4]. The main idea in the algorithm is to recursively decompose an addition/deletion operation on a region R into addition/deletion operations on its subregions, at the immediate lower level, so that each region is balanced. The advantage of this approach is that the load balancing and reading of the circuit can be done in parallel.

Local extraction step　Boolean mask manipulations are next performed locally on the different layers to derive new layers as specified in the technology file. The new layers include layers for the different devices. The rectangles in the device layers are subsequently grouped into maximal connected groups, which form the local devices. All rectangles, other than those in device layers, are grouped into electrically connected sets that form the local nets. The local nets and devices are collectively referred to as LCS (locally connected set) sets. These are labeled so that they are unique across processors and so that the processor number is a part of the label (the processor's address bits can be the d least significant bits of the label). For each layer and boundary of $R(p)$ a list of border segments is created. These segments are formed by the intersection of rectangles of the layer with the boundary. With each border segment, we have an associated LCS set that it belongs to. If a border segment is from a device layer then it is associated with the device it connects to. Similarly, if a border segment is from a non-device layer, then it is associated with the net it belongs to. All the rectangles in all layers are then cut so that only the portion of the rectangles within $R (p)$ is retained. These steps are done in a single scan-line algorithm. For each layer and boundary, the border segments are converted to maximal border segments by combining overlapping or abutting border segments. A single list is then constructed for each boundary by combining the maximal border segments for all the layers at the boundary. This list is then sorted lexicographically, first on the starting points of the segments, and second on the layer number. Each entry in the list points to the LCS set it belongs.

Merge step The lists constructed for each of the borders, and the LCS sets that touch a border are passed to a merge algorithm. The merge algorithm determines for each of the LCS sets a unique label that identifies its global connected component (GCS) set. It also determines the number of LCS sets that are part of the GCS set. The unique label of a GCS is chosen by the merge algorithm from the labels assigned to its LCS components.

We now present a simple algorithm for the merge problem on a hypercube multiprocessor of $P = 2^d$ processors. Other interesting algorithms for the problem are given in [5, 6]. The simple merge algorithm has d stages of message passing. Each stage involves sending and receiving a message at each processor followed by a computation step. The basic idea in this algorithm is that at each stage a processor doubles its area of knowledge in the circuit. Initially, a processor knows only about its region. After d stages a processor has knowledge about everything it needs to know in the entire circuit. The region of information of a processor in a certain stage of the merge algorithm is a rectangular region of the circuit. At any stage a processor maintains the following information: (1) List of connected sets in the information region that touch a border. These are called CCOMP sets. The CCOMP sets are specified by labels. (2) List of border segments for the borders of the information region. Each border segment points to the CCOMP set it is part of. (3) List of LCS sets at the processor that connect to at least a border of the information region. Each of them points to the CCOMP set it is a are part of. These LCS sets are called active LCS sets.

At each stage a processor communicates with another processor whose information region abuts the information region of the processor. The communication is said to be along the x axis (respectively, y axis) if the common border is perpendicular to the x axis (respectively, y axis). An example x axis communication and the communication phases on a 16-processor hypercube are shown in Figure 5.14. We now describe the work done in a particular stage by a processor P. Let Q be the processor that it communicates with in the stage.

First, send the border segments of the current information region of the processor, along with the CCOMP sets they point to, in a single message to processor Q. Wait for a similar message from Q. Next, combine the CCOMP sets of the corresponding common border segments of P and Q. Subsequently, the information region of P for the next stage is the combination of its current information region and that of Q. The new border segments are obtained by deleting the border segments along the common border and combining those sent by Q to those at P in order. The CCOMP sets for the new information region are those that are formed in the local extraction step that touch a border. For each active LCS set, the new set it belongs to after the unions in the local extraction step is next determined. If the new set is a CCOMP set for the new region, then the LCS set is retained in the active list. If not, the label of the new set is taken as the label of the GCS set corresponding to the LCS set. The LCS set is thereafter made inactive.

This completes the description of one stage of the merge algorithm. After d stages, each of the LCS sets gets a label denoting the GCS set to which it belongs. A processor is involved in d messages in this algorithm. The processor that has the LCS set with the unique label is said to own the GCS set. All LCS sets at a processor belonging to the same GCS set are

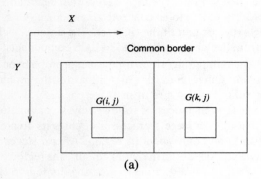

(a)

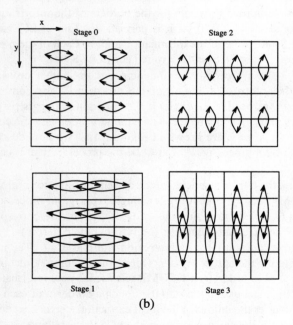

(b)

Figure 5.14 Example x-axis communication and stages of communication in merge algorithm

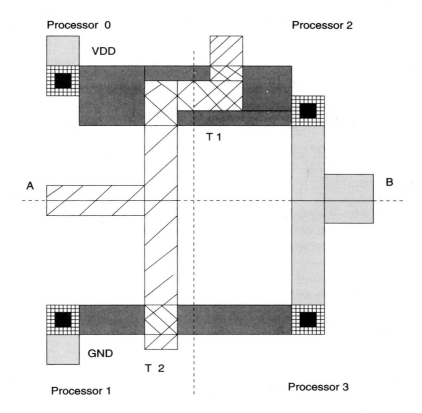

Figure 5.15 Example layout of inverter and parallel extraction

Processor 0	Processor 1	Processor 2	Processor 3
Lnet 1 (VDD)	Lnet 1 (A)	Lnet 1 (VDD)	Lnet 1 (B)
Lnet 2 (A)	Lnet 2 (GND)	Lnet 2 (A)	_____
Lnet 3 (B)	Lnet 3 (B)	Lnet 3 (B)	_____
Ltran 1 (T1)	Ltran 1 (T2)	Ltran 1 (T1)	_____

combined to form a single LCS set. This is useful for the subsequent steps. The local nets and devices for a four processor CMOS example is shown in Figure 5.15. Their final labels are shown in parentheses in the bottom figure.

Global netlist extraction At the end of the preceding steps, we have a list of local nets and devices at each processor. Also, for each local net and device, we have a label denoting its global component and the number of LCS sets comprising the global component. This information will be utilized in the parameter extraction phase to be described later. It should be noted that at this point the structural information about the circuit is obtained and may be output.

Overall algorithm An outline of the parallel netlist extraction algorithm entitled *DM-PARAL-LEL-NETLIST-AREA* (for distributed memory parallel netlist extraction using area decomposition) is given next.

Procedure *DM-PARALLEL-NETLIST-AREA;*

>   Read flattened mask layout;
>   Partition mask layout description by
>   (1) rectangular area (2) rectangular points
>   (3) slice area (4) slice points;
>
>   Assign partitions of mask rectangles to processors;
>   Rectangles touching borders of regions assigned to both processors
>   sharing a border;
>   FORALL processors in PARALLEL DO
>   Perform Boolean operations to derive new layers;
>   Identify local connected components;
>   Determine border segments;
>   END FORALL;

Merge Phase

>   FORALL processors in PARALLEL DO
>   FOR log(P) stages in P processor machine DO
>   Identify neighbor processor in current stage;
>   Merge LCS sets across processors in pair;
>   Create an extended region of local connected sets;
>   Create new border segments of extended region;
>   END FOR
>   END FORALL

Global netlist extraction
>   FORALL processors in PARALLEL DO
>   FOR each global connected component owned by processor DO
>   Report net for component;
>   Report devices for component;
>   END FOR
>   END FOR

End Procedure

TABLE 5.2 Runtimes (seconds) of Parallel Extraction Algorithm on the Intel iPSC/2™ Hypercube

Circuit	Rectangles	Serial (sec)	Area-Slice (sec)	Area-Rectangle (sec)	Point-Slice (sec)	Point-Rectangle (sec)
1	54,800	373.3	56.5	51.6	65.6	43.5
2	66,000	na	40.3	32.4	58.3	41.4
3	130,700	na	53.0	64.2	47.5	46.3
4	258,600	na	112.7	148.7	90.5	80.5
5	260,000	na	159.3	140.0	148.7	101.8

Implementation Belkhale and Banerjee have reported on the results of the implementation of the preceding parallel algorithm for extraction on an Intel iPSC/2™ hypercube [7, 8, 9]. Table 5.2 shows some example results on five benchmark circuits of the runtimes (in seconds) for various partitioning methods on a 16-processor Intel iPSC/2 hypercube. Except for the first circuit, the serial algorithm could not be run on one processor of the hypercube due to memory limitations. Some of the circuits have regular layouts, while others have portions with dense layouts and regions that are sparse. Hence equal-area-based partitioning methods do poorly on those circuits in terms of bad load balance. As can be seen from the results, the equal-points-based rectangular partitioning gives the best overall performance among all the circuits.

Several researchers have proposed similar parallel algorithms for circuit extraction. A parallel algorithm for speeding up the task of circuit extraction was proposed by Levitin [27]. The approach involved splitting the design into equal-sized horizontal slices, and assigning one slice to each processor. A sequential extraction algorithm [41] was executed on each slice. This approach had problems merging transistors across slice boundaries. The use of horizontal slices minimizes the amount of data required to be scanned at any scan-line stop for a vertical scan line moving from left to right. Using slices of equal size leads to poor load balancing among processors handling the slices if the density of the circuit varies. The algorithm was implemented on a VAXCluster™ distributed computing environment with communication through a common file server. Unfortunately, it did not achieve any performance improvements over the serial circuit extractor that served as its basis.

Tonkin has reported on a variant of the preceding algorithm for distributed memory multiprocessors by developing a parallel version [42] of a well-known sequential extractor called Goalie™ [40]. The basic approach was to divide the circuit into vertical slices such that they have equal numbers of edges, and edges crossing a slice boundary are split into separate edges. The original Goalie algorithm is run on each slice in parallel, generating edges for intermediate layers and assigning unique numbers to transistor regions. The results are merged using a merge algorithm similar to the one discussed previously by detecting edges at each boundary that belong to the same region, and merging the numbers associated with these regions. The parallel algorithm was implemented on a message-passing multiprocessor called HPC/VORX™. The author has reported speedups of about 7 to 13 on 16-processors for various circuits.

5.8.3 Shared Memory MIMD Parallel Algorithm

We will now describe a modified version of the preceding parallel algorithm for netlist extraction that is suitable for execution on a shared memory multiprocessor. The basic parallel algorithm is the same as the one described previously. We will only describe the modifications to the data partitioning phase and the merge phase in the shared memory environment.

The mapping of regions to processors is not a crucial issue in a shared memory environment since the entire chip image is stored in global shared memory. The circuit region is divided into different bins in the x dimension. The number of points that fall in each bin is determined and stored in an array. The entries in the array can then be used to determine the partitioning lines along the x dimension. The process can then be repeated in each resulting subregion, by the appropriate processors, to determine the partitioning lines along the y dimension. Figure 5.16 shows an approximate point based partitioning strategy.

The merge problem can be solved in an easy and interesting way using a parallel union-find algorithm and locking on a shared memory multiprocessor. As previously described, each processor computes the border segments for the four borders, with their associated LCS set labels. Each processor writes this information onto the shared memory. In the merge step, each processor looks at its top and right border segments. For each border segment a, it determines the corresponding border segment b in the processor at the other end of the border. It then does a union operation on the LCS sets of a and b. The union operations performed at different processors interfere, and hence locks are used to ensure correctness.

Consider the operation union(a, b), where a and b are two border segments. The data structure used by the algorithm consists of a union find data structure as shown in Figure 5.17. The first step in the algorithm is to determine the current roots x, y of LCS (a) and LCS (b) respectively. If x is same as y, the union algorithm returns. If $x \neq y$, the processor locks the roots in increasing order of their labels in order to avoid deadlock. Once the locks are obtained, the processor checks if x and y are still the roots. If x or y is not a root, the whole operation is continued from x, y after releasing the locks. If x and y are still the roots, a directed edge is added from x to y (or y to x) and the locks are released.

An outline of the parallel netlist extraction algorithm entitled *SM-PARALLEL-NETLIST-DATA* (for shared memory parallel netlist extraction using data decomposition) is given next.

Procedure *SM-PARALLEL-NETLIST-DATA;*

> Read flattened mask layout;
> Convert mask layout description in x-direction into bins
> Number of points in each bin is stored in array;
> Partition mask layout into vertical slices with
> approximately equal number of rectangles;
>
> Assign partitions of mask rectangles to processors;
> Rectangles touching borders of regions assigned to both processors;

Approximate partitioning into three subregions

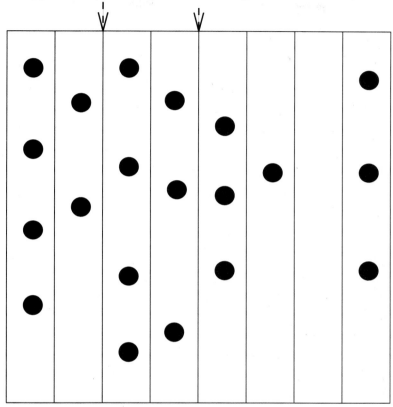

Region divided into buckets

Count array denoting number of entries per bucket

4	2	4	3	3	1	0	3

Figure 5.16 Point-based partitioning in a shared memory multiprocessor

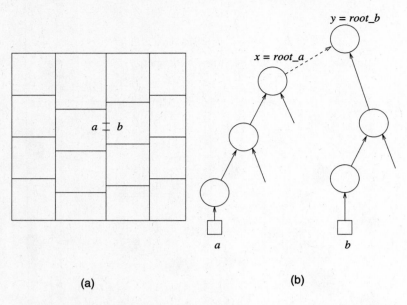

(a)   (b)

Figure 5.17 Merge algorithm on a shared memory multiprocessor.   (a) Processor partitioning. (b) Union-find data structure.

FORALL processors in PARALLEL DO
    Perform Boolean operations to derive new layers;
    Identify local connected components;
    Determine border segments;
END FORALL;

Merge Phase

FORALL processors in PARALLEL DO
    FOR log(P) stages in P processor machine DO
        Identify neighbor processor in current stage;
        Perform parallel union-find algorithm using locks to
        merge LCS sets across processors in pair;
        Create an extended region of local connected sets;
        Create new border segments of extended region;
        Update shared memory;
    END FOR
END FORALL

Global netlist extraction
FORALL processors in PARALLEL DO

TABLE 5.3 Runtimes (seconds) and Speedups of Parallel Extraction Algorithm on the Encore Multimax™ Multiprocessor

Circuit	Rectangles	1 Processor Runtime (speedup)	8 Processor Runtime (speedup)
1	54,800	196 (1.0)	43 (4.6)
2	66,000	221 (1.0)	41 (5.4)
3	130,700	305 (1.0)	63 (4.8)
4	258,600	691 (1.0)	137 (5.0)
5	260,000	985 (1.0)	190 (5.2)

```
        FOR each global connected component owned by processor DO
            Report net for component;
            Report devices for component;
        END FOR
    END FOR
```

End Procedure

Implementation   Belkhale and Banerjee have reported on the results of the shared memory parallel algorithm on an Encore Multimax™ shared memory multiprocessor [10]. Table 5.3 shows some example results on five benchmark circuits of the runtimes (in seconds) and speedups of the parallel algorithm on an eight processor Encore Multimax shared memory multiprocessor.

5.9 HIERARCHICAL NETLIST EXTRACTION

5.9.1 Overview

In this section we will describe a parallel algorithm for netlist extraction using a hierarchical decomposition that is suitable for execution on a shared memory MIMD parallel machine.

Hierarchical extractors exploit the repetitive information in this representation by extracting a cell that is used many times only once and appropriately modifying it wherever it is used [24, 36, 38, 41]. The main problem in hierarchical extraction, which is responsible for the overhead, is that the properties of a cell will change if it overlaps another cell or some base-level geometry. Some hierarchical extractors [41] forbid any overlapping of cells. However, this is inconvenient and unnecessarily restrictive. Other extractors like [24] transform the circuit with overlapping cells to a circuit in which there are no overlapping cells.

We will assume the second approach to hierarchical circuit extraction which has two steps: the analysis and transformation step and the actual extraction step. The first step involves transforming a circuit that has overlapping cells into one that does not have any overlapping cells. One way of achieving this involves looking at the subcells of each cell and instantiating a subcell A if it overlaps another subcell or geometry. The instantiation process involves replacing the cell A with its subcells and geometry. The whole process is repeated until there are no overlapping subcells in each of the cells. At the end of this step, cells that are not useful are discarded. A cell is useful if is the root cell or if it occurs as a subcell of a useful cell.

At the end of the first step, the task of extraction consists of extracting each cell that remains and appropriately combining the results using common node names. For each cell, the information available consists of its ports, the geometry in terms of rectangles, and ports of its subcells. The ports are represented as rectangles that have a span of zero along one dimension. With this representation, the extraction of a cell is done in a similar manner as for flat circuit extraction.

5.9.2 Shared Memory MIMD Parallel Algorithm

We will now describe a parallel algorithm for hierarchical extraction that is suitable for execution on a shared memory MIMD multiprocessor. We assume that the hierarchical circuit description is stored in global shared memory. The first step of hierarchical circuit extraction, the overlap analysis and transformation step, is parallelized by assigning cells to different processors dynamically from a list. The cells are ordered so that subcells of a cell occur before a cell. The amount of parallelism in this step is generally not more than a factor of 2. Fortunately, the second step is the most time consuming part of hierarchical circuit extraction. There are two approaches we could take for parallelizing this step.

One approach to parallelizing the second step involves dynamically assigning the extraction of cells to processors from a list. The list of cells could be sorted in decreasing order of the number of rectangles it contains. This algorithm corresponds to the LPT algorithm (largest processing time first) [21] for scheduling independent tasks on multiprocessors. The disadvantage with this approach is that some cells could be very large. A large cell assigned to a single processor will be a bottleneck for the whole computation, reducing the parallelism that can be obtained.

From the previous discussion, it is clear that we need to look at solutions that assign more processors to the extraction of a large cell. The assigned processors can extract the large cell by flattening the circuit and using the parallel algorithm for circuit extraction on flattened circuits described in the previous sections. However, since the speedups obtained in the parallel flattened circuit extraction algorithm will be less than linear, assigning many processors to the extraction of a cell could result in an increase in the overall time. It turns out that we can assign an optimal number of processors to extract each cell in the layout to minimize the overall extraction time. This problem is formulated as a general problem called *partitionable independent task scheduling (PITS)* problem [3].

The PITS problem consists of scheduling n independent tasks on p processors. Associated with each task T_i, $1 \leq i \leq n$, we have an estimate of the time taken by the task $\tau(T_i)$ on a single processor, and values $\sigma_j(T_i)$, $1 \leq j \leq p$, that give the speedups that can be obtained by running the task on j processors. The problem then is to schedule the collection of tasks on p processors so that the maximum completion time is minimized. For our application, the different tasks represent the different cells to be extracted. The time taken for extraction of a cell is estimated from the number of rectangles in the cell. The speedup function is assumed to be same for all the cells and is estimated by measuring the speedups obtained using the parallel algorithm on flattened circuits described in the previous section for different numbers of processors.

The *partitionable independent task scheduling* problem can be shown to be NP hard. Belkhale and Banerjee have proposed a heuristic that is used to solve the problem, which is guaranteed to produce results that are within twice the optimal [3] if the speedup curve is concave, which is true for most applications. The main idea in the algorithm is to construct a schedule and iteratively modify it by assigning some tasks to more processors. At any stage, for every task T_i, we have a number s_i that denotes the number of processors that has been currently allocated to T_i. During the course of the algorithm, the number of processors allocated to a task may be increased iteratively. Each increase is allowed only if it results in an "immediate" decrease in the schedule time. A task T_i assigned to $j = s_i > 1$ processors can be looked upon as a collection of j subtasks each having execution time $\frac{\tau(T_i)}{\sigma_j(T_i)}$. These subtasks are referred to as *split* tasks. The other tasks T_i, with $s_i = 1$, are referred to as *unsplit* tasks. Figure 5.18 shows an example task graph and its resultant scheduling on five processors. A detailed description of the partitionable independent task scheduling (PITS) algorithm appears in [3, 11].

An outline of the parallel hierarchical netlist extraction algorithm entitled *SM-PARAL-LEL-NETLIST-HIERARCHY* (for shared memory parallel netlist extraction using hierarchical decomposition) using the preceding scheduling algorithm is next.

Procedure *DM-PARALLEL-NETLIST-HIERARCHY;*

    Read hierarchical circuit description;
    Perform overlap analysis and transformation;
        IF two cells overlap
            THEN Flatten those cells;

    FOR each hierarchical independent cell DO
        Obtain estimate of extraction time by counting rectangles;
    ENDFOR

    Obtain Partionable Independent Task Schedule;
        Determines the number of processors s_i that should execute
        each task in parallel;

    FORALL processors in PARALLEL DO
        WHILE there are cells to extract DO
            Determine which s_i processors will participate in extraction;
            WHILE all processors in schedule not free DO
                Wait for them to be free;
            END WHILE
            Perform parallel netlist extraction among s_i processors

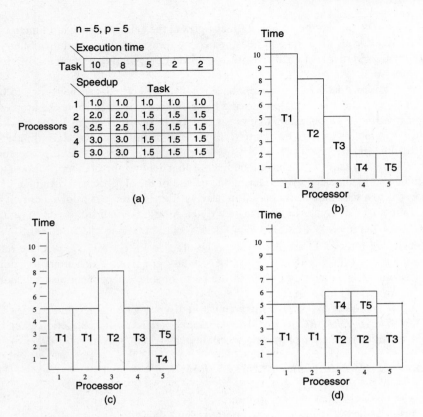

Figure 5.18 Example problem and the steps of the scheduling algorithm

     using parallel algorithm with area decomposition approach;
   END WHILE
END FORALL

End Procedure

Implementation The parallel algorithm for hierarchical netlist extraction just described has been implemented by Belkhale and Banerjee on an Encore Multimax™ shared memory multiprocessor [10, 11]. The authors have reported the results of the parallel algorithm on some example layouts and compared its performance with four other algorithms. These are the sequential flattened algorithm, the parallel flattened algorithm, the sequential hierarchical algorithm, the parallel hierarchical algorithm based on the LPT algorithm, and the parallel hierarchical algorithm based on the PITS algorithm. Table 5.4 shows some example results on five benchmark circuits of the runtimes (in seconds) of the different algorithms on a eight-processor Encore Multimax shared memory multiprocessor. In each case, the PITS-based

TABLE 5.4 Runtimes (seconds) of Various Sequential, Hierarchical, and Parallel Extraction Algorithms on the Encore Multimax™ Multiprocessor

Circuit (Rectangle)	Flat 1 Processor	Flat Parallel 8 Processors	Hierarchical Sequential 1 Processor	Hierarchical LPT 8 Processors	Hierarchical PITS 8 Processors
54,800	217	63	200	192	63
66,000	246	66	240	217	61
130,700	346	103	170	126	38
258,600	763	218	185	125	40
260,000	1062	268	1045	1030	222

algorithm performed the best (or close to the best), giving speedups of about 6 on eight processors. The parallel algorithm with LPT scheduling performed poorly in most of the cases.

5.10 PARAMETER EXTRACTION

The parameter extraction phase of circuit extraction involves device size extraction, parasitic capacitance extraction, and resistance extraction. This is the most time consuming part in circuit extraction. There are different models for parameter extraction, with varying accuracy and computational complexity. In the next section, we briefly describe two models, namely MEXTRA [20] and HPEX [38].

The rectangles of a net have parasitic capacitance with respect to substrate and also other overlapping or neighboring rectangles. The capacitance of a node (a set of electrically connected rectangles) with respect to the substrate can be accurately estimated for each connected region belonging to the same layer by determining its area A and perimeter P. This is usually determined as $C = \alpha A + \beta P$, where α and β are constants depending on the layer and the technology. The capacitances between two nodes from different nets caused by the overlap of rectangles are called overlap capacitances. This is not a simple function of area and perimeter, although many extractors report information about the regions of overlaps between rectangles [40]. Some tile based circuit extractors [36] also determine internodal capacitances between two long parallel edges close together, usually in the same layer. These are called parallel capacitances. In MEXTRA only the substrate capacitance is computed for each net by the preceding formula. However, in HPEX both substrate capacitance and resistance are computed.

In the following subsections, we will describe parallel algorithms for parameter extraction using two approaches.

- Area decomposition approach on flattened circuits

- Hierarchical decomposition approach on hierarchical circuits

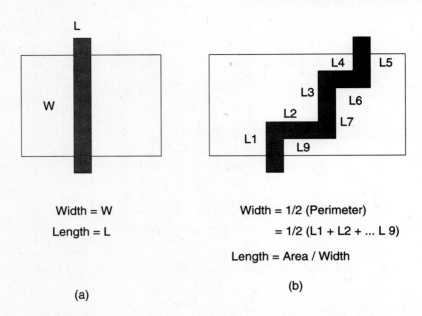

Width = W

Length = L

(a)

Width = 1/2 (Perimeter)

= 1/2 (L1 + L2 + ... L 9)

Length = Area / Width

(b)

Figure 5.19 CMOS transistor device extraction. (a) Simple rectangular transistor layout. (b) Nonrectangular transistor layout.

5.11 AREA PARTITIONED PARAMETER EXTRACTION

5.11.1 Overview

In this section we will describe a parallel algorithm for parameter extraction using an area decomposition approach that is suitable for execution on distributed memory and shared memory MIMD parallel machines. We will describe how two parameter extraction models can be interfaced to a parallel circuit extraction algorithm. The main theme of the section is to look at the general principles for interfacing any parameter model to the output of the netlist extraction phase of an extractor. Some of these models may require more information from the netlist extraction phase, but the issues will be the same. The main goal is to achieve a significant speedup in the parameter extraction phase, which is the most time consuming step in extraction. Also, with the increased computational power, we will be able to use more accurate and hence more time consuming models.

For device size extraction, we illustrate how they are computed for CMOS transistors. Other devices are handled in a similar fashion. The analog characteristics of a CMOS transistor are a function of length and width. For nonrectangular transistors an effective length and width can be computed using techniques like those of resistance extraction. However, a simpler alternative that is adopted in most systems including, MEXTRA and HPEX is to take one-half of the transistor's perimeter with diffusion as the effective width. The effective length is then calculated as the area of transistor divided by the effective width. Figure 5.19 shows the approach used in device extraction for CMOS transistors.

The rectangles of a net have resistance, creating an effective resistance between the terminals of the net. The most accurate method to determine resistances is to use the Laplace equation for the region of the net. However, this is very time consuming. An approximate approach involves identifying straight regions of the net, called branches. Simple analytical formulas can be applied for the evaluation of the resistance of branches. Once the straight regions are removed from a net, we have islands, each of which can be looked up in the library for its resistance, or some approximation can be used. This approach is used by many resistance extractors [18, 29, 38]

We now describe the resistance and capacitance model used in HPEX [38]. The rectangles of a net are first converted into a horizontally maximal nonoverlapping form. This is done by using a scan-line algorithm. The reason for this step is that this process will produce a unique representation for the net. The next step is to combine horizontally long rectangles in the vertical direction. In this step, two rectangles that are sufficiently longer in the x direction than in the y direction, are combined vertically if they abut on their horizontal edges. This step is accomplished by a similar scan-line algorithm as far as the first step. These two steps derive a set of rectangles for the net that gives an indication of the direction of the current. These two steps are illustrated in Figure 5.20.

The next step is to take each rectangle that is sufficiently longer in one direction than the other and cut it on its larger side, based on the intersections with other rectangles. Two overlapping rectangles from the intersections are merged into a single one. The next step is to find the branches of the net. Two rectangles are said to be electrically connected if they share more than one electrically connected point. A rectangle that connects to more than two rectangles, or to only one rectangle, is defined to be a knot. Also, the rectangles associated with the terminals of the devices are defined as ports. The rest of the rectangles are defined as branch rectangles. The knots and ports are then assigned unique numbers. A branch of a net is defined to be a path from a knot or port to another knot or port using only branch rectangles. The branches can be determined by a pass of the electrical connectivity graph. These steps are illustrated for the net of Figure 5.20.

The next step is to perform the resistances calculations for the branches. For this step, analytical formulas [38] are used for various configurations. These include formulas for a long straight rectangle, a cascade of rectangles in the same direction, corners, and bends. In the calculation for the resistance of a branch, the contributions of knots and ports are carefully approximated.

The calculation for substrate capacitance is done along with the resistance calculation. The capacitance of each knot and port is first determined. Then the capacitance of each branch is computed by adding the contributions of all its branch rectangles. The capacitance of a branch is lumped at its end points equally. Hence the result of parameter extraction is a distributed RC network for each net. To reduce the number of nodes in the resultant circuit output by the extractor, there is a node reduction phase in many extractors such as HPEX [38]. This involves finding an approximate equivalent small RC network for each net.

5.11.2 Distributed Memory MIMD Parallel Algorithm

Parallel parameter extraction is performed after parallel netlist extraction. We assume that the parallel netlist extraction has been performed on a flattened mask description by using some form of area decomposition of the chip area, distributing mask rectangles in various subareas

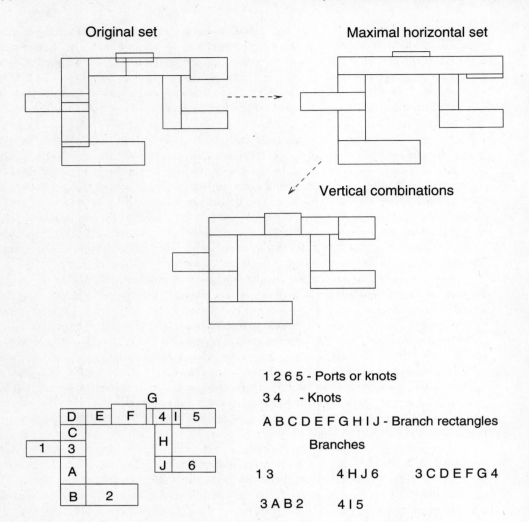

Figure 5.20 Steps in resistance extraction

to different processors, and performing the local netlist extraction, followed by the merge algorithm to determine the globally connected nets. We will now describe parallel algorithms for parameter extraction.

The issues in parallel parameter extraction are the same for both distributed memory and shared memory MIMD multiprocessors. For the local devices not connected to a boundary of an area decomposition, we have all the information for the device extraction. For the others, we do the following. If a local device is not owned by the processor, then its rectangles and other necessary information are sent to the processor that owns the global device. For example in CMOS technology, the necessary information consists of the abutting diffusion rectangles. If a local device is owned by the processor, it waits for messages to complete the information for the global device. The processor can then extract the device. A processor can determine when all the information for a device has been received because the number of local devices that comprise the global device is known from the merge algorithm. All communication between two processors in the preceding step can be done in a single message, since the information that needs to be sent is completely determined before the step. Thus communication can be very efficient.

The next step is the extraction of capacitances and resistances of nets. A general approach similar to device extraction could be followed. In other words, local nets touching the border but not owned by a processor can be sent to its owner which can then perform the detailed extraction of the net. This approach can be expected to distribute these nets equitably among processors, since the merge algorithm determines the label of a GCS in a random fashion from its constituent LCS labels. The problem, however, is that a net may take different amounts of time for extraction depending on its size, causing variation of load among the processors. For example, a processor that owns a power or ground net will have an excessive amount of load. Thus long nets pose a problem for this approach.

An examination of the problem reveals that parallelism can be achieved only if we can deal with the extraction of long nets in a distributed fashion. A global net with more than K rectangles is designated as a long net (K can be chosen to be around 100). The other global nets are designated as short nets. The merge algorithm is changed to determine for each GCS the number of rectangles in its set, similar to the way it determines the number of LCS in a GCS. The determination of whether a global net is a long or a short net is then made easily. Subsequently, for a short net we could use the approach describe previously for device extraction. For a long net, we need to design a way to extract it in a distributed fashion, so that it is as close to the original model as possible. This is the general approach that we have taken for the problem. We will now illustrate this approach for the models of MEXTRA and HPEX.

MEXTRA Model   The MEXTRA model only computes the substrate capacitance for the nets. It does not determine any resistances. The capacitance of a node (a set of electrically connected rectangles) with respect to the substrate can be accurately estimated for each connected region belonging to the same layer by determining its area A and perimeter P. This is usually determined as $C = c1 \cdot A + c2 \cdot P$ where $c1$ and $c2$ are constants depending on the layer and the technology. This is illustrated in Figure 5.21(a). Now suppose we have a global net G, which comprises of the local nets $L_1, ..., L_k$. For each of the local nets L_j we can compute its capacitance. This involves converting the rectangles stored in a local net into a nonoverlapping format, and then finding the contribution to the capacitance from each rectangle. However, the substrate capacitance of G is not just the sum C_{tot} of the substrate capacitances of its local nets, because of the possible overcounting of the perimeter components of the capacitance equation. This is illustrated in Figure 5.21(b). However, this overcounting can be resolved precisely by sending all the rectangles of L_j that touch the processor border to the processor owning G. The processor owning G can determine all those instances when a border rectangle B_1 of layer l belonging to L_i touches a border rectangle B_2 belonging to L_j of the same layer, where $i \neq j$. For each such instance, we subtract $2 * c2 * dist$ from C_{tot}, where β is the

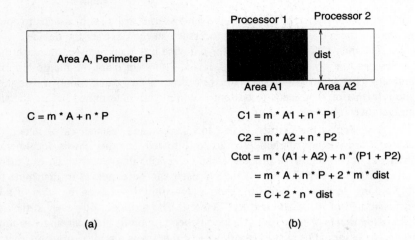

$$C = m * A + n * P$$

$$C1 = m * A1 + n * P1$$

$$C2 = m * A2 + n * P2$$

$$Ctot = m * (A1 + A2) + n * (P1 + P2)$$

$$= m * A + n * P + 2 * m * dist$$

$$= C + 2 * n * dist$$

(a)   (b)

Figure 5.21 Capacitance extraction in sequential and parallel MEXTRA.
(a) Extraction on one processor. (b) Extraction on two processors.

perimeter constant of the layer l and $dist$ is the length of the line of contact between B_1 and B_2. With this correction, we get the correct value of the capacitance for the global net G. Because of the accuracy of the method, we extract every global net, even if it is not a long net, in the precedingdistributed fashion. The communication in this step is done in an efficient manner, as in the previous step for extraction of devices.

HPEX Model The HPEX model computes both resistances and capacitances. Let G be a long global net comprising of the local nets $L_1, ..., L_k$. We now describe how it is extracted in a distributed fashion. For each local net L_i the rectangular formation and decomposition steps of Figure 5.20 are performed. The next step is to determine the knots and branch rectangles in L_i and assign numbers to the knots. In this step, the rectangles of L_i that touch a border are not classified as knots or branches, although they are counted in the connectivity calculations for other rectangles. The numbers assigned to the knots will contain the processor's address bits concatenated at the end. These steps are illustrated in Figure 5.22(a).

The next step is to consider those branches in L_i that start with a border rectangle and end with a knot or port or another border rectangle. These branches represent the incomplete branches of L_i. For example, in processor 0, the branch from knot 24 to the boundary is an incomplete branch. All the rectangles in the incomplete branches, including those at the end points, are then deleted from L_i and sent to the processor that owns G. Thus the knot 24 and all the rectangles in the incomplete branch are deleted from processor 0 and sent to the owner. This step is illustrated in Figure 5.22(b).

The rectangles in all the incomplete branches of G are received by the owner of G and combined into a set S. The rectangles in S may include some knots and ports. The set S is then transformed by the steps of Figure 5.20. In these steps, the rectangles that have been designated as ports or knots are not included. The new knots in S are subsequently determined and numbered. These steps are illustrated in Figure 5.22(c). The new knots determined are 1,

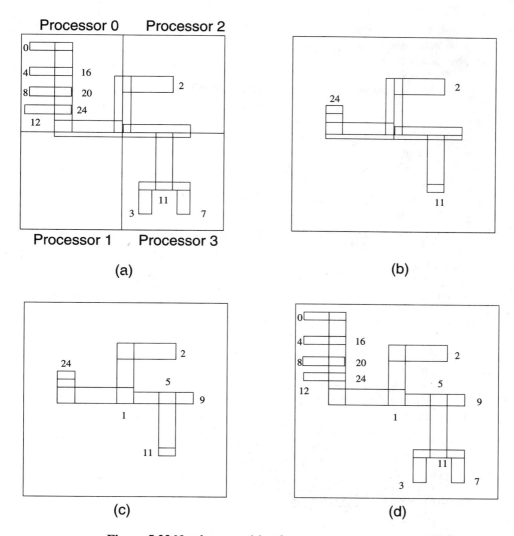

Figure 5.22 Net decomposition for parameter extraction in HPEX

5, and 9. The complete result is shown in Figure 5.22(d).

For each processor that contains a part of the global net G, a portion of S that is sufficient to complete its incomplete branches is sent back by the owner of G. On receiving this, these rectangles are included in the local net L_i. Once all the rectangles are received, the branches of L_i are determined. A processor computes the capacitance for each knot that it owns. It evaluates the resistance and capacitance of a branch if it owns one of the end points. The capacitance determined is lumped appropriately at the end points of the branch owned by the processor. A processor will report the capacitance of a port or knot only if it owns it. Similarly, the resistance of a branch is reported by a processor only if one end point is owned by the processor, and the number of the other end point is larger than it. This avoids duplication of information in the output.

The procedure described guarantees that the quality of the result is not compromised in any way by the parallel algorithm as compared to the sequential algorithm, since the same structure of knots and branches is obtained even though the global net was evaluated in a distributed manner. A simpler approach could have been used, which breaks each of the long global nets at the borders by inserting new knots. However, this approach may create inaccuracies in the direction of the current in the border rectangles. For example, when a long horizontal rectangle is split by a horizontal border line, the direction will be incorrectly assigned to be in the vertical direction.

It is easy to interface a node reduction phase, such as [38], at this stage. We will also be able to do the node reduction in parallel. The node reduction step for short nets or local nets that do not touch a border can proceed as before. However, for long nets node reduction can be done only for nodes that do not connect to a node not owned by the processor.

Overall Algorithm An outline of the parallel parameter extraction algorithm entitled *DM-PARALLEL-PARAMETER-HPEX-DATA* (for distributed memory parallel parameter extraction using HPEX models with data decomposition) follows.

Procedure *DM-PARALLEL-PARAMETER-HPEX-DATA;*

Read flattened mask layout;
Partition mask layout description among processors;

Perform parallel netlist extraction (described earlier)
FORALL processors in PARALLEL DO
   Perform local netlist extraction;
   Perform merge of connected components;
   Perform global netlist extraction;
END FORALL;

Global parameter extraction
FORALL processors in PARALLEL DO
  FOR each global connected component owned by processor DO
    IF number of rectangles $> K (= 100)$
      THEN break up long net into short nets
    FOR each short net L_i DO
      Form rectangles, Decompose, determine knots, branches;
      IF any rectangle of L_i touches a processor border
        THEN postpone processing of incomplete nets;
          Send rectangles of incomplete net to owner;
      Compute resistance of completed net;
      Compute capacitance of completed net;
    END FOR

END FOR
FOR each incomplete net owned by processor DO
    Receive rectangles of incomplete net;
    Form rectangle, decompose, determine, knots, branches;
    Compute resistance of incomplete net;
    Compute capacitance of incomplete net;
END FOR
END FORALL

End Procedure

Asynchronous Algorithm We will now describe an asynchronous distributed memory parallel algorithm for parameter extraction based on work reported by Ramkumar and Banerjee [33]. The programming model for the parallel algorithm assumes a concurrent object-oriented model of computation such as the ones provide by the CHARM [19, 25] and PROPERCAD2 systems described in Chapter 10 [32]. Conceptually, the PROPERCAD2 and CHARM systems maintain a pool of objects representing work that is created by the application program. Information is exchanged between these objects via messages. The objects in the work pool are distributed (and periodically balanced) across the available processors by the runtime system. All previous parallel algorithms for circuit extraction performed the extraction in several phases: a data distribution phase, a geometric extraction phase, a merge phase, and a parameter extraction phase. Such approaches involve synchronization at the start of each phase of the execution. This algorithm is different from other parallel approaches in that it is an asynchronous parallel algorithm using a coarse-grain data flow style of execution.

Data are initially distributed using area-based partitioning on each available processor as shown in Figure 5.23. Following that, each processor further subdivides its region based on a user-determined threshold (the maximum number of rectangles per region). The load is redistributed among the processors logically organized as a tree, as shown in Figure 5.24. The logical tree organization is used to perform the merge operations in the parallel extraction algorithm.

Once a circuit extraction object is created on a processor, a sequential algorithm for local geometric extraction is run on the region it represents to determine the nets and devices in that region. The nets and devices touching the border of the region they belong to are called *incomplete*. All other nets and devices are given unique identifiers and are available for parameter extraction. Portions of incomplete nets that can be processed without additional information are evaluated. The remaining incomplete nets and all incomplete devices are subjected to a *merge* algorithm in which they are combined with incomplete nets and devices from a region sharing a common border.

The merge algorithm proceeds in a hierarchical manner, at each stage of the merge, two adjacent regions are merged. Nets and devices that touch a common border of the two adjacent regions are combined. Following every stage of the merge algorithm, nets and devices that are completed become available for parameter extraction. Nets that are available for parameter extraction are load balanced *as and when they become complete* to ensure maximum utilization

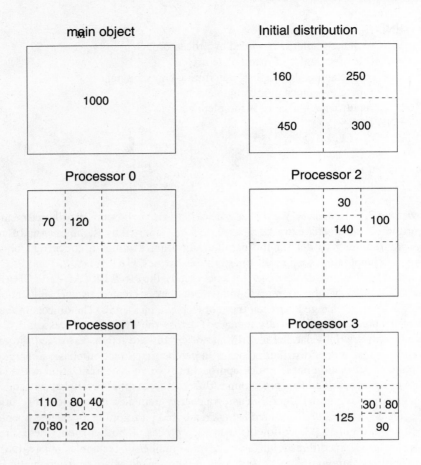

Figure 5.23 Example of data distribution on four processors

of processors.

Figure 5.25 illustrates the algorithm with a simple example. In Figure 5.25(a) we show a simple circuit that lies across two regions. Geometric extraction is performed in parallel on regions 1 and 2 and the nets are identified. Globally unique numbers are given to the nets. The incomplete nets are marked in Figure 5.25(b). Portions of the incomplete net whose results can be computed without additional information are processed and the results reported. The shaded region is then passed up to the parent object for merging. In the example, after the merge operation, net 1 subsumes net 3, and net 5 subsumes net 2. Finally, when the nets and devices are complete, they are also processed as shown in Figure 5.25(c).

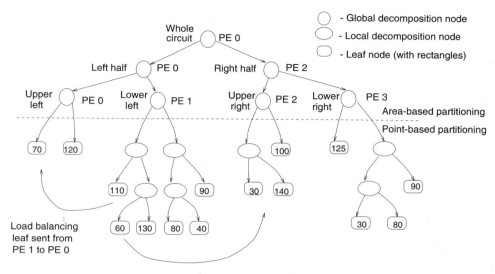

Figure 5.24 Load redistribution on tree of processors performing parallel extraction

TABLE 5.5 Runtimes (seconds) of Parallel HPEX Extraction Algorithm on Intel iPSC/2™ Hypercube

Circuit	Rectangles	1 Processor (sec)	4 Processors (sec)	8 Processors (sec)	16 Processors (sec)
1	54,800	373.3	107.6	59.6	43.5
2	66,000	na	106.4	60.3	41.4
3	130,700	na	156.8	78.1	46.3
4	258,600	na	na	163.2	80.5
5	260,000	na	na	220.7	101.8

Implementations The first parallel algorithm (synchronous algorithm) described has been implemented in the PACE extractor on an Intel iPSC/2™ hypercube by Belkhale and Banerjee [9]. Table 5.5 shows some example results on five benchmark circuits of the runtimes (in seconds) on varying numbers of processors on a 16-processor Intel hypercube using the equal-point-based rectangular partitioning method. Except for the first circuit, the serial algorithm could not be run on one processor of the hypercube due to memory limitations.

Ramkumar and Banerjee have reported an implementation of the second parallel extrac-

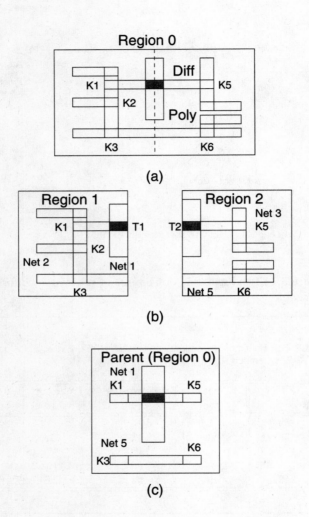

Figure 5.25 Example illustrating parallel extraction algorithm. (a) Layout region split at boundary. (b) Each processor extracts nets in parallel. (c) Parent processor extracts incomplete nets.

TABLE 5.6 Runtimes (seconds) of Parallel Extraction Algorithm PROPEREXT on NCUBE/2™ Hypercube

Circuit	Rectangles	8 Processors (sec)	16 Processors (sec)	32 Processors (sec)	64 Processors (sec)
1	54,800	16.3	8.0	6.8	4.4
2	66,000	47.7	38.2	34.0	34.7
3	130,700	97.1	84.3	80.5	75.0
4	258,600	na	41.8	34.0	28.6
5	260,000	na	na	59.7	48.9

tion algorithm (asynchronous algorithm) called PROPEREXT on an NCUBE/2™ hypercube. Table 5.6 shows the results of the parallel algorithm on an NCUBE/2 hypercube for several circuits. None of the circuits could be run on a single processor due to memory limitations, hence speedup results were not reported.

5.11.3 Shared Memory MIMD Parallel Algorithm

The preceding parallel algorithm can be very easily adapted to a shared memory environment where the entire mask layout information is kept in shared memory. The parameter extraction tasks on individual nets are kept as separate tasks in a shared task queue. The long nets are given higher priority over shorter nets. This simple scheduling algorithm gives good load balance in most cases. Again, there is a problem for one or two very long nets such as power, ground, or clock nets; hence, it would be desirable to decompose the tasks of solving each long net in parallel.

The strategy is again very similar to the previous algorithm. We assign each processor to a certain region of the chip, and therefore all rectangles of a long net in the appropriate region get assigned to each processor. We again perform rectangular decompositions similar to Figure 5.22 such that each processor determines the extraction parameters for the subnets in their region, and one of the designated processors performs extraction on the border rectangles on the net.

An outline of the parallel parameter extraction algorithm entitled *SM-PARALLEL-PARAMETER-HPEX-DATA* (for shared memory parallel parameter extraction using HPEX models with data decomposition) is given next.

Procedure *SM-PARALLEL-PARAMETER-HPEX-DATA;*

Read flattened mask layout;
Partition mask layout description among processors;

Perform parallel netlist extraction (described earlier)
FORALL processors in PARALLEL DO
    Perform local netlist extraction;

Perform merge of connected components;
Perform global netlist extraction;
END FORALL;

Global parameter extraction
FOR each global connected component DO
    Create a net extraction task;
    Insert in task queue;
    IF number of rectangles in net $> K$ (= 100) THEN
        Break up long net into short nets;
        Create short net extraction task;
        Insert in task queue;
END FOR

FORALL processors in PARALLEL DO
    WHILE there are nets in task queue DO
        Pick a net extraction task from task queue;
        Form rectangles, Decompose, determine knots, branches;
        IF any rectangle of L_i touches a processor border
            THEN postpone processing of incomplete nets;
                Create task for incomplete net;
        Compute resistance of completed nets;
        Compute capacitance of completed nets;
    END WHILE
END FORALL

End Procedure

Implementation The preceding parallel parameter extraction algorithm has been implemented by Belkhale and Banerjee [10] on an Encore Multimax™ shared memory multiprocessor. Table 5.3 given earlier shows some example results on five benchmark circuits of the runtimes (in seconds) and speedups of the parallel algorithm on a eight- processor Encore Multimax shared memory multiprocessor.

5.12 HIERARCHICAL PARAMETER EXTRACTION

5.12.1 Overview

In this section we will report on a parallel algorithm for parameter extraction using a hierarchical decomposition approach that is suitable for execution on a shared memory MIMD parallel machine.

Hierarchical extractors exploit the repetitive information in this representation by extracting a cell that is used many times only once and appropriately modifying it wherever it is used [24, 36, 38, 41]. We will suitably modify the hierarchical algorithm for netlist extraction described earlier for solving the parameter extraction problem. We assume that the hierarchical circuit extraction is performed in two steps: (1) transforming a circuit that has overlapping cells into one that does not have any overlapping cells and (2) subsequently performing the actual circuit extraction of each nonoverlapping cell.

5.12.2 Shared Memory MIMD Parallel Algorithm

We will now describe a parallel algorithm for hierarchical extraction that is suitable for execution on a shared memory multiprocessor. We assume that the hierarchical circuit description is stored in global shared memory. The first step of hierarchical circuit extraction, the overlap analysis and transformation step, is parallelized by assigning cells to different processors dynamically from a list. The second step involves the actual extraction of the individual cells.

One approach to parallelizing the second step involves assigning the extraction of cells to processors dynamically from a list. The list of cells could be obtained by sorting the cells in decreasing order of the number of rectangles it contains. This algorithm corresponds to the LPT algorithm (largest processing time first) [21] (LPT) for scheduling independent tasks on multiprocessors. The disadvantage with this approach is that some cells could be very large. A large cell assigned to a single processor will be a bottleneck for the whole computation, reducing the parallelism that can be obtained.

A second approach to parallelizing the second step is to assign more processors to the extraction of a large cell. The *partitionable independent task scheduling* (PITS) approach described in the related hierarchical algorithm for netlist extraction can be used here as well.

This algorithm has been implemented by Belkhale and Banerjee [10] on an Encore Multimax™ shared memory multiprocessor, and speedups of about 6.0 on eight processors have been reported on a variety of benchmark circuits.

5.13 HARDWARE ACCELERATORS

Numerous hardware accelerators have been proposed for speeding up the design rule checking problem. All work on flattened circuit descriptions and use data decomposition for parallel processing.representation. Many hardware accelerators that have been proposed for routing (discussed in Chapter 4) have also been programmed to perform design rule checking, since both problems involve local search strategies that map well on two-dimensional array processors. The basic idea for performing design rule checking in all the accelerators is based on the DRC algorithms on the pixelmap representation described earlier [2]. Consider a pixelmap representation of the layout as shown in Figure 5.3, and overlay a small square window (say 4×4) over the pixelmap so that each pixel is at some time the lower left corner of the window. At each such location some combination of pixels appears in the window, and a table lookup can reveal whether the window contains a rule violation. Since design rule checking is such a localized search operation, numerous researchers have mapped this basic operation into array processors. Figure 5.26 shows how the design rule checking can be performed on an array processor provided the mask layers are stored in a pixelmap representation.

Blank et al. [14] proposed the bit mapped processor shown in Figure 5.27 consisting of a three-dimensional data structure of bits in hardware that can support various local operations among its neighboring processors. It has been programmed to perform DRC using the window checking scheme. The ICL Distributed Array Processor (DAP™) consists of a 64×64 one-bit processing elements connected as a rectangular grid (four nearest neighbor connections)

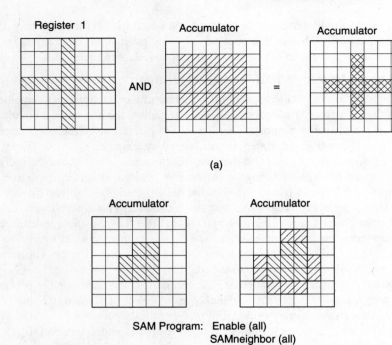

(a)

SAM Program: Enable (all)
                       SAMneighbor (all)

(b)

Figure 5.26 Design rule checking on array processors. (a) AND operation on masks. (b) EXPAND operation on masks. (Courtesy of Blank et al., *Proc. Design Automation Conf.*, ©IEEE 1981)

and two additional connections to the row and columns and operates in an SIMD fashion by which all processors perform the same instruction sequence. Adshead [1] has described how the DAP can be programmed to perform DRC. Rutenbar et al. have described algorithms for performing design rule checking on the Cytocomputer™ [34]. The Cytocomputer is a pipelined architecture of several identical stages each of which consists of a subarray processor that can perform operations on an individual pixel element and its four orthogonal and diagonal neighbors. Seiler has proposed a window processor that performs the design rule checking using rasterization hardware, a local checking hardware, and an error reporting hardware [37].

These hardware accelerators for design rule checking have all been based on the pixelmap representation, which is very inefficient in memory usage. Recently, Carlson and Rutenbar have proposed a scan line data structure processor for performing design rule checking [16].

5.14 SUMMARY

In this chapter, we have discussed parallel algorithms for applications dealing with layout analysis and verification. Three kinds of layout analysis tools were discussed: design rule

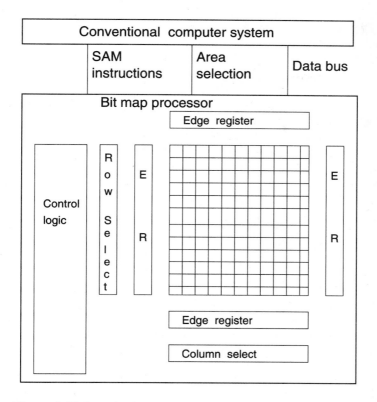

Figure 5.27 Organization of the Bit Mapped Processor Array (Courtesy of Blank et al., *Proc. Design Automation Conf.,* ©IEEE 1981)

checking, netlist extraction, and parameter extraction. For each problem, both shared memory and distributed memory MIMD parallel algorithms were discussed using a number of strategies for flattened and hierarchically specified layouts. We also discussed a massively parallel SIMD algorithm for design rule checking.

The parallel algorithm for design rule checking using area decomposition partitions a given chip layout by horizontal or vertical strips with an overlap of the maximum design rule interaction distance and performs DRC on each partition independently. The approach requires very little communication among the processors, and if each partition contains approximately the same number of rectangles, it gives good speedups. This approach is only suitable for flattened layouts, and is suitable for execution on shared memory and distributed memory MIMD multiprocessors.

The parallel algorithm for DRC using functional decomposition partitions the DRC tasks by the rules to be checked. Each rule can be potentially checked on the entire chip area by each processor. The approach is applicable to flattened and hierarchical circuits. However, the speedup of this approach is limited due to the fact that for many DRC operations we need to generate some common intermediate layers, which force a dependency on the application of the rules. This restricts the maximum parallelism available in the problem. The algorithm is suitable for shared memory and distributed memory MIMD multiprocessors.

A very efficient way to perform DRC in the sequential domain is to exploit hierarchical techniques. Parallel algorithms for hierarchical DRC essentially perform DRC tasks on individual cells in the hierarchical description of the circuit. The problem with this approach is that it is possible to get wide variances of load if we have cells of widely different sizes in a design. This can limit the speedups available in the problem. It is possible to use the partitionable independent task scheduling algorithm described for in the context of parallel hierarchical extraction to alleviate some of these problems [11]. The parallel hierarchical algorithm is suitable for shared memory and distributed memory MIMD multiprocessors.

The parallel algorithm for DRC using an edge based decomposition is suitable for SIMD massively parallel machines. The algorithm allocates each edge in the layout to a processor and performs DRC among processors owning adjacent edges. The approach gives good speedups, but is only applicable to flattened circuit designs.

In this chapter we also discussed parallel algorithms for netlist and parameter extraction. The parallel netlist and parameter algorithms based on data decomposition partition the chip area into subregions and perform local extraction within each region, followed by a merge algorithm to perform globally extraction. These algorithms are suitable for flattened layouts and can execute on both shared memory and distributed memory MIMD multiprocessors. Excellent speedups can be obtained through this method.

The parallel algorithm for hierarchical netlist and parameter extraction combines the benefits of hierarchy and parallelism to speed up the extraction process. In the simplest parallel hierarchical algorithm, each cell in the hierarchy is extracted independently on a different processor. This approach may give poor speedups if the load balance is not uniform, for example, if there are cells that are very big. A more efficient parallel hierarchical algorithm was proposed using the partitionable independent task scheduling method, in which a number of processors are assigned to solve the extraction problem of a hierarchical cell in parallel. This algorithm give excellent speedups and combines the benefits of hierarchy and parallelism effectively. The algorithms are suitable for shared memory and distributed memory MIMD multiprocessors.

We conclude this chapter with the following observations. The sequential algorithms for all the applications discussed have matured; hence parallel algorithms for the applications will become useful commercially. In fact, several industrial vendors have already started using such parallel algorithms. For example, Mentor Graphics has a parallel implementation of a circuit extractor called CHECKMATE™. An earlier version of the DRACULA™ program from Cadence Design Systems had a parallel implementation [31].

Future work in the area of parallel algorithms for layout analysis and verification will have to deal with changing technologies such as, non-Manhattan layouts. The scan line algorithms for edge-based representations can handle arbitrary polygons with some modifications. It remains to be seen how the parallel algorithms described in this chapter will have to be modified to include these changes.

5.15 PROBLEMS

5.1   Analyze the performance of the area partitioned distributed memory parallel algorithm for design rule checking, *DM-PARALLEL-DRC-AREA*. Assume a uniform distribution of rectangles on the chip area that contains $N \times N$ grid units and assuming equal area assigned to each processor. Assume P processors and a design rule interaction distance of $DRID$ units. Repeat your analysis assuming a clustered distribution of rectangles in the center of the chip. Account for load imbalances in the parallel algorithm assuming equal area. What would you do to balance the load? Give the advantages and disadvantages of your approach.

5.2   Design and implement a parallel hierarchical algorithm for design rule checking on a shared memory multiprocessor based on the algorithm *SM-PARALLEL-DRC-HIERARCHY*. Use the Sequent™ parallel programming library calls described in Chapter 2. Assume that the circuit mask description is specified in a hierarchical manner. Suppose some of the hierarchical cells are so large that they create a bottleneck in the processor executing the DRC task on that cell. Explain how you would speed up the parallel algorithm. HINT: Use the parallel algorithm for hierarchical extraction.

5.3   Design and implement a functional parallel design rule checking program for a shared memory multiprocessor based on the algorithm *DM-PARALLEL-DRC-FUNCTIONAL*. Implement the algorithm using dynamic self-scheduling, that is, without the use of a master processor.

5.4   Implement the SIMD parallel algorithm for design rule checking using the edge partitioned approach *SIMD-PARALLEL-DRC-EDGE*. Use the SIMD parallel programming library for the Thinking Machines CM-2™ Connection Machine described in Chapter 2.

5.5   Analyze the performance of the distributed memory parallel algorithm for netlist extraction using area decomposition, *DM-PARALLEL-NETLIST-AREA*. Use the method of equal number of points and a rectangular partitioning to decompose the chip area among processors. Compare the performance of this algorithm with the one using equal-area partitioning across processors. Assume uniform distribution of rectangles. Repeat the analysis with clustered distribution of rectangles, assuming highest density near the center of the chip. Assume R rectangles in an $N \times N$ chip area and P processors.

5.6   Implement the shared memory parallel algorithm for netlist extraction using area decomposition, *SM-PARALLEL-NETLIST-DATA*. Use the Sequent™ parallel programming library described in Chapter 2. Compare various load balancing strategies (static and dynamic) for the parallel algorithm.

5.7   The shared memory parallel algorithm for netlist extraction using hierarchy, *SM-PARALLEL-NETLIST-HIERARCHY*, allocates cells to groups of processors to perform netlist extraction in parallel on each cell. The allocation of the optimal number of processors to each cell is critical to the minimization of the execution time of the overall problem. The chapter has discussed a simple heuristic for solving the problem. Derive other more efficient heuristics for solving the problem, and analyze their performance compared to the simple heuristic discussed in the chapter.

5.8   Design and implement a distributed memory parallel algorithm for parameter extraction for the MEXTRA extraction model described in the chapter. Base your algorithm on the algorithm, *DM-PARALLEL-PARAMETER-HPEX-DATA*.

5.9   Design and implement a distributed memory parallel algorithm for parameter extraction using the HPEX extraction model, but exploiting the hierarchy of the circuit as well. The difficulty is in estimating the execution times and estimated speedups of individual cells.

5.16 REFERENCES

[1]   H. G. Adshead. Employing a Distributed Array Processor in a Dedicated Gate Array Layout System. *IEEE Int. Conf. Circuits Computers*, pages 411–414, Sept. 1982.

[2]   C. M. Baker. Artwork Analysis Tools for Integrated Circuits. Technical report, Massachusetts Institute of Technology, Cambridge, MA, 1980.

[3]   K. Belkhale and P. Banerjee. An Approximate Algorithm for the Partitionable Independent Task Scheduling Problem. *Proc. Int. Conf. Parallel Processing*, I:72–75, Aug. 1990.

[4]   K. P. Belkhale and P. Banerjee. Recursive Partitions on Multiprocessors. *Proc. 5th Distributed Memory Computing Conf.*, Apr. 1990.

[5]   K. P. Belkhale and P. Banerjee. Geometric Connected Component Labeling on a Hypercube Multiprocessor. *Proc. Int. Conf. Parallel Processing*, III:291–295, Aug. 1990.

[6]   K. P. Belkhale and P. Banerjee. Parallel Algorithms for Geometric Connected Component Labeling on Hypercube Multiprocessors. *IEEE Trans. Computers*, 41(6):699–709, June 1992.

[7]   K. P. Belkhale and P. Banerjee. Parallel Algorithms for VLSI Circuit Extraction. *IEEE Trans. Computer-aided Design Integrated Circuits Systems*, 10(2):604–618, May 1991.

[8]   K. P. Belkhale and P. Banerjee. PACE: A Parallel VLSI Circuit Extractor on the Intel Hypercube Multiprocessor. *Proc. Int. Conf. on Computer-aided Design (ICCAD-88)*, pages 326–329, Nov. 1988.

[9]   K. P. Belkhale and P. Banerjee. PACE2: An Improved Parallel VLSI Extractor with Parametric Extraction. *Proc. Int. Conf. Computer-aided Design*, pages 526–530, Nov. 1989.

[10]   K. P. Belkhale and P. Banerjee. A Parallel Algorithm for Hierarchical Circuit Extraction. *Proc. Int. Conf. Computer-aided Design*, Nov. 1990.

[11]   K. P. Belkhale, R. J. Brouwer, and P. Banerjee. Task Scheduling for Exploiting Parallelism and Hierarchy in VLSI CAD Applications. *IEEE Trans. Computer-aided Design Integrated Circuits Systems*, 12(5):557–567, May 1993.

[12]   J. B. Bentley and T. Ottman. The Complexity of Manipulating Hierarchically Defined Sets of Rectangles. Technical report, Computer Science Department, Carnegie-Mellon University, Pittsburg, PA, Apr. 1981.

[13]   G. E. Bier and A. R. Pleszkun. An Algorithm for Design Rule Checking on a Multiprocessor. *Proc. Design Automation Conf.*, pages 299–303, June 1985.

[14]   T. Blank, M. Stefik, and W. vanCleemput. A Parallel Bit Map Architecture for DA Algorithms. *Proc. 18th Design Automation Conf.*, pages 837–845, June 1981.

[15]   E. Carlson and R. Rutenbar. Design and Performance Evaluation of New Massively Parallel VLSI Mask Verification Algorithms in JIGSAW. *Proc. 27th Design Automation Conf.*, pages 253–259, June 1990.

[16]   E. Carlson and R. Rutenbar. A Scanline Data Structure Processor for VLSI Geometric Checking. *IEEE Trans. Computer-aided Design Integrated Circuits Systems*, pages 780–794, Sept. 1987.

[17]   E. C. Carlson and R. A. Rutenbar. Mask Verification on the Connection Machine. *Proc. Design Automation Conf.*, pages 134–140, June 1988.

[18]   K.W. Chiang. Resistance Extraction and Resistance Calculation in GOALIE2. *Proc. Design Automation Conf.*, pages 682–685, June 1989.

[19]   W. Fenton, B. Ramkumar, V. A. Saletore, A. B. Sinha, and L. V. Kale. Supporting Machine Independent Programming on Diverse Parallel Architecture. *Proc. Int. Conf. Parallel Processing*, Aug. 1991.

[20]   D. T. Fitzpatrick. MEXTRA: A Manhattan Circuit Extractor. Technical report, Department of Electrical Engineering, University of California, Berkeley, CA, Jan. 1982.

[21]   R. L. Graham. Bounds on Multiprocessing Timing Anomalies. *SIAM J. Appl. Math.*, 17:263–269, 1969.

[22]   F. Gregoretti and Z. Segall. Analysis and Evaluation of VLSI Design Rule Checking Implementation in a Multiprocessor. *Proc. Int. Conf. Parallel Processing*, pages 7–14, Aug. 1984.

[23]   A. Gupta. ACE: A Circuit Extractor. *Proc. 20th Design Automation Conf.*, pages 721–725, June 1983.

[24]   R. Hon and A. Gupta. *HEXT: A Hierchical Circuit Extractor*. Computer Science Press, Rockville, MD, 1983.

[25]   L. V. Kale. The Chare Kernel Parallel Programming System. *Proc. Int. Conf. Parallel Processing*, Aug. 1990.

[26]   U. Lauther. An O(N log N) Algorithm for Boolean Mask Operations. *Proc. 18th Design Automation Conf.*, July 1981.

[27]   S. Levitin. MACE: A Multiprocessing Approach to Circuit Extraction. Technical report, Department of Electrical Engineering, Massachusetts of Technology, Cambridge, MA, 1986.

[28]   J. Marantz. Exploiting Parallelism in VLSI CAD. *Proc. Int. Conf. Computer Design*, Oct. 1986.

[29]   S. P. McCormick. EXCL: A Circuit Extractor of IC Designs. *Proc. 21st Design Automation Conf.*, pages 624–628, June 1984.

[30]   M. E. Newell and D. T. Fitzpatrick. Exploiting Structure in Integrated Circuit Design Analysis. *Conf. Advanced Research in VLSI*, pages 84–92, 1982.

[31]   R. D. Nielson. Algorithmically Accelerated CAD. *VLSI Systems Design*, Feb. 1986.

[32]   S. Parkes, J. Chandy, and P. Banerjee. ProperCAD II: A Run-time Library for Portable, Parallel, Object-Oriented Programming with Applications to VLSI CAD. Technical Report CRHC-93-22/UILU-ENG-93-2250, University of Illinois, Coordinated Science Lab, Urbana, IL, Dec. 1993.

[33]   B. Ramkumar and P. Banerjee. ProperEXT: Portable Parallel Circuit Extraction. *Proc. Int. Parallel Processing Symp. (IPPS-93)*, Apr. 1993.

[34]   R. A. Rutenbar, T. N. Mudge, and D. E. Atkins. A Class of Cellular Architectures to Support Physical Design Automation. *IEEE Trans. Computer-aided Design Integrated Circuits Systems of Circuits and Systems*, CAD-3(4):264–278, Oct. 1984.

[35]   Y. Saad and M. H. Schultz. Topological Properties of Hypercubes. *IEEE Trans. Computers*, 37, No. 7:867–872, July 1988.

[36]   W. S. Scott and J. K. Ousterhout. Magic's Circuit Extractor. *IEEE Design Test Computers*, pages 24–34, Feb. 1986.

[37]   L. Seiler. A Hardware Assisted Design Rule Check Architecture. *Proc. 19th Design Automation Conf.*, pages 232–238, June 1982.

[38]   S. L. Su, V. B. Rao, and T. N. Trick. HPEX: A Hierarchical Parasitic Circuit Extractor. *Proc. 24th Design Automation Conf.*, pages 566–569, June 1987.

[39]   T. G. Symanski and C. J. Van Wyk. Layout analysis and verification. In B. Preas and M. Lorenzetti, editors, *Physical Design Automation of VLSI Systems*. Benjamin-Cummings Publishing Co., Menlo Park, CA, 1988.

[40]   T. G. Szymanski and C. J. Van Wyk. Goalie: A Space Efficient System for VLSI Artwork Analysis. *IEEE Design Test Computers*, 2(3):64–72, 1985.

[41]   G. M. Tarolli and W. J. Herman. Hierarchical Circuit Extraction with Detailed Parasitic Capacitance. *Proc. 20th Design Automation Conf*, pages 337–345, June 1983.

[42]   B. Tonkin. Circuit Extraction on a Message-based Multiprocessor. *Proc. 27th Design Automation Conf.*, pages 260–265, June 1990.

[43]   M. T. Yin. Layout Verification of VLSI Systems. *VLSI Systems Design*, July 1985.

CHAPTER **6**

Circuit Simulation

6.1 INTRODUCTION

Circuit simulation plays an important role in the design and verification of VLSI circuits. Circuit simulators are used to verify circuit functionality and to obtain detailed timing information before the expensive and time-consuming fabrication process takes place. Circuit simulation is one of the most heavily used CAD tools in terms of CPU time in the VLSI design cycle. Numerous researchers have therefore proposed parallel algorithms for solving the problem. An excellent review of parallel circuit simulation algorithms appears in [17].

In this chapter we will describe parallel algorithms for the circuit simulation problem. Section 6.2 will describe the problem and outline three different methods for circuit simulation: 1. direct methods, 2. nonlinear relaxation methods, and 3. waveform relaxation methods. Sections 6.3 through 6.7 deal with the direct method, Sections 6.8 through 6.10 deal with the nonlinear relaxation method, and Sections 6.11 through 6.13 deal with the waveform relaxation method of circuit simulation.

Section 6.3 will provide an overview of the direct method of circuit simulation. Section 6.4 will describe parallel algorithms for parallelizing the model evaluation phase of the direct method. Sections 6.5 through 6.7 discuss parallel algorithms for solving the linear system of equations in the direct method using different levels of parallelism and problem decomposition. Section 6.8 presents an overview of the nonlinear relaxation method of circuit simulation. Sections 6.9 and 6.10 will describe parallel algorithms for circuit simulation using the nonlinear relaxation method. Section 6.11 presents an overview of the waveform relaxation method of circuit simulation. Sections 6.12 and 6.13 discuss parallel algorithms for circuit simulation using the waveform relaxation method.

For each circuit simulation method, we describe different decomposition strategies. For each strategy, we discuss approaches to implementations on shared memory and distributed memory MIMD multiprocessors and massively parallel SIMD processors where appropriate. Finally, Section 6.14 will describe some work on hardware accelerators in circuit simulation.

6.2 CIRCUIT SIMULATION PROBLEM

The behavior of an electrical circuit can be accurately described by a set of equations involving node voltages, currents, charges and fluxes. The basic equations are formed from the Kirchhoff's Voltage Law (KVL) or Kirchhoff's Current Law (KCL), and the constitutive or branch equations. The branch equations can be grouped into three basic sets: (1) resistive, which relate the voltage to the current; (2) capacitive, which relate the voltage to the charge; and (3) inductive, which relate the current to the flux. The KVL and KCL equations are independent of the detailed equations that describe the individual devices in a circuit, but are determined entirely from the way in which the devices are connected together, which is the circuit topology. The KCL states that for any circuit node, the algebraic sum of currents incident at a node equals the rate of change of the algebraic sum of charges at a node. The KVL states that the sum of voltages across devices in any closed loop must be zero. There are many ways of expressing KVL and KCL equations. We will review only the ones that are well suited for electrical simulation of VLSI circuits.

The node equation formulation is the standard way of expressing KCL in circuit simulation. In this formulation, one equation is generated for each node in the circuit by stating that the algebraic sum of the resistive currents at a node is equal to the rate of change of the algebraic sum of charges at the node. A system of n nodes is described by a set of $n - 1$ equations for $n - 1$ nodes by setting an arbitrary node as reference node or ground node. For each node j of the circuit, except for the reference node, we form the following equation:

$$\frac{d}{dt} \sum_{\text{all capacitive elements at j}} q_{\text{element}} + \sum_{\text{all other elements at j}} i_{\text{element}} = 0$$

For example, for the circuit shown in Figure 6.1, the nodal equations are

$$c_1 \frac{dv_1}{dt} = -g_1(v_1(t) - v_in(t)) - g_2(v_1(t) - v_2(t)) - g_3((v_1(t) - v_3(t))$$

$$c_2 \frac{dv_2}{dt} = -g_2(v_2(t) - v_1(t))$$

$$c_3 \frac{dv_3}{dt} = -g_3(v_3(t) - v_1(t))$$

In general, the system of n equations that result have the following form:

$$C(v) \frac{dv}{dt} = -f(v(t), u(t))$$

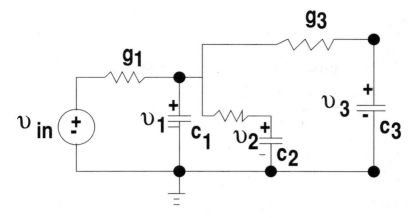

Figure 6.1 An example circuit for writing nodal equations (Courtesy of White and Sangiovanni-Vincentelli, *Relaxation Techniques for the Simulation of VLSI Circuits*, Kluwer Academic Publishers, 1987)

given initial node voltages, $v(0) = V$, where C = nodal capacitance matrix, f = vector of sums of resistive currents charging capacitances at each node, u = vector of input voltages, and v = vector of unknown node voltages. This set of first-order nonlinear ordinary differential equations has to be solved for the unknown node voltages, $v(t)$.

There are two basic approaches to solve the circuit simulation problem. The first, called the Direct Method, uses the following three basic steps: (1) An implicit integration method (backward Euler or trapezoidal rule) is used to convert the differential equations into a sequence of systems of nonlinear algebraic equations. (2) A damped Newton method is used to convert the nonlinear equations into linear equations. (3) The resulting sparse linear equations are solved using Gaussian elimination or LU decomposition.

While direct methods for circuit simulation have proved to be accurate, they have two limitations: (1) the solution time of the sparse linear equations becomes very expensive, and (2) waveform properties such as latency (certain circuit signal values do not change appreciably with time) and multirate behavior (signal values in different portions of the circuit change at different rates requiring different time steps) are difficult to exploit. MOS circuits, of which most VLSI chips are designed, exhibit a lot of latency and multirate behavior. Hence a second approach to solve circuit simulation has been proposed using relaxation based methods.

There are three forms of relaxation based methods.

1. Linear relaxation can be used in the third stage (solution of the linear system of equations) of the direct method to replace the Gaussian elimination method by an iterative method such as Gauss-Jacobi or Gaiss-Seidel method [22].

2. Nonlinear relaxation or iterated timing analysis, where the jth nonlinear equation in the second stage of the direct method (converting nonlinear equations to linear equations) is solved for the jth voltage variable while setting the other voltage variables to the previous iteration value (Gauss-Jacobi) or present iteration value (Gauss-Seidel). The equations are solved as part of a relaxation loop until the solution converges to a consistent solution. Then

the same process is repeated at the next time step.

3. Waveform relaxation method is applied at the differential equation level, at the first step of the direct method (solution of differential equations). The relaxation variables are entire voltage waveforms that are functions of time. By first guessing the waveform for all the voltage variables, each differential equation is solved in turn by assuming that the other voltages are fixed. The process stops when all the waveforms converge.

Although linear relaxation can be used in circuit simulation, it is often more effective to use relaxation in one of the earlier stages of the solution process. Hence circuit simulators using relaxation have been used mainly for nonlinear (iterated timing analysis) and waveform relaxation. The iterated timing analysis approach uses nonlinear relaxation to exploit circuit latency, and waveform relaxation exploits multirate behavior.

Researchers have investigated parallel algorithms for the direct methods and both forms of relaxation methods. In the following, we will review some of the main algorithms.

6.3 DIRECT METHOD OF CIRCUIT SIMULATION

We will now briefly describe the three basic steps in the direct method of solving the system of n equations that have the following form:

$$\frac{dq(v(t), u(t))}{dt} = g(v(t), u(t))$$

In the first step, an implicit integration method is used to convert the differential equations into a sequence of systems of nonlinear algebraic equations. The trapezoidal algorithm is frequently used which, given a time step h yields

$$\frac{q(v(t+h), u(t+h)) - q(v(t), u(t))}{h} = \frac{1}{2}[g(v(t+h), u(t+h)) + g(v(t), u(t))]$$

where $v(t)$, $u(t)$ and $u(t+h)$ are known, and the equation must be solved to compute $v(t+h)$.

In the second step, an iterative Newton-Raphson algorithm is used to convert these nonlinear equations into a set of linear equations. The Newton-Raphson iteration equation for solving a general nonlinear system of the form

$$F(x) = 0$$

is given by the equation

$$J_F(x^k)(x^{k+1} - x^k) = -F(x^k)$$

where (x^k) represents the value of x at iteration k, J_F is the Jacobian matrix of F with respect to x, and $F(x^k)$ is the Newton residue [17]. The linear system of equations then becomes

$$J_F(v^k(t+h))[v^{k+1}(t+h) - v^k(t+h)] = -F(v^k(t+h))$$

which can be solved by some form of Gaussian elimination.

In summary, the two most time consuming processes in the direct method to solving the circuit simulation problem are the model evaluation phase, which assembles the linear systems to be solved for each iteration of the Newton's method for each time point. The second is the linear system solution phase, which comprises the factorization of the Jacobian matrix and the solution of the linear system.

6.3.1 Model Evaluation

The model evaluation phase in the direct method assembles the linear systems to be solved for each iteration of the Newton's method for each time point and is a time-consuming phase of the direct method of circuit simulation. This requires the linearization of the nonlinear element characteristics and the addition of various currents, conductance, and charge values into the proper locations of the Jacobian matrix representing the matrix structure and the right-hand-side vector.

The device equations required to compute the contributions of the Jacobian matrix and the right-hand-side (RHS) vector are completely independent of one another and therefore can be parallelized. Figure 6.2 shows an example model evaluation of the Jacobian matrix and RHS vector for a simple circuit containing 3 elements, two resistances, $g1$ and $g2$, and a current source, J, and 3 non-ground electrical nodes, 1, 2, and 3. The KCL will result in forming a matrix equation relating the voltage variables $V1$, $V2$, and $V3$ to the element values. The element $g1$ connected between nodes 1 and 2 will be entered in matrix positions (1,1), (1,2), (2,1) and (2,2) with appropriate values $+g1$ or $-g1$. The element $g2$ connected between nodes 2 and 3 will be entered in matrix positions (2,2), (2,3), (3,2) and (3,3) with appropriate values $+g2$ or $-g2$. The current source J at node 2 will affect the right-hand side vector in row 2 and contribute a term $+J$. By looking at the circuit connectivity and the type of the element, it is possible to a priori know which locations of the matrix and right-hand side vector, the element contributions will be entered.

6.3.2 Solution of Linear Equations

Once the linear system of equations has been set up by the model evaluation phase of the direct method, the equations have to be solved. Because of the dependency relationships that exist in the factoring operations, parallelization is quite difficult. A circuit simulation problem is a special case of a sparse linear system solution in which pivoting or matrix reordering is avoided as much as possible. In most circuit simulation programs pivoting, is avoided because the linear equation is used as part of Newton's method for iterative solution of a nonlinear set of equations, and an occasional error during the iterative process does not affect the integrality of the result.

There are two basic forms of the LU factorization algorithm. They are called the source-row directed form and the target-row directed form and correspond to the $k - i - j$ and $i - k - j$ forms as characterized in [5]. Although these forms represent exactly the same set of arithmetic operations, they vary in operand access costs.

An outline of the source-row directed LU factorization algorithm entitled *LU-FACTOR-IZATION-SOURCE* is given next.

Procedure *LU-FACTORIZATION-SOURCE;*

```
FOR k = 1, n DO
    FOR j = k + 1, n such that a_kj ≠ 0 DO
        a_kj = a_kj/a_kk; /* Normalize */
    END FOR
```

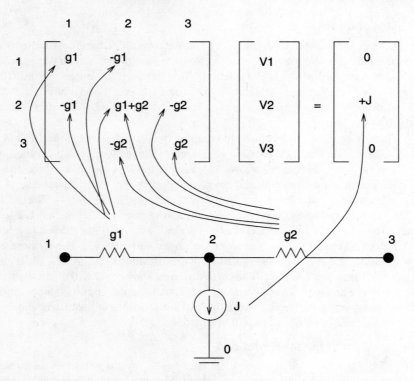

Figure 6.2 Model evaluation involves loading matrix and vector

FOR $i = k + 1, n$ such that $a_{ik} \neq 0$ DO
   FOR $j = k + 1, n$ such that $a_{kj} \neq 0$ DO
      $a_{ij} = a_{ij} - a_{ik} * a_{kj}$ /* Update */
   END FOR
   END FOR
END FOR

End Procedure

An outline of the target-row directed LU factorization algorithm entitled *LU-FACTOR-IZATION-TARGET* follows.

Procedure *LU-FACTORIZATION-TARGET;*

FOR $i = 1, n$ DO
   FOR $k = 1, i - 1$ such that $a_{ik} \neq 0$ DO
      FOR $j = k + 1, n$ such that $a_{kj} \neq 0$ DO
         $a_{ij} = a_{ij} - a_{ik} * a_{kj}$ /* Update */

      END FOR
    END FOR

    FOR $j = i + 1, n$ such that $a_{ij} \neq 0$ DO
      $a_{ij} = a_{ij}/a_{ii}$; /* Normalize */
    END FOR
    END FOR

End Procedure

The matrix A is processed according to the following order in the source row-directed method (the target-row method is similar). The row or column associated with the diagonal element a_{kk} is divided by the pivot element a_{kk}, and then each element a_{ij} is updated by subtracting the product of $a_{ik} \cdot a_{kj}$. The two basic operations in the algorithm are the normalize statement in the first loop and the update statement in the second loop. There are several levels of parallelism that can be exploited in LU decomposition.

    1. Fine-grain parallelism associated with each element level divide or update operation

    2. Medium-grain parallelism associated with row-level or column-level update operations

    3. Coarse-grain parallelism associated with independent pivots

Figure 6.3(a) shows an example of a sparse matrix. Figure 6.3(b) shows the row-level operations for its LU decomposition using the source-directed form. Figure 6.3(c) shows the row-level operations for its LU decomposition using the target-directed form.

In summary, the development of parallel algorithms for the direct methods for circuit simulation involves parallelization of the model evaluation phase and the linear system of equations solution phase.

We will describe various parallel algorithms for parallel model evaluation at various levels, element level, row level and matrix level, for both types of multiprocessors, shared memory and distributed memory.

We will then discuss various parallel algorithms for the sparse system solution at various levels, fine, medium and coarse, for both types of multiprocessors, shared memory and distributed memory.

6.4 MODEL EVALUATION

6.4.1 Overview

The model evaluation phase in the direct method assembles the linear systems to be solved for each iteration of the Newton's method for each time point. This requires the linearization of the nonlinear element characteristics and the addition of various currents, conductance, and charge values into the proper locations of the Jacobian matrix representing the matrix structure and the right-hand-side vector using basically a table-lookup method. The device equations required to compute the contributions of the Jacobian matrix and the (RHS) vector are completely independent of one another. An outline of the model evaluation algorithm entitled *MODEL-EVAL* is given next.

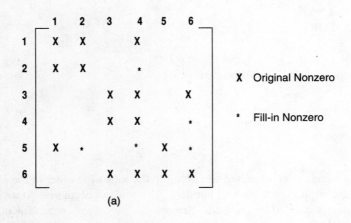

(a)

1. N1:   Normalize row 1
2. U12: Update row 2 using row 1
3. U15: Update row 5 using row 1
4. N2:   Normalize row 2
5. U25: Update row 5 using row 2
6. N3:   Normalize row 3
7. U34: Update row 4 using row 3
8. U36: Update row 6 using row 3
9. N4:   Normalize row 4
10. U45: Update row 5 using row 4
11. U46: Update row 6 using row 4
12. N5:   Normalize row 5
13. U56: Update row 6 using row 5

(b)

1. N1:   Normalize Row 1
2. U2:   Update Row 2 Using Row 1
3. N2:   Normalize Row 2
4. N3:   Normalize Row 3
5. U4:   Update Row 4 Using Row 3
6. N4:   Normalize Row 4
7. U5:   Update Row 5 Using Row 1, Row 2 and Row 4
8. N5:   Normalize Row 5
9. U6:   Update Row 6 Using Row 3, Row 4, and Row 5

(c)

Figure 6.3 Example of row level operations in sparse matrix factorization using the source and target row directed form. (a) A sparse matrix with fill-in locations shown. (b) List of row-level operations (source-directed). (c) List of row-level operations (target-directed). (Courtesy of Sadayappan and Viswanathan, *IEEE Trans. on Computers,* ⓒIEEE 1988)

Procedure *MODEL-EVAL;*

Read circuit elements and number of nodes;
Create Jacobian matrix and RHS vector of suitable size;

FOR each circuit element DO
   Determine element contribution on Jacobian matrix
     and RHS vector;
   Update Jacobian matrix and RHS vector;
END FOR

End Procedure

6.4.2 Shared Memory Parallel MIMD Algorithm

We will describe some methods for parallel model evaluation in shared memory MIMD multiprocessors. The accumulation of the Jacobian and the RHS vector requires synchronization because any location in the matrix or the RHS vector can have contributions from more than one device.

The first method is to have a lock for updating the matrix [9]. Before doing the element updates, the processors have to compete for a lock and execute the update as a critical section of code. Such a method has a lot of performance overhead since processors may be waiting for the lock. An outline of the model evaluation algorithm entitled *SM-PARALLEL-MODEL-EVAL-LOCKMATRIX* (for shared memory parallel model evaluation algorithm using element-based decomposition and locking at matrix level) is given next.

Procedure *SM-PARALLEL-MODEL-EVAL-LOCKMATRIX;*

Read circuit elements;
Partition circuit elements among processors;
Create shared Jacobian matrix and RHS vector;

FORALL processors in PARALLEL DO
   WHILE there are elements in own queue DO
     Pick next circuit element;
     Determine element contribution on Jacobian matrix;
     Wait for lock on matrix;
     Update shared Jacobian matrix and RHS vector;
   END WHILE
END FORALL

End Procedure

The second method is to use multiple locks, such as a lock per row of the matrix, and

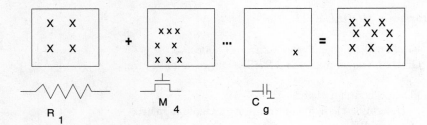

Figure 6.4 Templates for parallel model evaluation. (Courtesy of Saleh, Private Communication, 1992)

updates for appropriate elements of a row are performed while the row is locked [17]. An outline of the model evaluation algorithm entitled *SM-PARALLEL-MODEL-EVAL-LOCKROW* (for shared memory parallel model evaluation algorithm using element based decomposition and locking of row of matrix) is given below.

Procedure *SM-PARALLEL-MODEL-EVAL-LOCKROW;*

    Read circuit elements;
    Partition circuit elements among processors;
    Create shared Jacobian matrix and RHS vector;

    FORALL processors in PARALLEL DO
        WHILE there are elements in own queue DO
            Pick next circuit element;
            Determine element contribution on Jacobian matrix;
            Wait for lock on rows of matrix to be updated;
            Update shared Jacobian matrix and RHS vector;
        END WHILE
    END FORALL

End Procedure

The third method is a lockless approach based on barrier synchronization [1, 7]. In this case, a matrix template is allocated for each device in global memory. All the contributions for each device owned by a processor can be calculated and written to their respective private locations within each processor in parallel without any update. This is illustrated conceptually in Figure 6.4. After a single barrier synchronization point, the accumulation of the Jacobian matrix and the RHS vector is done in parallel. Each processor is assigned one or more elements of the matrix and must gather the set of contributions from the device matrix templates and updating the appropriate elements of the matrix. An outline of the model evaluation algorithm entitled *SM-PARALLEL-MODEL-EVAL-LOCKLESS* (for shared memory parallel model evaluation algorithm using element-based decomposition and without using locks) follows.

Procedure *SM-PARALLEL-MODEL-EVAL-LOCKLESS;*

Read circuit elements;
Partition circuit elements among processors;
Create shared Jacobian matrix and RHS vector;

FORALL processors in PARALLEL DO
   WHILE there are elements in own queue DO
      Pick next circuit element;
      Determine element contribution on Jacobian matrix;
      Update local copy of Jacobian matrix and RHS vector;
   END WHILE
   Accumulate local copies of Jacobian matrix and RHS vector
   into global shared copy;
END FORALL

End Procedure

In addition, consideration is given to the size of each basic model evaluation task and uniformity of tasks between different processors. For example, the multiple lock version is driven by a loop over all the devices, which is then synchronized in a manner described previously. The number of devices processed within each task in a parallel loop must be determined either statically or an runtime in order to minimize the cost of the synchronization points and balance the load across the machines.

Implementation We now describe the details of one parallel implementation using the lockless approach in the CAYENNE parallel algorithm for circuit simulation on a two-processor VAX 8800™ shared memory multiprocessor [1]. The Jacobian matrix structure is viewed as a three-dimensional structure. The third dimension of the structure is used to store each individual element contribution to a given circuit matrix as shown in Figure 6.5. For example, in the figure, the element G_1 has a contribution marked by the shaded boxes to the nodes i and j at the positions (i, i), (i, j), (j, j), and (j, i) as the first element in the third dimension at each of the matrix positions. The element G_2 has a contribution shown by the unshaded boxes at the nodes j and k at the matrix positions (j, j), (j, k), (k, k) and (k, j) as the second element in the third dimension at each of the matrix positions. There is no unused memory in this structure because there is a variable depth in the third dimension. The contributions for each matrix entry are subsequently summed and loaded in parallel in the circuit matrix. The matrix load is therefore performed in two successive phases. A dynamic task allocation is used over static allocation for the first phase of the load because the time needed to load each matrix element cannot be estimated exactly. The dynamic allocation is achieved through an array of tasks consisting of circuit elements to be loaded. An interlocked shared memory access is used to access the next array indexes representing the work to be used. Task allocation for

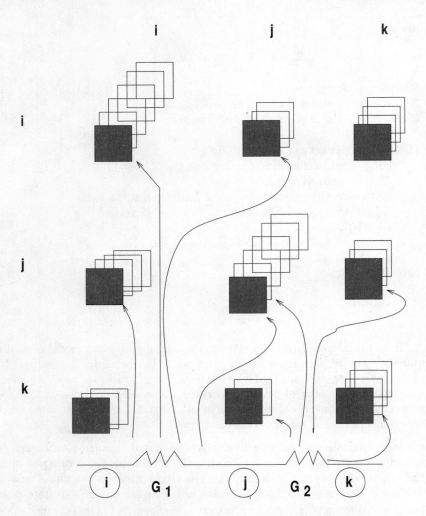

Figure 6.5 Three dimensional matrix structure for computing device templates (Courtesy of Bischoff and Greenberg, *Proc. Int. Conf. Computer-aided Design,* ©IEEE 1986)

the second phase of matrix load (accumulation) is done statically because the time required to perform these tasks would be almost equal.

Table 6.1 shows some example results on two benchmark circuits of the runtimes (in seconds) and speedups of the parallel algorithm for model evaluation on a two-processor VAX 8800™ shared memory multiprocessor.

TABLE 6.1 Runtimes (seconds) and Speedups of Parallel Model Evaluation Phase of a Circuit Simulation Algorithm on the VAX 8800™ Multiprocessor

Circuit	Nodes	Elements	1 Processor		2 Processors	
			Runtime	Speedup	Runtime	Speedup
ALU	200	1350	4260	1.0	2690	1.6
Control	160	530	750	1.0	440	1.7

6.4.3 Distributed Memory MIMD Parallel Algorithm

The parallel algorithms for model evaluation in distributed memory multiprocessors are based on the lockless approach for shared memory machines. The devices in the circuit are distributed statically to different processors such that the distribution of tasks of model evaluation is uniform across the processors. A matrix template is allocated for each device in its allocated processor. A global synchronization point is reached such that all processors completing their parallel model evaluation tasks report to one of the nodes acting as a scheduler, which in turn starts the accumulation phase of the matrix construction. Each processor is assigned a set of rows and is responsible for gathering the set of contributions from the device matrix templates stored in various processors. The accumulation of the matrix elements can be accomplished by a tree-based reduction algorithm rooted at the processor that owns the final matrix element.

An outline of the model evaluation algorithm entitled *DM-PARALLEL-MODEL-EVAL-ACCUM* (for distributed memory parallel model evaluation algorithm using element-based decomposition and accumulation of matrix) follow.

Procedure *DM-PARALLEL-MODEL-EVAL-ACCUM;*

Read circuit elements;
Partition circuit elements among processors;
Create local copies of Jacobian matrix and RHS vector
on each processor;

FORALL processors in PARALLEL DO
    WHILE there are elements in own processor DO
        Pick next circuit element;
        Determine element contribution on Jacobian matrix;
        Update local copy of Jacobian matrix and RHS vector;
    END WHILE
    Accumulate local copies of Jacobian matrix and RHS vector
    into global shared copy;
    Involves global reduction operations using sending messages;
END FORALL

End Procedure

No implementations of the distributed memory parallel algorithm have been reported.

6.5 ELEMENT PARTITIONED SOLUTION OF EQUATIONS

6.5.1 Overview

Once the linear system of equations has been set up by the model evaluation phase of the Direct method, the equations have to be solved. There are two basic forms of the LU factorization algorithm. They are called the source-row-directed form and the target-row-directed form as discussed in an earlier section.

In both the source- and target-row formulations of the LU factorization algorithm, there is an innermost loop performs the update and normalization operations. There is potential for parallel execution among the operations of LU decomposition of a sparse matrix. Figure 6.6(a) shows an example of a sparse matrix. The list of elementary divide and update operations is shown in Figure 6.6(b). The dependencies between the operations can be captured by the task dependency graphs shown in Figure 6.6(c), where the nodes represent an operation level tasks.

6.5.2 Shared Memory MIMD Parallel Algorithm

Given a parallel computation expressed as a task graph, one approach to scheduling its parallel execution is to use dynamic task queues onto which tasks are placed when their dependencies get satisfied and from which they are removed by a free processor. The disadvantage of this approach is the contention for a shared task queue which can easily offset any gain from parallel processing, especially for tasks of such fine grain size.

An alternative approach used in this application is to perform a one-time analysis and levelize the graph; where each task is associated with a level number that corresponds to the length of the longest path from any root task to it. Tasks of a levelized task graph are executed in order of increasing levels, with any two tasks at the same level being executed in parallel. Barrier synchronization is used to synchronize all processors at each level before proceeding to the next level.

An outline of the LU factorization algorithm entitled *SM-PARALLEL-LUFACT-ELEM* (denoting shared memory parallel LU factorization algorithm using element-based decomposition) follows:

Procedure *SM-PARALLEL-LUFACT-ELEM;*

Read in matrix elements and RHS vector;

Note sparse matrix nonzero entries;
Perform symbolic evaluation of equations below;
FOR $k = 1, n$ DO
    FOR $j = k + 1, n$ such that $a_{kj} \neq 0$ DO
        $a_{kj} = a_{kj}/a_{kk}$; /* Normalize */

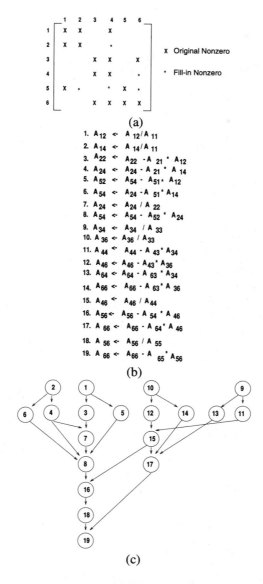

Figure 6.6 Example of element level parallelism in sparse matrix factorization. (a) A sparse matrix with fill-in locations shown. (b) List of element-level operations (source-directed). (c) Task graph for element-level operations. (Courtesy of Sadayappan and Viswanathan, *IEEE Trans. Computers,* ©IEEE 1988)

```
        END FOR

        FOR i = k + 1, n such that aᵢₖ ≠ 0 DO
            FOR j = k + 1, n such that aₖⱼ ≠ 0 DO
                aᵢⱼ = aᵢⱼ - aᵢₖ * aₖⱼ /* Update */
            END FOR
        END FOR
    END FOR
```

Create an elemental task node for every operation;
Levelize the task graph;
Partition tasks of task graph onto processors statically
    to give good load balancing such that at each level
    each processor has equal workload;

```
    FORALL processors in PARALLEL DO
        FOR each level L in task graph DO
            WHILE there are tasks in processor queue at level L DO
                Pick next task at level L;
                Execute operation and pass result to other nodes;
            END WHILE
            Barrier synchronize(level L);
        END FOR
    END FORALL
```

End Procedure

       Even though an idealized model of shared memory multiprocessor scheduling is feasible, may researchers have considered the model inappropriate for practical use due to prohibitive scheduling overheads. However, vector multiprocessors such as the Alliant FX/8™ that provide hardware-assisted scheduling of DO loops make the exploitation of fairly fine-grained parallelism possible.

Implementation Sadayappan and Viswanathan [15] have proposed a fine-grained parallel algorithm on an Alliant FX/8™ vector multiprocessor using a compiled/interpretive code approach. In this approach an ordered list of the entire set of elementary arithmetic operations required in the LU decomposition is obtained in a symbolic analysis phase where the task graphs are created. Good static scheduling is employed using a levelized approach. Tasks at each level are grouped into clusters and scheduled onto processors that are load balanced across processors statically. To exploit vectorization, the tasks in a task cluster are chosen to have the same primitive operation, so each task cluster represents a vector operation. Even though the concurrency of such an approach is high, the increased operand access times in the innermost loop accessing the sparse structure through a level of indirection of the pointers reduces the overall speedup. Experimental results on real circuits [15] have shown that speedups of about

5 on six processors can be achieved on an Alliant FX/8™ vector multiprocessor.

6.6 ROW PARTITIONED SOLUTION OF EQUATIONS

6.6.1 Overview

Consider the target-row directed LU decomposition algorithm, $LUFACT - TARGET$. The outermost i loop is independent since all target rows i can be updated simultaneously by the pivot source row k. Finally, with the outermost loop i, a row becomes a pivot row as soon as all prior rows have updated it. Hence parallelization at the row-level updates can be applied to distribute the tasks to multiple processors. In this approach each row-level update operation is an independent schedulable task.

Figure 6.7(a) shows an example of a sparse matrix. Figure 6.7(b) shows the row-level operations for its LU decomposition using the target row directed form. Figure 6.7(c) shows the task dependency graph of row-level operations using the target-row-directed form.

6.6.2 Shared Memory MIMD Parallel Algorithm

We will now describe a parallel algorithm for solving a linear system of equations using row-based decomposition that is suitable for execution on a shared memory MIMD multiprocessor. The algorithm is trivial if the matrices we are dealing with are full. However, since all circuit simulation problem matrices are sparse, compact sparse matrix storage schemes are typically used to save memory. In such schemes, only the nonzeros of the matrix along with the fill-ins (locations that will become nonzero due to some updates) are stored row by row in a single vector. An associated vector stores the corresponding column indexes. Auxiliary vectors point to the beginning of each row and its strictly upper triangular part. With this compact representation, even though the source elements involved in a row-level update are contiguously stored, the corresponding target-row elements are not necessarily so, since the target-row may have additional zeros that remain unaffected by the update with the given source row. A scatter-gather approach is used to solve such problems on vector processors with scatter-gather hardware. A target-row-directed approach is used. Before a row is updated, it is first scattered from its compact representation to a temporary full vector. All updates to the target-row by the relevant source rows are performed on the scattered target-row. For each source-row element involved in an update operation, the associated column indexes array provides the position of the corresponding target-row element in the temporary full vector. After all row updates to the target row are done, it is normalized and gathered back to its compact form. On machines such as the Alliant FX/8™, which has hardware support for scatter-gather, vectorization is possible. It is also possible to directly parallelize the preceding algorithm as follows. Each basic task involves the scattering of a target row, performing all the row updates on it, followed by a normalizing and gathering operation.

A second approach for exploiting row-level parallelism proposed by Sadayappan and Viswanathan is now presented [15]. As is obvious from the previous discussion, the cost of scatter-gather for each row-level update becomes prohibitive. In the context of repeated structurally identical factorization without numerical pivoting, the specific target-rows elements involved in a given row-level update can be computed a priori at compile time in a symbolic analysis phase. For any source-target row pair involved in a row-level update, an associated target indirection vector (TIV) contains the indexes of the compacted matrix of

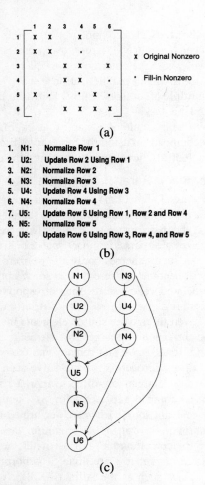

(a)

1. N1:   Normalize Row 1
2. U2:   Update Row 2 Using Row 1
3. N2:   Normalize Row 2
4. N3:   Normalize Row 3
5. U4:   Update Row 4 Using Row 3
6. N4:   Normalize Row 4
7. U5:   Update Row 5 Using Row 1, Row 2 and Row 4
8. N5:   Normalize Row 5
9. U6:   Update Row 6 Using Row 3, Row 4, and Row 5

(b)

(c)

Figure 6.7 Example of row-level parallelism in sparse matrix factorization using the target row directed form. (a) A sparse matrix with fill-in locations shown. (b) List of row-level operations (target-directed). (c) Task graph of row-level operations (target-directed). (Courtesy of Sadayappan and Viswanathan, *IEEE Trans. Computers,* ©IEEE 1988)

the relevant elements of the target row to be updated, in the same order as the corresponding source elements of a matrix. Thus, in the innermost loop, only one destination operand is indirectly accessed through the TIV vector, while the other two operands are a constant and a contiguous vector.

   The parallel algorithm proceeds as follows. For the sparse system of equations, a task graph is formed for the target-row-directed form, where the tasks are row-level updates. The graph is levelized in terms of the task-level dependencies as shown in Figure 6.7(c). The algorithm steps though the levels one by one, each step is separated by barrier synchronizations among the processors. For each level, all the tasks that constitute row-level operations (updates or normalization) are performed in parallel in vector mode by using the target indirection vector.

   An outline of the LU factorization algorithm entitled *SM-PARALLEL-LUFACT-ROW-TARGET* (denoting shared memory parallel LU factorization algorithm using row based decomposition using target-row directed scheme) is given next.

Procedure *SM-PARALLEL-LUFACT-ROW-TARGET;*

   Read in matrix elements and RHS vector;

   Note sparse matrix nonzero entries;

   Perform symbolic evaluation of row-level updates
      using targeted-row directed form below;

   FOR $i = 1, n$ DO
      FOR $k = 1, i - 1$ such that $a_{ik} \neq 0$ DO
         FOR $j = k + 1, n$ such that $a_{kj} \neq 0$ DO
            $a_{ij} = a_{ij} - a_{ik} * a_{kj}$ /* Update */
         END FOR
      END FOR

      FOR $j = i + 1, n$ such that $a_{ij} \neq 0$ DO
         $a_{ij} = a_{ij}/a_{ii}$; /* Normalize */
      END FOR
   END FOR

   Create a row-level task node for every row-level update;
   Levelize the task graph;
   Partition tasks of task graph onto processors statically
      to give good load balancing such that at each level
      each processor has equal workload;

   FORALL processors in PARALLEL DO
      FOR each level L in task graph DO
         WHILE there are tasks in processors queue at level L DO

TABLE 6.2 Normalized Speedups of Parallel Simulation Algorithm on the Alliant FX/8™ Multiprocessor

Circuit	Devices	Nodes	1 Processor Speedup	4 Processors Speedup	8 Processors Speedup
DAconvert	1388	124	1.0	3.72	5.32
Mem256K	1227	539	1.0	3.58	5.00
Mem64K	8689	2792	1.0	3.68	5.34

        Pick next task at level L;
        Since row is sparse, scatter row elements into vector;
        Execute all row operations in vector form;
        Gather row from vector form to sparse form;
        Store row in sparse form;
      END WHILE
      Barrier synchronize(level L);
    END FOR
  END FORALL

End Procedure

Implementation Sadayappan and Viswanathan reported on the implementation of this parallel algorithm on the Alliant FX/8™ vector multiprocessor [15]. They presented speedups of about 1.5 on six processors on the first algorithm using the scatter-gather approach. Experimental results on the second optimized algorithm using the compiled/interpretive approach and the target indirection vectors have shown speedups of 4.9 on six processors. Table 6.2 shows the normalized speedups of the second compile-time optimized algorithm on three benchmark circuits on the Alliant FX/8™ multiprocessor.

6.6.3 Distributed Memory MIMD Parallel Algorithm

In this section, we will describe a parallel algorithm for exploiting row-level parallelism that is suitable for execution on distributed memory multiprocessors based on work reported by Trotter and Agrawal [21]. We will discuss two approaches based on the source-row-directed and target-row-directed methods outlined earlier. In both schemes, the rows are mapped statically to different processors. The rows of the sparse matrix are distributed to the P different processors in a cyclic order, that is, processor 1 gets rows $1, P + 1, 2P + 1, ...,$ processor 2 gets rows $2, P + 2, 2P + 2,...,$ and so on. Each row therefore has a unique owner processor.

    In the source-row-directed algorithm which is based on the algorithm, $LUFACT - SOURCE$, described in Section 6.3.2, the algorithm identifies source rows that can be used to update different fan-out rows at the same time, using the directed graph to schedule the row operations, and to work out where to send the newly evaluated source row. The source rows are sent by the respective owning processors to the processors that need them. The various tasks in the directed graph are scheduled by assigning tasks to processors based on which row the task deals with. The source row is held in the owner processors' local memory and is used to update all the rows that the processor is responsible for. Once the operations are complete, the resultant source row is transmitted to other processors that may need it. The recipient processor may have to temporarily save the values if it is not ready to process them. An outline of the source directed LU factorization algorithm entitled *DM-PARALLEL-LUFACT-ROW-SOURCE* (denoting distributed memory parallel LU factorization algorithm using source-row-based method) is given next.

Procedure *DM-PARALLEL-LUFACT-ROW-SOURCE;*

Read in matrix elements and RHS vector;

Partition rows of matrix cyclically among processors;

Note sparse matrix nonzero entries;
Perform symbolic evaluation of row-level updates below;
FOR $k = 1, n$ DO
   FOR $j = k + 1, n$ such that $a_{kj} \neq 0$ DO
     Normalize row k;
     $a_{kj} = a_{kj}/a_{kk};$
   END FOR

   FOR $i = k + 1, n$ such that $a_{ik} \neq 0$ DO
     FOR $j = k + 1, n$ such that $a_{kj} \neq 0$ DO
       Update row i;
       $a_{ij} = a_{ij} - a_{ik} * a_{kj}$
     END FOR
   END FOR
END FOR

Create a row-level task node for every row-level update;
Partition tasks of task graph onto processors statically
   using cyclic distribution of ownership of rows;

FORALL processors in PARALLEL DO
   Use task graph to identify source rows that can be used
     to update different fan-out rows;
   Send source rows to other processors;
   Receive source rows from other processors;
   FOR each row-level tasks in owned by processors DO
     Since rows are sparse

Scatter source and target row elements into vector;
Execute all row operations in vector form;
Gather result row from vector form to sparse form;
Use task graph to check where to send the newly
    evaluated source row;
Send row results to respective processors;
END FOR
END FORALL

End Procedure

In the target-row-directed algorithm which is based on the algorithm, $LUFACT -$ $TARGET$, described in Section 6.3.2, the algorithm identifies target-row dependencies. Again, using a task dependency graph where the nodes are row operations, the tasks are statically scheduled on the processors such that all operations of a same level can be executed at a time. The target row is held in local memory of a processor. Source rows required for the target row are sent by the respective owning processors to the processor owning the target row, which can then update the target row. When the target row is fully evaluated, it can be used as a source row by other target rows. The order of the target row evaluations and the message communication is computed ahead of time to drive the scheduling and decomposition. An outline of the target-row directed algorithm entitled *DM-PARALLEL-LUFACT-TARGETROW* (denoting distributed memory parallel LU factorization algorithm using target-row-based method) follows:

Procedure *DM-PARALLEL-LUFACT-TARGETROW;*

Read in matrix elements and RHS vector;

Partition rows of matrix cyclically among processors;

Note sparse matrix nonzero entries;
Perform symbolic evaluation of row-level updates below;
FOR $i = 1, n$ DO
   FOR $k = 1, i - 1$ such that $a_{ik} \neq 0$ DO
     FOR $j = k + 1, n$ such that $a_{kj} \neq 0$ DO
      Update row i;
       $a_{ij} = a_{ij} - a_{ik} * a_{kj}$
     END FOR
   END FOR

   FOR $j = i + 1, n$ such that $a_{ij} \neq 0$ DO
     Normalize row i;
     $a_{ij} = a_{ij}/a_{ii};$
   END FOR

TABLE 6.3 Normalized Speedups of Parallel Circuit Simulation Algorithm on Simulated Multiprocessor

Circuit	Matrix Size	1 Processor Speedup	4 Processors Speedup	16 Processors Speedup	64 Processors Speedup
DRAM	2806	1.0	3.3	8.9	14.7
Omega	4212	1.0	2.5	4.2	4.5
MFR	5496	1.0	3.4	8.6	14.7
IIR	7310	1.0	3.6	10.7	22.4
Feb	11060	1.0	2.8	4.9	7.0

END FOR

Create a row-level task node for every row-level update;
Partition tasks of task graph onto processors statically
    using cyclic distribution of ownership of rows;

FORALL processors in PARALLEL DO
    FOR each row-level tasks in owned by processors DO
        Receive all the source rows for particular
        target row from processors owning them;
        Since rows are sparse
        Scatter source and target row elements into vector;
        Execute all row operations in vector form;
        Gather target row from vector form to sparse form;
        Send target row results to other processors
            needing result (for which this row is source);
    END FOR
END FORALL

End Procedure

Implementation Trotter and Agrawal have reported experimental evaluation of the schemes on a simulated multiprocessor in terms of processor utilizations [21]. Table 6.3 shows example results on five benchmark circuits of the speedups of the parallel algorithm on a simulated 64-processor distributed memory multiprocessor using the source-row-directed parallel algorithm. It should be noted that the simulated measurements estimated the speedups in terms of processor utilization through counting operations and ignored communication costs; hence an actual implementation on a real multiprocessor is expected to give lower speedups.

6.7 PIVOT PARTITIONED SOLUTION OF EQUATIONS

6.7.1 Overview

In the LU factorization algorithm for solving linear systems of equations, coarse-grain parallelism associated with independent pivots can be used as follows. For a given ordering of pivots, pivot a_{jj} is dependent on another pivot a_{ii} if a_{jj} must be factorized after a_{ii} to guarantee a correct solution. This can happen either when the matrix elements a_{ij} and a_{ji} are nonzero, or when there is a pivot a_{kk} such that a_{jj} depends on a_{kk} and a_{kk} depends on a_{ii}. Otherwise, the two pivots are termed independent, and factorization associated with each of them can be performed in parallel. Conflicts arising out of accumulation of the results of independent pivots can be handled using the lock-based approaches for shared memory multiprocessors or the lockless approaches for distributed memory multiprocessors described for the parallel model evaluation phase described in the preceding sections.

For uniprocessor applications, the goal of pivot ordering is to maintain sparsity to minimize the total number of matrix operations. The Markowitz algorithm produces a near optimal ordering by choosing at each stage in the process the pivot that has the lowest Markowitz count, which is defined as the product of the nonzero column entries and nonzero row entries, not including the element under consideration [17].

6.7.2 Shared Memory MIMD Parallel Algorithm

Numerous coarse-grain parallel algorithms based on independent pivot ordering have been reported. For a parallel processor, the goal of the ordering is to reduce the total time required to solve the decomposition by increasing the number of pivots that can be computed in parallel. A pivoting order so generated may not be the one with the fewest number of operations, hence a trade-off exists between the degree of parallelism and the number of additional operations introduced during the computation.

The quality of a particular ordering for coarse-grain parallelism can be measured by the longest directed path in an associated task dependency graph that reflects the pivot dependencies in the computation. Several ordering schemes have been proposed in the literature [20, 27].

Another approach to minimize fill-in is the notion of nested dissection of substructuring, which tends to produce matrices with a bordered block diagonal form (BBDF). The procedure to factorize the BBD form involves factorization of each diagonal block and then solving the connection matrix in the lower-right-hand corner associated with the border variables. This factorization algorithm exploits the inherent parallelism of the independent pivots contained in the diagonal blocks of a BBDF matrix. To reduce the parallel factorization time of the BBDF matrix, we would like to reduce the size of the diagonal blocks as well as the border. To achieve this, nested reordering schemes have been proposed as shown in Figure 6.8.

Numerous researchers have proposed shared memory parallel algorithms based on the preceding methods. We now describe one algorithm in more detail. This algorithm was originally developed by Cox et al. in the SUPPLE™ simulator [3].

Given a set of equations representing the circuit behavior the circuit is partitioned into subcircuits. The subcircuits can be obtained through user-defined directives, or by using a partitioner to partition the circuit recursively using an algorithm for graph partitioning

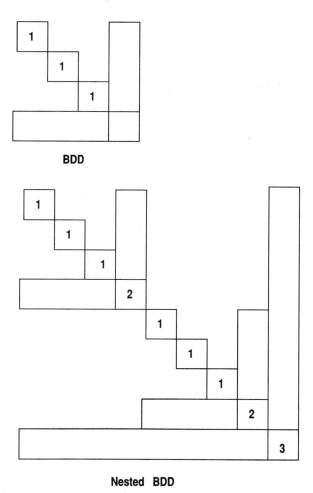

Figure 6.8 The bordered block diagonal (BBD) and nested BBD form
(Courtesy of Saleh et al. *Proc. IEEE,* ©IEEE 1989)

[11]. The circuit equations are subsequently reordered in the one-level BBD form shown in
Figure 6.8.

A parallel LU factorization step is used in each submatrices in the BBD form to remove
the internal variables from the equations that describe the subcircuit's interaction with the
rest of of the circuit. Each subcircuit can be loaded and partially LU factorized to the first
interconnect node independent of the other subcircuits. Subcircuit forward and backward
substitutions can also be performed independently. The solutions of these subcircuit equations
are then combined to form the global matrix. Since this resultant matrix is much smaller
than the original, the computation times for all phases of the nonlinear iteration phase can be

reduced.

An outline of the parallel routing algorithm entitled *SM-PARALLEL-LUFACT-PIVOT* (for shared memory parallel algorithm for LU factorization using pivot-based decomposition) follows:

Procedure *SM-PARALLEL-LUFACT-PIVOT;*

Read circuit description;
Partition circuit into subcircuits;
Form global Jacobian matrix and RHS;
Partition matrix into BBD form corresponding to subcircuits;

FORALL processors in PARALLEL DO
   WHILE there are subcircuits to solve DO
      Pick subcircuit from queue;
      Generate models, form Jacobian, RHS vector;
      Partially LU Factorize the submatrix;
      Partially solve the submatrix;
   END WHILE;
END FORALL

Combine solutions from submatrices to global matrix;
Complete LU factorization and solve;

End Procedure

It should be noted that in the total cycle of steps involved in the direct method of solution the execution times can be minimized by taking advantage of latency in the circuit. Specifically, we need to perform LU factorization only on those submatrices whose Jacobian has been modified. This is because the partial LU factorization of a converged subcircuit can be reused. The Jacobians of the subcircuits will remain constant under one of two conditions. First, the linearizations of all the nonlinear devices such as transistors must remain constant, which is true provides all the voltages and currents in the subcircuits are constant at reasonable tolerances. Second, the timestep must remain constant between iterations. In SUPPLE™ [3], the time step taken at any time point was determined by the average of the last 10 previous requested time steps, and was allowed to change if the average showed statistically significant variations.

Because of the subcircuit approach, the preceding algorithm can be implemented easily on a shared memory multiprocessor by maintaining a list of subtasks in a centralized scheduler. The scheduler assigns the tasks of factorizing independent diagonal submatrices to free processors.

Implementation Cox et al. have reported an implementation of the preceding parallel algorithm in the SUPPLE™ simulator that used implemented on a four-processor Sequent

Balance™ shared memory multiprocessor [3]. Speedups of about 3 on four-processors have been reported on some example circuits, such as inverter chains and clock driver circuits.

Remarks It has been reported that in the balanced partitioning scheme the speedup in the solution may degrade quickly due to the increased number of fill-ins. Numerous researchers have worked on the problem of partitioning or reordering the circuit matrices. Yeh and Rao [29] have proposed modifications of the basic node tearing partitioning scheme of Yang et al. [28]. The method uses a transformation of the circuit partitioning problem into a hypergraph partitioning problem and gives an algorithm to generate the partitions. Chang and Hajj have proposed an alternative partitioning algorithm [2] in which during the process of partitioning a circuit, instead of partitioning the into p equal parts for p processors, the sizes of parts are not necessarily kept equal, but instead the sizes and number of subcircuits are determined by minimality of the number of interconnection nodes and internal nodes in the largest subcircuit. The authors have showed that there exists an optimal level of partitioning that depends on the circuit structure, the number of processors used and the scheduling algorithm.

6.7.3 Distributed Memory MIMD Parallel Algorithm

We will now describe a distributed memory parallel algorithm for circuit simulation using pivot-level parallelism, based on the work of Yuan et al. [30]. The approach is similar in concept to the parallel algorithm described in the previous subsection. The simulation grid is partitioned using an incomplete nested dissection method dividing the matrix into independent blocks, isolated by multiple levels of separators. At each stage of the dissection process, a separator is found that divides the problem grid into two blocks. This procedure is recursively applied to each block until a block has been isolated for each processor. The circuit is partitioned or reordered into a hierarchical bordered block diagonal form (BBDF) shown in Figure 6.8(b) recursively using the heuristics of [18]. This is the difference with the SUPPLE™ algorithm [3] described earlier, which performed the partitioning on only a one-level BBD form. In the nested BBD form, we can judiciously choose the separators to balance the total number of blocks to have about the same size. The matrix structure and the mapping of the matrix to four-processors are shown in Figure 6.9. Each processor of a distributed memory machine handles one local block and its corresponding separators. The separators contain the interconnectivities among all the blocks, and each local block is independent of other blocks.

LU factorization is performed using a multifrontal method. Frontal methods have been introduced in the past to solve finite-element problems that are too large to reside in the main memory. In the distributed memory frontal method [12], each processor locally assembles the submatrix corresponding to its block of the dissected problem grid. Hence each processor is able to factor its own submatrix concurrently. Updates generated for locations in the matrix beyond those in the submatrix are maintained in a separate submatrix called the front. The processors assemble the front corresponding to the separators that were used to isolate the blocks. Interprocessor data dependencies manifest themselves in updates to the separators. Therefore, the processors may factor the blocks without communication. Updates to elements in separator fronts are stored in the processors that generate them. After the blocks have been factored, the partial updates of the separators are transmitted in long efficient messages to the processors that sum them. The two processors whose blocks were isolated by one of the final separators then cooperatively factor that separator's submatrix. This procedure is

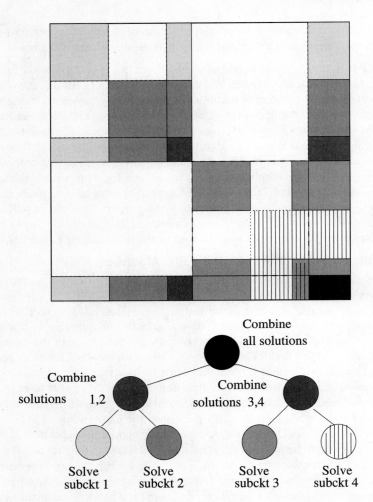

Figure 6.9 Nested BBDF and mapping to processors (Courtesy of Yuan et al, *Proc. Custom Integrated Circuits Conf.,* ©IEEE 1988)

repeated many times, each time doubling the number of cooperating processors until the initial separator is factored by all the processors. These steps are illustrated in Figure 6.9.

After partitioning the circuit into nested BBD form submatrices, the corresponding models related to each submatrix can also be partitioned and sent to the processors. With the distributed multifrontal method, each processor obtains a solution vector that includes the separators. In other words, the solutions representing the separators will be reproduced on multiple nodes. Since all the node voltages of any element are locally available to each processor after each Newton iteration, the model evaluation can be performed without any further communication. Each processor can independently produce its part of the Jacobian matrix. In this way, Newton iteration is performed concurrently the only communicating is done during the solution of sparse system of equations. Finally, after the Newton iteration the local truncation error and time-step calculations are also done on each processor. Then the processors communicate with each other to determine the next time step.

An outline of the parallel routing algorithm entitled *DM-PARALLEL-LUFACT-PIVOT* (for distributed memory parallel algorithm for LU factorization using pivot-based decomposition) is given next.

Procedure *DM-PARALLEL-LUFACT-PIVOT;*

Read circuit description;
Partition circuit into subcircuits;
Form Jacobian matrix and RHS;
Partition matrix into hierarchical nested BBD form
    corresponding to hierarchical partitioning;
Assign subcircuits and BBDF matrices to processors statically;
Replicate the solution vector on all processors;

FORALL processors in PARALLEL DO
    FOR log(P) steps DO
        Identify pairs of processors sharing separator;
        Receive assembled front from other processors;
        Receive truncation error, time-step
            from other processors;
        For subcircuit owned by processor
            locally assemble the submatrix corresponding to
            its block in the dissected problem grid;
        All node voltages available on all processor;
        Generate models, form Jacobian, RHS vector;
        Use distributed multifrontal method to solve matrix;
            Factor own submatrix independently;
            Updates generated for locations in matrix beyond
            those in submatrix maintained in front;
        Cooperate with processors to assemble front;
        Communicate truncation error, time-step
            to other processors;
        Combine solutions at separator;
        Send solutions one level up;
    END FOR
END FORALL

End Procedure

Implementation Yuan et al. have implemented the preceding distributed memory parallel algorithm in the PECSI™ circuit simulator on a hypercube [30]. The authors have reported on some circuit simulation results on several small benchmark circuits on an Intel iPSC/1™ hypercube of 16 processors and have demonstrated speedups of about 5 to 8. They have shown that the model evaluation part has nearly linear speedup, the matrix solution time did not show significant speedup, and the time-step control part of the algorithm produces significant communication overhead.

6.8 NONLINEAR RELAXATION FOR CIRCUIT SIMULATION

The direct methods described in the earlier section have proved to be accurate and reliable over a large class of circuits but suffer from two limitations. First, the sparse linear equation solution time grows faster than linearly with circuit size. Second, some waveform properties such as waveform latency and multirate behavior are hard to exploit. Waveform latency refers to any situation for which a signal value is not changing appreciably over some interval of time, as is true in most digital circuits. Multirate behavior refers to signal values changing at different rates over the same interval of time. Hence relaxation-based methods have been developed. The nonlinear relaxation methods exploit the latency property of waveforms and will be discussed in this section. The waveform relaxation methods exploit the multirate property of waveforms.

In the nonlinear relaxation methods using iterated timing analysis (ITA), the jth nonlinear equation is solved for the jth voltage variable while setting the other voltage variables to either the previous iteration value (Gauss-Jacobi), or the present iteration value if it has been computed (Gauss-Seidel). Specifically, given a nonlinear equation of the form

$$F(x) = (f_1(x), ..., f_n(x))^T = 0$$

at each step of the relaxation, the x_i element is updated by solving the implicit algebraic equation

$$f_i(x_1^k, ..., x_{i-1}^k, x_i^{k+1}, x_{i+1}^k, ..., x_n^k) = 0$$

for Gauss-Jacobi method, and

$$f_i(x_1^{k+1}, ..., x_{i-1}^{k+1}, x_i^{k+1}, x_{i+1}^k, ..., x_n^k) = 0$$

for the Gauss-Seidel method.

The solution of each nonlinear equation in either approach can be solved using a precise Newton-Raphson method at each step, but that is not required. It has been shown that the rate of convergence of the nonlinear relaxation is not reduced if, rather than solving the implicit algebraic systems at each step, only one iteration of the Newton method is used. Hence the equations are solved as part of a relaxation loop until the iteration converges to a consistent solution. Then a next time point is selected. Since the equations are recomputed, the computation for equations that are not changing with respect to time are skipped at each time point, thereby exploiting circuit latency.

The use of relaxation involves the partitioning of the circuit into subcircuits. The partitioning algorithm must consider the electrical coupling within the circuit, the derived convergence speed for the relaxation method, and parallel processing issues such as load balancing and degree of parallelism. For MOS circuits, the subcircuits are dc-connected or channel-connected sets of transistors, as shown in Figure 6.10.

The nonlinear relaxation-based methods have two general forms of parallelism: coarse-grain parallelism across subcircuits and fine-grain parallelism within the Newton iteration of a particular subcircuit. The problem with parallelizing the computations associated with a single Newton iteration is equivalent to the problem of parallelization of the direct methods discussed in the last section. In the case of relaxation-based methods, the subcircuits are usually small enough that the linear equation solution time is a small fraction of the total time. Therefore, parallel model evaluation is the only practical form of parallelism available at the fine-grain level. The coarse-grain parallelism is at the subcircuit level, and the degree of parallelism depends on the specific circuit structure and on the synchronization method, as explained later.

6.9 CIRCUIT PARTITIONED NONLINEAR RELAXATION

6.9.1 Overview

Nonlinear relaxation iterations can be defined in terms of a partial ordering of the subcircuits which is generated by extracting coupling information from the partitioner as shown in Figure 6.11. The subcircuit graph contains a vertex for each subcircuit and directed edges representing dependencies between subcircuits (flow of signals). In the classical Gauss-Seidel relaxation iteration, various subcircuits in the partial order are ordered into m ranks based on the distance in terms of directed edges from an input source. In the Gauss-Seidel relaxation iteration, a subcircuit can execute its kth iteration when all subcircuits of lower rank fanning into it have completed their k^{th} iteration and all subcircuits of higher rank have completed their $(k-1)^{st}$ iteration. The Gauss-Jacobi method is generated by placing all the subcircuits in a single rank and ignoring the directionality of the subcircuits within a single iteration.

6.9.2 Shared Memory MIMD Parallel Algorithm

The simplest form of parallelism is to process all the subcircuits in the same rank together. This leads to a multiple barrier approach, in which all subcircuits at a particular rank are evaluated in parallel by all the processors, which all synchronize at a barrier before proceeding to subcircuits of the next rank. The use of synchronization points between ranks suppresses the parallelism inherent in the relaxation scheme.

An outline of the parallel routing algorithm entitled *SM-PARALLEL-NONRELAX-CIRCUIT* (for shared memory parallel algorithm for nonlinear relaxation using subcircuit-based decomposition) is given next.

Procedure *SM-PARALLEL-NONRELAX-CIRCUIT;*
    Read in circuit description;
    Partition circuit into subcircuits;
    Rank subcircuits in order of evaluation in Gauss-Seidel
        relaxation iteration order;
    Assign subcircuits to processors statically by balancing
        workload at each rank;

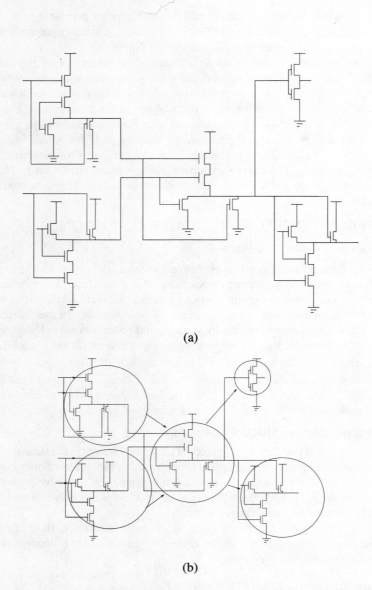

(a)

(b)

Figure 6.10 Subcircuit partitioning for MOS circuits. (a) Example MOS circuit. (b) Subcircuit partitioning. (Courtesy of Saleh, private communication, 1990.)

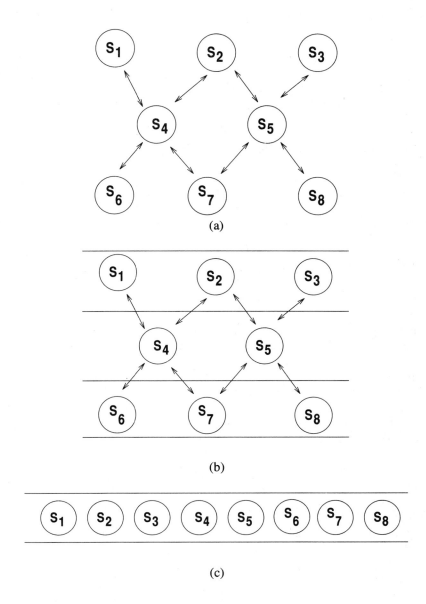

Figure 6.11 Example of partial ordering for Gauss-Seidel and Gauss-Jacobi Iterations. (a) Example subcircuit task graph. (b) Gauss-Seidel ordering ($m = 3$). (c) Gauss-Jacobi ordering ($m = 1$). (Courtesy of Saleh et al., *Proc. IEEE,* ©IEEE 1989)

        REPEAT Gauss-Seidel iteration
            FORALL processors in PARALLEL DO
                FOR each rank r DO
                    WHILE there are subcircuits s at rank r DO
                        Pick subcircuit s;
                        Solve subcircuit s for that iteration;
                    END WHILE
                    Barrier synchronize(rank r);
                END FOR
            END FOR ALL
        UNTIL convergence

End Procedure

Another approach to extract more parallelism is to alter the partial ordering in some static way, such as by moving subcircuits from one rank to another or by changing some dependencies into cross-iteration edges. Such alterations should be based on the number of processors available, the coupling of the subcircuits, the effect on the convergence, and sizes of subcircuits.

A third way to extract parallelism is to remove the multiple barriers between ranks, but use a single barrier synchronization at the end of each iteration. Within the iteration, subcircuits are processed in a data flow manner using queue-based approaches. On machines with hardware support for iteration indexes assignment, the following approach can be used. A list created a priori assigns all the tasks in one iteration to a set of processors. When a processor grabs a subcircuit task, it waits for the dependencies of the assigned tasks to be satisfied before proceeding with the task.

The amount of parallelism can be increased even further by eliminating the artificial barriers between iterations. This is achieved by "unrolling" the data dependence graph implied for each iteration over several iterations, as shown in Figure 6.12.

The complexity of such a scheme increases considerably, since convergence decisions and updates of global information that were originally performed at synchronization points are now distributed. Priority queues must be used to guarantee that tasks from earlier iterations always take precedence.

The simplified static scheduling methods mentioned here have a number of limitations when latency is exploited, since a static definition of a task graph cannot anticipate the subcircuits that will become latent at each time point. It also cannot anticipate the subcircuits that will become latent or activated due to fan-out scheduling. Updating the task graph at each time point is possible but represents a high overhead.

One variant of the classical scheme of static scheduling is an event-driven selective trace technique [16]. In this approach, whenever the value of an input node or any internal node of a subcircuit changes, an event is generated, due to which all if its fan-out subcircuits are scheduled dynamically to be processed. In this way, the effect of a change at the input

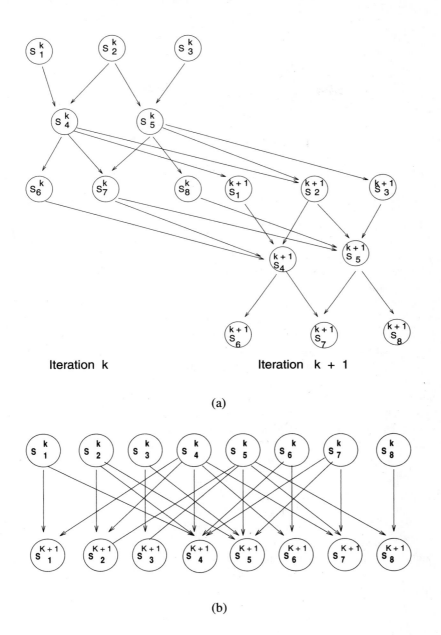

Iteration k   Iteration k + 1

(a)

(b)

Figure 6.12 Unrolled (a) Gauss-Seidel and (b) Gauss-Jacobi iterations
(Courtesy of Saleh et al., *Proc. IEEE,* ©IEEE 1989)

TABLE 6.4 Runtimes (seconds) and speedups of parallel circuit simulation algorithm on the Alliant FX/8™ Multiprocessor

	1 proc		8 proc	
Circuit	Runtime	Speedup	Runtime	Speedup
scdac	520.9	1.0	83.1	6.2
cramb	424.3	1.0	75.5	5.6
decpla	83.9	1.0	115.8	5.3
ckt3	1011	1.0	166.2	6.1

of the circuit may be traced as it propagates to other circuit nodes via fan-out tables and the event-driven scheduling algorithm. When the fan-outs of a subcircuit are scheduled, however, they are placed on a queue with a priority based on ranking due to the dominant edges of the Gauss-Seidel task graph.

We now describe various schemes for scheduling tasks corresponding to the evaluation of a particular node's voltage among processors. One scheme for scheduling tasks among the processors is to have one processor act as a centralized scheduler whose responsibility is to assign tasks to different processors. The problem with this approach is that the centralized scheduler constitutes a bottleneck.

A second scheme uses a distributed scheduler to implement a dynamic balance of tasks; each processor has a scheduler. Each scheduling processor places a task for processing on the queue of the processor with the least number of tasks in the queue at that time. The problem with this approach is that the distributed task allocation promotes contention for the global data structure that stores the number of tasks, which grows as the square of the number of tasks.

A third scheme is to use static task allocation to assign nodes to certain processors. It has been experimentally observed that the reduced runtime scheduling overhead and the lack of shared data contention improve the performance of the previous two methods. Speedups of about 20 were measured on 60 processors, but the speedup curves flattened out after a while since the load imbalances among subcircuit evaluations limited the speedups.

A final scheme that can be implemented is to use a single queue dynamic scheduling in which tasks are placed on and taken off a single centralized queue dynamically by processors. Even though this approach has the best load balancing, the centralized queue contention is high, hence the speedup curve shows a hump. That is, it starts to decrease after adding too many processors.

Implementation The preceding parallel algorithms for iterated timing analysis have been implemented in the PSPLICE program on the Sequent Balance™ multiprocessor and the Alliant FX/8™ multiprocessor [7, 16]. Table 6.4 shows some example results on four benchmark circuits of the speedups of the parallel algorithm on an Alliant FX/8™ shared memory multiprocessor.

Deutsch and Newton have reported another implementation of the preceding parallel algorithm in the MSPLICE program on the BBN Butterfly™ [8, 4]. Several scheduling schemes have been experimentally evaluated for the MSPLICE implementation on the BBN Butterfly using 10 processors. Experimentally, for the circuits that were tested, the scheduling algorithm using a single queue dynamic scheduling gave the maximum speedups among all schemes. On some example circuits, speedups of 7 on 10 processors were reported.

6.9.3 Distributed Memory MIMD Parallel Algorithm

We will now describe a distributed memory parallel algorithm for circuit simulation using nonlinear relaxation based on work reported by Ramamoorthy and Vij [14]. The first step is to partition the circuit into subcircuits which represent transistors that are connected by source-drain paths. The circuit is partitioned in the distributed memory multiprocessor such that each processor operates on a set of subcircuits and performs the same relaxation algorithm on its subcircuit. Consider the circuit shown in Figure 6.10. The nodes and their associated fan-in elements of each circuit partition are allocated to specific processors.

A single global variable *GlobalRemainingNets* is used to coordinate the processors at a given time point. It is incremented whenever a node is scheduled at this time point, and decremented when a node has finished being processed. When *GlobalRemainingNets* reaches zero, all processors move to the next time point of simulation. From the viewpoint of a single processor, we assume it has been allocated a set of electrical nodes M.

An outline of the *DM-PARALLEL-NONRELAX-CIRCUIT* (for distributed memory parallel algorithm for nonlinear relaxation using subcircuit-based decomposition) is given next.

Procedure *DM-PARALLEL-NONRELAX-CIRCUIT;*
Read in circuit description;
Partition circuit into subcircuits;

$t_n = 0$;
WHILE $(t_n <$ TSTOP) DO
   k = 0;
   WHILE *(GlobalRemainingNets* > 0) DO
      FORALL processors in PARALLEL DO
         FOR each node i in M (set of nodes in processor)
            that has been scheduled at time t_n DO
               FOR each fan-in element at i DO
                   Obtain its fan-in voltage using receive message,
                   $v_j^K, \mathrm{j} \neq \mathrm{i}, \mathrm{K} = \mathrm{k}$ or k+ 1;
               END FOR

               FOR each fan-in element at i DO
                   Compute its contribution to the nodal equation;

               Obtain v_i^{k+1} using a single Newton-Raphson step;

```
            IF (convergence achieved) THEN
                IF (v_{i,n} ≠ v_{i,n-1}) THEN
                    Schedule node i at t_{n+1};
                    Decrement GlobalRemainingNets;
                END IF
            ELSE
                Schedule i again at t_n;
                FOR all fan-out nodes of i DO
                    Increment GlobalRemainingNets;
                    Send message to the processors owning fan-out
                    nodes to schedule fan-out nodes;
                END FOR
            END IF

        END FOR
      END FORALL
    END WHILE ;
    k = k + 1;
  t_n = t_{n+1};
  END WHILE;
```

End Procedure

We now discuss some strategies for allocating subcircuits among processors. Three static allocation strategies have been proposed [14]. One simple strategy is to randomly allocate subcircuits to processors, while maintaining approximately the same number of nodes on each processor. A second strategy allocates nodes that are connected in a serial path to the same processor. This minimizes the interprocessor communication. Whenever more that one fan-out element is present, the other fan-out nodes are allocated to different processors. A third more involved strategy is to partition the nodes in the circuit among processors such that adjacent nodes in the circuit are placed on adjacent processors in the multiprocessor. Nodes can be allocated to processors dynamically as well. However, this causes a lot of movement of simulation data across processors; hence, even though this might give better load balance, the runtimes will be extremely large. Hence, dynamic node allocation is not practical on distributed memory multiprocessors.

Implementation Ramamoorthy and Vij have reported on an implementation of the preceding parallel algorithm on the Thinking Machines CM-5™ distributed memory multiprocessor [14]. Table 6.5 shows the runtimes and speedups of four benchmark circuits on a 128-processor CM-5.

TABLE 6.5 Runtimes (seconds) and Speedups of Parallel Circuit Simulation Algorithm on the CM-5™ Multiprocessor

Circuit	Devices	Nodes	1 Processor		128 Processors	
			Runtime	Speedup	Runtime	Speedup
adder	442	226	59	1.0	4.2	14.0
regfile	74,832	1,559	538	1.0	44.8	12.0
c7552	15,394	7,906	43,086	1.0	980	44.0
simd	37,939	18,860	694,916	1.0	17,372	40.0

6.10 POINT PARTITIONED NONLINEAR RELAXATION

6.10.1 Overview

We now describe a circuit simulation algorithm that is based on a Gauss-Jacobi form of nonlinear relaxation using a point-based parallel decomposition. In general, the system of n equations that is to be solved in order to perform circuit simulation have the following form:

$$\frac{d}{dt}q(v(t), u(t)) = -f(v(t), u(t))$$

For each time step, an initial guess of the voltages at the present time point is made on the basis of the voltages of the previous time points. The nonlinear set of equations

$$g_i(v_1^{k-1}, ..., v_i^k, ..., v_n^{k-1}) = 0$$

is repeatedly solved for each voltage v_i^k using the Newton-Raphson method until the relaxation iteration has converged. Each node voltage can be solved for independently, hence in parallel. After the relaxation iteration has converged, v_i^k becomes the new voltage at time $t + h$, and we can advance to the new time step.

It should be noted that in this algorithm, a point-based decomposition of nonlinear relaxation is used since the equations are completely decoupled from each other. This method can be contrasted with block-wise decomposition methods where the equations are grouped into subsystems and the decoupling operates between subsystems. It is well-known that the algorithms based on point-based decompositions converge much slower than algorithms based on block wise decompositions.

6.10.2 Massively Parallel SIMD Algorithm

We will now present a massively parallel algorithm for circuit simulation based on work reported by Webber and Sangiovanni-Vincentelli [23] that is suitable for execution on an SIMD machine.

In the parallel algorithm, each data type, specifically circuit nodes and devices such as transistors, resistors, capacitors, is mapped to a unique processor, and the interconnect between the nodes and devices is represented by pointers to the appropriate processors. Figure 6.13

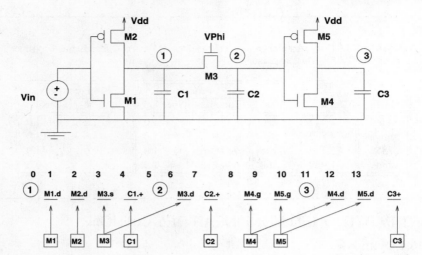

Figure 6.13 Example circuit and data structure on SIMD processor (Courtesy of Webber and Sangiovanni-Vincentelli, *Proc. Design Automation Conf.*, ©ACM 1987)

shows an example MOS circuit and its corresponding data distribution on a massively parallel processor. In the data structure, the first row is the processor number, and the second and third rows show the contents of the corresponding processor. The circles represent circuit nodes, the squares represent the devices, and the underlines represent the fan-out elements.

The parallel algorithm for circuit simulation is as follows. For each simulation time, a number of iterations are executed. For each iteration step, first all the node voltages from the processors containing the circuit nodes are sent to the processors containing the devices. This communication is performed efficiently by using the *scan* operator provided by SIMD parallel machines such as the Thinking Machines CM-2™ Second, all the devices are evaluated by selecting all the processors containing a given device model and executing the evaluation routine for that model. Third, each device sends the results of their computation back to the processors containing the circuit nodes. Fourth, all the processors containing circuit nodes are again selected, the code for completing the iteration step is executed, and the node voltages are updated. This process is repeated until the relaxation iteration converges and then advances to the next step.

In the massively parallel algorithm, a point-based decomposition is used in the nonlinear relaxation method that is known to cause slow convergence. If block decomposition is used, convergence is obtained much faster. However, for block wise decomposition, the solution of sparse matrices is required. This results in nonuniform data distributions that make the exploitation of fine-grain parallelism difficult in machines such as the Thinking Machines CM-2™. For ease of implementation, the point-based decomposition is used with the hope that, if the iterations are cheap enough, it is allowable to take a large number of iterations to make up for small convergence.

An outline of the massively parallel nonlinear relaxation algorithm entitled *SIMD-*

PARALLEL-NONRELAX-POINT (for massively parallel SIMD algorithm for nonlinear relaxation using point based decomposition) is given next.

Procedure *SIMD-PARALLEL-NONRELAX-POINT;*
    Read in circuit description;
    Map each circuit device and circuit node on different processor;
    REPEAT Gauss-Jacobi iteration
        FORALL processors in PARALLEL DO
            Select processors that own circuit nodes
                Send (voltages) to processors owning devices;
            FOR each device in circuit DO
                Select processors owning circuit devices;
                    Evaluate the device model;
            END FOR
            Select processors owning circuit devices;
                Send responses to processors owning circuit nodes;
            Select processors owning circuit nodes
                Calculate new node voltages;
        END FORALL
    UNTIL convergence

End Procedure

Implementation Webber and Sangiovanni-Vincentelli have reported on the implementation of the parallel algorithm on the Thinking Machines CM-2™ containing 16,000 bit serial processors and have compared the runtime of the algorithm on several benchmark circuits with implementations of circuit simulation using the direct and waveform relaxation methods on a DEC Microvax™ workstation. It was found that the execution time is roughly independent of the problem size in the Thinking Machines CM-2™ implementation since, as the problem size increased, more processors were added. Specifically, it took around 2000 seconds (for circuits with 100 to 500 nodes). The sequential implementations of the direct methods went from 100 to 70,000 seconds for circuits varying from 50 to 500 nodes, and the waveform relaxation methods went from 70 up to 15,000 for circuits from 50 to 500 nodes. Hence, for the largest circuits tried, the speedups of the massively parallel implementation over the best sequential implementation on a workstation were about 8.

6.11 WAVEFORM RELAXATION FOR CIRCUIT SIMULATION

The waveform relaxation method uses relaxation techniques at the differential equation solution level on the system of equations

$$\frac{dq(v(t), u(t))}{dt} = -f(v(t), u(t))$$

The relaxation variables are voltage waveforms that are functions of time. In each iteration entire waveforms are computed for each variable. Each subcircuit is solved for the output waveforms independently, given the input waveforms of the various nodes.

Specifically, in the Gauss-Jacobi algorithm for waveform relaxation, we solve the equations

$$v^{k+1} = f(v^k, \frac{dv^k}{dt}, u, t)$$

where v represents the unknown solution vector of node voltages, k is the waveform iteration number, u is a vector of external inputs, and t is the solution time. To compute the new voltage values for the solution vector, the Gauss-Jacobi algorithm uses the previous iteration's results for all input waveforms.

By contrast, the Gauss-Seidel waveform relaxation method uses a combination of results from current and previous iterations

$$v_i^{k+1} = f(v_{j<i}^{k+1}, v_{j \geq i}^k, \frac{dv_{j<i}^{k+1}}{dt}, \frac{dv_{j \geq i}^k}{dt}, u, t)$$

The Gauss-Seidel algorithm forces an ordering of the analysis and some serialization among subcircuits. It requires all subcircuits to be leveled and ordered based on their level (starting from primary inputs at level 0); that is, all level i subcircuits must be analyzed before any level $i + 1$ subcircuit.

The waveform relaxation (Gauss-Jacobi or Gauss-Seidel) algorithm begins by guessing a waveform for all the voltage variables. Then each differential equation is solved in turn assuming that all the other waveforms for the other variables are known. Once all the equations in the system have been processed, each solution is checked to use if the newly computed waveform is close enough to the previous waveform. The process is repeated until convergence is achieved. The procedure is illustrated in Figure 6.14.

The advantage of waveform relaxation is that it exploits the multirate property, because different time steps can be used in the solution of each differential equation.

6.12 WINDOW PARTITIONED WAVEFORM RELAXATION

6.12.1 Overview

The convergence speed of waveform relaxation methods depends on the coupling between the various equations in the system, the order in which the equations are processed and on the size of the interval over which the waveforms are computed. Waveform relaxation programs use the concept of windows to break the simulation interval into subintervals, and waveforms are computed for one window at a time [25].

A subcircuit evaluation in a full window technique begins executing only after all the waveforms from other fan-in tasks have been computed over the same interval. When a subcircuit has computed its internal waveforms, it checks to see if its fan-out subcircuits are ready for execution and, if so, they are scheduled for execution.

6.12.2 Shared Memory MIMD Parallel Algorithm

In parallel waveform relaxation using the full window technique, the largest-grain task consists of solving a subcircuit over an entire time window for one relaxation iteration. Since the full window technique represents a large amount of computation, the task scheduling is relatively

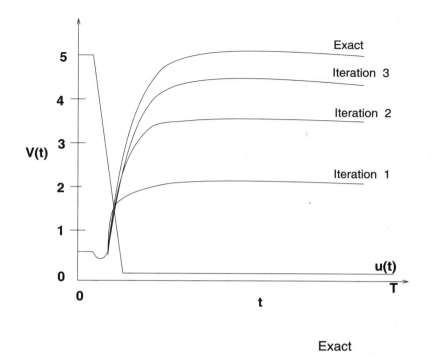

Figure 6.14 Iterative solutions for waveforms (Courtesy of White and Sangiovanni-Vincentelli, *Relaxation Techniques for the Simulation of VLSI Circuits*, Kluwer Academic Publishers, 1987)

inexpensive. The full window approach does not exploit the full degree of parallelism. This is a problem when the number of processors is large or when the task dependency graph is long and narrow such that, at a given point in time, not many processors can be kept busy.

As discussed earlier, a way to apply the waveform relaxation algorithm is to apply a Gauss-Jacobi version of waveform relaxation in which the relaxation makes use of the waveforms computed in the previous iteration for all the subcircuits [19]. The set of computations required to solve a subcircuit on an iteration over an entire time window is treated as a single task.

In a shared memory multiprocessor, all the subcircuits can be analyzed independently by various processors. Data exchange and task coordination occur only at window boundaries. Precedence constraints are imposed to preserve the strict Gauss-Seidel or Gauss-Jacobi pattern of waveform communication between tasks. Figure 6.15(a) shows the dependencies between subcircuits for an example circuit. Figures 6.15(b) and (c) show the task precedence graphs for the Gauss-Seidel and Gauss-Jacobi methods.

As can be seen, all the subcircuits can be solved in parallel in the Gauss-Jacobi method whereas in the Gauss-Seidel method only subcircuits whose fan-in subcircuits have completed can be evaluated in parallel.

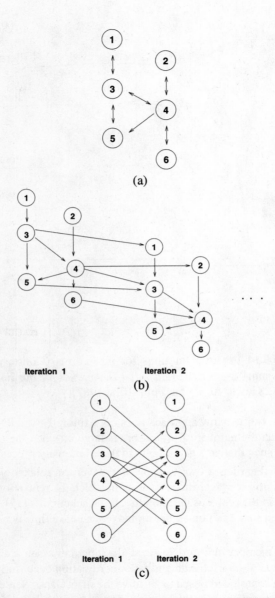

Figure 6.15 Data dependencies in the Gauss-Jacobi and Gauss-Seidel approach. (a) Subcircuit dependency graph. (b) Gauss-Seidel task precedence graph. (c) Gauss-Jacobi task precedence graph. (Courtesy of Smart and Trick, *Proc. Int. Conf. Computer-aided Design,* ©IEEE 1987)

Even though the Gauss-Jacobi method is slower than the Gauss-Seidel method in terms of convergence on a uniprocessor, since it has greater parallelism to be exploited, the overall speedups on the Gauss-Jacobi method can be more than the Gauss-Seidel method. The gains from parallel processing more than compensate for the loss due to slower convergence.

An outline of the parallel waveform relaxation algorithm entitled *SM-PARALLEL-WAVERELAX-FULL* (for shared memory parallel algorithm for waveform relaxation using full-window-based decomposition) follows:

Procedure *SM-PARALLEL-WAVERELAX-FULL;*

Read in circuit description;
Partition circuit into subcircuit;
Create shared data structure representing voltage waveforms;
(waveform = voltage values at all time steps);
Guess initial values of all nodes voltages on all time steps;

REPEAT
   FORALL processors in PARALLEL DO
      WHILE there are subcircuits to be processed DO
         Pick subcircuit;
         Read input waveforms for all input nodes to subcircuit;
            (voltages for all input nodes for all time steps)
         FOR each time step DO
            Solve subcircuit;
         Update output waveform for output nodes of subcircuit;
            (voltages for all output nodes for all time steps);
         IF output waveform of output nodes changed
            THEN Schedule this subcircuit for another evaluation;
      END WHILE
   END FORALL
UNTIL waveforms of all nodes converge;

End Procedure

Implementation Smart and Trick have reported results of a parallel waveform relaxation algorithm using the Gauss-Jacobi method of iterative solution on an Alliant FX/8™, which is a eight-processor shared memory multiprocessor [19].

The Gauss-Seidel and Gauss-Jacobi methods were incorporated in a unified manner in a multiprocessor version of the RELAX2.3™ program [26]. The set of computations required to solve a subcircuit on an iteration over an entire time window was treated as a single task. The task precedence graphs for both the Gauss-Seidel and Gauss-Jacobi methods were constructed in the presimulation phase of the program. During the simulation phase, processors obtained work from a central ready queue, and tasks were placed on the queue as soon as all their predecessor tasks finished executing. Tasks of different iterations could be active simultaneously provided their constraints were satisfied.

The queue was prioritized to favor tasks with lower iteration numbers, since convergence might be obtained on one of these iterations, making the higher-numbered iterations unnecessary. In a shared memory multiprocessor, a shared list of subcircuits can be maintained to allow any processor to compute the result for any subcircuit. A global queue can be used to represent the tasks for subcircuits. A locking mechanism prevents two processors from working on the same subcircuit by associating a lock per subcircuit.

Several circuits were simulated using both the Gauss-Seidel and Gauss-Jacobi methods on different numbers of processors. It was observed that on one processor the Gauss-Jacobi method was up to two times slower due to the slower convergence rate. Both methods show speedup with increasing number of processors. The Gauss-Seidel speedup flattened quickly due to the narrowness of the task precedence graphs. As the number of processors is increased, the Gauss-Jacobi performance surpassed the Gauss-Seidel method at around four processors.

6.12.3 Distributed Memory MIMD Parallel Algorithm

We will now describe a distributed memory parallel waveform relaxation algorithm using a modified Gauss-Seidel algorithm. The algorithm is based on work proposed by Johnson and Zukowski [10]. In this parallel algorithm, the given circuit is partitioned into dc-connected (source-drain paths of transistors) subcircuits, which are allocated statically to processors. In addition, the node waveforms are statically assigned to processors such that each processor contains a copy of all the waveforms needed for the analysis of the subcircuits allocated to that processor.

An outline of the parallel waveform relaxation algorithm entitled *DM-PARALLEL-WAVERELAX-FULL* (for distributed memory parallel algorithm for waveform relaxation using full-window-based decomposition) follows:

Procedure *DM-PARALLEL-WAVERELAX-FULL;*

Read in circuit description;
Partition circuit into dc-connected subcircuit;
Allocate partitions statically to processors;
Create data structures representing voltage waveforms
    on each processor for owned nodes;
Guess initial values of all nodes voltages on all time steps;
REPEAT
    FORALL processors in PARALLEL DO
        FOR all subcircuits owned by processor DO
            Pick subcircuit;
            Receive input waveforms for all input nodes to subcircuit;
            FOR each time step DO
                Solve subcircuit;
            Update output waveform for output nodes of subcircuit;
            Send output waveforms to processors

using Spread or Gather method;
   IF output waveform of output nodes changed
      THEN Schedule this subcircuit for another evaluation;
  END WHILE
 END FORALL
UNTIL waveforms of all nodes converge;

End Procedure

As a waveform changes on one processor, this change must be reflected on all copies on other processors. Two methods can be used to update the copies. The first method, called the *spread* method, is driven by the master processor (the unique processor on which a waveform is solved). As soon as a waveform is modified, messages with the waveform's new value are sent to all processors that contain external copies. The second method, called the *gather* method, is driven by the receiving processors. When a waveform is referenced, a message is sent to the processor holding the master copy requesting an updated version. The master then either sends its current version, which may be refused by the receiver if it is not current enough, or it waits until the version is updated. The *spread* method is more efficient in communication because it does not require the request message that the *gather* method does. However, the *spread* method is more memory intensive in that there must be enough storage for all externally generated inputs on every processor. The waveform relaxation algorithm guarantees that all computed waveforms from one iteration will be used during either the current iteration or the next; therefore, all transmitted data are eventually used. Hence the *spread* method is very effective.

The following static subcircuit allocation strategy can be used to distribute the subcircuits among processors. Communication among processors is reduced by generating chains of subcircuits. The sharing of waveform data among processors is dictated by the subcircuit fan-out and by the distribution of subcircuits that share data within the same processor. Hence, the assignment is determined by creating sequential chains from subcircuits of a partitioned network; each chain contains at most one subcircuit from each level as shown in Figure 6.16. A chain is built starting with a subcircuit that solves one or more output nodes. The next subcircuit added to the chain is selected from the subcircuits that drive the first subcircuit in the chain. If more than one subcircuit fans into the last subcircuit added to the chain, then the sub-circuit with the highest connectivity to the chain is selected. At each level the goal is to maximize connectivity of the elements within a chain. This process is repeated until all subcircuits are exhausted or a primary input is reached. Then a new output node is selected and a new chain is started. The workload on each processor can be balanced by grouping chains together to represent equal amounts of estimated work. Sometimes it may be necessary to truncate a chain before reaching the primary input to balance the workload.

Since several copies of the node voltage waveforms are spread across the processors, some synchronization is needed to ensure that effects from one phase of execution do not overwrite effects from another. The three phases of execution include the data structure initialization, the dc-solution, and the transient solution. Should one processor finish its

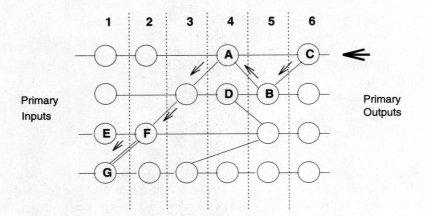

Figure 6.16 Chaining of subcircuits (Courtesy of Johnson and Zukowski, *IBM Jour. Res. Dev.*, 1991 ©International Business Machines Corporation)

initialization and begin its dc-solution, a solved waveform sent to a slower processor may get lost should the slower processor initialize the waveform copy after the update has been received. A very simple synchronization strategy can be enforced between phases. As a processor finishes work in a phase, its sends a "done" message to the host. When messages from all the processors have been received by the host, it sends "go" messages to all processors, which enter the next phase of computations.

In an attempt to increase the parallelism and improve the performance for circuits with significant sequential behavior, a *bounded chaotic algorithm* that favors Gauss-Seidel relaxation can be used. The relaxation is bounded so that no sub-circuit is permitted to be analyzed with input waveforms that are more than one iteration behind the current iteration. All subcircuits assigned to a processor that meets the Gauss-Seidel criteria are solved first. Then, if none of the remaining subcircuits meet this criteria, one subcircuit is chosen to be solved anyway, rather than waiting for updated input waveforms.

Implementation Johnson and Zukowski have implemented the preceding parallel algorithm on a 256 processor VICTOR™ multiprocessor which is an experimental message-passing multiprocessor developed at IBM Watson Research Center [10]. The speedups were estimated to be about 100 on 256 processors for large circuits compared to one processor of the VICTOR using the notion of parallel efficiency (actual speedups could not be measured since the large circuits did not run on one processor due to memory limitations).

6.13 PIPELINED WAVEFORM RELAXATION

6.13.1 Overview

A different approach to apply the waveform relaxation algorithm while still maintaining the strict ordering of the computation is to pipeline the waveform computation [26]. In this approach, one subtask would start computing the transient response for a subcircuit before waiting for the entire window to be completed. As soon as the first time point is generated,

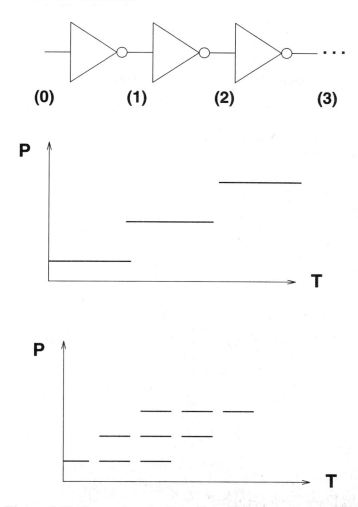

Figure 6.17 Time point pipelining in waveform relaxation (Courtesy of Saleh, Private Communication, 1992)

a second subtask can begin computing the first time point of the second subcircuit, while the first subtask computes the second time point of the first subcircuit. On the next step, a third subtask can be introduced, and so on, until very soon a set of subtasks begins to operate in a pipelined fashion on different subcircuits. This is illustrated in Figure 6.17.

6.13.2 Shared Memory MIMD Parallel Algorithm

Even though the time-point pipelining approach increases the potential parallelism, its limitation is the increased overhead and a complex thread of control. The scheduling of pipelines is quite expensive due to the checking process that has to check, after each computation of a time point, to see if other tasks have become eligible for execution.

We now describe a shared memory parallel algorithm for waveform relaxation using time-point pipelining. In the algorithm, a shared list of subcircuits can be maintained in global memory to allow any processor to compute the result for any subcircuit. A global queue can be used to represent the tasks for subcircuits. A locking mechanism can be used to prevent two processors from working on the same subcircuit by associating a lock per subcircuit. In the parallel waveform relaxation algorithm, one subtask would start computing the transient response for a subcircuit. Instead of waiting for the entire window to be completed, as soon as the first time point is generated, a second subtask can begin computing the first time point of the second subcircuit, while the first subtask computes the second time-point of the first subcircuit.

An outline of the parallel waveform relaxation algorithm entitled *SM-PARALLEL-WAVERELAX-TIMEPOINT* (for shared memory parallel algorithm for waveform relaxation using time-point-based decomposition) is given next.

Procedure *SM-PARALLEL-WAVERELAX-TIMEPOINT;*

Read in circuit description;
Partition circuit into subcircuit;
Create shared data structure representing voltage waveforms;
(waveform = voltage values at all time steps);
Guess initial values of all nodes voltages on all time steps;
FORALL processors in PARALLEL DO
    WHILE there are subcircuits left in task queue DO
        Pick a subcircuit s under lock;
        FOR each time-point t DO
            Create a task(subcircuit s, time t);
            Insert in global task queue;
        END FOR
    END WHILE
END FORALL

REPEAT
    FOR each time-point t DO
        FORALL processors in parallel DO
            WHILE there are subcircuits to be processed DO
                Pick subcircuit under lock;
                Read voltages of all input nodes to subcircuit
                    for current time-point t;
                FOR current time-point t DO
                    Solve subcircuit;
                Update voltage for output nodes of subcircuit
                    for current time-point t;
                IF output voltage for time-point changed
                    THEN schedule this subcircuit for another evaluation;

TABLE 6.6 Runtimes (seconds) and Speedups of Parallel Circuit Simulation Algorithm on the Sequent Balance 8000™ Multiprocessor

Circuit	Devices	1 Processor		9 Processor	
		Runtime	Speedup	Runtime	Speedup
Control	116	704	1.0	149	4.7
EPROM	348	745	1.0	182	4.1
CMOSram	428	3379	1.0	496	6.8

        Also schedule all fan-out subcircuits for evaluation;
   END WHILE
  END FORALL
  Increment time-point t+1;
 END FOR each time-point;
UNTIL waveforms of all nodes converge;

End Procedure

Although the original time-point pipelining idea was proposed for the Gauss-Seidel method, the idea has been generalized to apply to other relaxation methods, such as the Gauss-Jacobi method.

The time-segment pipelining uses a similar approach as time-point pipeling, except that it defines the solution for several time-points (a segment of the window) of a subcircuit as a basic task [6]. This approach reduces the overhead of scheduling by increasing the granularity of the tasks. The overhead is low because of the checking operation of whether other tasks have become eligible for execution.

Implementation White et al. have reported the implementation of the time-point pipelining algorithm on a Sequent Balance 8000™ shared memory multiprocessor [24]. Table 6.6 shows the runtimes and speedups of three benchmark circuits on the multiprocessor.

6.13.3 Distributed Memory MIMD Parallel Algorithm

We now describe a distributed memory parallel algorithm for waveform relaxation based circuit simulation using time-point pipelining. On a distributed memory multiprocessor, the list of subcircuits to be simulated is partitioned statically to different processors, so each processor has its own set of subcircuits to simulate. Each processor maintains a queue of tasks for its assigned subcircuits. Since there is no sharing of subcircuits, such an implementation does not have to pay the overheads for contention of shared resources. As soon as a subcircuit is simulated for a time-point, the owning processor sends messages to other processors to activate other fan-out subcircuits in their assigned partitions.

An outline of the parallel waveform relaxation algorithm entitled *DM-PARALLEL-WAVERELAX-TIMEPOINT* (for distributed memory parallel algorithm for waveform relaxation using time-point decomposition) follows:

Procedure *DM-PARALLEL-WAVERELAX-TIMEPOINT;*

Read in circuit description;
Partition circuit into dc-connected subcircuit;
Allocate partitions statically to processors;
Create data structures representing voltage waveforms
    on each processor for owned nodes;
Guess initial values of all nodes voltages on all time steps;
FORALL processors in PARALLEL DO
    FOR each time-point t DO
        FOR each subcircuit s owned by a processor DO
            Create a task(subcircuit s, time t);
            Insert in local task queue;
        END FOR
    END FOR
END FORALL

REPEAT
    FOR each time-point t DO
        FORALL processors in PARALLEL DO
            FOR all subcircuits owned by processor DO
                Pick subcircuit;
                Receive voltage of all input nodes to subcircuit
                    for current time step;
                Update voltage for output nodes of subcircuit
                    for current time step;
                Send output voltages to processors needing them;
            IF output voltage of output nodes changed
                THEN schedule this subcircuit for another evaluation;
                Also send messages to other processors to schedule
                    other fan-out subcircuits;
            END WHILE
        END FORALL
    END FOR
UNTIL waveforms of all nodes converge;

End Procedure

No implementations have been reported on distributed memory machines; however, the algorithm of Johnson and Zukowski described in the previous section [10] can be readily adapted to this algorithm.

6.14 HARDWARE ACCELERATORS

In this section we will discuss some approaches for designing special-purpose hardware or using the specialized hardware support of vector machines to solve the circuit simulation problem.

One approach to exploit fine-grain parallelism is used in machines with vectorization hardware such as the CRAY™, Alliant™, and CONVEX™ machines. The scatter-gather approach is used in conjunction with sparse matrix storage schemes in which the nonzeros of the matrix along with zero entries of the fill-ins are stored row by row in a single vector, with an associated vector that stores the corresponding column indexes. In the target-row-based LU decomposition approach, before a target row is updated, it is first scattered from its scattered representation to its temporary fill vector. All updates to the target row from the relevant source rows are performed on the scattered target row, after which the target row is gathered to its compact form.

It is possible to directly parallelize the algorithm by exploiting vectorization of the innermost loop using scatter-gather hardware support provided on vector machines. Experimental results on real circuits showed a vectorization speedup of about two times.

Nakata et al. have developed a hardware accelerator for speeding up the direct method for circuit simulation [13]. Their prototype consisted of four MC68020™ processors equipped with MC68881™ floating point coprocessors and 4 MB of memory. The processors were connected so as to allow each CPU to access data in its local memory via a local bus and to access the data in the other processor's memory via a global bus. The global bus was only used when processors wish to communicate with each other.

To parallelize the simulation, they adopted a divide and conquer method. The circuit to be simulated is divided into a set of subcircuits that is connected by an interconnection network. Each subcircuit and the network are allocated to a process, which is allocated statically to processors. The whole system can be viewed as a tree of processes, rooted by a process that represents the interconnection network of the modules at the highest level. Each stage of the algorithm is recursively composed of two phases. (1) a fanning out phase, in which each parent process calculates the values of the interfacing variables, and sends them to its children; (2) a fanning in phase, in which the children process calculate the values of the internal variables and send the correlated interphase values to the parent.

To support such a parallel simulation model, the subcircuit processes have to perform extra work, such as the computation of Norton equivalents and recomputation of internal variables, and the interconnection network process has to perform an extra matrix computation.

An implementation of the algorithm on the prototype machine demonstrated speedups of 3.3 on four processors for the input phase and 3.9 on four processors for the simulation phase.

6.15 SUMMARY

Circuit simulation has been a topic of great interest to the integrated circuit design community for many years. Exploiting parallel computation for circuit simulation is extremely important because the size of circuits to which circuit simulation has been applied has grown at a rate that far exceeds the increase in computational power due to technological improvement. A variety of techniques for parallel circuit simulation has been proposed by researchers over the last few years.

In this chapter we have reviewed several parallel approaches to circuit simulation. We described three basic approaches to solve the circuit simulation problem: (1) direct methods, (2) nonlinear relaxation methods, and (3) aveform relaxation methods. For each method we reviewed different approaches to decompose the problem for parallel solution. For each approach, we discussed parallel algorithms that are suitable for both shared memory and distributed memory MIMD multiprocessors and discussed SIMD algorithms where appropriate.

The parallel algorithms using direct methods are the most general and can be applied to any circuit. They are based on parallel solution techniques for linear algebraic systems. The direct methods constitute two parts: (1) the model evaluation part, which is relatively easy to parallelize, by assigning sets of devices to different processors and having each processor generate the model parameters of the matrices and vectors in parallel; and (2) the linear system solution phase, which is relatively hard to parallelize since these are sparse linear systems. There are some well-known parallel linear systems solution algorithms, and many of them are very efficient for parallel processing; but most are applicable to dense linear systems, or linear systems with well-defined sparse structures such as tridiagonal systems. For circuit simulation, since the systems are extremely sparse and irregular, parallelization is rather difficult. Among the approaches proposed, element-based parallelism is difficult to exploit on MIMD multiprocessors since the grain-size of the parallel tasks is extremely small. Row-based parallelism is easy to apply, but generates tasks of relatively medium grain. These methods do not generate appreciable speedups due to the small grain size of the computations. These methods are applicable mainly to shared memory MIMD multiprocessors. Pivot-based parallelism involves tasks of relatively large grain and is hence suitable for both shared memory and distributed memory MIMD multiprocessors. However, the issues with regard to identifying independent pivot-level parallelism are difficult. The amount of pivot-level parallelism is limited; hence such methods cannot give large speedups.

The major advantage of using direct methods is that they have proved to be accurate and reliable over a large class of circuits. There are, however, three major disadvantages. First, the sparse linear equation solution time grows faster than linearly with circuit size. Second, some waveform properties such as waveform latency and multirate behavior are hard to exploit. Hence, for large digital circuits that are based on MOS transistors, the direct methods constitute inherently slower approaches than relaxation-based methods, which have linear time complexity. Finally, direct methods are very hard to parallelize efficiently and get good speedups on large-scale parallel machines.

The nonlinear relaxation-based methods exploit the latency property of waveforms in MOS circuits. The parallel algorithms based on nonlinear relaxation solve the complete Newton-Raphson iteration of the nonlinear equation corresponding to one time-point for an entire subcircuit as a subtask. This approach has larger grain size compared to the grain sizes of tasks in parallel circuit simulation using the direct methods. It is therefore more suitable for parallel processing. This approach has been applied successfully to both shared memory and distributed memory MIMD multiprocessors, as well as SIMD massively parallel processors, with good speedups. Among the nonlinear relaxation approaches, the Gauss-Seidel relaxation methods are harder to parallelize, but converge faster than Gauss-Jacobi methods. For a very large number of processors, it is advantageous to use Gauss-Jacobi-based nonlinear relaxation methods since the advantages of more parallelism outweigh the increased time for convergence.

Waveform relaxation methods exploit the multirate property of waveforms and can give the least expensive approach to circuit simulation, faster than direct and nonlinear relaxation methods. Also, the parallelization of the circuit simulation problem is much easier using the waveform relaxation approach, since the grain size of tasks is even coarser than those obtained for the nonlinear relaxation approaches. A task in waveform relaxation constitutes the solution of complete voltage waveforms over an entire window for a subcircuit. This approach is therefore most suitable for large-scale parallelism. For distributed memory MIMD multiprocessors, for which the cost of sending messages is relatively high, but the cost of long messages is not significantly higher than the cost of short messages, the waveform relaxation approaches are the best. However, this approach has the disadvantage that its convergence properties depend a lot on the circuit characteristics and may take a large number of iterations to converge for some circuits.

6.16 PROBLEMS

6.1   Show how to apply parallelism to the model evaluation phase for the example circuit shown in Figure 6.1. Assume that each processor computes the model for each element in the circuit.

6.2   You are given a sparse matrix A corresponding to the Jacobian matrix in the direct method of circuit simulation of size 10×10. The nonzero elements are given in the following form (row, column, value): A = [(1,1,2.0), (1,3,4.0), (1,6,1.5), (2,2,1.3), (2,4,5.0), (2,8,2.0), (3,1,4.0), (3,3,2.0), (3,4,1.0), (3,10,5.0), (4,2,5.0), (4,3,1.0), (4,4,10.0), (4,6,6.0), (5,5,2.0), (5,6,8.0), (5,8,2.4), (6,5,8.0), (6,6,1.2), (6,7,4.0), (6,9, 2.0), (7,6,4.0), (7,7,3.0), (7,10,4.0), (8,2,2.0), (8,5,2.4), (8,8,4.0), (8,9,4.0), (9,6,2.0), (9,8, 4.0), (9,9,2.0), (9,10,3.0), (10,3,5.0), (10,7,4.0), (10,9,3.0), (10,10,0.5)] Solve the equation $A \cdot x = b$ for the unknown vector x, given known values of the b vector = [1.0, 2.0, 3.0, 0.5, 2.0, 0.6, 0.0, 3.0, 1.0, 0.0]. Use the source-row-directed and target-row-directed LU factorization algorithms.

6.3   For the LU factorization problem of Problem 6.2, construct the computation graph, and apply element-based parallelism and row-based parallelism to the graph.

6.4   Design and implement a shared memory parallel algorithm for the linear systems solution portion of the direct method of circuit simulation using row-based partitioning. Use a source-row-directed LU factorization algorithm. Use the Sequent™ parallel programming library described in Chapter 2.

6.5   Design and implement a distributed memory parallel algorithm for the model evaluation portion of the direct method of circuit simulation. Use the Intel iPSC™ library of message-passing parallel programming calls described in Chapter 2.

6.6   In the shared memory parallel algorithm for row-partitioned solution of equations, *SM-PARALLEL-LUFACT-SOURCEROW*, barrier synchronization is performed after each level of row tasks is performed. This can produce lot of overhead. Develop a scheme that performs static analysis of the task graph and assigns the tasks to processors and performed data-flow-based synchronization. Implement the algorithm on a distributed memory multicomputer.

6.7   For the example matrix given in Problem 6-2, apply pivot-based parallelism using the notion of bordered block diagonal form and nested block diagonal form.

6.8   Implement the shared memory parallel algorithm for linear system solution using pivot based parallelism, *SM-PARALLEL-LUFACT-PIVOT*. Use the Sequent™ parallel programming library described in Chapter 2.

6.9   Design and implement a shared memory parallel algorithm for nonlinear relaxation using circuit partitioning. Use the Sequent™ parallel programming library described in Chapter 2. Compare the performance of Gauss-Jacobi and Gauss-Seidel approaches on the relaxation on some real circuits.

6.10   In the shared memory parallel algorithm for nonlinear relaxation using circuit partitioning, *SM-PARALLEL-NONRELAX-CIRCUIT*, parallelism is inhibited by the barrier synchonization performed at each level of the circuit task graph in the Gauss-Seidel method. Show how the unrolling of iterations of the relaxation can exploit more parallelism. Implement the complex algorithm on a shared memory multiprocessor. What are the disadvantages of implementing this algorithm on a distributed memory multiprocessor?

6.11   Design and implement a distributed memory parallel algorithm for waveform relaxation using circuit partitioning and window-based partitioning. Use the Intel iPSC™ parallel programming library described in Chapter 2. Compare the performance of Gauss-Jacobi and Gauss-Seidel approaches on the relaxation on some real circuits.

6.17 REFERENCES

[1]   G. Bischoff and S. Greenberg. CAYENNE: A Parallel Implementation of the Circuit Simulator SPICE. *Proc. Int. Conf. Computer-aided Design*, pages 182–185, Nov. 1986.

[2]   M-C. Chang and I. N. Hajj. iPRIDE: A Parallel Integrated Circuit Simulator Using Direct Method. *Proc. Int. Conf. Computer-aided Design (ICCAD-88)*, pages 304–307, Nov. 1988.

[3]   P. Cox, R. Burch, D. Hocevar, and P. Yang. SUPPLE: Simulator Utilizing Parallel Processing and Latency Exploitation. *Proc. Int. Conf. Computer-aided Design (ICCAD-87)*, pages 368–371, Nov. 1987.

[4]   J. T. Deutsch and A. R. Newton. A Multiprocessor Implementation of Relaxation-Based Electrical Circuit Simulation. *Proc. 21st Design Automation Conf.*, pages 350–357, June 1984.

[5]   J. J. Dongarra, F. G. Gustavson, and A. Karp. Implementing Linear Algebra Algorithms for Dense Matrices on Vector Machines. *SIAM Review*, Vol. 26 no. 1:91–112, 1984.

[6]   D. Dumlegol, P. Ordent, J. Cockx, and H. De Man. The Segmented Waveform Relaxation Method for Mixed-Mode Switch Level Simulation of MOS Digital Circuits and its Hardware Acceleration on Parallel Computers. *Proc. Int. Conf. Computer-aided Design (ICCAD-86)*, pages 84–87, Nov. 1986.

[7]   K. Gallivan, P. Koss, S. Lo, and R. Saleh. A Comparison of Parallel Relaxation-based Circuit Simulation Techniques. *Proc. Electro 88 Meeting*, May 1988.

[8]   G. K. Jacob, A. R. Newton, and D. E. Pederson. An Empirical Analysis of Performance of a Multiprocessor-based Circuit Simulator. *Proc. 23rd Design Automation Conf.*, pages 588–593, June 1986.

[9]   G. K. Jacob, A. R. Newton, and D. O. Pederson. Direct Method Circuit Simulation Using Multiprocessors. *Proc. Int. Symp. Circuits Systems*, May 1986.

[10]   T. A. Johnson and D. J. Zukowski. Waveform Relaxation Based Circuit Simulation on the VICTOR (V256) Parallel Processor. *IBM J. Research Dev.*, 35(5/6):707–720, May/June 1991.

[11]   B. W. Kernighan and S. Lin. An Efficient Heuristic for Partitioning Graphs. *Bell Syst. Tech. J.*, 49:291–307, Feb. 1970.

[12]   R. Lucas, T. Blank, and J. Tieman. A Parallel Solution Method for Large Scale Systems of Equations. *Proc. Int. Conf. Computer-aided Design (ICCAD-86)*, pages 178–181, Nov. 1986.

[13]   T. Nakata, N. Tanabe, H. Onozuka, T. Kurobe, and N. Koike. A Multiprocessor System for Modular Circuit Simulation. *Proc. Int. Conf. Computer-aided Design (ICCAD-87)*, Nov. 1987.

[14]   C. V. Ramamoorthy and V. Vij. CM-SIM: A Parallel Circuit Simulator on a Distributed Memory Multiprocessor. Technical report, Computer Sciences Division, University of California, Berkeley, CA, May 1993.

[15]   P. Sadayappan and V. Viswanathan. Circuit Simulation on Shared Memory Multiprocessors. *IEEE Trans. Computers*, Vol. 37, no. 12:1634–1642, Dec. 1988.

[16]   R. Saleh. Nonlinear Relaxation Algorithms for Circuit Simulation. Technical report, Ph.D. thesis, Department of Electrical Engineering, University of California, Berkeley, CA, 1986.

[17]   R. A. Saleh, K. A. Gallivan, M. C. Chang, I. N. Hajj, D. Smart, and T. N. Trick. Parallel Circuit Simulation on Supercomputers. *Proc. IEEE*, 77(12):1915–1931, Dec. 1989.

[18]   A. Sangiovanni-Vincentelli, L-K. Chen, and L. O. Chua. An Efficient Heuristic Cluster Algorithm for Tearing Large-Scale Networks. *IEEE Trans. Circuits and Systems*, CAS-24 No. 12, Dec. 1977.

[19]   D. Smart and T. Trick. Increasing Parallelism in Multiprocessor Waveform Relaxation. *Proc. Int. Conf. Computer-aided Design (ICCAD-87)*, pages 360–363, Nov. 1987.

[20]   D. Smart and J. White. Reducing the Parallel Solution Time of Sparse Circuit matrices using Reordered Gaussian Elimination and Relaxation. *Proc. Int. Symp. Circuits Systems*, June 1988.

[21]   J. A. Trotter and P. Agrawal. Circuit Simulation Algorithms on a Distributed Memory Multiprocessor System. *Proc. Int. Conf. Computer-aided Design (ICCAD-90)*, pages 438–441, Nov. 1990.

[22]   R. S. Varga. *Matrix Iterative Analysis*. Prentice Hall, Englewoods-Cliffs,, NJ, 1962.

[23]   D. M. Webber and A. Sangiovanni-Vincentelli. Circuit Simulation on the Connection Machine. *Proc. 24th Design Automation Conf.*, pages 108–113, June 1987.

[24]   J. White, R. Saleh, A. Sangiovanni-Vincentelli, and A. R. Newton. Accelerating Relaxation Algorithms for Circuit Simulation Using Waveform Newton, Iterative Step Size Refinement and Parallel Techniques. *Proc. Int. Conf. Computer-aided Design (ICCAD-85)*, Nov. 1985.

[25]   J. White and A. Sangiovanni-Vincentelli. *Relaxation Methods for Simulation of VLSI Circuits*. Kluwer Academic Publishers, Norwell, MA, 1987.

[26]   J. White and A. Sangiovanni-Vincentelli. Partitioning Algorithms and Parallel Implementations of Waveform Relaxation Algorithms for Circuit Simulation. *Proc. Int. Symp. on Circuits and Systems*, pages 221–224, June 1985.

[27]   O. Wing and J. W. Huang. A Computational Model of Parallel Solution of Linear Equations. *IEEE Trans. Computers*, Vol. C-29:632–638, 1980.

[28]   P. Yang, I. N. Hajj, and T. N. Trick. SLATE: A Circuit Simulation Program with Latency Exploitation and Node Tearing. *Proc. Int. Symp. Circuits Systems (ISCAS-80)*, pages 353–355, Oct. 1980.

[29]   D. Yeh and V. B. Rao. Partitioning Issues in Circuit Simulation on Multiprocessors. *Proc. Int. Conf. Computer-aided Design (ICCAD-88)*, pages 300–303, Nov. 1988.

[30]   C. P. Yuan, R. Lucas, P. Chan, and Dutton R. Parallel Electronic Circuit Simulation on the iPSC System. *Proc. Custom Integrated Circuits Conf. (CICC-88)*, pages 6.5.1–6.5.4, May 1988.

CHAPTER 7

Logic and Behavioral Simulation

7.1 INTRODUCTION

The simulation of VLSI systems is performed at different levels of abstraction, ranging from architectural to gate- and switch-level to circuit and device simulation [44]. In the case of high-level behavioral simulation, we abstract largely from the actual implementation and model the system as an interconnection of functional blocks specified as subroutines in a high-level programming language. In gate- and switch-level simulation, circuits are modeled as the interconnection of Boolean gates and idealized transistors, respectively, while circuit simulators are based on more detailed physical device models. Corresponding to the level of abstraction, the time granularity in the different types of simulation varies: architectural simulation typically has a time resolution based on complete bus or machine cycles, and gate- and switch-level simulation is based on gate delays and clock cycles; circuit simulators in contrast compute complete continuous waveforms. The time granularity in the simulation is a significant parameter for the performance of parallel simulation schemes [8, 47].

Logic simulators are in widespread use as tools to analyze the behavior of digital circuits. Logic simulators are used in hardware design verification to verify the logical correctness and perform simple timing analysis of logic circuits. Logic simulators are also used for fault analysis when a test engineer may want to determine information about what faults are detected by a proposed test sequence.

Logic simulators rely on abstract models of the functioning of a digital system. They yield discrete value outputs and crude timing information [44]. For gate-level simulation,

407

circuits are described in terms of *primitive* logic gates. They are typically evaluated through table look-up or by calling a software function. Gate-level simulators are popular, because they can be implemented efficiently and because the gate model is in direct correspondence to the Boolean equation representation of digital designs. In contrast, a switch-level simulator operates directly on the transistor-level description of a circuit. The transistors are modeled to behave like switches, and the steady state of the transistor network is computed iteratively. Switch-level simulators can handle a larger class of circuits and design styles since phenomena such as bidirectional signal flow and charge sharing are modeled. Also, the simulation model is in close correspondence to the actual physical implementation; for example, a circuit description can be extracted from the layout and simulated directly.

Logic simulation is an extremely important part of the design and verification of any digital system. It takes large computing times; hence it is appropriate to investigate parallel algorithms for this problem.

The chapter is organized as follows. Section 7.2 gives an overview of the logic simulation problem and some sequential algorithms for logic simulation. Section 7.3 characterizes the different forms of parallelism in logic simulation. The functional parallelism approach is discussed in Section 7.4. The data parallelism approach is presented in Section 7.5. Section 7.6 discusses partitioning strategies that are common to all circuit parallel approaches. Section 7.7 describes a compiler-driven approach to circuit parallel logic simulation. Parallel synchronous event-driven simulation is described in Section 7.8. Section 7.9 describes parallel asynchronous event-driven simulation. Section 7.10 describes conservative asynchronous methods, while Section 7.11 discusses optimistic methods of event-driven simulation. Section 7.12 describes parallel algorithms for high- level behavioral simulation. We present a discussion on hardware accelerators for logic simulation in Section 7.13. We conclude the chapter in Section 7.14 with a summary of the different approaches to parallel simulation.

7.2 LOGIC SIMULATION PROBLEM

The input information to a logic simulator usually consists of (1) a description of the circuit to be simulated, which consists of the topology of the circuit and the circuit element types, along with a list of primary inputs and primary outputs and the specification of the delay parameters; (2) input data to be simulated; (3) initial values of memory states; if the initiate states of some devices are not known, an unknown value is assumed; and (4) signals to be monitored.

On the basis of the preceding inputs, a logic simulator performs the following steps. First, it reads the input information and sets up the data structures and the models for various circuit elements. Then, for each input vector, it calls a simulator module to simulate the logic circuit. Logic simulation can be classified as gate-level simulation or function-level simulation depending on the modeling level.

There are two basic approaches to controlling the gate evaluation process in logic simulation, compiled simulation and event-driven simulation [11].

7.2.1 Compiled Simulation

In the compiled simulation method, the logic behavior of a network is compiled into executable machine-level instructions. In such a method, all the gates in the circuit are evaluated for all

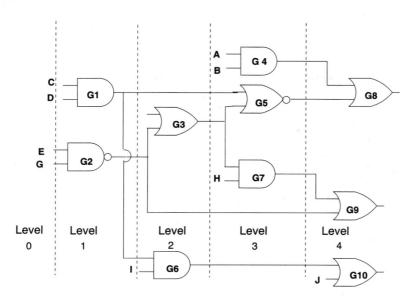

Order of evaluation: G1, G2, G3, G6, G4, G5, G7, G8, G9, G10

Figure 7.1 Example circuit showing logic levels and order of evaluation in compiled simulation

periods. A given logic network is levelized so that each gate is evaluated only once for a given input. Feedback lines are explicitly identified and broken.

The levelizing process assigns a level number to each element. All primary input lines and feedback lines are assigned the level 0. Subsequently, for any element not yet assigned a logic level such that all its inputs have been assigned a logic level, assign this element a level that is equal to 1 more than the maximum value of all its inputs. An example circuit and its levels are shown in Figure7.1. The order of evaluations of the gates is shown in the figure. Once the elements have been ordered, machine code can be generated. Usually, one computer word is used to specify the values of each signal in the circuit. For example, for an AND gate with four inputs, the machine code will be a sequence of instructions that will load the first signal value into an accumulator, subsequently AND the value with each of the other values, and then store the result. Similarly, code for other logic gates can be easily generated.

An outline of the compiled logic simulation algorithm *COMPILED-LOGIC-SIM* is given next.

Procedure *COMPILED-LOGIC-SIM;*

Read circuit description;
Break feedback loops;
Levelize gates into levels;
Generate compiled code for each gate;

Read in the initial value of each lines;
Read in next input vector and update values;
FOR each new input data DO
    FOR each level of logic circuit DO
        FOR each gate in level DO
            Execute compiled code for gate, i.e. simulate logic;
        END FOR
    END FOR
    IF new value of outputs of feedback
        lines same as old value
        THEN output results;
        ELSE set new input value of inputs of feedback lines
            same as new outputs;
END FOR

End Procedure

The main advantage of compiled simulation is that it is extremely fast, since the logic circuit is compiled into machine code on the machine the simulator runs on. There is no cost of interpreting the logic behavior of a circuit in the logic simulator. However, there are two disadvantages of compiled simulation. First, in typical simulations the percentage of gates that change their values is less than 10%. Hence compiled simulation performs a lot of useless work. The second disadvantage of compiled simulation is that it usually implies the zero delay or unit delay model (described in Section 7.2.3). It cannot handle arbitrary delay models in elements. Hence, most practical logic simulators are based on the concept of event-driven simulation, which will be discussed in the next subsection.

7.2.2 Event-driven Simulation

In the event-driven method, gates are only evaluated when there are *events*, that is, a change in the value of a signal. The output of a stable element i will change value only when one or more of its inputs change value. Hence element i needs to be simulated when an event occurs at one of its inputs. When an event does occur, every element to which this line fans out is called potentially active. If these potentially active elements are simulated, it is found that some of them are actually active, and others are not. A significant reduction in computation can be obtained by simulating only potentially active elements. Figure 7.2 shows an example circuit and an input change due to which a selected number of gates are simulated.

When an event i is simulated and it is determined that its output line j has changed state, then line j has to be scheduled to change at time $t_{current} + \Delta$, where Δ is some appropriate delay value of the gate. One way to mechanize the scheduling of events is to use a list of lists structure, where events occurring during the same event time t are stored in the same list. The headers of the lists for each time step are stored as a linked list that is ordered; that is, $t_i < t_j < t_k$. One problem with this mechanism is that scheduling an event to occur at time t requires a scan through the headers. Hence a second method is used, that of a timing wheel

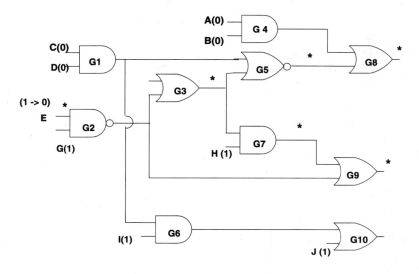

ORDER OF EVALUATION: G2; G3; G5; G7; G8

Figure 7.2 Example of event-driven simulation of a circuit.

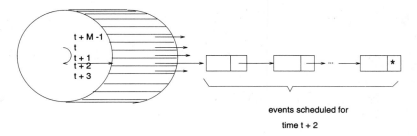

events scheduled for

time t + 2

Figure 7.3 Event scheduling using a timing wheel (Courtesy of Breuer and Friedman, *Diagnosis and Reliable Design of Digital Systems*, Computer Science Press, 1976)

as shown in Figure 7.3. Here the headers are stored in sequential words, and to schedule an event for time $t + \Delta$, the header for this list can be found by directly looking Δ units ahead of the current header. In the event $\Delta > M$, where M is the number of headers in the time wheel, typically 64, an entry is made in an overflow scheduler of the list structured variety.

An outline of the event-driven logic simulation algorithm, *EVENT-LOGIC-SIM* is given next.

Procedure *EVENT-LOGIC-SIM;*

Read logic circuit;

```
Read input vectors;
FOR each input vectors to be simulated DO
    Process new inputs;
    Update input nodes;
    Schedule connected elements on timing wheel;

    WHILE (elements left for evaluation) DO
        Evaluate element;
            IF ( change on output )
                THEN update all fanout nodes and schedule
                     connected elements on timing wheel;
    END WHILE
END FOR
```

End Procedure

7.2.3 Delay Models

Logic simulation deals with calculating the logic value of each signal line as a function of time. To do this correctly, delays within the circuit must be considered [11].

In the *zero delay model*, all gates are assumed to have zero delays, which is clearly an ideal case. In the *unit delay model*, all gates are assumed to have one unit delay, which assumes that the output of a gate will react to the input change after one time unit. Both of these delay models can be handled by compiled simulation using levelization of the circuit to ensure the correct order of evaluation of gates.

The *transport delay model* assumes that each gate and line has a unique delay that is added to the output of an idealized gate. Typically, the transport delay values are assigned multiples of some common unit, for example, 1 nanosecond (ns).

Often the exact transport delay through a device is not known. For example, the delay through a NOR gate may vary between 10 and 20 ns, as specified by the manufacturer in the form of a pair of delays, the minimum and maximum delays, Δ_m and Δ_M. In the *ambiguous delay model*, the minimum and maximum delays are specified for each gate, which define an ambiguous region of duration $(\Delta_M - \Delta_m)$ for which the output signal value of the gate is not defined.

Logic simulators often use a *rise/fall delay model* to characterize the different delays in responding to a 1/0 and a 0/1 transition at the output.

Finally, logic simulators use the notion of an *inertial delay model* to model the behavior of some minimum energy that is required to switch the device between states. In such a model, an input change must persist over a minimum duration called the inertial delay.

7.2.4 Multivalued Logic

For many logic simulation systems, two logic values (0, 1) are not sufficient. For example, in the presence of an ambiguous delay, during a region of time, the signal value of the output of a gate is not defined. Also, due to a race or hazard in the circuit, the value of a signal

Logic Value	Symbol
0	0
1	1
0 to 1 transition	0/1
1 to 0 transition	1/0
Unknown	u

NAND	0	1	0/1	1/0	u
0	1	1	1	1	1
1	1	0	1/0	0/1	u
0/1	1	1/0	1/0	u	u
1/0	1	0/1	u	0/1	u
u	u	u	u	u	u

Figure 7.4 Five-valued logic simulation model and truth table (Courtesy of Breuer and Friedman, *Diagnosis and Reliable Design of Digital Systems*, Computer Science Press, 1976)

may not be known. This situation also occurs when a circuit is initially powered up, called the unknown network state. For these reasons, logic simulators use multivalued logic. For example, Figure 7.4 shows a five-valued logic simulation model and the truth table of a NAND gate under that model. Using this model, it is possible to handle ambiguous delays and unknown initial network states of a circuit.

To provide more accurate circuit modeling, for example, static and dynamic hazards (temporary spikes in signals of the form 010 or 0101), more complex multivalued logic with up to nine values have been proposed [11].

7.3 PARALLEL LOGIC SIMULATION APPROACHES

We can classify the following types of parallelism in logic simulation.

1. Functional parallelism: During logic simulation, a number of different functions need to be executed, such as computing new output values, scheduling fan-out elements, and processing primary inputs and outputs. Some of these operations can be performed in a pipelined fashion by letting dedicated processors take care of specific functions. Thus the simulation algorithm is partitioned functionally.

2. Pattern parallelism: If a design is to be simulated with different sets of input patterns, each test pattern can run independently on one of the processors in a multiprocessor system. A copy of the whole design is simulated on each processor. Pattern parallelism is particularly attractive for vector processors where the main objective is to create long sequences of identical operations. Thus the sequence of input patterns for a circuit can be viewed as a vector.

3. Circuit or model parallelism: Since the electrical signals in a circuit propagate concurrently along many paths, different elements are active at the same time and can be computed by several processors in parallel. In this approach, the circuit is partitioned and each processor *owns* a subcircuit. Circuit parallelism can be further divided into several subapproaches.

3.1. Compiled approach: In this case, all the gates are evaluated at all time steps no matter whether evaluation is needed or not. Hence each processor in parallel simulates all gates in its partition for all time steps.

3.2. Event driven approach: In this case, only the gates whose inputs have changed in the present time step are evaluated. This is done by each processor on the gates in its partition in parallel. There are two subapproaches within event-driven simulation.

3.2.1. Synchronous approach: In this case, we require that all the necessary nodes be evaluated at a given time point before moving on to the next time point. The problem with this approach is that the parallelism in logic simulation is limited to within one time point at a time.

3.2.2. Asynchronous approach: In this case, different portions of the circuit are allowed to evaluate up to different points in time. Such an approach has the maximum scope for exploiting parallelism, since studies on statistics on logic simulation have shown that the circuit parallelism activity at a particular time instant is not that high [8, 47, 50]. However, if we allow processors to proceed ahead asynchronusly in time, there is a scope for more parallelism. The problem with such an approach is in guaranteeing causality constraints; that is, it is possible that an already processed event at a future time might have to be undone due to a late arriving past event. There are two basic methods to design such methods.

3.2.2.1. Conservative methods: In such methods, a parallel simulation is viewed as a series of sequential computations separated by synchronization messages and provides a deadlock avoidance method. Some variants of the method allow the processors to proceed until they deadlock. The deadlock is detected and broken repeatedly.

3.2.2.2. Optimistic methods: In this case, each processor is allowed to go ahead with its computations and to advance its local clock until a message is received that indicates an inconsistency. Then the processor state has to be rolled back to a point in time before the error.

While *functional parallelism* seems to be exploited best by special-purpose hardware, *pattern* and *circuit parallel* approaches lend themselves to an implementation in a loosely coupled distributed or a tightly coupled parallel environment. Typically, data parallel approaches take the least amount of recoding effort and can yield perfect linear speedup; however, their applicability is limited due to space and algorithm considerations. Circuit parallel approaches are geared to handle large designs that need to be partitioned; they involve complex preprocessing and usually require complete redesign of the simulation system. In the following sections, we will discuss each approach in detail.

7.4 FUNCTIONAL PARALLEL SIMULATION

7.4.1 Overview

One way to parallelize logic simulation is through functional decomposition of an event-driven simulation algorithm. The basic philosophy of event-driven simulation is to *evaluate*

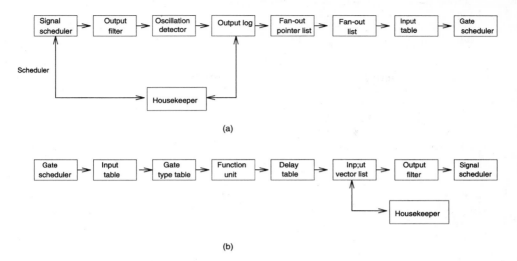

Figure 7.5 Functional decomposition of logic simulation. (a) Node or signal update phase. (b) Gate or element evaluation phase. (Courtesy of Agrawal and Dally, *IEEE Trans. Computer-Aided Design,* ©IEEE 1990)

(compute the output as a function of the inputs) a gate or functional unit if and only if an *event* (change in the value of the input signal) occurs at the gate inputs. All other gates or functional units are not processed. The basic event-driven simulation algorithm processes all events scheduled for one time step in two phases: (1) the node or signal update phase and (2) the gate or element evaluation phase.

During the node or signal update phase, each event scheduled for the current time is processed by updating the value of a specified signal and scheduling all the gates in the fan-out list of this signal for evaluation. Since several inputs of a gate can change state simultaneously, a check must be made to avoid scheduling the gate more than once. Processing the gates in two phases permits all input changes at one gate to be accumulated before the gate is evaluated. Each gate scheduled during a node update phase is evaluated during the evaluation phase. If the evaluation results in a new value of the gate output that differs from the previous output, an event is scheduled on the gate output signal. This event will be processed during some subsequent node update phase. Once all scheduled gates are evaluated, the simulator advances to the next time step and cancels any spurious events scheduled for this time step. The two phases can be combined into a single phase simulation if gates are evaluated immediately every time an input signal changes, rather than accumulating the changes in one time step.

To exploit parallelism in this algorithm, the simulation procedure can be partitioned into pipelined stages. The partitioning should be performed according to two criteria: load balancing and data access. To balance the computational load on each pipeline stage, the simulator can be partitioned into stages requiring about the same computation per event. Figure 7.5 shows the functional partitioning that has been used in the MARS™ hardware accelerator [2, 3, 4]. Even though the preceding decomposition of the logic simulation problem was for a special purpose hardware accelerator, the concepts of functional partitioning can be used in general-purpose parallel processors as well.

7.4.2 Shared Memory Parallel MIMD Algorithm

In a shared memory parallel algorithm, we will assume that there is a dedicated processor for each stage of the functional decomposition of the logic simulation problem. The data between the functional stages are passed between the processors through queues that are shared between pairs of consecutive processors in a pipeline. We describe below an example functional decomposition of the logic simulation problem as used in the MARS™ accelerator [2, 3, 4].

The *signal scheduler* stage sends all the scheduled events down the pipeline. Each event is filtered, logged and used to update gate inputs. The *output filter* receives event messages from the signal scheduler and processes them to remove spurious events. All uncanceled event messages are passed down the pipeline to the *oscillation detector*, which maintains a count of the number of times a signal has changed state during the current time step, and interrupts the housekeeper to signal an oscillation if any count exceeds a preset value. Transitions on monitored signals are recorded by the *output log unit*. The circuit topology is typically represented by the fan-out pointer and fan-out list data structures. For each signal the *fan-out list unit* contains a zero terminated list of fan-outs. The entries in the *fan-out pointer unit* consists of the pointers of the beginning of the fan-out list for each signal. For each message received, the *gate scheduler (GS)* pushes the specified gate number on the stack. To avoid scheduling a gate more than once, a bit vector (1 bit per gate) can be maintained indicating which gates are already scheduled. The bits are cleared when gates are removed from the stack. The gate scheduler transmits all scheduled gates to the *input type block*. For each gate number received, the input type block retrieves the input values for the gate and passes a message containing the gate number and input values on to the gate type unit.

The behavior of each gate is represented by the data structures in the gate type unit, the truth table, and the delay table units. Evaluating a gate is a three-step process. For each signal number and input value, the *gate type unit* appends the gate's type and forwards it to the *input type block,* which performs the table lookup, and forwards it the *delay type unit*, which evaluates the delay. The *input vector list unit* inserts additional events representing primary input changes into the message stream at the appropriate time.

Memory circuits are more efficiently modeled at the functional level than at the gate level. Functional memory gates can be processed by the *functional unit* in an alternative pipeline. The *memory detector block* differentiates between a logic gate and a memory block.

The preceding functional decomposition approach results in decomposing the logic simulation tasks into 14 subtasks, which can be executed in a pipelined manner.

The basic approaches to functional decomposition can be used in general-purpose parallel processors. An outline of the parallel logic simulation algorithm entitled *SM-PARALLEL-EVENT-LOGIC-SIM-FUNCTIONAL* (for shared memory parallel event-driven logic simulation algorithm using functional decomposition) follows:

Procedure *SM-PARALLEL-EVENT-LOGIC-SIM-FUNCTIONAL;*

Assign a processor to each subtask;

FORALL processors in PARALLEL DO
   IF (processor = 1)
     THEN act as signal scheduler;
     FOR each input vector DO
       Update input nodes;
       Schedule connected elements;
       Insert scheduled events on processor 2 queue;
   ENDIF
   IF (processor = 2)
     THEN act as output filter;
     WHILE there are events in input queue DO
       Pick next event on input queue;
       Process to remove spurious event;
       Insert events in processor 3 queue;
     END WHILE
   ENDIF
   IF (processor = 3)
     THEN act as oscillation detector;
     WHILE there are events in input queue DO
       Pick next event on input queue;
       Maintain count of times signal has changed;
       IF count > preset value
         THEN signal processor 14 (Housekeeper);
       Insert events in processor 4 queue;
     END WHILE
   ENDIF
   IF (processor = 4)
     THEN act as output log unit;
     WHILE there are events in input queue DO
       Pick next event on input queue;
       Monitor transitions on signals;
       Insert events in processor 5 queue;
     END WHILE
   ENDIF
   IF (processor = 5)
     THEN act as fan-out list pointer;
     WHInnnLE there are signals in input queue DO
       Pick next signal on input queue;
       Determine list of fan-outs for signal;
       Insert list of fan-outs in processor 6 queue;
     END WHILE
   ENDIF

```
IF (processor = 6)
    THEN act as fan-out pointer unit;
    WHILE there are signals in input queue DO
        Pick next signals on input queue;
        Determine pointers to beginning of fan-out
                list of signal;
        Insert pointers in processor 7 queue;
    END WHILE
ENDIF
IF (processor = 7)
    THEN act as gate scheduler unit;
    WHILE there are messages in input queue DO
        Pick next message on input queue;
        Determine which gate is to be scheduled;
        Insert gate in processor 8 queue;
    END WHILE
ENDIF
IF (processor = 8)
    THEN act as input type block;
    WHILE there are gates in input queue DO
        Pick next gate on input queue;
        Determine input values of gate;
        Insert gate and input values in processor 9 queue;
    END WHILE
ENDIF
IF (processor = 9)
    THEN act as gate type unit;
    WHILE there are gates in input queue DO
        Pick next gate on input queue;
        Determine gate type of gate;
        Insert gate and gate type in processor 10 queue;
    END WHILE
ENDIF
IF (processor = 10)
    THEN act as function unit block;
    WHILE there are gates in input queue DO
        Pick next gate on input queue;
        Determine whether gate is memory module or logic;
        IF logic gate
        THEN evaluate gate
        ELSE insert memory function in processor 11 queue;
        Insert gate and delay values in processor 12 queue;
    END WHILE
ENDIF
```

```
    IF (processor = 11)
        THEN act as memory function unit block;
        WHILE there are memory units in input queue DO
            Pick next memory function on input queue;
            Evaluate memory function;
            Insert memory function in processor 12 queue;
        END WHILE
    ENDIF
    IF (processor = 12)
        THEN act as delay type block;
        WHILE there are gates in input queue DO
            Pick next gate or memory function on input queue;
            Determine delay values of gate or memory;
            Insert output and delay values in processor 13 queue;
        END WHILE
    ENDIF
    IF (processor = 13)
        THEN act as input vector unit;
        WHILE there are signals in input queue DO
            Pick next input signal on input queue;
            Determine additional changes in signal values;
            Insert signal values in processor 1 queue;
        END WHILE
    ENDIF
    IF (processor = 14)
        THEN act as Housekeeper;
    ENDIF
END FORALL
End Procedure
```

Implementation No parallel implementations have been reported using the functional decomposition approach on any general-purpose shared memory multiprocessors.

The preceding functional decomposition approach has been implemented in the MARS™ hardware accelerator [2, 3, 4]. The MARS accelerator is described in detail in Section 7.12 on hardware accelerators. A similar approach to functional decomposition of the logic simulation problem was proposed by Abramovici et al. [1].

7.5 PATTERN PARALLEL SIMULATION

7.5.1 Overview

Pattern parallel simulation involves simulating the behavior of a circuit over a number of input patterns simultaneously. High degrees of parallelism can be achieved using this approach compared to other methods, since the synchronization overheads and communication

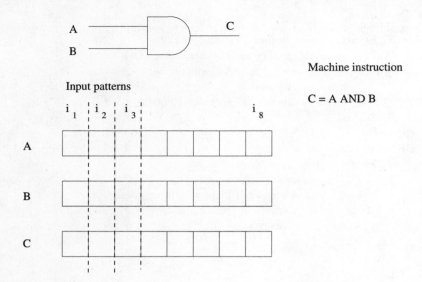

Figure 7.6 Word-level pattern parallelism

overheads are very low. The concept of pattern parallelism has been proposed by numerous researchers.

Word-parallel logic simulation utilizes bit-oriented logic operations to perform many gate evaluations simultaneously. If one word of a computer consists of b bits, b gate evaluations can be performed during the execution time of one machine instruction. We can therefore simulate b inputs patterns for a circuit at a time by assigning each input pattern behaviour to 1 bit.

Consider an AND gate having two inputs A and B as shown in Figure 7.6. Bit position i corresponds to the behavior of the circuit under input pattern i. If the value of A and B for the circuit behavior under input pattern i is stored in the ith bit of the words of A and B, then the AND of these two words will have the value of the output C of the gate in the ith bit of the resulting computer word C. If the word has b bits, then b different input problems can be handled simultaneously (in parallel), each in a different bit of the word. For example, suppose the word size of the computer is b; then bit position 0 can be used to represent the simulation for pattern 0, bit position 1 can represent the simulation under pattern 1, and bit position $b - 1$ can represent the simulation under pattern $b - 1$. Hence, if there are I inputs to process in the logic simulation problem, we must pack the input patterns into groups of b and execute the logic simulation over I/b passes.

This approach has been used in the HSS™ program [9] developed by Barzilai et al. at IBM, which simulated a single circuit on up to 32 patterns simultaneously using each bit position of a 32-bit machine word to represent the circuit behavior of a particular signal value for a different input combination.

The FSS™ program developed by Tan et al. [25] was designed to compute the expected signatures for circuits containing linear feedback shift registers (LFSR). By exploiting the superposition principle of linear systems, this program can divide the test sequences into 32 sections and simulate each sequence in 1-bit of a 32-bit representation of a word, and then combine the results to determine the signature that would result if the sections were simulated in sequence. This technique does not generalize to general circuits.

7.5.2 Pattern Parallel Approach for Combinational Circuits

Pattern parallelism is simple to exploit in logic simulation of combinational circuits with a zero-delay simulation model, where each logic gate is modeled as having zero delay. Pattern parallel simulation involves simulating the behavior of a circuit over a number of input patterns simultaneously on different processors.

Distributed Memory Parallel MIMD Algorithm An outline of the parallel logic simulation using pattern parallelism, *DM-PARALLEL-LOGIC-SIM-PATTERN* (for distributed memory parallel logic simulation using pattern parallelism), is given next.

>**Procedure** *DM-PARALLEL-LOGIC-SIM-PATTERN;*
>
>Read input pattern list;
>Partition I input patterns among P processors;
>Broadcast entire circuit structure to all processors;
>
>FORALL processors in PARALLEL DO
>　　Receive copy of entire circuit;
>　　Receive partitioned set of I/P input patterns;
>　　Partition I/P input patterns into W groups;
>　　　　(W is wordsize of processor)
>　　Simulate complete circuit for I/P inputs using
>　　　　conventional logic simulation algorithm on wordsizes
>　　　　of size W, reserving one input pattern per bit location;
>END FORALL

>**End Procedure**

7.5.3 Pattern Parallel Approach for Sequential Circuits

Pattern parallel logic simulation works for combinational circuits with zero delay models because no state information needs to be transmitted across frames of input patterns. However, for general combinational circuits with arbitrary multiple-delay simulation models and for sequential circuits, it is not easily possible to partition the input sequences into subsequences, since, in the worst case, the state of a circuit while simulating a particular input vector may depend on all previous inputs. An example of such a sequential circuit is a counter circuit.

Bryant has proposed a methodology [15] for partitioning input patterns into independent tests that is used as a formal method for verifying sequential circuits. In such a method, each simulation sequence checks a class of state transitions by the underlying sequential system. The simulation tests are designed with the following characteristics: (1) they focus on the operations of small regions of the circuit, and they assume only minimal initialization of the circuit, (2) there is no attempt to force all nodes out of the unknown values, (3) they directly manipulate and examine the states of internal nodes rather than observing the input-output behavior of the circuit, and (4) they simulate only short sequences of the circuit. Under such conditions, it is possible to partition the test patterns for sequential circuits into independent tests.

We now describe a parallel algorithm for simulation of synchronous sequential circuits using a pattern parallel approach based on the work reported by Kung and Lin [34]. The algorithm partitions a given input pattern sequence into subsequences of equal length and then performs the logic simulation with these subsequences in parallel. To solve the problem of state dependencies of sequential circuits among the subsequences, a multiple-pass strategy is developed and a detection mechanism is devised to minimize the number of simulation passes.

The basic idea is as follows. In synchronous sequential circuits, the values in the memory elements and the present inputs determine the outputs and new values of memory elements. The values of memory elements constitute the state vector s. A state vector is said to be completely specified if all its values are either 0 or 1 and is unspecified if all its values are indeterminate, denoted by X. Given a completely specified initial state vector s^b and a completely specified input sequence T, a logic simulation produces a completely specified output sequence and a completely specified state vector. On the other hand, when the initial vector is unspecified, the logic simulator in general can only determine an incompletely specified final state. However, with the same input sequence, the final state obtained from an unspecified initial state covers that obtained from the completely specified one. The implication of this observation is that with less information on the initial state, that is, more X's, the logic simulator can still produce a final state containing the actual one. Furthermore, given a more specified initial state, the final state would have less uncertainties, that is, less X's. This is the basis of parallel sequence logic simulation.

A given input vector sequence T can be viewed as a concatenation of a number of equal-length subsequences, $T_0|T_1|T_2|...|T_N$, where | denotes a concatenation operation. In the conventional logic simulation, the whole sequence is applied serially to simulate the circuit. In the parallel sequence simulation, these separate sequences are simulated in parallel. Since in a sequential circuit the responses may depend on preceding inputs, the correct results cannot be guaranteed by only one pass of parallel sequence simulation. However, the parallel sequence results will contain the correct result if the initial state for each subsequence is unspecified.

To obtain the correct results, multiple passes of simulation are used. At the beginning of each simulation pass, the final state of the previous subsequence becomes the initial state, as illustrated in Figure 7.7. This transporting of the states between two consecutive passes is formalized as follows. Define the extended state vector S as the vector of states of all subsequences, $s_0, s_1, ..., s_N$. An extended state vector in the simulation pass i is denoted by $S(i)$, and its initial and final extended state vectors are denoted by $S^b(i)$ and $S^f(i)$, respectively.

Clearly, when the number of simulation passes is equal to the number of subsequences, the correct states and responses of the entire sequence can be obtained. Fortunately, in most cases the parallel sequence simulation requires only a few passes to produce the correct result. A mechanism for detecting when a correct result has been obtained so that the simulation can

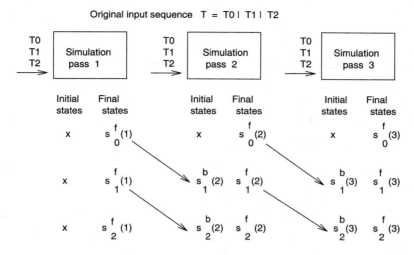

Original input sequence T = T0 | T1 | T2

Figure 7.7 Parallel sequence simulation (Courtesy of Kung and Lin, *Proc. European Design Automation Conf.*, ©IEEE 1992)

be terminated has been developed.

Distributed Memory MIMD Parallel Algorithm An outline of the parallel logic simulation using pattern parallelism for synchronous sequential circuits *DM-PARALLEL-SEQ-LOGIC-PATTERN* (for distributed memory parallel logic simulation for sequential circuit using pattern decomposition) is given next.

Procedure *DM-PARALLEL-SEQ-LOGIC-PATTERN;*

    Read input vector list;
    Partition I input patterns among P processors;
    Broadcast entire circuit structure to all processors;

    FORALL processors in PARALLEL DO
        Receive copy of entire circuit;
        Receive partitioned set of I/P input patterns;
            (processors' current subsequence);
        Initialize state vectors to all unknowns;
        WHILE states not converged DO
            Receive final state of previous input subsequence from
                appropriate processor owning previous subsequence;
            This state becomes current state of current subsequence;
            Simulate complete circuit for I/P inputs using
                conventional logic simulation algorithm on wordsizes
                of size W, reserving one input vector per bit location;
            Send final state of current subsequence to

processor owning next subsequence;
END WHILE
END FORALL

End Procedure

Implementation Bryant has reported a data parallel implementation [15] for the switch-level logic simulator COSMOS™, which operates on the Thinking Machines CM-2™ with 64K elements, with each processing element simulating the behavior of the circuit for one test sequence. Results have been reported on two simple circuits, a combinational ALU circuit and a sequential static RAM circuit for which the functional tests were obtained using the preceding methodology. The results showed speedups of 33,000 for the combinational circuit and about 2900 for the static RAM on a 64K processor CM-2 system.

Remarks The pattern parallel method of logic simulation is mainly applicable to combinational circuits with unit-delay models. It has been extended to handle synchronous sequential circuits using the multiple-pass algorithm. However, the number of passes required to converge in the worst case may equal the number of steps required to simulate the inputs of the original input sequence. This method cannot handle circuits with complex delay models. Since this method is not applicable to all circuits, we are forced to investigate other forms of parallelism in logic simulation.

7.6 CIRCUIT PARALLEL SIMULATION

In the uniprocessor event-driven simulation algorithm we perform the following steps for each active time step: (1) Update all scheduled nodes; (2) Evaluate all elements connected to the changed nodes. (3) Schedule all output nodes that change. One approach to parallel logic simulation is to use circuit-level parallelism (a given logic circuit is partitioned and each partition is assigned to a processor) and then use a conventional logic simulation algorithm on each partition.

The parallel version of the event-driven logic simulation algorithm would involve (1) performing the node update phase in parallel and (2) performing the element evaluation phase in parallel, making sure that all processors are done before continuing to the next time step.

The efficiency of parallel algorithms for logic simulation using circuit parallelism is critically dependent on the way the logic circuits are partitioned. Several researchers have reported algorithms for partitioning of logic circuits [18, 35, 40, 46]. Some example partitioning strategies are described below.

The first partitioning is called the natural partitioning: where gates are assigned to processors in the order in which they are read from the circuit input description. When a receiving processor gets its share of the number of gates equal to the total number of gates divided by the number of processors, the partition is considered full, and a new partition is generated.

A second partitioning strategy is to assign the gates randomly to processors based on a value returned from a random-number generator. Since for many circuits signal activity tends to be clustered, random partitioning offers the potential for relatively high degrees of processing concurrency.

A third strategy uses a levelizing procedure for the circuit, similar to the one described for compiled logic simulation. Partitioning by gate levels assigns gates with close levels to the same processor. Since some circuits exhibit consecutive waves of activity (for example, pipelined arithmetic units), partitioning based along circuit stages can take advantage of this behavior for a large number of input sequences. In this scheme, the circuit is traversed in level order, with gates being assigned to the same partition block until it is full.

Another partitioning strategy has been proposed by Levendel et al. [35] based on the notion of strings, which are defined as sets of connected gates with at most one fan-in and one fan-out. The goal is to assign fan-outs of a device to different blocks to maximize the likelihood of concurrent simulation activity resulting from a signal change on the driving output. This partitioning can be accomplished by traversing the circuit graph in a depth-first manner, starting from either a primary input or primary output, and traversing either successors or predecessors of gates.

A fifth partitioning strategy is called fan-out input cones; it has been proposed by [46]. Starting from each primary input, perform a breadth-first traversal of the circuit graph to identify all gates that can be reached from the input forming blocks. Gates in the circuit will obviously belong to multiple blocks. For each gate, compute the affinity of the gate to each block. The affinity of a gate to a block is defined to be the size of the intersection of the set of gates that are in its own cone of influence with the set of gates that are in each block. Assign the gate to the block with the most affinity.

A sixth partitioning strategy, called fan-in output cones, is performed in a manner similar to the previous method, but performing the search from the primary outputs backward through predecessors. Figure 7.8 shows the different partitioning methods on an example circuit.

The preceding partitioning strategies have been evaluated by Smith el al. [46]. on some ISCAS-85 combinational circuit benchmarks [13]. Using a simple mode of concurrency, the authors compared the effectiveness of the partitioning schemes. For a given simulation time unit, the total number of active gates in an event-driven simulation algorithm was measured to be A_{total}. In addition, the maximum number of active gates in a partition was measured to be A_{max}. The ratio A_{total}/A_{max} was defined to be the ideal concurrency which is a model of simulation concurrency ignoring inter processor communication costs. Experimental results showed that for the number of blocks set to 10 the ideal concurrency varied from 2.6 to 3.9 for natural partitioning, 3.3 to 5 for level partitioning, 4.5 to 8 for random partitioning, 4 to 7 for string partitioning, 4 to 6 for fanin cone partitioning, and 5 to 7 for fanout cone partitioning. Interprocessor communication was estimated as the average number of signals transferred by a single block. Experimental studies showed that the interprocessor communication varied from about 6000 for a large circuit (C7552) for natural partitioning, to 2000 for level order, and 10000 for random and string partitioning, and about 1500 for fan-in and fan-out partitioning.

From the studies it was concluded that the natural and level order partitioning strategies were poor in terms of both concurrency and interprocessor communication. While random partitioning yielded high concurrencies, the inter-processor communication was very high. The fan-out cones partitioning gets reasonably high concurrencies for less interprocessor communication.

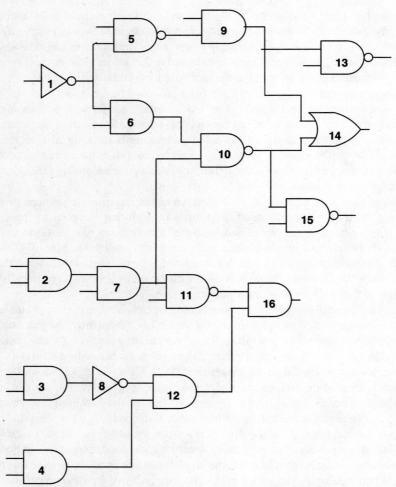

Natural partitions = [1, 5, 9,13][6, 10,14,15][2,7,11,16][3,8,4,12]
Level partitions = [1, 2, 3, 4][5,6,7,8][9,10,11,12][13,14,15,16]
Fan-out input cones = [1, 5, 6,9,13][2,7,10,11,14,15][3,8][4,12,16]
Fan-in output cones = [13, 9, 5,1][14,10,6,7,2][15,7,2][16,11,12,8,3,4]
Strings = [13, 9, 5,1][14,10,6][15][16,11,7,2][12,8,3][4]

Figure 7.8 Circuit partitioning strategies

These partitioning strategies do not take into consideration the cost of communication of a signal from one partition into another. During parallel simulation, even if one have concurrency between two gate evaluations that might point towards assigning them to different partitions, in practice, we may be better off by placing both gates in the same partition to avoid a costly communication cost. Recently, several partitioning strategies have been proposed by Patil et al. [40] and by Chamberlain and Franklin [18] that address the interprocessor communication cost explicitly during partitioning.

These partitioning strategies start with a levelized circuit graph. The algorithm estimates the cost of simulating the circuit by approximating the cost of simulating each gate, and the cost of interprocessor communication. The algorithm notes that if two gates are at the same level they can be simulated in parallel if they belong to different processors. The cost of simulating these two gates equals the sum of the costs of the gates if the gates are on the same processor and the maximum of the costs of the gates if they are assigned to different processors. However, when gates are assigned to different processors, the algorithm also adds the cost for communication to the evaluation of a gate if there is communication needed due to the placement of interacting gates on different processors. Initially, all gates are assigned to one processor. Gradually, individual gates are moved to other processors if the resultant total estimated execution time in the presence of communication goes down. If the choice is performed in a greedy manner, the algorithm runs quickly but can give suboptimal solutions.

A related simulated-annealing-based partitioning strategy was also devised so that some movements of gates to other processors were allowed, even though the cost increased temporarily with the hope that local optimas would be avoided. But the simulated annealing search takes an extraordinary amount of time to do the partitioning.

Experimental results of the partitioning strategies has been reported on a 16-processor hypercube with varying communication to computation cost ratio for gate evaluations [40]. The results on several ISCAS-85 combinational benchmark circuits [13] showed that the last two partitioning schemes outperformed the fan-in, fan-out and random partitioning schemes. Speedups of about 5 to 9 on 16 processors were reported on a variety of circuits with a simulated communication to computation cost ratio of unity. The speedup values were higher for lower costs and lower for higher communication costs.

In this section, we have discussed the issues regarding partitioning a given circuit to utilize the circuit or model parallelism in logic simulation. The partitioning approaches that are common to parallel logic simulation use circuit parallel approaches. Within the class of circuit parallel approaches we have the choice of using either compiled simulation or event-driven simulation. We will discuss the details of both approaches in the remaining sections.

7.7 COMPILED SIMULATION

7.7.1 Overview

A simple way to extract parallelism from logic simulation is to partition a logic circuit into as many parts as there are processors, let each processor get a portion of the circuit, and evaluate each gate in every simulation cycle using a compiled simulation technique (by generating compiled machine code for the portion of the circuit). This approach, called compiled parallel logic simulation, is effective for unit- or zero-delay simulation models only.

Basically, the approach involves rank ordering the gates in the circuit from primary inputs to primary outputs using the methods discussed in Section 7.2.1. Gates that are connected directly to primary inputs are assigned a rank of unity. Gates that receive inputs from outputs of gates that are at levels l or less are assigned level $l + 1$, and so on. In each simulation cycle, gates are simulated in increasing order of ranks to guarantee that all the input signals to a gate are correctly evaluated before evaluating the gate.

IBM has built three generations of logic simulation parallel machines all of which use compiled simulation techniques: the Logic Simulation Machine (LSM)™ [29], the Yorktown Simulation Engine™, and [41], the Engineering Verification Engine™ [24]. All the machines use the same basic architecture. The machines support logic simulation with three or four logic values, 0, 1, X, and high impedance, and zero- and unit-delay models. They consist of 64 to 256 processors, which are connected by a 64×64 or 256×256 crossbar switch that performs fast interprocessor communication. The logic circuit is partitioned into 4K gates each having about four to five inputs. The logic subcircuits are simulated by logic processors, and the memory elements are simulated by array processors. Since the simulator is compiled, and not event driven, the program counter in the controller advances through all the operations and memory without any branches; hence the pipelines are used optimally. All decisions are resolved at compile time, allowing the maximum possible speedup. Because the communication pattern is known at compile time, all speedup techniques and static load balancing techniques can be used.

7.7.2 Shared Memory Parallel MIMD Algorithm

We now describe a shared memory parallel compiled simulation algorithm based on work reported by Soule and Blank [48]. In compiled mode, since at every time step all the gates are evaluated, the parallel implementation involves statically partitioning the circuit among the processors and having each processor evaluate its own assigned gates at each step using compiled simulation techniques. The processors synchronize at the end of each time step to ensure that all the new values for all nets have been evaluated. Since each processor evaluates the same gates at every time step, the execution times are fairly predictable, and load balancing is easy. Unfortunately, since the activity of the circuits is typically low, even though we get some speedup, it may be meaningless since an event-driven algorithm would probably be able to get such speedups by evaluating less events.

An outline of the parallel compiled logic simulation algorithm, *SM-PARALLEL-COMP-ILED-LOGIC-SIM-CIRCUIT* (denoting shared memory parallel algorithm for compiled logic simulation using circuit partitioning), follows:

Procedure *SM-PARALLEL-COMPILED-LOGIC-SIM-CIRCUIT;*

Read logic circuit;
Partition logic circuit using heuristics;
Assign one subcircuit statically to each processors;
Create shared data structure of signal values;

FORALL processors in PARALLEL DO
    FOR each input pattern DO

TABLE 7.1 Normalized Speedups of Parallel Compiled Simulation Algorithm on Encore Multimax™ Multiprocessor

Circuit	Gates	1 Processor Speedup	8 Processors Speedup	16 Processors Speedup
func-mult	100	1.0	5.0	6.0
Inv-array	512	1.0	7.0	13.0
gate-mult	5000	1.0	6.9	12.8

```
       IF processor owns some primary inputs
           THEN Read inputs for current time;
                Process new inputs;
       FOR each level of logic circuit DO
           FOR each gate in level owned by processor DO
                Execute compiled code for gate, i.e. simulate logic;
                Update shared signal variables using locks;
           END FOR
           Barrier synchronize (level) ;
       END FOR


   END FOR
   END FORALL
```

End Procedure

Implementation Soule and Blank have reported results of the implementation of the preceding parallel compiled simulation algorithm on an Encore Multimax™ shared memory multiprocessor [48, 50]. Table 7.1 shows the normalized speedups of three benchmark circuits on the multiprocessor.

7.7.3 Distributed Memory Parallel MIMD Algorithm

The preceding parallel algorithm for compiled logic simulation can be implemented on any distributed memory multiprocessor by statically partitioning the logic circuit into groups of gates and assigning the partitions to different processors. Each processor goes through all gates in its partition and simulates all the gates in each clock cycle in order of increasing levels. When a gate outputs a signal that is the output of a gate in a different partition on a different processor, a message carrying the signal value is sent to that processor. All messages between the same set of processors are combined in the same message to reduce the cost of communication.

An outline of the parallel compiled logic simulation algorithm, *DM-PARALLEL-COMP-ILED-LOGIC-SIM-CIRCUIT* (denoting distributed memory parallel algorithm for compiled logic simulation using circuit partitioning) follows:

    Procedure *DM-PARALLEL-COMPILED-LOGIC-SIM-CIRCUIT;*

       Read logic circuit;
       Partition logic circuit using heuristics;
       Assign one subcircuit statically to each processors;

       FORALL processors in PARALLEL DO
         FOR each input pattern DO
           IF processor owns some primary inputs
             THEN Read inputs for current time;
           Receive other input changes from other processors;
           Process new inputs;

           FOR each level of logic circuit DO
             FOR each gate in level owned by processor DO
                Execute compiled code for gate, i.e. simulate logic;
                IF some fan-out of gate is on different processor
                  THEN save output value to be sent to processor;
           END FOR

           FOR each processor which owns one fan-out of
             one owned gate DO
             Send all newly evaluated outputs to processor;

           Barrier synchronize all processors at a particular level
             using a tree-based reduction of messages;

          END FOR

         END FOR
        END FORALL

    End Procedure

      No implementation of this parallel algorithm on a general-purpose distributed memory multiprocessor has been reported.

7.7.4 Massively Parallel SIMD Algorithm

We will now describe a massively parallel SIMD algorithm for compiled logic simulation based on the work reported by Kravitz et al. [33]. Boolean equations corresponding to a given logic network are mapped directly onto the processing elements of a massively parallel SIMD computer.

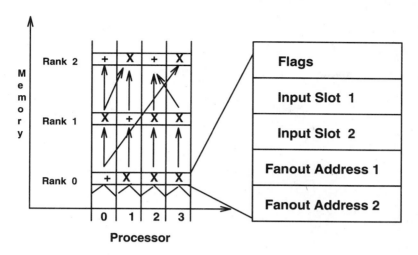

Figure 7.9 Compilation of Boolean model on SIMD massively parallel machine. (Courtesy of Kravitz et al, *IEEE Trans. Computer-Aided Design,* ©IEEE 1991)

The massively parallel algorithm for simulation consists of evaluating all the Boolean gates of the circuit at each step. The memory of the massively parallel machine is treated as a two dimensional array. Each entry in the array holds a data structure representing a two-input Boolean operator, AND or OR. All the Boolean operators comprising the simulation model for a circuit are loaded into the array. The arrangement of the operators is not random. The inputs to the operators in row k of the array are all produced in rows 0 to $k - 1$, or they are inputs to the simulation model. Likewise, the outputs of the operators in row k are consumed in rows $k + 1$ to R, where R is the top row of the array. The data structure representing each operator contains all the information needed to evaluate the operator. Figure 7.9 shows the arrangement of the Boolean model on the machine, and the data structure representing each operator is shown on the right. The atomic unit of computation is the processing of a single row of the array of Boolean operators. Processing of a row involves evaluating each Boolean operator using the data stored in its two input slots and fanning the results of the two fan-out addresses stored in the operator data structure. The flags in the operator data structure are used to select or disable processors from executing an instruction as is required in the SIMD style. The Boolean model is evaluated in rank order starting from rank 0. This is accomplished by levelizing the Boolean model before mapping them to processors. Communication occurs after the evaluation of each row of operators in order to distribute the results to succeeding rows. The mapping of the collection of the Boolean formulas onto the parallel machine is performed in two steps. First, the Boolean model for each unique subnetwork is mapped onto a processor-time rectangle - a rectangle of operators, with one dimension being ranks and the other, processors. Then the complete simulation model is created by packing the processor-time rectangles representing the Boolean models of the entire collection of subnetworks into a large processor time rectangle whose width is limited by the number of available processors.

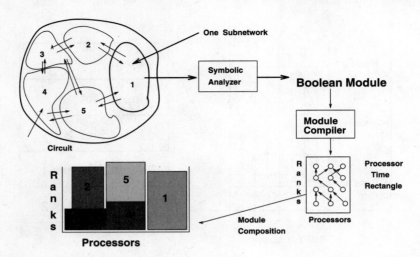

Figure 7.10 Example of model compilation (Courtesy of Kravitz et al, *IEEE Trans. Computer-Aided Design,* ©IEEE 1991)

Figure 7.10 shows such an example mapping.

Evaluating a step in the massively parallel simulator is a three-stage process. First, the inputs to the Boolean model are loaded into the input slots of all operators that require them. Second, the Boolean model is evaluated in several subphases as described previously. Finally, the new values of the outputs are compared with the old values to determine whether a stable state has been reached. To evaluate the circuit's response to an input change, the program performs a series of these steps until the network reaches a stable state. The parallelism in the simulation model is increased in various preprocessing steps, for example, by inserting fan-out trees to limit the amount of fan-out per processor to 2 and limiting the maximum fan-in per gate to 2.

The massively parallel SIMD algorithm for compiled simulation *SIMD-PARALLEL-COMPILED-LOGIC-SIM* is shown next.

Procedure *SIMD-PARALLEL-COMPILED-LOGIC-SIM;*

REPEAT
  REPEAT
    FORALL processors in PARALLEL DO
      Load inputs of Boolean model into input
        slots of processors;
      FOR each rank 0 to R step 1 DO
        Select processors (AND nodes)
          Evaluate AND nodes;
        Select processors (OR nodes)
          Evaluate OR nodes;

Communicate (node values to two fan-out processors)
END FOR
END FORALL
UNTIL(stable state has been reached per step)
UNTIL (end of simulation time)

End Procedure

Implementation Kravitz et al. [33] have demonstrated the feasibility of mapping a switch-level simulator COSMOS™ onto a massively parallel Thinking Machines CM-2™ Connection Machine with 32,000 processors. COSMOS™ preprocesses a transistor netlist into a set of Boolean formulas that captures the switch-level behavior of MOS circuits. These formulas were directly mapped onto the processing elements of the Connection Machine™. Experimental results of performance of this simulator has been reported on two benchmark circuits. For the two circuits, the average numbers of Boolean operations that were executed in parallel per rank were 300 and 3000, respectively, and the resultant speedup over COSMOS™ running on a VAX 8800™ was about two times.

7.8 SYNCHRONOUS EVENT-DRIVEN SIMULATION

7.8.1 Overview

In the previous section, we described a compiled approach to exploit circuit-level parallelism in parallel logic simulation. Another approach to utilize circuit parallelism in logic simulation is to use event-driven simulation. In the uniprocessor event-driven simulation algorithm, the following steps are performed for each active time step: (1) update all scheduled nodes, (2) evaluate all elements connected to the changed nodes, and (3) schedule all output nodes that change. This is actually performed in two separate phases, the node update phase and the element evaluation phase. An outline of the serial event-driven logic simulation algorithm, *EVENT-LOGIC-SIM* (denoting for event-driven logic simulation), is given next.

Procedure *EVENT-LOGIC-SIM;*

Read circuit description;

FOR each time step t DO

Node Update Phase

FOR each node n scheduled to change in time t DO
Update node n;
Activate all elements e connected to node n;
END FOR

Element Evaluation Phase

    FOR each activated element e DO
        Evaluate element e;
        FOR each output o of element e DO
            IF (change on output o) THEN
                Schedule fan-out node for output o to change
                    at time $t + delay(o)$;
            END IF
        END FOR
    END FOR
END FOR

End Procedure

     Within event-driven circuit parallel approaches, there are several subapproaches. We can perform synchronous or asynchronous event-driven simulation. In this section we will only discuss the synchronous parallel event-driven algorithms.

7.8.2 Shared Memory Parallel MIMD Algorithm

We will now describe a shared memory parallel algorithm for synchronous event-driven logic simulation based on work reported by Soule and Blank [48] and Soule [50]. A synchronous parallel event-driven simulation algorithm involves: (1) performing the node update phase in parallel and (2) performing the element evaluation phase in parallel. The intrinsic structure of the algorithm limits the extracted parallelism only to events occurring at the same time instance. Two global synchronizations are needed for each time instance, one after the node updates and one after the element evaluations, making sure that all processors have finished simulating the current time step before continuing to the next time step.

     This parallel algorithm can be implemented simply by having two centralized work queues, one for the node updates and another for the element evaluations, to distribute the load among the processors. Both phases of the parallel algorithm update both the queues. The node update phase removes items from the node update queue and adds items to the element evaluation queue. The element evaluation phase removes items from the element evaluation queue and adds items to the node update queue. Unfortunately, the speedups that can be obtained with this approach are limited due to the contention for the global queues. Since the grain sizes involved in simulation can be small (about 10 to 250 cycles on an ideal multiprocessor), the scheduling and removal of events can easily become a bottleneck to the performance of the algorithm. Consider the node update phase. To update a node, a processor must atomically remove an element from the global node update queue that specifies the node and the new value before it can do the actual update. It takes only a few instructions to perform the actual update, and most of the time is spent in accessing the global queue. A similar procedure is executed during the element evaluation.

     A better parallel algorithm for synchronous event-driven simulation uses a distributed work queue approach. Two different distributed queues are used, one for the node updates and another for the element evaluations. We will describe the distributed node queue in detail.

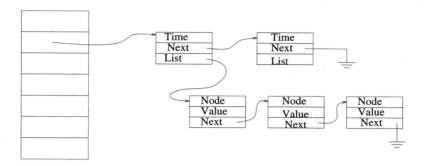

Figure 7.11 Distributed node hash table (Courtesy of Soule, Stanford University Tech. Report, 1992)

Both phases of the parallel algorithm update the node queue. The node update phase removes items from this queue, and the element evaluation phase adds items to the queue. The node queue is distributed by having one queue per processor. Each node has a preferred processor on whose queue it gets placed through a static function. Each queue is an array acting as a hash table, with each entry in the table being a list of times. Each time list in turn has a list of events or (node value) pairs as shown in Figure 7.11. Each queue has a lock associated with it to allow for exclusive access.

Load balancing in the node update phase is achieved in two parts. When a node is scheduled to be updated, it is scheduled on its preferred processor queue in the appropriate time list. This achieves a first cut at good load balancing. Then, during the execution of the node update phase, processors first update all the nodes in their own queues that are scheduled for the current time. When their queues become empty, the processors start checking the queues of the other processors for any remaining node updates. This completes the second part of the load balancing scheme.

The structure of the distributed element queue is simpler than the node update queue, since unlike the nodes that can be scheduled at any time in the future, the elements that are scheduled during the node update phase are all evaluated in the element evaluation phase of the current time instant. The element queue is also distributed with one queue per processor. Each queue has a lock to provide exclusive access. Each element is assigned to a preferred processor when a netlist is read; the assignment is done in a round-robin manner among the processors. During the element evaluation phase, the processors take elements from their own queues, evaluate them, and schedule any node changes as a result of the evaluation onto the distributed node queues. When the queues become empty, a processor is allowed to access the queues of other processors to ensure load balancing.

An outline of the parallel event-driven logic simulation algorithm, *SM-PARALLEL-EVENT-LOGIC-SIM-SYNCH* (denoting shared memory parallel algorithm for synchronous event-driven logic simulation), is given next.

Procedure *SM-PARALLEL-EVENT-LOGIC-SIM-SYNCH;*

Read circuit description;
Create N distributed node update queues;
Create N distributed element evaluation queues;

FORALL processors in parallel DO

  FOR each time step t DO

    Node Update Phase

    WHILE processor's own node queue not empty for time t DO
      Access node n scheduled to change at
        time t from own queue;
      Update node n;
      Activate all elements e connected to node n;
      Insert element e in appropriate element queue;
    END WHILE

    WHILE there are nodes in some queue for time t DO
      Access node n scheduled to change at
        time t from another processor's queue;
      Update node n;
      Activate all elements e connected to node n;
      Insert element e in appropriate element queue;
    END WHILE

    Barrier synchronize (time step t);

    Element Evaluation Phase

    Access element e scheduled to change at
      time t from own queue;
    Evaluate element e;
    FOR each output o of element e DO
      IF (change on output o) THEN
        Schedule fan-out node for output o to change
          at time $t + delay(o)$ on appropriate node queue;
      END IF
    END FOR
    END WHILE

    WHILE there are element in some queue for time t DO
      Access element e scheduled to change at
        time t from own queue;

             Evaluate element e;
             FOR each output o of element e DO
                IF (change on output o) THEN
                    Schedule fan-out node for output o to change
                        at time $t + delay(o)$ on appropriate node queue;
                END IF
             END FOR
          END WHILE
          Barrier synchronize (time step t);
        END FOR
      END FORALL

End Procedure

Some studies of the inherent parallelization in the logic simulation problem have been reported in the form of element and node concurrencies that show the parallelism available in the logic simulation problem, as opposed to the specifics of the parallel implementation. Even though the average concurrencies are quite high (about 100), speedups on parallel machines typically saturate at about 5 to 6. The reason for the poor speedups can be attributed to two factors. (1) There is poor load imbalance during the node update phase. A large variation in the grain size of computations of node updates was measured. Some of the nodes, such as, clock nodes, have very large fan-outs and have been observed to take about 30,000 cycles to perform an update, while others take about 30 cycles. (2) There is a large synchronization overhead due to the barrier synchronizations after the node update and element evaluation phases.

Several optimizations have therefore been suggested to improve the speedups. First, the high-fan-out nodes should be split into multiple nodes by changing the netlist so that certain nodes are duplicated; these intermediate nodes can be better load balanced among the processors. Second, the barrier synchronization after the node update phase can be removed. This is possible since, when a processor cannot find any available node updates, given N processors, at most $N - 1$ nodes will be changing (provided all the distributed queues have been checked by the idle processor). In this situation, the inputs of most elements that have been activated and placed in element queues will not depend on the changing nodes. Thus element evaluation can proceed even though all the node updates have not completed. During element evaluation, an element's inputs are checked to see if any are changing. If no inputs are changing, it is safe to proceed with normal element evaluation. If one or more nodes are changing, the element is requeued and another element is chosen and checked.

Implementation Soule et al [48, 50] have reported on an implementation of the preceding synchronous parallel algorithms for event-driven logic simulation on an Encore Multimax™ shared memory multiprocessor. In the simple algorithm using one centralized queue for all the node changes and one centralized queue for the activated elements, speedups of 2 were obtained on eight processors for several circuits. This was due to the contention for the global queues.

TABLE 7.2 Average Concurrency and Normalized Speedups of Parallel Simulation Algorithm on the Encore Multimax™ Multiprocessor

Circuit	Gates	Average Elem Concurrency	Average Node Concurrency	1 Processor Speedup	8 Processors Speedup
Multiplier	4,990	156	86	1.0	5.0
H-FRISC	5,060	139	87	1.0	3.7
NTT	11,555	222	74	1.0	5.1
R6000	12,207	256	82	1.0	4.0
Ardent	13,374	103	25	1.0	3.8
DASH	24,611	226	72	1.0	3.0

Results on the parallel algorithm for logic simulation with distributed queues have been much better. Table 7.2 shows the average element and node concurrencies and normalized speedups of several benchmark circuits on the Encore Multimax™ multiprocessor using the distributed queue algorithm, and using the optimizations discussed earlier (splitting high-fan-out nodes and removing the barrier synchronization after the node update phase).

7.8.3 Distributed Memory Parallel MIMD Algorithm

We will now describe a distributed memory parallel logic simulation algorithm for sequential circuits based on work reported by Mueller-Thuns et al. [37]. The parallel algorithm is applicable to a restricted class of sequential circuits consisting of zero-delay combinational gates and unit-delay latches and uses a loosely synchronous model that is suitable for execution on distributed memory multiprocessors. Hence the algorithm is less general than the parallel algorithm described in the previous section, which allows arbitrary delays in logic gates, as is required in most general logic simulators.

The circuits considered here contain two types of elements: zero-delay logic gates and latches with a unit delay. All feedback loops are required to contain at least one delay element. Thus the circuit can be uniquely levelized by assigning level zero to all primary inputs and latches. Computing the steady state of the circuit reduces to first evaluating the zero-delay combinational logic in one pass and then updating all latches for the next clock phases.

In a parallel simulation environment, the inputs of some element in the subcircuit of one processor may originate on a different processor. Thus, in a partitioning scheme that potentially cuts arbitrary signal lines, the processors need to be synchronized level by level.

An outline of the parallel event-driven logic simulation algorithm, *DM-PARALLEL-EVENT-LOGIC-SIM-SYNCH* (denoting distributed memory parallel algorithm for event-driven logic simulation using circuit partitioning and synchronous approach), is given next.

Procedure *DM-PARALLEL-EVENT-LOGIC-SIM-SYNCH;*

Read circuit description;
Partition circuit among processors;

FORALL processors in PARALLEL DO
    Each processor creates *maxlevel* queues corresponding
        to different ranks for scheduling events;
    FOR each input vector to be simulated DO
        FOR levels L = 1 to l = maxlevel DO
            Receive all needed signals (at rank L-1)
            Process new inputs among nodes in each processor;
            Update input nodes;
            Schedule affected elements on queue
            WHILE (elements left for evaluation on rank L) DO
                Evaluate element;
                IF (change on output) THEN
                    Update all fan-out nodes;
                    Schedule elements on queue at rank L+1
                ENDIF
                Send required signals for rank L+1 to other processors;
            END WHILE
            Synchronize processors at each level with each cycle;
        END FOR
    END FOR
END FORALL

End Procedure

We will now describe a more efficient parallel algorithm that uses a novel circuit partitioning scheme. The following requirements for partitioning a given circuit into a number of subcircuits can be identified in order to get good speedups from a parallel logic simulation algorithm:

- The partitioner should build connected circuit blocks of substantial size.

- It should cluster together events as much as possible and reduce the number of synchronizations needed.

- It should be efficient (preferably linear time) so that large designs can be handled.

An effective partitioning strategy is outlined next. The basic strategy of the partitioner is to assign the latches of the circuit to different processors and to ensure that each processor also owns the complete zero-delay fan-in cone of that latch. Thus all processors can compute a complete zero-delay cycle independently and need to synchronize on the clock boundary only.

Different ways of assigning the latches using some cost function are possible. One simple and fast algorithm is to simply start off with an arbitrary latch and grow fan-in cones in a depth-first search (DFS) manner until a specified size (measured in terms of number of latches) is reached. Clearly, this cone-finding step has complexity linear in the number of elements in the circuit, since each element is processed only once in a DFS manner. In a second pass, the cones are instantiated: since in the general case cones will overlap, some elements have to be replicated. It has been experimentally demonstrated by Mueller-Thuns et al. [37] that this is not a serious drawback for large systems; also, only a small fraction of all gates are active at any time, so not all replicated elements translate into extra work done.

Many variations and refinements are possible for this scheme; however, more complicated approaches, resulting in superlinear run-time, will be too costly for large designs (with, say, a million elements). Then a simpler scheme, run several times with different random starting points, will be preferable.

The proposed partitioning approach leads to a straightforward cycle by cycle simulation scheme. Synchronization is performed on the clock boundary only, instead of level by level. Assuming the typical maximum number of levels in a circuit to be on the order of 10 to 30, a considerable reduction in the number of synchronizations needed between processors is achieved.

An outline of the parallel event-driven logic simulation algorithm, *DM-PARALLEL-EVENT-LOGIC-CYCLE* (denoting distributed memory parallel algorithm for event-driven logic simulation using circuit partitioning and synchronous at the cycle-by-cycle approach), is given next.

Procedure *DM-PARALLEL-EVENT-LOGIC-CYCLE;*

Read circuit description;
Partition circuit using fan-in cones from latches;
Assign circuit partitions statically to processors;

FORALL processors in PARALLEL DO
    Each processor creates *maxlevel* queues corresponding
        to different ranks for scheduling events;
    FOR each input vector to be simulated DO
        Receive all needed signals from other processors;
        Schedule affected gates on queues;
        FOR levels L = 1 to l = maxlevel DO
            WHILE (elements left for evaluation on rank L) DO
                Evaluate element;
                IF (change on output) THEN
                    Update all fan-out nodes;
                    Schedule fan-out elements on queue at rank L+1
                ENDIF
            END WHILE
        ENDFOR
        Send required signals for next cycle to other processors;
    Synchronize processors at each cycle;

TABLE 7.3 Runtimes (seconds) and Speedups of Parallel Simulation Algorithm on an Intel iPSC/2™ Hypercube for 1000 Input Vectors

Circuit	Gates	1 Processor		8 Processors	
		Runtime	Speedup	Runtime	Speedup
s13207	7951	27.1	1.0	8.4	3.2
s15850	9772	29.8	1.0	9.4	3.2
s35932	16065	189.4	1.0	38.4	4.9
s38584	19253	148.7	1.0	30.9	4.8
s22179	22179	97.1	1.0	21.1	4.6

ENDFOR
END FORALL

End Procedure

A simple optimization can be performed on the preceding parallel algorithm. Due to the circuit partitioning approach, all signals that are transmitted between processors are the outputs of latches. Hence the signals need to be sent only when the latches are enabled. Then all signals owned by a particular clock can be grouped together and are sent only when the clock is active. For the special case of one system clock, the number of synchronizations is reduced by a factor of 2 (if the clock is inactive half the time).

It should be noted that the algorithm is only applicable to restricted classes of logic simulation on circuits consisting of zero-delay logic gates and unit delay memory elements (latches), assuming that all feedback loops have at least one unit-delay latch.

Implementation The distributed memory message-passing parallel algorithms have been implemented as a prototype logic simulation system by Mueller-Thuns et al. [37] on an Intel iPSC/2™ hypercube. Table 7.3 shows the runtimes and speedups of several ISCAS-89 sequential benchmark circuits [12] on an Intel iPSC/2™ hypercube multiprocessor. In the experiments the circuits were simulated with 1000 random input patterns.

7.9 ASYNCHRONOUS EVENT-DRIVEN SIMULATION

7.9.1 Overview

The parallel compiled mode simulation achieves good speedups but at the cost of extra work, whereas the parallel synchronous event-driven simulation does only necessary work, but achieves good speedups only when there are a lot of events at every time step. We will now investigate ways of designing parallel algorithms for asynchronous event-driven logic simulation.

Logic simulation is actually one application from a much broader class of applications called discrete event simulation. Researchers in that community have been working for many years to develop parallel algorithms for that general problem. We will first review some of the basic approaches that researchers have proposed to solve parallel discrete event simulation, an excellent discussion of which appears in [27].

A discrete event simulation model assumes that the system being simulated only changes at discrete points in simulated time. In asynchronous systems, events are not synchronized by a global clock, but occur at irregular time intervals. For these systems, few simulator events occur at each single point in simulated time; hence concurrent execution of events at different time points in simulated time is required. This introduces some interesting synchronization problems.

The reason parallel discrete event simulation (PDES) is difficult becomes evident if we examine the operation of a sequential discrete event simulator. Each event contains a time stamp and denotes a change in the state of the system.

The simulator typically removes the smallest time-stamped event from the event list and processes that event. Processing an event involves executing some simulator code to effect the appropriate change in state and scheduling one or more events into the simulated future. In this paradigm, it is crucial that we always select the smallest time-stamped event from the event list, E_{min}, as the one to be processed next. This is because if we were to select some other event containing a larger timestamp, say E_X, it would be possible for E_X to modify some state variables used by E_{min}, which would constitute a violation of the causality contraints of the physical system (the logic circuit in our case).

Most existing PDES strategies adopt a process model for simulation by constructing a set of logical processes, $LP1, LP2, ..., LPn$ to represent the physical processes (gates or clusters of gates in our case), $P1, P2, ..., Pn$. All interactions between physical processes are modeled by time-stamped messages between logical processes. PDES becomes difficult due to the complex sequencing constraints that get dictated by causality constraints that are highly data dependent.

PDES mechanisms broadly fall into two categories: (1) conservative and (2) optimistic. Conservative methods strictly avoid the possibility of a causality error by relying on some strategy to determine when it is safe to process an event. Optimistic approaches allow for causality errors to occur which are detected and recovered from by using a rollback mechanism.

7.9.2 Conservative Methods

We will now briefly review the basic concepts used in conservative methods of asynchronous simulation. The basic problem that such methods have to solve is to determine when it is safe to process an event. If a process contains an unprocessed event E_1 with time-stamp T_1 and no other with smaller time-stamp, and that process can determine that it is impossible for it to receive another event with time-stamp smaller than T_1, then the process can safely process E_1 because it can guarantee that doing so will not later result in a violation of the local causality constraint. Processes containing no safe events must block. This can lead to deadlock situations in which a set of processes block waiting on each other for processing safe messages.

Figure 7.12 shows an example of a deadlock situation, in which three processes A, B, and C are sending and receiving messages involving time-stamped events to and from each other and receiving messages from the external world. Process A has received a message from the external world with a time stamp 22 is stored in a nonempty queue. However, it has

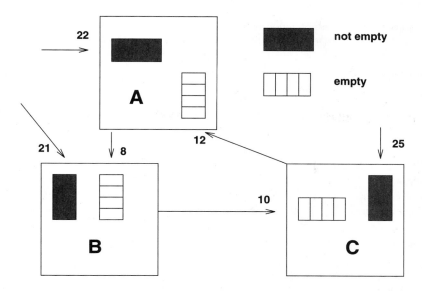

Figure 7.12 Deadlock situation in asynchronous PDES (Courtesy of Fuji-moto, *Comm. ACM,* ©ACM 1990)

processed a message from process C with time stamp 12; hence its empty queue has a time stamp of 12. Process A cannot process events from the non-empty queue corresponding to the external world (containing message 22), since its empty queue has a time stamp of 12. A process can only consume an event with a time stamp $E1$ if it can determine that no other event of lower time stamp can come later. Since there is no guarantee that process A will not receive a message of time stamp greater than 12 but less than 22 later from process C, process A has to block. Similarly, process B is waiting on a message from process A, since the last message from A had a time stamp of 8, even though there is an external event of time stamp 21, stored in its non-empty queue. Finally, process C is waiting on a message from process B since the last message from B had time stamp 10, even though it has a message from the external world with time stamp 25. Each process is waiting on the incoming link containing the smallest link value because the corresponding link value is empty. All three processes are blocked, even though there are event messages in other queues that are waiting to be processed.

Independently, Chandy and Misra [19] and Bryant [16] developed PDES algorithms with deadlock avoidance. These approaches require that we statically specify the links that indicate which processes can communicate with which other processes. To determine when it is safe to process a message, it is required that the sequence of time stamps on messages sent over a link be nondecreasing. This guarantees that the time stamp of the last message received on an incoming link is a lower bound on the time stamp of any subsequent message that will be later received. Each link has a clock associated with it that is equal to either the time stamp of the message at the front of the link if the queue has a message or the time stamp of the last message received on that link if that queue is empty. The process repeatedly selects the link with the smallest clock and, if there is a message in it, processes it. If the selected queue is empty, the process blocks. If a cycle of empty queues arises that has sufficiently small clock values, each process in that cycle might block and the simulation deadlocks, as shown in Figure 7.12.

Null messages are used to avoid deadlock situations. Null messages are used for synchronization purposes only and do not correspond to any activity in the physical system. Whenever a process finishes processing an event, it sends a null message along each of its output ports indicating lower bounds on the time stamps of next outgoing messages. A null message with time stamp T_{null} that is sent from LP_A to LP_B is essentially a promise by LP_A that it will not send a message to LP_B carrying a time stamp smaller than T_{null}. One way to determine the time stamp of null messages is to determine the clock values of each incoming link coupled with the minimum time-stamp increment for any message passing through the logical process. Whenever a process finishes processing an event, it sends a null message on each of its output ports indicating this bound. The receiver of this null message can now compute new bounds on its outgoing links and send this information on to its neighbors.

Let us show how the use of null messages can avoid the deadlock situation in Figure 7.12. For the set of events in the figure, process A would notice that the lowest incoming link has a time stamp of 12, so any message on that link will have at least that time stamp. Hence, it can send a null message to process B with a time stamp of 13, assuming it takes one time unit to process the message (this models a one unit gate delay for logic simulation process B). This will, in turn, allow process B to send a null message of time stamp 14 to process C, which will, in turn, send a null message of time stamp 15 to process A. This process will repeat until process B can pick a message from the nonempty queue with a time stamp of 21 and hence break the deadlock.

This mechanism will avoid deadlocks provided there are no cycles with a collective time-stamp increment across a cycle of a zero. This means we cannot perform zero-delay logic simulation for logic circuits with feedback in them. However, most logic simulation programs always assume a small gate delay, hence this is no problem for logic simulation.

Chandy and Misra also developed an alternative approach to parallel simulation that avoids the sending of null messages [19]. In this scheme, the computation is allowed to deadlock. A separate mechanism is used to break the deadlock. The deadlock can be broken by observing that the messages containing the smallest time stamp are always safe to process. Alternatively, we may use a distributed computation to compute a lower bound information to enlarge the set of safe messages. Unlike the deadlock avoidance approach, this mechanism does not prohibit cycles of zero time-stamp increment, although performance may be poor if such cycles exist.

Several other conservative methods to parallel simulation are possible [7, 39]. One approach is to use synchronous algorithms in which we iteratively determines which events are safe to process and then processes them. Barrier synchronizations are used to keep iterations from interfering from each other; hence such a technique can be used efficiently in shared memory multiprocessors. Thus the simulation moves through the phases of (1) processing events asynchronously and (2) performing some global synchronization to determine which events are safe to process.

We now discuss the methods used to determine if events are safe to process using the notion of a distance between processes. Distance provides a lower bound to the amount of simulated time that must elapse for an unprocessed event on one processor to propagate to another process. Lubachevsky [36] proposed the use of a moving simulated time window to reduce the overhead associated with determining when it is safe to process an event. The lower edge of the window is defined as the minimum time stamp of any unprocessed event. Only those unprocessed events whose time stamp resides within the window are eligible for processing. The purpose of the window is to reduce the search space we must traverse in determining if it is safe to process an event. Setting the window to the appropriate size requires application-specific information. If the window size is too small, very few events will be available for concurrent execution. If the window is too large, the search space again becomes very large, as in the conventional approach.

7.9.3 Optimistic Approaches

Another approach to asynchronous event-driven simulation is the use of optimistic methods. Optimistic methods detect and recover from causality errors. In contrast to conservative methods, optimistic methods need not determine when it is safe to proceed; instead they determine when an error has occurred and invoke a procedure to recover. One advantage of this approach is that it allows the simulator to exploit parallelism when causality errors might possibly occur.

Jefferson proposed the Time Warp mechanism based on the Virtual Time paradigm, which is the most well-known optimistic protocol [32]. In Time Warp, a causality error is detected when an event message (a straggler) is received that contains a time stamp smaller than that of the process' clock (that is, the time stamp of the last processed message). Recovery is accomplished by undoing the effects of all events that have been processed prematurely by the process receiving the straggler. An event may have done two things that have to be rolled back. It might have modified the state of the logical process, or it might have sent event messages to other processes. Rolling back the state can be achieved by periodically saving the process' state and restoring the state vector on rollback. Rollback from a previously sent message can be achieved by sending a negative or antimessage that annihilates the original message. If a process receives an antimessage, that process must roll back to undo the effect of processing the previous original message. Recursively repeating this procedure allows all the effects of the erroneous computations to be canceled.

Figure 7.13 illustrates the Virtual Time concept and shows the structure of a process named A. In Figure 7.13(a), process A has a local virtual clock of 181, which means that a message with receive time stamp 181 is being processed. The state of the logical process in our logic simulation example would correspond to all the signal assignments to the outputs of gates in that partition. The input queue contains all recent incoming messages sorted in order of virtual receive time. The output queue contains copies of messages that have been recently sent, kept in virtual time order. They are needed in case of a rollback, for which it will be necessary to know which messages have been sent and must be unsent. Figure 7.13(b) shows the situation when a new message with virtual receive time 135 arrives. Then all the work that was done by this process since 135 (in fact, since 121 the latest earlier event earlier than 135) must be undone. Hence the state queue is searched for a saved state prior to 135 and current state restored to that state at time 135. All future states are discarded. Finally, for

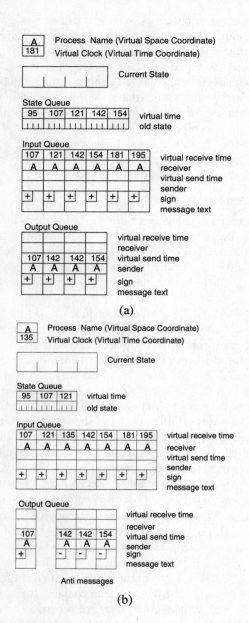

Figure 7.13 Virtual time concept. (a) Process A before rollback. (b) Process A after rollback. (Courtesy of Jefferson, *Proc. Int. Conf. Parallel Processing,* ©IEEE 1983)

all messages in the output queue after time 135, generate some new messages with the same times, but with a reverse sign (meaning an antimessage).

Numerous optimizations have been proposed on the basic technique. In lazy cancellation [28], processes do not immediately send an antimessage for any rolled back computation. Instead they see if a reevaluation of the computation regenerates the same messages, in which case there is no need to send antimessages. The lazy reevaluation or jump forward optimization [55] deals with comparisons of state vectors instead of messages to jump forward over rolled back events instead of reexecuting them if the state of the system is the same after processing the straggler message as before.

In the following sections we will review how these general approaches to asynchronous parallel discrete event simulation can be applied to the problem of parallel logic simulation.

7.10 CONSERVATIVE ASYNCHRONOUS EVENT-DRIVEN SIMULATION

7.10.1 Overview

In the domain of logic simulation, the physical processes are circuit elements (transistors, gates, and latches). One or more of these physical processes (circuit elements) can be combined into a logical process on which the simulator works. Each different type of logical process has a corresponding simulator code that simulates the gate-level circuits. Each of these logical processes has a local time associated with it that indicates how far each element has advanced in the logic simulation. Different logical processes can have different local times and advance independently of other elements.

7.10.2 Shared Memory Parallel MIMD Algorithm

We now describe a shared memory parallel logic simulation algorithm that uses the asynchronous optimistic approach of parallel discrete event simulation. The algorithm is based on work reported by Soule and Blank and Soule [48, 50]. We first describe an application of the Chandy-Misra-Bryant [16, 20, 19] algorithm to the problem of digital logic simulation. The simulated circuit consists of several circuit elements, gates, latches, and so on, called physical processes. One or more of these processes can be combined into a logical process, and the simulator works on these logical processes. Each logical process (set of gates) receives time-stamped event messages on its inputs and consumes these messages when all inputs are ready. As a result of consuming messages, the logic element advances its local time and possibly sends out one or more time stamped event messages on its outputs. Each input queue can hold any number of pending messages, ordered by time. Each wire in the circuit is represented as a list of events, and each input of an element just points to the event list of the corresponding wire.

As an example of an element evaluation, consider a two-input AND gate shown in Figure 7.14. Figure refand(a) shows the AND gate with a local time of 10, an event waiting on input 1 at time 20 (thus the value of input 1 is known between times 10 and 20), and no events pending on input 2. In this state the AND gate process is suspended, and it waits for an event message on input 2. When input 2 gets an event message with time stamp 15 shown in Figure 7.14(b), the AND gate becomes active, consumes the event on input-2, advances its local time to 15, and possibly sends an output message with time stamp 15 plus the delay of the AND gate (assumed to be unity) as shown in Figure 7.14(c).

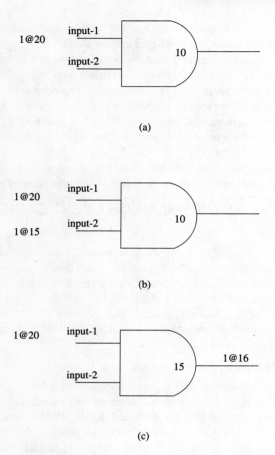

Figure 7.14 Example of element evaluation in Chandy-Misra-Bryant algorithm

In the main Chandy-Misra-Bryant (CMB) algorithm [16, 20, 19], when input events are consumed and the local time of a logical process is advanced, no messages are sent on an output wire unless the value of that output changes. This makes the CMB algorithm as efficient as event-driven simulation, but also makes it prone to deadlocks, in which no element can advance its local time, because each element has at least one input with no pending events or new information.

The CMB algorithm therefore cycles between two phases: the *compute phase*, when elements are advancing their local time, and the *deadlock resolution*, phase when the elements are being freed from deadlock.

In the parallel CMB algorithm, since each element is able to advance its local time independently of other elements, all elements can potentially execute concurrently. However, only when all inputs to an event become ready (have a pending event) is the element marked as available for execution and placed on a distributed work queue. The distributed work queue is implemented by having each processor own as many FIFO queues as number of processors, with each queue corresponding to one of the other processors. The processors remove elements from queues they own and add elements to queues that correspond to them. Hence each queue has only processor adding elements and another removing elements. The processors take these elements off the distributed work queue, execute them, update their outputs, and possibly activate other elements connected to the outputs. This process continues until a deadlock is reached, at which point a deadlock resolution procedure is invoked.

The outline of the basic deadlock detection scheme is as follows. Each processor starts out by processing elements in its own queue. Once its queue becomes empty, the processor starts querying the queues of other processors for more work. If all queues are checked and no new work is found, the processor assumes a deadlock and places itself on a list of deadlocked processors. If new work is found, the processor removes itself from the list of deadlocked processors. Only when all processors agree that a deadlock has occurred has an actual deadlock occurred, and control is passed to a deadlock resolution routine.

To resolve the deadlock, the minimum event time of all unprocesses events in the system, gmt, is computed. Subsequently, all elements with an input event of gmt are activated.

Prior to the execution of the parallel CMB algorithm, an initialization step is performed that initializes the generator and constant nodes. Generator nodes are nodes such as system clock, whose values are known for the entire simulation period, and constant nodes are nodes whose values do not change during the entire simulation period.

An outline of the parallel event-driven logic simulation algorithm, *SM-PARALLEL-EVENT-LOGIC-ASYNCH-CON* (denoting shared memory parallel algorithm for event-driven logic simulation using circuit partitioning with asynchrounous conservative techniques), follows:

Procedure *SM-PARALLEL-EVENT-LOGIC-ASYNCH-CON;*

Perform Initialization

Read circuit;
FOR all time steps DO
    FOR all generator and constant nodes DO
        Evaluate generator and constant nodes;
    END FOR
END FOR
Partition circuit among processors;

Simulation phase
FORALL processors in PARALLEL DO

Compute phase
    WHILE gmt < maximum-time DO
        WHILE (own element-queue not empty) DO
            Atomically remove element e from own queue;

     Check valid times and event times of all inputs;
     Call minimum of these times, t;
     t is the maximum time, that e can advance to;
     FOR each consumable input event v with time $\leq t$ DO
        Update input values to reflect consumption of v;
        Compute new output behavior;
     END FOR
     Update valid times on output wires;
     Update the element's local clock;
     Create output events for any changes in output values;
     Schedule for execution all elements connected
        to changed outputs;
   END WHILE
   IF own element queue empty THEN
     Look for more work from other processor queues;
     Atomically remove element from queue and perform
     above steps of simulation;
   IF all processor queues empty THEN
     Processor deadlocked;

Deadlock resolution phase

   Find the minimum time stamp, gmt of
     all unconsumed events;
   Activate all elements with an input event
     with time stamp gmt;
  END WHILE;
 END FORALL;

End Procedure

    The preceding parallel logic simulation algorithm alternates between compute and deadlock resolution phases. One way to bypass the deadlock problem is to send NULL messages that carry only time information and no value information, which would be sent after each element evaluation. Unfortunately, always sending a NULL message makes the algorithm so inefficient that it is not a good deadlock avoidance scheme.

    We will now describe the *selective* use of NULL messages to reduce the number of deadlocks that need to be processed based on work reported by Soule and Gupta [49, 50]. The approach involves the investigatation of some domain specific (logic simulation specific) causes behind deadlocks in logic simulation and provides solutions to them in the form of NULL messages that are selectively sent. In the logic simulation problem, deadlocks can be put into two categories: (1) those deadlocked due to some aspect of the circuit structure and (2) those deadlocked due to low activity levels. Some examples of sources of deadlocks and

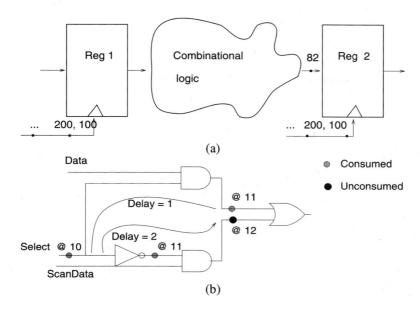

(a)

(b)

Figure 7.15 Examples of deadlocks in logic simulation. (a) Deadlock caused by a clocked register. (b) Deadlock caused by paths of different delays. (Courtesy of Soule, Stanford Univ. Tech. Report, 1992)

their proposed solutions will be discussed next and are illustrated in Figure 7.15.

The first cause of deadlocks can be attributed to register and generator nodes. In a typical synchronous circuit, enough time is allowed for the changes in the output of one set of registers to propagate all the way to the next set of registers in the data path and stabilize before the registers are clocked again. For example in Figure 7.15(a) the critical path of the combinational circuit is 82 ns, and the clock changes every 100 ns for everything to stabilize. $Reg1$ is clocked at the start of the simulation, and the events propagate through the combinational logic, generating an event at time 82, which is consumed by $Reg2$ since the clock is defined for all time. However the next event for $Reg2$ at time 100 is not consumed because the input to the latch is defined until time 82, not 100. This causes $Reg2$ to block and the deadlock resolution phase to enter. Such a deadlock can be prevented by taking advantage of the behavior of the latch. In the case of registers and latches, which constitute a large portion of the circuits in a design, we know that the output will not change until the next event. Hence the input to $Reg2$ will be the same until the next clock cycle (100).

Another example of deadlock behavior is when there are multiple paths with different delays as shown in the multiplexer circuit shown in Figure 7.15(b). There are two paths from the $Select$ line to the OR gate at the output. If the $Data$ and $ScanData$ lines are valid, an event on the $Select$ line could propagate through the two paths and generate events at times 11 and 12. The event at time 12 will not be consumed by the OR gate since its other input is only defined up to time 11 causing it to deadlock. Such a situation is due to the topology of the circuit and can be avoided by hiding the multiple paths by globbing the elements in multiple

TABLE 7.4 Normalized Speedups of Parallel Simulation Algorithm on an Encore Multimax™ Multiprocessor

Circuit	Gates	1 Processor Speedup	8 Processors Speedup	14 Processor Speedup
Multiplier	4,990	1.0	5.0	5.8
H-FRISC	5,060	1.0	7.0	8.2
NTT	11,555	1.0	6.0	7.5
R6000	12,207	1.0	6.0	7.2
Ardent	13,374	1.0	6.0	8.5
DASH	24,611	1.0	5.5	7.0

paths into a larger logical process or by taking advantage of the behavior of the circuit, for example, that the output of an OR gate is a 1 if one of the inputs is a 1, or the output of an AND gate is 0, m if one of the inputs is a 0.

Other sources of deadlocks such as those due to different order of node updates and unevaluated paths are discussed in [49].

The two basic approaches to remove the deadlocks are to exploit the element behavior of clocked registers, AND gates and OR gates, and the one level checking schemes, by which we propagate the time information one level of logic forward whenever latency occurs; that is, an element can use its local data in conjunction with the data of elements one level back to try to break any potential deadlock conditions.

Implementation Soule et al. [48, 49, 50] have reported an implementation of the preceding algorithms for parallel logic simulation using asynchronous conservative techniques on an Encore Multimax™ shared memory multiprocessor. Table 7.4 shows the normalized speedups of several benchmark circuits on an Encore Multimax with all the optimizations described earlier.

Soule et al. have also reported [49, 50] on the comparative performance of various parallel logic simulation algorithms on a shared memory multiprocessor: (1) synchronous parallel event-driven algorithm, (2) basic Chandy-Misra approach with event scanning to break deadlocks, (3) Chandy-Misra algorithms with NULL messages to break deadlocks, and (4) The Chandy-Misra algorithm with deadlock avoidance using the domain-specific techniques discussed previously. In all the circuits, the maximum speedups were obtained from method 4.

7.11 OPTIMISTIC ASYNCHRONOUS EVENT-DRIVEN SIMULATION

7.11.1 Overview

Researchers in the logic simulation area have also applied the circuit parallel approach to logic simulation using optimistic mechanisms based on the Virtual Time and Time Warp mechanism of rollback and recovery [31, 32]. We will now describe two parallel algorithms, one for distributed memory MIMD multiprocessors and another for shared memory MIMD shared memory multiprocessors.

7.11.2 Distributed Memory Parallel MIMD Algorithm

We will now describe a distributed memory parallel algorithm for logic simulation using the asynchronous optimitic approach based on work reported by Arnold and Terman [6]. Each processor in a parallel logic simulation is assigned the task of simulating one partition of the circuit. To maximize the processor utilization and minimize communication, the simulation load must be evenly distributed, and groups that need to pass signals frequently among themselves should be kept in one partition. Arnold and Terman [6] used a greedy algorithm based on clustering for assigning the partitions to processors, followed by an iterative improvement stage that moves groups from one partition to another if there is a lot of communication across the groups in two partitions.

Enforcing the precedence constraint represented by a node shared between two or more partitions requires additional communication. If the value of each input is known for all time, there would be no precedence constraint among the partitions and each partition could be simulated independently of others. Using this observation, the partitions can be decoupled by the use of *history buffers*, which for each partition store the value of each input node for all time. When a partition changes the value of an output node, it sends a message to the other partitions for which that node is an input. The receiving partitions use this information to update their *history buffers* and redo the simulation if necessary.

To correct a simulation to account for a change in the input history, a checkpointing and rollback strategy needs to be implemented. As the simulation progresses, a processor takes a checkpoint of the current state of the simulation that contains a record of the complete state of each partition: the value of every node, all pending events, and the current simulation time. From this checkpoint, the simulation state can be completely restored to the saved state at any future time, in effect rolling the simulation back to the time the checkpoint was taken. The ideal checkpointing strategy would achieve a balance between the amount of resimulation due to rollback (by increasing checkpoint frequency) and minimizing storage overhead (by decreasing checkpoint frequency).

One successful strategy is use an approach that varies the checkpointing frequency with time. Following each resynchronization and rollback, a checkpoint is taken every time step for the first several steps. As the simulation progresses, the number of time steps between echeckpoints is increased exponentially up to some maximum period.

An outline of the parallel event-driven logic simulation algorithm, *DM-PARALLEL-EVENT-LOGIC-ASYNCH-OPT* (denoting distributed memory parallel algorithm for event-driven logic simulation using circuit partitioning and asynchronous optimistic approach), is given next.

Procedure *DM-PARALLEL-EVENT-LOGIC-ASYNCH-OPT;*

Read circuit description;
Partition circuit among processors;
Create history buffers at each dependence node

common among circuit partitions (output node of some);

FORALL processors in PARALLEL DO
   Initialize history buffers
   FOR each gate DO
      FOR each input and output node in gate DO
         FOR all time steps DO
            IF node is primary input
               THEN read input value;
               ELSE guess a value for node,
                  e.g. set to value 0 for all time;
            Store value as history buffer;
         END FOR
      END FOR
   END FOR

   WHILE (element needs evaluation) DO
      Pick next element for evaluation;
      Evaluate element;
      IF (change on output) THEN
         Update all fan-out nodes;
         Schedule fan-out elements on queue;
      Receive updated input signals from other processors;
      IF received signal different from history buffer THEN
         Rollback simulation to last checkpointed state;
         Redo simulation for all time steps for element;
         Send cancellation messages to other processors;
         Schedule affected gates on queues;
      Save simulation state in history buffers;
      Send output signals to other processors;
   END WHILE
END FORALL

End Procedure

Implementation Arnold and Terman have reported an implementation of a parallel switch level timing and logic simulator called PRSIM using the preceding parallel algorithm [6]. The simulation model was based on Terman's sequential switch level simulator called RSIM [52].

    In the RSIM model for timing simulation of MOS transistors, transistors are represented by ideal switches and a series resistor representing the conductance of the transistor when on. Associated with the capacitance of the various electrical nodes of the circuit, it is possible to use RC timing models to predict the times at which events would occur into the future.

    The circuit to be simulated is divided into N partitions, each composed of one or more dc-connected or channel-connected groups of transistors. The value of a electrical node is determined by a single group. Nodes that connect to gates of transistors in a group are called inputs, and nodes in the group that control transistors in other groups are called outputs.

In a switch-level simulation, each group can be considered as a unit similar to a logic gate in logic simulation. The evaluation procedure of a logic gate is replaced by an evaluation procedure of a group of transistors. Given the values of logic values at the input nodes to a group, the values of the logic values and the times at which they occur can be determined using simple RC models within each group [52]. A precedence constraint between two partitions can occur when one partition determines the value of a node that is an input to another partition. Then the computation of the dependent partition must always lag behind the original partition to ensure that the correct input value is used. This is analogous to the case in logic simulation when a gate can be evaluated only after all the gates feeding it are evaluated.

PRSIM was implemented on a BBN Butterfly™ multiprocessor and speedups of about 4 were measured on six processors for simulating a 64- bit adder. Three factors resulted in the speedups being less than linear: (1) the extra simulation necessary as a result of rollback, (2) the processor imbalance of load due to improper static load balancing; third, the synchronization overheads associated with parallel processing.

In the PRSIM simulator, no collection of old events was done to reclaim storage of events that would never be rolled back to. Hence only small circuits were run on the simulator.

7.11.3 Shared Memory Parallel MIMD Algorithm

We will now describe a shared memory parallel logic simulation algorithm that applies the Virtual Time/Time Warp paradigm more rigorously based on work reported by Briner [14]. Several optimizations are used on top of the Virtual Time/Time Warp paradigm described in Section 7.9.3.

The first optimization deals with minimizing storage requirements by collecting storage for old events. One way to achieve this is through global synchronization, that is an expensive process. Another way to accomplish this objective is through the notion of a global virtual time which is the minimum among all the processors' local virtual times; this computation can be achieved in a tree-based manner among processors. Using this global virtual time as a bound on the time beyond which no event needs to be saved for recovery, we can reclaim storage for such old events.

Another optimization deals with the use of a bounded window technique. Using a very tight bound on the global virtual time, processors are prevented from progressing beyond a a certain time frame ahead of the global virtual time. That is, the maximum difference between the local virtual time and global virtual time is bounded. This prevents processors from doing extra work too much ahead into the future, which may have to be rolled back. This helps the processors that are behind the others to concentrate on advancing the global time of the systems. Care must be taken in choosing the window size appropriately. If the window size is too small, for example, equal to 1, then the simulation becomes a version of a synchronous simulation. If the size is too large, the scheme behaves as if there is no bounded window, except that the overhead of implementing the bounded window increases.

An outline of the parallel event-driven logic simulation algorithm, *SM-PARALLEL-EVENT-LOGIC-ASYNCH-OPT* (denoting shared memory parallel algorithm for event-driven logic simulation using circuit partitioning and asynchronous optimistic approach), is given next.

   Procedure *SM-PARALLEL-EVENT-LOGIC-ASYNCH-OPT;*

   Read circuit description;
   Partition circuit among processors;
   Create one separate timing wheel (queue) per processor;
   Set global virtual time GVT = 0;
   Set Local Virtual Time (LVT) = 0 for all processors;

   FORALL processors in PARALLEl DO
      WHILE (events needs evaluation) DO
         Pick next event for evaluation;
         Evaluate gate corresponding to event;
         IF (change on output) THEN
            Update all fan-out nodes;
            Send cancellation events to other processors;
         IF cancellation messages received from
               other processors THEN
            Rollback simulation to last checkpointed state;
            Redo simulation for all time steps from
               checkpoint to final step for element;
            Schedule affected gates on queues;
         Checkpoint simulation state;
         IF (LVT - GVT) < window THEN
            Increment LVT;
         ELSE Wait; do not increment LVT;
      END WHILE
      Set GVT = Minimum(all LVTs of all processors);
      Reclaim storage for all states less than GVT;
   END FORALL

   End Procedure

Implementation Briner has implemented the preceding parallel logic simulation algorithm
with various optimizations and investigated the performance of the algorithm on a BBN
GP1000 multiprocessor [14]. Table 7.5 shows the normalized speedups of several benchmark
circuits on various processors of the BBN multiprocessor.

   Experiments have been reported on varying the window size of the bounded window
optimization. For an example circuit, with a window size of 1, the speedup obtained was
4.5 on 32 processors, a speedup of 11 was obtained with a window size of 400 (the best), a
speedup of 8 was obtained with a window size of 1000, and a speedup of 6 was obtained with
unbounded windows.

   Various versions of checkpointing have been implemented and studied. In the interprocessor synchronization approach, all components, ports, and events on the same processor

TABLE 7.5 Normalized Speedups of Parallel Simulation Algorithm on an Encore Multimax™ Multiprocessor

Circuit	Gates	1 Processor Speedup	16 Processors Speedup	32 Processors Speedup
Adder	400	1.0	4.5	6.5
QRS	1,000	1.0	5.0	7.0
CCArray	32,000	1.0	14.0	20.0

have the same time frame. If an event arrives at a processor with a simulation time earlier than the last dequeued message, the entire processor is rolled back. In the intercomponent synchronization approach, only those nodes and ports directly connected to each component have the same time frame. Thus only an event associated with a component can cause a rollback. The cost of a rollback is much less in intercomponent synchronization than interprocessor synchronization. Some measurements of speedups of a real circuit (a 64-bit adder) on the BBN multiprocessor showed speedups of about 6.5 for intercomponent synchronization versus 4.5 for interprocessor synchronization on 32 processors.

Results have also been reported on two versions of event cancellation. In aggressive cancellation, following an event that has to be rolled back, an anti-message is immediately send to other processors to cancel the effect of the event. In lazy cancellation, the cancellation of the event is delayed until the event is known to be canceled. This delay is good if the event is definitely not going to be canceled. However, if the event is canceled, the other processor will have to rollback further and start later than it would have had to do otherwise. For some real measurements, speedups were reported to be better with lazy cancellation (speedup of 8 on 32 processors) than for aggressive cancellation (speedup of 7.5 on 32 processors), but not significantly better.

7.12 HIGH-LEVEL BEHAVIORAL SIMULATION

7.12.1 Overview

While most hardware and software simulators have been targeted at logic level gates with some extensions to handle memory elements, there is a lot of recent interest in high-level simulation. Behavioral simulation languages such as Verilog™ and VHDL™ [5] are becoming industry standard. System-level simulations of complex digital designs are often performed in Verilog or VHDL. We will provide a brief overview of the VHDL language and its use in modeling digital systems. [1]

In VHDL, a given logic circuit is represented as a *design entity*. The logic circuit can be as complicated as a microprocessor or as simple as an AND or OR gate. A *design entity* consists of two types of descriptions: the *interface description* and, one or more, *architectural*

---

[1] Portions of this section have been adapted from J. R. Armstrong, *Chip Level Modeling with VHDL*, Prentice Hall, 1989

bodies. Consider the interface description for a circuit that counts the number of 1's in an input vector of length 3:

```
entity COUNTER is
  port(A: in BIT_VECTOR(0 to 2); C: out BIT_VECTOR(0 to 1);
end COUNTER;
```

The interface description names the entity and describes its inputs and outputs. The description of interface signals includes the mode of the signal (in or out) and the type of the signal (3-bit or 2-bit vectors). The interface description defines only the inputs and outputs of the design entity, basically. The specification of the behavior of the entity is done by the *architecture body*. A behavioral description of the counter is given next:

```
architecture BEHAVIOR of COUNTER is
  begin
    process(A)
     variable NUM: INTEGER range 0 to 3;
    begin
      NUM := 0;
      for I in 0 to 2 loop
        if A(I) = '1' then
          NUM := NUM + 1;
        end if;
      end loop;
      case NUM is
       when 0 => C <= '00';
       when 1 => C <= '10';
       when 2 => C <= '01';
       when 3 => C <= '11';
      end case;
    end process;
end BEHAVIOR;
```

The preceding behavioral body describes the operation of the algorithm, perfectly; but its relevance to real hardware is weak. We can continue the design of the counter to the logic design stage and determine the logical outputs of the two bits of the counter $C1$ and $C0$ as

$$C1 = A1.A0 + A2.A0 + A2.A1 = MAJ3(A)$$

$$C0 = A2.\bar{A}1.\bar{A}0 + \bar{A}2.\bar{A}1.A0 + A2.A1.A0 + \bar{A}2.A1.\bar{A}0 = OPAR3(A)$$

From these equations it can be noted that $C1$ is the majority function (MAJ3) of 3 variables, and $C0$ is the odd-parity (OPAR3) function of 3 variables. We can therefore specify the architecture body of the counter in a structural form as follows:

```
architecture STRUCTURAL of COUNTER is

begin
  C(1) = MAJ3(A);
  C(0) = OPAR3(A);
end STRUCTURAL;
```

This assumes the existence of the MAJ3 and OPAR3 gates at the hardware level that the functions MAJ3 and OPAR3 must have been declared and defined, previously.

This may be done for the MAJ3 function as follows:

```
entity MAJ3 is
  port (X: in BIT_VECTOR() to 2): Z: out BIT)
end MAJ3;

architecture STRUCTURAL of MAJ3 is

component AND2
  port (I1,I2: in BIT; O: out BIT)
end component;

component OR3
  port (I1, I2, I3: in BIT; O: out BIT)
end component;

begin
 G1: AND2
      port map (X(0), X(1), A1);
 G2: AND2
      port map (X(0), X(2), A2);
 G3: AND2
      port map (X(1), X(2), A3);
 G4: OR3
      port map (A1, A2, A3, Z);
end STRUCTURAL;
```

The preceding assumes that the components AND2 and OR3 exist, that is, the functions for AND2 and OR3 have been declared previously. This can be accomplished for the AND2 gate as follows.

```
entity AND2 is
  port (I1, I2: in BIT; O: out BIT)
```

```
end AND21

architecture BEHAVIOR of AND2 is
  begin
    O <= I1 and I2;
end BEHAVIOR;
```

Having introduced the VHDL language through an example, we now highlight some key features of the language. The first feature is the notion of a *block*, that is a basic element of a VHDL description. A block is a bounded region of text that contains a declaration section and an executable section. Thus, the architectural body itself is a block. However, within an architectural body, internal blocks (two blocks A and B) can exist. Such a block structure supports a natural form of design decomposition. Furthermore, a guard condition can be associated with a block. When a guard condition is TRUE, it enables certain types of statements inside the block. These are useful for describing sequential logic.

Another feature in VHDL is that of a *process*. Process represents a fundamental method by which concurrent activities in digital circuits are modeled. A process is described by the keyword *process (A)*. The vector *A*, in this instance, is said to make up the sensitivity list of the process. Whenever a signal in the sensitivity list changes, the process is activated; and the statements within the block are executed. For example, three concurrent processes corresponding to three logic blocks or gates in a circuit can be described as:

```
LOGIC_BLK1: process (X1,X2,X3)
                variable YINT: BIT;
                begin
                   YINT:=  X1 and X2;
                   Z1 <= YINT or X3 after 30 ns;
                end process LOGIC_BLK1;

LOGIC_BLK2: process (X4, X5)
. . . . .

LOGIC_BLK3: process (Z1,Z2)
. . . .
```

In digital systems, a logical process will frequently pause its execution while waiting for a time-period to elapse or an event to occur. Once the time-period has elapsed or the awaited event has occurred, execution of the process resumes. This is illustrated as follows:

```
process
. . . .               (Begin process execution)
```

```
    . . . .

wait for time T
     or
wait until event E
    . . . .            (Resume process execution)
    . . . .
end process    (End process execution)
```

The use of the wait mechanism implies a sequential behavior of the logic. The form of the wait construct in VHDL is: WAIT ON sensitivity-list UNTIL condition-clause FOR time-out. For example, the statement

```
wait on X,Y until (Z=0) for 100 ns;
```

would suspend a process until either X or Y change, then the expression Z=0 is evaluated, and if TRUE, the process will resume. Regardless of the conditions, the process will resume after a delay of 100 ns.

In the previous discussion, we have provided an introduction to the high-level modeling of digital systems using VHDL. The reader is referred to [5] for more details.

It should be pointed out that the same ideas of parallel discrete event simulation (PDES) described in Section 7.9 are directly applicable to parallel behavioral simulation. A process construct in VHDL maps to the notion of a logical process in PDES. We can therefore use either synchronous or asynchronous parallel behavioral simulation ideas to speed up behavioral simulation. The issues of partitioning different components of a behavioral model to different processors is very similar to the partitioning methods discussed for parallel logic simulation. We can also use either conservative or optimistic asynchronous methods of parallel discrete event simulation to behavioral simulation.

7.12.2 Distributed Memory MIMD Parallel Algorithm

We will now describe a distributed memory parallel MIMD algorithm for behavioral simulation based on work reported by the Jade Simulations International Corporation™ [21]. The basic idea in this parallel algorithm is to use the Time Warp model of asynchronous optimistic parallel discrete event simulation [32] described in Section 7.9.3.

We will discuss the main ideas in mapping a VHDL simulator on to Time Warp [32]. The two main VHDL constructs of interest are signals and processes. Processes in the VHDL construct correspond to the notion of a Time Warp logical process. Hence each VHDL process is mapped to a Time Warp process. Each update of a signal waveform will require that a message be sent from the driver of the signal to all processes that are sensitive to the signal, or can potentially read from it. If there are multiple drivers for a signal than all updates to the waveform are sent to a single Time Warp process, where the resolution is done. If parts of a waveform are canceled as a result of inertial or transport delays, an antimessage or cancellation message is sent on the Time Warp system, to delete the waveforms in the receiving processes.

Since the message communication constitutes overhead in such parallel simulators, it is important to perform optimizations in message communication. The need for optimization in message communication becomes obvious if we enumerate the types of messages used in the Time Warp system in order from most expensive to least expensive.

- From machine to machine over a local area network

- From machine to machine over high speed link, for example, hypercube channels

- From machine to machine via shared memory

- From Time Warp process to time warp process on the same machine

- From Time Warp process to time warp process within a cluster

- From a Time Warp process back to itself

If the VHDL processes all have a lot of computing to perform (for example, several milliseconds of computation per event), there is no problem with achieving good speedups during parallel simulation. However, in practice, the scheduled events have very little computing associated with them, for example, evaluation of a concurrent signal assignment. Instead of executing such lightweight operations with the overhead of a full send, we can amortize the message overhead by grouping together multiple VHDL processes into a single Time Warp process. Messages in and out of such a grouping will constitute a full message passi with the usual overheads. Messages internal to a grouping can be processed in a more efficient way.

There are two ways to do such a grouping. The simplest way is to group processes together into a cluster. A cluster is a Time Warp facility that says that all entities in a cluster must be in the same machine. The advantage is that the processes on a cluster share memory. Hence a message sent from one process to another in a cluster can be retrieved by an operation from shared memory, that incurs much less overhead than actually sending a message across machines. Note that at this level, the underlying time wrp system is still handling the event list scheduling, and the individual processes are still independent coroutines with their own stack which is maintained by Time Warp.

A second more complex way of grouping processes is to construct a complete copy of a VHDL simulator within a single Time Warp process. This embedded simulator will be almost identical to a standard sequential simulator and will be implemented as efficiently as the sequential one. In particular, it will need to maintain its own event list and schedule processes from it. The central loop of the embedded simulator will consist of taking the next event off the event list, repeatedly.

Implementation The preceding parallel algorithm has been implemented by the Jade Simulations International Corporation [21] on top of the *Sim++* simulation system that is a C++ runtime environment for distributed simulation using Time Warp [32]. No experimental results have been reported.

7.12.3 Massively Parallel SIMD Parallel Algorithm

We will now describe a massively parallel SIMD algorithm for behavioral simulation using a synchronous parallel simulation approach. The algorithm is based on work reported reported by Vellandi and Lightner [53].

The basic approach to massively parallel simulation is to assign each data independent concurrent computational unit in the VHDL specification to a different processor in a massively parallel SIMD system. Figure 7.16 shows the division of the simulation task into component model processors, node model processors, and delay element processors. These processors send data between themselves. It is assumed that there are N model components and M nodes; hence there are N component model processors and M node processors. For each N component, there are M pointers representing nodes that connect to the component's inputs. Also, for each N component, there are M pointers representing nodes that connect to the component's outputs. In addition, there are altogether $N \times M$ delay element processors representing unique delays that can be set between each component output and each node to represent delay statements in VHDL.

The simulation is performed by executing each task in parallel among processors in the massively parallel SIMD system. If a processor does not have any work to perform at an instant, it sits idle. The simulation proceeds as follows. First, all new values are input to the component models, and the model code fragments are executed to completion. New values generated by the component model processors will be added to temporary storage in the delay elements. When there are multiple drivers of a node, the resultant signal value on a node has to be obtained via signal conflict resolution. All new values for a given time step are calculated by the node model processors according to certain signal conflict resolution functions, and the values are then made available to the component model inputs for the next repetition of the three phases. Each phase of computation is performed by a different type of processor in the .SIMD machine, under lock step centralized control.

Extraction of parallelism from a VHDL specification can be done in two ways. We can use the explictly parallel constructs of VHDL that are specified in the language. Each statement or group of statements inside such a parallel construct represents an independent code fragment that can be executed to completion. One concern is to properly handle statements with sensitivity lists or guards. This is handled by replicating the guards on all parallel statements.

In addition, it is possible to further decompose the model functions and extract some implicit parallelism. Extraction of implicit parallelism from VHDL statements can be performed by standard data dependence analysis (true, anti and output dependence) used in parallelizing compilers [42, 56]. This can be achieved by building a graph involving the statements and variables/signals in the VHDL program. The nodes in such a graph represent statements in the VHDL model, and edges represent data and control dependencies among the statements. From the graph, we can determine the maximally strongly connected components with no outgoing arcs and assign each component (group of statements) as an independent code fragment to be assigned to a different processor.

Once the tasks for different independent VHDL statements are allocated to different processors in the SIMD parallel machine, the simulation proceeds using three phases of

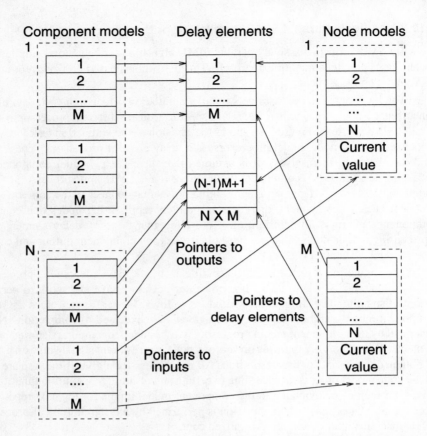

Figure 7.16 Mapping of VHDL simulation tasks to SIMD processors (Courtesy of Vellandi and Lightner, *Proc. European Design Automation Conf.*, ©IEEE 1993)

standard discrete event simulation techniques: (1) model evaluation, (2) delay evaluation and event list manipulation, and (3) signal operations and node update.

    An outline of the massively parallel behavioral simulation algorithm, *SIMD-PARALLEL-BEHAV-SIM* (denoting massively parallel SIMD algorithm for behavioral simulation using a synchronous approach), is given next.

Procedure *SIMD-PARALLEL-BEHAV-SIM*;

Read VHDL input description;
Extract explicit and implicit parallelism;
Determine which code fragments in VHDL code are independent;

Assign each independent code fragment to different processor;

FORALL processors in parallel DO

  REPEAT
    FOR given time step DO
      Barrier synchronize;
      Begin phase 1;
      IF component model processor THEN
        Load signal values;
        Evaluate component model code fragments to completion;
        Add new values of model evaluation
            to delay element processor buffers;
      ENDIF

      Barrier synchronize;
      Begin phase 2;
      IF delay element processor THEN
        Evaluate delay of element in buffer;
        Insert new events on event list;
        Deschedule events if necessary;
        Pick next time step;
      ENDIF
      Barrier synchronize;

      Begin phase 3;
      IF node model processor THEN
        Calculate new values of node for next time step;
        Resolve signal values;
        Make values available to component model
            processor input;
      ENDIF
    UNTIL end of time;
  END FORALL

End Procedure

Implementation Vellandi and Lightner have reported an implementation of the preceding massively parallel algorithm on a Thinking Machines CM-2™ system [53]. In their implementation, a given VHDL program was analyzed by a parallelizing compiler called LAMPO™, which extracted all the parallelism, both explicit and implicit, in the model functions. They subsequently performed the processor assignment and code generation in C*, the data parallel language for the CM-2. The C* source code, the model functions, and connectivity of the circuit were linked to a parallel logic simulator written in C* on the CM-2 system to form an executable simulator. No actual runtimes were reported on the CM-2 for the VHDL models.

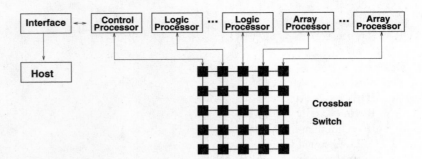

Figure 7.17 IBM logic simulation machine architecture (Courtesy of Burggraff et al, *Proc. Int. Conf. Computer Design,* ©IEEE 1983)

Instead, speedups of an ideal MIMD simulator were estimated for VHDL models of several circuits. The circuits ranged from adders and counters to general synchronous sequential logic. Speedups ranged from 1.4 to 10.4 for the different circuits on the ideal simulator.

7.13 HARDWARE ACCELERATORS

Several research projects have investigated the use of dedicated hardware accelerators for VLSI simulation. We will review some of them in this section.

IBM has built three generations of simulation engines that use circuit parallel algorithms using the compiled synchronous approach. The machines are the Logic Simulation Machine (LSM)™ [29], the Yorktown Simulation Engine™, [41], and the Engineering Verification Engine™ [24]. All the machines use the same basic architecture. The machines support logic simulation with three or four logic values, 0,1, X, and high impedance, and zero- and unit-delay models. It consists of 64 to 256 processors, which are connected by a 64 × 64 or a 256 × 256 crossbar switch that performs fast interprocessor communication. Figure 7.17 shows the architecture of the Logic Simulation Machine [29, 51].

The logic circuit is partitioned into 4K gates each having about four to five inputs. The logic subcircuits are simulated by logic processors, and the memory elements are simulated by array processors. Since the simulator is compiled and not event-driven, the program counter in the controller advances through all the operations and memory without any branches; hence the pipelines are used optimally. All decisions are resolved at compile time, allowing the maximum possible speedup. Because the communication pattern is known at compile time, all speedup techniques and static load balancing techniques can be used.

The EVE™ accelerator is in production use at IBM. It uses more than 200 special-purpose processors. They are either logic processors that evaluate arbitrary four-input one-output logic functions or so-called array processors that simulate memory elements (the so-called arrays). The processors are connected by a full 256-to-256 crosspoint switch that is scheduled statically for interprocessor communication. The design to be simulated is partitioned automatically among the processors based on the rank ordering of the logic. EVE can simulate up to 1.8 million gates and 50 Mbytes of storage. Its peak performance is rated at 2.2 billion gate evaluations per second; typical real performance lies at about 80% of the peak performance.

Another widely used commercial accelerator for gate-level simulation is the Logic Evaluator LE-series™ offered by Zycad Corporation [22]. It uses a synchronous approach to circuit parallel logic simulation and a bus-based multiprocessor architecture with up to 16 processors that implements scheduling and evaluation in hardware. The Zycad LE1032 accelerator exhibits a peak performance of 3.75 million gate evaluations per second on each processor, and 60 million gate evaluations per second on 16 processors. The system can handle up to 1 million gates.

Finally, there have been several hardware accelerators that use the functional parallel approach to parallel logic simulation. To exploit parallelism in this algorithm, the simulation procedure can be partitioned into pipelined stages. Such an approach has been used in the MARS™ hardware accelerator [2, 3, 4]. Figure 7.5 showed the partitioning that was used in the MARS hardware accelerator. The signal scheduler stage sends all the scheduled events down the pipeline. Each event is filtered, logged, and used to update gate inputs. The output filter receives event messages from the signal scheduler and processes them to remove spurious events. All uncanceled event messages are passed down the pipeline to the oscillation detector, which maintains a count of the number of times a signal has changed state during the current time step and interrupts the housekeeper to signal an oscillation if any count exceeds a preset value, for example, 15. Transitions on monitored signals are recoreded by the output log. The circuit topology is represented by the fan-out pointer and fan-out list data structures. For each signal the fan-out list contains a zero-terminated list of fan-outs. The entries in the fan-out pointer consist of the pointers of the beginning of the fan-out list for each signal. Each fan-out is represented by a gate number (16 bits) and a pin number (2 bits, since gates are restricted to be only four-input gates). For each message received, the gate scheduler (GS) pushes the specified gate number on the stack. To avoid scheduling a gate more than once, a 64K-bit vector (1 bit per gate) is maintained, indicating which gates are already scheduled. The bits are cleared when gates are removed from the stack. The gate scheduler transmits all scheduled gates to the input type block. For each gate number received, the input type block retrieves the input values for the gate and passes a message containing gate number and input values on to the gate type unit. The behavior of each gate is represented by the data structures in the gate type unit, the truth table and the delay table units. The MARS system supports a maximum of 256 logic primitives (AND, NAND, and so on). For each gate, its primitive type (8 bits) is held in the gate type table. Shifted left 8 bits, this type is a pointer to the beginning of a 256-input combination by 2-bit truth table. The exhaustive truth table contains 256 gate primitives with four inputs per gate. The delay for each gate is held in the delay table. For unit-delay simulation model, a 0 or a 1 is stored. (For multiple-delay models, the delay time unit contains separate 8-bit rise and fall delays for each gate. Note that for multiple delay models the signal scheduler is implemented as a 4096-slot time wheel.) Evaluating a gate is a three step process. For each signal number and input value, the gate type unit appends the gate's type and forwards it to the input type block, which performs the table lookup and forwards it the delay type unit, which evaluates the delay. The input vector list unit inserts additional events representing primary input changes into the message stream at the appropriate time. Memory circuits are more efficiently modeled at the functional level than at the gate level. MARS supports the functional modeling of memories by using the physical memory of one of the processing elements. Functional memory gates are processed in an alternative pipeline.

The memory detector block differentiates between a logic gate and a memory block. This functional decomposition approach results in decomposing the logic simulation tasks into 15 subtasks, which when executed in a pipelined manner has been demonstrated to speed up logic simulation more than 100 times over software logic simulation running on a Sun 3/260™ system. The hardware of the MARS™ system consists of 15 processing elements connected to a crossbar switch. The processors are microprogrammed engines with special message-passing and table manipulation capabilities. The simulation algorithm is partitioned among the processors. In contrast to other accelerators, MARS has general-purpose features such as multiple delay simulation and spike and race analysis. The performance of the MARS hardware accelerator has been rated at 1 million gate evaluations per second.

A similar hardware accelerator using a functional decomposition of the logic simulation problem was proposed in the Logic Simulation Machine™ by Abramovici et al. [1]. They functionally decomposed the tasks in logic simulation into several subtasks: (1) advance timestep, (2) retrieve current event, (3) update configuration of source, (4) determine fan-out, (5) update configuration of fan-out, (6) evaluate gate, (7) schedule next event, and (8) insert new event in event list. Using a paper design, the authors showed through simple theoretical analysis that their algorithm would run about 60 times faster than existing logic simulation software on general-purpose machines.

Algorithms and implementations of logic simulation on vector processing machines are discussed in [43, 38, 30]. The common theme in all these approaches is to note that a vector processor has the facility to execute operations on vectors extremely fast; hence the contributions of these algorithms are in mapping a logic simulation problem into a vector processing problem. Several simulation techniques have been developed for (1) zero-delay simulation of combinational circuits, (2) zero delay simulation of synchronous sequential circuits, and (3) simulation with delay considerations. For simulation of combinational circuits, a vector-parallel *time-first evaluation* algorithm is used; all the computation in the time direction is performed for each gate. A sequence of states on a signal line is treated as a pattern vector, and the gate evaluation (AND, NAND, NOR, or other) is performed by vector logical operations on pattern vectors. For simulation of synchronous sequential circuits, the simulation procedure is vectorized by a gate grouping technique, which is based on a *space-first evaluation* algorithm in which simulation is performed by incrementing the time by a certain step and computing the state of all gates in the circuit at each time period. For simulations with sophisticated delay models, a conventional event-driven algorithm is modified by vectorizing all the procedures associated with event fetch, propagation evaluation, and the like, that are scheduled to occur in the same period.

For switch-level simulation, several special-purpose hardware engines have been proposed and built [23, 26, 45]. All the architectures are based on the iterative MOSSIM™ algorithm for switch-level simulation [17]. Recently, some researchers have mapped the switch-level simulation algorithm on hardware accelerators for logic simulation such as the Yorktown Simulation Engine™ [10].

More recently, there has been a lot of activity in hardware emulation systems based on field-programmable gate arrays (FPGAs). Companies such as Quickturn Systems™, have products in which a large number of FPGA chips are connected together. Such emulation systems read in a netlist of a design and convert the chip design gates into a prototype design.

The prototype design is synthesized into the information needed to program the FPGAs to perform the relevant functions.

The Quickturn RPM emulation system [54] uses a large number of XILINX™ FPGAs on a printed circuit board. Each FPGA is connected to all its nearest neighbors in a regular array of signal routing channels. Several such boards are connected together in a system. RPM uses Sun workstations to run the configuration software and automatically generates the prototype interconnection information from the chip netlist. All connections for in-circuit emulation of the prototype are made electronically by programming the FPGAs. In addition to the core reprogramming logic hardware, the RPM includes an internal logic analyzer for monitoring the outputs, a stimulus generator, and an interface cabling system for connection to the target system.

7.14 SUMMARY

We began this chapter by giving background information on the logic simulation problem. In particular, we stressed the significance of simulation at various levels of abstraction for the design of VLSI circuit. We then identified the different types of parallelism inherent in simulation. We discussed both shared memory MIMD and distributed memory MIMD parallel algorithms for logic simulation based on each approach and reported on results of implementations where appropriate.

We classified the following types of parallelism in logic simulation. *Functional parallelism* deals with the exploitation of parallelism in logic simulation by assigning different functions associated with logic simulation to different processors. *Input data parallelism* assigns different sets of input patterns to each processor on the entire circuit. *Circuit or model parallelism* exploits the parallelism by assigning portions of a circuit to different processors and simulating the circuit partitions in parallel. In the *compiled circuit parallel approach*, the simulation code for the gates in the circuit partition assigned to each processor is compiled into machine code, and all the gates are evaluated at all time steps whether they are needed or not. In the *event-driven circuit parallel approach*, only those gates whose inputs have changed in the present time step are evaluated. There are two subapproaches within event-driven simulation. In the *synchronous approach*, we require that all the necessary nodes be evaluated at a given time point before moving on to the next time point. The problem with this approach is that the parallelism in logic simulation is limited to within one time point at a time. In the *asynchronous approach*, different portions of the circuit are allowed to evaluate up to different points in time. Such an approach has the maximum scope for exploiting parallelism. The problem with such an approach is in guaranteeing causality constraints. There are two basic ways to design such methods. In *conservative methods*, a parallel simulation is viewed as a series of sequential computations separated by synchronization messages. Suitable deadlock avoidance methods or deadlock detection and recovery methods have to be used. In *optimistic methods*, each processor is allowed to go ahead with its computations and to advance its local clock until a message is received that indicates an inconsistency. Then the processor state has to be rolled back to a point in time before the error.

While *functional parallelism* seems to be exploited best by special-purpose hardware, *pattern parallel* and *circuit parallel* approaches lend themselves shared memory and distributed memory MIMD multiprocessors. Typically, pattern parallel approaches take the least amount of recoding effort and can yield perfect linear speedup; however, their applicability is limited due to space and algorithm considerations. Pattern parallel algorithms are mainly restricted to combinational circuits with zero-delay gates.

Circuit parallel approaches are geared to handle large designs that need to be partitioned; they involve complex preprocessing and usually require complete redesign of the simulation system. Synchronous event-driven circuit parallel logic simulation gives reasonably good speedups on shared memory MIMD multiprocessors. These algorithms are not that complex.

The best speedups are obtained through asynchronous circuit parallel logic simulation algorithms. Both forms of asynchronous algorithms, conservative and optimistic, can give good speedups and are suitable for both shared memory and distributed memory MIMD multiprocessors. The algorithms are, however, much more complicated to implement than the simple synchronous parallel algorithms.

7.15 PROBLEMS

7.1   Analyze the performance of a parallel compiled simulation on a shared memory multiprocessor. Assume N gates, P processors, L levels of gates in a combinational circuit, and I input vectors. Also assume that the ratio of computation of a logic evaluation to the synchronization cost to be α.

7.2   For the circuit shown in Figure 7.1, apply compiled parallel logic simulation; assume you have three processors and a suitable partitioning of the gates to processors. What would be the expected speedup?

7.3   For the circuit shown in Figure 7.2, apply synchronous event-driven parallel logic simulation; assume that you have three processors and a suitable partitioning of the gates to processors. What would be the expected speedup?

7.4   Design and implement a distributed memory parallel algorithm for the functional approach to parallel simulation based on the shared memory version, *SM-PARALLEL-EVENT-LOGIC-SIM-FUNCTIONAL*. Use the Sequent™ parallel programming library described in Chapter 2.

7.5   Design and implement a distributed memory parallel algorithm for pattern parallel logic simulation for combinational circuits. Extend the scheme to sequential circuits using parallel sequence simulation. Use the Intel iPSC™ parallel programming library described in Chapter 2.

7.6   Analyze the performance of the parallel sequence simulation algorithm on a distributed memory multiprocessor. Assume N gates, P processors, and I input patterns. Also assume that the ratio of computation of a logic evaluation to the communication cost to be α.

7.7   Implement a circuit partitioner that partitions a given circuit by different strategies: (1) level order, (2) input cones, (3) output cones, and (4) minimizing communication by performing a min-cut partitioning. Compare the expected maximum concurrency that you can expect on a distributed memory multiprocessor and synchronous event-driven simulation for some example circuits using each of the preceding partitioning methods for some random inputs.

7.8   Implement a distributed memory parallel algorithm for logic simulation using circuit level partitioning and synchronous event-driven simulation. Compare the performance with a compiled simulation approach.

7.9   Implement a massively parallel SIMD algorithm for compiled logic simulation for combinational circuits based on the algorithm *SIMD-PARALLEL-COMPILED-LOGIC-SIM*. Use the Thinking Machines CM-2™ parallel programming library described in Chapter 2. Assign one gate to each processor. You may assume unlimited fan-out capability for each gate.

7.10   In the shared memory parallel algorithm for synchronous event-driven simulation, there is a lot of overhead involved in locking and unlocking event queues for dynamic load balancing. Implemement both centralized and distributed event queue methods and compare the performance in the context of parallel logic simulation for some example circuits.

7.11   We described a distributed memory parallel algorithm for synchonous event-driven simulation that synchronizes processors at clock cycles instead of at each level, *DM-PARALLEL-EVENT-LOGIC-CYCLE*. What are the advantages and disadvantages of this approach? Analyze the speedup of the parallel algorithm, assuming N gates, P processors, and L levels, I inputs. Also assume that the ratio of computation of a logic evaluation to the barrier synchronization cost to be α.

7.12   Construct a case for five processes to deadlock similar to Figure 7.12 during a conservative approach to asynchronous parallel simulation. Then apply deadlock avoidance approach using null messages and deadlock detection and recovery (without null messages) to show how the deadlock in your case is avoided or resolved.

7.13   Implement a shared memory parallel algorithm for conservative asynchronous logic simulation. Use the Sequent™ parallel programming library described in Chapter 2. Implement both deadlock avoidance and deadlock detection and recovery approaches.

7.14   Implement a distributed memory parallel algorithm for optimistic asynchronous logic simulation. Use the Intel iPSC™ parallel programming library described in Chapter 2. Implement using Time Warp concepts, but with simple garbage collection strategies.

7.15   For the virtual time example of optimistic asynchronous parallel logic simulation shown in Figure 7.13, assume a new message arriving with time stamp 170, instead of the message with time stamp 135. What action needs to be taken? If instead of this message, a new message with time stamp 192 arrives, what action needs to be taken?

7.16 REFERENCES

[1]   M. Abramovici, Y. H. Levendel, and P. R. Menon. A Logic Simulation Machine. *IEEE Trans. Computer-aided Design Integrated Circuits Systems*, CAD-2(2):82–93, Apr. 1983.

[2]   P. Agrawal and W. J. Dally. A Hardware Logic Simulation System. *IEEE Trans. Computer-aided Design Integrated Circuits Systems*, 9(1):19–29, Jan. 1990.

[3]   P. Agrawal, W. J. Dally, A. K. Ezzat, W. C. Fischer, H. V. Jagdish, and A. S. Krishnakumar. Architecture and Design of the MARS Hardware Accelerator. *Proc. 24th Design Automation Conf.*, pages 108–113, June 1987.

[4]   P. Agrawal, W. J. Dally, W. C. Fischer, H. V. Jagdish, A. S. Krishnakumar, and R. Tutundjian. MARS: A Multiprocessor-based Programmable Accelerator. *IEEE Design Test Computers*, 4(5):28–36, Oct. 1987.

[5]   J. R. Armstrong. *Chip-level Modeling with VHDL.* Prentice Hall, Englewoods Cliffs, NJ, 1989.

[6]   J. M. Arnold and C. T. Terman. A Multiprocessor Implementation of a Logic-level Timing Simulator. *Proc. Int. Conf. Computer-aided Design*, pages 116–118, Nov. 1985.

[7]   R. Ayani. A Parallel Simulation Scheme Based on Distance between Objects. *Proc. SCS Multiconference Distibuted Simulation*, pages 113–118, Mar. 1979.

[8]   M. L. Bailey and L. Snyder. An Empirical Study of On-chip Parallelism. *Proc. 25th Design Automation Conf.*, pages 160–165, June 1988.

[9]   Z. Barzilai, J. L. Carter, B. K. Rosen, and J. D. Rutledge. HSS – A High Speed Simulator. *IEEE Trans. Computer Aided Design INtegrated Circuits Systems*, pages 601–617, July 1987.

[10]   Z. Barzilai, L. Huisman, G. M. Silberman, D. T. Tang, and L.S. Woo. Fast Pass-Transistor Simulation for Custom MOS Circuits. *IEEE Design Test Computers*, pages 71–81, Feb. 1984.

[11]   M. A. Breuer and A. D. Friedman. *Diagnosis and Reliable Design of Digital Systems.* Computer Science Press, Rockville, MD, 1976.

[12]   F. Brglez, D. Bryan, and K. Kominski. Combinational Profiles of Sequential Benchmark Circuits. *Proc. IEEE Int. Symp. Circuits Systems*, June 1989.

[13]   F. Brglez and H. Fujiwara. A Neutral Netlist of 10 Combinational Benchmark Circuits and a Target Translator in FORTRAN. *Proc. Int. Symp. Circuits Systems*, June 1985.

[14]   J. Briner. Parallel Mixed Level Simulation of Digital Circuits using Virtual Time. Technical report, Ph.D. Thesis, Department of Electrical Engineering, Duke University, Durham, NC, 1990.

[15]   R. Bryant. Data Parallel Switch-level Simulation. *Proc. Int. Conf. Computer-aided Design (ICCAD-88)*, Nov. 1988.

[16]   R. E. Bryant. Simulation of Packet Communications Architecture Computer Systems. Technical Report MIT-LCS-TR-188, Laboratory of Computer Science, Massachusetts Institute of Technology, Cambridge, MA, 1977.

[17]   R. E. Bryant. A Switch-level Model and Simulator for MOS Digital Systems. *IEEE Trans. Computers*, C-33(2):160–177, Feb. 1984.

[18]   R. Chamberlain and M. A. Franklin. Discrete Event Simulation on Hypercube Architectures. *Proc. Int. Conf. Computer-aided Design (ICCAD-88)*, Nov. 1988.

[19]   K. M. Chandy and J. Misra. Asynchronous distributed simulation via a sequence of parallel computations. *Comm. ACM*, 24(11):198–206, Apr. 1981.

[20]   K. M. Chandy and J. Misra. Distributed Simulation: A Case Study in Design and Verification of Distributed Programs. *IEEE Trans. Software Eng.*, SE-5(5):44–452, Sept. 1979.

[21]   Jade Simulations Int. Co. Implementation Issues of Jade's VHDL Simulator. Technical report, Calgary, Alberta, Canada, 1989.

[22]   ZYCAD Co. Zycad Logic Evaluator LE-1000 series –Product Description. Technical report, St. Paul, MN, 1987.

[23]   W. J. Dally and R. E. Bryant. A Hardware Architecture for Switch-level Simulation. *IEEE Trans. Computer-aided Design Integrated Circuits Systems*, pages 239–250, July 1985.

[24]   L. N. Dunn. IBM's Engineering Design System Support for VLSI Design and Verification. *IEEE Design Test Computers*, pages 30–40, Feb. 1984.

[25]   S. B. Tan et al. A Fast Signature Simulation Tool for Built-in Self Testing Circuits. *Proc. 24th Design Automation Conf.*, June 1987.

[26]   E. H. Frank. Exploiting Parallelism in a Switch-level Simulation Machine. *Proc. Design Automation Conf.*, pages 209–215, June 1986.

[27]   R. M. Fujimoto. Parallel Discrete Event Simulation. *Comm. ACM*, 33(3):30–53, Oct. 1990.

[28]   A. Gafni. Rollback Mechanisms for Optimistic Distributed Simulation Systems. *Proc. SCS Multiconference Distributed Simulation*, pages 61–67, July 1988.

[29]   J. K. Howard, L. Malm, and L. M. Warren. Introduction to the IBM Los Gatos Logic Simulation Machine. *Proc. IEEE Int. Conf. Computer Design: VLSI in Computers*, pages 580–583, Oct. 1983.

[30]   N. Ishiura, H. Yasuura, and S. Yajima. High-speed Logic Simulation on Vector Processors. *IEEE Trans. Computer-aided Design Integrated Circuits Systems*, CAD-6, no. 3:305–321, May 1987.

[31]   D. Jefferson. Virtual Time. *Proc. Int. Conf. Parallel Processing*, pages 384–394, Aug. 1983.

[32]   D. Jefferson. Virtual Time. *ACM Trans. Programming Languages Systems*, pages 404–425, July 1985.

[33]   S. A. Kravitz, R. Bryant, and R. Rutenbar. Massively Parallel Switch-level Simulation: A Feasibility Study. *IEEE Trans. Computer-aided Design Integrated Circuits Systems*, 10(7), July 1991.

[34]   C. P. Kung and C. S. Lin. Parallel Sequence Fault Simulation for Synchronous Sequential Circuits. *Proc. European Design Automation Conf.*, pages 434–438, Mar. 1992.

[35]   Y. H. Levendel, P. R. Menon, and S. H. Patel. Special-purpose Computer for Logic Simulation Using Distributed Processing. *Bell System Tech. J.*, 61(10):2873–2910, Dec. 1982.

[36]   B. D. Lubachevsky. Efficient Distributed Event-driven Simulation of Multiple Loop Networks. *Comm. ACM*, pages 111–123, Jan. 1989.

[37]   R. B. Mueller-Thuns, D. G. Saab, R. F. Damiano, and J. A. Abraham. Portable Parallel Logic and Fault Simulation. *Proc. Int. Conf. Computer-aided Design (ICCAD-89)*, pages 506–509, Nov. 1989.

[38]   S. Nagashima, T. Nakagawa, and S. Miyamoto K. Omota. Hardware Implementation of VELVET on the Hitachi S-810 Supercomputer. *Proc. Int. Conf. Computer-aided Design (ICCAD-86)*, Nov. 1986.

[39]   D. M. Nicol. The Cost of Conservative Synchronization in Parallel Discrete Event Simulations. Technical Report ICASE-90-21, Institute for Computer Applications in Science and Engineering, NASA Langley Research Center, Hampton, VA, June 1989.

[40]   S. Patil, P. Banerjee, and C. Polychronopolous. Efficient Circuit Partitioning Algorithms for Parallel Logic Simulation. *Proc. Supercomputing Conf.*, pages 361–364, Nov. 1989.

[41]   G. Pfister. The Yorktown Simulation Engine: Introduction. *Proc. 19th Design Automation Conf.*, pages 51–54, June 1982.

[42]   C. D. Polychronopoulos. *Parallel Programming and Compilers*. Kluwer Academic Publishers, Norwell, MA, 1988.

[43]   R. Raghavan, J. P. Hayes, and W. R. Martin. Logic Simulation on Vector Processors. *Proc. Int. Conf. Computer-aided Design (ICCAD-88)*, Nov. 1988.

[44]   A. E. Ruehli and G. S. Ditlow. Circuit Analysis, Logic Simulation, and Design Verification for VLSI. *Proc. IEEE*, 71(1), Jan. 1983.

[45]   M. Smith. A Hardware Switch-level Simulator for Large MOS Circuits. *Proc. 24th Design Automation Conf.*, June 1987.

[46]   S. P. Smith, W. Underwood, and M. R. Mercer. An Analysis of Several Approaches to Circuit Partitioning for Parallel Logic Simulation. *Proc. Int. Conf. Computer Design (ICCD87)*, pages 664–667, 1987.

[47]   L. Soule and T. Blank. Statistics for Parallelism and Abstraction Level in Digital Simulation. *Proc. 24th ACM/IEEE Design Automation Conf.*, June 1987.

[48]   L. Soule and T. Blank. Parallel Logic Simulation on General Purpose Machines. *Proc. Design Automation Conf.*, pages 166–171, June 1988.

[49]   L. Soule and A. Gupta. Characterization of Parallelism and Deadlocks in Distributed Digital Logic Simulation. *Proc. 26th Design Automation Conf.*, pages 81–86, June 1989.

[50]   L. P. Soule. Parallel Logic Simulation: An Evaluation of Centralized-time and Distributed-time Algorithms. Technical report, Computer Systems Lab, Stanford University, Stanford, CA, 1992.

[51]   R. Malm T. Burggraff, A. Love and A. Rudy. The ibm los gatos logic simulation machine hardware. *Proc. Int. Conf. Computer Design (ICCD)*, pages 584–587, Oct. 1993.

[52]   C. Terman. RSIM: A Logic Level Timing Simulator. *Proc. Int. Conf. Computer Design*, pages 437–440, Oct. 1983.

[53]   B. Vellandi and M. Lightner. Parallelism Extraction and Program Restructuring of VHDL for Parallel Simulation. *Proc. European Design Automation Conf. (EDAC-93)*, Mar. 1993.

[54]   S. Walters. Computer-aided Prototyping for ASIC-based Systems. *IEEE Design Test Computers*, 8(2):4–10, June 1991.

[55]   D. West. Optimizing Time Warp: Lazy Rollback and Lazy Reevaluation. Technical report, Department of Computer Science, University of Calgary, Alberta, Canada, Jan. 1988.

[56]   M. J. Wolfe. Optimizing Compilers for Supercomputers. Technical Report CSRD-82-329, Center for Supercomputing Research and Development, University of Illinois, Urbana, IL, Oct. 1982.

476

CHAPTER **8**

Test Generation and Fault Simulation

8.1 INTRODUCTION

Once a digital circuit is designed and fabricated, the circuit needs to be tested for the presence of absence of physical defects or faults. Generating test patterns for testing digital circuits consumes a significant portion of the design time. Automatic test pattern generation (ATPG) deals with this problem automatically for a given circuit description. The process of generation of test patterns for digital logic involves a search through all possible input values or sets of input values to find one that causes the output of a good circuit to differ from that of one containing a fault. Algorithms for ATPG in the past were focussed on ways to produce tests for combinational circuits. Even this problem is known to be NP complete [34] and can, in practice, take large computing times. Excellent discussions of the ATPG problem and algorithms appear in [13, 48].

The problem becomes even more difficult for sequential circuits. Design for test methods, such as level sensitive scan designs [27], convert a sequential circuit into a combinational circuit in the test mode to reduce the complexity of test generation. However, this is done at a cost to the area, gate count, and delay increase of the digital circuit and an increase in the test application time at a tester, since all the test patterns have to be serially shifted in into the scan chain before each test vector can be applied. Hence ATPG for sequential circuits is also becoming very attractive. ATPG tools for sequential circuits require even more computing times, often on the orders of weeks on a fast workstation for a large circuit. Several researchers have therefore started investigating parallel algorithms for automatic test generation.

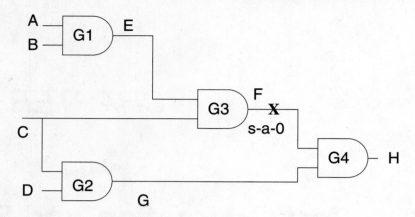

Figure 8.1 Example circuit for illustrating test generation

The objective of a fault simulation algorithm is to find the fraction of total faults (also referred to as the *fault coverage*) that are detected by a given set of input vectors. Often a fault simulation procedure is integrated within an automatic test pattern generation system.

The chapter is organized as follows. Section 8.2 gives an overview of the test generation problem. Section 8.3 outlines the basic methods of exploiting parallelism in automatic test generation. Parallel algorithms for test generation using fault decomposition are discussed in Section 8.4. A parallel algorithm for test generation using heuristic decomposition is described in Section 8.5. Section 8.6 presents parallel algorithms for ATPG based on search-space-parallel decomposition. Functional parallel decomposition is presented in Section 8.7. Finally, Section 8.8 describes parallel algorithms for ATPG using circuit decomposition.

Section 8.9 gives an overview of the fault simulation problem and Section 8.10 outlines the different forms of parallelism that can be exploited in the problem. Section 8.11 describes parallel algororithms for fault simulation using fault decomposition. Parallel algorithms for fault simulation based on input pattern decomposition are presented in Section 8.12. Section 8.13 presents parallel algorithms for fault simulation based on circuit decomposition. Section 8.14 discusses a parallel algorithm for fault simulation using a pipelined decomposition. Hardware accelerators for test generation and fault simulation are discussed in Section 8.15. A chapter summary is given in Section 8.16.

8.2 TEST GENERATION PROBLEM

In this section we consider algorithms for generating tests for single stuck-at faults. These are physical failures that cause a node in the circuit to behave as if it were stuck at a logic 0 or logic 1. The single stuck-at fault model is a simplification of the types of faults found in real circuits, but empirical evidence shows that for most common implementation technologies it provides very high coverage for physical faults.

Consider the circuit shown in Figure 8.1. The inputs to the circuit, A, B, C, and D, are called *primary inputs* where we apply the test patterns. The outputs of the circuit (only one in this circuit, H) are called *primary outputs* and are the only places we can observe the effects of these tests. The test pattern generation task is to find a set of input patterns (for combinational circuits) or a sequence of input patterns (for sequential circuits) that will fully test the circuit, that is, will separate the good circuit from the faulty circuit. A failure is revealed if at least one primary output is different in the faulty circuit and good circuit.

The set of input patterns that detects all or a large fraction of all the faults in a circuit is called the *test set*. The test set must be reasonably small so that it is economically possible to apply them to all circuits produced. A testing procedure that uses all possible input patterns will, of course, reveal faulty circuits, but such *exhaustive testing* can be prohibitive for large circuits. For example, in the example circuit shown in the figure, the set of all possible combinations of inputs, ABCD = 0000, 0001, ..., 1111, would be an exhaustive test of the circuit.

For large circuits there are two basic approaches to automatic test pattern generation (ATPG): (1) *algorithmic or deterministic* test pattern generation and (2) *statistical or pseudo-exhaustive* test pattern generation. In the algorithmic approach, a specific ATPG algorithm is used to generate a test for each fault in the circuit. This may involve searching an entire solution space. In the pseudoexhaustive approach, we select test patterns at random and uses fault simulation to determine the faults detected by the pattern. Test patterns are selected and added to the test set if they detect any previously undetected faults until some required fault coverage is reached. The second method finds tests for easy-to-detect faults quickly, but becomes less and less efficient as the easy-to-detect faults are removed from the fault list and only the hard-to-detect faults remain. An efficient combined method for solving the ATPG problem is to use statistical methods to find tests for the easy-to-detect faults on the fault list and to switch to an algorithmic method to find tests for the remaining hard-to-detect faults. In either this method or the purely algorithmic method, a significant portion of the computation time will be spent generating tests for the hard-to-detect faults deterministically. This is where parallel processing can be really useful.

In a deterministic test generation environment, a fault simulator helps in finding out the additional faults that are detectable by the same vector sequence. This helps reduce the effort required in test generation and also the test length. The test length determines the test application time and the memory necessary to store the vectors. Figure 8.2 shows the interplay between the test pattern generator and the fault simulator in a deterministic test pattern generation environment. We start with a fault list, which is normally constructed by collapsing equivalent faults. The test pattern generator selects a fault from the fault list and tries to generate a test. If the test pattern generator is successful in generating a test, fault simulation is carried out on the entire fault list and the detected faults are deleted from the fault list. The test pattern generator may fail to generate a test if the fault is redundant or some prespecified resource constraint is exceeded (for example, the backtrack or time limit per fault).

8.2.1 Basics of Automatic Test Pattern Generation

Consider the circuit shown in Figure 8.1. To detect the fault line F stuck-at-0 (s-a-0), the first step in deterministic test generation is to *sensitize* the fault, which involves setting the line to the opposite value so that the good circuit and faulty circuit have different values at the fault location.

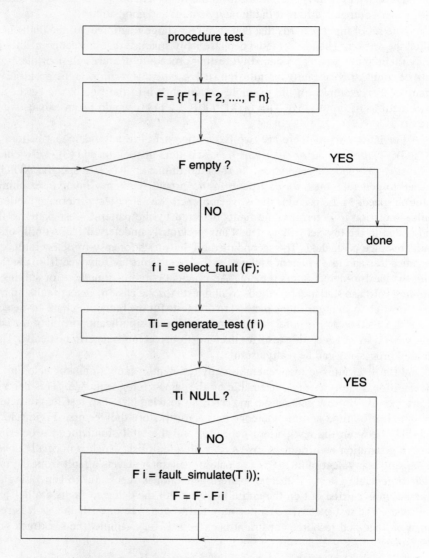

Figure 8.2 Integrated deterministic test generation/fault simulation

The next step is to *propagate* the effect of the fault to a primary output. In the figure, the fault will be propagated through the gate H. Hence the input G to gate H has to be set to 1 so that any value at F can propagate through H.

Finally, we need to perform *justification* of the assigned internal line values by applying suitable input patterns to the primary inputs. For example, $A = 1, B = 1, C = 1, D = 0$.

The primary output H in the circuit is now different in the good (=1) and faulty circuits (=0). Hence the input pattern is a test vector for the fault line F stuck-at-0.

We will now describe automatic test pattern generation algorithms to perform the procedure outlined.

8.2.2 ATPG Algorithms for Combinational Circuits

The D algorithm proposed by Roth and Roth et al. [86, 87] was the first true algorithm for ATPG that can be viewed as an algorithm to search a space of input vectors to find one that detects a fault. The algorithm uses a five-valued logic, which consists of the logic values 0 and 1, an unknown value X, and two additional values D and $\overline{D}$. A D value signifies a value of 1 in the good circuit and a 0 in the faulty circuit (the definition of the $\overline{D}$ is opposite). Each gate in the circuit has two *D-cubes* associated with it, the *primitive D-cube of a fault (pdcf)*, and a *propagation D-cube (pdc)*. A *pdcf* is a set of inputs that produces an error signal on the output of the gate if it contains a fault. A *pdc* specifies the input values necessary to propagate an error signal to the output. Figure 8.3 shows the pdcf's and pdc's of a two-input AND gate.

The D-algorithm's basic operation is the repeated intersection of the D-cubes necessary to perform the tasks required to test for a specific fault. This operation can also be viewed as a search problem in a search graph. The search graph for the D-algorithm contains all the nodes of the circuit arranged as a tree. For the circuit shown in Figure 8.1, the space consists of nodes A, B, C, D, E, F, G, H. The D-algorithm searches this nine-node space for each fault considered. All circuit nodes are initially set to the unknown state X. Figure 8.4 illustrates the search process on the example circuit. In the search process, suppose we try to first propagate the D at line H through gate $G4$ before justifying the inputs to gate $G3$. Hence we begin by setting G to 1, which is justified by setting C to 0. Then, when we try to justify a D at line F, we need to set C to a 1 which is a conflict. To resolve this conflict, we backtrack through the search tree until we reach node C so that it can be set to the opposite value.

Goel proposed the PODEM algorithm for ATPG [38] by viewing the problem as a search problem in the primary input space. While the D-algorithm includes every circuit node (internal and primary inputs) in the search graph, PODEM only considers the primary inputs. All other nodes in the circuit are some function of the primary inputs. Hence, when we choose inputs as nodes in the search space, we will not have hidden conflicts and each node can be assigned independently. Further, suppose that we have a set of primary input assignments, and another primary input has been assigned a value that causes a conflict. We would try only one other value at this input (the complement of the current value) to determine if the current assignment will ever be compatible with the goal. If the complementary also conflicts, then the goal cannot be achieved with the existing input assignments; hence a large portion of the search space can be pruned off.

We will now illustrate the working of the PODEM algorithm for the circuit shown in Figure 8.1. Figure 8.5 shows the search graph of the PODEM algorithm. Again the goal is to

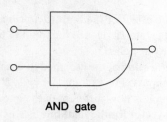

AND gate

pdcf

Input	Output
1 1	D
0 1	D̄
1 0	D̄

pdc

Input	Output
1 D	D
D 1	D
1 D̄	D̄
D̄ 1	D̄
D D	D
D̄ D̄	D̄

Figure 8.3 D-cubes for AND gate

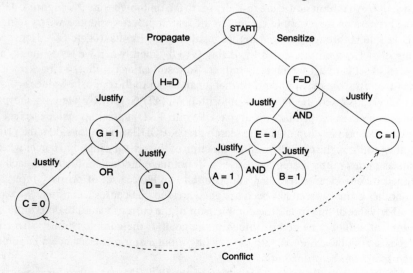

Figure 8.4 D-algorithm search graph

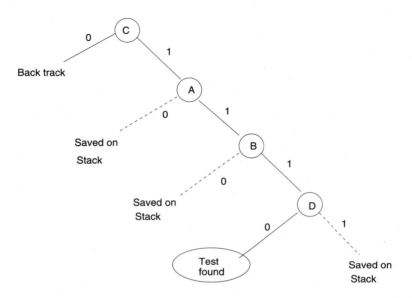

Figure 8.5 PODEM algorithm search space

find a test for line F stuck-at-0; hence the first goal is to set line F in the good circuit to 1. PODEM tries to identify a value to be assigned to a primary input. It does so by *backtracing* from line H to the primary input. Backtracing is the process of working backward in the circuit from a current goal (of setting a node to a certain value) to determine an input assignment. Suppose that due to the backtracing the input C is set to 0. This step is followed by a *forward implication step*, which is like a traditional logic simulation; it determines the values of all internal nodes of the circuit due to this input assignment. It is checked if the simulation reveals any conflicts with the current goal, which is to set line F to 1. If there are no conflicts, then the procedure tries to find another input to assign a value to. In this case, the forward implication with $C = 0$ gives rise to $F = 0$, which conflicts with the goal, hence we backtrack and set $C = 1$. The process repeats until a test is found or when it finds that it cannot backtrack anymore; that is, it has tried all possible input combinations explicitly or implicitly. The other input assignments are $C = 1, A = 1, B = 1$, and $D = 0$, which is the test.

   An outline of the PODEM test generation algorithm *PODEM-COMB-ATPG* (denoting PODEM ATPG algorithm for combinational circuits) follows:

   Procedure *PODEM-COMB-ATPG*;
        Read circuit topology;
        Read list of faults;
        Compute controllability and observability;
        Select a fault;
        Determine initial objective;
        WHILE (objective not met) DO
            Apply backtrace (until new primary input assignment made);

Perform forward implication (of all assigned inputs);
Store circuit state (as value of node on stack);
IF (D objective satisfied)
THEN
    IF (D or Dbar propagated to output)
    THEN exit(test);
    ELSE Find easiest observable element(set new objective);
  ELSE return to D(set new objective);
ENDWHILE
End Procedure

The PODEM algorithm will eventually try all the primary input combinations, either explicitly or implicitly, until it finds a test, or it hits a backtrack limit, or it has exhausted all combinations (hence has identified the fault as redundant).

8.2.3 Guidance Heuristics for Combinational ATPG

Several heuristics are used in the implementation of the search process. First, there is a heuristic for backtracing to select a path back to a primary input, starting from an internal node value assignment objective. Regardless of the search space used, if the paths we choose result in conflicts, we will have to waste computation time resolving them. Suppose all the inputs to a gate must be set to a particular value (for example, all inputs set to 1 for an AND gate to produce output 1) to achieve a particular goal. Then we are better off in trying to set the *hardest* input to a 1 first, rather than the easiest. Since the hardest choice is most likely to fail, the failure is most likely to occur sooner, and hence there is less time spent on finding the failure. Conversely, if the hardest succeeds, the others are likely to succeed also. On the other hand, if any one of the input values needs to be set to a particular value (e.g. any input set to 1 for an OR gate to produce output of 1), then choose the easiest one to control. Similarly, for choosing the gate to drive a D to a primary output, choose the easiest to observe gate.

In summary, we need to compute controllability and observability measures for various lines in the circuit to help guide the search process [11]. One simple cost measure is based on the level of the gate and the number of its inputs. Gates with higher levels and larger number of inputs are harder to control. Another very popular measure is the SCOAP heuristic [39], which computes separate controllabilty and observability numbers for values of 0 and 1. Other measures such as CAMELOT [12] have also been proposed.

8.2.4 ATPG Algorithm for Sequential Circuits

Most sequential circuit test generation algorithms use the iterative logic array (ILA) model for synchronous sequential circuits and use modified versions of the combinational circuit test generation algorithms such as PODEM and the D-algorithm. For example, the implementations reported in [21, 56, 58] are based on the D-algorithm, and the implementations reported in [55, 67] are based on PODEM. The algorithm reported in [6] does not use an ILA model but uses a cost function to guide the search for a test vector. The algorithm reported in [35] uses the Boolean cover of the sequential machine (representing the next state logic) for test generation.

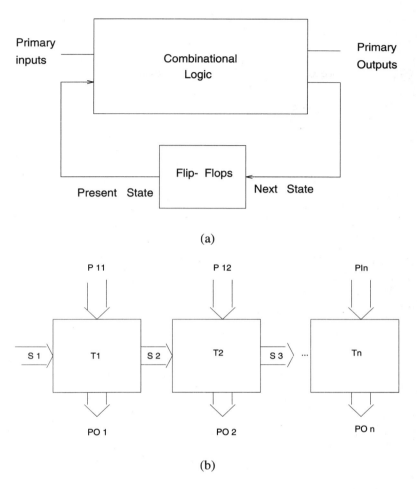

Figure 8.6 Sequential Circuit and Iterative Logic Array Model. (a) Sequential circuit model. (b) Iterative array model.

We now describe the details of one algorithm for test pattern generation for synchronous sequential circuits that is based on PODEM and uses the conventional techniques of *forward-time processing (FTP)* and *reverse-time processing (RTP)* [56] for test generation.

A conceptual model of a synchronous sequential circuit is shown in Figure 8.6(a) and its ILA interpretation is shown in Figure 8.6(b). The lines collectively labeled PI are the primary inputs and the lines labeled as PO are the primary outputs. The lines labeled PS are the present state lines and the lines labeled NS are the next state lines. The next state lines feed into a bank of memory elements (usually D-type flip-flops) and emerge as the present state lines. Thus the logic values on the present state lines assume the values of the next state lines at the next clock. It is assumed that there is an implicit single-phase clock. To represent the sequential machine as an ILA, the state lines at the output of the memory elements are "cut" and the machine is unrolled across time frames. The present state lines are referred to as *pseudo-inputs (PSI)* and the next state lines are referred to as *pseudo-outputs (PSO)* in the ILA model. Thus the pseudo-outputs of one time frame form the pseudo-inputs of the next time frame. Using this ILA model, any conventional combinational test generation algorithm can be used with a few modifications. Thus, the time complexity of a sequential machine is transformed into space complexity by an ILA.

We now describe how test generation is performed using the ILA representation of a sequential circuit. First, a fault is injected into each time frame. The five-valued logic $(0, 1, D, \overline{D}, X)$ used by combinational test pattern generation algorithms is inadequate for sequential circuits since it does not take care of the repeated effect of faults across time frames. Also, the five-valued logic results in overspecification of signal values, which may make justification of signal values more difficult. Thus a nine-valued logic [63] is used that results in a minimal specification of signal values, which are represented as a pair of logic values denoting the good circuit and fault circuit values. Since each of the circuits (good and faulty) can assume three logic values $(0, 1, X)$, we have nine logic values. Thus a value 1/0 denotes a value 1 in the good circuit and a value 0 in the faulty circuit (called a D in the five-valued logic). A value $1/X$ indicates that the good circuit value is 1 and the faulty circuit value is unspecified (or a *don't-care*).

The first phase in the test generation process consists of *forward-time processing (FTP)*; the test vectors are generated in the order in which they are applied. In the FTP phase, the fault is propagated across time frames until it reaches a primary output. Testability measures are used to guide the propagation so that the FTP phase can be accomplished using as few time frames as possible. The FTP phase results in an assignment of values to the pseudo-inputs and primary inputs in the time frames necessary to propagate the fault. The vector specifying the pseudo-input values in the time frame in which the fault is first excited specifies the initial state S_0 in which the machine should be for the fault propagation and excitation to be successful.

The *reverse-time processing (RTP) phase* or the *state justification phase* is triggered by the initial state vector S_0 generated by the FTP phase. The purpose of the RTP phase is to generate a sequence of vectors that results in the initial state S_0. Since these vectors are generated in an order opposite to the order they are applied, it is called the reverse-time processing phase. The RTP phase starts with the initial state S_0 and keeps going back in time until an all-unknown state or a reset state is reached. Some test pattern generators may also try to utilize the state generated by a test vector sequence generated for the previous fault [47]. Also, the algorithm reported in [55] tries to generate the vector sequence necessary to reach the initial state directly from the partial state transition graph. We assume that the PODEM algorithm generates vectors during the RTP phase. Given a next-state vector that has to be realized at the end of the current time frame, only one physical time frame has to be used to generate the present state vector and the input vector. The present state vector forms the next-state vector for the next RTP step, and the process stops when the present state vector is an all-unknown state or a reset state.

We now illustrate the process of test generation of sequential circuits with the example circuit shown in Figure 8.7(a). The example has been taken from [59]. We assume that we are trying to generate a test for the fault at the output of gate $g5$, which is assumed to be stuck at 0.

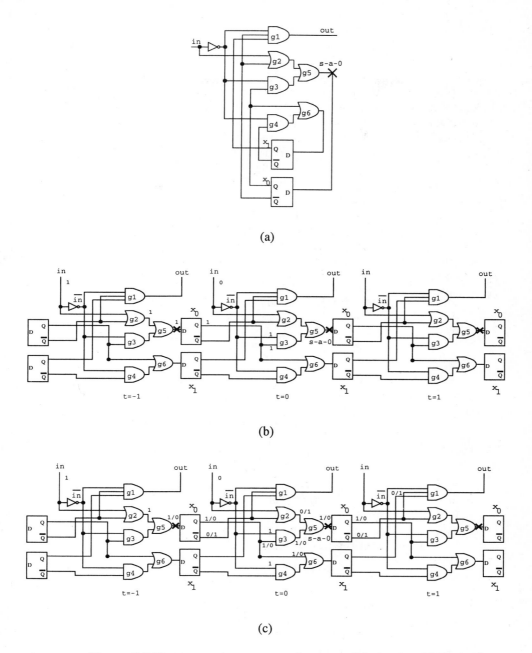

Figure 8.7 Test generation on example sequential circuit. (a) Example sequential circuit. (b) Iterative array model of circuit. (c) More assignments on iterative model. (Courtesy of Mathew, Private Communication, 1994)

In Figure 8.7(b), we illustrate the time frame expansions. To activate the fault, let us suppose that the only alternative left is to make the output of $g3 = 1$. To do this, the inputs of gate $g3$ must have logic value 1. The upper input is easy to justify at the primary input in. The lower input requires a 1 at the output of flip-flop x_0. This requires the x_0 flip-flop to be set to logic value 1 in the previous time frame, or clock period ($t = -1$). This can be done by obtaining a logic value 1 at gate $g2$, which, in turn, can be obtained by setting the primary input in to 1 in the time frame $t = -1$. In Figure 8.7(c), we simulate forward the logic values set on the primary inputs. The resultant values are shown. The fault is present in all time frames. Therefore, the fault effect is activated even in time frame $t = -1$. These values propagate to the fault site in time frame $t = 0$ where the fault is again activated and sent to the flip-flop x_0. The fault is not yet at a primary output. Therefore, we have to propagate the fault effect forward into another time frame ($t = 1$). In doing so, the fault effect reaches the input of gate $g1$ in time frame $t = 1$. The fault is not yet detected. What remains to be done is to produce a logic value 1 on the other two inputs of gate $g1$ in time frame $t = 1$. This is left as an exercise to the interested reader.

An outline of a sequential circuit test generation algorithm *PODEM-SEQUENTIAL-ATPG* is given next.

Procedure *PODEM-SEQUENTIAL-ATPG;*
    Read circuit topology;
    Read list of faults;
    Compute controllability and observability;
    Select a fault;
    Forward-time-processing(0);
    Reverse-time-processing(0);
End Procedure

Procedure *Forward-time-processing(currenttime)*
    Apply fault at site;
    Save assignments on stack for currenttime);
    Propagate fault to a Primary Output;
    IF (success in propagation)
    THEN report pseudo-input assignments on all time frames;
    ELSE Forward-time-processing(currenttime + 1);
End Procedure

Procedure *Reverse-time-processing(currenttime);*
    Determine initial objective (state S0, current-time);
    Apply PODEM-backtrace (until new primary input assignment made));
    Perform forward implication (of all assigned inputs);
    Save assignments on stack of current time;
    IF (any conflict)
        THEN PODEM-backtrack;

IF (all pseudo-inputs of previous time frame = X)
    THEN exit (test found);
    ELSE Reverse-time-processing(currenttime - 1)
End Procedure

8.2.5 Guidance Heuristics for Sequential Circuit ATPG

Since the problem of test generation for sequential circuits can be expected to be harder than that for combinational circuits, the testability measure used can have a significant impact on the overall performance. The testability measure used should result in as few assignments on the primary inputs as possible and also should lead to shorter test sequences to reduce test generation time. The testability measure should bias the assignment of values so that very few pseudo inputs are assigned values. The combinational SCOAP [39] heuristic has been widely used for test generation for combinational circuits and has been shown to be very efficient for most combinational circuits. A slightly modified version of the sequential SCOAP heuristic can be used for the sequential circuit ATPG [75]. The algorithm for computing this measure iterates through the SCOAP values along feedback paths until either the controllability/observability values stabilize or an iteration limit is exceeded. When the iterations are started, the controllability of pseudo-inputs and the observability of pseudo-outputs are set to infinity (some high integer value).

Another measure that is useful in pruning the search space and reducing the memory requirements for test generation is an estimate of the number of time frames necessary to generate a test for a fault. The *sequential depth* [89] of a node is the minimum number of flip-flops between any primary input and the node under consideration. Since this particular definition does not take into account the effect of intervening logic, we can define the *logical sequential depth* as the minimum number of time frames necessary to realize a logic value on a particular line. We can also define the *observation depth* as the minimum number of time frames necessary to observe the fault effect on a particular line at any primary output. The minimum number of time frames necessary to generate a logic value 0 will be called 0-sequential depth, and the corresponding value for logic value 1 will be called 1-sequential depth. The algorithm used to compute the sequential depth values iterates through the network until the values stabilize or the iteration limit is exceeded [75].

8.3 PARALLEL TEST GENERATION APPROACHES

In this section we will broadly classify the different decomposition approaches to exploit parallelism in test generation.

8.3.1 Fault Parallelism

Fault parallelism refers to the evaluation of the test patterns for the given fault set in parallel by dividing the fault set equally among n processors. Each processor can now generate tests for its own fault set independently. But this method suffers from a serious drawback as far as the overall test length and runtime are concerned. In an integrated test generation/fault simulation (TG/FS) environment, test generation and fault simulation are interleaved to reduce the overall runtime and to produce a compact test set. The method involves selecting a fault from a fault list, generating a test on it, and subsequently performing fault simulation on that derived test vector to remove other faults from the fault list, before repeating the process of generating another test for the next fault in the fault list.

A parallel implementation of test generation should also include fault simulation. Each processor performs fault simulation on the test vectors derived during its own test generation phase and by other processors. Communication among processors for fault simulation can be reduced or eliminated altogether by dividing the fault sets into independent fault sets [7]. This reduces the likelihood of a test vector derived by one processor being a test for a fault on some other processor.

The main advantage of fault parallelism is that the communication overhead is very low, and it is possible to achieve linear speedups when the number of processors is very small compared to the number of faults. But the main disadvantage is that faults that are hard to detect for the uniprocessor algorithm (that is, faults that require a large number of backtracks on the uniprocessor) remain undetected even in the parallel implementation.

8.3.2 Heuristic Parallelism

Almost all test generation algorithms use some heuristics to guide test generation. Experiments reported in [74] suggested that there is no clear cut advantage of using one heuristic over the other. We can exploit *heuristic parallelism* by letting each processor use a different heuristic to guide the search for the same fault.

The main advantages of this method are that the recoding effort is very low, and the communication overheads are low. But the main disadvantage of this method is that the parallelism is limited by the number of heuristics available for search (at most five to six). Also, by using different heuristics there is no guarantee that the search spaces are disjoint. This may lead to redundant work. Also, no improvement is possible if a fault remains undetectable for all the heuristics.

8.3.3 Search Space Parallelism

A way to view the test generation process is as a search in a search space of primary inputs that can be each assigned 0/1 values in different time frames. We typically perform depth-first search on that large search space, with backtracks in input assignments when we encounter conflicting input assignments. *Search space parallelism* refers to evaluating the functions associated with several choice points in parallel. This can be modeled also as an AND/OR type of parallelism of a search space as described in [24]. In the case of test generation, this essentially means that we are searching different portions of the search space concurrently. Each processor can be allocated a portion of the search space, either statically or dynamically, and the search for the test vector can proceed concurrently. A brute-force method of dividing the search space might entail useless search in nonsolution areas by some processors. A heuristics-based method aimed at increasing the probability of searching in a solution area would be more desirable, but the search spaces may not be disjoint in such a situation.

The advantage of search-space parallelism is that the processors search different parts of the search space and therefore do not perform redundant work. Parallel processing is used to speed up the test generation of a particular fault. This is especially important when we have *hard-to-detect* faults, that require a large number of backtracks to perform the search.

An additional advantage of this scheme is that the communication overhead can be kept low and a large number of processors can be utilized efficiently. Superlinear speedups might be possible due to search anomalies [54, 97]. The disadvantage is that the coding is difficult.

8.3.4 Functional Parallelism

Functional parallelism can be exploited in algorithms that use divide and conquer methods to solve certain problems. In such methods, a task is divided into a series of subtasks, all of which have to be completed and the results merged.

The disadvantage of the technique is that the subtasks can be executed in parallel if they do not access or modify any common variables. If they have common variables, execution of the functional-parallel subtasks becomes complicated due to variable binding conflicts. The overheads due to variable binding conflicts may essentially reduce the functional-parallel tasks to sequential execution due to consistency checking, and the like. As an example of how parallelism may be used in a test generation environment, consider the objectives of exciting the fault and then propagating the fault to a primary output. Both objectives are mandatory to generate a test for a fault. Thus we can try to realize these two objectives in parallel by using functional parallel techniques. However, both objectives will depend on some common primary input assignments or signal values in the internal lines of the logic circuit, which may lead to variable binding conflicts. The result of this problem is that the speedups achievable using the functional parallel approach to test generation are very limited.

8.3.5 Circuit Parallelism

Another approach to parallel test generation is based on circuit decomposition. In all the parallel approaches discussed so far, each processor keeps a copy of the entire circuit. For extremely large circuits, the memory of each processor may not be enough to store the entire circuit. In a circuit decomposed approach, each processor keeps a partition of the circuit and performs various operations (such as backtracing, justification and implication) on its own subcircuit to satisfy various test generation objectives. With this approach, it is extremely hard to achieve efficient speedups.

A different way to use circuit decomposition in the test generation is to speed up one time-consuming component of test generation. One major component of run time in test generation is forward implication. Every primary input assignment is followed by forward implication, which takes $O(n)$ time in the worst case (n is the number of lines in the logic circuit). This makes backtracks expensive and the test generation process has to be aborted when a test cannot be generated after a certain backtrack limit. We can exploit parallelism in this simulation of the implication phase using a *circuit decomposed* approach by using parallel logic simulation methods on different parts of a circuit. The circuit can be partitioned across processors so that each processor simulates a part of the circuit. The partitioning strategy should minimize communication and maximize concurrency.

In the following sections, we will discuss the details of each approach to parallel test generation.

8.4 FAULT PARALLEL TEST GENERATION

8.4.1 Overview

The simplest way to parallelize an automatic test pattern generation algorithm is to divide the fault list among the processors. Each processor then generates tests for each fault on its portion of the fault list until tests for all the faults have been generated. Such a scheme has been proposed by Chandra and Patel [18]. This scheme results in each processor having a completely separate task in that it performs the entire test generation procedure on its own.

If fault simulation is not a part of a test generation system, that is, only a deterministic test pattern generation program is used, the problem of partitioning faults for test generation is relatively straightforward. To obtain the maximum amount of speedup on a multiprocessor, the work load must be balanced on all processors at all times. A simple dynamic allocation scheme in which an idle processor requests a target fault from some other processor would suffice. It is then very easy to obtain linear speedups as reported in [18].

However, Patil and Banerjee have reported [77] on the inefficiency of this procedure since many of the faults in the fault list can be detected through fault simulation. It is well known that the task of fault simulation is much easier than test generation. Hence, most test generation systems use a test generation/ fault simulation loop in which each test generation step is followed by a fault simulation step to detect additional faults from the fault list. The purpose of this step is twofold. First, since the complexity of fault simulation is much less than that of test generation, the fault simulation step saves the effort in test generation for faults having the same test vector. Second, the overall test length is reduced due to the additional faults detected during the fault simulation phase. The overall test generation time for the fault set is therefore much less if fault simulation is used.

8.4.2 Fault Parallel Approach for Combinational Circuits

We will now describe parallel algorithms for test generation for combinational circuits using a fault parallel approach. Due to the use of fault simulation, the problem of fault partitioning in a parallel TG/FS environment becomes nontrivial. A simple dynamic scheme in which each processor is allocated one target fault at a time reduces to the case where no fault simulation is used at all. Thus, for fault simulation to be useful, each processor has to be allocated more than one fault at a time. Patil and Banerjee have addressed this problem in [77].

The best allocation strategy should minimize the overall runtime and test length. An ideal allocation would be such that (1) if a test vector for fault f_i can also be a test for f_j then they are assigned to the same processor and (2) the load on all processors is balanced. If fault f_i is assigned to processor p_i and fault f_j is assigned to processor p_j and both have a common test vector, then p_i and p_j might end up doing some redundant work, that could otherwise have been avoided on the uniprocessor by using fault simulation. Two faults are called *compatible* if a vector exists which can detect both the faults. It should be noted that a compatibility relationship is much weaker than a *fault dominance or equivalence* relationship [13]. If fault f_i is dominant over f_j or f_i is equivalent to f_j, then f_i and f_j are compatible but not vice versa.

As an example, consider the six faults shown in Figure 8.8. An edge between f_i and f_j means that fault f_i is compatible with fault f_j. It should however be noted that compatibility

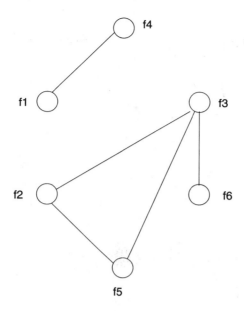

Figure 8.8 Compatible fault sets

is not a transitive relation, that is, if f_i is compatible with f_j, and if f_j is compatible with f_k, it does not mean that f_i and f_k are compatible. For our example, we will assume that if fault f_i is compatible with faults f_j and f_k, at least one vector exists that is a test for all the faults f_i, f_j, f_k, which in the general case may not be possible. Also, we will assume that whenever the test generator generates a test for a fault f_i, it generates a vector that detects not only fault f_i, but also all faults that are compatible with f_i. These assumptions are only for illustration purposes and may not hold true in the general case. Assume that the faults are processed on the uniprocessor in the order, $f_1, f_2, ..., f_6$. Now assume that it takes 10 time units to generate a test for a fault, and after each test generation step it takes R time units for fault simulation, where R is the number of remaining faults. Therefore, if the faults are considered in the order f_1 followed by f_2, and so on, it takes 10 time units to generate a test for f_1 and 5 time units to do fault simulation for the remaining faults. Fault f_4 is deleted from the fault list, assuming it is detected during fault simulation. It takes 10 time units to generate a test for f_2 and 3 time units for fault simulation and faults f_3 and f_5 are deleted from the fault list. It takes another 10 time units to generate a test for the fault f_6 and the TG/FS process terminates. Thus the total time for TG/FS on the uniprocessor is $(10 + 5 + 10 + 3 + 10 = 38)$ time units and the test length is 3.

Next, let us assume there are two processors p_1 and p_2 performing test generation and fault simulation. Let faults f_1, f_2, f_6 be assigned to p_1 and faults f_3, f_4, f_5 be assigned to p_2. Using the compatibility relationships shown in Figure 8.8, p_1 takes 30 time units to complete TG/FS for its own fault list and p_2 takes 12 time units for its own fault list. Thus the overall completion time is 30 time units and the test length is 4. Here, it has been assumed that the processors are computing test vectors independent of each other and have no knowledge of vectors generated by other processors. This restriction will be relaxed later. Now consider another assignment. Let f_1, f_4, f_6 be assigned to p_1 and f_2, f_3, f_5 be assigned to p_2. The completion time now is 22 time units and the test length is 3, same as that on the uniprocessor. Since f_2, f_3, f_5 belong to the same *compatible fault set*, they were assigned to the same processor thus reducing the overall runtime.

We formally define a compatible fault set as follows. A set of faults is called a *compatible fault set* if for every pair of faults belonging to the same fault set there exists at least one test vector that detects both the faults. Thus, all faults in a compatible fault set are pairwise compatible. A compatible set is a complete subgraph in the graph shown in Figure 8.8 (or a clique). A complete subgraph is one in which there is an edge between any two distinct vertices that belong to the subgraph. Finding out whether two faults f_i and f_j have a test vector in common is a computationally hard problem and is as difficult as test generation itself. In the worst case, it might be necessary to enumerate all possible test vectors for f_i to find out whether there is a vector that detects f_j also. Since our objective is to find out compatible fault sets without actually using test generation and fault simulation, approximate heuristic methods have to be used. If heuristic methods are used, it cannot be guaranteed that two faults belonging to the same partition or set will have a test vector in common. Due to this reason, the partitions generated by any of the heuristic partitioning methods will be referred to as *pseudo-compatible fault sets*. Assigning each pseudo-compatible fault set to a different processor results in a shorter runtime and test length due to more faults being detected during the fault simulation phase.

As the number of processors is increased, since we consider minimization of the overall runtime for TG/FS as our primary objective, some pseudo-compatible fault sets may have to be split across processors to keep the load balanced. Thus, with an increase in the number of processors, it can be expected that the test length is also increased. The heuristic partitioning algorithms presented in this section try to minimize this increase. As the number of processors approaches the number of faults, it can be expected that the test length approaches the number of faults also (since we assume the primary objective is to reduce the runtime).

Apart from using better partitioning methods to reduce the test lengths, test length can also be reduced by broadcasting the vectors generated on one processor (through test generation) to all other processors. These test vectors can be used during the fault simulation process by each processor to reduce the test length as long as the associated overheads are not high. Due to the approximate nature of the fault partitioning techniques used, it is still very likely that a test vector generated for a target fault f_i assigned to processor p_i is also a test for a fault f_j assigned to processor p_j. Thus, if we communicate the test vector to processor p_j then it does not have to generate a test for fault f_j. Since each processor is using test vectors generated on its own and those sent by other processors, the number of test vectors used for fault simulation by each processor may be greater than or equal to the number of vectors used for fault simulation on the uniprocessor. It can so happen that the fault simulation phase dominates the overall runtime and each processor ends up spending about the same time as the uniprocessor. Also, the communication overhead is increased and the multiprocessor may quickly run out of buffer space for messages because of test vectors arriving from other processors at a rate faster than the fault simulation rate. This can cause further degradation in performance. Thus we have to find an optimal value of some communication parameter p_c, called the *communication cutoff factor*, that results in a small test length without producing a severe degradation in runtime.

Partitioning methods that are used as a preprocessing step before the actual TG/FS phase will be referred to as *static* partitioning methods. A static partitioning method may not result in balanced workloads on all the processors. A *dynamic* load balancing technique may have to be used to keep the processor loads balanced at runtime. A good partitioning method to exploit fault parallelism should do the following:

- Avoid potential increase in test length by assigning all faults in the same compatible fault set to the same processor

- Control the degree of communication based on an optimal value of the communication cutoff factor p_c

- Use dynamic load balancing if necessary to keep the load balanced on all processors

- Use a static partitioning technique which requires a very small computation time when compared to the overall TG/FS time

Static Fault Partitioning Methods   All the methods described next can be used in the static partitioning or the preprocessing step to initially assign faults to the processors before the parallel TG/FS process is started. Each method assigns n_f/N faults to each processor where n_f is the total number of faults and N is the number of processors. Since each processor is assigned roughly an equal number of faults, if the number of sets generated by any of the following methods is greater than the number of processors, multiple sets are assigned to each processor. This may sometimes require splitting the sets between two processors.

Natural order partitioning   Faults are assigned in groups of n_f/N in the order in which they appear in the global fault list, which is often ordered for different reasons.

Random partitioning   Faults are assigned randomly to the processors. This method is used for comparison with other approaches.

Input cones partitioning   This method assumes that all compatible faults lie in the same fan-out cone of an input. Since each processor has to be assigned approximately n_f/N faults, each processor is allocated a bucket of size n_f/N. A depth-first search is conducted starting from the inputs, where each input is selected in some arbitrary order. In the process of traversal from some other input, if it is found that a node (or fault) has already been visited, the depth-first search does not proceed any further for that node since faults in the fan-out cone of that node have already been assigned. Thus faults belonging to more than one topological input cone will be assigned to only one processor. During the traversal of the circuit using depth-first search, the parity of the gates during the search is taken into account. For example, if a s-a-0 fault was selected at the input of an inverting gate, then a s-a-1 fault will be selected at the output. This approach tries to avoid assigning a s-a-0 and a s-a-1 fault on the same line to the same processor (since a s-a-0 and a s-a-1 fault on the same line cannot be detected by the same test vector). As the bucket for a processor becomes filled during the depth-first traversal, another processor is selected for assignment. Thus input cones may be split across processors during the depth-first traversal.

Output cones partitioning   This method is similar to that for input cones except that the depth-first search traversal of the network is performed starting at the outputs and proceeding toward the inputs.

Mandatory constraint propagation (MACP) partitioning   A set of constraints is derived based on the testing requirements imposed by each fault. Two faults are considered compatible if their testing constraints match; that is, the testing requirements do not conflict. A preprocessing phase is used in which the flow dominators of all the gates are generated [93]. A gate G is a dominator of a gate g if all paths from g to any output in the logic circuit pass through G. Starting at the fault site and by using backward and forward implication, a set of uniquely implied logic values is generated. The initial assignments that trigger backward and forward implication are based on both the excitation and propagation requirements of a fault. For example, if we are testing for a stuck-at-0 fault at the output of a gate, then a logic value 1 will be required at the gate output to excite the fault. This procedure also gives a set of faults in the vicinity of a fault α which may be detected by a test for α. All such faults are put in the same *pseudo-compatible fault set* as α (*pseudo-compatible* since two faults in the same set may not really be compatible). The next step tries to generate more constraints from the global flow dominator information. If G is a dominator of g and we are testing for a fault α of g, then it must be observed at G. Also, all inputs of G that are not reachable from the fault site must be set to noncontrolling values. A test for a fault at the output of g thus must detect at least one fault at the output of G (either s-a-0 or s-a-1). Backward and forward implication is performed for G and its inputs. This is repeated for all dominators G of g, and additional faults are added to the pseudo-compatible set for α.

Dynamic Fault Partitioning   If faults f_i and f_j are in the same pseudo-compatible fault set, it is very likely that they have a common test vector. But the heuristic procedures given preceding do not guarantee that two faults will be compatible if they are included in the same pseudo-compatible set (by definition). All faults belonging to the same pseudo-compatible fault set are assigned to the same processor. It can be seen that finding pseudo-compatible fault sets by mandatory constraint propagation requires much more computation time than any of the methods discussed so far. All partitioning methods presented in this section require $O(n)$ computation time, where n is the number of lines in the logic network, except partitioning by MACP, which takes $O(n^2)$ time, which is equivalent to one pass for fault simulation. From the preceding discussion, it would seem that partitioning by MACP is the best static partitioning method. However, due to its computational complexity, it may take a large amount of preprocessing time for large circuits.

It is easy to see that partitioning by input cones has some inherent advantages over partitioning by output cones if we consider the test generation process itself. During test generation, starting at the fault site, sensitized paths are created that fan out from the fault site toward the output. Thus, additional faults will be detected during fault simulation along these sensitized paths. Since partitioning by input cones will lump all these faults in the same set, it can be expected that partitioning by input cones will do better than partitioning by output cones on the average.

Also, the partitioning methods presented may have a tendency to lump all the hard-to-detect or redundant faults into the same set. Thus a processor may end up spending too much time on such faults, resulting in skewed workloads. Since it is difficult to come up with an a priori estimate of how difficult it is to generate a test for a particular fault, additional load balancing is done at runtime by using techniques described in the next section. If a processor ends up spending too much time on redundant or hard-to-detect faults, it will be left with a backlog of faults yet to be processed. In such a case, the faults will be reallocated to processors that are idle if the dynamic load balancing technique detailed in the next section is used, thus improving the overall system performance. The dynamic load balancing technique would be effective irrespective of what the backtrack limit is.

The number of faults is often a very poor estimate of the workload. It has been found that even if an equal number of faults is allocated to different processors the variation in work load (measured as the amount of time spent doing fault simulation and test generation) is often substantial. Since it is very difficult to judge a priori how difficult it is to generate a test for a particular fault, a static work load allocation scheme may result in unbalanced workloads. Some processors may become idle before others. However, a dynamic workload distribution scheme may result in excessive communication, which may offset any performance gains due to dynamic load balancing.

Distributed Memory MIMD Parallel Algorithm We will now describe a distributed memory parallel algorithm for test generation of combinational circuits that uses fault parallelism, based on work reported by Patil and Banerjee [77]. The algorithm uses a combination of static and dynamic fault partitioning. In this parallel algorithm, initially, the fault list is distributed using one of the static partitioning schemes described earlier. If a processor is done with test generation of all faults in its own fault list, it broadcasts a request for additional work from other processors. Each processor receiving such a message sends the number of faults still to be processed (an estimate of the remaining workload) to the processor requesting work. The processor requesting work then sends an explicit work request message to the processor having the largest fault list. The processor having the largest fault list then splits its own fault list in half and sends it off to the requesting processor. When splitting the fault list, care is taken to ensure that faults are partitioned according to the static partitioning criterion used initially; for example, if the static fault partitioning criterion was partitioning by input cones, the idle processor gets faults that are in the same input cone.

Termination detection is very simple in this scheme. When all the fault lists have been exhausted, all processors will try to request work from each other. When a particular processor finds that all other processors have exhausted their own fault lists, it terminates. This particular load distribution and distributed termination detection algorithm result in high message traffic only at the end of the TG/FS process.

An outline of the parallel test generation algorithm *DM-PARALLEL-COMB-ATPG-FAULT* (denoting distributed memory parallel algorithm for test generation of combinational circuits using fault decomposition), is given next.

Procedure *DM-PARALLEL-COMB-ATPG-FAULT;*
Partition fault lists statically among processors;

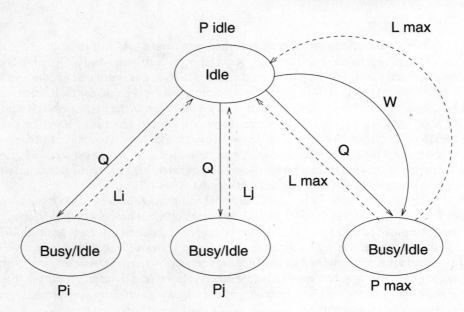

Figure 8.9 Dynamic load balancing

```
FORALL processors in PARALLEL DO
    REPEAT
        WHILE processor's own fault list not empty DO
            Select a fault f_i from own fault list;
            Perform ATPG to determine test t_i for fault f_i;
                t_i = PODEM-COMBINATIONAL-ATPG(f_i);
            Fault simulate on Own fault list for test t_i;
            Remove detected faults from own fault list;
            Check Messages from other processors for load balance;
        END WHILE
        IF processor fault list empty THEN
            Get work from other processors
            Query other processors for fault list
            Receive half fault list of most loaded processor
    UNTIL all faults detected or aborted
END FORALL
End Procedure
```

Figure 8.9 shows the dynamic load balancing process. The processor labeled p_{idle} is the idle processor and p_{max} is the processor having the largest fault list. Q are query messages broadcast by p_{idle} and the messages shown with dashed edges are messages that contain the length of the remaining fault list. W is the work request message sent to processor p_{max}. Finally, processor p_{max} splits its own fault list into half and sends one portion to p_{idle}

TABLE 8.1 Quality (Fault Coverage and Test Length), Runtimes (Seconds), and Speedups, of Parallel Test Generation Algorithm on an Intel iPSC/2™ Hypercube

Circuit	1 Processor			16 Processors		
	Coverage	Length	Runtime (Speedup)	Coverage	Length	Runtime (Speedup)
c432	99.2	71	6.8 (1.0)	99.1	213	1.6 (4.1)
c499	98.9	72	9.2 (1.0)	98.9	196	1.7 (5.3)
c880	100.0	85	9.1 (1.0)	100.0	258	1.6 (5.6)
c1355	99.5	145	38.0 (1.0)	99.1	371	5.2 (7.3)
c3540	96.8	206	235.8 (1.0)	94.3	615	31.4 (7.5)
c5315	99.2	161	150.4 (1.0)	99.1	673	23.5 (6.4)
c7552	97.7	251	437.0 (1.0)	96.4	812	56.1 (7.8)

(indicated by the message labeled $L_{max}/2$).

Implementation   Patil and Banerjee have reported an implementation of the preceding parallel algorithm using PODEM as a deterministic test pattern generator and a deductive fault simulator on a 16-processor Intel iPSC/2™ hypercube [76, 77]. The SCOAP [39] heuristic was used for guidance in the test generation process. The ISCAS-85 combinational benchmark circuits [15] were used to evaluate the parallel algorithm.

The first set of results reported by Patil and Banerjee was for the uniprocessor and the parallel processor results for some of the ISCAS-85 circuits *when no fault simulation was used.* Even though random partitioning was used to partition the faults, the results show almost linear speedups. However, the uniprocessor results were much inferior to those obtained by the uniprocessor by using test generation and fault simulation, both in terms of the test lengths and runtimes. Hence we can conclude that this simple method of fault partitioning and independent test generation on different processors is not an efficient use of parallel processors.

We now report on some results where fault simulation is always used with deterministic test pattern generation. It was reported that except for partitioning by MACP, most partitioning methods (which constitute a preprocessing overhead) take a negligible time compared to the total test generation time. However, for large circuits, partitioning by MACP takes time that is comparable to that of test generation. The results with MACP partitioning and input cones partitioning were similar; hence the extra time spent for MACP is probably not worth it. Table 8.1 shows the runtimes and speedups of several ISCAS-89 sequential benchmark circuits [14] on an Intel iPSC/2™ hypercube multiprocessor using partitioning by input cones.

The test lengths are higher than the uniprocessor in all cases. No communication for test vectors was allowed, and a combination of static and dynamic load balancing was used. The fault coverage figures were similar to those on one processor.

In summary, the partitioning by input cones had the best performance for the test length, and random partitioning had the best performance from the speedup viewpoint, even though it had the worst performance for the test length. These results are in some sense

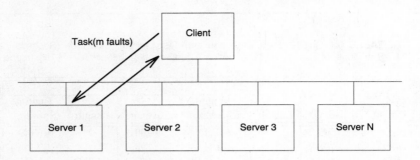

Figure 8.10 Client-server model for parallel test generation

counterintuitive, since we would expect that speedup should be higher for the partitioning method, which produces a lower test length. If we assign equal weights to test length and speedup, partitioning by input cones and MACP turned out to be the best partitioning methods. However, considering the large amount of preprocessing time required by MACP, which is an order of magnitude higher than the total TG/FS time on a multiprocessor, partitioning by input cones turns out to be the best partitioning method.

In some related work, Fujiwara and Inoue [31, 32] have presented an implementation of a fault parallel test generation algorithm in a loosely coupled distributed network of workstations. The implementation involved the client-server model of computation shown in Figure 8.10. In the network, the client processor requests a remote server process to execute a task (consisting of test generation on a cluster of faults). When a server finishes its assigned task, it sends the result (test vectors, a set of faults that are detected, a set of faults that are proved to be redundant, and a set of faults that were aborted due to excessive backtrackings) to the client and requests a new task. The client updates the fault table, and provides a new task by extracting a new cluster of undetected faults to the server. The client service discipline is first-come, first-served. The granularity of computation (the number of faults given to a server) determines the speedup. If the granularity is decreased in order to exploit more parallelism, then servers complete the tasks more rapidly, and hence send requests to clients more frequently. This increases the communication and reduces the speedup.

Fujiwara and Inoue have analyzed the effects of static and dynamic allocation of target faults to processors, the optimal granularity (grain size of target faults), and the speedup ratio using some simple models of computations and communication in a network of workstations, and using a simple model of test generation times [31, 32]. For the homogeneous case in which all servers are uniform, and when the processing and communication times are assumed to be the same for all the faults, if the test generation process is applied to each fault with no fault simulation, the total processing and communication time becomes a monotone decreasing function of the number of target faults m; hence, the best performance is obtained when each server receives all target faults only once from each client, that is, when $m = M/N$. However, it may often occur that a test pattern generated for one fault can also be a test pattern for other faults, which can be detected through fault simulation. To analyze this case, the authors have introduced the notion of the ratio of newly processed faults (faults that get detected or proved to be redundant during a pass of test generation for m faults) to target faults and derived expressions of optimal granularity in both cases of static and dynamic task allocation. The authors validated their theoretical analysis with an implementation of the fault partitioned parallel algorithm test generation/fault simulation on a network of 15 SUN 3/50™ workstations (one for client and $N = 14$ for servers). For an example circuit (c7552 from the ISCAS-85 benchmark), the maximum speedup was measured to be 7.0 for a grain size of about 25 faults using static allocation of tasks, out of a problem size of 500 faults.

Shared Memory MIMD Parallel Algorithm The parallel algorithm for fault simulation of combinational circuits using fault partitioning [77] can be implemented very easily in a shared memory parallel environment, even though no such implementation has been reported. In such an approach, the entire circuit structure and list of faults can be kept in shared memory. Each processor atomically removes a fault from the global fault list that is not yet detected, or proved redundant, or previously aborted and tries to generate a test for it using a conventional ATPG algorithm. If the fault is proved redundant in the test generation process, it is marked as such in the global list of faults. If the test generation process gets aborted due to excessive backtracks, the fault is marked aborted in the list of faults. If a test is found, fault simulation is performed on the global list of undetectable faults for the test pattern. After the fault simulation, the global fault list is updated to reflect the faults that are newly detected or proved redundant. The process is repeated until all faults are detected, proved redundant, or aborted by the test generator.

An outline of the parallel test generation algorithm *SM-PARALLEL-COMB-ATPG-FAULT* (denoting shared memory parallel algorithm for test generation of combinational circuits using fault decomposition) is given next.

Procedure *SM-PARALLEL-COMB-ATPG-FAULT;*
    Read circuit and list of faults;
    Create shared copy of circuit on all processors;
    Create global shared queue of fault list;
    FORALL processor in PARALLEL DO
        WHILE undetected fault remains in global fault queue DO
            Atomically select a fault f_i from fault queue;
            Perform ATPG to determine test t_i for fault f_i;
                t_i = PODEM-COMBINATIONAL-ATPG(f_i);
            Copy list of faults not detected from
                shared queue under locks to local list;
            Fault simulate on local fault list for test t_i;
            Mark detected/redundant/aborted faults
                in shared fault queue under locks;
        END WHILE
    END FORALL
 End Procedure

The preceding algorithm can cause a lot of contention for the global fault list among processors. The algorithm can be modified as follows. When a processor goes to get the next undetected fault from the shared fault list, instead of getting a single fault, it gets a set of m

faults that are not detected and stores them in a local fault list. The processor tries to generate tests for all the faults in its list before visiting the shared global queue. It picks the first fault from the local list and generates a test for it using a conventional ATPG algorithm. Once such a test is found, fault simulation is performed on the local list of undetectable faults (from the cluster of m faults). Once all faults in its local list of faults are detected, proved redundant, or aborted, the processor updates the global fault list under locks, and grabs the next group of m undetected faults.

An outline of the parallel test generation algorithm *SM-PARALLEL-COMB-ATPG-FAULT-SET* (denoting shared memory parallel algorithm for test generation of combinational circuits using fault parallelism, and using sets of faults at a time) follows:

> **Procedure** *SM-PARALLEL-COMB-ATPG-FAULT-SET;*
>   Read circuit description and fault list;
>   Create shared copy of circuit on all processors;
>   Create global shared queue of fault list;
>   FORALL processors in PARALLEL DO
>   WHILE undetected fault remains in global fault list DO
>   Copy a group of m undetected faults
>   from global fault list under locks into local list;
>   WHILE undetected fault remains in local fault list DO
>   Select a fault f_i from local fault list;
>   Perform ATPG to determine test t_i for fault f_i;
>   Fault simulate on local fault list for test t_i;
>   Remove detected faults from own fault list;
>   END WHILE
>   Update shared global fault list under locks;
>   END WHILE
>   END FORALL
> **End Procedure**

The preceding algorithm still produces some contention for access to the global fault list every time a set of m faults is picked up by a processor. This can be prevented by a modified algorithm based on the algorithm for distributed memory multiprocessors. In this algorithm, each processor receives a static partition of the fault list, which will be stored in a separate queue per processor to avoid contention of a global fault list among processors. The dynamic load balancing can be implemented easily as follows.

When a processor is finished with its own fault list on its own queue, it can read all the other processor's fault lists from shared memory, since each is maintained as a separate shared queue in main memory. When the idle processor identifies the queue with the longest remaining fault list, it obtains exclusive control of that queue through locks, splits the queue in half, takes half the fault list for itself, and returns the remaining half to the other processor. The other processor can return to its normal work on this reduced fault list.

An outline of the parallel test generation algorithm *SM-PARALLEL-COMB-ATPG-FAULT-LOCAL* (denoting shared memory parallel algorithm for test generation of combinational circuits using fault parallelism keeping local queue) follows:

Procedure *SM-PARALLEL-COMB-ATPG-FAULT-LOCAL;*
   Read circuit description and fault list;
   Partition fault lists statically among processors;
   Create N fault lists (queues), one per processor;
   FORALL processors in PARALLEL DO
      REPEAT
         WHILE processor's own fault list not empty DO
            Select a fault f_i from own fault list;
            Perform ATPG to determine test t_i for fault f_i;
               t_i = PODEM-COMBINATIONAL-ATPG(f_i);
            Fault simulate on Own fault list for test t_i;
            Remove detected faults from own fault list;
         END WHILE
         IF processor fault list empty
         THEN get work from other processors
            Check other processors for fault list
            Remove half fault list of most loaded processor
      UNTIL all faults detected or aborted
   END FORALL
End Procedure

No implementations of any of the preceding parallel algorithms for shared memory multiprocessors have been reported for combinational circuits.

8.4.3 Fault Parallel Approach for Sequential Circuits

We will now describe a fault parallel approach for ATPG on sequential circuits based on work reported by Patil, Banerjee and Patel [80].

   We assume that each processor selects a different fault from the fault list and generates a test vector sequence for the faults in parallel. If we assume that the test generation is performed without any fault simulation, this simple approach is satisfactory. However, all deterministic test pattern generators use fault simulation to detect other faults detected by a given test vector sequence. For sequential circuits, each test generation step generates a *sequence* of test vectors, which needs to be simulated from a given initial state for fault simulation. Hence the procedures for test generation/fault simulation on each processor cease to be independent. This is illustrated in Figure 8.11 for four processors. Each processor i generates a test vector sequence t_i. At the end of test generation for all the faults, the test vector sequences are concatenated into one combined sequence and then fault simulated. This is necessary to correctly deal with propagation of state information in sequential circuits across time frames.

Shared Memory Parallel MIMD Algorithm We now discuss a shared memory parallel test generation algorithm for sequential circuits using fault parallelism based on work reported by Patil, Banerjee and Patel [80]. In the fault parallel approach, each processor picks up a fault for test generation from a global fault list and tries to generate a test for the fault in parallel. The processors then synchronize at a barrier, and all the test vectors generated for all the p faults are fault simulated. Thus all the test vectors generated at the end of the test generation

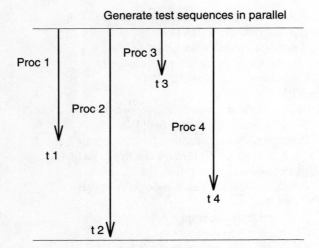

Fault Simulate (t1; t2; t3; t4 sequence)

Figure 8.11 Fault parallel test generation for sequential circuits

step are simulated by all processors in the *same sequence*. To ensure that the times taken for test generation for faults being processed in parallel are the same, the fault list is sorted according to a test length estimate.

We describe the test length estimate (the number of time frames necessary to generate a test for a fault) in more detail later. The *sequential depth* [89] of a node is the minimum number of flip-flops between any primary input and the node under consideration. Since this particular definition does not take into account the effect of intervening logic, we define the *logical sequential depth* as the minimum number of time frames necessary to realize a logic value on a particular line. We also define the *observation depth* as the minimum number of time frames necessary to observe the fault effect on a particular line at any primary output. The minimum number of time frames necessary to generate a logic value 0 will be called 0-sequential depth, and the corresponding value for logic value 1 will be called 1-sequential depth. The algorithm used to compute the sequential depth values iterates through the network until the values stabilize or the iteration limit is exceeded.

The fault partitioning strategies detailed in [77] are not used since the partitioning strategies were based on tracing out the region of influence of a fault effect. Due to the presence of feedback paths in a sequential circuit, it is very likely that a majority of lines are reachable by the fault effect. This would require inclusion of a large portion of the circuit in a partition and cause a skew in processor workloads.

An outline of the parallel test generation algorithm *SM-PARALLEL-SEQUENTIAL-ATPG-FAULT* (denoting shared memory parallel algorithm for test generation of sequential circuits using fault decomposition) is given next.

Procedure *SM-PARALLEL-SEQUENTIAL-ATPG-FAULT;*

TABLE 8.2 Quality (Coverage and Test Length), Runtimes (Seconds), and Speedups, of Parallel Test Generation Algorithm on the Encore Multimax™ Multiprocessor

Circuit	1 Processor			8 Processors		
	Coverage	Length	Runtime (Speedup)	Coverage	Length	Runtime (Speedup)
s298	90.9	208	2014.5 (1.0)	85.4	34	209.4 (9.6)
s1494	38.7	58	6384.1 (1.0)	44.9	43	920.0 (6.9)
s13207	93.6	111	6775.5 (1.0)	93.7	222	909.1 (7.5)
s35932	99.2	485	46181.5 (1.0)	99.1	616	7089.4 (6.5)

Read circuit and list of faults;
Create global shared queue of fault list
    sorted by estimated test generation time
FORALL processor in PARALLEL DO
    WHILE undetected fault remains in global fault list DO
        Select a fault f_i from fault queue;
        Perform ATPG to determine set of test
            vectors TV_i for fault f_i;
            TV_i = PODEM-SEQUENTIAL-ATPG(f_i);
        Write test vectors to shared memory;
        Barrier synchronize ();
        Concatenate test vectors from all processors;
        Partition list of faults not detected
            in shared queue among processors;
        Fault simulate on local fault list for
            concatenated test sequence $TV_1, TV_2, ...TV_P$;
        Remove detected faults from shared fault queue;
    END WHILE
    ENDFOR
End Procedure

Implementation An implementation of the preceding algorithm for test generation of sequential circuits has been reported by Patil, Banerjee and Patel on an Encore Multimax™ shared memory multiprocessor [80]. Table 8.2 shows the runtimes and speedups of several ISCAS-89 sequential benchmark circuits [14] on the multiprocessor.

Distributed Memory Parallel MIMD Algorithm We will now describe a distributed memory parallel MIMD algorithm for test generation of sequential circuits based on fault parallelism. The algorithm is based on work reported by Agrawal et al. [2].

The basic idea in the algorithm is to distribute a given fault list for a sequential circuit evenly over all processors of a distributed memory multicomputer. Each processor performs a complete sequential ATPG algorithm pass using forward and reverse time processing on faults on its fault list. The ATPG process is performed with a small fixed per fault CPU time limit within a pass. Faults requiring more time are abandoned for later passes. During each pass, each processor independently generates test sequences for the assigned faults through test generation and fault simulation. At the end of a pass, each processor simulates the entire fault list with its own vectors and broadcasts the list of undetected faults to all other processors. Processors then combine these fault lists to create a list of faults that were not detected by all processors. This list is again divided equally, and the next pass begins with a larger per fault time limit for test generation. The process stops when either the required fault coverage is obtained or the overall process time limit is reached.

An outline of the parallel test generation algorithm *DM-PARALLEL-SEQUENTIAL-ATPG-FAULT* (denoting distributed memory parallel algorithm for test generation of sequential circuits using fault decomposition) is given next.

> **Procedure** *DM-PARALLEL-SEQUENTIAL-ATPG-FAULT;*
> Read circuit and list of faults;
> Passnumber = 0;
> REPEAT
>   Passnumber = Passnumber + 1;
>   Update time limit per fault for pass;
>   Partition list of undetected faults
>   equally among all processors;
>   FORALL processors in PARALLEL DO
>   WHILE own undetected fault list not empty DO
>   Select a fault f_i from own fault list;
>   Perform ATPG to determine set of test
>   vectors TV_i for fault f_i under time limit;
> TV_i = PODEM-SEQUENTIAL-ATPG(f_i);
>   Fault simulate own undetected fault list
>   using test sequence TV_i;
>   Remove detected faults from undetected fault list;
>   IF time limit exceeded for fault f_i THEN
>   Retain fault f_i in undetected fault list;
>   END WHILE
>   Broadcast list of undetected faults
>   END FORALL
>   Compile list of undetected faults in all processors;
> UNTIL all faults detected or process time limit;
> **End Procedure**

Implementation   Agrawal et al. have implemented the preceding parallel algorithm for test generation on a network of SUN SPARC 2™ workstations connected through an Ethernet [2]. The test generator used in each processor was an existing well-known test generator called GENTEST [22] which is based on a time-frame expansion method, and the PROOFS

TABLE 8.3 Result Quality (Fault Coverage and Test Length), Runtimes (Seconds), and Speedups, of Parallel Test Generation Algorithm on Network of SUN SPARC 2™ Workstations

Circuit	1 Processor			12 Processors		
	Coverage	Length	Runtime (Speedup)	Coverage	Length	Runtime (Speedup)
s526	76.4	2582	65,487 (1.0)	81.2	5925	8,855 (7.4)
s820	89.2	465	26,279 (1.0)	85.9	558	2,836 (9.3)
s1488	88.4	373	31,432 (1.0)	88.8	724	6,473 (4.9)
s5378	76.2	436	2,022,275 (1.0)	73.4	1157	11,201 (180)

differential fault simulator [68]. Table 8.3 shows the runtimes and speedups of several ISCAS-89 sequential benchmark circuits [14] on a network of 12 workstations (SPARC 2).

As can be seen, excellent speedups can be obtained from this approach; however, the size of the test vector set increases dramatically with this approach. The superlinear speedup in one of the circuits, s5378, is due to the different ordering of the test search space solution among multiple processors.

Another implementation of a similar fault parallel approach to test generation of sequential circuits has been reported by Krauss on a network of 100 Hewlett-Packard/9000™ workstations [51]. The sequential test pattern generator used is ESSENTIAL [89]. Speedups of between 27 and 92 have been measured on a set of ISCAS-89 sequential benchmark circuits.

8.5 HEURISTIC PARALLEL TEST GENERATION

8.5.1 Overview

As discussed earlier, heuristics are used to guide deterministic ATPG algorithms. The test generation process involves backtracking on primary input assignments when a particular input combination gives a conflict. It has been reported that, instead of usingone set of testability measures to continue the test generation process, when the ATPG algorithm starts backtracking, it is often useful to switch to other heuristics. Research has indicated that many heuristics will produce a test for a given fault within some computation time limit when other heuristics have failed to do so [19, 74]. These complementary heuristics can be used in a multiprocessor system to aid ATPG.

8.5.2 Distributed Memory MIMD Parallel Algorithm

We will now describe a parallel algorithm for test generation using heuristic decomposition based on the algorithms proposed by Chandra and Patel [18]. The basic approach is to have each processor in a multiprocessor use *different* testability measures, hoping that they will choose different primary input assignments. Each processor performs an independent ATPG algorithm and terminates the search when the processorff finds a test.

The parallel heuristics approach has the potential of achieving superlinear speedups due to the anomalies in the ordering of the heuristics for different faults. For example, suppose the time limit for each of the five heuristics in the uniprocessor algorithm is 10 seconds. That is, if a heuristic fails to find a test within 10 seconds, the heuristic is discarded and the next heuristic is tried. If the five heuristics are tried in sequential order and only the last heuristic can find a test in 5 seconds, the uniprocessor test generation algorithm will find a test in 45 seconds. A concurrent parallel heuristics method with five processors searching in parallel will find a test in 5 seconds, giving a speedup of 9 on five processors.

An outline of the parallel test generation algorithm using heuristic decomposition entitled *DM-PARALLEL-PODEM-ATPG-HEURISTIC* (denoting a distributed memory parallel algorithm for ATPG using heuristic decomposition) is given next.

Procedure *DM-PARALLEL-PODEM-ATPG-HEURISTIC;*
    Read circuit topology;
    Read list of faults;
    WHILE fault list not empty DO
      Select a fault f_i;
      FORALL processors p in PARALLEL DO
        Perform ATPG(f_i, use DIFFERENT heuristic p);
        IF some processor finds a test for fault
          THEN quit ATPG for fault f_i;
      END FORALL
    ENDWHILE
End Procedure

The main disadvantage of the concurrent heuristic method is that there is no way to ensure that the search space of each processor is disjoint. Even if the heuristics used by the processors differ, they might lead the ATPG algorithm down the same path to the nonsolution, and a test may not be found in the allocated time, even though one exists. Another disadvantage is that, since typically the number of available heuristics is limited to about five or six, this method of parallelization is not scalable to large number of processors.

Implementation The preceding algorithm for parallel test generation using heuristic parallelism was implemented on a network of workstations by Chandra and Patel [18]. The implementation combined the heuristic parallelism with fault parallelism. In such a combined scheme, the system was assumed to have $k \times h$ processors, where h is the total number of heuristics available, and k is the number of different fault lists which are executed on different clusters. If k equals 1, each processor computes a test for the same fault using one of the h heuristics. Whenever, a processor succeeds in generating a test for a fault, it sends a message to the other processors in the cluster, and they stop processing the fault. A new fault is selected from the fault list and the process repeats again.

Experimental results were reported on a network of five SUN 3/50™ workstations. Table 8.4 shows some example results on several benchmark circuits of the runtimes (in seconds) and speedups of the parallel algorithm using the combined method on five workstations on the network.

TABLE 8.4 Runtimes (Seconds) and Speedups of Parallel Test Generation on Network of Workstations

Circuit	Faults	1 Processor		2 Processors	
		Runtime	Speedup	Runtime	Speedup
c432	524	99.2	1.0	47.2	2.1
c499	758	608.6	1.0	101.4	6.0
c880	942	58.1	1.0	52.4	1.1
c2670	2595	1751.6	1.0	509.2	3.4
c7552	7552	4958.6	1.0	2709.6	1.8

8.5.3 Shared Memory MIMD Parallel Algorithm

It is trivial to extend the preceding parallel algorithm for a shared memory multiprocessor. Basically, the list of faults would be kept in shared memory. Processors would select a fault from the list, and try different heuristics for the test generation process. When one processor finds a test, all the processors terminate the ATPG process. This can be achieved by checking a shared flag in the main ATPG loop by each processor.

An outline of the shared memory parallel test generation algorithm using heuristic decomposition entitled *SM-PARALLEL-PODEM-ATPG-HEURISTIC* (denoting a shared memory parallel algorithm for ATPG using heuristic decomposition) is given next.

Procedure *SM-PARALLEL-PODEM-ATPG-HEURISTIC;*
    Read circuit topology;
    Read list of faults;
    Create shared list of faults;
    WHILE fault list not empty DO
        Select a fault f_i;
        FORALL processors p in PARALLEL DO
            Perform ATPG(f_i, use DIFFERENT heuristic p);
            IF some processor finds a test for fault
                THEN quit ATPG for fault f_i;
        END FORALL
    ENDWHILE
End Procedure

No shared memory implementations of this parallel algorithm have been reported.

8.6 SEARCH SPACE PARALLEL TEST GENERATION

8.6.1 Overview

The PODEM test generation algorithm treats test generation as a branch and bound search on the n-dimensional Boolean input space of a logic circuit. A conceptual representation of the

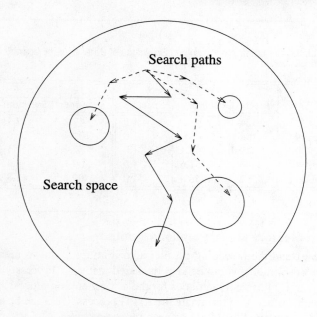

Figure 8.12 Parallel search in search space of test generation

search space is shown in Figure 8.12. The big outer circle indicates the entire search space of size 2^n, where n is the number of primary inputs of the logic circuit. The smaller circles inside the big circle indicate subspaces containing a test for the particular fault under consideration. The solid directed path indicates the path taken by the test generation algorithm to find a test for the fault. The length of the path is proportional to the time taken to find the test for the fault. The dotted paths indicate alternative paths that could have been taken to generate a test in shorter time. Even though a test may exist for a fault, the search may have to be terminated after a predecided backtrack or time limit to save on time.

Each processor can be allocated a portion of the search space, either statically or dynamically, and the search for the test vector can proceed concurrently. A bruteforce method of dividing the search space might entail useless search in nonsolution areas by some processors. A heuristics-based method aimed at increasing the probability of searching in a solution area would be more desirable but the search spaces may not be disjoint in such a situation. The advantage of search parallelism is that communication overhead is very low and a large number of processors can be utilized efficiently. Also, the backtracks per processor can be reduced.

8.6.2 Search Parallel Approach for Combinational Circuits

In this section we will study parallel algorithms using the search-parallel approach for the PODEM algorithm for combinational circuits. Techniques to parallelize the PODEM algorithm borrow some concepts from parallelizing pure depth-first-search (DFS), examples of which appear in [54, 84, 85, 97].

We now describe a parallel branch and bound algorithm for test generation that searches

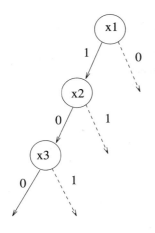

val	input	tried
1	x1	0
0	x2	0
0	x3	0

Figure 8.13 Decision tree used in PODEM

different portions of the search space concurrently. The algorithm is based on work reported by Patil and Banerjee [79] and Arvindam et al. [9].

The decision tree used by PODEM is shown in Figure 8.13. A 0 or a 1 along a solid edge indicates the current assignment to a primary input. It is a binary tree maintained as a stack in which each edge corresponds to a 0 or a 1 assignment to a primary input. Each stack entry has a three fields, a *val* field storing the current assignment to a primary input, an *input* field identifying the primary input, and a *tried* field indicating whether the alternative value at the primary input has been tried. The dashed edges indicate unexplored subspaces. The algorithm proceeds in a depth-first manner to implicitly enumerate the search space for a test vector. If a conflict occurs during this process, the algorithm backtracks to a previous choice point to try another alternative (points with a 0 in the *tried* field). It has been shown experimentally in [74] that it is very unlikely that a fault that has not been detected by a heuristic with a lower backtrack limit will be detected by increasing the backtrack limit. There is a very fundamental reason for this observation. When a conflict occurs, the assignment that gave rise to the conflict need not necessarily be the assignment made at the previous choice point. A blind backtrack to the previous choice point may lead to more fruitless backtracks. Hence the algorithm would perform much better if we were to backtrack to the point that gave rise to the conflict. It is, however, very difficult to determine which previous assignment gave rise to the conflict. The proposed parallel implementation tries to divide the search space so that intermediate choice points are skipped by one processor, while at the same time the skipped choice points are evaluated by some other processor. This leads to a much better fault coverage figure for hard-to-detect faults compared to the uniprocessor implementation. Also, the search space is divided so that all processors are searching disjoint subspaces at all times. Since the size of the search space is exponential in the number of primary inputs, many processors can be utilized efficiently.

Figure 8.14 shows how a decision tree belonging to processor i would be split between processor i and another processor j. The choice points are alternately split between processor

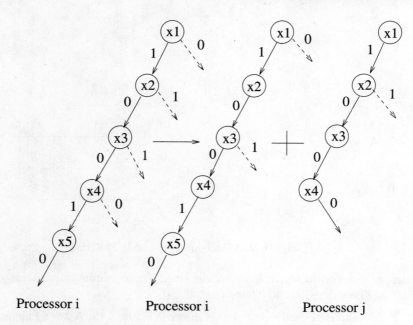

Figure 8.14 Splitting search spaces

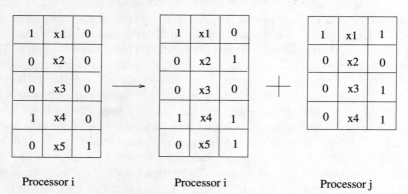

Figure 8.15 Stacks after splitting

i and processor j so that each processor has roughly an equal number of choice points. The exact mechanism by which these search spaces are allocated is described in the next section. A 0 in the *tried* field of a stack entry for a processor indicates that the processor has been allocated the particular choice point. Figure 8.15 shows the stacks after splitting.

Distributed Memory MIMD Parallel Algorithm We will now describe a distributed memory parallel algorithm for test generation of combinational circuits using search space parallelism. The algorithm is based on work reported by Patil and Banerjee [79].

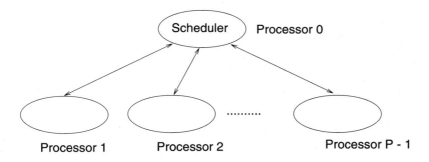

Figure 8.16 Use of centralized scheduling in parallel search

A dynamic search-space allocation strategy is used to keep the load balanced at all times. The processors in a multiprocessor are numbered from 0 to $(P-1)$, as shown in Figure 8.16. One processor (processor 0) is used for scheduling (known as a *scheduler*), while processors 1 to $(P-1)$ carry out test generation using parallel branch and bound (known as *processing* nodes). Initially, the circuit description and information about the heuristic to be used are broadcast to all processors. For each fault, the gate under test and the type of fault (s-a-1 or s-a-0) is also broadcast to all processors. The processors communicate with the scheduler to get more work or to inform the scheduler of special conditions.

An outline of the parallel algorithm for test generation called *DM-PARALLEL-COMB-ATPG-SEARCH-CENT;* (denoting a distributed memory parallel algorithm for test generation of combinational circuits using search parallel decomposition with a centralized scheduler) follows:

Procedure *DM-PARALLEL-COMB-ATPG-SEARCH-CENT;*
Read circuit and list of faults;
Compute controllability and observability measures;
Select a fault;
FORALL processors in PARALLEL DO
   WHILE test not found DO
     IF processor is Master THEN
       IF WORK-REQUEST message received from processor p_{idle};
       Broadcast QUERY message to all processors;
       Receive workload on each processor;
       Identify busiest processor p_{busy};
       Send SPLIT-WORK message to p_{busy} to split its stack
         and give half to p_{idle};
     ELSE if processor is Slave THEN
       Check messages from other processor;
       IF a TESTFOUND, NOTEST or ABORT message received
         THEN Terminate search;
       Execute one iteration of PODEM search loop;
       IF a test is generated for the given fault THEN

           Report test;
           Send TESTFOUND messages to all processors;
           Terminate search;
       IF backtrack limit is exceeded THEN
           Terminate search;
           Check if other processors terminated;
           Last processor to terminate sends ABORT messages;
       IF local search space is exhausted THEN
           Send a WORK-REQUEST messages to Master;
           Received half search space from most loaded processor;
       IF QUERY message received from Master processor
           Send current workload to Master;
       IF a SPLIT-WORK(p_{idle}) message is received from Master processor
           THEN split stack and send half to processor p_{idle};
       IF all search spaces exhausted and no test found
           THEN Send NOTEST messages;
   END WHILE
   END FORALL
   End Procedure

     The function of the master scheduler is to coordinate the activities of the remaining slave processors. It receives messages from the slave processors and carries out actions based on the type of message. After gate under test and the fault type (s-a-1 or s-a-0) are broadcast to each processor, the scheduler maintains a list of slave processors that are busy generating a test for the current fault. This list is maintained in the form of a queue and is called a *donor queue*. Initially, processor 1 starts generating a test for the fault assuming it has the whole search space. At the beginning of test generation for a particular fault, the donor queue is initialized to include processor 1. The remaining processors do not send an explicit message for requesting work, but send a NOTEST message indicating that the search space is empty and that they require more work.

     Dynamic load balancing is implicit in the scheduling algorithms given previously. The scheduling processor is not allowed to execute PODEM to make sure that its does not become a bottleneck as the number of processors is increased. The algorithhm described uses a centralized scheduler.

     We can design an algorithm in which the scheduling operation is distributed. In such an algorithm, the processor that is looking for work queries all other processors for their workload and then gets a portion of the search space from the most loaded processor. An outline of the parallel algorithm for test generation called *DM-PARALLEL-COMB-ATPG-SEARCH-DIST* (denoting a distributed memory parallel algorithm for test generation of combinational circuits using search-parallel search space decomposition with distributed scheduling) follows:

Procedure *DM-PARALLEL-COMB-ATPG-SEARCH-DIST;*
Read circuit and list of faults;

Compute controllability and observability measures;
Select a fault;
FORALL processors in PARALLEL DO
   WHILE test not found DO
      Check messages from other processor;
      IF a TESTFOUND, NOTEST or ABORT message received
         THEN Terminate search;
      Execute one iteration of PODEM search loop;
      IF a test is generated for the given fault THEN
         Report test;
         Send TESTFOUND messages to all processors;
         Terminate search;
      IF backtrack limit is exceeded THEN
         Terminate search;
         Check if other processors terminated;
         Last processor to terminate sends ABORT messages;
      IF local search space is exhausted THEN
         Search for remaining search spaces among other processors;
         Send a WORK-REQUEST messages to processor with
           largest search space;
      IF all search spaces exhausted and no test found
         THEN Send NOTEST messages;
      IF a WORK-REQUEST message is received from a processor
         THEN split the stack and send half to the processor
   END WHILE
   END FORALL
   End Procedure

Implementation   The PODEM-based test generator using parallel branch and bound has been implemented by Patil and Banerjee on a 16-processor Intel iPSC/2™ hypercube using the centralized scheduling algorithm [78, 79]. The hard-to-detect (HTD) faults were first filtered out using a uniprocessor implementation of PODEM. A backtrack limit of 25 was used for the uniprocessor algorithm, and all faults dropped by a particular heuristic were classified as HTD faults. To demonstrate that the efficiency of the parallel algorithm is independent of the testability measure used, both random selection (heuristic RANDOM) and the SCOAP heuristic were used.

The faults dropped by the RANDOM and SCOAP heuristics were used as HTD faults for obtaining speedup numbers. For a fair comparison with the uniprocessor results, the total backtrack limit over all processors was kept the same as the backtrack limit for the uniprocessor implementation. In the parallel implementation, the backtrack limit per processor was kept at 25. For example, since the total backtrack limit over four processors is $3 \times 25 = 75$ (one processor acts as a scheduler and does not take part in test generation), the uniprocessor backtrack limit was increased to 75. Similarly, for comparison with the eight-processor results,

TABLE 8.5 Runtimes (Seconds) and Speedups of Parallel Test Generation on the Intel iPSC/2™ Hypercube for Hard-to-detect (HTD) Faults

Circuit	HTD Faults	1 Processor		16 Processors	
		HTD Coverage	Runtime (Speedup)	HTD Coverage	Runtime (Speedup)
c432	5	0.00	14.0 (1.0)	20.00	1.2 (11.6)
c1355	14	14.29	58.2 (1.0)	28.57	7.8 (7.5)
c2670	203	31.53	952.8 (1.0)	56.65	92.7 (10.3)
c6288	24	20.83	519.1 (1.0)	91.67	18.4 (28.2)
c7552	434	35.48	2859.6 (1.0)	75.12	374.1 (7.6)

the uniprocessor backtrack limit was 175, and for the 16-processor results, the uniprocessor backtrack limit was 375. The parallel and the uniprocessor algorithms with the scaled-up backtrack limits were run on the ISCAS-85 circuits [15] for the HTD faults. It was observed from the experiments that the parallel implementation performs much better than the uniprocessor version in most cases, both with respect to the HTD fault coverage and the time per HTD fault.

Table 8.5 shows some example results on several ISCAS-85 combinational benchmark circuits of the runtimes (in seconds) and speedups of the parallel algorithm for test generation using the SCOAP heuristic on the Intel iPSC/2™ hypercube multiprocessor.

The speedups were on the average about 10 on 16 processors, with the lowest being 7 and the highest being 28. In some cases, the speedups were superlinear due to search anomalies, e.g., c6288 showed a speedup of 28 on 16 processors. The message passing overheads were low since messages are passed only to get work and to inform the scheduler of completion. Due to the nondeterminism introduced by parallel execution, sometimes increase in the number of processors can cause a small increase or decrease in the fault coverage. On the average, the parallel implementation performed much better than the uniprocessor implementation.

It should be pointed out here that for the special case of redundant faults, the parallel algorithm will have to search through the *same* nodes as the serial algorithm before proving the fault to be redundant. This is because for redundant faults, the entire search space will have to be implicitly enumerated. Thus the speedup for redundant faults will be at most N, where N is the number of processors.

A related parallel search method to search different portions of the decision tree of an ATPG algorithm in parallel was proposed in [61], but the search-space allocation strategy did not use any heuristics to increase the probability of searching in a solution area. This approach may result in fruitless search for an input vector in a nonsolution area even though a solution may exist. A dedicated processor was used that scheduled partially specified test vectors for test generation on multiple processors.

Recently, Arvindam et al. [9] have reported a parallel implementation of a similar parallel algorithm for ATPG on a network of SUN™ workstations. They reported results on the ISCAS-85 combinational circuits [15] with the total backtrack limit set equal for both the serial and parallel algorithms at about 25,000 bactracks. Speedups of about 3.5 to 8 (superlinear) were reported on four processors.

Shared Memory MIMD Parallel Algorithm We now describe a shared memory MIMD parallel algorithm for test generation that is based on a modification of the preceding algorithm for distributed memory multiprocessors. In such an algorithm, each processor keeps a local stack of the search space and executes iterations of the PODEM search loop. When a processor exhausts its independent search space, it requests work from another processor. The donor processor then splits its search stack and gives half of its search space to the requesting processor. An outline of the parallel test generation algorithm *SM-PARALLEL-COMB-ATPG-SEARCH* (denoting shared memory parallel algorithm for test generation of combinational circuits using search parallel decomposition) is given next.

Procedure *SM-PARALLEL-COMB-ATPG-SEARCH;*
Read circuit and list of faults;
Select a fault;
FORALL processors in PARALLEL DO
  WHILE test not found DO
    Check shared flags TESTFOUND,NOTEST, ABORT;
    IF TESTFOUND, or ABORT, or NOTEST flags are set
      THEN terminate search;
    Execute one iteration of PODEM search loop;
    IF a test is generated for the given fault THEN
      Report test; Set TESTFOUND flag; terminate search;
    IF backtrack limit is exceeded THEN
      Set ABORT flag; terminate search;
    IF local search space is exhausted THEN
      Search for remaining search spaces of other processors;
      Set a WRK-REQ flag in processor with
        largest search space;
    IF all search spaces exhausted and no test found
      THEN Set NOTEST flag;
    IF a WRK-REQ flag is set from a processor
      THEN split the stack and give it to the processor
  END WHILE
END FORALL
End Procedure

We now describe another shared memory MIMD parallel algorithm for test generation of combinational circuits using search parallelism. The algorithm is based on work reported by Venkatraman, Seth, and Agrawal [96].

The test generation algorithm is based on Boolean satisfiability, and not on PODEM. While PODEM is based on the structural properties of the circuit, Boolean satisfiability is

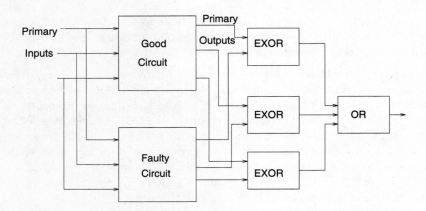

Figure 8.17 Boolean difference formulation (Courtesy of Venkataraman, Seth and Agrawal, Univ. of Nebraska Tech. Report, 1992)

based on the functional properties of the circuit. Given a line stuck type fault, the Boolean satisfiability approach constructs a formula representing the Boolean difference between the good and the faulty circuit. An input assignment that satisfies the formula is a test for the fault and, conversely, any test for the fault satisfies the formula. The formula in conjunctive normal form, or CNF, is composed of clauses with two literals (2CNF) and three literals (3CNF). Finding a satisfiability solution for 2CNF clauses is referred to as 2SAT, and a satisfying solution for 3CNF is 3SAT.

We now describe how a CNF formula can be associated with a logic circuit. For example, a two-input OR gate, with inputs A and B and output C, would contribute two CNF terms, $\bar{A} + C$ and $\bar{B} + C$, and a 3CNF term $A + B + \bar{C}$. The formula for the entire circuit is obtained by a conjunction of the terms for individual gates.

The construction of the Boolean difference formula can now be understood with respect to the circuit in Figure 8.17. It can be verified that the output of the circuit is true if and only if the input assignment is a test for the fault. Thus a CNF of the circuit in the figure is the Boolean difference formula. The formula for the faulty circuit can be derived from the fault-free circuit by renaming variables for the wires that are affected by the fault, the wires that are in the forward cone of the fault site.

The solutions to the 2SAT and 3SAT problems are obtained using heuristics. An implication graph is constructed from the 2CNF clauses by creating nodes for each distinct literal in the 2CNF, and two edges $(\bar{A}, B)$, and $(\bar{B}, A)$, representing the implications $\bar{A} \Rightarrow B$ and $\bar{B} \Rightarrow A$ for each conjuctive clause $(A + B)$. To find a satisfying assignment, the variables are bound to true or false in this graph so that the assignment leads to a conflict-free assignment in the implication graph and does not falsify any 3SAT clauses. Since there are an exponential number of 2SAT solutions to try, heuristics are employed to speed up the search for one that also satisfies the 3CNF clauses. The heuristics are used to order the variables in some way to perform the search for a consistent set of assignments.

At this point, the ATPG algorithm resorts to an ordered search of inputs to which various assignments are made until a consistent set of assignments is found that makes the output of the circuit in Figure 8.17 true. We can therefore modify the shared memory parallel algorithm for test generation using PODEM described at the beginning of this section to produce a parallel algorithm using Boolean satifiability.

The search-space partitioning among processors in a parallel processing system is very similar to the algorithm described earlier. In the static partitioning, the search space is split into equal-sized disjoint subspaces, and each subspace is assigned to one processor. The variables are ordered by some heuristics of the serial algorithm. If 2^n processors are available, each processor is assigned the subspace defined by a unique assignment to the first n variables. It is supplied with its own implication graph and 3CNF clauses. After these initial assignments, it can explore the subspace assigned to it independently to find a test.

In the dynamic partitioning approach, each processor is given a complete copy of the implication graph, and the set of 3CNF clauses so that it can proceed independently to find a solution. When one processor finds a solution, it stops all other processors. When all processors exhaust their search spaces without a solution, the fault is declared to be redundant. In the dynamic algorithm, whenever a processor becomes available, a processor having work splits its search space by scanning its set of assignments for the first available *choice point*. A choice point is a variable that has been bound to a value, and the alternative value is yet to be tried. The donor processor splits the work at this choice point and passes the partial assignment list (up to the choice point) to the new processor. After this, the donor processor adjusts its search space to reflect this reduced work. The free processor, on receiving the work, initializes the implication graph with the partial assignment list and assigns the alternative value to the choice point. Then the free processor carries out the implications of these assignments to re-create the starting state of the implication graph. After initialization, a processor starts exploring its search space looking for a test.

An outline of the parallel test generation algorithm *SM-PARALLEL-COMB-ATPG-SEARCH-BOOL* (denoting shared memory parallel algorithm for test generation of combinational circuits using search parallel decomposition and Boolean satisfiability) is given next.

Procedure *SM-PARALLEL-COMB-ATPG-SEARCH-BOOL;*
Read circuit and list of faults;
Select a fault;
Construct 2CNF, 3CNF clauses,
and implication graph;
FORALL processors in PARALLEL DO
   WHILE test not found DO
     Check shared flags TESTFOUND,NOTEST, ABORT;
     IF TESTFOUND, or ABORT, or NOTEST flags are set
       THEN terminate search;
     Execute one iteration of BOOLEAN search loop;
     IF a test is generated for the given fault THEN
       Report test; Set TESTFOUND flag; terminate search;

IF search limit is exceeded THEN
    Set ABORT flag; terminate search;
IF local search space is exhausted THEN
    Search for remaining search spaces of other processors;
    Set a WRK-REQ flag in processor with
        largest search space;
IF all search spaces exhausted and no test found
    THEN Set NOTEST flag;
IF a WRK-REQ flag is set from a requesting processor
    THEN split the search space at choice point
        and give it to requesting processor
        Donor processor passes partial assignment list
        (upto the choice point) to the new processor;
        Donor processor adjusts its search space;
IF requesting processor THEN
    Initialize implication graph with partial assignment;
    Assign alternate value to choice point;
    Perform implications of assignments;
    Start exploring its search space;
  END WHILE
END FORALL
End Procedure

Implementation   Venkatraman et al. have reported an implementation of the preceding algorithm on a Sequent Symmetry™ shared memory multiprocessor [96]. Table 8.6 shows some example results on several ISCAS-85 combinational benchmark circuits [15] of the result quality (hard-to detect faults that are detected or proved redundant), the runtimes (in seconds), and the speedups of the parallel algorithm for test generation using a combination of different heuristics on the Sequent multiprocessor.

8.6.3 Search Parallel Approach for Sequential Circuits

We will now describe a search parallel algorithm for sequential circuit test generation based on work reported by Patil, Banerjee, and Patel [80]. We briefly review the uniprocessor algorithm for synchronous sequential circuits, which was presented earlier in Section 8.2. A conceptual model of a synchronous sequential circuit is shown in Figure 8.6(a) and its ILA interpretation is shown in Figure 8.6(b). The lines collectively labeled PI are the primary inputs and the lines labeled as PO are the primary outputs.

We now describe how test generation is performed using the ILA representation of a sequential circuit. First, a fault is injected into each time frame. A nine-valued logic [63] is used, which results in a minimal specification of signal values, which are represented as a pair of logic values denoting the good circuit and fault circuit values.

The first phase in the test generation process consists of *forward-time processing (FTP)*; the test vectors are generated in the order in which they are applied. In the FTP phase, the fault is propagated across time frames until it reaches a primary output. Testability measures

TABLE 8.6 Result Quality (HTD Faults Detected or Proved Redundant), Runtimes (Seconds) and Speedups of Parallel Test Generation on Sequent Symmetry for Hard-to-detect (HTD) Faults

	HTD	1 Processor		6 Processors	
Circuit	Faults	HTD det. + red.	Runtime (speedup)	HTD det. + red.	Runtime (speedup)
c432	12	11	99.8 (1.0)	12	8.0 (12.3)
c499	20	20	32.5 (1.0)	20	3.8 (8.5)
c2670	94	94	275.3 (1.0)	94	123.5 (2.2)
c6288	10	7	226.8 (1.0)	10	43.9 (5.1)
c7552	650	628	2100.5 (1.0)	650	887.9 (2.4)

are used to guide the propagation so that the FTP phase can be accomplished using as few time frames as possible. The FTP phase results in an assignment of values to the pseudo-inputs and primary inputs in the time frames necessary to propagate the fault. The vector specifying the pseudo-input values in the time frame in which the fault is first excited specifies the initial state S_0 in which the machine should be for the fault propagation and excitation to be successful.

The *reverse-time processing phase* or the *state justification phase* is triggered by the initial state vector S_0 generated by the FTP phase. The purpose of the RTP phase is to generate a sequence of vectors that results in the initial state S_0. Since these vectors are generated in an order opposite to the order in which they are applied, it is called the reverse-time processing phase. The RTP phase starts with the initial state S_0 and keeps going back in time until an all-unknown state or a reset state is reached. The PODEM algorithm is used to generate vectors during the RTP phase. Given a next-state vector that has to be realized at the end of the current time frame, only one physical time frame has to be used to generate the present state vector and the input vector. The present state vector forms the next-state vector for the next RTP step and the process stops when the present state vector is an all-unknown state or a reset state.

Shared Memory MIMD Parallel Algorithm We now discuss a parallel algorithm for sequential circuit ATPG based on search parallelism on a shared memory MIMD multiprocessor, based on work reported by Patil, Banerjee, and Patel [80]. It was shown in [79] that only a small percentage of faults (less than 10%) required parallel search (these were referred to as hard-to-detect or HTD faults). The remaining faults were detected using very few backtracks. The parallel branch and bound algorithm proposed in [79] has been extended to sequential circuits. However, since the size of the search space for sequential circuits is orders of magnitude higher than that for combinational circuits, more careful splitting of search space is required, as outlined next.

Conceptually, the parallel branch and bound technique is shown in Figure 8.18. All processors cooperate with each other in generating a test (if one exists) for the same fault. The decision trees before and after search-space splitting are shown. A node labeled $(x_n : i)$

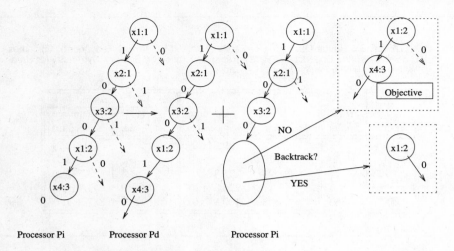

Figure 8.18 Search space allocation in sequential circuit ATPG

indicates that primary input (or pseudo-input during the RTP phase) x_n in time frame i has been assigned a value shown along the solid edge. The dashed edges indicate alternative values that have yet to be assigned.

An idle processor p_i requests work from a busy processor p_d. The processor p_d splits the search space between itself and p_i such that the number of choice points (or backtrack points) assigned to each processor is roughly equal. The treatment of the node at the leaf of the decision tree varies, depending on the test generation state of processor p_d. The splitting shown in Figure 8.18 may result in disjoint or overlapping search spaces, depending on the test generation state of processor p_d. In the case of disjoint splitting, processor p_d is made to take a path disjoint from that of processor p_i by taking the alternative choice at the terminal node. The test generation state is indicated by a flag that indicates whether the last step executed by a processor was a backtrace or a backtrack.

If the last step executed was a backtrace, it means that the processor has reached a consistent set of assignments (locally), which may lead to a test. In such a case, forcing the processor p_i to take a disjoint path may lead to fruitless search since the assignments made by processor p_d may be mandatory. In such a case, processor p_d stores the last choice point encountered during backtrace. When the search space is split between p_i and p_d, the terminal node is not split. Instead, only the choice points are split equally between p_i and p_d. Processor p_i uses the choice point stored by p_d as an initial objective to direct the search in a different direction.

If the last step executed by p_d was a backtrack, the search space is split in a disjoint fashion. The conditional splitting of the terminal node is shown in Figure 8.18. If the last step executed by processor p_d was a backtrack, processor p_i takes an alternative path at node $x_1 : 2$. If the last step executed by p_d was not a backtrack (it was a backtrace) p_i takes the same path as p_d, but with a temporary backtrace objective stored by p_d, which helps it in searching in a different solution area. This strategy helps in reducing useless search in nonsolution areas.

However, it should be noted that choice points are split in both cases, and the resultant search spaces allocated to both processors are in general smaller.

An outline of the shared memory parallel test generation algorithm *SM-PARALLEL-SEQUENTIAL-ATPG-SEARCH* (denoting shared memory parallel algorithm for test generation of sequential circuits using search parallel decomposition) is given next.

Procedure *SM-PARALLEL-SEQUENTIAL-ATPG-SEARCH;*
Read circuit and list of faults;
Select a fault;
FORALL processors in PARALLEL DO
   WHILE in PODEM loop DO
      Check shared flags TESTFOUND, ABORT, NOTEST;
      IF TESFOUND, ABORT, or NOTEST flags set THEN
         Report test;
         Set TESTFOUND;
         Terminate search;
      IF backtrack limit is exceeded
         THEN set ABORT flag in shared memory;
      IF search space is exhausted
         THEN search for other processor's search stacks;
            Set a WRK-REQ flag on most loaded processor;
      IF a WRK-REQ request is received by setting flag
         THEN split the stack and send it to the processor
            Note special conditions in splitting process;
            IF last step executed was backtrace THEN
               Do not split terminal node;
               Only split choice points;
            ELSE if last step was a backtrack
               Split search space in disjoint fashion;
   END WHILE
   END FORALL
End Procedure

In the preceding algorithm, the search space allocation takes place in a distributed fashion. This results in a better utilization of the available processors and prevents a single processor from becoming a bottleneck. It should be noted that this can be achieved because we have a shared memory multiprocessor, in which it is easy for an idle processor to look at the sizes of the workpool on each processor.

The idle processor p_i requests work from a processor p_d whose stack (or search space) has been split the least number of times. This ensures that p_i gets the largest chunk of work possible. Otherwise, p_i might exhaust the allocated search space and may need to request work repeatedly to remain busy, which may increase the synchronization overhead and increase the idle time. During the parallel search step, only the dynamic information (circuit state, and

TABLE 8.7 Result Quality (Coverage of Hard-to-detect Faults), Runtimes (Seconds) and Speedups of Parallel Test Generation on the Encore Multimax™ Multiprocessor

Circuit	HTD Faults	1 Processor		8 Processors	
		HTD Coverage (%)	Runtime (Speedup)	HTD Coverage (%)	Runtime (Speedup)
s208	35	34.29	225.6 (1.0)	31.43	47.8 (4.72)
s298	42	40.48	1938.9 (1.0)	42.86	136.1 (14.2)
s349	34	5.88	310.9 (1.0)	35.29	32.2 (9.6)
s713	22	81.88	280.9 (1.0)	81.88	56.5 (5.0)
s35932	297	43.10	11342.5 (1.0)	43.10	9206.0 (1.3)

the like) need be replicated across all processors while the static circuit graph is shared by all processors, thus reducing the memory overhead. The parallel search can take place under either a backtrack limit or a time limit. If a backtrack limit is used, each processor maintains its own backtrack limit counter in the shared memory. When the sum of backtracks across all processors exceeds the specified backtrack limit, test generation is aborted. Similarly, if a time limit is used, a shared *timeout* flag indicates whether the time limit is exceeded. All processors check the timeout flag periodically and also check their local clock. If a processor finds that the timeout flag has been set, it aborts test generation for the current fault. The timeout flag is set by the first processor that finds that its local clock has exceeded the time limit.

Implementation   Patil, Banerjee, and Patel have reported an implementation of the preceding parallel algorithm for sequential circuit test generation on an Encore Multimax shared memory multiprocessor [80]. Table 8.7 shows some example results on several ISCAS-89 sequential benchmark circuits [14] of the hard-to-detect fault coverages, the runtimes (in seconds), and speedups of the parallel algorithm for test generation on the Encore Multimax™ multiprocessor. It can be noted from the table that, depending on the circuit, we get superlinear speedups (for example circuit $s298$ gets speedup of 14 on eight processors), or get very poor speedups (for example, circuit $s35932$ gets speedup of 1.3 on eight processors). Such behavior is due to parallel search anomalies in search-space problems. It should be noted that the quality of the results is also different in the parallel algorithm over the serial algorithms due to search anomalies.

Distributed Memory MIMD Parallel Algorithm   We will now describe a distributed memory parallel algorithm for sequential circuits using a combination of fault parallelism and search parallelism that is based on work reported by Ramkumar and Banerjee [83]. The programming model for the parallel algorithm assumes a concurrent object-oriented model of computation such as the ones provide by the CHARM [29, 46] and PROPERCAD2 systems [73]. Conceptually, the PROPERCAD2 and CHARM systems maintain a pool of objects representing work that is created by the application program. Information is exchanged between these objects via messages. The objects in the work pool are distributed (and periodically balanced) across the available processors by the runtime system.

An outline of the parallel test generation algorithm *DM-PARALLEL-SEQUENTIAL-ATPG-SEARCH* (denoting distributed memory parallel algorithm for test generation of sequential circuits using search parallel decomposition) follows:

Procedure *DM-PARALLEL-SEQUENTIAL-ATPG-SEARCH;*
    Read circuit and list of faults;
    Initially create one object per fault
    Distribution of objects performed by runtime system;
    All processors maintain a bit vector (one bit per fault) and
        a count per fault for managing time/backtrack limits
    Every object carries a *depth bound* = # of PI/PSI's
        to be assigned in parallel

    FORALL processors in parallel DO
        WHILE there are objects to be executed in processor DO
        Select a object P for fault F;
        IF bit for F in bit vector is set
            THEN discard P;
        IF count for F indicates time/backtrack limit exceeded
            THEN discard P;
        IF number of PI/PSI's assigned for fault F
            is less than *depth bound*
        THEN
                Get next PI/PSI according to chosen heuristic;
                Create one object for two assignments to next PI/PSI;
                Terminate object P;
        ELSE
                Perform test generation *sequentially*
                using best available uniprocessor algorithm;
                IF test vectors found for F *or* F aborted THEN
                    Set bit for fault F on local processor;
                IF test vectors found THEN
                     Run fault simulator;
                     Set bits in bit vector for all faults covered;
                     Broadcast bit vector to all other processors;
                     Update count for Fault F;
                     Broadcast count to all other processors;
        END WHILE

        IF message is bit vector (due to broadcast) THEN
            Bitwise OR bit vector with local processor bit vector;

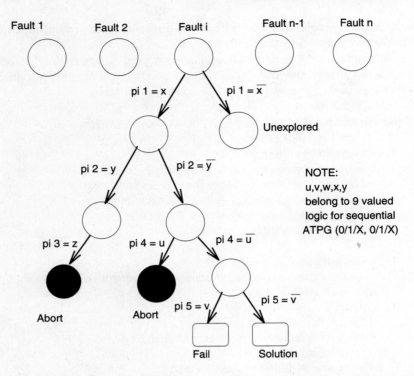

Figure 8.19 Typical search space created by the parallel test generator

```
        IF message is a count for Fault F THEN
            Update local copy of count for Fault F;
    END FORALL
End Procedure
```

In the parallel algorithm, illustrated in Figure 8.19, initially only one process is created per fault. Note that the destination processor for the test generator objects is not provided. The underlying kernel on the distributed memory multiprocessor is responsible for load balancing these objects.

When an object for fault F is picked up for execution, the next primary or pseudo-input pi to be assigned is identified (together with its assigned value v and the time frame in which the assignment was made), based on heuristics defined in the uniprocessor code. Typically, this is one iteration of the PODEM loop in which no backtracks are permitted. Two objects are then created: one carries the assignment v to pi and the second object carries the assignment $pi = $ complement of v. The two objects thus represent two disjoint regions of the search space defined by the choice point at pi on the stack. The creation of objects in this manner is carried on recursively. At any node N in the search tree, object P representing N carries the sequence of assignments to primary or pseudo-inputs carried by its parent object together with the assignment made to the *next* primary or pseudo-input at N. Assignments made in the parallel search space are not *backtrackable*. Should the current set of assignments lead to a conflict, the object simply terminates. The recursion terminates at a predefined depth in the search space.

When the recursion is terminated, each leaf node L in the parallel search space represents a sequence of assignments to primary or pseudo inputs made along the path from the root of the search tree to L. The uniprocessor test generator is then invoked with these assignments to primary or pseudo-inputs marked as fixed nonbacktrackable assignments. Objects representing these nodes in the search space are the *leaf* objects in the parallel search tree. The remainder of the search is then performed sequentially until a user-specified time limit or backtrack limit has been reached.

To ensure that wasted effort is minimized, each processor maintains (1) one count per fault to maintain the total elapsed time (or backtracks) for the fault across all the processors, and (2) a bit vector with 1 bit per fault to identify the faults that have been covered or aborted and are no longer to be processed. Whenever an object is picked up for evaluation, the bit vector is first checked to ensure that the object represents useful work. In addition, the count is checked to ensure that the time limit for the fault has not elapsed. If the object is not redundant, execution continues as outlined previously. As soon as an object has been executed, the count for a given fault is updated (either elapsed time or backtracks). Whenever a *leaf* object for a fault is executed, the value of the count for that fault is broadcast to the other processors. Whenever a vector sequence is found for a fault, a fault simulator is invoked (using random fill-in of X assignments) to cover as many faults as possible. The bits representing all the covered faults in the local processor's bit vector are set, and the bit vector is broadcast to all the other processors.

The data-flow style of execution is very effective in overcoming the cost of communication incurred by periodic broadcasts of the fault counts and the fault bit vector. This is because computation is overlapped with communication whenever possible, thereby yielding a very high utilization of the available processors.

An interesting feature of the parallel algorithm is that the programmer can influence the order in which messages in the work pool are picked for processing by assigning priorities to them. We now describe the use of priorities to guide the parallel search and control wasted computation in detail.

In test generation for sequential circuits, fault ordering has been shown to have a significant effect on the total execution time [67]. As a result, a preprocessing pass is often used to determine a good fault ordering. In the parallel algorithm, we therefore create one object per fault in the fault set and assign them priorities that reflect the ordering from such a preprocessing pass.

Three parameters control the amount of processing time devoted to a fault. Every object created for a given fault is assigned a priority, a time slice and a bound on the depth of the parallel search space. Initially, the priority of a fault is determined by the fault ordering. The initial time slice assigned to each fault is an arbitrary constant, typically 1 second (unless the user specified bound is smaller). The depth of the parallel search space for a fault is initially zero, that is, no OR parallelism is exploited in the first time slice.

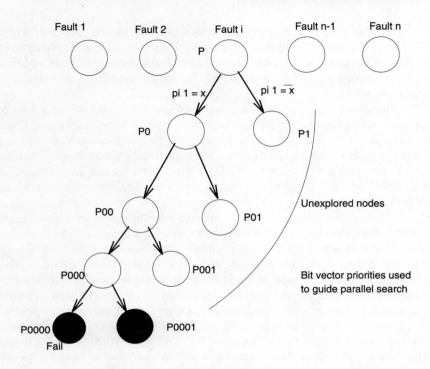

Figure 8.20 Use of priorities to guide the parallel search

Every fault is assigned a time slice t_1. If no solution is found within that time slice, the time slice is increased to $min(T, t_2)$ where $t_2 = c * t_1, c > 1$. However, at the same time, the priority of the fault is decreased such that it has lower priority than all the priorities of faults with a current time slice of t_1. In this scheme, 0 is the highest priority available. Initially, fault i in the fault ordering is assigned priority i. If there are N faults in the fault set, when the time slice t_1 is exhausted for i, the priority of i is changed to $N + i$, now with time slice t_2. Furthermore, when the time slice is increased, the fault is recognized to be a hard-to-detect fault. At this point, the fault becomes a candidate for parallel search, and the maximum depth of the parallel search space is increased by a user-defined constant. This process is repeated iteratively until the user-specified overall time limit for each fault is reached. At this point the execution terminates.

We now focus our attention on parallel search in the search space for a given fault. As mentioned earlier, a major problem encountered in parallel test generation is the presence of search anomalies. These anomalies result in a wide variation in execution time and fault coverage from run to run. For parallel test generation to become practical, it is extremely important to be able to provide consistently good speedups and quality comparable to that of a uniprocessor run.

To provide consistent speedups, priorities are assigned to nodes in the order that they are visited by the underlying uniprocessor test generator. Bit vectors are used to represent priorities; two bit vectors are compared using lexicographic ordering. In lexicographic ordering, bits are compared from left to right, and bit 0 has higher priority than bit 1. For example, the bit vector 00100 has higher priority than 01. The assignment of priorities to nodes in the search space for a fault is illustrated in Figure 8.20. The use of priorities in this manner for combinatorial search was proposed in [88, 97].

This assignment of priorities ensures that the available processors focus their effort in the leftmost, bottommost region of the search space. This maximizes the likelihood that the search is performed in a region that would have been explored during uniprocessor search. To minimize any wasted computation in the upper region of the search space, a technique called *delayed release* [88] is used. To illustrate this, consider the nodes with priorities P1, P01, and P001 in Figure 8.20. Processes representing these nodes are not released into the work pool until a leaf object is encountered. This is accomplished by carrying these objects down the left branch of the search space and releasing them only when a leaf object is encountered. Thus, available processors pick objects with the highest priority, that is, nodes toward the left and bottom of the search space.

We described earlier how progressive time limits are handled when no search-space parallelism is exploited. The presence of search-space parallelism presents an interesting problem in the implementation of progressive time limits. Recall that several objects representing different nodes in the search space for the same fault may be present in the work pool. One or more of these objects may even be under execution by different processors.

Whenever a time slice is completed for a fault F without finding a solution, a high-priority message is broadcast to all the processors notifying them of the time spent on F. Furthermore, the state of the current object is saved and the object is deposited in the work pool with lower priority, as described earlier.

But what about the other object created for fault F (for example, the objects with priority P1, P01 and P001 in Figure 8.20)? Recall that whenever a object is picked up by a processor, a check is made to determine whether the object represents useful work. At the same time, if it is determined that the current time slice for the object has expired, the object is redeposited into the work pool with the lower priority. There remains the problem of ensuring that the priorities of all the objects created for fault F do not change relative to each other. For example, if the objects in Figure 8.20 are all reassigned a lower priority, it is necessary to replace priority $P\alpha$ with $(P + N)\alpha$, where N is the total number of faults in the fault set, and α is an arbitrary bit string. Since the overall time limit T imposed by the user is known, the number of steps in the progression is also known. Thus, preallocating the necessary number of bits to represent the fault priorities $P + kN \leq T, k = 0, 1, \ldots$, is sufficient.

Recently, Parkes, Banerjee, and Patel have reported [72] a different distributed memory MIMD parallel algorithm using search-space parallelism based on the HITEC algorithm for test generation of sequential circuits [67] To understand the parallel algorithm, it is important to clarify the underlying algorithm used in HITEC.

The most successful combinational and sequential ATPG algorithms are based on the PODEM algorithm, itself a descendant of the D algorithm. PODEM differs from the D algorithm in the set of potential assumptions that the algorithm will consider. Whereas the D algorithm will assume values on internal nodes, PODEM will assume values only on primary inputs; this reduces the number of backtracks the algorithm may have to execute, speeding the overall process. The extension of PODEM to sequential circuits is straightforward. The sequential circuit is modeled as an infinite iterative array of identical copies of the combination portion of the circuit. The latch outputs of each time frame form the latch inputs of the next time frame.

HITEC uses an extension of the PODEM approach. It uses the notion of a *targeted D-frontier*. Since the calculation of all implications of an assignment is NP complete, test generation algorithms only compute a subset of all implications. One way of maximizing the size of this subset is to maintain a D-frontier, the set of nodes closest to the primary outputs that have a D or $\bar{D}$ value. For each element of the frontier set, the set of *dominators* is found; that is, the set of single assignments required to justify the frontier element. The dominator sets for each element are then intersected; the result of the intersection is a set of implications that is necessary to justify every possible propagation path to a primary output.

HITEC does not perform the intersection operation. Instead, the frontier element most likely to propagate to a primary output is identified and a D or $\bar{D}$ value is *assumed* on that node. The number of implications that can be derived from this assumption is much larger than the implications resulting from the intersection of every possible propagation path. However, since a value is being assumed, this operation is a bactrackable decision; if further processing determines that the assignment cannot be propagated or justified, it must be backtracked and another element of the frontier chosen. If all elements of the frontier are exhausted without generating a test, a prior assignment must be backtracked or, if none exists, the fault is untestable because the fault effect is not observable.

The parallel algorithm for test generation uses *fault-parallelism* and *decision-parallelism* (see Figure 8.21.)

Fault-parallel execution is simply the process of partitioning the set of undetected faults among the available processors and running the test generation algorithm in parallel. Implementation of fault parallelism is relatively easy, since test generation for different faults is by and large independent.

In *decision-parallel* execution, when a backtrackable decision is made, rather than performing a depth-first search of the alternatives, new test generator objects are created in parallel to explore the alternatives. In PODEM, the only decisions are input assignments, so the object graph for each fault is a binary tree. In HITEC, backtrackable decisions are also made on the targeted D-frontier; therefore, each node in the search graph is either an input assignment with two out-edges representing the alternative assignments or a D assignment with N out-edges, where N is the number of nodes in the D frontier when one was targeted.

Only one significant change is required to HITEC heuristics to implement decision parallelism. The change stems from the ability to pass information up the search tree in serial depth-first search. When a backtrack occurs in a depth-first search, information gained in detecting the backtrack can be passed up the search tree to influence the backtracking process itself. HITEC utilizes such information when a state-justification failure occurs. When such a condition occurs, a flag is set indicating that any decision alternatives that do not change the state-justification target should be backtracked immediately. When a decision alternative results in a different state for justification, normal operation resumes.

When decision parallelism is used, a breadth-first-like search is employed. Since decision alternatives no longer execute strictly in sequence, there is no way to pass the flag

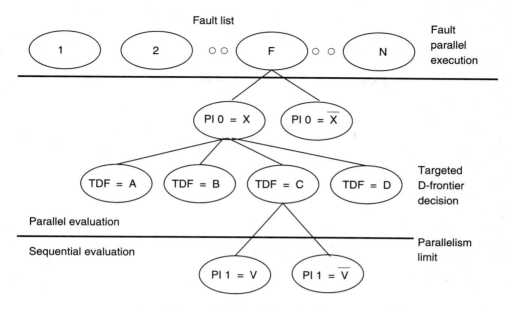

Figure 8.21 Parallelism in parallel HITEC

among them. Fortunately, this information is closely related to the failed states array already maintained by the fault database. In fact, it is easy to show that for those cases where the flag is set, the backtracked state must be in the failed states array. Checking the failed states array is actually more accurate, since a backtrack that does change the state may simply change it to another failed state, a condition that the original HITEC algorithm does not detect. Since the amount of processing required to check the failed states array is more than that required to simply to test a flag, the choice of which technique to use dependents on the relative amount of time required to check the array versus that required to perform the useless work of exploring nonsolution alternatives.

Implementation   Ramkumar and Banerjee [83] have reported an implementation of the preceding parallel algorithm for sequential circuit test generation on an Intel iPSC/860™ hypercube. Table 8.8 shows the results of the fault coverage, runtimes (in seconds), and the speedups of the parallel algorithm.

  The second parallel algorithm using HITEC has been implemented by Parkes, Banerjee and Patel [72] on top of the portable object-oriented parallel programming environment called ProperCAD II [73] described in Chapter 10. Speedups of about 4.5 on eight processors have been reported on the algorithm on an Intel iPSC/860™ hypercube.

8.7 FUNCTIONAL PARALLEL TEST GENERATION

8.7.1 Overview

Functional parallelism arises in algorithms using a divide and conquer type of approach in which a task is divided into a series of subtasks, all of which have to be completed. These

TABLE 8.8 Runtimes (Seconds) and Speedups of Parallel Test Generation on the Intel iPSC/860™ Hypercube

		1 Processor		8 Processors	
		Fault	Runtime	Fault	Runtime
Circuit	Faults	Coverage	(Speedup)	Coverage	(Speedup)
s386	384	100.0	187.1 (1.0)	100.0	30.1 (6.2)
s713	581	98.8	30.7 (1.0)	98.8	7.6 (4.0)
s1196	1242	100.0	15.6 (1.0)	100.0	4.1 (3.8)
s1238	1355	100.0	24.0 (1.0)	100.0	4.9 (4.9)
s5378	4603	75.3	6201.3 (1.0)	72.7	940.3 (6.6)

subtasks can be executed in parallel if they do not access or modify any common variables. If they have common variables, execution of the AND-parallel subtasks becomes complicated due to variable binding conflicts. The overheads due to variable binding conflicts may essentially reduce the AND-parallel tasks to sequential execution due to consistency checking and the like. In a logic circuit, reconvergent fan-out is one source of variable binding conflict.

Most serial ATPG algorithms developed thus far are difficult to parallelize through functional parallel techniques. The few subtasks that can be identified, such as fault sensitization, path sensitization, and justification, are not independent. That is, action taken to perform one of these processes may change the circuit state such that it has a side effect or causes an inconsistency in another process. Two goals cannot be justified simultaneously unless they consist of assigning values to two separate basis nodes. One way to allow parallelism in justification is to perform justification for goals in different faults simultaneously.

8.7.2 Distributed Memory MIMD Parallel Algorithm

We now describe a distributed memory parallel algorithm for test generation using functional parallelism based on work reported by Motohara et al. [61]. The fault list of the circuit is divided into groups of related faults. An example group of related faults includes those in a particular fan-out cone. Each group of faults is sent to a cluster of processors that includes a test generator and a fault simulator. The test generator takes the first fault and generates a test for it using the PODEM algorithm with a limited number of backtracks. If a test is not generated, it is considered as a hard-to-detect fault. If a test is found, it is sent to a fault simulator node, which runs a concurrent fault simulator on its group of faults. The faults that are detected by fault simulation are removed from the fault list. This technique reduces the size of both the remaining fault list to be processed by the ATPG algorithm and the test set itself.

An outline of the parallel test generation algorithm *DM-PARALLEL-COMB-ATPG-FUNC* (denoting distributed memory parallel algorithm for test generation of combinational circuits using functional parallel decomposition) is given next.

Procedure *DM-PARALLEL-COMB-ATPG-FUNC;*

Partition fault lists into related faults, e.g. fan-out cones;
Assign a partition of faults to a cluster (pair) of processors;
FORALL clusters of processors in PARALLEL DO
   REPEAT
      WHILE cluster's own fault list not empty DO
         IF (processor = test generator) THEN
            Select a fault f_i from own fault list;
            Perform ATPG to determine test t_i for fault f_i;
            t_i = PODEM-COMBINATIONAL-ATPG(f_i);
         IF (processor = fault simulator) THEN
            Fault simulate on Own fault list for test t_i;
            Remove detected faults from own fault list;
      END WHILE
   UNTIL all faults detected or aborted
END FORALL
End Procedure

An extension to this scheme involves a dynamic allocation of the test generation and fault simulation tasks to the processors of a cluster. Suppose the fault list is again partitioned into groups of related faults and each sublist is assigned to a cluster of processors. The test generation processors in the cluster take faults from the list and perform deterministic ATPG using the PODEM algorithm on them. When a test is found, it is passed to a fault simulation processor, which performs fault simulation with it. If the faults being processed are easy-to-detect faults, the number of processors in the cluster doing ATPG and fault simulation will be roughly equal. If an ATPG processor runs into a hard-to-detect fault and begins to backtrack a lot, the number of tests being generated will decrease and the fault simulation processors will idle. If the system stops ATPG on the hard-to-detect faults after a certain number of backtracks, the work done thus far in searching the solution space will be wasted. A better solution is to take an idle fault simulation processor and put it to work generating a test for a hard-to-detect fault using search parallel decomposition of the search space. This method keeps the processors busy and minimizes wasted processing.

Implementation Motohara et al. [61] implemented a version of AND-parallel functional decomposition on a distributed memory multicomputer system called LINKS-1 consisting of 50 processors connected as a tree of processors, each of which was a Z8000 and had 1 Mbyte of memory. Figure 8.22 shows the system configuration of the various processors in a distributed computer system to perform the various subtasks.

In this scheme, the number of test generator nodes and fault simulator nodes per cluster was statically determined and was set to roughly equal numbers. In the system, the *fault table divider* processors were responsible for dividing the fault table prior to test pattern generation. The *fault table manager* processors manage fault subtables given by the FTD to each cluster of processors. The *test generator* processors perform the ATPG on the subfault list, and the *fault simulator* processors perform fault simulation on the fault subtables. Speedups of about 25 to 30 were obtained on 50 processors for two example circuits.

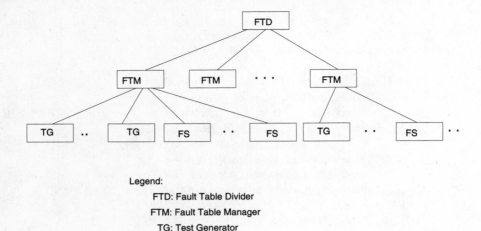

Legend:
FTD: Fault Table Divider
FTM: Fault Table Manager
TG: Test Generator
FS: Fault Simulator

Figure 8.22 System configuration for functional parallel test generation (Courtesy of Motohara et al., *Proc. Int. Conf. Computer-aided Design,* ©IEEE 1986)

8.7.3 Shared Memory MIMD Parallel Algorithm

The parallel test generation algorithm described previously used a very coarse-grain approach to generate functional parallel tasks. We now describe a fine-grain functional parallel approach to parallel test generation that has been proposed for sequential circuits and is suitable for execution on shared memory multiprocessors. The functional parallel algorithm is based on work reported by Patil [75].

A main bottleneck in any sequential circuit test generation algorithm is memory usage. Due to the time-space transformation of the sequential circuit into an iterative logic array, the memory usage increases with the test sequence length for a single fault. Due to memory limitations, conventional sequential circuit test generation algorithms defer justification of values on pseudo-inputs until all requirements on the current time frame have been satisfied. This might impede early detection of conflicts since some of the assignments already made may be unjustifiable. This will not be discovered until the processing for the current time frame is completed and another time frame is expanded.

As an example, consider a sequential circuit in the reverse-time processing phase. Given the required next state vector (values to be realized on the pseudo-outputs), the test generation algorithm tries to come up with a primary input assignment and a present state vector (assignments to the pseudo-inputs) that will give rise to the next-state vector. However, the assignments on the pseudo-inputs are delayed until all the requirements for the current time frame have been satisfied. This is an example of a space-time trade-off for which early detection of a conflict is sacrificed to save space. If, instead of waiting for all assignments in the current time frame, the justification was performed all the way backward in time as soon as a value to a pseudo-input is assigned, it is very likely conflicts can be discovered early during

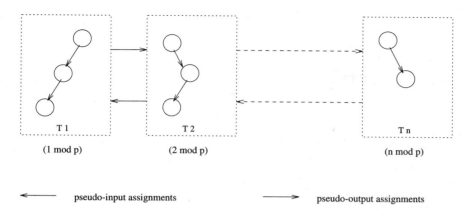

Figure 8.23 Distributed backtracking

the test generation process, resulting in an effective pruning of the search space. Since a uniprocessor implementation would require physically expanding all the time frames at once, this method is normally not used due to memory limitations. Let us now examine how this can be accomplished on a multiprocessor by distributing time frames *across* processors.

Figure 8.23 shows each time frame in the ILA model of a sequential circuit and the decision tree associated with each time frame during test generation. Suppose we have p processors and we are trying to generate a test for a fault that requires n time frames. Thus we can assign $\lceil n/p \rceil$ time frames to each processor where a processor is assigned time frame i if (i mod p) equals the processor ID (where the processor IDs are assumed to be from 0 to $p - 1$). This results in a cyclic assignment of time frames to processors, in which consecutive time frames are assigned to different processors. Since the test generation algorithms proceed through time frames in sequence (that is, for two consecutive assignments, as a result of a procedure such as backtrace, either assignments are made in the same time frame or in neighboring time frames). This assignment should be able to initiate concurrent waves of activity as opposed to an assignment of time frames in which a block of consecutive time frames are assigned to the same processor. Given this particular assignment of time frames where time frame i is assigned to processor (i mod p), let us see how test generation can proceed in parallel. The pseudo-outputs and pseudo-inputs can be considered to be communication channels by which signal requirements are exchanged. During the test generation process, if an assignment is made on a pseudo-input in time frame i by a processor owning the time frame, the processor owning time frame ($i - 1$) tries to justify the required value at the corresponding pseudo-output in time frame ($i - 1$). Thus, activity in time frame i and ($i - 1$) can proceed concurrently. The activity in time frame i proceeds in an optimistic fashion, that is, as if the values assigned at the pseudo-inputs have been realized. Similarly, justification objectives may be initiated due to assignments made on the pseudo-inputs in time frame ($i - 1$), giving rise to activity in time frame ($i - 2$). This is an example of concurrent waves of activity initiated backward in time. Concurrent activity can also occur forward in time during the FTP phase of test generation.

In cases for which the required objectives cannot be met, a backtrack message has to be communicated which forces an alternative value to be assigned to a pseudo-input. Also, in the process of justifying the objective value at a particular pseudo-output in time frame i, additional values may be implied at other pseudo-outputs, and this has to be communicated to the processor with time frame $(i + 1)$, which can update the corresponding values on the pseudo-inputs in time frame $(i + 1)$.

Consider Figure 8.23 again. The arrows between time frames in the figure indicate the backward and forward flow of information. The forward flow of information (time frame t_i to t_{i+1}) is due to pseudo-output assignments occurring in time frame t_i, and the backward flow of information (from t_i to t_{i-1}) is due to pseudo-input assignments occurring in time frame t_i. Thus it can be seen that implementation of the distributed backtracking method is very complex and will need very complicated distributed rollback and recovery schemes, such as the ones used in optimistic approaches to parallel event-driven simulation [45]. An efficient termination detection algorithm is also needed to evaluate whether all the assignments are consistent and whether there are no outstanding unjustified assignments. In most test generation algorithms, the testability measures are chosen such that assignments to pseudo-inputs are avoided as much as possible, unless the assignments are mandatory to realize some condition. This will result in large idle times across processors since the concurrent activity is initiated by assignments at the pseudo-inputs. The concurrency will also be limited by the inherently sequential waves of activity across time frames and high synchronization overheads. A complex distributed backtracking mechanism is needed to make sure that the entire search space is explored [24]. The deficiencies of this approach are very similar to those encountered during the implementation of AND parallelism.

An outline of the parallel test generation algorithm *SM-PARALLEL-SEQUENTIAL-ATPG-FUNC* (denoting shared memory parallel algorithm for test generation of combinational circuits using functional parallel decomposition) follows.

Procedure *SM-PARALLEL-SEQUENTIAL-ATPG-FUNC;*
Read circuit and list of faults;
REPEAT
   Select a fault f_i from own fault list;
   FORALL processors in PARALLEL DO
      Try to generate a test for fault f_i;
      WHILE objectives not met DO
         Expand time frames;
         Create new objectives in time frame i;
         Assign time frame i to processor (i mod P);
         IF (processor = i mod (P)) THEN
            Perform Forward-time-processing(i);
         IF (processor = i mod (P)) THEN
            Perform Reverse-time-processing(i);
         Propagate assignments between processors
            and time frames;
      END WHILE
      TV_i = test vector set for f_i;

Partition fault list among processors;
Fault simulate on Own fault list for test t_i;
Remove detected faults from own fault list;
END FORALL
UNTIL all faults detected or aborted
End Procedure

Owing to the difficulties described, an actual implementation of this system resulted in very little speedups [75].

8.8 CIRCUIT PARALLEL TEST GENERATION

8.8.1 Overview

We will now finally describe a parallel test generation method is based on circuit decomposition. In all the parallel approaches discussed thus far, each processor has a copy of the entire circuit. For extremely large circuits, the memory on each processor may not be large enough to store the entire circuit. In a circuit decomposed approach, each processor keeps a partition of the circuit and performs various test generation operations, such as justification and implication, on its own subcircuit to satisfy various test generation objectives.

Researchers have investigated various circuit partitioning strategies for logic simulation [81, 91]. Results have been presented on several partitioning schemes for logic simulation: natural, random, level-wise, input cones, output cones, and string-wise. The results indicated that for simulation, random partitioning performs best for concurrency but worst in interprocessor communication. Partitioning by fan-in and fan-out cones offers the best trade-off between concurrency and interprocessor communication, with fan-out cones being slightly better.

The optimum partitioning for ATPG will depend on the algorithm used. PODEM uses a simulation like process for justification; hence partitioning by fan-out cones may be best. However, the circuit activity in the D-algorithm tends to be along circuit levels, as during the advance of the D-frontier [86, 87]. Using the D-algorithm, partitioning by gate levels may produce better results. In any case, the partitioning must be done carefully to reduce interprocessor communication and to increase concurrency.

8.8.2 Distributed Memory MIMD Parallel Algorithm

We will now discuss a parallel algorithm for test generation using the circuit partitioned approach that is suitable for execution on distributed memory MIMD multicomputers. The algorithm is based on work reported by Bell et al. and Klenke et al. [10, 49]. In such a parallel algorithm, the system begins by assigning gates to any one of N partitions according to some heuristic, where N is the number of processors in the system. The partitions are generated using a simulated annealing algorithm that optimizes for reduced interpartition communications or good load balancing across partitions. The system then performs a D-algorithm based ATPG procedure on the partitioned circuits. The parallel implementation comprises two main procedures, one running on a master processor and another on the slave processors. A master processor has complete centralized control over the ATPG algorithm. The methods in the slave processors are used to initiate tasks that carry out the master processor's tasks. These tasks are the operations necessary to carry out the D-algorithm, such as propagation, justification, implication, and consistency.

The master processor is initialized with a test-cube stack, which is an array of test-cubes containing the circuit node values $(0,1,X, D, \overline{D})$. Processing of a fault begins in the master by placing a primitive D-cube of failure for the target fault in a test cube and pushing it in the stack. The master then sends the test cube with the PDCF in it to the partition in which the faulty gate resides. The slave processors also maintain a test-cube stack for the fault. Each slave processor carries out a propagation to either a primary output or its partition boundary. During this propagation, each assignment of a propagation D cube (PDC) to a gate in the partition results in pushing a test cube on the appropriate test-cube stack. Backtracking is accomplished by popping a test cube off the stack, choosing the next available PDC, assigning it to the gate and pushing the updated test cube. Each slave processor maintains a history of past operations, while the master processor maintains a history of the operations that it assigns to the slaves and their results.

When a slave processor propagates an assignment to the edge of its assigned partition, it returns the final state to the master processor. This test cube is pushed on the master's test-cube stack and then the master determines the list of the current D-frontiers. Depending on what value appears as the next D-frontier in this list, the master sends the current test cube to the appropriate slave processor object for another propagation.

When the fault site has been propagated to a primary output, the current test cube is sent to all the slaves in which a consistency operation is indicated. The slave processors decide which gates need to be made consistent and place the necessary singular covers on the appropriate gates, making decisions and backtracking when necessary. When all consistencies are complete in the slaves, the test generation is complete.

Whenever an assignment is made to a test cube, implication is then performed, which assigns values to all nodes in the circuit that are implied by that assignment. This process may involve other nodes in other slaves, hence messages must be sent to the other slaves. This process is similar to parallel logic simulation on partitioned circuits.

An outline of the parallel event-driven logic simulation algorithm, *DM-PARALLEL-COMB-ATPG-CIRCUIT* (denoting distributed memory parallel algorithm for test generation of combinational circuits using circuit partitioning) is given next.

Procedure *DM-PARALLEL-COMB-ATPG-CIRCUIT;*
    Read circuit and list of faults;
    Partition circuit into subcircuit by cones, etc.;
    Assign each subcircuit to a slave processor;
    Assign entire circuit to master processor;

    FORALL processors in PARALLEL DO
      IF (processor = Master) THEN
        Select fault from fault list;
        Create initial objective;
        WHILE objective not met DO
          IF objective in slave processor p corresponding to partition

THEN Send message containing objective to processor p;
IF message received from processor q THEN
Note results and create new objectives;
END WHILE
END IF

IF (processor = slave) THEN
Receive new objective from master;
WHILE objective not met and
new objectives within boundary DO
Execute some steps of D-algorithm;
Propagation, backtracing, etc.
Determine new objectives;
IF new objectives reach boundary of subcircuit THEN
Send message to other slaves and master about
new objective;
END WHILE
END IF
END FORALL
End Procedure

Another distributed memory parallel algorithm for test generation of combinational circuits and full-scan sequential circuits (which can be viewed as combinational circuits with respect to the test generation complexity) has been recently proposed by Chan [17]. The basic approach used in this algorithm is to partition the logic of a given circuit into a set of logic partitions by the fan-in cones of the outputs. The objective is to minimize the logic overlapping among the logic partitions. Figure 8.24 shows an example partitioning of a given circuit into three parts. Partition A contains the logic rooted by output pins $O1$ and $O2$. Partition B contains logic rooted by output pin $O3$. Partition C contains logic rooted by output pin $O4$.

After the logic partitions are generated, combinational ATPG is executed on each partition and the list of faults on that partition independently on a different processor. The logic partitioning process consists of two phases: logic cones generation and logic cones merging.

The logic cones generation generates one logic cone for each primary output (a circuit primary output pin or a scan latch data input) in a circuit. This is done by tracing back from each primary output toward primary inputs (circuit primary inputs or scan latch outputs) and marking all the gates that are traced. Each cone generated has a list of primary inputs, primary outputs, and gates.

The cones are sorted according to the number of gates stored in them. The second phase merges these logic cones into logic partitions. Two cones C_i and C_j are merged if the intersection of primary inputs I_i and I_o between two different cones is greater than some threshold, I_t. The threshold I_t starts at large value, for example, 100%, and then gradually decreases to a very small value, for example, 1%. The merging of two cones results in a new cone that replaces C_i and C_j by C_k, which contains the union of the primary inputs, primary

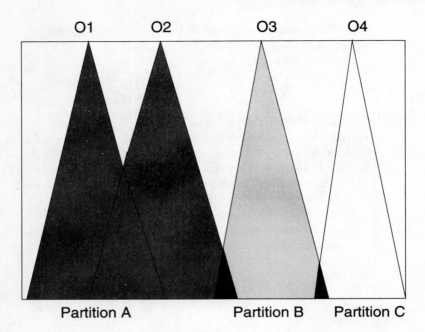

Figure 8.24 Logic partitioning by cones (Courtesy of Chan, *Proc. Application Specific Integrated Circuits Conf.,* ©IEEE 1992)

outputs and gates of each cone. The basic idea of the algorithm is to merge those cones that are most close to each other into larger cones very early in the merging process. As soon as a cone's size exceeds some threshold that corresponds to the minimum number of gates in a partition, it is written out as a logic partition. This process ensures that logic cones that have less overlapping logic will have less chance of being merged together, and vice versa.

After the logic partitions are generated, the faults associated with each logic partition can be divided into disjoint fault sets. An independent ATPG process can be created on each fault subset on a logic partition to create fine-grain ATPG tasks on a network of workstations. Each ATPG task then performs an integrated test generation and fault simulation pass on faults in its own set and the logic circuit in each partition.

It should be noted that in the preceding algorithm the test generation process of a *particular fault* is not speeded up by the circuit parallel ATPG technique, but the speedup comes mainly from the fault parallelism, in that each processor is determining the tests for different faults in parallel.

Implementation The first circuit parallel algorithm for ATPG described previously, *DM-PARALLEL-COMB-ATPG-CIRCUIT*, has been implemented by Bell et al. and Klenke et al. [10, 49]. The parallel algorithm has been developed in C++ around the ES-KIT multiprocessor, which is a 16-processor machine with a two-dimensional mesh interconnection. The parallel implementation of this algorithm gave poor speedups for speeding up the test generation process for single faults. In fact, the runtimes on eight processors were actually more than

TABLE 8.9 Result Quality (Test Length), Runtimes (Seconds), and Speedups, of Parallel Test Generation Algorithm on Network of Hewlett-Packard-9000™ and SUN SPARC™Workstations

Circuit	Gates	1 Processor			6 Processors		
		Length	Runtime	Speedup	Length	Runtime	Speedup
1	25088	1751	1206.1	1.0	1965	296.1	4.1
2	27772	1191	1412.9	1.0	1203	309.1	4.6
3	29406	1373	1519.2	1.0	1398	428.4	3.5

the runtimes on a single processor. The authors used fault partitioning in addition to circuit parallelism in order to keep all the processors busy. Fault partitioning did not decrease the time required to process a single fault, but it did result in speedups for processing an entire fault list. It was observed that the runtimes decreased as the number of faults processed in parallel increased up to a point and then the runtimes leveled off. In general, it was found that the optimum number of faults to process in parallel was about two to three more than the number of partitions.

The second parallel algorithm described, which partitions logic circuits into cones and performs ATPG on each partition independently, has been implemented by Chan on a network of 12 SUN SPARC™ and Hewlett Packard-9000™ workstations [17]. Results have been reported on several ISCAS-85 benchmark circuits [15] and on some large ASIC chip designs. The circuits were partitioned into six circuit partitions and one fault set per partition. On a single processor, the ATPG was run on the entire circuit and on the complete fault set. On six processors, each processor ran a single logic partition and its fault set. Table 8.9 shows the resulting quality in terms of test length, runtimes and speedups of several ISCAS-89 sequential benchmark circuits [14] on a network of 6 SUN SPARC™ and Hewlett-Packard-9000™ workstations. Fault coverage numbers were not reported.

8.8.3 Massively Parallel SIMD Algorithm

We will now describe a massively parallel SIMD algorithm using circuit parallel decomposition of the test generation problem based on work reported by Kramer [50]. The test generation system is divided into two sections, the *test generator*, which derives all tests for a particular fault, and the *test merger*, which compresses the test sets derived to one near-minimal test set.

The system is based on circuit partitioning by which each gate in the circuit is instantiated on a set of processors of an SIMD parallel machine. Gates in the circuit are built up of collections of processor cells. The output cell for each gate contains pointers to the input cells for other gates. These pointers comprise the topological description of the circuit and are used to direct messages to their proper destinations. The contents of these messages are the values present on the circuit node (a node is the output of a gate). Associated with each of these values is a tag, in which each bit position represents one logical state of the circuit, that is, one unique combination of inputs. The test generation is performed by exhaustive enumeration of the values of every circuit node for all primary input combinations, taking into account the fact that particular lines may have a faulty behavior. Specifically, a fault will be active as a D (or D-bar) on the appropriate line when for the normal circuit the node is a 1 (0) but under fault it is a 0 (1). Each gate processor performs the task of exhaustive simulation of all possible input combinations. The information regarding the states of the output of the gate for these input combinations is sent to the other gate processors that represent the fan-out from this gate in the form of a message. Once all the node-value set messages are received by a gate for all its inputs, the gate can evaluate its output. Using this procedure, the test generator determines all input vectors that will detect a particular fault.

After all the tests are generated, the test merger creates a compressed list of tests to cover all the faults. The test merger combines all the tags for all the tests into one large matrix. Each column of the matrix represents a possible test, and each row represents a single fault. The test that covers the largest number of faults is found and removed from the matrix, and at the same time all the rows (faults) that are covered by this test are removed. This process is repeated on the smaller matrix recursively until the matrix is empty.

Another massively parallel SIMD algorithm for test generation has been recently proposed by Mayer et al. [60]. The algorithm considers one fault at a time and generates a test for it by parallelizing each step in the FAN algorithm for test generation [33]. Each gate in the network is mapped to a processor. Parallelization is achieved by several gates simultaneously doing backtrace or forward propagation. The steps in the parallel algorithm are as follows. In the algorithm, the setting up of multiple objectives, for example, in trying to push a D toward a primary output (PO), set up an initial objective so that the D is propagated down multiple levels instead of a single level. During the parallel backtrace step, all gates in the same level (from the primary inputs PI) work in parallel to propagate the objectives backwards toward the PIs. After a PI is set to a value, simulation is necessary to determine the implication of the assignment. During the parallel forward implication step, all gates in the same level work in parallel to propagate the values forward toward the POs. If a PI assignment that has been simulated does not propagate a D to a PO, the algorithm has to determine if there is a possibility of making additional PI assignments leading to a test. For this purpose, a check is performed to determine if a path of unknown values (X) only exists from the D-frontier to a PO. If it does not, backtracking is needed. This X-path check is performed in parallel. Starting from all nodes in the D-frontier, a trace toward the POs is performed to determine an X-path.

An outline of the massively parallel SIMD algorithm for test generation *SIMD-PARAL-LEL-COMB-ATPG-CIRCUIT* (denoting massively parallel SIMD algorithm for test generation of combinational circuits using circuit decomposition) follows:

    Procedure *SIMD-PARALLEL-COMB-ATPG-CIRCUIT;*
    Read circuit and list of faults;
    Map each gate to a processor.
    REPEAT
       Select a fault;
       In setting up an initial objective, multiple
           objectives are set up;
       FORALL processors in PARALLEL DO

> WHILE objectives not met DO
>   FOR each level L = 0 to maxlevel DO
>   Select processors owning gates on current level L;
>   Perform parallel backtrace;
>   Send signal values to gate processors
>   owning fan-ins of current gates;
>   ENDFOR
>   FOR each level L = 0 to maxlevel DO
>   Select processors owning gates on current level L;
>   Perform forward implication;
>   Send signal values to gate processors
>   owning fan-outs of current gates;
>   ENDFOR
>   FOR each level L = D-frontier to Primary-Output DO
>   Select processors owning gates on current level L;
>   Perform X-path check toward primary output;
>   Send X values to gate processors
>   owning fan-outs of current gates;
>   ENDFOR
>   IF no X-paths exist, backtracking is needed;
>   END WHILE
> END FORALL
> UNTIL all faults detected or aborted
> **End Procedure**

Implementation   Kramer reported an implementation of the first approach to massively parallel test generation using exhaustive enumeration on the Thinking Machines CM-1™ system consisting of 16,000 processors [50]. This approach gave good speedups on some example circuits. For one example circuit, the runtime on a Symbolics 3600™ machine was about 5 hours, whereas the time on the Thinking Machines CM-1 was about 10 seconds. The limitation of this approach is that this method can handle circuits that have a small number of primary inputs, for example, less than 12. Beyond that the exponential size of the tags makes the approach impractical.

No implementation results have been reported on the second approach to SIMD parallel ATPG, which parallelizes each step of the test generation process.

8.9 FAULT SIMULATION PROBLEM

The objective of a fault simulation algorithm is to find the fraction of total faults (also referred to as *fault coverage*) that is detected by a given set of input vectors. Figure 8.25 illustrates the task of fault simulation[68]. Each column corresponds to a test vector, and each row corresponds to a machine. There is one good machine and m faulty machines corresponding to different faulty lines, n test vectors, and $(m + 1)n$ machine states. The task of fault simulation is to find all the primary output values of the $(m + 1)n$ machine states and to

	V $_1$	...	V $_j$	...	V $_n$
Good	G 1	...	G j	...	G n
Fault 1	F 1,1	...	F 1,j	...	F 1,n
Fault 2	F 2,1	...	F 2,j	...	F 2,n
.	.	...	.	...	.
Fault i	F i,1	...	F i,j	...	F i,n
.	.	...	.	...	.
Fault m	F m,i	...	F m,j	...	F m,n

Figure 8.25 Task of Fault Simulation (Courtesy of Niermann, Cheng and Patel, *IEEE Trans. Computer-aided Design*, ©IEEE 1992)

determine which faulty machines have output values different from the good machine.

In its simplest form, a fault is injected into a logic circuit by setting a line or a gate to a faulty value and then the effect of the fault is simulated using logic simulation. Sophisticated methods such as *deductive* [8], *concurrent* [95], and *word-parallel* [90] fault simulation have been proposed that have been able to reduce the time considerably for fault simulation. Most fault simulation algorithms are typically of $O(n^2)$ time complexity, where n is the number of lines in the circuit. Studies have shown that there is little hope of finding a linear-time fault simulation algorithm [40].

Fault simulation algorithms may be used in two different environments: either in a deterministic test generation environment or in a random pattern test generation environment. In a deterministic test generation environment, the fault simulator helps in finding out the additional faults that are detectable by the same vector sequence. This helps reduce the effort required in test generation and also the test length. The test length determines the test application time and the memory necessary to store the vectors. Figure 8.2 shows the interplay between the test pattern generator and the fault simulator in a deterministic test pattern generation environment.

We start with a fault list which is normally constructed by collapsing equivalent faults. The test pattern generator selects a fault from the fault list and tries to generate a test. If the test pattern generator is successful in generating a test, fault simulation is carried out on the entire fault list and the detected faults are deleted from the fault list. The test pattern generator may fail to generate a test if the fault is redundant or some prespecified resource constraint is exceeded (for example, the backtrack or time limit per fault).

In a random pattern environment, the fault simulator helps in evaluating the fault

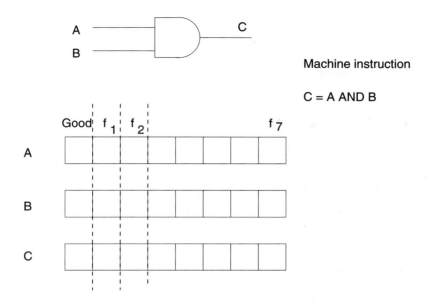

Figure 8.26 Word-level fault parallelism

coverage of a set of random patterns. In either of the two environments, fault simulation can consume a significant amount of time, especially random pattern testing for which millions of vectors may have to be simulated. Thus, parallel processing can be used to reduce the fault simulation time significantly.

We will now describe the sequential algorithms for deductive, concurrent, and word-parallel fault simulation.

8.9.1 Word-parallel Fault Simulation

Word-parallel simulation utilizes bit-oriented logic operations to perform many of gate evaluations simultaneously. If one word of a computer consists of b bits, b gate evaluations can be performed at a time. Parallel simulation can be classified as fault-parallel or pattern-parallel simulation. The former simulates b fault classes for one input pattern at a time by assigning one fault case to 1 bit. The latter simulates b inputs patterns for one fault at a time by assigning each fault case to 1 bit.

Let us first discuss the fault-parallel algorithm. Consider an AND gate having two inputs A and B as shown in Figure 8.26. Bit position 0 in words A, B, C corresponds to the good machine simulation. If the value of A and B for the circuit behavior under fault f_i is stored in the ith bit of the words of A and B, then the AND of these two words will have the value of the output C of the gate in the ith bit of the resulting computer word C. If the word has b bits, then b different problems can be handled simultaneously (in parallel), each in a different bit of the word. Suppose the word size of the computer is b then bit position 0 can be used to represent the good machine simulation, bit position 1 can represent the simulation under line A stuck at 0, bit position 2 can represent the simulation under line A stuck at 1, bit position 3

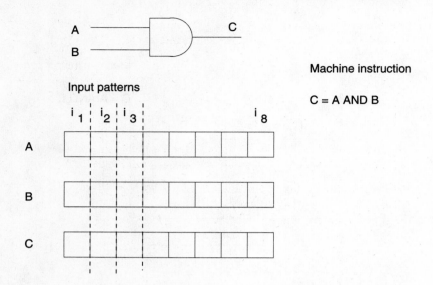

Figure 8.27 Word-level pattern parallelism

can represent the simulation under line B stuck at 0, and so on. Hence, if there are m faults to process in the fault simulation, we need to pack the faults into groups of $b-1$ and execute the fault simulation over $m/(b-1)$ passes. For each of these passes, we have to repeat the good machine simulation so that we can check if the faulty machine value is different from the good machine value to report the fault coverage.

In a similar manner, we can perform a pattern-parallel fault simulation. In this case, if the word size of the computer is b, then each bit position can represent the behavior of the circuit for a different input pattern (up to b different input patterns can be simultaneously represented and evaluated using one instruction). Consider an AND gate having two inputs A and B as shown in Figure 8.27. Bit position i corresponds to the behavior of the circuit under input pattern i. If the value of A and B for the circuit behavior under input pattern i is stored in the ith bit of the words of A and B, then the AND of these two words will have the value of the output C of the gate in the ith bit of the resulting computer word C. Pattern-parallel fault simulation first performs good machine simulation for b input patterns and then performs fault simulation for a particular fault for the same b input patterns and compares the resultant outputs. If the faulty output differs from the good machine simulation in at least 1 bit position (one input pattern), the fault is marked as detected.

Recently, a new fault simulation algorithm has been proposed called parallel pattern single fault propagation (PPSFP) [98] that is can be applied to compiled simulation or event-driven simulation techniques. A compiled logic simulator compiles a given circuit description into machine code by levelizing a given circuit and simulating all gates in sequence in order of increasing levels. Compiled simulation achieves fast simulation time since it can apply compiler optimizations to the machine code that is executed without any branches in sequence. All gates are simulated at all clock cycles. Faults can be introduced into the compiled simulation model by either modifying the code or by inserting branches to and from a description of the faulty logic. Execution of this modified code produces an output that may or may not differ from the good machine. If the outputs differ, the fault is detected. In the PPSFP approach for compiled driven techniques, the given combinational circuit is rank ordered and simulated using compiled simulation techniques for N patterns in the fault-free case and subsequently for a single fault for the same N patterns. This is repeated for each undetected fault. Then the next set of N patterns are chosen, and the process is repeated for the undetected faults.

An outline of the sequential algorithm for the pattern parallel single fault propagation algorithm *FAULTSIM-COMPILED-PPSFP* is given next.

> **Procedure** *FAULTSIM-COMPILED-PPSFP;*
>   Read circuit and list of faults;
>   Rank order the circuit in terms of levels;
>   Primary inputs are at level 0, other gates are at
>   level one higher than the maximum level of its inputs.
>   Read input patterns;
>
>   WHILE there are more input patterns remaining DO
>   Pick next N patterns;
>   WHILE there are undetected faults remaining DO
>   Simulate the fault-free network for
>   N patterns for some N using compiled simulation;
>   Pick an undetected fault;
>   Inject fault into fault-free network.
>   Fault simulate for the same N patterns
>   using compiled simulation;
>   Determine if the fault is detected by any of
>   the N patterns
>   ENDWHILE
>   ENDWHILE
> **End Procedure**

We now describe a PPSFP event-driven simulator using the notion of selective tracing [13]. The fault-free circuit is first simulated and all internal signal values are stored. Next a fault simulation is performed by propagating the faulty values from the fault sources to the primary outputs. Since the fault-free values of all lines have been computed and stored in the previous step, we can avoid the waste of simulating the gates whose faulty input values are the same as the fault-free ones. In PPSFP, faults are processed one by one in the second step of selective tracing.

An outline of the sequential algorithm for the pattern parallel single fault propagation algorithm *FAULTSIM-SELECTIVE-TRACE-PPSFP* follows:

> **Procedure** *FAULTSIM-SELECTIVE-TRACE-PPSFP;*

WHILE there are more input patterns remaining DO
Pick next N patterns;
WHILE there are undetected faults remaining DO
    Simulate the fault-free network for N
       patterns for some N using event-driven algorithm;
    Store all signal values for all N patterns;
    Pick an undetected fault;
    Inject it into fault-free network.
    Fault simulate for the same N patterns from fault
       from fault source to output using event driven algorithm;
    Only simulate gates different from good machine simulation;
    Determine if fault is detected by any of the patterns
  ENDWHILE
ENDWHILE
End Procedure

The advantages of using PPSFP fault simulation over conventional fault simulation methods have been outlined in [98]. In summary, it has been shown that word-level parallel simulation combined with selective tracing can be as efficient as deductive or concurrent fault simulation.

8.9.2 Deductive Fault Simulation

Deductive fault simulation is based on the concept that if the inputs to a logic element and the effect of faults on the circuit for these input values are known, the output of the element under all faulty conditions can be deduced. This is accomplished using the concept of fault list propagation.

To illustrate this concept, consider an AND gate having inputs $a = 0$, $b = 1$, and $c = 1$ as shown in Figure 8.28(a). Then the output d has value 0. If there is a fault on line a, the value of line a will be 1; then the entire list of faults on line a will appear at output line d, provided the lines b and c remain at values 1, which are the fault-free values. If a fault that appears on line a also appears on either lines b or c, the values on lines b or c will be different from 1 (equal to 0), hence the effect of the fault list propagation from line a will be terminated due to a 0 at a different input of the AND gate. Therefore, the faults that cause an error at line d are the fault $ds - a - 1$ and any fault in line a, represented as the fault list L_a, that is not in list L_b or L_c. We can represent the this condition as

$$L_d = \{d\, s - a - 1\} \cup \{L_a \cap \overline{L_b} \cap \overline{L_c}\}$$

The deductive fault simulation algorithm involves a good machine simulation of all the gates in the circuit in level order and simultaneously, the corresponding propagation of the fault lists using the following simple rules.

Rule 1. If the value ψ of an element in the normal circuit is 0(1), let $E(x_1, x_2, ..., x_n)$ be a sum of products or product of sums Boolean expression for $\psi(\overline{\psi})$ in terms of the inputs to the element $x_1, x_2, ..., x_n$. If the value of an input variable x_i in the normal circuit is 0, replace all appearances of x_i in E by L_{x_i} and all appearances of $\overline{x}_i$ by $\overline{L}_{x_i}$; if the value of an input variable x_i in the normal circuit is 1, replace all appearances of x_i in E by $\overline{L}_{x_i}$ and

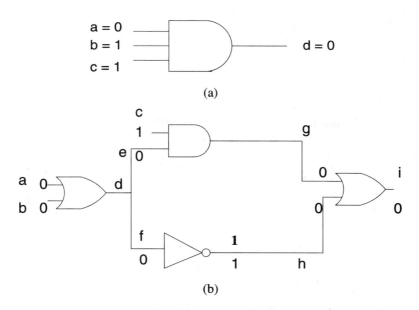

Figure 8.28 Illustration of deductive simulation. (a) AND gate. (b) Example circuit.

all appearances of $\bar{x}_i$ by L_{x_i}. Also replace products in the expression by $\cap$ and sums in the expression by $\cup$.

Rule 2. If d is the element output, add d_1 (d_0) to the fault list obtained if the value of d = 0 (= 1). Figure 8.28(b) shows an example circuit and the logic values of various gates for one input vector. Any fault in fault list L_i corresponding to line i of the figure will be detected by the test vector (a, b, c) = (1, 1, 0). The fault list propagation for this circuit and this set of input combinations are given as follows:

$$L_a = \{\, a_1 \,\}, L_b = \{b_1\}, L_c = \{c_0\}$$
$$L_d = L_a \cup L_b \cup d_1 = \{a_1, b_1, d_1\}$$
$$L_e = L_d \cup e_1 = \{a_1, b_1, d_1, e_1\}$$
$$L_f = L_d \cup f_1 = \{a_1, b_1, d_1, f_1\}$$
$$L_g = L_e \cap \bar{L}_c \cup g_1 = \{a_1, b_1, d_1, f_1, g_1\}$$
$$L_h = L_f \cup h_0 = \{a_1, b_1, d_1, f_1, h_0\}$$
$$L_i = L_g \cup L_h \cup i_1 = \{a_1, b_1, d_1, f_1, g_1, h_0, i_1\}$$

Now assume that the input c changes from 1 to 0. Instead of evaluating all the lists, the lists can be computed in an event driven manner similar in philosophy to event-driven logic simulation discussed in Chapter 7. That is, noting the lines and lists that change, only update the corresponding lists.

The faults lists can be stored either as ordered or unordered linked lists. The computation of set union and intersection for linked lists can be very time consuming; hence a characteristic bit vector representation is used. Using this representation, the insertion or deletion of a fault is done by either storing a 1 or a 0 in the appropriate bit. Set union or intersection are done by simple AND or OR word operations. Hence all list operations become very fast (linear time). However, this representation requires more memory than the linked list representations.

8.9.3 Concurrent Fault Simulation

Ulrich and Baker proposed another method of fault simulation called concurrent fault simulation [95]. An excellent overview of this technique is presented in [13]. Like deductive simulation, this is also a one-pass process. It basically simulates multiple faulty machines concurrently by maintaining a list of fault effects for each primitive gate in the circuit. In concurrent fault simulation, those elements in the faulty circuit that do not agree in terms of input and/or input values with the same element of the fault-free circuit are explicitly simulated.

Consider a single output n-input combinational element E. At a particular simulation time t for fault f, this element has input values $a_1^f, a_2^f, \ldots, a_n^f$ and output value b^f, where $f = 0$ refers to a faulty circuit. Consider the set of faults $F' \subset F$ (where F is the set of all single stuck-at faults in the circuit), such that for each $f \in F'$, either $b^f \neq b^0$ or $a_j^f \neq a_j^0$ for some input j. That is, for each fault $f \in F'$, either an input or the output b is in error. We can now associate with b a super fault list in which each entry of the list is of the form

$$f; a_1^f; a_2^f; \ldots, a_n^f; b^f$$

This is illustrated in Figure 8.29(a).

In concurrent simulation, the faulty and good circuits are processed and scheduled concurrently. Each entry in the super faulty list S is processed separately. When an event occurs during concurrent simulation, an entry is placed in the scheduler at the appropriate time. This entry is a 4-tuple consisting of (1) the name of the element E to be simulated, (2) the name of the fault causing the simulation, (3) the name of the input line on which an event occurred that caused E to be scheduled, and (4) the new value on this line.

Figure 8.29(b) shows an example of a concurrent simulation on a small example circuit. For each gate, the corresponding input vectors in the fault-free case are marked on the figure, and the behavior under fault is shown as a list next to them. The reason that the input vector is stored along with its entry in the fault list is because each element E^f is actually simulated one at a time because there is any activity associated with it. If a gate has some activity due to faults i, j, and k, three separate copies of c are simulated, and these entries are placed in the scheduler's list S. Because each entry in S is processed separately and its inputs are known, fast simulation techniques can be used.

8.10 PARALLEL FAULT SIMULATION APPROACHES

In this section we will review the parallelism available in the fault simulation problem.

8.10.1 Fault Parallelism

Exploiting parallelism in fault simulation is relatively simple. At the beginning of fault simulation, we have n_t patterns that have to be simulated against n_f faults. We can exploit *fault parallelism* by partitioning n_f faults across the available processors. It is possible to obtain almost linear speedups in the case of fault parallel implementations. The problem is that for each partition of faults. We have to perform a good machine simulation. Depending on the partitioning of the faults, the fault activity of each partition for a particular input vector may be not uniform across all partitions. This gives poor load balance.

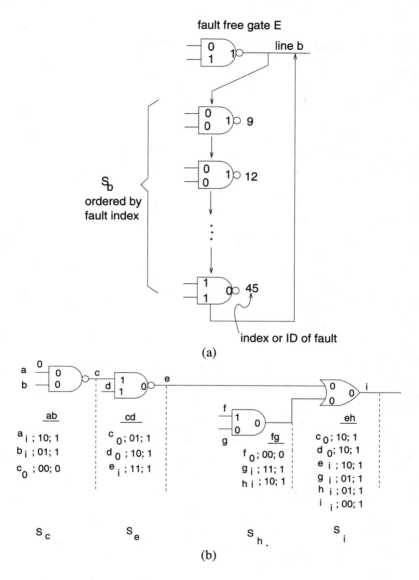

Figure 8.29 Concurrent fault simulation. (a) Super fault lists for a gate. (b) An example concurrent fault simulation. (Courtesy of Breuer and Friedman, *Diagnosis and Reliable Design of Digital Systems*, Computer Science Press, 1976)

8.10.2 Pattern Parallelism

We can exploit *input pattern parallelism* by partitioning the n_t patterns for combinational circuits. It may not always be possible to exploit pattern parallelism. For sequential circuits, the future behavior of the circuit depends on past input patternsl; hence the patterns have to be simulated in sequence. Also, in a test generation/fault simulation environment only one test vector is available at the beginning of each fault simulation step. It is possible to obtain almost linear speedups in the case of pattern parallel implementations.

8.10.3 Circuit Parallelism

We can exploit circuit decomposition methods of parallelism by speeding up each pass by using parallel logic simulation techniques. The parallelism available here is strongly dependent on the circuit topology and the partitioning strategy used. The communication overheads can be very high.

8.10.4 Pipelined Approach

A pipeline-type approach can be used in which all gates at a particular logic level form a stage of a pipeline. Either faults or patterns can then be pipelined through the logic circuit. In the case of sequential circuits, since the test vectors have to be applied in sequence, it is not possible to exploit pattern parallelism. Also, due to the presence of feedback paths through memory elements, the speedups possible through pipelined parallelism may be severely limited.

8.10.5 Combination of Approaches

The word-level parallel fault simulation technique attempts to reduce the computation time by performing gate evaluations for multiple fault-cases or pattern-cases at a time using bit-wise logical operations of a computer. The former is called fault-parallel simulation, and the latter is called pattern-parallel simulation. By simply extending the unit of gate evaluation from a single word of a single processor to multiple words of a parallel processor, we can obtain extended fault-parallelism or pattern-parallelism. Let w be the number of bits in a computer word of a single processor, and f and p be referred to as the fault and pattern parallelism factor, representing the number of faults or patterns simulated at a time.

It has been noted that due to fault dropping, the number of undetected faults drops exponentially with the number of vectors applied. This is illustrated in Figure 8.30. As is shown in part (a) a lot of undetected faults exist in the early passes. Because the number of undetected faults decreases as simulation proceeds, the fault-parallelism factor f becomes extremely small in later passes. However, if we attempt to simulate with a large pattern-parallelism factor p as shown in part (b), to get a large effective word length in the later passes, many wasteful simulations need to be performed in the early passes for the faults that might be dropped if simulated with a small p. Hence, it is better to apply fault-parallelism for the early passes, and pattern-parallelism for the later passes. It may be possible to dynamically combine the two approaches as well.

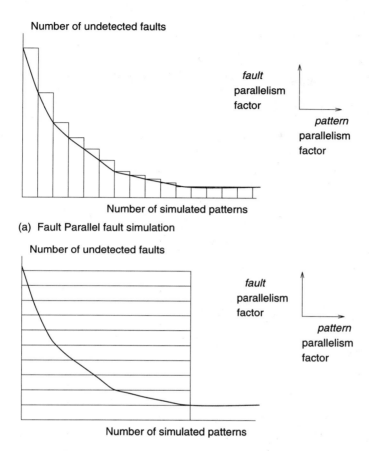

Figure 8.30 Fault-parallel and pattern-parallel fault simulation. (a) Fault parallel fault simulation. (b) Pattern parallel fault simulation. (Courtesy of Ishiura et al., *IEEE Trans. Computer-aided Design,* ©IEEE 1987)

8.11 FAULT PARALLEL FAULT SIMULATION

8.11.1 Overview

The most straightforward approach to parallel fault simulation is to partition the fault list among various processors, and let each processor perform fault simulation on the entire circuit for the complete set of input vectors for its own fault lists.

8.11.2 Distributed Memory MIMD Parallel Algorithm

We will now describe a distributed memory parallel algorithm for fault simulation using the fault parallel approach based on work reported by Duba et al. [25]. The algorithm involves the client-server model of computation shown in Figure 8.10. A fault list is maintained in the client process. Each fault has a status flag, which can be in one of three states: UNTRIED, DETECTED, UNDETECTED. If a fault is marked UNTRIED, it means that no fault simulation has been performed on that fault for the input set. If a fault is marked DETECTED, it means that a fault simulation has been performed on the fault, and it has been determined that the fault is detected. Similarly, if the fault is marked UNDETECTED, it means that the fault is not detected by this input set.

The client processor requests a remote server processor to execute a task (consisting of fault simulation on a cluster of faults) and to return its result (set of faults that are detected, and a set of faults that were not detected) to the client. When a server finishes its assigned tasks, it sends the result to the client and requests a new task. The client updates the fault table and provides a new task by extracting a new cluster of untried faults to the server. Client service discipline is first-come, first-served.

An outline of the parallel fault simulation algorithm *DM-PARALLEL-FSIM-FAULT-CENT* (denoting distributed memory parallel fault simulation using fault decomposition with centralized control) is given next.

> **Procedure** *DM-PARALLEL-FSIM-FAULT-CENT;*
> Read circuit description;
> Read list of faults under consideration;
> For each fault create status flags
>   (UNTRIED, DETECTED, UNDETECTED);
> Initialize list of faults; set to UNTRIED
> Read input patterns;
> Assign one processor as Client and P-1 processors as Servers;
> Broadcast circuit copy to all servers;
>
> FORALL processors in PARALLEL DO
>   WHILE there are no UNTRIED faults in list DO
>   IF (processor = Client) THEN
>   Receive fault simulation results from a server;
>   FOR each fault in result DO
>   Update flag to DETECTED or UNDETECTED;
>   Send a new partition of UNTRIED faults to server processor;
>   ELSE IF (processor = Server) THEN
>   Receive a partition of UNTRIED faults from Client;
>   Perform fault simulation on set of faults on complete input set;
>   Sends fault simulation results to the client;
>   Requests client for a new partition of UNTRIED faults;
>   ENDIF
>   ENDWHILE
> END FORALL
> **End Procedure**

The granularity of computation (the number of faults given to a server) determines the speedup. If the granularity is decreased in order to exploit more parallelism and provide more load balance, servers complete the tasks more rapidly and hence send requests to clients more frequently. This increases the communication and reduces the speedup.

By keeping the granularity of the computation of each fault simulation pass low (by performing fault simulation on a small set of faults m), we can get good load balance. However, there are two disadvantages. First, for each fault simulation pass, we have to perform a good machine simulation to compare with the value of the fault simulation. By increasing the number of passes, the number of good machine simulations is increased; this constitutes redundant work. Second, in the preceding algorithm, there is contention for use of the single client process to distribute the faults to the server processes.

One way to reduce the effect of the contention is to have the processors perform fault simulation in parallel using separate fault lists, without using an explicit client-server discipline. In this approach, P separate fault lists are created for P processors. Faults are placed in the different fault lists through some static fault partitioning method. Processors access faults from their own fault lists to extract the next set of m faults and mark the status of the faults as DETECTED or UNDETECTED in their own fault lists. If a processor's fault list becomes empty, it queries the fault lists of other processors to look for more work. The fault list of the processor that has the largest number of faults that are marked UNTRIED is split in half and copied to the idle processor's list, and the process is resumed. Note that in this algorithm there is good load balance, almost as good as for the previous algorithm; however, the contention for accessing the fault lists is restricted to the last phase of the parallel algorithm, where processors try to query each other for distributing their workload.

An outline of the parallel fault simulation algorithm *DM-PARALLEL-FSIM-FAULT-DIST* (denoting distributed memory parallel fault simulation using fault decomposition with distributed control) follows:

Procedure *DM-PARALLEL-FSIM-FAULT-DIST;*
Read circuit description;
Read list of faults under consideration;
Read list of input vectors;
Partition list of faults statically among processors;
For each fault create status flags
   (UNTRIED, DETECTED, UNDETECTED);
Initialize list of faults; set to UNTRIED
Read input patterns;
Broadcast circuit copy to all servers;
FORALL processors in PARALLEL DO
   WHILE there are no UNTRIED faults in system DO
      WHILE processor's own fault list not empty DO
         Select a set of m faults from own fault list;
         Perform fault simulation on set of faults;
         Update DETECTED / UNDETECTED flag on own fault list;
         Check Messages from other processors for load balance;
      END WHILE

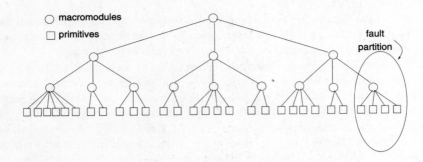

Figure 8.31 Hierarchical fault partitioning (Courtesy of Duba et al., *Proc. Design Automation Conf.*, 1988, ©IEEE 1988)

```
        IF processor own fault list empty THEN
            Get work from other processors
            Query other processors for fault list
            Receive half fault list of most loaded processor
    END WHILE
    END FORALL
    End Procedure
```

Implementation Duba et al. [25] have reported an implementation of the client-server method of parallel fault simulation using a fault decomposing approach. The fault simulation was based on a concurrent hierarchical fault simulator called CHIEFS. CHIEFS features a hierarchical fault partitioning technique that increases fault simulator performance by reducing the total amount of computation required to perform the simulation. This technique is based on the hierarchical circuit description and high-level functional definitions for the higher-level macromodules in the circuit description.

Initially, the circuit description is automatically partitioned using hierarchical information into subcircuits, each of which contains a small subset of all possible faults, as shown in Figure 8.31. During simulation, the circuit description is reconfigured so that the current fault partition is simulated at the primitive level and all other fault-free parts of the circuit are simulated at the highest possible levels. This is achieved by substituting the high-level functional description for subcircuits wherever possible in the fault-free areas. After the fault simulation is performed, the circuit is reconfigured; faults in the next partition are injected, and the previous partition is now set to fault-free. This reconfiguration process is repeated until all the partitions have been fault simulated.

The architecture of the loosely coupled system on which the parallel algorithm was developed on a client-server model. The system consisted of a client and several servers on a network of workstations employing the TCP protocol. The remote procedure call (RPC) facility of the network file system was used to support a mechanism by which a client machine can request a remote server machine to execute a procedure and return results to the client.

The preceding parallel algorithm called DCHIEFS was implemented on a network of eight SUN workstations. The algorithm was evaluated on three example circuits such as array multipliers and control units, each having three levels of hierarchy. Speedups of about 5 to 6 were reported on eight processors.

Recently, Markas et al. [57] have reported a distributed fault simulation algorithm on a heterogeneous network of workstations connected through a local area network. Results have been reported on a nonhierarchical fault simulator, using different fault partitioning methods.

8.11.3 Shared Memory MIMD Parallel Algorithm

We will now describe a shared memory parallel algorithm for fault simulation using the fault parallel approach. In this approach, a master fault list is maintained in shared memory. Each fault has a status flag, which can be in one of three states: UNTRIED, DETECTED, and UNDETECTED, as discussed earlier. Processors access the shared fault list and copy a set of m UNTRIED faults from the master list into a local list. Fault simulation is performed on the input vector set for the local list of faults. At the end of fault simulation, the processor accesses the shared fault list, updates the fault entries of the faults that were simulated by it in this pass to DETECTED or UNDETECTED, and extracts another set of m UNTRIED faults.

An outline of the parallel fault simulation algorithm *SM-PARALLEL-FSIM-FAULT-GLOBAL* (denoting shared memory parallel fault simulation using fault decomposition with global fault list) is given next.

> **Procedure** *SM-PARALLEL-FSIM-FAULT-GLOBAL;*
> Read circuit description;
> Read list of faults under consideration;
> Read input patterns;
> Create shared fault list in shared memory;
> For each fault create status flags
>   (UNTRIED, DETECTED, UNDETECTED);
> Initialize list of faults; set to UNTRIED
> FORALL processors in PARALLEL DO
>   WHILE there are no UNTRIED faults in list DO
>   Access shared list of faults from shared memory under lock;
>   Extract a new partition of UNTRIED faults
>   Copy list of faults to local fault list of processor;
>   Perform fault simulation on local set of faults on complete input set;
>   Access shared list of faults;
>   Update entries of faults to DETECTED or UNDETECTED;
>   ENDWHILE
> END FORALL
> **End Procedure**

By keeping the granularity of the computation of each fault simulation pass low (by performing fault simulation on a small set of faults m), we can get good load balance. However, there are two disadvantages for the corresponding distributed memory algorithm. First, for each fault simulation pass, we have to perform a good machine simulation to compare the value of the fault simulation to. By increasing the number of passes, the number of good machine simulations is increased; this constitutes redundant work. Second, in the preceding algorithm, there is contention for the shared list of faults each time a new partition of faults is extracted from the list by a processor. The relative cost of acquiring the shared list of faults, extracting a set of faults from it, and updating the status of the faults becomes comparable to the cost of fault simulation itself for small sets of faults.

One way to reduce the effect of the contention is to have P separate fault lists for P processors. Faults are placed in the different fault lists through some static fault partitioning method. Processors access faults from their own fault lists to extract the next set of m faults and mark the status of the faults as DETECTED or UNDETECTED in their own fault lists. If a processor's fault list becomes empty, it queries the fault lists of other processors to look for more work. The fault list of the processor with the largest number of faults UNTRIED is split in half and copied to the idle processor's list, and the process is resumed. Note that in this algorithm there is good load balance, almost as good as the previous algorithm; however, the contention for accessing the fault lists are restricted to the last phase of the parallel algorithm.

An outline of the parallel fault simulation algorithm *DM-PARALLEL-FSIM-FAULT-LOCAL* (denoting distributed memory parallel fault simulation using fault decomposition using local fault lists) is given next.

> **Procedure** *DM-PARALLEL-FSIM-FAULT-LOCAL;*
> Read circuit description;
> Read list of faults under consideration;
> Read list of input vectors;
> Partition list of faults statically among processors;
> For each fault create status flags
>   (UNTRIED, DETECTED, UNDETECTED);
> Initialize list of faults; set to UNTRIED
> Read input patterns;
> FORALL processors in PARALLEL DO
>   WHILE there are no UNTRIED faults in system DO
>   WHILE processor's own fault list not empty DO
>   Select a set of m faults from own fault list;
>   Perform fault simulation on set of faults;
>   Update DETECTED / UNDETECTED flag on own fault list;
>   END WHILE
>   IF processor own fault list empty THEN
>   Get work from other processors
>   Query other processors for fault list
>   Copy half fault list of most loaded processor
>   END IF
>   END WHILE
> END FORALL
> **End Procedure**

No implementations of the preceding parallel algorithms have been reported.

8.12 PATTERN PARALLEL FAULT SIMULATION

8.12.1 Overview

We will now describe some parallel algorithms for fault simulation using input pattern decomposition. The given input pattern set is decomposed into several subsets. Each processor of a parallel machine gets a copy of the entire circuit and the entire fault set and a subset of the inputs patterns. Each processor performs fault simulation on its subset of input patterns. This approach is easily applicable to combinational circuits when no state information is carried across different input vectors. This approach cannot be applied easily to sequential circuits, since the state of a circuit depends in the worst case on all the input patterns that are applied in sequence.

8.12.2 Pattern Parallel Approach for Combinational Circuits

We will first describe a pattern parallel approach to fault simulation for combinational circuits. This approach is relatively easy because there is no state information is carried across different vectors.

Shared Memory MIMD Parallel Algorithm In this section we will present a shared memory parallel algorithm for fault simulation using pattern parallelism based on work reported by Ostapko et al. [69]. The parallel algorithm for fault simulation uses data parallel compiled simulation techniques similar to the PPSFP fault simulation approach described in earlier [98]. A compiled logic simulator compiles a given circuit description into machine code by levelizing a given circuit and simulating all gates in sequence in order of increasing levels for all input patterns. During the simulation process, only 1 bit is needed for describing the logic value of a signal. Since the machine instruction supports the bit-wise logic operations performed by the logic being simulated, for example, AND, OR, and NOT, up to b input patterns can be simulated simultaneously assuming a b bit machine word. Faults can be introduced into the compiled simulation model by either modifying the code or by inserting branches to and from a description of the faulty logic. Execution of this modified code produces an output that may or may not differ from the good machine. If the outputs differ, the fault is detected. We now describe a parallel algorithm that can exploit the parallelism among the multiple processors of a multiprocessor and the b-way parallelism of the existing fault simulator, such as the PPSFP simulator described earlier.

It must be noted that to evaluate the fault coverage of a given set of test patterns each fault can be treated independently of the others. The fact that a certain pattern detects a certain fault is not related to the same pattern detecting other faults. The choice is between splitting the circuit's compiled model into several modules all of which can be simulated in parallel or replicating the full model on different processors. The first approach increases the amount of communication and synchronization activity and hence limits parallelism. Hence, for compiled fault simulation, it is better to keep the circuit model as one entity and replicate it on several processors. Once it is decided to keep the model as a single entity, there is a choice of whether to distribute the faulty models or the input patterns among the processors. In the pattern parallel approach, the patterns are distributed to different processors. Each processor then simulates the same set of 32 input patterns, assuming a word size $b = 32$ of the processors. These input patterns are applied to successive faulty models until all faults have been evaluated.

The details of the algorithm are described next. Each processor gets the current set of 32 input patterns and simulates the results of a fault-free run using compiled simulation. Each processor then gets a fault from the global fault list resident in shared memory, modifies the compiled circuit model, and simulates the faulty circuit for the 32 input patterns. If the faulty output differs from the fault-free output, the fault has been detected and is marked as such in the global fault list. Otherwise, the fault is returned to the list being constructed for simulation by the next set of 32 input patterns, and a new fault is taken from that list. In this scheme, a good machine simulation occurs once for every input pattern on possibly all processors. This approach serves to balance the processor utilization since certain faults are detected very quickly, while others require a large number of input patterns.

An outline of the parallel fault simulation algorithm *SM-PARALLEL-FSIM-COMB-PAT-TERN* (denoting shared memory parallel fault simulation using input pattern decomposition) is given next.

Procedure *SM-PARALLEL-FSIM-COMB-PATTERN;*
Read circuit, list of faults, inputs;
Create a Global Input Pattern List; Create a Global Fault List;
FORALL processors in PARALLEL DO
   Each processor works on entire circuit on own input patterns;
   WHILE MaxFault > 0 and PatternNumber $\leq$ MaxPattern DO
      PatternNumber = Get_Next_32Patterns (Global Pattern List)
      Simulate Good Machine and Store Results;
      FaultNumber = Get Next Fault (Global Fault List);
      WHILE FaultNumber $\leq$ MaxFault DO
         Create Faulty Machine;
         Simulate and Compare with Good Machine
            for all patterns in PatternNumber;
         Record Detected Faults;
         FaultNumber = Get Next Fault (Global Fault List)
      ENDWHILE
      Synchronize: Wait for all processors;
      IF (processor = 1) Update global fault list;
   ENDWHILE
End Procedure

A second version of this algorithm is to simulate a fault in a processor for several sets of input patterns. This would require the storage of several good machine simulations with no resulting improvement in the ratio of the good to faulty machine simulations. Another alternative is to have one processor simulate the good machine and store the result in global memory for the other processors to use for comparison with the outputs of their faulty models. This also improves the ratio of faulty to good machine simulations.

A final version of the parallel algorithm is to simulate a faulty circuit-compiled model on one processor for a large number of input pattern sets. The fault list is then kept in global memory, and each processor accesses it to obtain a fault. Each processor obtains a fault-free response for a set of 32 input patterns and then runs the faulty model and looks for fault detection at the outputs. If the fault is not detected by this set of input patterns, the process (fault-free evaluation followed by faulty model simulation) is repeated with a new set of 32 input patterns. If, on the other hand, the processor succeeds in detecting the fault, the appropriate entry in the global list if updated and a new fault is chosen from the list and the whole process is repeated.

Implementation   Ostapko et al. implemented the preceding pattern parallel fault simulation algorithm for combinational circuits on the VM/EPEX™ environment for the RP3 shared memory multiprocessor, which was a research prototype multiprocessor developed at IBM [69]. Speedups of about 3.9 on four processors were measured on some circuits.

Distributed Memory MIMD Parallel Algorithm   We will now discuss a distributed memory parallel algorithm for fault simulation using input pattern partitioning that is based on work by Warshawsky and Rajski [99]. The parallel fault simulator is based around a uniprocessor fault simulator, which is an event driven and not a compiled simulator. Hence not all gates are evaluated at all times. The entire circuit and fault set are simulated on each processor, but each processor gets a subset of the input vector set. This requires the duplication of the circuit description and temporary structures for simulation in each node. Hence such an approach requires more memory than do others. In terms of processing time, this method does not repeat any processing, as in fault set partitioning. Each test vector is simulated only once. Furthermore, the simulation of each vector can proceed independently of others, so no communication is required, although features such as fault dropping make a small amount of communication necessary.

The parallel algorithm is novel in the handling of fault dropping during fault simulation. Most fault simulation algorithms use fault dropping or other methods to dynamically reduce the amount of processing required for each vector. In a distributed simulator using input pattern partitioning and no communication, the simulator on each processor would only be able to drop those faults that it detects and, as a result, would perform more work than necessary. Furthermore, with no communication it is not possible to control the load balancing dynamically.

An outline of the parallel fault simulation algorithm *DM-PARALLEL-FSIM-COMB-PAT-TERN* (denoting distributed memory parallel fault simulation using input decomposition) follows:

Procedure *DM-PARALLEL-FSIM-COMB-PATTERN;*
Read circuit description;
Perform preprocessing;
Read list of faults;
FORALL processors in PARALLEL DO
    WHILE there are input vectors left to simulate DO
        Receive next group of input vectors;

        Initialize primary inputs with the test vectors;
        Perform fault-free simulation;
        Perform fault simulation;
        Place detected faults in an output queue for distribution
           to other processors;
        Check input queue for faults detected externally;
        Perform fault dropping based on new faults covered
           by this pass;
    ENDWHILE
  END FORALL
Report fault coverage and undetected faults;
End Procedure

We now provide a model to analyze the pattern parallel fault simulation algorithm based on work reported by Warshawsky and Rajski [99]. Let us define a function $\phi(f_r)$ to represent the amount of work that must be done to simulate a single vector given, that the size of the remaining fault set after fault dropping is f_r. Then the expected time to fault simulate N input vectors on a uniprocessor is $W(N) = \sum_{n=1}^{N} \phi(f_r(n-1))$. There have been several studies on empirically relating the amount of fault simulation work with the size of the remaining fault set. One such approximate function is $\phi(f_r) = B_1 \cdot f_r + B_2$. The values of the coefficients B_1 and B_2 for some example circuits can be experimentally determined.

Numerous researchers have also reported experimental measurements on the fault dropping behavior, using which it is possible to obtain a linear approximation to the function $f_r(n) = \frac{A_1}{n+1} + A_2 + A_3 \cdot (n+1)$, again, in terms of experimentally obtained coefficients.

Let us now estimate the execution time of a parallel algorithm for fault simulation using input pattern decomposition, where N/p vectors are statically allocated to each processor for simulation. The estimated runtime on p processors is $W_p(N) = \sum_{n=1}^{N/p} \phi(f_r(n_l + n_e))$, where n_l represents the number of input vectors simulated locally, and n_e represents the number of input vectors simulated by the other $p-1$ processors for which the processor in question can perform dropping. In all cases, when simulating the nth vector on a particular processor, that processor has already simulated $n-1$ vectors, so $n_l = n - 1$. The quantity n_e depends on whether there is communication and the latency of communication. If there were ideal communication, each processor would synchronize after each vector; hence the estimate for $n_e = (n-1)(p-1)$. If we assume that in the time for a communication, δ vectors can be simulated, then $n_e = (n-1)(p-\delta-1)$. Using this simple analysis, the the following simple expression for the speedup function can be derived: $S_p(N) = \frac{W(N)}{W_p(N)}$.

Implementation   The preceding parallel algorithm was implemented on a network of SUN/4 workstations. Table 8.10 shows the results of the runtimes (in seconds) and the speedups of the parallel fault simulation algorithm on several ISCAS-85 combinational benchmark circuits on 10 workstations. Each fault simulation was run over 512,000 random input vectors.

TABLE 8.10 Runtimes (Seconds) and Speedups of Parallel Fault Simulation on a Network of SUN/4™ Workstations

Circuit	1 Processor		10 Processors	
	Runtime	Speedup	Runtime	Speedup
2670	500	1.0	51	9.8
7552	1312	1.0	141	9.3
13207	1819	1.0	192	9.47
15850	2603	1.0	275	9.47
38584	6140	1.0	661	9.3

8.12.3 Pattern Parallel Approach for Sequential Circuits

We now describe an input pattern parallel fault simulation algorithm for sequential circuits. The basic approach is to partition the input pattern set into N sets assuming N processors and have each processor perform fault simulation on the entire fault list (with fault dropping) on its input patterns. A given input vector sequence T can be viewed as a concatenation of a number of equal-length subsequences, $T_0|T_1|T_2|...|T_N$, where | denotes a concatenation operation. In the conventional logic simulation, the whole sequence is applied serially to simulate the circuit. In the parallel sequence simulation, these separate sequences are simulated in parallel. Since in a sequential circuit the responses may depend on preceding inputs, the correct results cannot be guaranteed by only one pass of parallel sequence simulation. However, the parallel sequence results will contain the correct result if the initial state for each subsequence is unspecified.

In the parallel fault simulation, a processor i gets assigned input patterns T_i, for which it performs fault simulation, but has to perform true value simulation of all the preceding patterns (that is, those that are in time sequence *before* it, $T_0|T_1|T_2|...|T_{i-1}$). This is needed to set up the states of the storage elements for the time step prior to T_i. While this may seem like redundant work on each processor, the main point to be noted is that the true value simulation is only a small portion of the total computation, and the main cost is in fault simulation.

Distributed Memory MIMD Parallel Algorithm We will now describe a distributed memory parallel algorithm for fault simulation of sequential circuits using a pattern parallel approach based on work reported by Kung and Lin [52].

An outline of the parallel fault simulation algorithm *DM-PARALLEL-FSIM-SEQ-PATTERN* (denoting distributed memory parallel fault simulation of sequential circuits using input pattern decomposition) follows.

Procedure *DM-PARALLEL-FSIM-SEQ-PATTERN;*
Read circuit description;
Perform preprocessing;
Read list of faults;
Distribute true value simulation patterns to processors;

(Processor i gets $T_0|T_1|T_2|...|T_{i-1}$).
Distribute fault simulation patterns to processors;
(Processor i gets T_i)
FORALL processors in PARALLEL DO
   Perform true value simulation with own true pattern set;
   All storage element states are saved at beginning
   of current fault simulation input pattern;
   WHILE fault simulation patterns are not empty DO
      Get next group of input vectors from T_i;
      Perform fault-free simulation;
      Perform fault simulation;
      Place detected faults in an output queue for distribution
         to other processors;
      Check input queue for faults detected externally;
      Perform fault dropping based on new faults covered
         by this pass;
   ENDWHILE
END FORALL
Report fault coverage and undetected faults;
End Procedure

No implementation results of this algorithm have been reported.

8.13 CIRCUIT PARALLEL FAULT SIMULATION

8.13.1 Overview

In the circuit partitioned approach, a subset of circuit elements (gates and lines) is allocated to a processor, and simulation for that portion of the circuit is done entirely by that processor. When one processor needs information about a circuit node or line that is not in its own subset of the circuit, it must communicate with the processor that does contain the element. Hence a large amount of communication bandwidth is required.

This method has the advantage that each processor need only store the circuit description and temporary structures for a fraction of the complete circuit, and hence it is possible to implement this strategy on processors with fairly small amounts of memory per processor. The other advantage of this approach is that we can use this method without any special modifications for combinational and sequential circuits, contrary to the methods of fault partitioning and input pattern partitioning, which work best for combinational circuits and have to be modified to apply them to sequential circuits. This is because, in the circuit partitioned approach, the circuit is simulated in sequence for all the input patterns; hence any state information propagation across time frames is correctly handled.

8.13.2 Distributed Memory MIMD Parallel Algorithm

In this section, we will describe parallel fault simulation using circuit decomposition based on work reported by Levendel, Menon and Patel [53]. The parallel algorithm is suitable for distributed memory multiprocessors.

In this parallel algorithm, one processor performs as a master and the others as slaves. The circuit to be simulated is partitioned into subcircuits and each subcircuit is simulated in a separate processor. The circuit is partititioned by a depth-first method using a *strings* approach, as discussed in Chapter 7 on logic simulation. Subcircuits in different processors become active as signal values proceed from primary inputs to primary outputs. As simulation progresses, data are transferred between subcircuits as the logic values on the signal connection between two subcircuits change. The information that is exchanged consists of the true value of the node and the faulty values represented as a bit vector, which is as long as the total number of faults in the circuit. No actual implementation of this algorithm on a real parallel machine has been reported. However, the problem with this algorithm is that there is a need for communication and/or synchronization at every level. This is because the partitioning can potentially cut arbitrary lines.

We will now describe a distributed memory parallel algorithm for fault simulation using circuit decomposition for sequential circuits based on work reported by Mueller-Thuns et al. [62]. A standard concurrent fault simulation algorithm can be used as the serial algorithm executing on each processor. The circuit is partitioned into zero-delay fan-in cones of latches, as reported in the circuit parallel scheme for parallel logic simulation in Chapter 7.

A *zero-delay fan-in cone* of a latch is defined recursively as all zero-delay elements fanning into the latch and their zero-delay fan-in cones. The goal of this partitioning strategy is to assign latches of the sequential circuit to different processors and to ensure that each processor also owns the complete zero-delay fan-in cone of that latch. Thus all processors can compute a complete zero-delay cycle independently and need to synchronize only on the clock boundaries.

The proposed partitioned approach leads to a cycle by cycle synchronous logic simulation scheme by which for each input vector at each processor, the following steps are performed. First, all the signals needed from other processors are received. Second, the affected gates are scheduled. Third, for all the levels in the partition, the gates at each level are evaluated and its fan-out gates scheduled. Finally, all the required signals for the next cycle are sent to other processors.

To process the activity of receiving signals from the input buffers and writing out values to the output buffers, two new gate types, the *receive gate* and the *send gate*, are introduced. When a new vector of signals arrives from another processor, it is immediately propagated to the correct pins of the receiving gate. The receive gates propagate the changes, if any, to the circuit. Thus, if a signal from processor A is connected to several gates from processor B, it will be only sent once, and a receive gate in processor B will take care of fanning it out. Similarly, the send gate writes new signal values to the buffers that will be transmitted to other processors.

The preceding algorithm is extended to perform parallel fault simulation by maintaining lists of fault effects for each primitive element (gate) in the circuit. The send gates introduced previously collect all the faults visible on the boundary of the subcircuit. If the send gate corresponds to a primary output, the faults are detected; otherwise, the faults need to be sent to the connected processors. The array of signal values exchanged for good machine simulation gets replaced by an array of pairs containing both the signal values and the list of faults visible at a particular pin. To avoid allocating worst-case buffer space for each pin, one large buffer for all the output channels of a processor is provided and partitioned dynamically. For transmitting fault information, three steps are performed. (1) The faults associated with each send gate are counted. (2) The buffer is partitioned for fault information. (3) The fault information is packed into the buffer. A *fault array* is maintained to keep track of which faults have been detected and can therefore be dropped.

An outline of the parallel fault simulation algorithm *DM-PARALLEL-FSIM-CIRCUIT* (denoting distributed memory parallel fault simulation using circuit decomposition) follows.

> **Procedure** *DM-PARALLEL-FSIM-CIRCUIT;*
> Read circuit;
> Read list of faults;
> Read input patterns;
> Partition circuit into zero-delay fan-in cones;
> Assign subcircuit cones to processors;
> FORALL processors in PARALLEL DO
>   FOR all vectors being simulated DO
>   Receive all needed signals and fault lists
>   from other processors;
>   Schedule affected gates;
>   FOR level l = 1 to maximum_level DO
>   Evaluate gates and faults at rank l;
>   Schedule fan-out elements;
>   ENDFOR
>   Send required signals and fault lists
>   for next cycle to other processors;
>   Update fault array, perform fault dropping;
>   ENDFOR
> END FORALL
> **End Procedure**

We will now describe a different parallel fault simulation algorithm using circuit partitioning for combinational and sequential circuits based on work reported by Ghosh [36]. The novelty in this algorithm is in the *asynchronous* nature by which the fault simulation tasks on the circuit partitions are executed. It borrows concepts from asynchronous parallel event-driven simulation [30] and applies them to the fault simulation problem.

A model M representing a component C of the circuit consists of a behavioral description of C and a list of faults. Associated with every input and output port p of C is a *fault-list(p)*, which is a linked list of records that contain the effects of faults outside of C at the port p. Each record contains the logical value, assertion time fault identifier. When a new signal is asserted at one or more input ports $p_1, p_2, ..., p_n$ of model M, it is initiated for execution. First, the activation time of the model t_1, is computed as the minimum assertion times among all its ports. The significance of the activation time is that the model may execute at time $t = t_1$

TABLE 8.11 Runtimes (Seconds) and Speedups of Parallel Fault Simulation Algorithm on Intel iPSC/2™ Hypercube

Circuit	Gates	1 Processor		8 Processors	
		Runtime	Speedup	Runtime	Speedup
s13207	7,951	199.5	1.0	55.4	3.6
s15850	9,772	310.9	1.0	66.1	4.7
s35932	16,065	102.7	1.0	13.9	7.4
s38584	19,253	315.7	1.0	71.8	4.4
s22179	22,179	148.7	1.0	27.5	5.4

with absolute certainty. This is similar to the conservative method of asynchronous parallel discrete event simulations [30]. When t_1 exceeds the value of the previous activation time of M, the model M is executed. As part of the execution of M, all those fault list entries at the input ports $p_1, ..., p_n$ with assertion times less than t_1 are identified and simulated one at a time. For a fault list entry at p_j characterized by $\{V_1, t_{x1}, f_{d1}\}$ (where V_1, t_{x1}, f_{d1} are the logical value assertion time and fault identifier respectively), V_1 is asserted at p_j, the model is executed, and the value V_2 is generated at time $t_1 + \delta$, where δ is the propagation delay of M. The output along with the fault identifier is stored in the output fault list of that port, and the corresponding input fault list entry is deleted. Other fault entries whose assertion times exceed t_1 cannot be executed. This algorithm proceeds asynchronously among various processors.

An extension of this basic algorithm to sequential circuits creates the problem of deadlocks, similar to deadlocks in asynchronous parallel discrete event simulation [30]. The approach proposed by the author is to have the user identify feedback cycles in the circuit graph and break them and provide the NODIFS simulator with an acyclic graph on which the asynchronous simulations are run.

Implementation Mueller-Thuns et al. [62] have reported an implementation of the preceding algorithm, *DM-PARALLEL-FSIM-CIRCUIT*, on an Intel iPSC™ hypercube multicomputer for several ISCAS-89 sequential circuit becnhmarks [14]. Table 8.11 shows the runtimes and speedups of several ISCAS-89 sequential benchmark circuits on the Intel iPSC/2™ hypercube multicomputer. In the experiments the circuits were simulated with 1000 random input patterns.

A related parallel algorithm for fault simulation on a hypercube-based distributed memory multiprocessor has been reported by Nelson [66]. In this approach the circuit is first levelized. Subsequently, the circuit is partitioned into as many groups as there are levels in the circuit. The gates in each level are fault simulated by a unique processor in the hypercube using deductive fault simulation. Reasonably good speedups were obtained for some example circuits.

Ghosh [36] has implemented the asynchronous parallel fault simulation algorithm called NODIFS for combinational and sequential circuits on an experimental parallel processor system called ARMSTRONG™ at Brown University. Even though the parallel algorithm was novel, the experimental results on speedups were extremely poor on real circuits.

8.13.3 Shared Memory MIMD Parallel Algorithm

We now describe a shared memory parallel algorithm for fault simulation of sequential circuits using circuit partitioning based on work reported by Patil, Banerjee, and Patel [80]. The basic event-driven deductive fault simulator for synchronous sequential circuits uses a levelized circuit graph and processes the events in level order. This makes the evaluation of the events very efficient since each gate will be evaluated exactly once. In conventional event-driven simulation algorithms, since events may be processed in any arbitrary order, a gate may be evaluated more than once (as many times as the number of inputs of the gate). In the case of deductive fault simulation, it is critical that a gate be reevaluated as few times as possible since the cost of computing the fault list at a gate output can be very high (since each such evaluation will involve a series of list intersection and merge operations).

A circuit partitioned approach is used in parallel fault simulation. Various techniques have been proposed in the past for parallel logic simulation using circuit partitioning [91, 92]. The most obvious (and least efficient) technique is to maintain a single global event queue from which different processors obtain events for processing. The processors synchronize at each gate level before proceeding to evaluate the events scheduled for the next gate level. Although this technique would ensure that the processor loads are balanced at all times, the contention for the single event queue can limit the speedups severely. It has been observed that it may not be possible to obtain speedups of more than 2 to 3 for logic simulation [92]. To tackle this problem, a distributed event-queue approach was suggested in [92] that allows event updates to be done in parallel without the need to lock a global event queue. The proposed parallel fault simulation algorithm also uses distributed event queues, but is different from the approach suggested in [92] in the sense that the circuit partitioning is done statically.

The need for an event queue can be dispensed with by using a *compiled code* simulation approach in which a gate is evaluated irrespective of whether the inputs of the gates have changed. However, even though the speedups obtained over the corresponding uniprocessor algorithm may be close to linear, the overall runtimes will still be much higher than that for the corresponding parallel event-driven simulation algorithm because of the extra computation involved for gates whose outputs have not changed.

Another approach is to evaluate the gates in an asynchronous fashion, that is, process the events as they arrive instead of synchronizing at each gate level before proceeding to the next level. This method gets rid of the barrier synchronization needed at each gate level. However, this might entail reevaluating a gate a number of times. In a logic simulation environment, for which the process of reevaluating a gate is basically a table look-up operation, the overheads are bound to be low. Also, since the number of logic values possible at the output of a logic gate is very low, the probability that a gate output is going to change and initiate further events is also low. Thus optimistic asynchronous approaches such as the time warp [45] and the Chandy-Misra [20] algorithms may be well-suited for logic simulation. However, in deductive fault simulation, since the effect of all the faults is evaluated concurrently, the probability that a gate output is going to change is very high. Since re-evaluation of gate outputs is going to be more expensive than in the case of logic simulation, the performance gains will not be very high. Thus an efficient parallel algorithm should avoid reevaluating the gates by constraining events to be evaluated in level order.

The parallel fault simulation approach of Patil, Banerjee, and Patel [80] first assigns gates statically to each processor. Thus, normally, a processor that *owns* the gate will process an event associated with that gate. After the initial static assignment, a dynamic assignment of events takes place when processors become idle. Due to the efficiency of the dynamic allocation, it was found that the static assignment of gates has very little effect on the performance of the parallel fault simulator as long as roughly an equal number of gates are assigned to each processor. Once the gates are assigned to each processor, each processor generates a list of gates assigned to itself. Also, the list is partitioned into L separate lists where L is the number of levels in the logic circuit. A list for level l for a processor p contains all gates at level l that are assigned to processor p. Barrier synchronization takes place at each level of the logic circuit so that all processors are done with processing gates at level l before proceeding with level $(l+1)$. Each gate has a shared flag associated with it that is set when that particular gate is scheduled for evaluation and reset when the gate has been evaluated.

Thus, if a gate g owned by processor p is to be scheduled for evaluation, the processor generating the event sets the flag associated with that gate instead of making an entry in the event list for processor p, which would require locking of the event list. The gate evaluation flags can be set by different processors without the need to lock the data structure for that gate. Before a processor begins evaluating the gates scheduled for evaluation at level l, the processor goes through the list of gates owned at processor l and generates an event list for all gates whose evaluation flag is set. Thus this event list generation can proceed concurrently. Once the event list is generated, the evaluation of gates at level l begins. The dynamic load balancing strategy (discussed next), however, necessitates that the event queue be locked when an event is deleted from the queue for processing. But the contention for the queue is very low since other processors will be accessing the queue only when they become idle. Also, a count is maintained that shows the number of events left unprocessed at level l by processor p.

Even though an equal number of gates are assigned to different processors, it is very likely that the processor workloads are skewed due to unequal activity in different portions of the logic circuit. This is taken care of by a dynamic load balancing strategy that supplements the static allocation. When a processor p_i exhausts all events owned by itself at level l, it starts looking into the event lists owned by other processors. Then p_i determines processor p_d that owns the largest unprocessed event list at level l. If the length of the event list owned by p_d is greater than a threshold MIN-EVENTS, processor p_i gains access (by locking) to the event queue owned by p_d and divides the events scheduled for evaluation on p_d equally between itself and p_d. If the number of events left is less than MIN-EVENTS, processor p_i simply waits at the barrier for all processors to complete evaluation of gates scheduled at level l.

The uniprocessor version of the deductive fault simulator incorporates efficient memory retrieval techniques that are based on updating the reference counts associated with dynamic lists generated by different gates. However, in a parallel environment, the reference counts may be updated by different processors, which would require mutual exclusion. Instead of using reference counts, the parallel algorithm contains a list of gates at each level whose fault lists can be retrieved. These memory retrieval lists at each level are also divided equally among different processors so that memory retrieval can proceed in parallel. Also, the deductive fault simulation is preceded by a phase in which the state of the good circuit is evaluated. It has been shown in [37] that the fault simulation activity decreases almost exponentially with the number of test vectors since fewer faults per vector are detected as the number of vectors is increased. Thus the good circuit simulation dominates the computation time as the number of vectors is increased, and it becomes necessary to speed up the good circuit simulation. The state of the good circuit is also evaluated in parallel using techniques very similar to those used for parallel fault simulation.

An outline of the parallel fault simulation algorithm *SM-PARALLEL-FSIM-CIRCUIT* (denoting shared memory parallel fault simulation using circuit decomposition) follows:

> **Procedure** *SM-PARALLEL-FSIM-CIRCUIT;*
> Read circuit;
> Read list of faults;
> Read list of inputs;
> Partition gates in logic circuit;
> Initially statically assign partitions to processors;
> FORALL processors in PARALLEL DO
>   FOR all vectors being simulated DO
>   FOR level L = 1 to maximum_level DO
>   Each processor creates event list at level L
>   on *owned gates* by looking at set flags
>   FOR each event on event list at level L DO
>   IF processor's event list at level L empty
>   THEN Perform dynamic load balancing to take
>   half events of most loaded processor;
>   Each processor evaluates gates on
>   *owned event list* at rank l;
>   Schedule fan-out elements, i.e.
>   Set flags of associated gates;
>   ENDFOR
>   ENDFOR
>   Update fault array, perform fault dropping;
>   ENDFOR
> END FORALL
> **End Procedure**

As an example, consider the synchronous sequential circuit shown in Figure 8.32. The circuit is first levelized starting from the pseudo-inputs and the primary inputs. Thus the circuit has seven levels, denoted by L_1 through L_7. The vertical lines in Figure 8.32 are the points for barrier synchronization during the fault simulation process. Thus, all gates at a particular level can be evaluated in parallel since all the inputs of any gate at that level would have been evaluated. For example, gates 14 and 15 can be evaluated in parallel when level L_3 is evaluated. Also, memory retrieval at each level can take place in parallel. For example, after evaluation of gate 20 at level L_5, memory associated with fault lists for gates 18 and 19

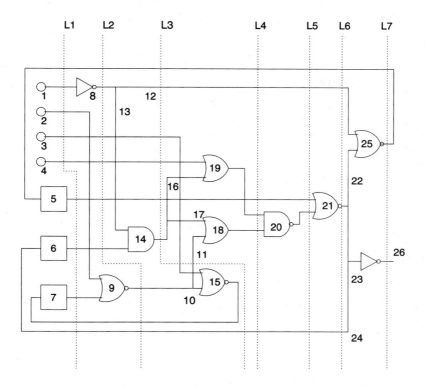

Figure 8.32 Parallel fault simulation

can be returned to the free pool. The minimum time to evaluate a given circuit in parallel depends on the time required to evaluate the gates along the critical path in the logic circuit.

Implementation Patil et al. have reported an implementation of parallel fault simulation on several ISCAS-89 sequential benchmark circuits [14] on an Encore Multimax™ shared memory multiprocessor with eight processors [80]. Table 8.12 shows some example results on several ISCAS-89 sequential benchmark circuits of the runtimes (in seconds) and speedups of the parallel algorithm for fault simulation on the Encore Multimax™ multiprocessor. It should be noted that the input vectors applied were vectors obtained from a deterministic test generator and are not random input vectors as reported in other results.

8.13.4 Massively Parallel SIMD Algorithm

We will now present a massively parallel SIMD algorithms for fault simulation based on work reported by Narayanan and Pitchumani [64, 65]. The fault simulation algorithm is based on the parallel pattern single fault propagation (PPSFP) algorithm described earlier [98]. In the PPSFP approach, the given combinational circuit is rank ordered and simulated using compiled simulation techniques for N patterns in the fault-free case and subsequently for a single fault for the same N patterns. This is repeated for each undetected fault. Then the next set of N patterns is chosen, and the process is repeated for the undetected faults.

TABLE 8.12 Runtimes (Seconds) and Speedups of Parallel Fault Simulation Algorithm on the Encore Multimax™ Multiprocessor

Circuit	Gates	Vectors	1 Processor		8 Processors	
			Runtime	Speedup	Runtime	Speedup
s444	474	713	121.0	1.0	51.0	2.4
s5378	4,603	856	771.8	1.0	160.0	4.8
s13207	7,951	111	194.9	1.0	42.4	4.6
s35932	16,065	86	1118.4	1.0	177.1	6.3

The PPSFP single fault simulation algorithm can be mapped to a massively parallel SIMD machine such as the connection machine by mapping each gate of the circuit onto a processing element (PE) called the *gate PE*. Also, each point-to-point connection in the circuit is mapped to a unique PE called the *link PE*.

The parallel algorithm for massively parallel fault simulation *SIMD-PARALLEL-FSIM-PPSFP-CIRCUIT* (denoting an SIMD parallel algorithm for fault simulation using circuit decomposition) follows:

Procedure *SIMD-PARALLEL-FSIM-PPSFP-CIRCUIT;*
Read in Circuit Description;
Map each gate, primary input/output to gate-PE;
Map each connection to link-PE;
Perform Preprocessing such as rank ordering;
FORALL processors in PARALLEL DO
    WHILE input vectors remaining AND undetected faults
        Load next group of N input vectors;
        Initialize primary inputs with the test vectors;
            (Patterns stored as vector of N bits)
        Perform fault-free simulation for N input patterns;
           FOR level = 1 to max_level DO
              Select ALL link-PEs at current level;
                  Link PEs read logic values from source gate-PEs;
                  Link PEs send logic values to destination gate-PEs;
              Select gate-PEs at current level;
                  Gate-PEs combine logic values they receive
                      using appropriate reduction operations;
        ENDFOR
        Inject one fault into network;
        Perform fault simulation;
           FOR level = 1 to max_level DO
              Select ALL link-PEs at current level;

> Link PEs read logic values from source gate-PEs;
> Link PEs send logic values to destination gate-PEs;
> Select gate-PEs at current level;
>> Gate-PEs combine logic values they receive
>> using appropriate reduction operations;
> Increment current level and repeat above steps;
> ENDFOR
> Compare outputs of fault-free and faulty networks;
> ENDWHILE
> END FORALL
> Report fault coverage and undetected faults;
> **End Procedure**

The preceding algorithm simulates all the gates in level 1 simultaneously, then all gates in level 2, and so on. In reality, the operation of the combining operation at the gate PEs during the simulation is broken up into a small number of steps, one for each type of gate type, such as AND or OR. Also, inverting functions such as NAND and NOR that are not really associative are computed by first computing the noninverting combining operation such as AND or OR and then by inverting the result. The rank ordering keeps only the essential PEs active at each step.

Implementation Narayanan and Pitchumani have implemented the above massively parallel algorithm on the Thinking Machines CM-2™ system [64, 65]. The algorithm has been evaluated on several ISCAS-85 combinational benchmark circuits [15]. For one circuit, c1355, about 1715 processing elements were used, and it resulted in a gate evaluation rate of 330,000 gate evaluations per second.

8.14 PIPELINED FAULT SIMULATION

8.14.1 Overview

We finally discuss another approach to parallel fault simulation using a pipelined decomposition that has been presented by Ozguner et al. [70]. Parallelism is achieved by partitioning the circuit so that different processors compute fault lists for each subcircuit. In this method, a pipeline-type approach can be used in which all gates at a particular logic level form a stage of a pipeline. The different input patterns are then pipelined through the logic circuit. In the case of sequential circuits, since the test vectors have to be applied in sequence, it is not possible to exploit input pattern parallelism. Also, due to the presence of feedback paths through memory elements, the speedups possible through pipelined parallelism may be severely limited.

8.14.2 Distributed Memory MIMD Parallel Algorithm

The distributed memory parallel algorithm for fault simulation using the pipelined approach works as follows. Different processors compute fault lists for each subcircuit in a pipelined manner. Since the circuit must be processed level by level from the inputs to the outputs, the computational dependencies in the fault simulation can be modeled by a task precedence graph as shown in Figure 8.33(a). Each vertex in the task precedence graph represents a

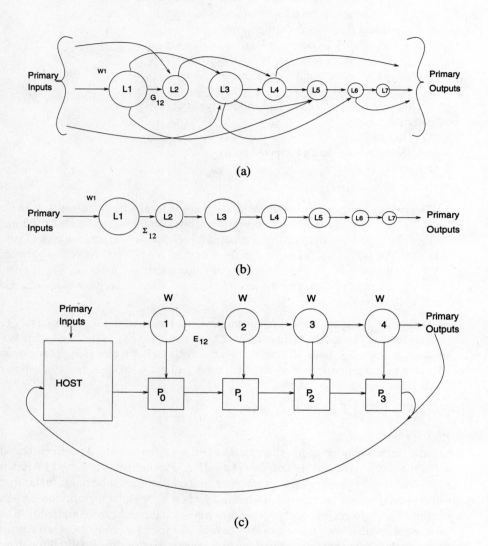

Figure 8.33 Parallel fault simulation using pipelined decomposition. (a) Task precedence graph in deductive fault simulation. (b) Edge-collapsed task precedence graph.(c) Mapping of task graph on ring of processors. (Courtesy of Ozguner et al., *Proc. 3rd Conf. Hypercube Concurrent Computers Applications*, ©ACM 1988)

computational task associated with fault simulation for the gates in a single level of the logic circuit for one input test pattern. A directed edge e_{ij} from vertex v_i to vertex v_j in the task precedence graph indicates that at least one of the gates at level L_j has an input from a gate at level L_i. The weight associated with each vertex represents the fault simulation time for the corresponding level of the logic circuit for one test pattern.

In a levelized logic circuit, there may be fan-outs from the outputs of the gates at level L_i to the inputs at level L_j, for $j = i + 1, ..., N_L$, where N_L indicates the number of levels in the circuit. In the next step, the task precedence graph is collapsed into a edge-collapsed graph in which all directed edges from vertex v_i to the succeeding vertices of the TPG are collapsed into a single directed edge $E_{i,i+1}$, thus resulting in a directed chain *TPG* as shown in Figure 8.33(b).

Hence the fault simulation problem modeled using edge-collapsed task precedence graph can be pipelined into a linear array of processors by assigning the simulation of each level (vertex of the task precedence graph) to a processor of the linear array. Concurrency is achieved by starting the simulation for the next test pattern on a processor, while processors in the succeeding stages finish computations for the current test pattern.

This parallel algorithm requires as many processors as there are levels in a circuit, which for some deep circuits may be very large. Moreover, the simulation rate of this algorithm is limited by the bottleneck processor that is assigned the level that requires the maximum simulation time.

The total simulation time in the parallel algorithm is minimized by balancing the simulation loads of each processor that is proportional to the number of gates assigned to that processor. Load balancing is achieved by mapping a logic circuit with N_L levels and N_G gates to P processors by assigning approximately N_G/P gates per processor, with all the gates in the partition being in succeeding levels. This load balanced mapping of the task graph on four processors is shown in Figure 8.33(c).

An outline of the parallel fault simulation algorithm *DM-PARALLEL-FSIM-PIPE* (denoting distributed memory parallel fault simulation using pipelined decomposition) is given next.

> **Procedure** *DM-PARALLEL-FSIM-PIPE;*
> Read circuit description;
> Rank order the circuit into levels;
> Configure processors as a linear array;
> Map one level of gates to one processor;
> Read list of faults;
> FORALL processors in PARALLEL DO
>   Each processor p works on level(p) of gates;
>   WHILE there are input vectors left to simulate DO
>   Receive next set of inputs from previous processor, p-1;
>   Perform fault-free simulation on level(p) gates;
>   Perform fault simulation on level(p) gates;
>   IF (processor owns output level) THEN
>   Report detected faults;

Send fault-free and faulty outputs of gates
in current level to next processor, p+1;
ENDWHILE
END FORALL
Report fault coverage and undetected faults;
End Procedure

Implementation Ozguner et al. [70] implemented this parallel algorithm on an Intel iPSC/2™
hypercube. Speedups of about 3.5 to 4 were reported on eight processors on two sample
circuits.

8.15 HARDWARE ACCELERATORS

There have been several hardware accelerators proposed for test generation and fault simulation. Chakradhar et al. [16] have proposed a massively parallel algorithm for test generation
using a neural network model of a logic circuit. In this method, a combinational digital circuit
is represented as a bidirectional network of neurons. The circuit function is coded in the firing
thresholds of neurons and the weights of the interconnection links. This neural network is
suitably configured for solving the ATPG problem. A fault is injected into the neural network
and an energy function is constructed with a global minimum at test vectors. The ATPG
algorithm is implemented on the neural network as a directed search technique augmented
by probabilistic relaxation. No actual neural network hardware has been implemented. The
algorithm has been verified through simulations on a serial computer. Preliminary results on
example circuits showed the feasibility of the approach.

Hirose et al. [41] have proposed a test generation algorithm based on fast parallel logic
simulation using circuit partitioned methods on a special-purpose simulation processor called
SP developed by Fujitsu Ltd. [28]. In this system, the circuit is divided topologically among
several processors called gate processors. Faults are injected into the circuit, and a depth-first
search similar to that of PODEM searches the entire input space to find an input that detects
the injected faults. In this approach, given a combinational circuit C that has faults F, a
test generation circuit $S(C, F)$ is synthesized on a host computer and is simulated on the SP
simulation processor through circuit partitioned techniques. Figure 8.34 shows the concept
behind the approach. The fault injector is embedded onto the circuit C so that it injects single
stuck-at faults successively. The input searcher searches the inputs to expose the faults. The
output checker detects if a fault is detected or not for an input pattern. The strategy controller
controls the timing of the input searcher and the fault controller. The input searcher executes a
depth-first search in the input vector space, which is implemented as a one-dimensional array
of registers with carry. Figure 8.35 shows an example circuit with a single stuck-at-1 fault.
First, the inputs (S, A, B) of the circuit are set to (X, X, X), which is the set of all input patterns,
and through logic and fault simulation it is determined if the output can detect the fault. The
set is partitioned into (1, X, X) and (0, X, X). Since (1, X, X) does not detect the fault, the (0,
X, X) pattern is applied (simulate a backtracking). The same procedure is repeated for all the
inputs by changing the values from X to 1 to 0 until finally the entire search space is explored.
This method searches the space in a predetermined order, as opposed to the PODEM algorithm

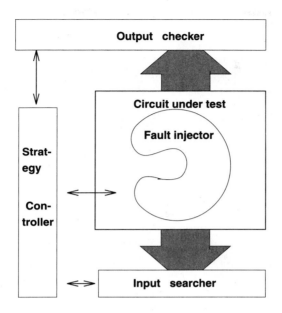

Figure 8.34 Test generation accelerator (Courtesy of Hirose et al., *Proc. Int. Test Conf.,* ©IEEE 1988)

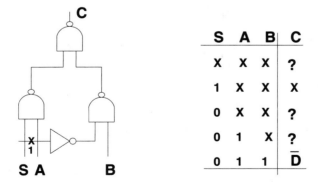

S	A	B	C
X	X	X	?
1	X	X	X
0	X	X	?
0	1	X	?
0	1	1	$\overline{D}$

Figure 8.35 Depth-first search on accelerator (Courtesy of Hirose et al., *Proc. Int. Test Conf.,* ©IEEE 1988)

[38] for which heuristics are used to decide the order and values of signal assigments to inputs. Since the SP is an ultra-high-speed event-driven logic simulator simulating 800 million gate evaluations per second, this method of test generation becomes practical.

Several research projects have investigated the use of dedicated hardware accelerators for logic simulation. Most of the accelerators have been used for fault simulation as well. The hardware accelerators for logic simulation were discussed in Chapter 7. For completeness, we are reviewing the same machines and highlighting how they have been used for performing fast fault simulation.

IBM has built three generations of simulation engines that use circuit parallel algorithms using the compiled synchronous approach. The machines are the Logic Simulation Machine (LSM)™ [42], the Yorktown Simulation Engine™ [82], the Engineering Verification Engine™ [26]. All the machines use the same basic architecture. The machines support logic simulation with three or four logic values, 0, 1, X, and high impedance, and zero- and unit-delay models. It consists of 64 to 256 processors, which are connected by a 64 to 256 size crossbar switch that performs fast interprocessor communication. The logic circuit is partitioned into 4K gates each having about four to five inputs. The logic subcircuits are simulated by logic processors, and the memory elements are simulated by array processors.

The EVE™ accelerator is in production use at IBM. It uses more than 200 special purpose processors. They are either logic processors that evaluate arbitrary four-input one-output logic functions or so-called array processors that simulate memory elements (the so-called arrays). The processors are connected by a full 256-to-256 crosspoint switch that is scheduled statically for interprocessor communication. The design to be simulated is partitioned automatically among the processors based on the rank ordering of the logic. EVE can simulate up to 1.8 million gates and 50 Mbytes of storage. Its peak performance is rated at 2.2 billion gate evaluations per second; typical real performance lies at about 80% of the peak performance.

Fault simulation can be performed on these machines using the following compiled fault simulation algorithm. The given logic circuit is partitioned into groups of 4K gates, and each partition is mapped onto a logic processor. The partitioned circuit is rank ordered and simulated using compiled simulation techniques for N patterns in the fault-free case. Subsequently, a single fault is selected from the global fault list and injected into the circuit. The circuit model is modified in the processor where the fault is injected. The modified circuit model is simulated for the same N patterns. This is repeated for each undetected fault. Then the next set of N patterns is chosen, and the process is repeated for the undetected faults.

Another widely used commercial accelerator for gate-level simulation is offered by Zycad [23]. It uses a synchronous event-driven approach to circuit parallel logic simulation and a bus-based multiprocessor architecture with up to 16 processors that implement scheduling and evaluation in hardware. It exhibits a peak performance of 16 million gate evaluations per second and can handle up to 1.1 million gates. Fault simulation is performed on these machines by invoking a concurrent fault simulation algorithm on the logic partitions on each processor.

Finally, there have been several hardware accelerators that use the functional parallel approach to parallel logic and fault simulation. To exploit parallelism in this algorithm, the simulation procedure can be partitioned into pipelined stages. Such an approach has been used in the MARS™ hardware accelerator [3, 4, 5] which was discussed in Chapter 7. The accelerator was used to implement a multipass concurrent fault simulator [1]. Each pass of the concurrent fault simulator was partitioned into pipelined stages with the following tasks: (1) signal scheduler, (2) oscillation detector, (3) output logger, (4) fan-out pointer processors, (5) fan-out list processors, (6) fault data structure processors, (7) injected input fault keeper, (8) gate table and truth table processor, (9) event detector, (10) delay unit, (11) input vector list processor, and (12) injected output fault keeper, with the output of stage 12 fed back to stage 1. The performance of the MARS hardware has been reported to be about five to six times faster than a software fault simulator run on a SUN 3/260™ workstation [1].

Algorithms and implementations of fault simulation on vector processing machines are discussed in [43, 44, 71, 94]. The common theme in all these approaches is to note that a vector processor has the facility to execute operations on vectors extremely fast, hence the contribution of these algorithms is in mapping a fault simulation problem into a vector processing problem. Parallel simulation utilizes bit-oriented logic operations to perform a lot of gate evaluations simultaneously. If one word of a computer consists of b bits, b gate evaluations can be performed at a time. Parallel simulation can be classified as fault-parallel or pattern-parallel simulation. The former simulates b fault classes for one input pattern at a time by assigning one fault case to 1 bit. The latter simulates b inputs patterns for one fault at a time by assigning each fault case to 1 bit. In each method, by simply extending the unit of gate evaluation from a word to a vector consisting of multiple words, we can achieve extended pattern parallelism or extended fault parallelism as shown in Figure 8.36. Ozguner et al. [71] proposed a scheme for pattern-parallel vectorized fault simulation on a CRAY YMP™ vector machine.

The efficiency of the pattern-parallel or fault-parallel vectorized techniques increases with long vector lengths. However, in many cases, long vector lengths cannot be obtained because of fault dropping. Ishiura et al. proposed a dynamic two-dimensional parallel fault simulation technique [43], by which large vector lengths were obtained by utilizing both pattern and fault parallelism. However, it was noted that, due to fault dropping, the number of undetected faults drops exponentially with the number of vectors applied. Hence it is better to apply fault parallelism for the early passes and then pattern parallelism for the later passes. By dynamically adjusting the two parallelism factors complementarily from pass to pass, the authors proposed a dynamic fault simulation algorithm. This is illustrated in Figure 8.37. This method was implemented on a Fujitsu FACOM VP-200™ vector processor that accelerated fault simulation by a factor of 20 over conventional methods.

8.16 SUMMARY

In this chapter, we discussed parallel algorithms for test generation and fault simulation of combinational and sequential circuits. The parallel algorithms for test generation were based on fault parallelism, circuit parallelism, search parallelism, functional parallelism, and heuristic parallelism. The parallel algorithms for fault simulation were based on fault parallelism, input pattern parallelism, circuit parallelism, and pipelined parallelism.

Fault parallel test generation refers to the evaluation of the test patterns for the given fault set in parallel. In this method, the fault set is divided equally among n processors. Each processor can now generate tests for its own fault set independently. This method has the advantage that the approach is independent of the actual ATPG and fault simulation algorithm

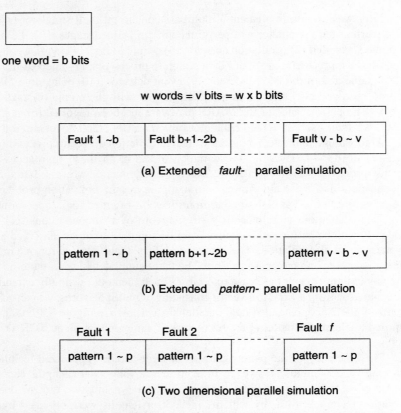

(a) Extended *fault-* parallel simulation

(b) Extended *pattern-* parallel simulation

(c) Two dimensional parallel simulation

Figure 8.36 Fault, pattern, and two-dimensional vectorized fault simulation. (a) Extended *fault*-parallel simulation. (b) Extended *pattern*-parallel simulation. (c) Two-dimensional parallel simulation. (Courtesy of Ishiura et al., *IEEE Trans. Computer-aided Design*, ©IEEE 1987)

used and is therefore the easiest to use. Excellent speedups can be achieved with a dynamic partitioning of the fault list using a multipass approach. In such an approach, each pass of test generation and fault simulation is performed using a fixed time limit per fault. The time limit is increased in successive passes, so the easier faults are detected in earlier passes and harder faults are detected in later passes. The main disadvantage of this approach is that the test set size increases significantly over serial algorithms. The approach is applicable to both combinational and sequential circuits.

Heuristic parallel test generation involves letting each processor use a different heuristic to guide the search for the same fault. But the main disadvantage of this method is that the parallelism is limited by the number of heuristics available for search (at most five to six). Also, by using different heuristics there is no guarantee that the search spaces are disjoint. This may lead to redundant work. Also, no improvement is possible if a fault remains undetectable for all the heuristics.

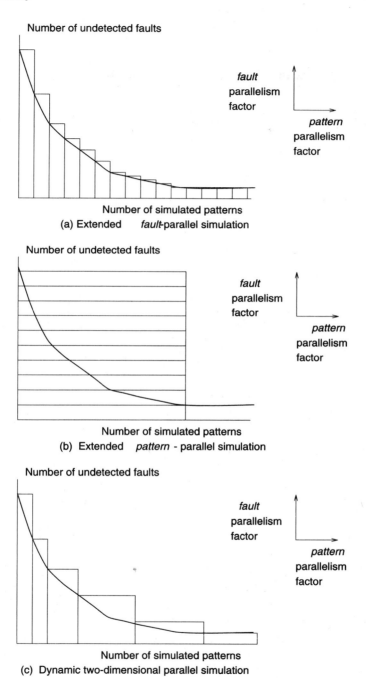

Figure 8.37 Fault, pattern, and two-dimensional vectorized simulation (Courtesy of Ishiura et al., *IEEE Trans. Computer-aided Design,* ©IEEE 1987)

Search space parallel test generation assigns disjoint search spaces to multiple processors to search for a test vector or test vector sequence of a particular fault. Each processor can be allocated a portion of the search space, either statically or dynamically, and the search for the test vector can proceed concurrently. The advantage of this approach is that the really hard to detect faults are detected by a truly parallel test generation strategy; hence this approach reduces the runtime for particularly hard faults. The other advantage is that, when integrated with a fault simulation phase after each test generation phase, the test set size can be kept almost as small as the corresponding serial algorithm. The disadvantage of this approach is that not all faults are hard to detect, and many faults are detected with a few number of backtracks, for example 10 if good heuristics are used.

Functional parallel test generation uses a divide and conquer type approach by which a task is divided into a series of subtasks, all of which have to be completed. These subtasks can be completed in parallel if they do not access or modify any common variables. If they have common variables as they do in test generation, execution of the AND-parallel subtasks becomes complicated due to variable binding conflicts. The overheads due to variable binding conflicts may essentially reduce the AND-parallel tasks to sequential execution due to consistency checking, and the like. Hence this approach is not very attractive for parallel test generation.

In all the parallel approaches discussed so far, each processor keeps a copy of the entire circuit. For extremely large circuits, the memory of each processor may not be able to store the entire circuit. In a circuit decomposed approach, each processor keeps a partition of the circuit and performs various operations (such as backtracing, justification and implication) on its own subcircuit to satisfy various test generation objectives. While this approach is attractive for really large circuits, it is extremely hard to achieve efficient speedups with this method.

For test generation, it appears that the most successful approach to parallelization is to use a combination of fault parallelism (for the first phase to detect easy faults) and search parallelism to detect the hard faults. In any case, we should include fault simulation as part of the test generation process for efficiency.

In this chapter, we also described various approaches to parallel fault simulation: fault parallel, pattern parallel, circuit parallel, and pipelining.

We can use fault parallel fault simulation by partitioning a list of faults across the available processors and having each processor perform fault simulation on all the input vectors for each sublist. It is possible to obtain almost linear speedups in the case of fault parallel implementations. The problem is that for each partition of faults we have to perform a good machine simulation. Depending on the partitioning of the faults, the fault activity of each partition for a particular input vector may not be uniform across all partitions. This approach can also give poor load balance due to widely different fault dropping characteristics. One way to provide better load balance is to partition the fault list into smaller sized partitions, but then the good machine simulation (which represents wasted work) increases significantly.

Pattern parallel fault simulation involves partitioning the input patterns and letting each processor perform fault simulation on the entire fault list but for a subset of the input patterns in parallel. This approach gives excellent speedups; however, it is restricted to combinational circuits. The approach cannot be used in sequential circuits since the future behavior of a sequential circuit depends on all previous vectors. The approach can be used if we can identify independent subsets of patterns even in sequential circuits or if we use an iterative approach to solve the simulation problem until convergence.

In all previous approaches, the entire circuit structure is kept in all memories of the parallel processors. For large circuits, the memory limitations on each processor can limit the size of circuits the fault simulation can run on. Circuit parallel fault simulation involves partitioning a given circuit among processors and having all processors cooperate in the fault simulation of all faults and all inputs together. The advantage of this approach is that it is memory efficient and can handle very large circuits. However, the communication overheads of this approach are quite high, and it is difficult to get good speedups.

In summary, for parallel fault simulation, the fault parallel approach is a general approach applicable to both combinational and sequential circuits. For very large circuits, we should use circuit parallel approaches. For medium-sized combinational circuits, the pattern parallel approach is the best.

Given the problem that the user is trying to solve, the best approach to parallel test generation and fault simulation is different. The chapter has shed light on the issues involved so as to assist the user in making an informed decision.

8.17 PROBLEMS

8.1   List the different approaches for parallel test generation. Give the advantages and disadvantages of each approach.

8.2   List the different approaches for parallel fault simulation. Give the advantages and disadvantages of each approach.

8.3   Analyze the performance of a fault parallel approach to test generation regarding the expected speedup on this approach. Assume that the circuit has G gates, F faults, and P processors. Assume some empirical complexity measures of fault simulation and test generation described in the papers by Fujiwara and Inoue [31, 32] for the analysis.

8.4   Analyze the performance of a search space parallel approach to test generation regarding the expected speedup on this approach. Assume that the circuit has G gates, F faults, and P processors. Assume some empirical complexity measures of fault simulation and test generation described in the paper by Patil and Banerjee [79] for the analysis.

8.5   Implement a fault parallel approach to test generation using an ATPG program and a fault simulation program of your choice on a distributed memory MIMD multicomputer. Use the Intel iPSC™ parallel programming library described in Chapter 2.

8.6   Implement a circuit parallel approach to fault simulation using the PPSFP algorithm on a shared memory MIMD multiprocessor. Use the Sequent™ parallel programming library described in Chapter 2.

8.7   For the circuit shown in Figure 8.7, apply search parallel test generation to show how two processors would split up the search space and solve the test generation problem in parallel.

8.8   For the circuit shown in Figure 8.7, apply circuit parallel fault simulation using deductive simulation techniques to show how two processors would split up the circuit and solve the fault simulation problem in parallel.

8.9   Apply circuit level parallel fault simulation to the circuit shown in Figure 8.32. Assume
        a shared memory MIMD parallel algorithm using two processors. Show which processors
        simulate which gates assuming a levelized solution with dynamic load balancing.

8.18 REFERENCES

[1]   P. Agrawal, V. Agrawal, K. T. Cheng, and R. Tutundjian. Fault Simulation in a Pipelined
        Multiprocessor System. *Proc. Int. Test Conf. (ITC-89)*, pages 727–734, Aug. 1989.

[2]   P. Agrawal, V. D. Agrawal, and J. Villodo. Sequential Circuit Test Generation on a Distributed
        System. *Proc. 30th Design Automation Conf. (DAC-93)*, June 1993.

[3]   P. Agrawal and W. J. Dally. A Hardware Logic Simulation System. *IEEE Trans. Computer-
        aided Design Integrated Circuits Systems*, 9(1):19–29, Jan. 1990.

[4]   P. Agrawal, W. J. Dally, A. K. Ezzat, W. C. Fischer, H. V. Jagdish, and A. S. Krishnakumar.
        Architecture and Design of the MARS Hardware Accelerator. *Proc. 24th Design Automation
        Conf.*, pages 108–113, June 1987.

[5]   P. Agrawal, W. J. Dally, W. C. Fischer, H. V. Jagdish, A. S. Krishnakumar, and R. Tutundjian.
        MARS: A Multiprocessor-based Programmable Accelerator. *IEEE Design Test Computers*,
        4(5):28–36, Oct. 1987.

[6]   V. D. Agrawal, K. T. Cheng, and P. Agrawal. CONTEST: A Concurrent Test Generator for
        Sequential Circuits. *Proc. 25th Design Automation Conf.*, June 1988.

[7]   S. B. Akers, C. Joseph, and B. Krishnamurthy. On the Role of Independent Fault Sets in the
        Generation of Minimal Test Sets. *Proc. Int. Test Conf.*, pages 1100–1107, Oct. 1987.

[8]   D. B. Armstrong. A Deductive Method for Simulating Faults in Logic Circuits. *IEEE Trans.
        Computers*, C-21:462–471, May 1972.

[9]   S. Arvindam, V. Kumar, V. N. Rao, and V. Singh. Automatic Test Pattern Generation on Parallel
        Processors. Technical Report TR-90-29, Computer Science Dept, University of Minnesota,
        Minneapolis, MN, May 1990.

[10]   R. H. Bell, R. H. Klenke, J. Aylor, and R. D. Williams. Results of a Topologically Partitioned
        Parallel Automatic Test Pattern Generation System on a Distributed Memory Multiprocessor.
        Proc. Application Specific Integrated Circuits Conf., Sept. 1992.

[11]   R. G. Bennetts. *Design of Testable Logic Circuits*. Addison-Wesley, Reading, MA, 1984.

[12]   R. G. Bennetts and et al. CAMELOT: A Computer-aided Measure for Logic Testability. *Proc.
        IEEE Autotestcon*, pages 177–189, Sept. 1981.

[13]   M. A. Breuer and A. D. Friedman. *Diagnosis and Reliable Design of Digital Systems*.
        Computer Science Press, Rockville, MD, 1976.

[14]   F. Brglez, D. Bryan, and K. Kominski. Combinational Profiles of Sequential Benchmark Circuits. *Proc. IEEE Int. Symp. Circuits Systems*, June 1989.

[15]   F. Brglez and H. Fujiwara. A Neutral Netlist of 10 Combinational Benchmark Circuits and a Target Translator in FORTRAN. *Proc. Int. Symp. Circuits Systems*, June 1985.

[16]   S. Chakradhar, M. L. Bushnell, and V. D. Agrawal. Towards Massively Parallel Automatic Test Generation. *IEEE Trans. Computer-aided Design Integrated Circuits Systems*, pages 981–994, Sept. 1990.

[17]   T. Chan. Distributed Automatic Test Pattern Generation. *Proc. Application Specific Integrated Circuits Conf. (ASIC-92)*, Sept. 1992.

[18]   S. Chandra and J. H. Patel. Test Generation in a Parallel Processing Environment. *Proc. Int. Conf. Computer Design (ICCD-88)*, pages 11–14, Oct. 1988.

[19]   S. J. Chandra and J. H. Patel. Experimental Evaluation of Testability Measures for Test Generation. *IEEE Trans. Computer-aided Design Integrated Circuits Systems*, 8:93–98, Jan. 1989.

[20]   K. M. Chandy and J. Misra. Asynchronous Distributed Simulation via a Sequence of Parallel Computations. *Comm. ACM*, 24(11):198–206, Apr. 1981.

[21]   W.-T. Cheng. The BACK Algorithm for Sequential Circuit Test Generation. *Proc. Int. Conf. Computer Design*, pages 66–69, Oct. 1988.

[22]   W. T. Cheng and T. Chakraborty. Gentest - An Automatic Test Generation System. *IEEE Computer*, 22:43–49, Apr. 1989.

[23]   ZYCAD Co. Zycad Logic Evaluator LE-1000 series –Product Description. Technical report, St. Paul, MN, 1987.

[24]   J. S. Conery. The AND/OR Process Model for Parallel Interpretation of Logic Programs. Technical Report UCI-CS-83-204, Department of Computer Science, University of California, Irvine, CA, June 1983.

[25]   P. A. Duba, R. K. Roy, J. A. Abraham, and W. A. Rogers. Fault Simulation in a Distributed Environment. *Proc. 25th Design Automation Conf.*, pages 686–691, June 1988.

[26]   L. N. Dunn. IBM's Engineering Design System Support for VLSI Design and Verification. *IEEE Design Test Computers*, pages 30–40, Feb. 1984.

[27]   E. B. Eichelberger and T. W. Williams. A Logic Design Structure for LSI Testing. *Proc. 14th Design Automation Conf.*, pages 462–468, June 1977.

[28]   F. Hirose et al. Simulation Processor SP. *Proc. Int. Conf. Computer-aided Design*, pages 484–487, Nov. 1987.

[29]   W. Fenton, B. Ramkumar, V. A. Saletore, A. B. Sinha, and L. V. Kale. Supporting Machine Independent Programming on Diverse Parallel Architecture. *Proc. Int. Conf. Parallel Processing*, Aug. 1991.

[30]   R. M. Fujimoto. Parallel Discrete Event Simulation. *Comm. ACM*, 33(3):30–53, Oct. 1990.

[31]   H. Fujiwara and T. Inoue. Optimal Granularity of Test Generation in a Distributed System. *IEEE Trans. Computer-aided Design Integrated Circuits Systems*, pages 885–892, Aug. 1990.

[32]   H. Fujiwara and T. Inoue. Optimal Test Granularity of Test Generation in a Distributed System. *Proc. Int. Conf. Computer Aided Design*, Nov. 1989.

[33]   H. Fujiwara and T. Shimono. On the Acceleration of Test Generation Algorithms. *IEEE Trans. Computers*, C-32(12):1137–1144, Dec. 1983.

[34]   H. Fujiwara and S. Toida. The Complexity of Fault Detection Problems for Combinational Logic Circuits. *IEEE Trans. Computers*, C-31(6):555–560, June 1982.

[35]   A. Ghosh, S. Devadas, and A. R. Newton. Test Generation for Highly Sequential Circuits. *Proc. Int. Conf. Computer-aided Design (ICCAD-89)*, Nov. 1989.

[36]   S. Ghosh. NODIFS: A Novel, Distributed Circuit Partitioning Based Algorithm for Fault Simulation of Combinational and Sequential Digital Designs on Loosely Coupled Parallel Processors. Technical report, LEMS, Division of Engineering, Brown University, Providence, RI, 1991.

[37]   P. Goel. Test Generation Costs Analysis and Projections. *Proc. 17th Design Automation Conf.*, June 1980.

[38]   P. Goel. An Implicit Enumeration Algorithm to Generate Tests for Combinational Logic Circuits. *IEEE Trans. Computers*, C-30(3):215–222, Mar. 1981.

[39]   L. H. Goldstein and E. L. Theigpen. SCOAP: Sandia Controllability/Observability Analysis Program. *Proc. 17th Design Automation Conf.*, pages 190–196, 1980.

[40]   D. Harel and B. Krishnamurthy. Is There Hope for Linear Time Fault Simulation? *Proc. Fault Tolerant Computing Symp.*, pages 28–33, June 1987.

[41]   F. Hirose, K. Takayama, and N. Kawato. A Method to Generate Tests for Combinational Logic using an Ultra-high Speed Logic Simulator. *Proc. Int. Test Conf.*, pages 102–107, Sept. 1988.

[42]   J. K. Howard, L. Malm, and L. M. Warren. Introduction to the IBM Los Gatos Logic Simulation Machine. *Proc. IEEE Int. Conf. Computer Design: VLSI in Computers*, pages 580–583, Oct. 1983.

[43]   N. Ishiura, M. Ito, and S. Yajima. High-speed Fault Simulation Using a Vector Processor. *Proc. Int. Conf. Computer-aided Design (ICCAD-87)*, pages 10–13, Nov. 1987.

[44]   N. Ishiura, H. Yasuura, and S. Yajima. High-speed Logic Simulation on Vector Processors. *IEEE Trans. Computer-aided Design Integrated Circuits Systems*, CAD-6, no. 3:305–321, May 1987.

[45]   D. Jefferson. Virtual Time. *ACM Trans. Programming Languages Systems*, pages 404–425, July 1985.

[46]   L. V. Kale. The Chare Kernel Parallel Programming System. *Proc. Int. Conf. Parallel Processing*, Aug. 1990.

[47]   T. P. Kelsey and K. K. Saluja. Fast Test Generation for Sequential Circuits. *Proc. Int. Conf. Computer-aided Design*, pages 354–357, Nov. 1989.

[48]   T. Kirkland and M. R. Mercer. Algorithms for Automatic Test Pattern Generation. *IEEE Design Test Computers*, pages 43–55, June 1988.

[49]   R. H. Klenke, R. D. Williams, and J. Aylor. Parallel Processing Techniques for Automatic Test Pattern Generation. *IEEE Computer*, pages 71–84, Jan. 1992.

[50]   G. A. Kramer. Employing Massive Parallelism in Digital ATPG Algorithms. *Proc. Int. Test Conf.*, pages 108–114, Oct. 1983.

[51]   P. Krauss. Parallel Automatic Test Pattern Generation Using Large Workstation Networks. Technical report, Technical University of Munich, Department of Electrical Engineering, Munich, Germany, Mar. 1993.

[52]   C. P. Kung and C. S. Lin. Parallel Sequence Fault Simulation for Synchronous Sequential Circuits. *Proc. European Design Automation Conf.*, pages 434–438, Mar. 1992.

[53]   Y. H. Levendel, P. R. Menon, and S. H. Patel. Parallel Fault Simulation Using Distributed Processing. *Bell Systems Tech. J.*, 62(10):3107–3137, December 1983.

[54]   G. J. Li and B. W. Wah. MANIP-2: A Multicomputer Architecture for Evaluating Logic Programs. *Proc. Int. Conf. Parallel Processing*, pages 123–130, Aug. 1985.

[55]   H. K. T. Ma, S. Devadas, A. R. Newton, and A. Sangiovanni-Vincentelli. Test Generation for Sequential Circuits. *IEEE Trans. Computer-aided Design Integrated Circuits Systems*, 7(10):1081–1093, Oct. 1988.

[56]   S. Mallela and S. Wu. A Sequential Test Generation System. *Proc. Int. Test Conf.*, pages 57–61, Oct. 1985.

[57]   T. Markas, M. Royals, and N. Kanopoulos. On Distributed Fault Simulation. *IEEE Computer*, pages 40–52, Jan. 1990.

[58]   R. Marlett. EBT: A Comprehensive Test Generation Technique for Highly Sequential Circuits. *Proc. 15th Design Automation Conf.*, pages 332–338, June 1978.

[59]   B. Mathew. Private communication. 1994.

[60]   P. Mayor, V. Pitchumani, and V. Narayanan. A Parallel Algorithm for Test Generation on the Connection Machine. *Proc. Int. Test Conf. (ITC-89)*, page P.9, Sept. 1989.

[61]   A. Motohara, K. Nishimura, H. Fujiwara, and I. Shirakawa. A Parallel Scheme for Test Pattern Generation. *Proc. Int. Conf. Computer-aided Design*, pages 156–159, Nov. 1986.

[62]   R. B. Mueller-Thuns, D. G. Saab, R. F. Damiano, and J. A. Abraham. Portable Parallel Logic and Fault Simulation. *Proc. Int. Conf. Computer-aided Design (ICCAD-89)*, pages 506–509, Nov. 1989.

[63]   P. Muth. A Nine-valued Circuit Model for Test Generation. *IEEE Trans. Computers*, C-25:630–636, June 1976.

[64]   V. Narayanan and V. Pitchumani. A Massively Parallel Algorithm for Fault Simulation on the Connection Machine. *Proc. 26th Design Automation Conf.*, pages 734–737, June 1989.

[65]   V. Narayanan and V. Pitchumani. A Parallel Algorithm for Fault Simulation on the Connection Machine. *Proc. Int. Test Conf. (ITC-88)*, pages 89–93, September 1988.

[66]   J. F. Nelson. Deductive Fault Simulation on Hypercube Multiprocessors. *Proc. 9th AT&T Conf. Electronic Testing*, Oct. 1987.

[67]   T. M. Niermann. Techniques for Sequential Circuit Automatic Test Generation. Technical report, Coordinated Science Lab, University of Illinois, Urbana, IL, Mar. 1991.

[68]   T. M. Niermann, W. T. Cheng, and J. H. Patel. PROOFS: A Fast, Memory-efficient Sequential Circuit Fault Simulator. *IEEE Trans. Computer-aided Design Integrated Circuits Systems*, 11(2):198–207, Feb. 1992.

[69]   D. Ostapko, Z. Barzilai, and G. M. Silberman. Fast Fault Simulation in a Parallel Processing Environment. *Proc. Int. Test Conf.*, Oct. 1987.

[70]   F. Ozguner, C. Aykanat, and O. Khalid. Logic Fault Simulation on a Vector Hypercube Multiprocessor. *Proc. 3rd Int. Conf. Hypercube Concurrent Computers Applications*, II:1108–1116, Jan. 1988.

[71]   F. Ozguner and R. Daoud. Vectorized Fault Simulation on the CRAY X-MP Supercomputer. *Proc. Int. Conf. Computer-aided Design (ICCAD-88)*, Nov. 1988.

[72]   S. Parkes, P. Banerjee, and J. Patel. ProperHITEC: A Portable, Parallel, Object-Oriented Approach to Sequential Test Generation. *Proc. 31st Design Automation Conf.*, June 1994.

[73]   S. Parkes, J. Chandy, and P. Banerjee. ProperCAD II: A Run-time Library for Portable, Parallel, Object-Oriented Programming with Applications to VLSI CAD. Technical Report CRHC-93-22/UILU-ENG-93-2250, University of Illinois, Coordinated Science Lab, Urbana, IL, Dec. 1993.

[74]   S. T. Patel and J. H. Patel. Effectiveness of Heuristic Measures for Automatic Test Pattern Generation. *Proc. 23rd Design Automation Conf.*, pages 547–552, 1986.

[75]   S. Patil. Parallel Algorithms for Test Generation and Fault Simulation. Technical report, Coordinated Science Lab, University of Illinois, Urbana, IL, Sept. 1990.

[76]   S. Patil and P. Banerjee. Fault Partitioning Issues in an Integrated Parallel Test Generation Fault Simulation Environment. *Proc. Int. Test Conf.*, pages 718–727, Aug. 1989.

[77]   S. Patil and P. Banerjee. Performance Trade-offs in a Parallel Test Generation Fault Simulation Environment. *IEEE Trans. Computer-aided Design Integrated Circuits Systems*, 10(12):1542–1558, Dec. 1991.

[78]   S. Patil and P. Banerjee. A Parallel Branch and Bound Approach to Test Generation. *Proc. 26th Design Automation Conf.*, pages 339–345, June 1989.

[79]   S. Patil and P. Banerjee. A Parallel Branch and Bound Approach to Test Generation. *IEEE Trans. Computer-aided Design Integrated Circuits Systems*, 9(3):313–322, Mar. 1990.

[80]   S. Patil, P. Banerjee, and J. Patel. Parallel Test Generation for Sequential Circuits on General Purpose Multiprocessors. *Proc. 28th Design Automation Conf. (DAC-91)*, June 1991.

[81]   S. Patil, P. Banerjee, and C. Polychronopolous. Efficient Circuit Partitioning Algorithms for Parallel Logic Simulation. *Proc. Supercomputing Conf.*, pages 361–364, Nov. 1989.

[82]   G. Pfister. The Yorktown Simulation Engine: Introduction. *Proc. 19th Design Automation Conf.*, pages 51–54, June 1982.

[83]   B. Ramkumar and P. Banerjee. A Portable Parallel Algorithm for Test Generation. *Proc. Int. Conf. Computer-aided Design (ICCAD-92)*, Nov. 1992.

[84]   V. N. Rao and V. Kumar. Parallel Depth First Search, Part I: Implementation. *Int. J. Parallel Programming*, 16(6), 1987.

[85]   V. N. Rao and V. Kumar. Parallel Depth First Search, Part II: Analysis. *Int. J. Parallel Programming*, 16(6), 1987.

[86]   J. P. Roth. Diagnosis of Automata Failures: A Calculus and a Method. *IBM J. Research Dev.*, 10:278–291, July 1966.

[87]   J. P. Roth, W. G. Bouricius, and P. R. Schneider. Programmed Algorithms to Compute Tests to Detect and Distinguish between Failures in Logic Circuits. *IEEE Trans. Computers*, EC-16(5):567–580, Oct. 1967.

[88]   V. A. Saletore. Machine Independent Parallel Execution of Speculative Computations. Technical report, University of Illinois, Urbana, IL, 1991.

[89]   M. H. Schultz and E. Auth. ESSENTIAL: An Efficient Self-learning Test Pattern Generation Algorithm for Sequential Circuits. *Proc. Int. Test Conf.*, Aug. 1989.

[90]   S. Seshu. On an Improved Diagnosis Program. *IEEE Trans. Electronic Computers*, EC-14:76–79, 1965.

[91]   S. P. Smith, W. Underwood, and M. R. Mercer. An Analysis of Several Approaches to Circuit Partitioning for Parallel Logic Simulation. *Proc. Int. Conf. Computer Design (ICCD87)*, pages 664–667, 1987.

[92]   L. Soule and T. Blank. Parallel Logic Simulation on General Purpose Machines. *Proc. Design Automation Conf.*, pages 166–171, June 1988.

[93]   R. E. Tarjan. Finding Dominators in Directed Graphs. *SIAM J. Computing*, pages 62–89, 1974.

[94]   E. Ulrich and et al. High-speed Concurrent Fault Simulation with Vectors and Scalars. *Proc. 20th Design Automation Conf.*, pages 709–712, Aug. 1983.

[95]   E. G. Ulrich and T. Baker. Concurrent Simulation of Nearly Identical Digital Networks. *Computer*, 7:39–44, April 1974.

[96]   S. Venkatraman, S. Seth, and P. Agrawal. Parallel Test Pattern Generation Using Boolean Satisfiability. Technical Report CSE 92-023, University of Nebraska, Department of Electrical Engineering, Lincoln, NB, Dec. 1992.

[97]   B. W. Wah, G. J. Li, and C. F. Yu. Multiprocessing of Combinatorial Search Problems. *IEEE Computer*, 18(6):93–108, June 1985.

[98]   J. A. Waicukauski, E. B. Eichelberger, D. O. Forlenza, E. Lindbloom, and T. McCarthy. Fault Simulation for Structured VLSI. *VLSI Systems Design*, pages 20–32, Dec. 1985.

[99]   A. Warshawsky and J. Rajski. Distributed Fault Simulation with Vector Set Partitioning. Technical report, VLSI Design Laboratory, McGill University, Montreal, Canada, 1991.

CHAPTER **9**

Logic Synthesis and Verification

9.1 INTRODUCTION

The goal of computer-aided design systems is the automated synthesis of a VLSI chip from a behavioral description. Logic synthesis fits between register transfer level (RTL) specification of a digital design and the netlist of gates specification. It provides the automatic synthesis of near-optimal logic netlists, for which the goal is minimum delay, minimum area, or maximum testability. Logic synthesis is usually considered as dealing with all facets of pure combinational logic, including its optimization, design for testability, and verification.

The logic synthesis area is usually divided into two-level synthesis (PLAs) and multilevel synthesis. Two-level logic minimization has been used to synthesize PLAs for control logic. Because of the architecture inherent to PLAs, optimization methods focus almost exclusively on minimizing the number of product terms. The other method of implementing logic, which is useful for both control and data-flow logic, is multilevel logic. Many efficient algorithms for two-level logic minimization exist, such as ESPRESSO [6], MINI [29], and PRESTO [8]. Similarly, many algorithms for multilevel logic optimization exist, such as SOCRATES [18], MIS [3], SYLON-XTRANS [35, 42, 41], and BOLD [2]. An excellent review of multilevel logic synthesis appears in [7].

Logic verification tools compare the logic design of integrated circuits at different levels to make sure that, in the synthesis process, no logic errors have been introduced. For example, in a silicon compiler environment where a design is translated or synthesized into a lower level from a higher-level description, logic verification is usually performed between the functional

591

level (before logic synthesis) and the gate level (after logic synthesis).

Logic synthesis and verification for medium-sized circuits have large computing times and memory requirements. For larger circuits of the future, sequential algorithms will not be able to address their complexity. Parallel processing is fast becoming an attractive solution to reduce the large amounts of time spent in VLSI circuit design. Recently, researchers have therefore started to investigate parallel algorithms for problems in logic synthesis and verification.

This chapter will discuss some of the work on parallel algorithms for logic synthesis and verification. Section 9.2 describes the two-level synthesis problem. Parallel algorithms for two-level synthesis are presented in Section 9.3. Section 9.4 describes the multilevel synthesis problem. Section 9.5 presents parallel algorithms for multilevel synthesis using circuit partitioning. A second approach to parallel multilevel synthesis based on the MIS approach is presented in Section 9.6. Another approach to parallel synthesis based on the transduction method is presented in Section 9.7. Section 9.8 describes the logic verification problem. Sections 9.9 and 9.10 discuss parallel algorithms for logic verification using two approaches, one based on implicit enumeration and another based on tautology checking. Section 9.11 concludes with a summary of the various algorithms described in the chapter.

9.2 TWO-LEVEL SYNTHESIS

The logic synthesis area is usually divided into two-level synthesis and multilevel synthesis. Two-level logic minimization has been used to synthesize programmable logic arrays (PLA) for control logic. Because of the architecture inherent to PLAs, optimization methods focus almost exclusively on minimizing the number of product terms. Programmable logic arrays are often used to implement logic functions for the control logic of microprocessors. There is a straightforward mapping between the two-level description of logic functions into physical layout; hence their synthesis can be automated. Figure 9.1 shows an example PLA.

The logic cover of a PLA can be represented by a pair of matrices called input and output matrices. For example, for the following two-level functions

$$f_1 = x_3 \bar{x_6}$$

$$f_2 = x_2 \bar{x_4}$$

$$f_3 = \bar{x_1}$$

$$f_4 = x_1 \bar{x_6} + x_1 x_5 + x_6$$

we can identify six unique product terms, each of which can be implemented by a unique row in a PLA shown in Figure 9.1. The product terms are $x_3\bar{x_6}$, $x_2\bar{x_4}$, $\bar{x_1}$, $x_1\bar{x_6}$, x_1x_5 and x_6. A common representation of a PLA is called the PLA personality, which consists of two matrices, one having entries, 0, 1, and *, corresponding to the AND plane programming of the PLA, and the other having entries 0 and 1, corresponding to the OR plane of the PLA. Every

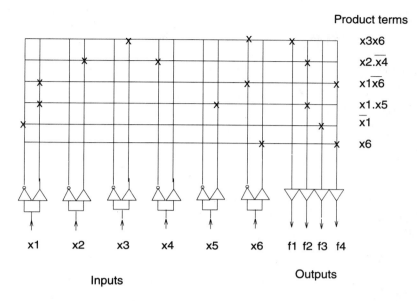

Figure 9.1 Programmable logic array physical implementation (Courtesy of Brayton et al., *Logic Minimization Algorithms for VLSI Synthesis*, Kluwer Academic Publishers, 1984)

input to the logic function (each column of the input matrix) corresponds to a pair of columns in the left part of the physical array of the PLA. Every implicant, or equivalently every row of the input and output matrices, corresponds to a row of the physical array of the PLA. Every input row corresponds to a logical product of some set of inputs. The implementation of a particular switching function is obtained by programming the PLA (by placing or connecting appropriate devices in the array in the input or output column position specified by the 1 or 0). The input and output arrays are referred to as the AND plane and OR plane respectively. The following two matrices correspond to the PLA implementation shown in Figure 9.1.

```
*   *   1   *   *   0      1   0   0   0
*   1   *   0   *   *      0   1   0   0
1   *   *   *   *   0      0   0   0   1
1   *   *   *   1   *      0   0   0   1
0   *   *   *   *   *      0   0   1   0
*   *   *   *   *   1      0   0   0   1
```

In CMOS technology, where it is easier to implement the negative logic of a function, we usually implement the PLA using a NOR-NOR form, where the devices that are programmed constitute the n-channel transistors of a NOR gate.

Given a set of two-level functions, we often want a minimal two-level representation in order to minimize the area of the PLA. There are many two-level circuit minimizers. Examples include MINI [29], PRESTO [8], and ESPRESSO programs [6, 5]. Among these, ESPRESSO is the most widely available. We will discuss that algorithm in more detail in the next section and then describe a parallel algorithm based on that algorithm.

9.3 TWO-LEVEL SYNTHESIS USING ESPRESSO APPROACH

9.3.1 Overview

ESPRESSO is a collection of heuristic two-level logic minimization algorithms [6]. A user desiring minimization of a two-level programmable logic array (PLA) specifies the on-set F and the don't-care set D as a list of cubes (implicants) to ESPRESSO. The ESPRESSO minimization involves the following basic routines: COMPLEMENT, EXPAND, ESSENTIAL, IRREDUNDANT, and REDUCE. An overview of the ESPRESSO algorithm for two-level minimization is given next.

Procedure *ESPRESSO(F,D*
    F refers to ON set of function;
    D refers to OFF set of function;
    R refers to don't care set of function;
    Cost(F) considers number of cubes in F
        and number of literals to implement F;
    R = COMPLEMENT(F+D); /* Compute complement */
    F = EXPAND(F,R); /* Initial expansion */
    F = IRREDUNDANT(F,D); /* Initial irredundant */
    F = ESSENTIAL(F,D); /* Detecting essential primes */
    F = F - E; /* Remove essentials from F */
    D = D + E; /* Add essentials to D */
    WHILE Cost(F) keeps decreasing DO
        WHILE Cost(F) keeps decreasing DO
            F = REDUCE(F,D);
            F = EXPAND(F,R);
            F = IRREDUNDANT(F,D);
        ENDWHILE
        F = LASTGASP(F,D,R);
    ENDWHILE
    F = F + E; /* Add essentials to F */
    RETURN F;
End Procedure

The key procedures of the ESPRESSO algorithm will be discussed briefly next. The *COMPLEMENT* procedure complements a given function, that is, generates an off-set of a function, given the on-set and don't-care set. The computation of the complement is done by recursive decomposition of the function based on Shannon's expansion.

$$\overline{f} = x_j \overline{f_{x_j}} + \overline{x_j}\,\overline{f_{\overline{x_j}}}$$

At each node of the binary recursion tree, the "splitting" variable, x_j, is chosen so that the cofactors in this expression become successively more unate (a function is unate if it contains only the positive or negative terms of each variable, not both). The recursion continues until at each leaf of the recursion tree a unate function is encountered.

The *EXPAND* procedure, using several heuristics, generates a limited set of prime cubes of a given function. A cube from an ordered list of cubes is expanded into a prime cube to cover as many nonprime cubes, following it in the ordered list, as possible, and as many minterms of the original function as possible. The direction of the expansion is guided by a set of heuristics. Since each cube in an initial cover is replaced by at most one prime cube and the cubes covered by the expanded cubes are removed, the size of the cover after EXPAND is always less than or equal to the initial cover size.

The *IRREDUNDANT* procedure generates a minimal set of prime cubes sufficient to realize a function. This involves finding a set of relatively essential prime cubes, partially redundant prime cubes, and totally redundant prime cubes. Totally redundant prime cubes are removed from the cover. From the partially redundant cubes, a minimal set of cubes is found heuristically that, along with the set of relatively essential prime cubes, is sufficient to realize the function.

The *REDUCE* procedure facilitates improvement over the local minimum obtained by the procedure IRREDUNDANT. REDUCE takes, in turn, each prime cube and reduces it to the smallest cube contained in it such that the resultant cover still realizes the function. The reduction of the cubes is done in a heuristic order.

The EXPAND, IRREDUNDANT, and REDUCE procedures are sequentially iterated until no further improvement is seen in the cover size.

As an example of an iteration of the ESPRESSO procedure, consider the following function to be minimized.

$$F_i = \bar{b}c + \bar{a}c + a\bar{b}\bar{c}$$

The REDUCE procedure takes each prime cube and reduces it to a smaller cube by adding a literal. For example, if we add literal a to the cube $\bar{b}c$, we have the following transformation.

$$F_i = \bar{b}c + \bar{a}c + a\bar{b}\bar{c} \Rightarrow F_i = a\bar{b}c + \bar{a}c + a\bar{b}\bar{c}$$

The subsequent EXPAND procedure expands the set of cubes in many directions. For example, if we expand cube $a\bar{b}c$ by removing literal c from the cube, we have the following transformation.

$$F_i = a\bar{b}c + \bar{a}c + a\bar{b}\bar{c} \Rightarrow F_i = a\bar{b} + \bar{a}c + a\bar{b}\bar{c}$$

The subsequent IRREDUNDANT procedure tries to remove redundant cubes, finds cube $a\bar{b}\bar{c}$ to be redundant, and hence removes it.

$$F_i = a\bar{b} + \bar{a}c + a\bar{b}\bar{c} \Rightarrow F_i = a\bar{b}c + \bar{a}c$$

At each change of the expressions for F_i, we need to check for Boolean equivalence, using a tautology procedure.

9.3.2 Shared Memory MIMD Parallel Algorithm

In this section, we will describe a shared memory parallel algorithm for two-level minimization using ESPRESSO, based on work reported by Galivanche and Reddy [25]. We will now describe the parallel algorithms for each of the main procedures of the EXPRESSO algorithm described previously.

The procedure *COMPLEMENT* can be parallelized as follows. In the COMPLEMENT procedure, the function to be complemented is recursively decomposed into two subfunctions along a splitting variable. Since the computation of the complement of each subfunction can proceed independently, the complement of each subfunction is computed on a different processor. After each recursive decomposition, a new processor is allocated to work on one subfunction, and the old processor continues to work on the other subfunction. Thus the allocation of processors to work on these subfunctions is done until no more processors are left out of the total number of processors. The allocation of processors is done in a controlled way so as to divide the work equally among the processors. An outline of the *SM-PARALLEL-COMPLEMENT* algorithm (denoting shared memory parallel algorithm for complementation) is given next.

> **Procedure** *SM-PARALLEL-COMPLEMENT(F,D)*;
>   Create COMPLEMENT task queues for each of N processors;
>   Call COMPLEMENT(F,0,N,0,0) on processor 0;
>   FORALL processors in PARALLEL DO
>   WHILE not done DO
>   Pick next COMPLEMENT task off own queue;
>   Execute COMPLEMENT() at appropriate level
>   of recursion;
>   END WHILE
>   END FORALL
> **End Procedure**

> **Procedure** *COMPLEMENT(F,i,N,parent,il)*;
>   Read Inputs:
>   F : a two-level cover;
>   i : current level of recursion
>   N : number of processors
>   parent : information about the parent process
>   il : level in the recursion tree of the complementation

IF (F is unate) THEN
    Call UNATE-FUNCTION-COMPLEMENTER(F,D);
    Send results back to parent process;
ELSE
    Choose a splitting variable;
    j ← SELECT-SPLIT(F);
    Create two functions to be complemented;
    F_{x_j} ← COFACTOR(F, x_j);
    $F_{\overline{x_j}}$ ← COFACTOR(F, $\overline{x_j}$);
    IF $(i \leq (log_2(N) - 1))$ THEN /* Start new process */
        Start a new task on new processor;
        Assign complementation of $F_{\overline{x_j}}$
          to the new processor;
        Call COMPLEMENT($F_{\overline{x_j}}$,i+1,N,newparent,i+1)
        on new processor;
        Call COMPLEMENT(F_{x_j}),i+1,N,parent,il) on own processor;
        Wait for the child processor to send an answer back;
        Merge results of both parts of decomposition;
        Send the answer back to parent processor;
    ELSE /* Perform serial complementation */
        Evaluate COMPLEMENT(F_{x_j});
        Evaluate COMPLEMENT($F_{\overline{x_j}}$);
    ENDIF
  ENDIF
End Procedure

Figure 9.2 shows the allocation of the complement tasks among four processors.

In the parallel algorithm of the *EXPAND* procedure, the cubes are ordered, prior to processing, using the same heuristics as in EXPRESSO. Multiple cubes are then expanded concurrently. Concurrent expansion of multiple cubes has the potential problem of creating two or more identical prime cubes. This is shown in Figure 9.3. In case (a), two cubes $p1$ and $p2$ can expand to cover each other, which forms two identical prime cubes. To avoid this, while expanding $p2$, a check is made to see if $p2$ is covered by some other expanding cube; then the expansion of $p2$ can be stopped, and a different cube can be expanded. However in case (b), before $p2$ is detected as covered, $p2$ may expand to cover $p3$, in which case the expansion of $p2$ should not be stopped. In case (c), $p2$ expands to cover the same implicant $p3$ as that covered by the expansion of $p1$; hence the expansion of $p2$ can be stopped. Identical prime cubes affect the parallelism in two forms. First, the computations in the IRREDUNDANT procedure are unnecessarily increased. Second, if an essential prime cube has an identical prime cube in the cover, it would not be detected as an essential prime cube.

To overcome these problems, the following strategy is used to parallelize the EXPAND operation. Let p be a cube that is being expanded concurrently with some other cubes. A periodic check is done during the expansion of p to find whether p is covered by any other

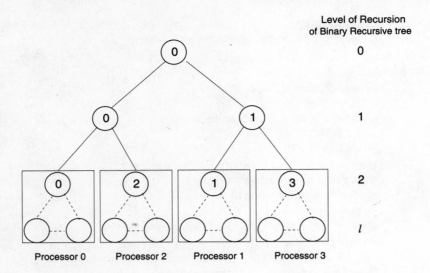

Figure 9.2 Decomposition of complement tasks in parallel algorithm

expanded cube. If p is found covered, one of the following is done. If p did not cover any other cubes at the time it is found to be covered, the expansion of p is stopped and p is removed from the ONSET. This avoids the formation of potential duplicate prime cubes. If p is covered by some other prime cubes in the cover, since it is not known whether p is covering the same cubes as the expanding cube covering p, expansion of p is continued, but the prime cube resulting from the expansion of p is assigned to a set of *temporary identical prime cubes*, T_d. At the end of the EXPAND procedure, any duplicate cubes in T_d are removed and each prime cube in T_d is checked to find whether it is identical to any other prime cube not in T_d. An outline of the *SM-PARALLEL-EXPAND* algorithm (denoting shared memory parallel algorithm for expansion of cubes) follows:

Procedure *SM-PARALLEL-EXPAND(F,D)*
Order cubes for expansion using same heuristics as ESPRESSO;
Create a task queue of cubes for expansion;
FORALL processors in PARALLEL DO
   WHILE some cubes exist for expansion DO
      Pick a cube p from queue;
      Expand cube p concurrently;
      Check if cube p is covered by any other cube;
      IF p is covered by some other prime cubes THEN
         p is expanded, but expanded cube is assigned to
         set of *temporary identical prime cubes*, T_d;
      END IF
   END WHILE
END FORALL

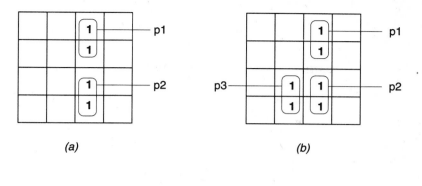

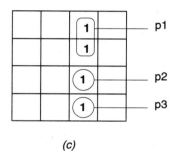

Figure 9.3 Creation of identical prime cubes during Parallel EXPAND (Courtesy of Galivanche, University of Iowa ECE Dept. Tech. Report, 1986)

Remove duplicate cubes in T_d;
Each prime cube in T_d is checked whether it is identical
to any of the other prime cubes not in T_d;
End Procedure

We now describe a parallel algorithm for the *REDUCE* procedure. Prior to executing this procedure, cubes are all prime and are arranged in a heuristic order. After the reduction of the prime cube to the smallest cube contained in it, the cover will have a new set of cubes. The reduction of the next set of cubes will have to be done with respect to the next set of cubes. A cube is reduced to its smallest size by removing some of the minterms that are already contained in the other cubes of the cover. When multiple cubes are reduced concurrently, there is a possibility of each cube reducing to its smallest size by deleting the minterms common among them, thus potentially resulting in a cover that no longer realizes the function. Figure 9.4 shows an example of concurrent reduction of cubes whereby the cubes $p1$ and $p2$ are individually reduced, hence deleting a minterm marked * common to both of them. Case (a) shows the cubes before the reduction process, and case (b) shows the cubes after the reduction process.

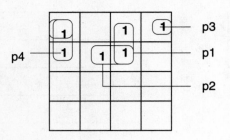

(a) Original cubes

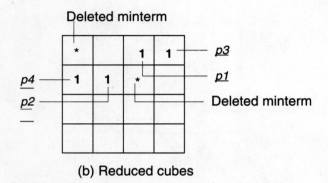

(b) Reduced cubes

Figure 9.4 Example of concurrent reduction of cubes. (a) Original cubes. (b) Reduced cubes. (Courtesy of Galivanche, University of Iowa ECE Dept. Tech. Report, 1986)

To overcome this problem, the following strategy is used in parallelizing the REDUCE operation. Whenever a prime cube p is selected for reduction, all other prime cubes that are currently being reduced and are above p in the ordered list of cubes are considered nonexistent for the purpose of reducing p. This strategy may result in some of the reducible cubes remaining unreduced or not reduced as much as they could have been. An outline of the *SM-PARALLEL-REDUCE* algorithm (denoting shared memory parallel algorithm for reduction of cubes) is provided next.

Procedure *SM-PARALLEL-REDUCE(F,D)*
Order cubes for expansion using same heuristics as ESPRESSO;
Create a task queue of cubes for expansion;
FORALL processors in PARALLEL DO
    WHILE some cubes exist for reduction DO
        Pick a cube p from queue;
        Reduce to smallest cube;
        Do not consider existence of other prime cubes above p;
    END WHILE

END FORALL
End Procedure

We finally provide an outline of the *SM-PARALLEL-IRREDUNDANT* algorithm (denoting shared memory parallel algorithm for identification of irredundant cubes) next.

Procedure *SM-PARALLEL-IRREDUNDANT(F,D)*
Order cubes for irredundant cover using ESPRESSO heuristics;
Create a task queue of cubes for irredundant cover;
FORALL processors in PARALLEL DO
    WHILE cubes exist for cover DO
        Pick cube p from queue;
        Determine if cube p is relatively essential;
            partially redundant, or totally redundant;
        IF cube p is totally redundant THEN
            Remove cube p from cover;
        IF cube p is essential THEN
            Keep cube p in cover;
        IF cube p is partially redundant THEN
            Determine if this cube along with essential cubes
                adds to the cover;
    END WHILE
END FORALL ;
End Procedure

An outline of the overall parallel ESPRESSO algorithm for two-level minimization *SM-PARALLEL-TWO-LEVEL-SYNTHESIS-ESPRESSO* (denoting a shared memory parallel algorithm for two-level synthesis using the ESPRESSO algorithm) follows:

Procedure *SM-PARALLEL-TWO-LEVEL-SYNTHESIS-ESPRESSO(F,D)*
FORALL processors in PARALLEL DO
    R = SM-PARALLEL-COMPLEMENT(F+D); /* Compute complement */
    F = SM-PARALLEL-EXPAND(F,R); /* Initial expansion */
    F = SM-PARALLEL-IRREDUNDANT(F,D); /* Initial irredundant */
    F = SM-PARALLEL-ESSENTIAL(F,D); /* Detecting essential primes */
    Lock data structure;
        Update F = F - E; /* Remove essentials from F */
        Update D = D + E; /* Add essentials to D */
    Unlock data structure;

    WHILE Cost(F) keeps decreasing DO
        WHILE Cost(F) keeps decreasing DO
            F = SM-PARALLEL-REDUCE(F,D);

TABLE 9.1 Result Quality, Runtimes (Seconds), and Speedups, of Parallel ESPRESSO Algorithm on the Encore Multimax™ Multiprocessor

| | 1 Processor | | | 10 Processors | | |
| | NP | NL | Runtime (speedup) | NP | NL | Runtime (speedup) |
Circuit	NP	NL	Runtime (speedup)	NP	NL	Runtime (speedup)
bc0	178	2079	526 (1.0)	177	2088	172 (3.1)
cps	162	2808	781 (1.0)	162	2806	142 (5.5)
ti	213	2572	1081 (1.0)	213	2572	252 (4.3)
tial	579	5131	1536 (1.0)	579	5130	202 (7.6)
vg2.c	174	1184	2563 (1.0)	174	1184	440 (5.8)
exep.c	131	1680	5819 (1.0)	131	1714	1102 (5.3)
x7dn.c	746	4918	7030 (1.0)	746	4918	987 (7.1)

```
        F = SM-PARALLEL-EXPAND(F,R);
        F = SM-PARALLEL-IRREDUNDANT(F,D);
      ENDWHILE
      F = LASTGASP(F,D,R);
    ENDWHILE
  END FORALL
  F = F + E; /* Add essentials to F */
  RETURN F;
End Procedure
```

Implementation The preceding parallel PLA minimization algorithm has been implemented on an Encore Multimax™ shared memory multiprocessor by Galivanche and Reddy [25]. Results have been obtained on 105 example PLAs. The quality of the circuits was measured in terms of the number of product terms (NP) and the number of literals (NL). It was found that the quality of the results of the multiple processor runs were within ±2.5% of the results of an uniprocessor run of ESPRESSO. Table 9.1 shows the result quality, runtimes, and speedups of several benchmark circuits on an Encore Multimax™ multiprocessor. It is clear from the table that reasonably good speedups were obtained at no significant loss in quality of the results.

9.4 MULTI-LEVEL LOGIC SYNTHESIS

Automated multilevel logic synthesis has had two approaches: rule based and algorithmic approaches. The IBM LSS™ system [11] used rule-based local transformations, which used a set of ad hoc rules that were fired when certain patterns were found in the network of logic gates. A rule transforms a pattern for a local set of gates and interconnections into another equivalent one. Since rules need to be described, and hence must know about each gate type, the rule-based approach usually requires that the description of the logic be confined to a limited set of gates types such as AND, OR, and NAND. These rules have limited optimization capability. Other examples of rule based systems are those in use at NEC and Trimeter.

The algorithmic approach to logic synthesis uses two phases: a technology-independent phase based on techniques for manipulating general Boolean functions, and a technology mapping step in which the design described in terms of generic Boolean functions is mapped into a set of gates that can be implemented in the design method of choice (gate arrays, standard cells, macro cells). Examples of algorithmic approaches are MIS [3], BOLD [2], Tranduction [35], and those in use at Synopsis and AT&T.

Recently, there has been a trend to combining the technology-independent activity using algorithmic methods and the technology mapping activity using rule-based methods. Examples of such approaches is SOCRATES [18].

9.5 SYNTHESIS USING PARTITIONING APPROACH

9.5.1 Overview

An obvious way of speeding up the logic synthesis application is to generate a large number of logic partitions of a given circuit and to synthesize each partition independently. The results of the individual partitions can then be merged back. Unfortunately, such an approach has the problem that with increasing number of partitions, even though the synthesis time goes down, the quality of the overall network degrades. Specifically, it has been shown that even if the individual partitions are synthesized perfectly, such that they are each completely irredundant, the resultant network can still have redundancies when the synthesized partitions are reconnected to form a larger network. This is because each synthesis procedure of a partition only synthesizes within a partition by treating it as an independent block. It does not take any global information into consideration during minimization. A good partitioning algorithm that can guarantee minimum degradation in the network quality is desirable. Examples of existing partitioning algorithms are ones proposed by Kernighan and Lin [31], Fidducia and Mattheyses [24], Donath [20], Dey et al. [19], Cho et al. [10], and that of De and Banerjee [14].

We will now describe some partitioning algorithms for multilevel circuits. A multilevel logic network can be viewed as a directed acyclic graph (DAG) in which each node corresponds to a variable y_i with its logic function in sum-of-products and/or factored form. An arc corresponds to the direct dependence of the variables. The primary inputs (PI) and primary outputs (PO) form the sources and sinks of the graph. A partitioning algorithm partitions a given DAG of the entire circuit into DAGs of smaller circuits such that each subcircuit can be synthesized independently.

The graph partitioning problem has been addressed by researchers in numerous disciplines. Given a graph of nodes and arcs, the objective is to partition the nodes into two or more graphs such that the total cost of the arcs between nodes in different partitions is minimized. The optimum graph partitioning problem is known to be NP complete [26]. We will discuss several partitioning algorithms in the following.

Kernighan-Lin Partitioning Algorithm An efficient heuristic for partitioning a graph based on the group migration method has been proposed by Kernighan and Lin to reduce the total cost of the cut between two partitions [31]. Such a heuristic can be used to reduce the number of connections across the cut if the cost of each connection is considered unity.

The details of the *group migration method* based on the Kernighan-Lin's algorithm [31] are given next. Let us consider a node ν in the partition Π_i. The gain obtained in moving the node ν to the other partition, Π_j, is denoted as $total\_gain(\nu, \Pi_j)$. The loss achieved by moving the node ν from the partition Π_i is denoted as $total\_gain(\nu, \Pi_i)$. Thus the net gain of moving ν from Π_i to Π_j is expressed in the following equation:

$$net\_gain(\nu) = total\_gain(\nu, \Pi_j) - total\_gain(\nu, \Pi_i)$$

For every node in Π_1 and Π_2, the net_gain is computed. Then a pair of nodes *(a, b)*, *a* $\in \Pi_1$ and $b \in \Pi_2$, is chosen such that the gain for swapping them is maximum. This pair of nodes is swapped. This procedure is repeated until no such pair is found that yields a positive gain by swapping themselves. The algorithm for group migration based on Kernighan-Lin's algorithm follows:

Procedure *Group Migration(*Π_1, Π_2*)*
    FOR all nodes $\nu \in (\Pi_1 \cup \Pi_2)$
        Compute net_gain(ν);
    gain = 1.0 /* Anything nonzero will do */

    WHILE (gain $\neq$ 0) /* partition is improving */
        Find a $\in \Pi_1$ and b $\in \Pi_2$ such that
            best_gain = net_gain(a) + net_gain(b) - edge_cost({a,b}) is maximum
        IF (best_gain $\neq$ 0) /* some gain in swapping */ THEN
            Swap a and b
            gain = best_gain
            FOR all nodes $\nu \in (\Pi_1 \cup \Pi_2)$
                compute net_gain(ν);
        ENDIF
    ENDWHILE
End Procedure

The complexity of this algorithm grows as the cube of the number of nodes. A more efficient algorithm using a complex data structure has been proposed by Fidducia and Mattheyses with linear time complexity. Details of the algorithm can be found in [24].

Cluster-based Partitioning Algorithm A partitioning approach based on the seed clustering method has been reported in [10]. This method generates *k* seeds for *k* partitions and then the remaining nodes are clustered around the seeds to generate *k* partitions. This method satisfies some constraints on the number of internal nodes and primary inputs/outputs of each block by moving nodes from one partition to another. The details of the *seed-clustering algorithm* of Donath [20] are given next. A similar approach has also been used in [10]. We describe the partitioning algorithm for generating two partitions of a given network. If we need more than two partitions, we recursively partition the resulting blocks until we reach the desired number of partitions.

The seed clustering method starts with finding two seeds for two partitions. All primary inputs and primary outputs are grouped into a set called *boundary vertices*, B. All the vertices connected to a primary input or output and having only one input (that is, inverter and buffer) are also considered boundary nodes and are included in B. The rest of the nodes, $C = N - B$, are called *candidate nodes* for seeds, where N denotes the set of all the nodes of the network. The distance of the shortest path, $dist(c, b)$, from a vertex $c \in C$ to every $b \in B$ is computed. The length of each edge is considered to be 1 if it is driven by a node that has more than one input and 0, otherwise. The $mindist$ is calculated as

$$mindist(c) = MIN_{b \in B}(dist(c, b)) \ \forall c \in C$$

Then $\psi \in C$ is chosen as a seed if

$$mindist(\psi) = MAX_{c \in C}(mindist(c))$$

Then ψ is put into the set of boundary nodes, B, and the same procedure is repeated to obtain another seed.

After the seed generation process, we have two seeds, ψ_1 and ψ_2. The clustering process starts around the seeds. These two seeds are placed in the two partitions, partition Π_1 and partition Π_2. All the other nodes of the network are put in a *free-list*. Then one partition is picked at a time, and all the nodes are considered that are in the *freelist* and have at least one arc between them and a node in that partition. For each such node, the gain of including that node in the partition is obtained. The node whose inclusion results in the maximum gain is included in that partition and removed from the *freelist*. Then the other partition is considered and the same procedure is repeated. The clustering procedure terminates when there are no nodes left in the *freelist*. Since nodes are placed in the partitions alternately, both the partitions are expected to be of equal complexity if the nodes are assumed to be of equal complexity. The algorithm for seed clustering follows:

> **Procedure** *Seed Clustering(seed1, seed2, Network)*
> $\Pi_1 = \{seed1\}$; /* partition1 contains only seed1 */
> $\Pi_2 = \{seed2\}$; /* partition2 contains only seed2 */
> FOR all nodes ν in Network other than seed1 and seed2
> Put ν in free_list;
> WHILE (free_list $\neq$ NULL)
> IF (($\nu_a \in$ free_list) AND ($\{\nu_a, \mu\}$ is an edge, $\mu \in \Pi_1$) AND
> (total_gain (ν_a, Π_1) is MAXIMUM))
> THEN put ν_a in Π_1
> IF (($\nu_b \in$ free_list) AND ($\{\nu_b, \mu\}$ is an edge, $\mu \in \Pi_2$) AND
> (total_gain(ν_b, Π_2) is MAXIMUM))
> THEN put ν_b in Π_2
> ENDWHILE
> **End Procedure**

Corolla-based Partitioning Algorithm Recent work has been reported on a circuit partitioning method based on the analysis of reconvergent fan-out [19]. In this approach, a *corolla* is defined as set of overlapping fan-out regions. The circuit is partitioned into a set of nonoverlapping corollas. Since the circuits can have a large number of reconvergent fan-out regions, a reconvergence zone may contain the entire circuit. Hence a heuristic method is applied to choose the corollas. The details of the partitioning algorithm are given next.

Figure 9.5(a) shows a multilevel combinational circuit, and Figure 9.5(b) shows the corresponding directed graph representation of the circuit. A node in the circuit is called a *fan-out stem* if it has an outdegree greater than 1. A stem node s is called a *reconvergent fan-out stem* if there are more than one disjoint paths from the node to another node. A *closing reconvergent node* of a reconvergent stem s is one that does not drive any other reconvergent node of s. In the figure, node a is a stem, and nodes o, p, q, v are closing reconvergent nodes of a. The primary stem region of a reconvergent stem s consists of all nodes that are located on all the paths from s to any of its closing reconvergent nodes and all the output edges of these nodes. In Figure 9.5(b), the primary stem region of stem a consists of the nodes, $a, c, d, e, f, g, h, i, j, k, l, m, n, o, p, q, r, s, v$, and all their output edges.

The partitioning algorithm partitions the circuit graph initially into *petals*. Let s be a reconvergent fan-out stem. Each petal in s, $P(s)$, is a biconnected component of the primary stem region of s with the directions of the edges ignored. (A biconnected component is defined as follows. Let G be a connected undirected graph. Then the graph G is biconnected if, for every distinct triple of vertices v, w, a, there exists a path between v and w not containing a.) Figure 9.5(c) shows the petals of the example circuit. Petals are said to overlap if they have some common nodes. A corolla is a collection of overlapping petals. However, any two corollas are nonoverlapping or disjoint.

The preceding partitioning algorithm was implemented in the COROLLA system [19].

Don't-care-based Partitioning Algorithm None of the work described previously addressed the don't-cares of the block as an aspect to be included in the measure of the quality of a partition. As described before, even though each logic partition can be synthesized for 100% irredundancy, after connecting each re-synthesized partition, the resultant circuit is not guaranteed to be 100% irredundant. We will now describe a partitioning method that takes into account an estimate of the don't-cares of a given partition set [14].

The cost function used to measure the amount of gain of including a gate in a partition consists of a weighted sum of two parts: (1) *cluster gain*, which measures the increase in the number of internal gates and primary inputs due to inclusion of the gate in the partition; and (2) *don't-care gain* , which estimates the sizes of the don't-care sets at the boundaries of all the partitions due to inclusion of the gate in the partition. The cluster gain is used for area minimization by encouraging sharing of common gates within a partition. The don't-care gain is used to minimize the sizes of the don't-care sets at boundaries of each partition so that ignoring these don't-care sets during the synthesis of each partition will not overlook too much global information and will hence produce a good synthesis of each partition. Specifically, if the synthesized partitions are completely irredundant individually, they will continue to be almost completely irredundant when the partitions are connected together. The sizes of the don't-care sets are estimated through probabilistic testability measures.

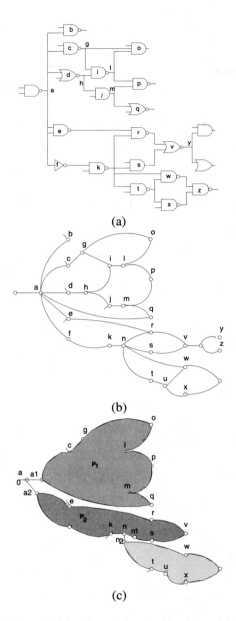

Figure 9.5 Example circuit and its partitioning. (a) Example multilevel circuit. (b) Directed acyclic graph representation of circuit. (c) DAG partitioning into petals. (Courtesy of Dey et al.,*Proc. Design Automation Conf.,* ©IEEE 1990)

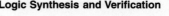

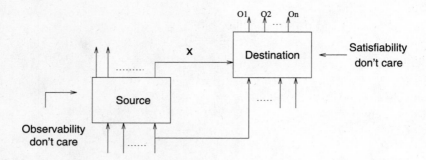

Figure 9.6 Don't-care sets for an arc between two partitions

We now describe the estimation of don't-care-based cost functions. Due to bisectioning a network, there will be some arcs between two partitions. Also, some primary inputs will be shared by both the blocks, which may result in reconvergent fan-out between the two blocks. Due to these reconvergences, there will be some redundancy when two blocks are merged even if each block is individually 100% irredundant. As an example, let us consider only one arc x between two blocks in Figure 9.6. According to the signal flow direction along that arc, we mark one block as the *source* and other block as the *destination*. During the synthesis process of the *destination* block, the *satisfiability* don't-care sets [1] need to be considered due to the fact that all possible combinations of x and other primary inputs are not possible due to reconvergence. The *satisfiability* don't-care set is expressed as [1]

$$DIV_x = x\overline{F_x} + \overline{x}F_x = x \oplus F_x$$

where F_x is the representation of x.

During the synthesis process of the *source* block, we need to consider the *observability* don't-care set, which can be expressed as

$$DT_x = \bigcap_{\forall j} DT_{xj}$$

where

$$DT_{xj} = (Oj)_x (Oj)_{\overline{x}} + \overline{(Oj)_x} \; \overline{(Oj)_{\overline{x}}}$$
$$= ((Oj)_x \equiv (Oj)_{\overline{x}})$$

where $(Oj)_x$ is the cofactor of Oj with respect to x.

With the exception of small circuits, the exact computation of don't-care sets becomes prohibitively expensive with present computational resources. Thus we have to resort to heuristic methods that measure the size of the don't-care set at each arc and use these measures as the cost of the arcs to be minimized during the partitioning algorithm. Details of the heuristic methods appear in [13, 14].

Using the don't-care-based cost function, large logic circuits can be partitioned into smaller subcircuits, which when synthesized individually and merged together to form a large circuit produce circuits with very few remaining redundancies. The partitioning algorithm performs bipartitioning (or bisectioning) at one time. To have more partitions, we subsequently bipartition recursively each bipartitioned block. Each step of the bipartitioning algorithm comprises of seed-clustering and group-migration phases.

Partitioning for Equal Synthesis Times   The primary objective of partitioning is to retain the logic minimization potential as much as possible. To achieve that, the partitions need to capture the gross structural features of the given circuit. We can have a secondary objective during partitioning of a logic circuit to include the times for synthesizing the subcircuits. Since we plan to synthesize the partitions in parallel, the completion time of the parallel synthesis procedure is bounded by the largest completion among all the partitions. Hence, in order to reduce the completion time of the parallel synthesis procedure, we need to minimize the largest completion time for synthesis among all the partitions.

To minimize the maximum completion time for synthesis among all the partitions, we need to have some estimate of the completion time for synthesis during partitioning. But the synthesis time of a circuit depends on many factors, such as the size of the circuit, the synthesis algorithm used, the number of primary inputs and outputs, and the complexity of the logic expressions of nodes in the circuit.

We now describe an empirical model of the synthesis time expressed as a function of the size of the circuit. The size of the circuit is measured by the initial literal count of the circuit. Let us assume that the synthesis time (T) is proportional to some power of the size of the circuit (S) as follows.

$$T = \beta \star S^{\alpha}$$

To determine the values of α and β empirically, an experiment was reported in [12]. Synthesis was performed using MIS-II on 27 benchmark circuits of various sizes and collected the runtimes for synthesis and the original sizes of the circuit in terms of the literal count. Using a statistical method of *least-square line fitting* on these data, the value of α was computed to be 1.58 and the value of β to be 0.00047.

A cost function is used to guide the partitioning process and discern the best move among all possible moves. The average size of a partition, AS, is computed as follows.

$$AS = \sum_{\text{for all nodes in circuit}} S(node) / N$$

where

$$S(node) = \beta \star (literal\_count(node))^{\alpha}$$

and N is the number of partitions. Let us denote AI to be the average number of inputs to each partition. Since AI cannot be exactly determined a priori, it is approximated as

$$AI = \text{number of primary inputs} / 2$$

Let us consider a node η that we want to put in a partition π. Let us denote DI_{π} to be the change in the number of inputs of the block π caused by moving η into π and $PS(\pi)$ to be the size of the partition π prior to moving the node η to π. Then the cost of moving the node η to the partition π is expressed as follows:

$$\text{cost}(\eta, \pi) \; = \; C_1 \star (DI_\pi / AI) - (1 - C_1) \star (S(\eta)/AS) \star SIGN(AS - PS(\pi) - S(\eta))$$

where $SIGN(val)$ = -1.0 if val < 0, otherwise it is 1.0.

The cost function given in the preceding equation has two parts. The first part penalizes a move if it introduces a lot of additional inputs to the block. Hence this part encourages the acceptance of a node that forms a good cluster. The second part of the cost function encourages a move of a large-sized node into the block as long as the block size does not exceed AS after the node is moved. On the other hand, if the size will exceed AS, it penalizes that move. This part of the cost function encourages the formation of equal-sized partitions.

9.5.2 Distributed Memory MIMD Parallel Algorithm

We now describe a distributed memory MIMD parallel algorithm for logic synthesis using partitioning based on work reported by De and Banerjee in [12]. In this approach, a combinational circuit is first partitioned into N partitions using a partitioning algorithm that takes into account circuit clustering and equal synthesis times, as described previously. The partitioning is performed on a single processor.

After the partitioning is performed, individual partitions are distributed to different processors. When a partition is picked up by a processor, that partition is synthesized by a combinational synthesis algorithm. After the completion of synthesis on all the partitions, all the synthesized partitions are merged to form the synthesized circuit.

The major limitation of the this one-pass approach is that the quality of the circuit is not optimal because the synthesis is performed on only one partition at a time. There will be no sharing of common logic among the nodes that are in different partitions. This can potentially degrade the quality of the resultant synthesized circuit. Also, very large circuits cannot be resynthesized to improve the quality because of prohibitive runtimes and memory requirements. Hence it is desirable to use an iterative procedure to improve the quality of the circuit. The main idea is to allow synthesis among certain constrained sets of nodes that are in different partitions at one time, and this procedure is repeated a certain number of times. This iterative procedure is explained with an example in Figure 9.7 with four partitions. The partitions are numbered from 1 to 4 in the figure.

Figure 9.7(a) shows the first phase of the iteration. This is the same as the one pass approach described in the last subsection; each partition is synthesized independently. In this phase, a node η in a particular partition can share logic with only the nodes in the same partition as η. After the first phase, we obtain the synthesized version of the four partitions of the circuit. In the second phase, shown in Figure 9.7(b), we bipartition each of the four partitions obtained in the last phase and mark them as A and B. Then the partitions $1A$ and $2A$ are merged to form the new partition 1, and the partitions $1B$ and $2B$ are merged to form the new partition 2. Similarly, the partitions $3A$ and $4A$ are merged to form the new partition 3, and the partitions $3B$ and $4B$ are merged to form the new partition 4. Now these new partitions (1 to 4) are synthesized independently. In this phase, one-half of the nodes of partition 1 is synthesized with one-half of the nodes of partition 2, and the other half of the nodes of partition 1 is synthesized with the other half of the nodes of partition 2. This will

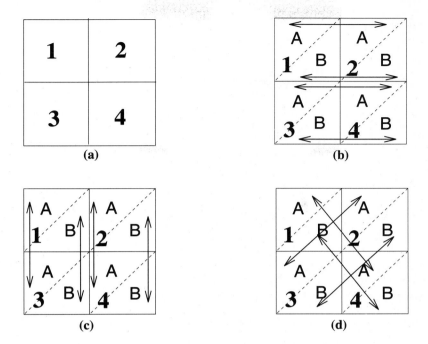

Figure 9.7 Example of iterative approach for synthesis using the partitioning approach with four partitions

allow some logic sharing among the nodes in partitions 1 and 2. The same is true for partitions 3 and 4. This can potentially improve the quality of the circuit, but will never degrade the quality. In the third phase, as shown in Figure 9.7(c), each partition is bipartitioned again. But this time partitions $1A$ and $3A$ ($1B$ and $3B$) are paired, and partitions $2A$ and $4A$ ($2B$ and $4B$) are paired, and the same procedure is repeated. In the fourth phase, as shown in Figure 9.7(d), partitions $1A$ and $4A$ ($1B$ and $4B$) are paired, and partitions $2A$ and $3A$ ($2B$ and $3B$) are paired and the same procedure is repeated.

In this iterative approach, the pairing of different partitions for different phases needs to be generated. We assume that the number of partitions, N, is a power of 2, that is, $N = 2^k$ where k is a positive integer. We need to generate the pairing in such a way that each partition is paired with different partitions in different phases of this iterative approach. Also, in any phase, any particular partition is involved in only one pairing. Then it is obvious that the number of phases is the same as the number of partitions, N. Also, the number of pairings in any phase is N. For example, for four partitions the pairings at different phases are given as

Phase 1: [(1A, 1B), (2A, 2B), (3A, 3B), (4A, 4B)]
Phase 2: [(1A, 2A), (1B, 2B), (3A, 4A), (3B, 4B)]
Phase 3: [(1A, 3A), (1B, 3B), (2A, 4A), (2B, 4B)]
Phase 4: [(1A, 4A), (1B, 4B), (2A, 3A), (2B, 3B)]

TABLE 9.2 Comparison of Quality (Literal Count) and Runtimes (Seconds) of the Iterative Approach of Partitioned Logic Synthesis with MIS 2.2

Circuit	Initial Literal Count	MIS 2.2 1 Processor		Iterative partitioned			
				1 Proc		8 Proc	
		Literal	Time	Literal	Time (speed)	Literal	Time (speed)
des	7657	4024	2,784.00	4659	3185.4 (1.0)	4659	652.4 (4.9)
k2	3,063	n	n	1,692	989.4 (1.0)	1692	210.8 (4.7)
C7552	6144	2691	652.60	2893	1225.3 (1.0)	2893	241.6 (5.1)
C6288	4800	3729	1,037.20	3652	1566.8 (1.0)	3652	241.6 (5.1)
C5315	4386	2010	241.70	2320	884.7 (1.0)	2320	168.1 (5.3)
dk2ber	1314	n	n	840	370.6 (1.0)	840	77.4 (4.8)

It should be noted that phase 1 is the same as the one pass approach, that is, all the individual partitions are synthesized independently. The complete algorithm for generating all the phases of the iterative approach is described in [12].

Implementation The preceding parallel algorithm for logic synthesis using the iterative approach of partitioning and resynthesis has been implemented by De and Banerjee [12] on a network of SUN/4™ workstations. The underlying synthesis algorithm used on each partition was MIS 2.2.

In Table 9.2, we compare the literal counts (in sum-of-products form) and the runtimes (on a uniprocessor SUN/4™ workstation) obtained by running MIS 2.2 with those obtained by running the iterative approach using eight partitions on eight processors. The runtimes for the iterative approach on any circuit include the initial partitioning time, parallel partitioning-merge-synthesis times at different phases (on a uniprocessor, done one by one sequentially), and the final merge time. An n in the table means it either ran out of memory or it could not finish in 40 hours.

We can observe from the results in the table that the quality of the synthesized circuit obtained by the iterative approach is not as good as that obtained by applying MIS 2.2 on the entire circuit, whenever it is possible to run MIS 2.2 on the entire circuit. But for two circuits, *k2* and *dk2ber*, MIS 2.2 could not run on the whole circuit. The speedup results are very good for most of the circuits.

In summary, in this section we described a parallel algorithm for logic synthesis using the partitioning approach whereby a given circuit is partitioned into as many parts as there are processors, and each partition is synthesized on a different processor. The approach has three advantages. First, it is possible to get excellent speedups by partitioning the circuit into as many parts as there are processors. Second, the approach is independent of the logic synthesis algorithm used, the MIS approach [3] or the transduction approach [35]. Hence it is possible to use the best sequential algorithms for logic synthesis available at the moment. Finally, the approach minimizes the memory requirements needed in the synthesis algorithm. Hence it is possible to run synthesis on really large circuits. The main disadvantage of this approach is that the quality of the synthesized circuit deteriorates significantly with increasing number of partitions.

In the following sections, we will describe parallel algorithms for multilevel logic synthesis by parallelizing the underlying logic synthesis algorithm itself so that it runs on the entire circuit. In the next section, we will describe parallel algorithms for logic synthesis using the MIS approach. In a later section, we will describe parallel algorithms for multilevel synthesis using the transduction method.

9.6 SYNTHESIS USING MIS APPROACH

9.6.1 Overview

In this section, we will describe a parallel algorithm for logic synthesis that is based on iterative factoring and simplification of nodes in a multilevel circuit. These procedures form the core of the MIS approach to logic synthesis [3], which is one of the most popular logic synthesis systems. We will first review some basic definitions used in the MIS approach of logic synthesis.

A *variable* is a symbol representing a single coordinate of the Boolean space. A *literal* is a variable or its negation. A *cube* is a set C of literals such that $x \in C$ implies $\bar{x} \notin C$. An *expression* is a set f of cubes. The *support* of an expression f is the set of literals that is present in the sum-of-product expression of F. For example,

$$F = af + bf + ag + cg + ade + bde + cde$$

is a sum-of-products expression for the function F, where ade is a cube, and the support of F is $\{a, b, c, d, e, f, g\}$

The *primary divisors* of an expression f form a set of expressions

$$D(f) = \{f/C | C \text{ is a cube}\}$$

The *kernels* of an expression f are the set of expressions

$$K(f) = \{g | g \in D(f) \text{ and } g \text{ is cubefree}\}$$

In other word, the kernels of an expression f are the cube-free primary divisors of f. The cube C used to obtain kernel $k = f/C$ is called the *co-kernel* of k. For example, the expression $a + b$ is a multiple cube (the cubes are a and b) divisor of the expression F in the preceding example. After division, the expression F can be represented as

$$F = de(a + b) + f(a + b) + ag + cg$$

A Boolean network is a directed acyclic graph (DAG) in which each node i is associated with 1) a variable y_i and 2) a representation f_i of a logic function. In the graph, an arc connects node i to node j if $y_i \in sup(f_j)$. The *fan-in* of a node i is the set of all the nodes pointing to node i. The *fan-out* of a node i is the set of all nodes that node i points to. The *transitive fan-in* of a node i is the set of all the nodes that has a directed path to node i in the graph. The *transitive fan-out* of a node i is the set of nodes to which there is a directed path from node i. The *satisfiability don't-care* set of a node i is defined to be

$$DSAT_i = y_i \overline{f_i} + \overline{y_i} f_i = y_i \oplus f_i,$$

where y_i is the variable representing the node i and f_i is the logic function for that node. The *fan-out don't-care* set of a node i is defined to be

$$DT_i = \bigcap_{j \in FO_i} DTF_{ji}, \text{where}$$

$$DTF_{ji} = ((f_j)_{y_i} \equiv (f_j)_{\overline{y_i}}) = (f_j)_{y_i}.(f_j)_{\overline{y_i}} + \overline{(f_j)_{y_i}}.\overline{(f_j)_{\overline{y_i}}}$$

where FO_i denotes the fan-out of the node i and $(f_j)_{y_i}$ denotes the expression when the value of y_i is 1.

We will now explain various transformations used in the MIS system to synthesize a multilevel logic circuit. The aim of *kernel extraction* is to search for multiple-cube common divisors and extract those divisors. For example, given the equations in a Boolean network

$$F = af + bf + ag + cg + ade + bde + cde$$

$$G = af + bf + ace + bce$$

$$H = ade + cde$$

the best multiple-cube divisor that can be found is $a + b$. After creating a new node X for the common divisor in the network, the equations in the network become

$$F = deX + fX + ag + cg$$

$$G = ceX + fX,$$

$$H = ade + cde$$

$$X = a + b$$

The original network had 33 literals, and the modified network after the kernel extraction has 22 literals.

The aim of *cube extraction* is to search for single-cube common divisors and extract those divisors. For example, given the equations in a Boolean network

$$F = af + bf + ag + cg + ade + bde + cde$$

$$G = af + bf + ace + bce$$

$$H = ade + cde$$

the best multiple-cube divisor that can be found is $a + b$. After creating a new node X for the common divisor in the network, the equations in the network become

$$F \ = \ deX + fX + ag + cg$$

$$G \ = \ ceX + fX$$

$$H \ = \ ade + cde$$

$$X \ = \ a + b$$

The original network had 16 literals. After the cube extraction, the number of literals in the modified network is 15.

   Resubstitution is used to check whether an existing function itself is a divisor of other functions. For example, suppose the network is

$$x \ = \ ac + ad + bc + bd + e \ \text{ and } \ y = a + b$$

   The function y itself is a divisor of the function x. Therefore, it can be used to simplify the function x, which can be rewritten as

$$x \ = \ y(c + d) + e$$

   Each node of a Boolean network is a Boolean function expressed in the sum-of-products format (two-level logic). Hence, two-level minimization algorithms such as ESPRESSO [6] can be used to minimize each node of the Boolean network. That process is called *simplification*. Two-level minimization can be made more powerful in the context of multilevel circuits by using various don't-care sets arising due to the multilevel structure, as discussed in this section.

9.6.2 Distributed Memory MIMD Parallel Algorithm

We will now describe a distributed memory parallel algorithm for logic synthesis using the MIS approach based on work reported by De and Banerjee in [15]. The programming model for the parallel algorithm assumes a concurrent object-oriented model of computation such as the ones provide by the CHARM [23, 30] and PROPERCAD2 systems [36]. Conceptually, the PROPERCAD2 and CHARM systems maintain a pool of objects representing work that is created by the application program. Information is exchanged between these objects via messages. The objects in the work pool are distributed (and periodically balanced) across the available processors by the runtime system.

Workload Partitioning In this parallel algorithm, the given logic circuit is partitioned into subcircuits in order to distribute the various synthesis tasks among various processors. It should be noted that the partitioning is used for the purpose of *distribution of work* among different processors, and not for synthesizing each partition independently. Since the partitioning is used only for distribution of work among different processors, the partitioning algorithm does not have any effect on the quality of the synthesized circuit. Hence a very simple partitioning strategy, such as one based on input cones of the primary outputs, can be used for this purpose.

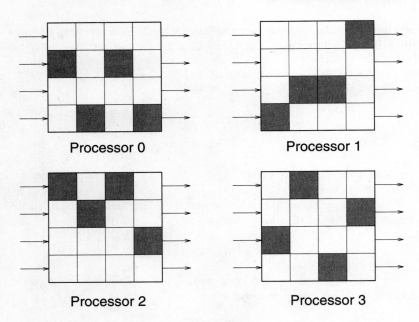

Processor 0

Processor 1

Processor 2

Processor 3

Figure 9.8 Partitions of a circuit and the ownership of each processor

For each circuit partition, one *partition_object* is created as depicted in Figure 9.8. Processes that perform various operations on these objects are distributed to different processors using load balancing methods. Typically, a large number of small partitions are created such that load balancing is good. But it is ensured that the amount of computation required by each partition is roughly an order of magnitude higher than that of the communication time for sending a message between objects. We will denote the object for a partition p as *partition_object* p. Each processor has a copy of the circuit, but has the responsibility for the shaded regions of the circuit. Effectively, we can say that each processor *owns* some parts of the circuit as shown in Figure 9.8.

A large number of small partitions are created such that load balancing is good, while making sure that the amount of computation required by each partition is roughly an order of magnitude higher than that of the communication time for sending a message between objects. The runtime system automatically distributes these objects to different processors.

Version Consistency A major problem that has to be dealt with in such a parallel algorithm is the fact that different processors may perform different optimizations simultaneously on the circuit. Hence, to provide some coherence or consistency mechanism among various applications of these optimizations in parallel, the concept of *version number* of the nodes is used. Every node in the Boolean network has a *version number* attached to it. Whenever the functionality of a node changes due to some transformation, the version number of that node increases by 1. In addition, a particular processor is designated as the *master* processor, which has to give permission before any transformation can take place. Whenever any processor finds a possible transformation on a node η, it asks for permission from the master processor for that transformation and it provides the *version number* of η in the request. When the *master* processor picks up the request, it checks if the *version number* provided in the request is the same as the current *version number* of η. If the condition is satisfied, then it gives the permission because the functionality of η has not changed since it was checked for the possible transformation. Otherwise, the permission is denied.

Parallel Algorithm for Kernel Extraction We will now describe a parallel algorithm for the *kernel extraction* process whose objective is to search for multiple-cube common divisors and extract those divisors. For example, given the equations in a Boolean network

$$F = af + bf + ag + cg + ade + bde + cde \tag{9.1}$$

$$G = af + bf + ace + bce \tag{9.2}$$

$$H = ade + cde \tag{9.3}$$

the best multiple-cube divisor that can be found is $a + b$. After creating a new node X for the common divisor in the network, the equations in the network become

$$F = deX + fX + ag + cg \tag{9.4}$$

$$G = ceX + fX \tag{9.5}$$

$$H = ade + cde \tag{9.6}$$

$$X = a + b \tag{9.7}$$

To perform the best kernel extraction, it is necessary to generate the kernels for all the nodes. Then the intersection of different subsets of the kernels generates possible factors, out of which the best factor is chosen to create a new node in the circuit.

In the parallel algorithm, the kernels for the nodes can be generated in parallel. A message is sent to all the *partition_objects* to generate the kernels of the nodes in that partition. The *partition_object(i)* will generate the kernels for all the nodes in partition i. Then it will broadcast that information to all the processors.

Finding useful intersections of kernels is facilitated with a concept called the *co-kernel cube* matrix, as described in [38]. A row in this matrix corresponds to a kernel (and its associated co-kernel), and a column corresponds to a cube that is present in some kernel. The entry at position (i, j) is nonzero if kernel i contains the cube j.

For example, consider the equations given above. The kernels (co-kernels) of the equation F are *de + f + g (a)*, *de + f (b)*, *a + b + c (de)*, *a + b (f)*, *de + g (c)*, and *a + c (g)*. The kernels (co-kernels) of G are *ce + f (a, b)*, and *a + b (f, ce)*, and the only kernel of H is *a + c (de)*. The expressions F and G are also kernels (because they are cube-free), but they are not listed. The expression H is not a kernel because it is not cube-free.

TABLE 9.3 Example Co-kernel Cube Matrix

			a	b	c	de	f	g	ce
			1	2	3	4	5	6	7
F	a	1	.	.	.		5	1	3	.
F	b	2	.	.			6	2	.	.
F	de	3	5	6	7	.	.	.	.
F	f	4	1	2	.	.	.	.	.
F	c	5	.	.	.		7	.	4	.
F	g	6	3	.	4	.	.	.	.
G	a	7	.	.	.	.	8	.	10
G	b	8	.	.	.	.	9	.	11
G	ce	9	10	11	.	.	.	.	.
G	f	10	8	9	.	.	.	.	.
H	de	11	12	.	13	.	.	.	.

The co-kernel cube matrix can be constructed from these expressions using the algorithm described in [38]. For each kernel (co-kernel), there is a row in the matrix (total of 11). The *unique* cubes from all the kernels are a, b, c, ce, de, f, and g; these cubes are used to label the columns of the matrix. The product of a co-kernel for a row and a kernel-cube for a column yields a cube of some expression. For reference, the cubes of the original expressions are numbered from 1 to 13. The cube number of the cube resulting from the product of the co-kernel for row i and the kernel-cube for column j is placed at position (i, j) in the co-kernel cube matrix. For example, the co-kernel a when multiplied by the kernel $de + f + g$ yields the cubes numbered 5, 1, 3 (which are ade, af, and ag). Note that there is often more than one way to form each cube in an expression. For example, cube 1 (af) is created by the co-kernel a multiplying the kernel $de + f + g$ and by the co-kernel f multiplying the kernel $a + b$. The co-kernel cube matrix for the expressions in Equations 9.1- 9.3 is given in Table 9.3.

In a parallel environment, the creation of the co-kernel cube matrix is a more involved process. If we want to create the co-kernel cube matrix in all the processors, they have to be the same in all the processors. In the sequential algorithm, when a new kernel (co-kernel) is generated, a new row is assigned for that kernel, and the row number corresponding to that kernel is noted in a table. Similarly, when a *unique* kernel-cube is generated, a new column is assigned for that cube and the column number corresponding to that cube is noted in a table.

Since the kernels are generated in parallel and then broadcast to all the processors, the order in which the kernels are received may be different in different processors. For example, one processor may receive the kernels in the order F, G, and H. In that case, the co-kernel cube matrix will be the same as that given in Table 9.3. But if another processor receives the kernels in the order G, H, and F, the co-kernel cube matrix in that processor will look like the one given in Table 9.4, which has a different labeling for the rows and the columns. To perform rectangular covering in parallel, we need to make the co-kernel cube matrix in all the processors the same irrespective of the order in which they receive the kernel informations.

TABLE 9.4 Co-kernel Cube Matrix for Different Ordering

			ce	f	a	b	c	de	g
			1	2	3	4	5	6	7
G	a	1	10	8	.	.	.	.	.
G	b	2	11	9	.	.	.	.	.
G	ce	3	.	.	10	11	.	.	.
G	f	4	.	.	8	9	.	.	.
H	de	5	.	.	12	.	13	.	.
F	a	6	.	1	.	.	.	5	3
F	b	7	.	2	.	.	.	6	.
F	de	8	.	.	5	6	7	.	.
F	f	9	.	.	1	2	.	.	.
F	c	10	.	.	.	.	.	7	4
F	g	11	.	.	3	.	4	.	.

TABLE 9.5 Using Labeling for Consistent Co-kernel Cube Matrix

			a	b	c	de	f	g	ce
			1	2	3	4	5	6	1003
F	a	1	.	.	.	5	1	3	.
F	b	2	.	.	.	6	2	.	.
F	de	3	5	6	7	.	.	.	.
F	f	4	1	2	.	.	.	.	.
F	c	5	.	.	.	7	.	4	.
F	g	6	3	.	4	.	.	.	.
G	a	1001	.	.	.	.	8	.	10
G	b	1002	.	.	.	.	9	.	11
G	ce	1003	10	11	.	.	.	.	.
G	f	1004	8	9	.	.	.	.	.
H	de	2001	12	.	13	.	.	.	.

To make the row and column labeling consistent in all the processors, the following strategy can be used. For each node, an interval of labels is assigned. For example, we can assign the intervals [1–1000], [1001–2000] and [2001–3000] to the nodes F, G, and H, respectively. So any kernel (co-kernel) generated for the node G will be labeled as a row in the co-kernel cube matrix with a number starting from 1001. Hence the labeling of the rows will be consistent in all the processors irrespective of the order in which the kernels are received.

For column labeling, a similar strategy is used. The unique kernel cubes generated for each node will be numbered initially using a number from the interval assigned to that node.

For example, the kernel cube a will be labeled as 1 while generating kernels for F, 1001 while generating kernels for G, and 2001 while generating kernels for the node H. When the same kernel cube arrives in a processor with a different label, it will choose the minimum of the labels to label the column corresponding to that kernel cube. Hence, after kernels of all the nodes are received, the label of the column corresponding to the kernel cube a will be 1 irrespective of the order in which kernels are received. The co-kernel cube matrix will finally look like the one given in Table 9.5. But in any intermediate time, the labeling can be different in different processors. For example, if the kernels of the nodes are received in the order H, G, and F, the column labeling for the kernel cube a will change from 2001 to 1001 to 1.

A rectangle of the co-kernel cube matrix identifies an intersection of kernels; this kernel intersection is a common subexpression in the network. The columns of the rectangle identify the cubes in the subexpression, and the rows of the rectangle identify the particular functions that the subexpression divides. The entries covered by the matrix correspond to cubes from the original network. For example, the prime rectangle ({3, 4, 1003, 1004}, {1, 2}) in Table 9.5 (shown in italics) identifies the subexpression $a + b$, which divides the function F and G. The cubes numbered 1, 2, 5, 6, 8, 9, 10, and 11 from the original set of functions are covered by this rectangle. The corresponding factorization is given in Equations 9.4-9.7. Another rectangle is ({3, 2001}, {1, 3}), which identifies the subexpression $a + c$ and divides the functions F and H.

The *weight* of a rectangle of the co-kernel cube matrix is chosen to reflect the number of literals in the network if the corresponding subexpression is inserted in the network. A minimum-weighted rectangle cover of the co-kernel cube matrix then corresponds to a simultaneous selection of a set of subexpressions to add to the network in order to minimize the total number of literals in the network.

Let w_j^c be the number of literals in the kernel cube for column j. If a rectangle (R, C) is used to identify a subexpression, then a new function is formed using the columns of C. This new function has $\sum_{j \in C} w_j^c$ literals. The rows of the rectangle indicate that the expressions that will be divided by the subexpression. After algebraic division by the subexpression, each expression consists of a sum of the corresponding co-kernel cubes multiplying the literal for the new expression. Let w_i^r be the number of literals in the co-kernel for row i plus 1. Therefore, the number of literals in the affected functions after extraction of the rectangle is $\sum_{i \in R} w_i^r$. Therefore, the weight of a rectangle (R, C) of the co-kernel cube matrix is defined as

$$w(R, C) = \sum_{i \in R} w_i^r + \sum_{j \in C} w_j^c$$

The *value* of a rectangle measures the reduction of the number of literals in the network if the particular rectangle is selected. The number of literals after the rectangle is selected is the weight of the rectangle as defined previously. Let V_{ij} be the number of literals in the cube that is covered by position (i, j) of the co-kernel cube matrix. Then the number of literals before the extraction of the rectangle is simply $\sum_{i \in R, j \in C} V_{ij}$. Hence the value of a rectangle

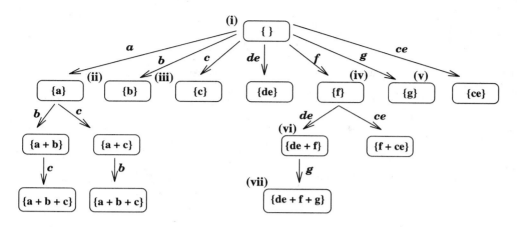

Figure 9.9 Conceptual search space for finding the maximum-valued rectangle

(R, C) of the co-kernel cube matrix is defined as

$$v(R, C) = \sum_{i \in R, j \in C} V_{ij} - w(R, C)$$

The rectangle covering is performed by generating all possible rectangles and selecting the maximum-valued rectangle as described in [38].

The search for the maximum-valued rectangle can be performed in parallel. The procedure is conceptually illustrated in Figure 9.9 and illustrated with the help of the *co-kernel cube matrix* in Figure 9.10. A processor is designated as the *master* processor. After the generation of all the kernels, the *master* processor creates an object called *kernel_extract_object* to compute the maximum-valued rectangle by generating all prime rectangles.

When a new *kernel_extract_object* is created, the following information is passed: the submatrix of the co-kernel cube matrix (M), the rectangle generated so far ($rect$) and the index of the column from which onward it should search for new prime rectangles ($index$). For the root *kernel_extract_object*, M is the co-kernel cube matrix itself, $rect$ is a empty rectangle, and the value of $index$ is 0 as shown in Figure 9.10(i). Conceptually, it is the root of the search tree as shown in Figure 9.9(i), corresponding to the null subexpression. The responsibility of this *kernel_extract_object* is to generate all prime rectangles with fewer rows but more columns that $rect$. This is performed by adding columns with labels more than or equal to $index$ to $rect$. Conceptually, it is equivalent to generating all possible subexpressions that can be multiple cube common divisors to the given set of equations by adding more kernel cubes (columns of M) to the given subexpression (represented by $rect$) to the *kernel_extract_object*. It also computes the value of $rect$ and records the information if it is the best rectangle seen by this object.

If the number of columns in the submatrix M is less than a user-defined threshold, all possible prime rectangles are generated by applying the sequential algorithm described in [38].

Otherwise, new child objects are created and the search space is divided among those child objects. Each column c with a label greater than *index* is examined as a column to include in the rectangle. If the column has only a single element, it cannot create a nontrivial rectangle, so only columns with two or more elements are of interest. The submatrix $M1$ of the original matrix M is created by selecting only the rows where column c has a nonzero value, and a new rectangle *rect1* is formed from the columns of the old rectangle *rect* and the rows for which c has a nonzero value. Any column of the submatrix $M1$ (including c) that is now all nonzero can also be added to the rectangle. At this point, *rect1* represents a new prime rectangle of the matrix, and $M1$ is a new submatrix to be searched for more prime rectangles. At this point, a new *kernel_extract_object* is created with following arguments: the submatrix $M1$, the new rectangle *rect1*, and the index c->column. For example, by adding column *1* to the empty rectangle in the root object, we create a new rectangle *rect1* with one column and six rows $(3, 4, 6, 9, 10, 11)$, as shown in Figure 9.10(ii). This object receives the submatrix $M1$, the rectangle *rect1* as shown in Figure 9.10(ii), and the value of the parameter *index* will be 1. Conceptually, it is equivalent to adding the kernel cube a to the null subexpression in the root object as shown in Figure 9.9(ii). The label of an edge in Figure 9.9 represents the kernel cube that will be added to the subexpression at the source node of that edge. For example, by adding the kernel cube de to the subexpression f in node (iv), a new subexpression $de + f$ is generated in node (vi), and by adding the kernel cube g to that, another new subexpression $de + f + g$ is generated in node (vii) in Figure 9.9. Similarly, the effects of adding columns 2, 5, and 6 to the empty rectangle at the root are shown in Figure 9.10 (iii), (iv), and (v) respectively. The corresponding nodes in the conceptual domain in Figure 9.9 are (iii), (iv), and (v), respectively.

If a *kernel_extract_object* generates prime rectangles by using the sequential algorithm, it reports the best rectangle seen by that object to its parent after the computation is performed. If it creates child objects, it waits for them to report the best rectangles seen by them, and then computes the best rectangle by picking the best of them. It subsequently reports that information to its parent. The root *kernel_extract_object* finally reports the best rectangle information to the *master* processor.

When the *master* processor receives the information regarding the maximum-valued rectangle, it computes the subexpression corresponding to that rectangle from the co-kernel cube matrix. It also determines the expression that can be divided by that subexpression. It broadcasts that information to all other processors. All the processors perform the divisions. All the kernels of the affected expressions are removed from the co-kernel cube matrix. The *version numbers* of the affected nodes are incremented by 1. The *partition_objects* corresponding to the partitions in which those affected nodes reside are sent messages to generate kernels again for those nodes. A new node is created for the subexpression and it is allocated to a suitable partition. Then a message is sent to that *partition_object* to create kernels for that node. Then the *master* processor creates a *kernel_extract_object* for searching for more kernels to be extracted. At this point, it does not wait for the re-generation of the kernels of the affected nodes. But the *kernel_extract_object* will be created with lower priority than the message for kernel re-generation. Therefore, it is very likely that kernels for the affected nodes will be regenerated before the *kernel_extract_object* is picked up by some processor, but it is not guaranteed. This strategy is used to remove synchronizing barriers at

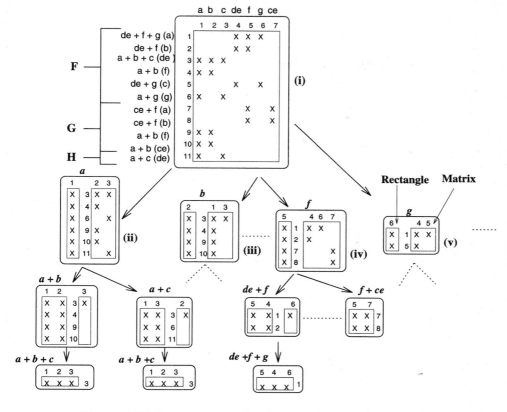

Figure 9.10 Example of performing kernel extraction by creating *kernel_extract_objects*

every stage of kernel extraction.

An outline of the *DM-PARALLEL-KERNEL-EXTRACT* algorithm (denoting distributed memory parallel algorithm for kernel extraction) is given next.

Procedure *DM-PARALLEL-KERNEL-EXTRACT;* Partition nodes among processors;
FORALL processors in parallel DO
    FOR each node in partition owned by processor DO
        Generate kernels in parallel;
        Construct kernel-cokernel matrix
            using nodes in own partition;
        Use consistent labeling approach;
    FOR each node in partition owned by processor DO
        Create kernel-extract-objects;
        WHILE circuit keeps improving DO
            IF circuit changed THEN

Reconstruct Kernel-Cokernel matrix;
Perform parallel search for best kernel;
Create a new node, assign to same processor;
FOR each node to be divided by best kernel DO
Ask Master processor for permission to
update node (use version number);
Perform factoring on node;
END FOR
END WHILE
END IF
END FORALL
End Procedure

Parallel Cube Extraction The aim of *cube extraction* is to search for single-cube common divisors and extract those divisors. For example, given the equations in a Boolean network

$$F = abc + abd + eg, \quad G = abfg \text{ and } H = bd + ef \qquad (9.8)$$

the best single cube common divisor can be found is ab. After creating a new node X in the network, the equations in the modified network become

$$F = Xc + Xd + eg, \quad G = Xfg, \quad H = bd + ef \text{ and } X = ab \qquad (9.9)$$

To perform the cube extraction, all possible cube intersections are generated and the common cube that reduces the literal count of the network maximally is extracted as the common subexpression.

To perform all possible cube intersections, a *cube-literal matrix* is formed at all the processors. Unlike kernel generation, we do not distribute the job of creating the *cube-literal matrix* to different objects. The creation of the *cube-literal matrix* is a relatively inexpensive process. Each expression is already expressed in sum-of-products form. As a result, all the cubes of the expressions are immediately available, they just needed to be filled up in the *cube-literal matrix*. So each processor creates its *cube-literal matrix* independently.

Every expression (and the associated literals) in the network is assigned a unique number, called *node-id*, when it is created in the Boolean network. That number is the same in all processors. Each expression in the Boolean network is assigned an interval, and all the cubes in that expression are labeled by numbers from that interval. The reason for using this strategy is to ensure that all the processor will create the same *cube-literal* matrix irrespective of the order in which information for different expressions is filled up. This approach is similar to the method used for labeling the kernel matrix in the parallel kernel extraction procedure.

The *cube-literal matrix* is created by using the following method. Each row of the *cube-literal matrix* corresponds to a cube in an expression in the network, and the row is labeled by the cube number of the cube. Each column of the matrix corresponds to a *unique* literal, and it is labeled by the *node-id* of that literal. The position (i, j) in the *cube-literal matrix* is set to a 1 if cube i contains literal j. A rectangle in the cube literal matrix identifies

TABLE 9.6 Consistent Cube-literal Matrix

		a	b	c	d	e	f	g
		1	2	3	4	5	6	7
F_1	1	*1*	*1*	1	.	.	.	.
F_2	2	*1*	*1*	.	1	.	.	.
F_3	3	.	.	.	.	1	.	1
G_1	1001	1	1	.	.	.	1	1
H_1	2001	.	1	.	1	.	.	.
H_2	2002	.	.	.	.	1	1	.

a cube that can be extracted from the network [4]. The columns of the rectangle identify the literals in the common cube, and the rows identify the cubes (and expressions) that will be affected if this common cube is extracted.

For example, consider the set of expressions in Equation 9.8. Let us assume that we have assigned the intervals [1–1000], [1001–2000], and [2001–3000] to the nodes F, G, and H, respectively. The *cube-literal matrix* for the expressions in Equation 9.8 is shown in Table 9.6.

Following the construction of the *cube-literal matrix*, the *master* processor creates a *cube_ext- ract_object* to generate all possible prime rectangles and find the maximum-valued rectangle. The algorithm is almost identical to that of kernel extraction. For example, one prime rectangle is ($\{1, 2\}, \{1, 2\}$) (shown in italics), corresponding to the extracted cube ab.

After the root *cube_extract_object* finds the maximum-valued rectangle, it reports that to the *master* processor. The *master* processor extracts the common cube and determines the set of expressions that this common cube will divide. It then broadcasts that information to all the processors. All the affected cubes are removed from the *cube-literal matrix* and the new cubes are entered. The *version number* of the affected nodes is incremented by 1. The *master* processor then creates a *cube_extract_object* to search for more cube extraction. The master processor does not wait for all the processors to finish the update for creating the object. But the priority of the *cube_extract_object* will be lower than that of the update message.

An outline of the *DM-PARALLEL-CUBE-EXTRACT* algorithm (denoting distributed memory parallel algorithm for cube extraction) is given next.

Procedure *DM-PARALLEL-CUBE-EXTRACT;*
Read circuit;
Partition nodes among processors;
FORALL Processors in PARALLEL DO
    FOR each node in partition owned by processor DO
        Generate cubes in parallel;
        Construct cube-literal matrix
            using nodes in own partition;
    FOR each node in partition owned by processor DO

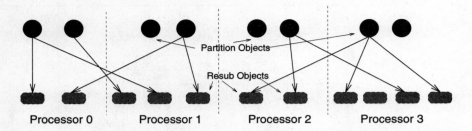

Figure 9.11 Creation of objects for resubstitution

        Create cube-extract-objects;
    END FOR
    WHILE circuit keeps improving DO
        IF circuit changed THEN
            Evaluate cube-literal matrix;
        Perform parallel search for best cube;
        FOR each node to be divided by best cube DO
            Ask Master processor for permission to
                update node (use version number);
            Perform cube factoring on node;
        END FOR
    END WHILE
  END FORALL
End Procedure

Parallel Resubstitution The *resubstitution* operation is used to check whether an existing functions itself is a divisor of other function. For example, suppose the network is

$$x = ac + ad + bc + bd + e \text{ and } y = a + b$$

The function y itself is a divisor of the function x. Therefore, it can be used to simplify the function x, which can be rewritten as

$$x = y(c + d) + e$$

The resubstitution operation can be performed in parallel. The *partition_objects* creates the *resub_objects* for each node in that partition. These objects are distributed across all the processors as shown in Figure 9.11.

    The responsibility of *resub_objects*(η) is to search for possible resubstitution by other nodes in the node η. We will restrict our search to algebraic divisors because the search for Boolean division is very expensive. A node ν can be an algebraic divisor of the node η if the *support* of ν is a subset of the *support* of η. Hence the *resub_objects*(η) restricts its search for divisors to the nodes whose *supports* are subsets of the *support* of η. Anytime it finds a divisor

ν and the division is going to reduce the literal count of the network, it requests permission from the *master* processor. In the request, it supplies the *version numbers* of the divisor ν and η.

When the *master* processor receives that request, it checks if the *version numbers* mentioned in the request are the same as the current *version numbers*. If so, it performs the resubstitution and increments the *version number* of the resubstituted node η. It then broadcasts the information to all other processors. Since the functionality of the node η has changed, the *master* processor creates a new *resub_object* for the node η.

An outline of the *DM-PARALLEL-RESUB* algorithm (denoting distributed memory parallel algorithm for resubstitution) follows:

Procedure *DM-PARALLEL-RESUB;*
Read circuit;
Partition nodes among processors;
FORALL Processors in PARALLEL DO
   FOR each node i owned by processor DO
     Create resubstitution-object(i, all other nodes);
   END FOR
   WHILE circuit keeps improving DO
     IF circuit changed THEN
       Evaluate Kernel-cokernel matrix;
     FOR each node to be resubstituted by i DO
       Ask Master processor for permission to
         update node (use version number);
       Perform resubstitution on node;
     END FOR
   END WHILE
END FORALL
End Procedure

Parallel Node Simplification   During multilevel logic synthesis, the sum-of-products form of each expression in a Boolean network needs to be minimized. Two-level minimization can be made more powerful in the context of a multilevel network by providing the minimizer with various don't-care sets derived from the structure of the network.

The *satisfiability don't-care* set of a node i is defined to be

$$DSAT_i \;=\; y_i \overline{f_i} + \overline{y_i} f_i \;=\; y_i \oplus f_i,$$

where y_i is the variable representing the node i and f_i is the logic function for that node. The *fan-out don't-care* set of a node i is defined to be

$$DT_i \;=\; \bigcap_{j \in FO_i} DTF_{ji}, \text{ where}$$

$$DTF_{ji} = ((f_j)_{y_i} \equiv (f_j)_{\overline{y_i}}) = (f_j)_{y_i} \cdot (f_j)_{\overline{y_i}} + \overline{(f_j)_{y_i}} \cdot \overline{(f_j)_{\overline{y_i}}}$$

where FO_i denotes the fan-out of the node i and $(f_j)_{y_i}$ denotes the the expression when the value of y_i is 1. The size of the don't-care sets determines how thorough and how fast the minimization process will be.

In a sequential algorithm for simplification, only one node is simplified at one time. As a result, the *satisfiability* don't care set of any other node can be used in the simplification process, and the result will still be correct. Similarly, the *fan-out* don't-care sets can also be used without any constraint (except that the simplification process may become very time consuming) because only one node in the network can change its function at one time.

When node simplifications are performed in parallel, many nodes may be simplified concurrently, and there will be some constraints on which don't-cares can be used to ensure the result to be correct. For example, consider the set of expressions

$$X = a\overline{b} + \overline{a}b \text{ and } Y = ab + \overline{ab}$$

If both node are simplified concurrently and they use each other's satisfiability don't-care sets, then the result will be

$$X = \overline{Y} \text{ and } Y = \overline{X}$$

which is wrong. But if they are simplified one at a time, that will never happen. Then we would have

$$X = a\overline{b} + \overline{a}b \text{ and } Y = \overline{X} \qquad \text{or} \qquad X = \overline{Y} \text{ and } Y = ab + \overline{ab}$$

This simple example shows that if two nodes are being simplified concurrently they should not use each other's satisfiability don't-care sets.

To make concurrent node simplification possible, we introduce the concept of *locking* a node. A node is said to be *algebraically locked* if no change in functionality is allowed to that node. A node is said to be *Boolean locked* if simplification of that node is not allowed, but all algebraic operations such as kernel extraction, cube extraction, and resubstitution are allowed.

Conceptually, the satisfiability don't-care of any node can be used for simplification of another node as long as it does not form a cycle in the network. But if a large don't-care set is supplied to the two-level minimizer, the simplification process will be very expensive. Hence, some don't-care filters have been proposed in [39]. One popular filter is the *subset support filter* for which the satisfiability don't-care of only those nodes is considered whose *support* is a subset of the *support* η, where η is the node to be minimized. Another popular heuristic is to collect transitive fan-in nodes of η up to i_i level and their transitive fan-outs up to o_i level, except for those nodes that are in the transitive fan-out of η, and use their satisfiability don't-care sets in the minimization of η, where i_i and o_i are user-specified parameters.

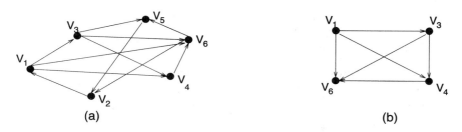

Figure 9.12 (a) Example of SDG; (b) largest acyclic vertex set of that SDG

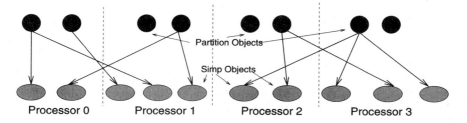

Figure 9.13 Creation of objects for simplification

Given the heuristic/filter to be used for the use of a satisfiability don't-care set, we can compute a set of nodes for every node η in the network whose satisfiability don't-care sets will be used for the simplification of η. From that information, we can generate a directed graph, called the satisfiability don't-care graph (SDG), denoted by (V, A). The vertex set of this graph consists of the nodes in the network. There exists a directed arc $(v_i, v_j) \in A$, v_i and $v_j \in A$, if the satisfiability don't-care set of the node v_j will be used in the simplification of the node v_i. An example of a SDG is shown in Figure 9.12(a).

We now make some observations about the SDG graph. A set of nodes Γ in a Boolean network can be simplified concurrently without any other constraint if they do not form any cycle in the corresponding SDG and if only a satisfiability don't-care set is used to simplify those nodes. To perform the simplification of the nodes in parallel, it is desirable to find the largest set of nodes such that simplification of those nodes can be performed concurrently. This problem can be reduced to finding the largest set of nodes in the corresponding SDG such that they do not form any cycle among themselves. It turns out that the *largest acyclic vertex set* problem is an NP-hard problem. The proof is provided in [15]. Since that problem is computationally intractable, the following heuristic method can be used.

Each *partition_object* creates a *simp_object* for each node in that partition. The *simp_object*(η) is responsible for simplification of the node η. Those simplification objects are distributed across different processors as shown in Figure 9.13.

Whenever a message is sent to a *simp_object*(η), the latter asks for permission from the *master* processor for the simplification of η. Initially all the nodes are unlocked. The *master* processor picks up the requests for permission one at a time. When it picks up the request for simplification for the node η, it checks if η is *Boolean locked*. If it is, the *master*

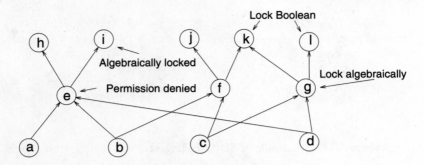

Figure 9.14 Algebraic and Boolean locking of nodes during simplification

processor denies permission and ask the *simp_object*(η) to try later. Otherwise, if the don't-care type chosen by the user includes the fan-out don't-care, it checks the fan-outs of η to see if any one of them is *algebraic locked*. If so, the *master* processor denies permission and asks the *simp_object*(η) to try later (as shown for the node e in Figure 9.14). Otherwise, it *Boolean locks* all the fan-outs of η (as shown for the node g in Figure 9.14). Then it checks if the satisfiability don't-care set is chosen in the don't-care type. If it is not chosen, permission is sent to *simp_object*(η) and η is *algebraic locked*. If it is chosen, it computes the list, *satis_DC_list*, of nodes whose satisfiability don't-care sets should be used for the simplification of η using the heuristic technique chosen by the user. From the *satis_DC_list*, it removes all the nodes that are *algebraically locked* at that time. It then sends the permission along with the *satis_DC_list* to the *simp_object*(η) and it *algebraically locks* the node η.

All the processors update the functionality of η when they receive the result from the *simp_object*(η). The *master* processor does some other tasks in addition. It unlocks the *algebraic lock* of η. Also, if the fan-in don't-care set was used, it unlocks the *Boolean locks* of the fan-outs of η.

It is apparent from the description of the simplification procedure that the first node to receive permission can use all the don't-care sets it asks for. The next node cannot use the satisfiability don't-care set of the first node if it asks permission before the simplification of the first node is completed. Hence for better simplification, we have assigned different priorities to different *simp_objects*. The priorities are assigned proportional to the size of the nodes (in terms of the literal count). If two *simp_objects* ask permission from the *master* processor simultaneously, the one with higher priority will be picked up first.

At any time, a processor p will have a list of messages to be processed. Some of them will be the permission from the *master* processor for simplification for some node, and some will be new *simp_object* creations (and other synthesis objects as well). These messages will be sorted according to decreasing value of the priorities, and the highest-priority message will be picked up for processing. Hence it will process simplification of a high-priority node (after it receives the permission) before creation (and asking permission) of a low priority node. As a result, the low-priority will not prematurely ask permission for simplification. When the message for creation for a low-priority node is picked up, the synthesis of some high-priority nodes is already completed. Hence the satisfiability don't-care sets of those nodes will be available for use. This can potentially improve the quality of node simplification. An outline of the *PARALLEL-NODE-SIMPLIFY* algorithm (denoting distributed memory parallel algorithm for node simplification) is given next.

Procedure *PARALLEL-NODE-SIMPLIFY;*
FORALL processors in parallel DO
  IF processor = Master THEN
    IF request for permission for node η received THEN
      IF (η is Boolean locked) THEN
        Send denial to SIMP-OBJ(η);
      IF fan-out DC to be used THEN
        IF any fan-out(η) is algebraic-locked THEN
          Send denial to SIMP-OBJ(η);
        ELSE Boolean lock fan-outs of η;
      IF satisfiability DC to be used THEN
        Compute sat-DC-list using heuristics;
        Removed algebraic locked from sat-DC-list;
        Send permission and sat-DC-list to SIMP-OBJ(η);
    IF received message after simplification of η THEN
      IF fan-out DC to be used THEN
        Boolean unlock fan-outs of η;
      Algebraic unlock η;
      Update expression for η;
  ELSE /* if processor not master */
    WHILE there are simplification objects DO
      Pick SIMP-OBJ(η) from queue;
      Request permission to Master processor;
      IF permission denied THEN
        Lower priority and request permission again;
      ELSE
        $D = \phi$;
      IF fan-out DC to be used THEN
        $D = D \cup$ fan-out-dont-care set;
      IF satisfiability DC to be used THEN
        FOR each node ν in sat-DC-list DO
          $D = D \cup$ sat-dont-care set of ν;
        Perform two level simplification;
        $\eta =$ ESPRESSO (η, D);
        IF any improvement THEN
          Report new expression for η to all processors;
        ELSE inform Master processor to unlock nodes;
  END IF
 END FORALL
End Procedure

Overview of the Parallel Algorithm In the previous subsections, we have described the parallel algorithm for each individual logic transformation. In this section, we will describe how the entire system works with all the transformations.

After the circuit is read, the partitions are formed and the *partition_objects* are created. The partition objects create the *simp_objects*. Then the simplification process proceeds as described previously.

When all of the nodes in a partition π are simplified, the *partition_object*(π) is sent a message to generate kernels for the nodes in π. All the processors are sent messages to fill up the *cube-literal matrix* (used for cube extraction) with the cubes of the nodes in π. Also, *partition_object*(π) is sent a message to create the *resub_objects* (responsible for resubstitution) for the nodes in π. Priorities are assigned to different transformations. The initial priorities are ordered as (highest to lowest) simplification, kernel extraction, cube extraction and resubstitution. A processor p will pick up a message of priority pr and process that request if there is no message with priority higher than pr waiting to be processed. For example, a processor will not pick up any message regarding kernel generation or kernel extraction if some other message regarding simplification is waiting to be processed in that processor.

After the *master* processor receives kernels of all the partitions, it creates the *kernel_extract_objects* for all the partitions. It also creates all the *cube_extract_objects* after it fills up cubes of all the nodes.

Whenever the *master* processor performs any logic transformation, it invalidates the kernels and the cubes of the affected nodes in the *co-kernel cube matrix* and *cube-literal matrix*, respectively, if the data are present. All the processors do the same when they receive the instruction from the *master* processor. Then messages are sent to the corresponding *partition_objects* to regenerate the kernels of the affected nodes. Similarly, messages are sent to reinsert the cubes of the affected nodes in the *cube-literal matrix* in all of the processors.

From this description, it is clear that, unlike the MIS algorithm, we do not have any separate phase for regeneration of kernels for the affected nodes. The regeneration of the kernels of the affected nodes is done *asynchronously*. The same thing is true for cube extraction.

After one kernel extraction, another *kernel_extract_object* is created immediately, hence we do not wait for the regeneration of kernels of the affected nodes. Therefore, we do not have any synchronizing barrier at every step of the kernel extraction process. The *kernel_extract_object* has lower priority than the kernel generation messages. It is possible that the regenerated kernels may arrive at the middle of the kernel extraction, making some generated rectangles in the kernel extraction algorithm invalid. Thus the computed maximum-valued rectangle may not be the maximum-valued rectangle in the modified *co-kernel cube matrix*. But we go ahead with that rectangle because computing the maximum-valued rectangle at every step to find a rectangular cover is a heuristic method, and compromising the maximum-value property at some stages of the covering process does not necessarily compromise quality. The cube extraction algorithm is implemented similarly.

If the priority of kernel extraction is kept always higher than that of cube extraction, the

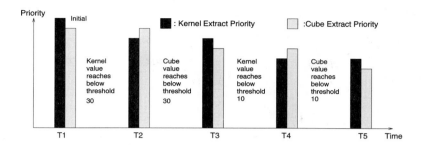

Figure 9.15 Example of priority adjustments of kernel and cube extraction

system will tend to perform almost all the kernel extractions before any cube extraction. This may lead to local minima. It is therefore advised that kernel extraction and cube extraction should be used in an interleaved fashion. For example, it is recommended that a high *threshold* (for example, 30) should be chosen, and kernel extraction should be performed using that threshold, which implies that only kernels that result in savings of at least 30 literals will be extracted. Subsequently, cube extraction will be performed with that threshold. After all kernel extractions and cube extractions with threshold 30 have been performed, the *threshold* should be reduced (for example, to 10) and the process repeated. Finally, the *threshold* can be reduced to 0, and the process repeated again.

The preceding method can be emulated by using a priority allocation as shown in Figure 9.15 and by maintaining two thresholds, *kernel_threshold* and *cube_threshold*. Initially, both of the thresholds are set to high values (for example, 30) and the priority of kernel extraction is set to be higher than that of cube extraction (time $T1$ in Figure 9.15). Hence initially, mostly kernel extractions will be performed. Whenever the gain from kernel extraction reaches below the *kernel_threshold*, the priority of the kernel extraction process is reduced below that of the cube extraction process, and the *kernel_threshold* is reduced to a lower value (for example, 10). Now mostly cube extractions will be performed because they are of higher priority (time $T2$ in Figure 9.15). Whenever the gain from cube extraction reaches below the *cube_threshold*, the priority of the cube extraction process is reduced such that it goes below the priority of the kernel extraction process and reduces the *cube_threshold* to a lower value (for example, 10). Now, again, mainly kernel extractions will be performed because they are of higher priority (time $T3$ in Figure 9.15). This procedure continues until both thresholds reach 0. Note that this procedure accomplishes the goal of interleaving kernel and cube extraction *without* the use of synchronizing barriers in the parallel algorithm.

Implementation The above parallel algorithm has been implemented by De and Banerjee [15] on an Intel iPSC/860™ hypercube. Table 9.7 shows the runtimes and speedups of several benchmark circuits on an Intel iPSC/860™ hypercube multiprocessor. It is clear from the table that reasonably good speedups were obtained at no significant loss in quality of results.

In summary, in this section we described a parallel algorithm for logic synthesis based on the MIS approach. Each major synthesis step of MIS, kernel extraction, cube extraction, resubstitution, and node simplification, was parallelized or results of the parallel algorithm on a real distributed memory multicomputer showed excellent speedups with minimal degradation

TABLE 9.7 Quality (Literal Count), Runtimes (Seconds), and Speedups, of Parallel Synthesis Algorithm on Intel iPSC/860™ hypercube

		1 Processor		8 Processors	
	Initial	Final	Runtime	Final	Runtime
Circuit	Literal	Literal	(speedup)	Literal	(speedup)
duke2	1775	459	66.3 (1.0)	464	18.1 (3.7)
misex3	1675	511	102.8 (1.0)	464	21.4 (4.8)
i8	4626	1151	80.5 (1.0)	1162	20.4 (4.0)
dalu	3588	1277	131.4 (1.0)	1286	32.2 (4.1)
c499	616	598	32.8 (1.0)	599	6.2 (5.3)

in result quality.

9.7 SYNTHESIS USING TRANSDUCTION APPROACH

9.7.1 Overview

In this section, we will describe parallel algorithms for logic synthesis using the transduction approach. We will first briefly review the transduction method of logic synthesis [35, 42, 41]. We will consider loop-free multilevel networks consisting of only simple gates such as AND, OR, NAND, NOR and NOT gates. However, it is conceptually trivial to extend the methods discussed in this section to handle more complex gates as well.

Let g be the number of gates in a multilevel network, $V = v_1, v_2, ..., v_g$ be the set of gates in the network, and $C = c_{ij}$ be the set of connections, where c_{ij} connects the output of gate v_i to an input of gate v_j. A gate v_i is an *immediate predecessor* of v_j if there exists a connection c_{ij}. Conversely, v_j is an *immediate successor* of v_i if c_{ij} exists. Let $IP(v_i)$ and $IS(v_i)$ be the set of all immediate predecessors and immediate successors of the gate v_i, respectively. When there is a sequence of gates $v_{k_1}, v_{k_2}, ..., v_{k_t}$ such that $v_{k_{b+1}} \in IS(v_{k_b})$ for all $b = 1, 2, ..., t - 1$, then v_{k_t} is a *successor* of v_{k_1}. Similarly defined, v_{k_1} is a *predecessor* of v_{k_t}. In the transduction method, we frequently need to consider connections the same way as gates. Hence these definitions apply to connections as well. For example, we say that c_{ij} is an immediate predecessor of v_j.

A network can be viewed as a graph consisting of nodes arranged in levels as done in compiled logic simulation. Each node represents either a gate or a connection. The level number (or just 'level' for short) of a gate or a connection in a network can be defined from either the primary inputs or the primary outputs. Formally, its level with respect to the primary inputs is defined to be 0 if it is a primary input or 1 + (the maximum level among its immediate predecessors) if it is not a primary input. Similarly, the level of a gate or a connection with respect to the primary outputs is defined to be 0 if it is a primary output, or, 1 + (the maximum level among its immediate successors) if it is not a primary output. Figure 9.16 shows an example of a network in which the gates and connections are arranged according to their levels with respect to the primary inputs.

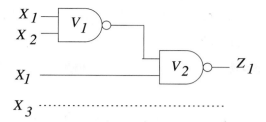

Figure 9.16 Example circuit for illustrating transduction method

The transduction method [35] is based on the concept of sets of permissible functions. The output function of a gate can be any member of its set of permissible functions without changing the primary outputs of the network. Hence, conceptually, sets of permissible functions are equivalent to observability don't-cares.

There are two types of permissible functions, the *maximum set of permissible functions (MSPF)* and the *compatible set of permissible functions (CSPF)*. As its name suggests, the MSPF of a gate or connection contains the largest set of functions that the output of a gate can take without changing the primary outputs. On the other hand, the CSPF of a gate or a connection is a subset of its MSPF, calculated based on some ordering of the connections in the network. However, the computation time needed for CSPF is much shorter than that required for MSPF, although it is less effective. The computations of MSPFs and CSPFs for gates and connections in a multilevel network can be found in [41].

Briefly, an *output function* of a gate in a network is the set of values output by the gate for all combinations (2^n for n inputs) of the primary input variables. The output function at a gate v_i, $f(v_i)$, can be expressed as a vector of Boolean values. For example, in Figure 9.16, where $n = 3$, we can write $x_1 = (01010101)$, $x_2 = (00110011)$, and $x_3 = (00001111)$ to express all possible combinations of the primary inputs. For the NAND-gate v_1, with x_1 and x_2 as its input, we can compute $f(v_1) = (11101110)$. For the NAND gate v_2, with x_1 and v_1 as its inputs, we can compute $f(v_2) = (10111011)$. Instead of formally giving the definitions of the CSPF and MSPF, we give an example. Since the output z_1 must remain unchanged, MSPF(v_2) = f(v_2) = (10111011). For the first input combination represented by the leftmost bit position in the vector, $x_1 = 0$, $f(v_2) = 1$. Since v_2 is a NAND-gate, and x_1 is 0, $f(v_2)$ is always 1 regardless of the value of $f(v_1)$, hence the first bit of MSPF(v_1) = * (don't-care). Similarly, the remaining MSPF bits of v_1 can be computed, and this vector is found to be (*1*0*1*0). There are explicit ways of computing MSPFs of gates and connections.

Given a multilevel network, it is possible to compute the output function of each gate or connection for all possible input combinations in a symbolic way by traversing the network from the primary inputs to the primary outputs in order of increasing levels with respect to the primary inputs. The procedure for computing the MSPFs or CSPFs, subsequently, involves traversing the gates in a reverse direction, from outputs to inputs, and applying some rules for each type of gate. For each gate, its MSPF (or CSPF) can be computed using the MSPFs (or CSPFs) of its immediate successors. For each input connection of a gate, its MSPF (or CSPF) can be computed using the MSPF (or CSPF) of its immediate successor, as well as the output

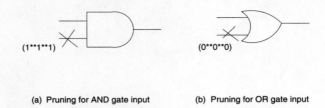

(a) Pruning for AND gate input   (b) Pruning for OR gate input

Figure 9.17 Example of pruning of connections. (a) Pruning for AND gate input. (b) Pruning for OR gate input.

functions of the other input connections that are connected to the same gate. For example, in the preceding circuit, the MSPF of v_1 was computed using the MSPF of its successor, v_2, and the output function of the other input to the gate, x_1. It is important to note that the MSPF or CSPF of a gate (or connection) can be computed using the MSPF or CSPF, respectively, of its immediate successor(s) only.

With the MSPFs or CSPFs of gates and connections in a multilevel network, we can perform a series of transformations and reductions to the network. We will use the term, *set of permissible functions (SPF)* as a general name for both MSPF and CSPF. SYLON-XTRANS [42, 41] consists of four main transformations: gate substitution, gate merging, generalized gate substitution, and gate input reduction. It also prunes redundant connections in a network.

Let us first describe the pruning operation. A connection is defined to be redundant if its removal from the circuit does not change the circuits functionality. In terms of the transduction terminology, a connection is redundant if its MSPF/CSPF is a string of all 1s and don't-cares at an input to an AND/NAND gate or if its MSPF/CSPF is a string of all 0s and don't-cares at an input of an OR/NOR gate. This is illustrated in Figure 9.17. This is because the presence/absence of the input connection does not affect the gate output, from the definition of the MSPF. Hence those inputs can be pruned from the network.

We will briefly describe each of the other transformations. In *gate substitution*, we search for a pair of gates, v_i and v_j, such that the output function of v_i is a member of the SPF of v_j. In this case, we can replace all the output connections of v_j by new connections from v_i. The gate v_j can then be removed from the network. Figure 9.18 gives an example of the gate substitution transformation.

In *gate merging*, we search for a pair of gates, v_i and v_j, such that the intersection of their SPF is nonempty. We then try to synthesize a new gate, v_k, whose SPF is the intersection of the SPFs of v_i and v_j. This is achieved by connecting the inputs of v_k to a minimal set of existing gates in the network through the connectability condition [42, 41]. The condition states that the input of the synthesized gate will be connected to a minimal set of outputs of the existing gates in the network, under the restriction that the successors of the two gates to be merged are not allowed to connect. After this, v_i and v_j can both be deleted from the network. Figure 9.19 gives an example of the gate substitution transformation.

A more general version of gate substitution is *generalized gate substitution*. In this transformation, we search the network for a candidate gate, v_i, whose output can replace an output connection of another existing gate, v_j. This is possible if the output function of v_i is a member of the SPF of the corresponding output connection of v_j. If each output connection

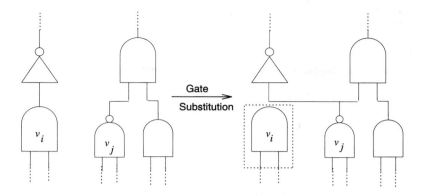

Figure 9.18 Example of gate substitution

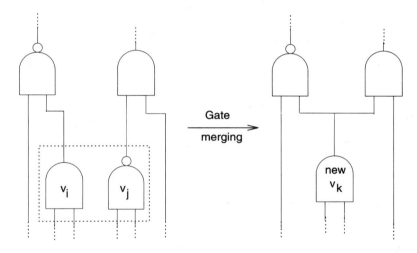

Figure 9.19 Example of gate merging

of v_j can be replaced by an appropriate connection from another gate in the network, we can then perform the replacements and remove v_j from the network.

Finally, in gate input reduction, we try to reduce the number of inputs to a gate. Here, for every gate v_i in the network, we try to synthesize a new gate, v_m, that also has the same SPF as v_i. The inputs to v_m are from the outputs of a minimal set of gates in the network. Such connections can be found using the connectability condition [42, 41]. The condition states that the input of the synthesized gate will be connected to a minimal set of outputs of the existing gates in the network, under the restriction that the successors of the two gates to be merged are not allowed to connect. If the number of inputs to v_m is less than that to v_i, we can then replace v_i by v_m and thus reduce the number of connections in the network.

Generally, these transformations are iterated until no further improvement can be made to a network. However, the performances of generalized gate substitution and gate input reduction decrease rather rapidly after a constant number of iterations (once or twice). Hence, in the SYLON-XTRANS synthesis system [42], they are combined into a single procedure and applied to the network for only a constant number of times. In this procedure, generalized gate substitution is applied to a gate first. If this is successful, the procedure will proceed to process other gates. Gate input reduction will only be tried on the gate if generalized gate substitution fails. With these transformations, SYLON-XTRANS is able to produce near optimal networks [42, 41].

An outline of the transduction method of logic synthesis algorithm *MULTILEVEL-SYNTHESIS-TRANSDUCTION* is given next.

Procedure *MULTILEVEL-SYNTHESIS-TRANSDUCTION;*
    Read circuit;
    Evaluate output functions from primary inputs to primary outputs;
    Evaluate CSPFs from primary outputs to primary inputs;
    WHILE circuit keeps improving DO
      WHILE circuit keeps improving DO
        IF circuit changed THEN
          Evaluate output functions and CSPFs;
        IF redundant link found THEN
          Perform gate pruning;
      END WHILE
      WHILE circuit keeps improving DO
        IF circuit changed THEN
          Evaluate output functions and CSPFs;
        Perform gate substitution transformation;
      END WHILE
      WHILE circuit keeps improving DO
        IF circuit changed THEN
          Evaluate output functions and CSPFs;
        Perform gate merging transformation;
      END WHILE
      WHILE circuit keeps improving DO
        IF circuit changed THEN
          Evaluate output functions and CSPFs;
        Perform generalized gate substitution transformation;
      END WHILE
      WHILE circuit keeps improving DO
        IF circuit changed THEN
          Evaluate output functions and CSPFs;
        Perform gate input reduction transformation;
      END WHILE
    END WHILE
End Procedure

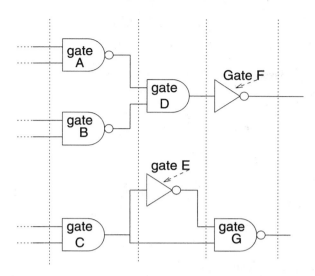

Figure 9.20 Example of parallel evaluation

9.7.2 Shared Memory MIMD Parallel Algorithm

We will now describe a shared memory parallel algorithm for logic synthesis using the transduction method that is based on work reported by Lim et al. [32]. In the following sections, we will describe how the various transduction procedures can be applied to a single partition in parallel.

Parallel computation of functions The approach to parallel computation of output functions and compatible set of permissible functions (CSPFs) is conceptually similar to the parallel methods of logic simulation. From the definition of the level of a gate given in the previous section, it can be seen that gates and connections in the same level with respect to the primary inputs can have their output functions computed in parallel. Similarly, the CSPFs of gates and connections in the same level with respect to the primary outputs can be computed in parallel too.

Suppose we want to compute the output functions of the gates and connections of a network in parallel. We start with the primary inputs and distribute them evenly among the processors for parallel computation. After this, we distribute the connections that are connected to these inputs and process them in parallel. Next we pick those gates in the network whose input connections have all been processed, distribute them, and compute their output functions in parallel, too. This is repeated until every gate and connection has been processed. An exit is located after this so that the slave processors involved in the computation can return to the slave pool. Figure 9.20 gives an example of parallel gate evaluation.

Obviously, the processors need to be synchronized before the gates and connections are distributed to them. Between two consecutive synchronizations, the processors are actually processing a level of gates or connections with respect to the primary inputs. During the parallel processing of such a level, a processor may sometimes complete its job before others. When this happens, the processor will identify which of the other processors has the most unprocessed gates and connections left, remove half of that processor's unprocessed items, and process them. This load balancing strategy minimizes the amount of idleness at each processor.

An outline of the *SM-PARALLEL-TRANSDUCTION-OUTPUT-FUNCTION* algorithm (denoting shared memory parallel algorithm for output function evaluation in the transduction method) follows:

Procedure *SM-PARALLEL-TRANSDUCTION-OUTPUT-FUNCTION;*
    Partition the circuit into levels from primary inputs
    to primary outputs;
    Insert gates of each level into separate queue;
    FOR each level L = 1 to maxlevel DO
        FORALL processors in PARALLEL DO
            WHILE there are gates on level L DO
                Pick gate of level L from queue;
                Perform output function evaluation;
            END WHILE
        END FORALL
    END FOR
End Procedure

Using a similar approach, we can also compute the CPSFs of gates and connections by starting with the primary outputs. An outline of the *SM-PARALLEL-TRANSDUCTION-CSPF* algorithm (denoting shared memory parallel algorithm for CSPF evaluation in the transduction method) is given next.

Procedure *SM-PARALLEL-TRANSDUCTION-CSPF;*
    Partition the circuit into levels from primary inputs
    to primary outputs;
    Insert gates of each level into separate queue;
    FORALL processors in PARALLEL DO
        FOR each level L = maxlevel down to 1 DO
            WHILE there are gates on level L DO
                Pick gate of level L from queue;
                Perform CSPF evaluation;
            END WHILE
            Barrier Synchronize processors (L);
        END FOR
    END FORALL
End Procedure

Parallel Pruning As discussed earlier, a connection is pruned if it is proved to be redundant. In terms of the transduction terminology, a connection is redundant if its MSPF/CSPF is a string of all 1s and don't-cares at an input to an AND/NAND gate or if its MSPF/CSPF is a string of all 0s and don't-cares at an input of an OR/NOR gate. Pruning can be performed with either CSPF or MSPF. We will first describe how pruning with CSPF is performed in parallel.

The procedure for parallel pruning with CSPF is a modification of the procedure for parallel computation of CSPFs, which was described in the previous section. In this procedure, we check for the redundancy of a connection immediately after its CSPF has been computed. Hence, after the CSPFs of every gate and connection in a partition have been computed in parallel, we know which of the connections are redundant. The master in charge of minimizing this partition will then remove these connections. A single processor is used to remove the redundant connections because we need to adjust only a few pointers in the program's data structures during each removal, which can be performed very quickly. Hence it is not worth parallelizing. After removing the connections, the master initiates the recomputation of the CSPFs for the next iteration of the procedure. This is repeated until no further redundant connections can be found.

On the other hand, in the procedure for parallel pruning with MSPF, we do not wait until the MSPFs of all the gates and connections have been computed before performing any removal. This is because, after a connection has been removed, we need to recompute the MSPFs. Hence a lot of work will be wasted if we were to compute all the MSPFs first. In this procedure, we let the processors compute the MSPFs of gates and connections in parallel, similar to the procedure used for the computation of CSPFs. However, after a processor has computed the MSPF of a connection and has determined that the connection is redundant, it informs the other processors to halt. The master processor will then remove the redundant connection, while the slaves return to the slave pool. After this, the master processor initiates the recomputation of the MSPFs for the next iteration of the procedure.

An outline of the *SM-PARALLEL-TRANSDUCTION-PRUNING* algorithm (denoting shared memory parallel algorithm for gate/line pruning in the transduction method) is given next.

Procedure *SM-PARALLEL-TRANSDUCTION-PRUNING;*
    Partition the circuit into levels;
    Insert gates and connections of each level
       into separate queue;
    FORALL processors in PARALLEL DO
      FOR each level L = maxlevel down to 1 DO
         WHILE there are gates or connections on level L DO
           Pick gate or connection of level L from queue;
           Perform CSPF evaluation;
           Check for redundancy;
           IF redundant THEN
                Obtain lock on circuit;
                Remove gate/connection and fan-in circuits;
                Release lock;

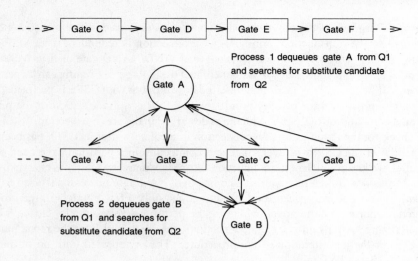

Figure 9.21 Example of parallel gate subsitution

                    END WHILE
                    Barrier Synchronize processors (L);
                END FOR
            END FORALL
        End Procedure

Parallel Gate Substitution The main idea of gate substitution is to search a given network for pairs of gates such that in each pair one gate can substitute for the other. However, as the network needs to be loop-free, the substitute gate must not be a successor of the gate to be substituted. Hence to minimize the chance of this happening, the substitute gate and the substituted one were chosen to be as near as possible to the primary inputs and primary outputs, respectively.

To explain how parallel gate substitution works, we will describe an iteration of the procedure. In each iteration, we try to generate, in parallel, a set of pairs of gates, (v_i, v_j), such that in each pair the gate v_i can substitute for the corresponding gate v_j. Each processor p will mark a *unique* gate, v_{j_p}, in the circuit. (We use 'unique' in the sense that each processor chooses a different gate.) This v_{j_p} is obtained by scanning the circuit, starting with the primary outputs, for the first gate that has not yet been marked by any processor. After this, the processor will then search the circuit for another gate v_{i_p} that can substitute for v_{j_p}. This search begins with the primary inputs. If the search is successful, the processor will halt the other processors working on the same circuit. Figure 9.21 gives an example of the parallel gate substitution transformation.

After each iteration of the procedure, the output functions and CSPFs of the gates and connections in the network are computed before proceeding to the next iteration.

An outline of the *SM-PARALLEL-TRANSDUCTION-GATESUB* algorithm (denoting shared memory parallel algorithm for gate substitution transformation in the transduction method) follows:

Procedure *SM-PARALLEL-TRANSDUCTION-GATESUB;*
    WHILE circuit keeps improving DO
        FORALL processors in PARALLEL DO
            WHILE there are gates or connections in the queue DO
                Pick unique unmarked gate v_j from
                    the queue starting from primary outputs;
                Mark gate v_j;
                FOR each gate v_i searching from primary inputs to outputs DO
                    Check if gate v_i can substitute gate v_j;
                    IF gate substitution possible THEN
                        Obtain lock on circuit;
                        Substitute gate v_j with gate v_i;
                        Release lock;
             END WHILE
        END FORALL
    END WHILE
End Procedure

Parallel Gate Merging Gate merging is an iterative improvement procedure similar to gate substitution. In each iteration of the procedure, the processors in parallel search for a pair of gates (v_i, v_j) and try to synthesize a third gate, v_k, to replace them. The inputs to the newly merged gate v_k have to be selected from the outputs of existing gates. However, the inputs to v_k must not come from successors of v_i and v_j (to maintain the loop-free condition of the transduction procedure). Hence to increase the probability of being able to synthesize v_k, the search for v_i and v_j is started from the primary outputs, and also the search for the inputs to v_k is started from the primary inputs.

    To describe how the parallel search works, we will describe an iteration of the gate merging procedure. Every processor p will each mark a unique gate, v_{i_p}, in the circuit. This v_{i_p} is obtained by scanning the circuit, starting with the primary outputs, for the first gate that has not been marked by any processor. Beginning with the primary outputs, the respective processor will search for another gate v_{j_p} such that its CSPF intersects with that of v_{i_p}. After obtaining the pair (v_{i_p}, v_{j_p}), the processor tries to synthesize a third gate v_{k_p} that can replace both v_{i_p} and v_{j_p}. If this is successful, the processor will then inform the other processors working on the same circuit to halt. The processor will perform the gate merging operation. On the other hand, if the processor cannot find a suitable v_{j_p} for the gate v_{i_p} or is unable to synthesize v_{k_p} for both v_{i_p} and v_{j_p}, it will look for another v_{i_p} and repeat the searching process. After each iteration of the procedure, the output functions and CSPFs of the gates and connections in the circuit are recomputed before proceeding to the next iteration.

    An outline of the *SM-PARALLEL-TRANSDUCTION-GATEMERGE* algorithm (denoting shared memory parallel algorithm for the gate merging transformation in the transduction method) follows:

Procedure *SM-PARALLEL-TRANSDUCTION-GATEMERGE;*
WHILE circuit keeps improving DO
    FORALL processors in PARALLEL DO
        WHILE there are gates remaining in the queue DO
            Pick unique unmarked gate v_j from
                the queue starting from primary outputs;
            Mark gate v_j;
            FOR each gate v_i searching from primary inputs to outputs DO
                Check if gate v_i can be merged with gate v_j;
            IF gate merging possible THEN
                Obtain lock on circuit;
                Merge gates v_j with gate v_i to
                    synthesize new gate v_k;
                Release lock;
        END WHILE
    END FORALL
END WHILE
End Procedure

Similar parallel algorithms have been developed for generalized gate substitution and gate input reduction [32].

Implementation Lim et al. have implemented the preceding parallel algorithm for logic synthesis using the transduction method on an Encore Multimax™ shared memory multiprocessor [32]. The implementation combined a partitioned approach to parallel logic synthesis with a parallel algorithm for transduction. Large networks were partitioned into several smaller partitions in order to solve very large circuits under memory constraints. The algorithm then exploited interpartition parallelism (synthesizing different partitions in parallel) and intrapartition parallelism (synthesizing a given partition in parallel among many processors). Processors were dynamically assigned to different partitions depending on the workload on a given logic partition at a time.

The algorithm has been evaluated on a large set of MCNC and ISCAS logic synthesis benchmark circuits. The quality of the synthesis results is similar to that produced by the SYLON-XTRANS algorithm. Speedup results af about 6 to 7.5 were measured on eight processors. Table 9.8 shows the performance of the parallel implementation in terms of runtimes (in seconds) and the quality of the synthesized circuits (measured in terms of gate counts and connections).

9.7.3 Distributed Memory MIMD Parallel Algorithm

We will now describe a distributed memory parallel algorithm for logic synthesis using the transduction method based on work reported by De et al. [17, 16]. The programming model for the parallel algorithm assumes a concurrent object-oriented model of computation such as the ones provide by the CHARM [23, 30] and PROPERCAD2 systems [36]. Conceptually, the PROPERCAD2 and CHARM systems maintain a pool of objects representing work that

TABLE 9.8 Quality (Gate/Connections), Runtimes (Seconds), and Speedups, of Parallel Synthesis Algorithm on the Encore Multimax™ Multiprocessor

		1 Processor		8 Processors	
Circuit	Initial Gate/Connection	Final Gate/Connection	Runtime (speedup)	Final Gate/Connection	Runtime (speedup)
C432	198/411	166/345	4911 (1.0)	166/345	832 (5.9)
C499	526/942	493/892	5231 (1.0)	493/892	697 (7.5)
C880	342/688	313/632	1535 (1.0)	313/632	219 (7.0)
C1908	599/1220	448/914	6219 (1.0)	453/940	1173 (5.3)

is created by the application program. Information is exchanged between these objects via messages. The objects in the work pool are distributed (and periodically balanced) across the available processors by the runtime system.

Workload Partitioning In the parallel algorithm, the logic network is divided into a set of nonoverlapping partitions, however, the partitioning is for *parallelization purposes only*, and the transformations and the optimizations are performed on the entire network. This is similar to the distributed memory parallel algorithm for logic synthesis using the MIS approach dscribed in Section 9.6.2.

For each partition, one *object* is created as depicted in Figure 9.8. Processes that perform various operations on these objects are distributed to different processors using load balancing methods. Typically, a large number of small partitions are created such that the load is equally balanced. But it is ensured that the amount of computation required by each partition is roughly an order of magnitude higher than that of communication time for sending a message between objects. We will denote the object for a partition p as *partition_object* p. Each processor has a copy of the network, but has the responsibility for the shaded regions of the network. Effectively, we can say that each processor owns some parts of the network.

Version Consistency For optimization purposes, we need to evaluate the output functions at each gate and connection in the network. The output functions need to be expressed in terms of the primary inputs of the network. The output functions are computed using binary decision diagrams (BDD) instead of the bit vector representation described earlier to save memory [9].

A major problem we must to deal with is the fact that since different processes perform different optimizations simultaneously on the network, the output functions and the CSPFs keep changing. It is important to provide some coherence or consistency mechanism among various applications of these optimizations in parallel. To do this, we keep a tag with each BDD, called the *version*. Also, with each gate and connection, we keep the current version number of the output function and the CSPF. A BDD is valid if its version number is current. Any transformation in the network changes the output functions and the CSPFs in some parts of the network. The version numbers are used to prevent any illegal transformation done using an invalid BDD. Initially, the versions of output functions and the CSPF are set to 1. If, due to

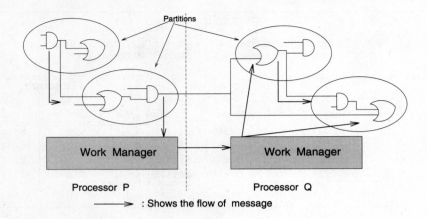

Figure 9.22 Evaluation of output functions and the flow of messages

any transformation, the output function or CSPF of a gate or connection becomes invalid, the corresponding version number attached to it is incremented by 1. This method is similar to the version consistency used in the distributed memory parallel algorithm for logic synthesis using the MIS approach.

Parallel Evaluation of Output Functions   The evaluation of output functions starts from the primary inputs of the network. The output function of a gate can be evaluated if valid output functions of its fan-ins are available. Any gate whose fan-ins are primary inputs only can be evaluated without any constraints. Gates that have fan-ins from other partitions cannot be evaluated unless the output function of those fan-ins arrives from the other partitions.

   After the output function of a gate ζ is evaluated in a partition, it is checked if its output function is needed in any other partition. If the other partition that needs the output function is in the same processor, that *partition_object* is informed about the availability of the output function of ζ. But if it is in a different processor, the current *partition_object* invokes a *work manager* in the current processor, which in turn transmits the BDD to the *work manager* of the destination processor and then the *work manager* in the destination processor sends a message to the corresponding processes in that processor about the availability of the output function of ζ. We use the *work manager* to ensure that only one copy of the BDD is sent across the processor boundary. The procedure is illustrated in Figure 9.22.

   Whenever a *partition_object* receives a message about the availability of the output function of a gate ζ, it checks to make sure that it is a valid BDD. It then checks for the gates in this partition that are waiting for the availability of the output function of ζ. Gates that have all the output functions of their fan-ins available can now be evaluated.

   An outline of the *DM-PARALLEL-TRANSDUCTION-OUTPUT-FUNCTION* algorithm (denoting distributed memory parallel algorithm for output function evaluation in the transduction method) is given next.

Procedure *DM-PARALLEL-TRANSDUCTION-OUTPUT-FUNCTION;*
   Partition the circuit into large number of partitions;

```
        Assign partitions of subcircuits to processors;
        FORALL processors in PARALLEL DO
            WHILE there are subcircuits in own processor DO
                Receive output functions from other processors;
                Pick a subcircuit;
                Check if all inputs have valid evaluated output functions;
                IF invalid THEN
                    insert subcircuit back in queue;
                FOR each level L = 1 to maxlevel within subcircuit DO
                    WHILE there are gates on level L DO
                        Pick gate of level L from queue;
                        Perform output function evaluation;
                        Send output functions to other processors;
                    END WHILE
                END FOR
            END WHILE
        END FORALL
    End Procedure
```

It is clear from the preceding description that the parallel evaluation of the output function is performed using an asynchronous message-driven data-flow computational model. The parallel algorithm does not have any synchronizing barriers at each level of gates, as was needed in the previous shared memory parallel algorithm; hence this parallel algorithm is expected to scale well with a large number of processors.

Parallel Evaluation of CSPF   The flow of evaluation of CSPF moves from the primary outputs to the primary inputs. If the output function of a primary output is available, its CSPF can be calculated immediately. If no *external don't-care* [1] is specified for that primary output, the CSPF is the same as the output function; otherwise, the CSPF is the union of the output function and the external don't-care.

The CSPF of an input connection to a gate can be computed if the output functions of all the input connections to that gate are available as well as the CSPF of that gate. Then the CSPF of the input connection is computed as a function of the type of gate, the CSPF of the gate output, the output functions of the sibling connections, and the output function of the connection itself [41]. The CSPF of a gate can be computed if the CSPF of all the output connections are available. The CSPF of a gate is the set intersection of the CSPFs of its output connections [41].

The partitions that have any primary outputs start evaluation of the CSPF at the primary outputs. After evaluation of an input connection, it is checked to see if it is connected to the output of a gate that is in a different partition and the partition is in the same processor; then that *partition_object* is informed about the availability of the CSPF of the connection. If the partition is in a different processor, the CSPF is transmitted to the other processor through the *work managers* of the two processors, similar to the case of the evaluation of output functions. The procedure is explained in Figure 9.23.

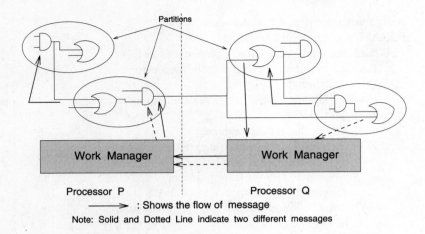

Figure 9.23 Evaluation of CSPF and the flow of messages

Again, it is clear from the description of the parallel algorithm that the parallel evaluation of the CSPF proceeds in an asynchronous message-driven data-flow computational model with no barriers.

An outline of the *DM-PARALLEL-TRANSDUCTION-CSPF* algorithm (denoting distributed memory parallel algorithm for CSPF evaluation in the transduction method) follows:

Procedure *DM-PARALLEL-TRANSDUCTION-CSPF;*
    Partition the circuit into a large number of partitions;
    Assign partitions of subcircuits to processors;
    FORALL processors in PARALLEL DO
       WHILE there are subcircuits in own processor DO
          Receive CSPFs from other processors;
          Pick a subcircuit;
          Check if all outputs have valid evaluated CSPFs;
          IF invalid THEN
             insert subcircuit back in queue;
          FOR each level L = maxlevel down to 1 within subcircuit DO
             WHILE there are gates on level L DO
                Pick gate of level L from queue;
                Perform CSPF evaluation;
                Send CSPF to other processors;
             END WHILE
          END FOR
       END WHILE
    END FORALL
End Procedure

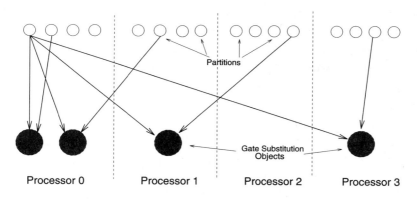

Figure 9.24 Creation of objects for gate substitution

Parallel Gate Substitution Gate substitution is one of the transformations provided in the transduction method. The main idea of gate substitution is to search a given network for pair of gates such that in each pair one of the gates can substitute for the other. However, as the network needs to be loop-free, the substitute gate must not be a successor of the gate to be substituted. Hence to minimize the chance of this happening, the substitute gate and the substituted one should be as near as possible to the primary inputs and outputs, respectively.

Let us denote p as the number of *partition_objects* created. Then the *partition_object* x will create another p objects, called *gate_sub_objects*. They are denoted as the pair (x, y), $x = 1, \ldots, p, y = 1, \ldots, p$. The *gate_sub_object* denoted by (i, j) is responsible for substitution of any gate in the *partition_object* i by any gate in the *partition_object* j. Note that there will be another *gate_sub_object* (j, i) created whose job is the complement of the job of (i, j). Hence the number of *gate_sub_objects* created will be p^2. We have already mentioned that it is preferable to have the partition i close to the primary outputs and the partition j close to primary inputs to maximize the chance of finding a gate substitution pair. Hence we adjust the priorities of the different *gate_sub_object* to achieve that (the priorities are used to direct the underlying runtime system to process certain messages with higher priority). The procedure is depicted in Figure 9.24.

Now consider the *gate_sub_object* (i, j). A gate g_1 in the partition i can be substituted by a gate g_2 in the partition j if the output function of the gate g_2 is a subset of the CSPF of the gate g_1. Then the *gate_sub_object* (i, j) will need valid CSPF of all the gates in the partition i and output functions of the gates in the partition j.

When the *gate_sub_object* denoted by (i, j) is activated by a message, it starts by collecting the output functions and the CSPFs that it needs. Some output functions and CSPFs may not be available at that time, so it will ask the *work manager* in this processor to get the BDD and inform it when that is available. If this processor does not own the portion of the network that contains the gate for which BDD has been asked, the *work manager* on the requesting processor will ask the *work manager* in the requested processor to send the BDD. After this *gate_sub_object* has collected all the available "valid" BDDs, it does pairwise comparisons to find out any possible gate substitution. If any gate substitution is possible, it sends a message to a particular processor, designated to be the *master* processor for deciding about any change in the network, asking permission for this gate substitution. The message also contains the version numbers of the output function and the CSPF used for checking the gate substitution. When it is finished with all comparisons, it asks *partition_object i* to inform it if CSPF of any gate in the partition i changes and it asks *partition_object j* to inform it if the output function of any gate in the partition j changes.

Whenever an output function or CSPF arrives from any other processor or the current version gets computed in this processor, the *work manager* checks the list to find out if any object has asked for this BDD. If so, it sends a message to the corresponding objects.

Whenever a *gate_sub_object* (i, j) receives a message about the availability of an output function of gate g_2 in the partition j, it then compares this with the valid CSPFs available at the gates in the partition i. If any substitution is possible, it then sends a message asking for permission for that gate substitution, as explained earlier. Similar operations are performed if this object receives a message about the availability of the CSPF of a gate in partition i.

An outline of the *DM-PARALLEL-TRANSDUCTION-GATESUB* algorithm (denoting distributed memory parallel algorithm for the gate substitution transformation in the transduction method) follows:

Procedure *DM-PARALLEL-TRANSDUCTION-GATESUB)* ;
Partition circuit into subcircuits;
FOR each subcircuit i DO
   FOR each subcircuit j DO
      Create a gate substitution object (i,j);
      Assign gate substitution object(i,j) to a processor;
   END FOR
END FOR
FORALL processors in PARALLEL DO
   WHILE there are gate_sub_objects(i,j) on processor DO
      IF message sent for gate_sub_object (i, j) THEN
         Collect CSPFs of all gates in partition i
         Collect OutFunct of all gates in partition j
         IF any CSPF or OutFunct is not available
            THEN request *work manager* to get it
         Perform pairwise comparison of available CSPFs and OutFunct
         IF possible gate substitution found
            THEN ask *master* processor for permission
         Ask partition i to inform if any CSPF changes in partition i
         Ask partition j to inform if any OutFunct changes in partition j
      ENDIF
      IF gate_sub_object(i,j) receives a new CSPF THEN
         Compare this CSPF with all available OutFunct of partition j
         IF possible gate substitution found
            THEN ask *master* processor for permission
      ENDIF

IF gate_sub_object(i,j) receives a new output function THEN
    Compare this OutFunct with all available CSPFs of partition i
    IF possible gate substitution found
        THEN ask *master* processor for permission
ENDIF
End Procedure

When the *master* processor receives the request for permission for a gate substitution, it first checks if both gates in the gate substitution pair exist. Then it checks if the current version of the output function and the CSPF of the substitute gate and the substituted gate respectively are the same as that mentioned in the message. The version check is performed to make sure that the requested gate substitution is still legal, that is, no other transformation performed on the network has affected this gate substitution. The master processor then broadcasts a message to all other processors to perform this gate substitution in their copy of the network and then itself performs the substitution. It is through this centralized update that coherence is maintained in data updates, and it is guaranteed that no errors are made in the optimization process.

After the substitution is performed, the output functions of all the *successors* of the substituted gate will be invalid, as well as the CSPFs of the *predecessors* of the substitute gate. This is shown in Figure 9.25(a). But if the output functions are reevaluated in the region where they are marked, then the CSPFs of all the gates in the transitive fan-ins of that region will get invalidated. Since in this approach there are no synchronizing barriers to decide when to start reevaluation of the output functions and the CSPFs, the reevaluation can start any time in any order. Hence the invalidation of the output function and the CSPFs are marked as shown in Figure 9.25(b). Invalidation of the output function or the CSPF is done by incrementing the current version number attached to the corresponding gates and connections such that any BDD in the system with lower version number will be considered invalid.

After the invalidation of the output functions and the CSPFs, the corresponding *partition_objects* are sent a message to reevaluate the BDDs. After they have reevaluated the BDDs, they will inform the corresponding *gate_sub_objects* to check for more gate substitutions because the BDDs have changed.

Parallel Gate Merging Gate merging is another transformation used in the transduction method based on an iterative improvement procedure. In this transformation, a search is performed for a pair of gates (g_1, g_2), and we attempt to synthesize a third gate g_3 that can replace both the gates. Two gates, g_1 and g_2, are mergeable if the intersection of the CSPFs of the two gates is nonempty. Then an attempt is made to form a third gate with four simple gate types: AND, OR, NAND, and NOR. For each gate type, an attempt is made to connect the inputs of the gate from the minimal set of outputs of the existing gates in the network. If the search succeeds in forming such a gate, both gates g_1 and g_2 can be replaced by the new gate. However, to maintain the loop-free condition of the network, the inputs of the new gate, g_3, must not come from the successors of g_1 and g_2. Hence to maximize the chance of gate merging, gates g_1 and g_2 should be close to the primary outputs.

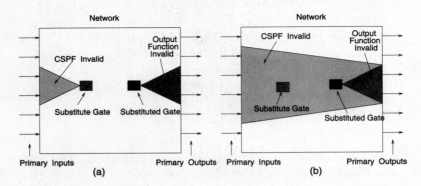

Figure 9.25 Invalidation of output function and CSPF due to gate substitution

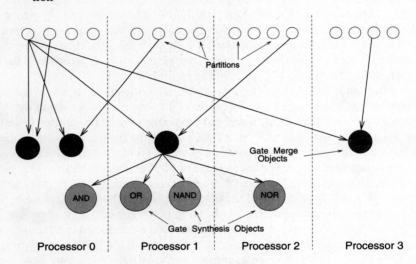

Figure 9.26 Creation of gate merge objects and creation of objects for gate synthesis

Let p denote the number of partitions. For each partition pair (i, j), an object is created of type *gate_merge_object*. The *gate_merge_object* denoted by (i, j) is responsible for testing for any gate merging between any gate in the partition i and any gate in the partition j. In addition, a number (equal to p) of *gate_merge_objects* will be created, one for each partition to check for any possible gate merging in the same partition. So, in total, $\binom{p}{2} + p$ objects are created. The procedure is depicted in Figure 9.26.

Now consider a *gate_merge_object* denoted by (i, j). The gate g_1 in the partition i can be merged with the gate g_2 in the partition j if the intersection of the CSPFs of these two gates is nonempty. Hence, this *gate_merge_object* will need valid CSPF of all the gates in the partition i and the partition j.

A *gate_merge_object* behaves in almost the same manner as a *gate_sub_object* if it does not find any CSPF. It sends a request to the *work manager* in the current processor, which sends a message to the *work manager* of the corresponding processor if needed. Whenever that CSPF is available, the *work manager* will inform this object. If this object is finished with searching for gate merging pairs with available CSPFs, it requests the corresponding *partition_objects* to inform this object whenever the CSPFs in those partitions change. The procedure is illustrated in Figure 9.19.

If any *gate_merge_object* finds a pair of gates (g_1, g_2) that have nonempty intersection of their CSPFs, then it creates 4 new objects, called *gate_synthesis_objects*, for each of four types of simple gates, AND, OR, NAND, and NOR. A *gate_synthesis_object* has the responsibility of synthesizing a gate of the type supplied to it whose output function is a member of the intersection of the CSPFs of the pair of gates that are to be merged. The input of the synthesized gate will be connected to a minimal set of outputs of the existing gates in the network, under the restriction that the successors of the two gates to be merged are not allowed to connect.

An outline of the *DM-PARALLEL-TRANSDUCTION-GATEMERGE* algorithm (denoting distributed memory parallel algorithm for the gate merging transformation in the transduction method) is given next.

Procedure *DM-PARALLEL-TRANSDUCTION-GATEMERGE;*
Partition circuit into subcircuits;
FOR each subcircuit i DO
    FOR each subcircuit j DO
        Create a gate merging object (i, j);
        Assign gate merging object (i, j) to a processor;
    END FOR
END FOR
FORALL processors in PARALLEL DO
    WHILE there are gate_merge_objects (i, j) on processor DO
        IF GM object (i, j) receives evaluation message THEN
            Collect CSPFs of all the gates in partition i
            Collect CSPFs of all the gates in partition j
            IF any CSPF is not available
                THEN request *work manager* to get it
            Perform pairwise comparison of available CSPFs
                to find any possible gate merging
            IF possible gate merging found between gate g_1 and g_2
                THEN Create 4 new gate synthesis objects,
                    one for each gate type: AND, OR, NAND and NOR
            ENDIF
            Ask partition i to inform if any CSPF changes in partition i
            Ask partition j to inform if any CSPF changes in partition j
        ENDIF
        IF GM object (i, j) receives a new CSPF of partition i THEN
            Compare this CSPF with all available CSPFs of partition j

IF possible gate merging found between gate g_1 and g_2
    THEN create 4 new gate synthesis objects,
        one for each gate type: AND, OR, NAND and NOR
ENDIF

IF GM object (i, j) receives a new CSPF of partition j THEN
    Compare this CSPF with all available CSPFs of partition i
IF possible gate merging found between gate g_1 and g_2
    THEN create 4 new gate synthesis objects,
        one for each gate type: AND, OR, NAND and NOR
ENDIF
End Procedure

Whenever a *gate_synthesis_object* is activated by a message, it first checks to see if both gates exist and if they have the same CSPF version number as they had when they were checked for merging. Then it makes a list of all the gates that are not successors of both gates that are to be merged. Let us denote this list as the *possible_input_list*. For every gate ζ in the *possible_input_list*, it tries to connect that gate to the input of the synthesized gate if a valid output function ζ is available. If it is possible to connect the gate, it first puts ζ in a *partial_input_list* and then checks if the new gate synthesis is complete; that is, the output function of the new gate is already a member of the intersection of the CSPFs of the gate pairs to be merged. If it has already been realized, it first minimizes the number of input connections to the new gate and then asks the *master* processor for permission to perform this gate merging. If the synthesis process is not complete, it remembers the partial output function that has been produced so far. If a valid output function of any gate in *possible_input_list* is not available, it requests the *work manager* in the current processor to inform itself whenever it is available. After going through the *possible_input_list*, if it cannot synthesize the gate and it has no new output function to receive from the *work manager*, it terminates itself.

When a *gate_synthesis_object* receives an output function, it again checks to see if both gates that are to be merged exist and if they have the same CSPF version number. It then checks if the output function can be connected to the synthesized gate. If it is possible to connect to the synthesized gate, it checks for all the gates in a *partial_input_list* to ensure that the version number of the output functions has not changed. If there is no change, it simply adds this new connection and updates the partial output function and *partial_input_list*. If any change has happened, it has to discard the partial output function and perform the computations again.

When the *master* processor receives a message asking permission for a gate merging transformation, it checks for the existence of the gates to be merged and the correct versions of the CSPF. It then checks for the existence of the immediate predecessors of the synthesized gate the correct versions of their output functions. If all the conditions are satisfied, it broadcasts a message to all other processors to perform this gate merging and performs the gate merging itself. Due to a gate merge, the invalidation of output functions and CSPF will be performed similarly to the case of gate substitution described earlier.

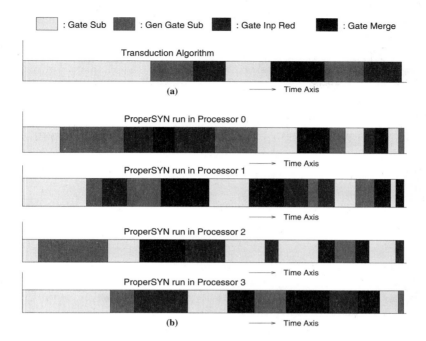

Figure 9.27 Comparison of sequence of transformations

Parallel Pruning The parallel pruning procedure *prunes* a connection to a gate if the connection is found *redundant*; that is, removal of the connection will not change the output function of any primary output. When the CSPF is computed for a connection, the *redundancy* of that connection is checked. If it is found *redundant*, permission is asked from the *master* processor. If the *master* processor finds it valid, it broadcasts a message to other processors and then performs the pruning.

Implementation De et al. have implemented the preceding asynchronous parallel algorithm in the ProperSYN system on on Intel iPSC/860™ hypercube multicomputer [17, 16].

In the previous subsections, we discussed the parallel algorithms for each transformation performed in the ProperSYN system. In this subsection, we will give the overview of the entire system. We should mention that the ProperSYN system is not the same algorithm as the transduction system. In the transduction system, the user specifies the *order* in which different transformations are to be applied at the beginning and the transformations are applied strictly in that order, one after the other. A typical run of the transduction method is shown in Figure 9.27(a).

In the case of ProperSYN, although the same transformations are used as in the transduction method, the applications of different transformations are intermixed. Different priorities are assigned to the different transformations according to their cost to performance ratio to guide the synthesis process. The priorities are assigned to the different transformations in the following decreasing order: *gate substitution, generalized gate substitution, gate input reduc-*

TABLE 9.9 Quality (Gate/Connections), Runtimes (Seconds), and Speedups, of Parallel Synthesis Algorithm on the Encore Multimax™ Multiprocessor

| | | 1 Processor | | 8 Processors | |
| | Initial | Final | Runtime | Final | Runtime |
Circuit	Gate/Connection	Gate/Connection	(speedup)	Gate/Connection	(speedup)
bw	207/480	104/267	217 (1.0)	109/262	42 (5.2)
rd73	136/322	83/185	234 (1.0)	92/208	29 (8.0
apex7	241/474	176/372	1,478 (1.0)	177/375	223 (6.6)
apex6	765/1432	615/1224	15,419 (1.0)	620/1231	1842 (8.3)
duke2	468/1206	292/745	12,190 (1.0)	305/775	1686 (7.2)
misex3c	473/1202	314/821	15,257 (1.0)	320/835	1907 (7.9)

tion, and *gate merging*. There are no *synchronizing barriers* at the end of each transformation. Each transformation is applied repeatedly until there are no more changes in the network. To keep coherence in the network, for any possible transformation, a permission is asked from the *master* processor as described previously.

The algorithms have been evaluated on a large set of MCNC and ISCAS benchmark circuits. The quality of the circuits synthesized were comparable to SYLON-XTRANS [42] and MIS 2.2 [3, 22]. Table 9.9 shows the performance of the parallel implementation in terms of runtimes (in seconds) and the quality of the synthesized circuits (measured in terms of gate counts and connections) on an Intel iPSC/860™ hypercube.

9.8 LOGIC VERIFICATION

Logic verification tools compare the logic design of integrated circuits at different levels to make sure that, in the synthesis process, no logic errors have been introduced. For example, in a silicon compiler environment where a design is translated or synthesized into a lower level from a higher-level description, logic verification is usually performed between functional level (before logic synthesis) and gate level (after logic synthesis).

Some formal verification techniques have been proposed in the past [21, 37], but only a few have been applied to real circuits due to the computational complexity of the problem. In PROTEUS [40], a number of efficient heuristics have been developed and implemented. The PROTEUS systems includes four basic approaches: verification by justification, by cube comparison, by exhaustive simulation, and verification by cover generation and simulation.

In the following sections we will describe several parallel algorithms for logic verification using various approaches. In each case we will first describe the sequential algorithm and then the shared memory MIMD and distributed memory MIMD parallel algorithms.

9.9 VERIFICATION USING ENUMERATION APPROACH

9.9.1 Overview

This section describes the LOVER approach for verifying the equivalence of two combinational logic circuits [34]. Let A and B be the two circuits whose equivalence have to be verified. A cube c from $C_A{}^{ON}$ (the ON-set cover of circuit A) is enumerated and simulated on B to check if B produces a 1 at its output. If so, another enumeration/simulation process continues, with another cube from $C_A{}^{ON}$. If, on the contrary, a 0 appears, the verification is completed with the conclusion that A and B are not Boolean equivalent. If an x (unknown) appears, c is split into smaller cubes and resimulated until a known value appears at the output of B. Cube splitting and simulation are implicitly exhaustive. The process continues until all cubes from $C_A{}^{ON}$ have been simulated. A similar process for $C_A{}^{OFF}$ (the OFF-set cover of circuit A) is then carried out. This method is called the two-set/two-phase approach because there are two sets (the ON-Set and OFF-set) that are explicitly verified, and the operation is performed over two phases (enumeration and simulation). This approach gives a large degree of freedom in the LOVER approach to verification; many different kinds of simulation and verification can be used. Since simulation is a relatively well understood area, the emphasis in this section will be placed on the enumeration algorithms.

The LOVER-PODEM approach uses the decision tree concept in the PODEM test generation algorithm [33, 34]. A decision tree for LOVER-PODEM is shown in Figure 9.28. In general, two decision trees are required: one for the ON-set verification and one for the OFF-set verification.

Each node in the decision tree represents a primary input (PI) assignment. Initially, all primary inputs are assigned unknown values. Given an initial objective; that is, to set a primary output line to a 1 or 0 (for ON-set or OFF-set verification), a path is traced from the objective line backward to a primary input to obtain a primary input (PI) assignment. After each new PI assignment, the circuit is simulated using the current set of PI assignments to see if the value at the target line has been set up. If not, the backtrace process continues. If the desired value has been achieved, a cube in the corresponding ON or OFF set is found and is simulated on the other circuit. If the opposite value has been set up, the algorithm backtracks to the last PI assignment, tries an alternative value, and flags the node to indicate that both assignments have been tried. If the alternative has been tried, the node is removed, and the backtrack process continues until an unflagged node with a possible alternative is reached. The backtrack process is also applied when a desired value has been set up at the target line. This is different from the PODEM test generation for which the enumeration process terminates when the desired value is set up at the target line. When the decision tree is found to be empty in the backtrack process, the total input space for the corresponding set has been implicitly but exhaustively enumerated.

9.9.2 Shared Memory MIMD Parallel Algorithm

We will now describe two parallel algorithms for logic verification, one using static decomposition of tasks and the other using dynamic decomposition based on work reported in [34].

The static decomposition scheme works as follows. Let A and B be the two circuits that need verification. Let n_i (n_o) denote the number of inputs (outputs) to the circuits. The

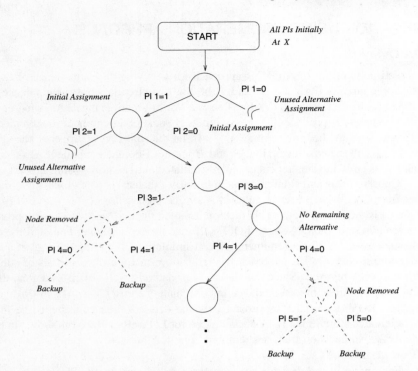

Figure 9.28 Decision tree in LOVER-PODEM (Courtesy of Ma et al., *Proc. Design Automation Conf.,* ©ACM 1987)

circuits are partitioned into single-output cones, each of which can be verified individually. Furthermore, for each set verification, the tasks of enumeration and simulation with proper synchronization can be performed in parallel. The simulation tasks follow the enumeration tasks on every increment of a fixed number of cube enumerations. For 32-vector parallel simulation, an increment contains 32 enumerated cubes. For single vector serial simulation, an increment is an enumerated cube.

Using the preceding static decomposition of tasks, a total of n_{task} parallel tasks are created, where $n_{\text{task}} = n_o \times 2 \times 2$. For convenience, each task is denoted as $task(type, i, j)$, where the $type = enum$ or sim indicates whether the task is an enumeration or simulation task, $i = 0$ or 1 indicates whether it is an ON-set or OFF-set verification problem, and $j = 1$, 2,...,n_o denotes the cone circuit under consideration. These tasks are executed on P processors.

We now describe a second parallel algorithm using dynamic decomposition of work, which addresses the load imbalance problems of the static method. In this method, whenever a new PI assignment is made in the enumeration process, two disjoint input spaces are implicitly developed for the decision tree corresponding to the 0 and 1 values of the newly assigned input and old values of all the previously assigned inputs. Since these inputs spaces are disjoint, they can be enumerated in parallel in two processors.

Disjoint input spaces are continually generated by all the processors doing the enumeration every time a new PI assignment is made. After a processor performs a PI assignment, it picks one of the disjoint spaces and continues enumeration on that space. As soon as a processor completes enumeration on its own space, it picks ups another branch that corresponds to a previously generated input space by other processors. This process continues until the entire input space is enumerated. The selection of a new input space by a processor entails an initialization overhead. It is desirable to select the largest unenumerated input space available that corresponds to the space with the minimum number of assigned primary inputs.

The preceding schemes are implemented as follows. The decision tree is an ordered list of nodes and is implemented as a stack. Each processor owns a separate stack that corresponds to the input space currently being enumerated by it. Whenever a new PI assignment is made, a new unflagged node is pushed onto the top of the stack. Whenever a backtrack step is made, the node on the top of the stack is examined. If the node is unflagged, the alternative value is assigned to the corresponding input and the node is flagged to indicate that both choices have been tried. Enumeration of a particular input space is completed until the stack becomes empty. The selection of a new input space by a processor is done by popping nodes from the bottom of the stack of another processor and pushing them onto the processor's own stack. This popping and pushing process continues until the first unflagged node is reached. This unflagged node is flagged and the corresponding input is assigned the alternative value, creating a new disjoint space on which the processor enumerates. The popping of nodes begins from the bottom of the stack rather than the top so as to obtain the largest unenumerated space to minimize the initialization overhead.

An outline of the *SM-PARALLEL-LOGIC-VERIFY-ENUM-DYN* algorithm (denoting a shared memory parallel algorithm for logic verification using implicit enumeration and dynamic decomposition) follows:

Procedure *SM-PARALLEL-LOGIC-VERIFY-ENUM-DYN*;
Read two combinational circuits;
Create decision tree as an ordered list of nodes
represented as a stack S for circuits 1 and 2;
Create separate stacks S_i for each processor P_i;
FORALL processors in PARALLEL DO
   WHILE (enumeration not finished) DO
      IF (output not set) THEN
         Find new pi assignment;
         Push an unflagged node on top of stack S1;
         Simulate the current set of pi assignments;
      ELSE
         IF (output is 1) THEN
            A cube from ON-set is generated for circuit 1;
            Simulate circuit 2 for cube and compare;
            IF different outputs THEN circuits unequal, exit;
         ELSE
            A cube from OFF-set is generated for circuit 1;
            Simulate circuit 2 for cube and compare;

```
                    IF different outputs THEN circuits unequal, exit;
                ENDIF
            ENDIF
            IF (an unflagged node is found) THEN
                Flag node;
                Assign alternative value to the primary input;
                Simulate current set of pi assignments;
            ELSE
            select:
                select a nonempty stack S2 of another processor;
                WHILE (node at bottom of S2 is flagged
                        AND S2 is not empty) DO
                Pop the node and push on top of S1;
                Assign the pi value corresponding to that node;
            ENDWHILE
            IF (an unflagged node is found) THEN
                Pop the node and push on top of S1;
                Flag the node;
                Assign alternative value to the primary input;
                Simulate the current set of pi assignments;
            ELSE
                goto select;
            ENDIF
        END FORALL
        End Procedure
```

Circuits with an arbitrary number of outputs can be efficiently verified using the dynamic scheduling scheme described by using all the processors to verify each output and verifying the outputs sequentially. However, in this approach there is an overhead of selecting new input spaces by various processors. Hence a more efficient dynamic scheduling scheme is to have each processor pick an output, enumerate and simulate over the entire input space. If a processor runs out of unverified outputs it then helps the processors that have not completed their outputs via dynamic scheduling.

Implementation Both the static and dynamic work decomposition schemes have been implemented on a Sequent Balance 8000™ shared memory multiprocessor by Ma et al. [34]. Experimental results showed speedups of about 6 on eight processors for some ISCAS combinational circuit benchmarks on the static scheme. The speedups using this scheme saturates at about 6 because the speedup is governed by the time taken to perform the longest enumeration task on the largest single output cone in the circuit.

The dynamic scheduling scheme showed speedups of about 7.7 to 7.9 on eight processors on the same ISCAS benchmark circuits. Excellent load balancing results were reported in the dynamic scheme compared to the static section.

TABLE 9.10 Runtimes (Seconds) and Speedups, of Parallel Verification Algorithms on Sequent Balance 8000

Circuit	Inputs/ Outputs	Static		Dynamic	
		1 Processor Runtime (speedup)	8 Processors Runtime (speedup)	1 Processor Runtime (speedup)	8 Processors Runtime (speedup)
C880	60/26	136,800 (1.0)	29,107 (4.7)	39,240 (1.0)	5,040 (7.9)
C432	36/7	61,200 (1.0)	10,032 (6.1)	12,040 (1.0)	15,480 (7.9)

Table 9.10 shows the performance of the parallel implementation in terms of runtimes (in seconds) and speedups for the two schemes on the Sequent Balance 8000 multiprocessor.

9.10 VERIFICATION USING TAUTOLOGY APPROACH

9.10.1 Overview

Logic verification of two logic functions G and H can be formulated as a tautology problem [27]. The tautology problem determines if a given Boolean function evaluates to 1 for all possible input combinations. Given functions G and H that need to be compared and the function D representing the set of inputs that cannot occur, the logic verification problem is precisely stated as answering the question if

$$F(v) = D(v) + G(v).H(v) + \overline{G}(v) \cdot \overline{H}(v) \equiv 1$$

for all $v \in 2^n$, where 2^n represents the set of all possible inputs.

We will now describe a sequential algorithm for solving the tautology problem (deciding if $F \equiv 1$) for a multilevel function based on the simulation method [27]. The algorithm uses a recursive divide and conquer algorithm called ML-TAUTOLOGY shown later. Processing begins by testing for various special cases in a procedure called SPECIAL-CASES. In this procedure, the outputs of a cover F are scanned: if they are set to 0 or all set to 1 then a 0 or 1 is returned correspondingly. Otherwise, a value of -1 is returned. In the 1-level algorithm (applicable to two-level circuits such as PLAs), other attributes such as special unate properties are checked and, if they exist, that allows the recursion tree to be trimmed. If an answer cannot be determined by the SPECIAL-CASES procedure, then this procedure returns a -1. If the SPECIAL-CASES procedure returns a 0 or 1, the tautology question is answered at that level of recursion. If the SPECIAL-CASES procedure returns a -1, Shannon's expansion is used to express the function in terms of the cofactors.

$$F = x_j \cdot F_{x_j} + \overline{x_j} \cdot F_{\overline{x_j}}$$

where F_{x_j} denotes the cofactor of F with respect to the variable x_j, and $F_{\overline{x_j}}$ denotes the cofactor of F with respect to the variable $\overline{x_j}$. An input variable is heuristically chosen to be a splitting variable by the routine SELECT-SPLIT. The routine COFACTOR is called twice, which creates the two covers by cofactoring F with respect to x_j and $\overline{x_j}$. In the multilevel algorithm, the cofactoring procedure copies the cover F to create new multilevel covers F_{x_j} and $F_{\overline{x_j}}$ and asserts the primary input x_j to a 1 or 0. The SIMULATE procedure then propagates the value towards the primary outputs through logic simulation. An outline of the sequential algorithm for *ML-TAUTOLOGY* is given next.

> **Procedure** *ML-TAUTOLOGY*;
>   Input: F - a multilevel cover;
>   Output: Returns 1 if F is tautology otherwise returns 0;
>   r ← SPECIAL-CASES(F);
>   IF (r $\neq$ -1) THEN RETURN(r);
>   j ← SELECT-SPLIT(F);
> F_{x_j} ← COFACTOR(F, x_j);
> $F_{\overline{x_j}}$ ← COFACTOR(F, $\overline{x_j}$);
> F_{x_j} ← SIMULATE(F, x_j);
> $F_{\overline{x_j}}$ ← SIMULATE(F, $\overline{x_j}$)
>   IF (ML-TAUTOLOGY(F_{x_j}) = 0) THEN RETURN(0);
>   IF (ML-TAUTOLOGY($F_{\overline{x_j}}$) = 0) THEN RETURN(0);
>   RETURN(1);
> **End Procedure**

An example of the tautology process for a simple function is shown in Figure 9.29.

9.10.2 Distributed Memory MIMD Parallel Algorithm

We now describe a parallel algorithm for multilevel tautology using the preceding recursive divide and conquer sequential algorithm. The parallel algorithm has been proposed by Hachtel and Moceyunas [28] and is described next. The parallel algorithm is similar to the serial algorithm up to the last call to COFACTOR. After the last call to COFACTOR, the algorithm branches to follow a parallel processing path or a serial processing path, based on the number of processors or the current level of recursion. If the number of processors is greater than or equal to the maximum number of nodes in the tree at the next level of the recursion, a parallel processing path is taken. Otherwise, the parallel algorithm takes the serial processing path and behaves exactly like the serial algorithm. In the concurrent processing path, a new processor is allocated to work on one of the subfunctions, and the old processor continues to work on the other subfunction. Thus the allocation of processors to work on these subfunctions is done until no more processors are left out of the total number of processors. The allocation of processors is done in a controlled way so as to divide the work equally among the processors.

Let m be the label of the current processor and n be the label of the new processor. Processor m sends the cover $F_{\overline{x_j}}$ to processor n. Processor m calls the SIMULATE procedure and then the DM-PARALLEL-TAUT procedure with F_{x_j} as the input cover, and, similarly, processor n calls the SIMULATE and the DM-PARALLEL-TAUT procedures with $F_{\overline{x_j}}$ as the input cover. Like the serial algorithm, if either function is not found to be a tautology, then the cover F is not a tautology. If both are found to be the tautology, then F is a tautology. Note

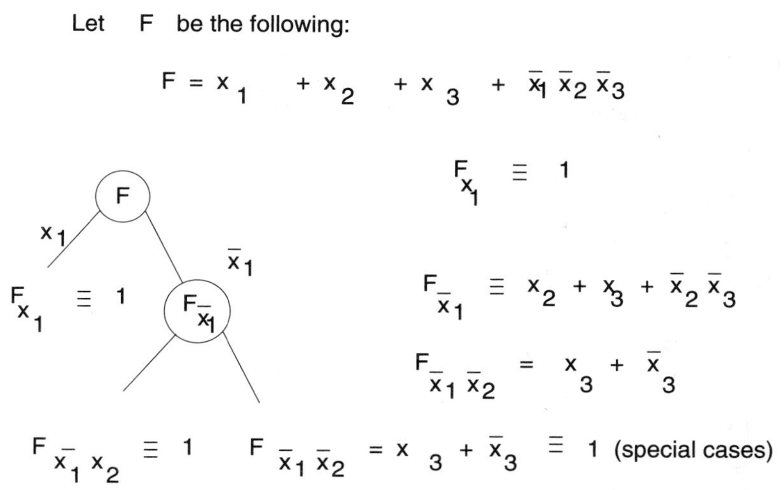

Let   F   be the following:

$$F = x_1 + x_2 + x_3 + \bar{x}_1\,\bar{x}_2\,\bar{x}_3$$

$$F_{x_1} \equiv 1$$

$$F_{\bar{x}_1} \equiv x_2 + x_3 + \bar{x}_2\,\bar{x}_3$$

$$F_{\bar{x}_1\,\bar{x}_2} = x_3 + \bar{x}_3$$

$$F_{\bar{x}_1\,x_2} \equiv 1 \qquad F_{\bar{x}_1\,\bar{x}_2} = x_3 + \bar{x}_3 \equiv 1 \text{ (special cases)}$$

Figure 9.29 Example tautology application on a function (Courtesy of Hachtel and Moceyunas, *Proc. Int. Conf. Computer-aided Design,* ©IEEE 1987)

that the answer produced by processor n must be sent back to its parent processor m, which must wait for this result.

An outline of the *DM-PARALLEL-LOGIC-VER-TAUT* algorithm (denoting a distributed memory parallel algorithm for logic verification using tautology checking) follows:

Procedure *DM-PARALLEL-LOGIC-VER-TAUT*;
    Read multilevel circuit;
    Generate multilevel cover, F;
    Create PARALLEL-ML-TAUTOLOGY task queues for each processor;
    Call TAUTOLOGY(F,0,N,0,0) on processor 0;
    FORALL processors in PARALLEL DO
        WHILE not done DO
            Pick next TAUTOLOGY task off own queue;
            Execute TAUTOLOGY() at appropriate level
                of recursion;
        END WHILE
    END FORALL
End Procedure

Procedure *TAUTOLOGY(F,i,N,parent,il)*;
    Read Inputs:
    F : a multilevel cover;
    i: current level of recursion

N : number of processors
parent : information about the parent process
il : level in the recursion tree of the tautology

r ← SPECIAL-CASES(F);
IF (r ≠ -1) THEN RETURN(r);
j ← SELECT-SPLIT(F);
F_{x_j} ← COFACTOR(F, x_j);
$F_{\overline{x_j}}$ ← COFACTOR(F, $\overline{x_j}$);

IF ($i \leq (log_2(N) - 1)$) THEN
 Start a new task on a new processor;
 Send $F_{\overline{x_j}}$ to the new processor;
 Call $F_{\overline{x_j}}$ ← SIMULATE(F, $\overline{x_j}$) on new processor;
 Call TAUTOLOGY($F_{\overline{x_j}}$,i+1,N,newparent,i+1)
 on own processor;
 F_{x_j} ← SIMULATE(F, x_j)
 IF (TAUTOLOGY(F_{x_j}),i+1,N,parent,il) = 0) THEN
  IF (il ≠ i) RETURN(0);
  Send a 0 back to the parent processor;
 ENDIF
 Wait for the child processor to send an answer back;
  IF (il ≠ i) RETURN(answer);
  Send the answer back to parent processor;

 ELSE /* Perform serial tautology */
  F_{x_j} ← SIMULATE(F, x_j);
  $F_{\overline{x_j}}$ ← SIMULATE(F, $\overline{x_j}$)
  IF (TAUTOLOGY(F_{x_j}) = 0) THEN RETURN(0);
  IF (TAUTOLOGY($F_{\overline{x_j}}$) = 0) THEN RETURN(0);
 ENDIF
 RETURN(1);
End Procedure

An example of the decomposition of the tautology tasks for a four processor parallel machine is shown in Figure 9.30.

Implementation Hachtel and Moceyunas have analyzed the performance and speedups of this parallel algorithm using models of simulation costs and communication costs for various multiprocessor architectures [28]. They have also reported speedups of 5.5 on a 32-processor Intel iPSC/2 hypercube and speedups of 3.0 on an eight-processor network of SUN/3™ workstations for various circuits.

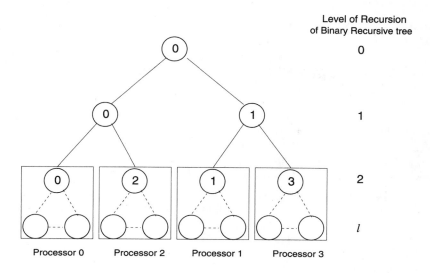

Figure 9.30 Decomposition of tautology tasks in parallel algorithm

9.11 SUMMARY

In this chapter we have reviewed parallel algorithms for logic synthesis and verification. We described parallel algorithms for two-level synthesis based on the EXPRESSO sequential algorithm. We next described parallel algorithms for multilevel synthesis based on three approaches. The first approach used circuit partitioning, the second used the MIS approach, and the third used the transduction method. We finally described parallel algorithms for logic verification of two-level and multilevel logic using two approaches, implicit enumeration and tautology checking.

The parallel algorithm for two-level logic synthesis essentially involved parallelizing each procedure within the ESPRESSO sequential algorithm: the complementation of cubes, the reduction of cubes, the expansion of cubes, and elimination of redundant cubes. To preserve the correctness of the cover of the circuit, several interesting heuristics were described to prevent simultaneous elimination of cubes during parallel reduction and creation of multiple identical cubes during parallel expansion of cubes. Good speedups were reported on the parallel algorithm using the parallel algorithm with slight degradation in circuit quality.

The parallel algorithm for logic synthesis using the partitioning approach initially partitioned a given circuit into as many partitions as there are processors. Subsequently, it performed bipartitioning, merging and resynthesis of each partition with different pairings of processors in an iterative manner. The approach has three advantages. First, it is possible to get excellent speedups by partitioning the circuit into as many parts as there are processors. Second, the approach is independent of the logic synthesis algorithm used, the MIS approach [3] or the transduction approach [35, 42]. Hence it is possible to use the best sequential algorithms for logic synthesis available at the moment. Finally, the approach minimizes the memory requirements needed in the synthesis algorithm. Hence it is possible to perform logic synthesis on very large circuits. The main disadvantage of this approach is that the quality of the synthesized circuit deteriorates significantly with an increasing number of partitions.

The parallel algorithm for logic synthesis using the MIS approach involved parallelizing each synthesis procedure within the MIS system. Specifically, we described parallel algorithms for kernel and cube generation, kernel and cube extraction, resubstitution, and node simplification. A key feature of the algorithm is in the use of partitioning of the circuit for workload distribution, while the logic synthesis is performed on the entire network. Consistency is maintained among concurrent updates to the network due to various transformations by using the notion of version numbering on the nodes in the circuit. Excellent speedups were reported using the parallel algorithm with very little degradation in circuit quality. The MIS approach is one of the best-known methods of multilevel logic synthesis, and is known to produce circuits of excellent quality, and is also very efficient in time and memory requirements. Hence the parallel algorithm for logic synthesis using the MIS approach has very high practical value.

We also described a parallel algorithm for logic synthesis using the transduction method, which is another popular method for logic synthesis. The advantage of the transduction approach is that it can produce circuits of excellent quality, but the disadvantage is that it has large computing and memory requirements. The parallel algorithm involved parallelizing each procedure used in the transduction method. Specifically, we described parallel algorithms for the evaluation of output and permissible functions and for various transformations such as pruning, gate substitution, and gate merging. Good speedups were reported using the parallel algorithm with slight degradation in circuit quality.

We finally described two parallel algorithms for logic verification. The first algorithm was based on an implicit enumeration approach, and the algorithm used a recursive decomposition of the search space of verification for all possible input combinations implicitly. The dynamic decomposition of the search space gave excellent load balance and speedups.

The second parallel algorithm for logic verification was based on tautology checking. Again, the algorithm was based on a recursive divide-and-conquer decomposition of the search space of input combinations. The parallel algorithm gave excellent speedups.

The chapter reviewed parallel algorithms for logic synthesis and verification for combinational circuits. In the future, we need to develop parallel algorithms for sequential circuit synthesis and verification.

9.12 PROBLEMS

9.1   Develop distributed memory parallel algorithms for reduction, complementation, and irredundant cover operations in the ESPRESSO approach of two-level logic synthesis. Implement the algorithms on an Intel iPSC message-passing multicomputers using the libraries described in Chapter 2.

9.2   For the example function shown below

$$F_i = \bar{b}c + \bar{a}c + a b \bar{c}$$

execute the steps of a parallel algorithm for two-level synthesis assuming two processors. Perform the steps of EXPAND, REDUCE, and IRREDUNDANT-COVER in parallel.

9.3   Analyze the distributed memory MIMD parallel algorithm for kernel extraction in the multi-level logic synthesis problem using the MIS approach.

9.4   Design and implement shared memory parallel MIMD algorithms for kernel extraction, cube extraction and resubstitution operations in the MIS approach. Use the Sequent™ shared memory programming library described in Chapter 2.

9.5   In the distributed memory parallel algorithm for logic synthesis using the transduction method, we described the use of version numbers for maintaining version consistency. The algorithm described in the chapter uses a centralized scheme with a single master processor. What is the problem with this approach and how can you fix it? Give an algorithm and an implementation to resolve the problem.

9.6   We have described parallel algorithms for logic synthesis using partitioning and using the MIS approach. Give an algorithm for combining the two approaches. What are some difficulties and advantages?

9.7   Design and implement a distributed memory MIMD algorithm for logic verification using the implicit enumeration approach. Use the Intel iPSC™ parallel programming library described in Chapter 2.

9.8   In this chapter, we have only described MIMD parallel algorithms for logic synthesis. Develop a massively parallel algorithm for logic synthesis using the MIS approach and data parallel techniques. Assign a gate and a connection to each virtual processor. If new gates and connections are created, assign them to new processors. Implement the algorithm on the Thinking Machines CM-2™ parallel processor using the parallel programming library described in Chapter 2.

9.13 REFERENCES

[1]   K. A. Barlett, R. K. Brayton, G. D. Hachtecl, R. M. Jacoby, C. R. Morrison, R. L. Rudell, A. Sangiovanni-Vincentelli, and A. R. Wang. Multilevel Logic Minimization using Implicit Don't Cares. *IEEE Transactions on Computer-aided Design*, CAD-7(6):723–740, June 1988.

[2]   D. Bostick, G. D. Hachtel, R. Jacoby, M. Lightner, P. Moceyunas, C. R. Morrison, and D. Ravenscroft. The Boulder Optimal Logic Design System. *Proc. Int. Conf. Computer Aided Design*, pages 62–65, Nov. 1987.

[3]   R. Brayton, R. Rudell, A. Sangiovanni-Vincentelli, and A. Wang. MIS: A Multiple-level Logic Optimization System. *IEEE Trans. Computer-aided Design Integrated Circuits Systems*, CAD-6(6):1062–1081, Nov. 1987.

[4]   R. Brayton, R. Rudell, A. Sangiovanni-Vincentelli, and A. Wang. Multilevel Logic Optimization and the Rectangular Covering Problem. *Proc. Int. Conf. Computer-aided Design*, pages 66–69, Nov. 1987.

[5]   R. K. Brayton and et al. ESPRESSO-II: A New Logic Minimizer for Programmable Logic Arrays. *Proc. Custom Integrated Circuits Conf.*, pages 370–376, June 1984.

[6]   R. K. Brayton, G. D. Hachtel, C. T. McMullen, and A. L. Sangiovanni-Vincentelli. *Logic Minimization Algorithms for VLSI Synthesis*. Kluwer Academic Publishers, Norwell, MA, 1984.

[7]   R. K. Brayton, G. D. Hachtel, and A. L. Sangiovanni-Vincentelli. Multilevel Logic Synthesis. *Proc. IEEE*, 78(2), Feb. 1990.

[8]   D. W. Brown. A State Machine Synthesizer. *Proc. 18th Design Automation Conf.*, pages 301–304, June 1981.

[9]   R. E. Bryant. Graph-based Algorithms for Boolean Function Manipulation. *IEEE Trans. Computers*, pages 677–691, Aug. 1986.

[10]   H. Cho, G. Hachtel, M. Nash, and L. Setiono. BEAT_NP: A Tool for Partitioning Boolean Networks. *Proc. Int. Conf. Computer-aided Design*, pages 10–13, Nov. 1988.

[11]   J. Darringer, D. Brand, J. Gerbi, W. Joyner, and L. Trevillyan. LSS: A System for Production Logic Synthesis. *IBM J. Research Dev.*, 28(5):537–545, Sept. 1984.

[12]   K. De and P. Banerjee. Parallel Logic Synthesis Using Partitioning. *Proc. Int. Conf. Parallel Processing*, Aug. 1994.

[13]   K. De and P. Banerjee. PREST: A System for Logic Partitioning and Resynthesis. *IEEE Trans. VLSI Systems*, 1(4):514–525, Dec. 1993.

[14]   K. De and P. Banerjee. Logic Partitioning and Resynthesis for Testability. *Proc. Int. Test Conf.*, Oct. 1991.

[15]   K. De and P. Banerjee. Parallel Algorithms for Logic Synthesis Using the MIS Approach. Technical report, Coordinated Science Lab, University of Illinois, Urbana, IL, Oct. 1993.

[16]   K. De, B. Ramkumar, and P. Banerjee. A Portable Parallel Algorithm for Logic Synthesis using Transduction Method. *IEEE Trans. Computer-aided Design Integrated Circuits Systems*, May 1994.

[17]   K. De, B. Ramkumar, and P. Banerjee. ProperSYN: A Portable Parallel Algorithm for Logic Synthesis. *Proc. Int. Conf. Computer-aided Design (ICCAD-92)*, Nov. 1992.

[18]   A. J. de Geus and W. Cohen. A Rule-based System for Optimizing Combinational Logic. *IEEE Design Test Computers*, pages 22–32, August 1985.

[19]   S. Dey, F. Berglez, and G. Kedem. Corolla Based Circuit Partitioning and Resynthesis. *27th Design Automation Conf.*, pages 607–612, 1990.

[20]   W. E. Donath. The Partitioning of Computer Logic. In G. N. Rabbat, editor, *Advances in VLSI Computer-aided Design*, England, 1984. JAI Press.

[21]   W. E. Donath and H. Ofek. Automatic Identification of Equivalence Points for Boolean Logic Verification. *IBM Technical Disclosure Bulletin*, 18(8), Jan. 1976.

[22]   Electronics Research Laboratory, University of California, Berkeley. *Octtools Distribution 3.0, Volume 3*, August 1989.

[23]   W. Fenton, B. Ramkumar, V. A. Saletore, A. B. Sinha, and L. V. Kale. Supporting Machine Independent Programming on Diverse Parallel Architecture. *Proc. Int. Conf. Parallel Processing*, Aug. 1991.

[24]   C. M. Fiduccia and R. M. Mattheyses. A Linear-time Heuristic for Improving Network Partitioning. *Proc. 19th Desigh Automation Conf.*, pages 175–181, 1982.

[25]   R. Galivanche and S. M. Reddy. A Parallel PLA Minimization Program. *Proc. Design Automation Conf.*, pages 600–607, 1987.

[26]   M. R. Garey and D. S. Johnson. *Computers and Intractability: A Guide to the Theory of NP-Completeness*. W. H. Freeman and Co., New York, NY, 1979.

[27]   G. D. Hachtel and R. M. Jacoby. Verification Algorithms for VLSI Synthesis. *IEEE Trans. Computer-aided Design Integrated Circuits Systems*, 7(5):616–640, May 1988.

[28]   G. D. Hachtel and P. H. Moceyunas. Parallel Algorithms for Boolean Tautology Checking. *Proc. Int. Conf. Computer-aided Design*, pages 422–425, Nov. 1987.

[29]   S. J. Hong, R. G. Cain, and D. L. Ostapko. MINI: A heuristic approach for logic minimization. *IBM J. Research Dev.*, 18:443–458, Sept. 1974.

[30]   L. V. Kale. The Chare Kernel Parallel Programming System. *Proc. Int. Conf. Parallel Processing*, Aug. 1990.

[31]   B. W. Kernighan and S. Lin. An Efficient Heuristic Procedure for Partitioning Graphs. *Bell System Technical Journal*, 49:291–307, 1970.

[32]   C. F. Lim, P. Banerjee, K. De, and S. Muroga. A Shared Memory Parallel Algorithm for Logic Synthesis. *Proc. 6th Int. Conf. VLSI Design*, Jan. 1993.

[33]   H. K. T. Ma, S. Devadas, and A. Sangiovanni-Vincentelli. Logic Verification Algorithms and their Parallel Implementation. *Proc. Design Automation Conf.*, pages 283–290, June 1987.

[34]   H. T. Ma, S. Devadas, and A. Sangiovanni-Vincentelli. Logic Verification Algorithms and Their Parallel Implementation. *IEEE Trans. Computer-aided Design Integrated Circuits Systems*, 8(2):181–189, Feb. 1989.

[35]   S. Muroga, Y. Kambayashi, H. C. Lai, and J. N. Culliney. The Transduction Method - Design of Logic Networks Based on Permissible Functions. *IEEE Trans. Computers*, pages 1404–1424, Oct. 1989.

[36]   S. Parkes, J. Chandy, and P. Banerjee. ProperCAD II: A Run-time Library for Portable, Parallel, Object-Oriented Programming with Applications to VLSI CAD. Technical Report CRHC-93-22/UILU-ENG-93-2250, University of Illinois, Coordinated Science Lab, Urbana, IL, Dec. 1993.

[37] P. Roth. Hardware Verification. *IEEE Trans. Computers*, C-26:1292–1294, 1977.

[38] R. L. Rudell. *Logic Synthesis for VLSI Design*. PhD thesis, Department of Electrical Engineering, University of California, Berkeley, CA, 1989.

[39] A. Saldhana, A. Wang, R. Brayton, and A. Sangiovanni-Vincentell. Multilevel Logic Simplification Using Don't cares and Filters. *Proc. 26th Design Automation Conf.*, pages 277–282, June 1989.

[40] R. S. Wei and A. Sangiovanni-Vincentelli. PROTEUS: A Logic Verification System for Combinational Circuits. *Proc. Int. Test Conf.*, Sept. 1986.

[41] X. Xiang. *Multilevel Logic Network Synthesis Systems, SYLON-XTRANS*. PhD thesis, University of Illinois, Department of Computer Science, Urbana, IL, 1990.

[42] X. Q. Xiang and S. Muroga. SYLON-XTRANS: A Multi-level Logic Network Synthesizer. *Int. Workshop Logic Synthesis*, 1989.

CHAPTER 10

Conclusions and Future Directions

In view of the increasing complexity of VLSI circuits of the future, the requirements on VLSI CAD tools will continuously increase. Parallel processing for CAD applications is becoming gradually recognized as a popular vehicle to support the increasing computing requirements of future CAD tools. Recent research on parallel CAD applications have been reported for a wide variety of applications such as placement, routing, layout verification, circuit simulation, test generation, fault simulation, and logic synthesis. The book has discussed most of these parallel algorithms.

Parallel processing for VLSI CAD has become a reality in industry as well. Hardware vendors such as Sun Microsystems, Solbourne, Hewlett-Packard and Digital have already announced products with multiple CPUs in a single workstation. Software CAD vendors such as Cadence Design Systems and Mentor Graphics have announced products such as PDRACULA™ (parallel design rule checker and circuit extractor) and PARADE™ (parallel cell placement) that use multiprocessing to accelerate CAD tasks. A major limitation with almost all previous work is that the parallel algorithms have been targeted to run on specific machines like an Intel iPSC™ hypercube-based message-passing distributed memory multicomputer or an Encore Multimax™ shared memory multiprocessor. Such work, although interesting, is not usable by the rest of the VLSI CAD community since the algorithms are not portable to other machines.

A second serious problem also presents itself in the design of parallel algorithms. The software development cycle for parallel algorithms is considerably longer than for sequential algorithms. This has two important implications. The first is they are considerably more costly to develop than sequential algorithms. This is exacerbated by the lack of portability across parallel machines. The second implication is a more pragmatic. Given the fast pace of progress in the development and improvement of sequential algorithms for CAD applications for a given application, sequential algorithms frequently outperform parallel algorithms due to the longer development time of the latter; for example, parallel test pattern generation. The latest version of HITEC [32], a uniprocessor test pattern generation program for sequential circuits is already comparable in performance and is slightly better in quality of results than a recent parallel algorithm for test pattern generation [35].

A related issue in the development of parallel algorithms is that certain approaches are inherently parallelizable and others are extremely difficult parallelize. More often than not, the trade-off between these two approaches is the quality of results. Algorithms that are easy to parallelize most often give results that are not as good as the best sequential algorithms.

Cell placement is a good example. The quadrisection algorithm [42] is easily parallelizable and is significantly faster than algorithms based on simulated annealing. Unfortunately, it cannot produce results comparable to TimberWolf [39], a sequential technique that uses simulated annealing (and a host of related tricks). An interesting possibility would be to use a hybrid of these two (and possibly other) techniques, where; for example, quadrisection could be used for decomposition of the layout area into regions, and TimberWolf would be used for placement in a given region. However, to experiment with such techniques, it should not be necessary to rewrite the software entirely. Any attempt to rewrite TimberWolf [39] will not only be extremely time consuming; it is also unlikely to be comparable in performance. However, if it is possible to decouple the parallel and sequential algorithms and provide a well-defined interface between the two, the TimberWolf software (say a recent version TW 7.0) can be substantially reused, making it practical to experiment with hybrid schemes such as these.

It would be presumptuous to assume that it will be trivial to interface the parallel algorithm with the sequential algorithm as described above. For this to be practical, it is imperative that sequential algorithms be written in a modular fashion. Fortunately, object-oriented programming in C++ (or even disciplined C programming) goes a long way in realizing this requirement. Many CAD vendors are already rewriting many of their well-established CAD applications using such disciplined, modular programming methods due to the benefits offered in program design and maintenance.

The most important questions that need to be addressed in the development of parallel algorithms are therefore: how can we design parallel algorithms that are truly portable across parallel machines and how can we exploit good sequential algorithms in the design of parallel algorithms, and how can parallel algorithms keep pace with future developments in sequential algorithms. These are the main objectives of a new project to be discussed next.

But, before we discuss the project, it is important to discuss some related projects in portable parallel programming.

10.1 PORTABLE PARALLEL PROGRAMMING

Recently, due to the overabundance of parallel machines, there have been several attempts to develop machine independent (portable) parallel programming.

One of the early attempts at machine independence was the development of the "Argonne macros" [7] aimed at porting parallel programs across shared memory machines. This attempt, although significant in the direction it chose to take, did not go far enough, restricting its attention to a single type of architecture, portability across shared memory parallel machines.

The VMMP project [15] is designed for developing portable and efficient software on both shared and nonshared memory machines. VMMP supports different information sharing abstractions, as shared objects. On VMMP, shared objects are located at one central site and access involves blocking and an RPC-type protocol. The execution model of VMMP is a *blocked workers* model.

Strand™ is a new programming language built from scratch expressly for parallelism and multiprocessing, the only such commercially supported language running on multiple platforms [21]. Strand approaches parallel computation via implicit parallelism, where the underlying parallel operations are concealed from the programmer, making his programming job much easier; the compiler relieves him of the onerous management of nondeterminism, race conditions, synchronization, intertask and interprocessor communication, and task scheduling. A Strand program is a collection of clauses, much like a Prolog program, that relies on a single-assignment rule for storage and an underlying computational model for handling synchronization and partitioning of tasks onto multiple processors. It uses recursion, lists, and tuples in place of arrays.

Linda™ [30] is represents a relatively radical approach to concurrent processing. In Linda, shared data are represented by a shared *tuple space* to which all functions have access. Elements in the tuple space are key-value pairs which are accessed via pattern matching on the key. This formulation has particular benefit in logic programming. Linda has been ported on shared memory and distributed memory message-passing machines.

The Reactive Kernel/Cosmic Environment™ [3] also supports machine independent programming by providing communication mechanisms on both shared memory and message-passing parallel machines.

A significant amount of related work has been performed in concurrent object-oriented computing. The Actor model for concurrent computing, first proposed by Hewitt [19] and subsequently refined and codified by Agha [1, 2], is a message-driven computational model targeted towards fine-grain platforms. A number of pure actor languages have been implemented [1, 17, 29, 40, 44], most of which are predominantly functional; that is, side-effect free, and untyped. Implementations of the majority of these approaches have targeted fine-grain concurrency on massively-parallel MIMD architectures. Of particular note is the HAL language of Houck and Agha [20], which was implemented on top of the Charm™ programming system [16] and applicable to medium-grain problems and architectures.

Chien [13] recognized the need for a multiaccess interface to augment the serial interface of Actors and proposed aggregates as collections of actors that present a unified, multiaccess interface. Key to aggregates is support for efficient intraaggregate addressing. Chien developed an actor language, *Concurrent Aggregates*, which in addition to the features of actors, aggregates, and intraaggregate addressing, provides support for first-class continuations and first-class messages. The Concert system[14, 26] is a compiler and runtime support system for a version of Concurrent Aggregates on stock hardware.

Charm/Charm++™ [16, 23, 24] was developed specifically to address the need for a portable, parallel language realizable across a wide variety of shared-memory and message-passing architectures. Charm differs from other actor languages in that it is derived from imperative languages, C and C++, and targeted to medium-grain architectures rather than the fine-grain architectures of other approaches. Charm represents an extension of the C programming language with extensions to support actor- and aggregate-like characteristics. With a few exceptions, most of the the imperative constructs of C are retained. Recently, with the introduction of Charm++, the C-language model of Charm has been extended to a C++-based interface. Charm provides developer-visible models for the operation of the underlying runtime system in the areas of load-balancing and prioritized message delivery. Strategies in both areas can be selected from a set of alternatives at linktime. Of particular note is work with lexicographically-ordered message priorities applied to search problems [25]. Charm provides a library of object types with parallel semantics such as read-only variables, distributed computation types such as accumulators, and distributed mappings.

The Actor model is not the only model of concurrent object-oriented computing. Gannon and Lee [18] developed pC++, an extension of C++ with support for distributed data structures. The flavor of pC++ is much that of High-Performance FORTRAN™ (HPF). pC++ provides support for distributed collections of arbitrary types, array-based and tree-based, with full support for the C++ mechanisms of derivation and dynamic-binding.

Compositional C++, or CC++, proposed by Chandy et al. [10] takes an alternate approach to parallelism; where in pC++ processor control is implicit in the parallel data structures, in CC++ parallelism is achieved though imperative constructs which cause particular code fragments to be executed concurrently on different processing threads. CC++ also provides a number of synchronization primitives necessary for a thread-oriented programming interface.

The Experimental Systems Kernel, or ES-Kit, of Leddy and Smith [28] is implemented via modifications to an existing C++ compiler and as such tries to stay true to the spirit and syntax of C++. In ES-Kit, pointers are extended to address a global namespace and remote execution is represented by the execution of a method call though a pointer to a nonlocal address. Object distribution is either automatic or under program control via the C++ placement syntax [41]. The fundamental parallelism constructs in ES-Kit are remote procedure calls (RPCs) and futures [4].

The Amber system [12], derived from Presto [5], is an extension of C++ targeted specifically toward a workstation cluster running the Topaz operating system [6]. In Amber, the approach is to explicitly locate a shared datum on a particular node and then to cluster Topaz threads on that node. When access is made to a remote node, the runtime system traps to the Amber kernel and the thread of control is transferred to the processor on which the data value resides.

COOL, developed by Chandra et al. [9], is also based on thread-explicit extensions to C++, in this case targeted towards shared memory architectures in general. COOL provides a full-range of classical synchronization constructs.

In addition to language-based approaches, a number of library-based approaches have been pursued. Some are based up on an object model [11, 22] while others implement a simple message-passing interface [8, 43].

One of the most attractive aspects of library-based approaches is that they are at least to a first approximation compatible with existing compilers and other development tools. Again, we consider C and C++ libraries.

ACT++ is a C++ library-based implementation of the actor paradigm developed by Kafura and Lee [22]. ACT++ implements an Actor base class which supports the actor model primitives, *new*, *send*, and *become*. Additionally, ACT++ supports an RPC-style of actor method invocation [1]. ACT++ supports the use of normal (non-actor) C++ objects, but only as private, nonshared acquaintances of an actor. ACT++ is targeted toward medium-grain architectures, but implementation details on parallel architectures have not been reported.

The Paragon project of Chase et al. [11] is implemented via a C++ library for support of distributed data structures. Support is provided for distributed arrays through partitioning and replication.

PVM™, developed by Sunderam et al. [43] is a widely used library for parallel programming on local area network-connected processors and, recently, a number of parallel architectures. The library provides C and FORTRAN interfaces for synchronous and asynchronous message passing and provides support for heterogeneity of processing elements, data representation and processing power. Included tools provide particularly strong support for easy machine configuration, debugging, and performance analysis.

p4™, developed by Butler et al. at Argonne National Laboratory [8], provides a similar message-passing interface to that of PVM and also adds an interface for shared memory. In addition to supporting network-connected processors, p4 provides support for a wide range of parallel platforms.

10.2 OVERVIEW OF THE PROPERCAD PROJECT

Two important questions that need to be addressed in the development of parallel algorithms for CAD are how we can design parallel algorithms for CAD that are truly portable across parallel machines and how we can exploit good sequential algorithms in the design of parallel algorithms for CAD. The ProperCAD project (**P**ortable **o**bject-oriented **p**arallel **e**nvironment for **CAD**) at Illinois by Banerjee et al. [38, 36, 34] tries to address these goals. We now describe how it is possible to design parallel algorithms keeping these objectives in mind.

The approach to parallelism taken in this research is the development of a runtime library that provides, simultaneously, a high-level, object-oriented abstraction to application programmers and an underlying runtime implementation that utilizes to the maximum extent and highest efficiency possible the resources available to the program. This approach facilitates the incremental application of parallel constructs to develop a parallel application while maintaining compatibility and code-sharing with the serial implementation. [1] This approach differs from previous work in a number of ways:

Targets The target architectures are existing platforms supporting medium-grain parallelism. Likewise, the target applications are those that require medium-grain parallelism; that is, those that perform a moderate amount of serial work between parallel invocations. While it is difficult to quantify the characteristics which make an application medium-grain, the library shows its tendency toward medium-grain parallelism in as much as it

---

[1] Since the runtime library is simply a library written in an existing language, serial programs are degenerate cases of parallel programs.

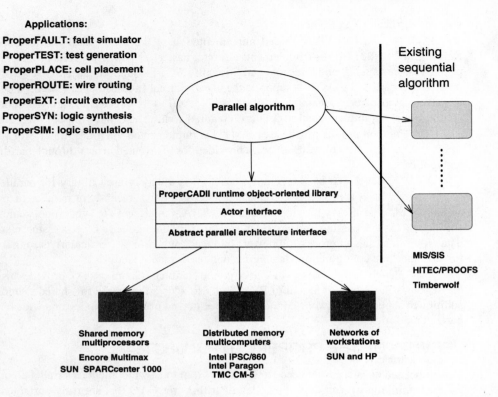

Applications:

ProperFAULT: fault simulator
ProperTEST: test generation
ProperPLACE: cell placement
ProperROUTE: wire routing
ProperEXT: circuit extracton
ProperSYN: logic synthesis
ProperSIM: logic simulation

Figure 10.1 Overview of the ProperCAD II project

provides a set of parallel constructs that can be used to express parallelism while not
precluding the use of native constructs provided in the native language, C++.

In contrast, in fine-grain parallel languages, typically all constructs are implicitly parallel.

C++ An overriding constraint was that the implementation be in C++. No extensions were
considered since these would prohibit the use of existing compilers and debuggers.

Portability The wide variety of extant medium-grain parallel architectures makes the issue of
portability extremely important; an implementation that is difficult to port would have
little chance of success.

To simultaneously maximize the portability and efficiency of the ProperCAD II library,
two distinct interfaces were designed (see Figure 10.1). The upper level of the library, the actor
interface (AIF), provides a high-level interface, one that assists the application developer in
limiting complexity through abstraction and encapsulation, without limiting parallelism. The
actor interface is based closely on the Actor paradigm and supports such advanced features as
aggregates and meta-programmability.

The lower level of the library, the abstract parallel architectures (APA), provides a set of interfaces and implementations that can be used to describe and utilize resources needed by any parallel application across a wide variety of architectures. Such resources include processor threads, synchronization primitives, and memory management techniques. The APA is used by the AIF to express parallelism but may also be used by application programs.[2]

10.2.1 Actor Interface

The fundamental object in an Actor paradigm is the actor, an object that communicates with other actors by sending messages. All actions that an actor performs are in response to messages; thus, the model is message driven. When a message is received, the receiving actor may perform a number of actions in response; possible actions are the creation of a new actor, the sending of a message to an existing actor, and the changing of the actor's behavior.

Of particular note is lack of explicit sequencing primitives in the Actor model. Instead, synchronization is implicit and derives from the message reception serialization property of the model: while an actor is processing a message, it may not receive another; actors are single threaded with respect to message reception. Because there are no explicit synchronization primitives, an actor processing a message cannot block or suspend itself in anticipation of a future event. Instead, when the processing of a message is complete, the actor returns control of the processor to the runtime library, implicitly becoming available for any pending messages. This limited synchronization control is key to the concurrency of Actors and is very beneficial in terms of portability. Concurrency in parallel applications is often lost because the interface to a message-passing system may require an ordering on message sends and receives. Also, since an actor can not suspend execution implicitly in the middle of a computation, all the context needed to restart the computation upon message reception must be explicitly moved off the runtime stack. While this puts more burden on the designer, the elimination of the need for the runtime system to deal with stack and register manipulation has obvious positive affects on portability.

Actors   In the ProperCAD II library, actor types are derived from a common class, `Actor`, provided by the library. Other than the base class, there are few restrictions on the structure of actor classes. Like all other C++ classes, they may have public, protected, and private members, may be derived from other types including other actor types, and may be used as class members.

ActorNames   `ActorNames` serve the role of pointers and references for `Actor` instances but are valid in the global namespace of a running program, independent of the number, type, and interconnection of threads executing the application.

ActorMethods, Continuations, and Messages   The member interface for `Actor` classes has been extended to include the concept of *actor methods*, which, when executed via *continuations,* fill the role of parallel function calls. An actor method is a nested class derived from the templated `ActorMethod` library class, which supports the creation of a

---

[2] Such use may limit the architectures on which an application may run; the APA does not try to abstract away the characteristics of the underlying hardware but instead provides a uniform interface across a wide variety of hardware and software implementations.

continuation. When such a continuation is subsequently called, an asynchronous invocation of the C++ member function of the same name is scheduled.

Actor methods are implemented using two abstractions, `Messages` and `Continuations`, both of which are provided by the library. The interaction between the classes comprising these abstractions results in a statically typed interface to application code; the classes encapsulate all the type information necessary to transport the method operand to a distant processor.[3] `Messages` are first-class values that are passed as arguments to actor method calls. `Continuations` play the role of a bound actor method pointer; when called, using function-call syntax, execution of the appropriate member function is scheduled. Actual execution occurs asynchronously with respect to the calling actor but is serialized with respect to the target actor.

Continuation calls differ from C++ member function calls in a few key ways, reflecting their parallel nature:

Continuation execution occurs asynchronously. When an actor method is invoked via a continuation, a request (message) is passed to the runtime system and dispatched to the location of the target actor. This is the sole construct in the runtime library for expressing parallelism and subsumes such task-parallelism operations as `fork` and `join`.

Continuation calls take a single argument. This requirement is an artifact of the library implementation and could be hidden in a compiler implementation via a compile-time transformation. In cases when multiple arguments would be used by a C++ member function, it is sufficient to wrap the argument vector in a minimal C structure.

Continuation calls do not return a value. The lack of a return value is a result of the asynchronous nature of continuation execution. This restriction is unavoidable in a strict actor paradigm but may be loosened by using a compiler that performs continuation lifting to implement what is essentially a remote-procedure call (RPC).

Beyond the characteristics mentioned, continuation execution is virtually synonymous with member function execution. When the result of an `ActorMethod` invocation is scheduled to run on a particular processor, the member function of the same name is invoked by the runtime system with the datum passed to the continuation as the function parameter.

NewActorMethods   `NewActorMethods` implements the Actor `new` primitive; for actor types, they fill the role of a C++ *new-expression* [41]. Creation of actors typically differs from creation of common C++ objects in that actors are often distributed over available processors to maximize resource utilization. Declaration and usage of `NewActorMethods` is similar in most respects to that of `ActorMethods`.

Aggregates   An aggregate is a collection of one or more actors which share a common name. Messages sent to an aggregate name are directed by the runtime system to a member actor or *representative*. Application aggregate types are derived from the library class `Aggregate`. In contrast to actors, which always exist on exactly one processor, aggregates may have representatives distributed across multiple processors. This makes it possible for other actors and ordinary C++ objects to directly execute member functions on aggregate instances

---

[3] The runtime library contains no type switch statements and assigns no type enumerations of its own; all type information is based up on the type information provided by the C++ compiler.

in those cases where a local representative exists; such access is facilitated by the runtime library.

Distributions   Distribution of aggregate representatives is specified via a `Distribution`, an object that specifies the number and location of the representatives of an aggregate. The interface of the abstract `Distribution` class is general enough to represent both enumerated and algorithmically-computed distributions. The library provides distribution classes that facilitate the most commonly used sharing abstractions found in medium-grain applications. Unlike the original definition of aggregates [13], the library provides meta-programming functionality whereby representative selection may be performed in an application-specific manner. On medium-grain architectures, such selection is important to achieve efficient processor utilization.

Implementation and Meta-programmability   The runtime support of the actor interface is meta-circularly implemented via a number of library-supplied aggregates that implement such operations as continuation scheduling and name resolution. Any of the system aggregate types may be used as a base class in an application, and thus the runtime system may be customized in an application-specific manner. Additionally, the system aggregates provide object-level interfaces that allow limited meta-programmability, for example, scheduling and load balancing, without the need to resort to derivation.

10.2.2 Abstract Parallel Architecture

The abstract parallel architecture (APA) comprises a model of a parallel computer and a set of objects that represents a reification of that model. The APA provides abstractions for thread (processor), memory, and communication management and has been architected to provide a standard interface across all platforms with no significant overhead. Moreover, the internal interfaces have been aggressively factored in such a way that code is shared to the maximum extent possible within the zero-overhead requirement. This factoring facilitates portability by minimizing the amount of code that must be changed to support new operating system interfaces. The APA is self-sufficient and has been designed to be usable apart from the actor interface.

The APA thread subsystem manages a set of virtual processing elements represented by instances of the `Thread` class. Thread objects are collected into sets characterized by the means by which they are interconnected. These sets are represented by the library classes `Process`, `ProcessGroup`, and `Cluster`. The relationships between the threads and sets are depicted in Figure 10.2.

Threads   The fundamental unit of computation is the `Thread`, defined as an allocated processing element. A thread may or may not represent individual processors; under operating systems with multiprocessing support, a thread represents an operating-system scheduled entity.[4]

Processes   Threads that share a complete address space are collected into a container called a `Process`. Since all `Threads` in a `Process` share the same address space, all

---

[4] Having more threads than processors provides no performance improvement but is useful when debugging a program on a uniprocessor workstation.

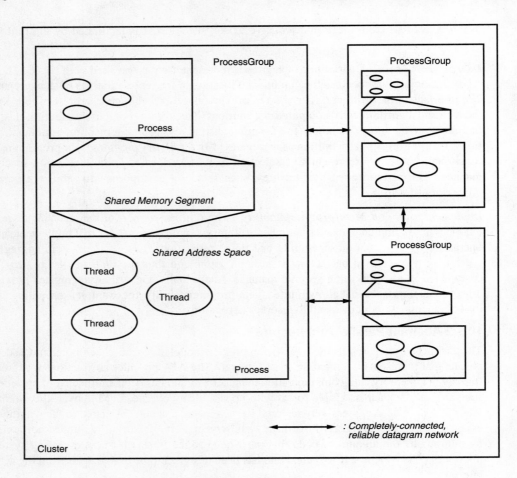

Figure 10.2 APA thread management classes

pointers are valid across `Thread` boundaries within a `Process`. This model is applicable, for example, to Mach threads.

ProcessGroups   `Threads` that share at least a portion of their address space are collected into a container called a `ProcessGroup`. Since all `Threads` in a `ProcessGroup` do not necessarily share identical address spaces, pointers may not be valid across `Process` boundaries; addresses are guaranteed to be valid if and only if they point into a shared-memory segment. This model is applicable, for example, to *Unix* `fork`-based multiprocessing systems.

Clusters   All threads in a program are collected into a `Cluster` object. To the user of the APA, it appears that `ProcessGroups` are interconnected by a completely connected, reliable, unordered, datagram network. All `Threads` in the APA can communicate in some way; either through shared-memory if they are in the same `ProcessGroup`or via a reliable,

TABLE 10.1 APA Triples for Various Machines

Machine	APA Configuration
Figure 10.2 architecture	3/2/3
16 Node Intel iPSC	16/1/1
Four-processor Sun 4/600MP	1/4/1
Two 4-processor Sun 4/600MPs connected by Ethernet)	2/4/1
Intel 64 fat node Paragon	64/1/4

datagram network.

The utility of this architecture can be demonstrated by considering the mapping of contemporary architectures to the model. Table 10.1 shows the number of each type of thread management object for a number of common parallel architectures. The first number in each triple represents the number of ProcessGroups per Cluster, the second the number of Processes per ProcessGroup, and the last the number of Threads per Process; the total number of threads can be calculated by forming the product of the triple elements. Of particular interest are the last two rows in the table, an IP-connected pair of Sun multiprocessors and an Intel Paragon™ with *fat nodes*.[5] In contrast to most previous work, the APA can represent machines which are hybrids of message-passing and shared-memory architectures. The APA is not restricted to architectures that can be expressed by triples of the form above (uniform numbers of Processes per ProcessGroup).

The APA can support shared memory multiprocessors such as the Encore Multimax™, the Sequent Symmetry™, and the SUN SPARCCenter 1000™, distributed memory message-passing multicomputers such as the Intel iPSC/860™ hypercube, the Intel Paragon™, the Thinking Machines Corporation CM5™, and the IBM PowerParallel SP-1™, and also distributed networks of workstations connected via a local area network. Most of the ports have been completed and a few are under way.

10.3 EXAMPLE PORTABLE PARALLEL APPLICATIONS

We now report on some promising initial success with the portable parallel applications for CAD in the ProperCAD project by Banerjee et al. [38, 36, 34]. Successful implementations of several CAD applications have been reported on the ProperCAD environment: *ProperHITEC*, a test generator for sequential and combinational circuits and *ProperPLACE*, placement for combinational circuits.

10.3.1 Automatic Test Pattern Generation

The first application for the ProperCAD environment was automatic test pattern generation for sequential circuits and has been reported by Parkes et al. [33]. The parallel algorithm is based on the algorithm, described in Section 8.6.3 of Chapter 8, that combines fault-parallelism with search parallelism.

---

[5] The Paragon is a mesh-connected multicomputer; when configured with fat nodes each node contains four processors connected by shared-memory.

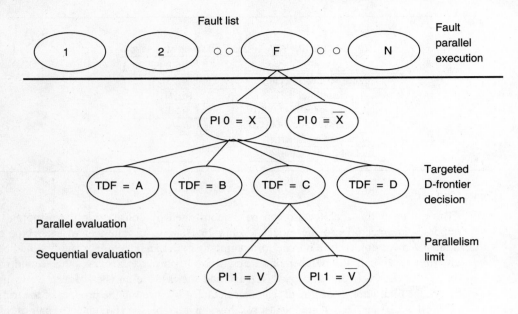

Figure 10.3 Parallelism in `ProperHITEC`

The `HITEC/PROOFS` package for sequential test generation and fault simulation exhibit performance and quality among the best in the field [31], and was therefore chosen as the basis for the development of an efficient and effective parallel test generator. `HITEC` is a descendant of an extension to the PODEM approach. The extensions, roughly in decreasing order of significance, are targeted D-Frontier, enhanced state justification, fault simulation, and variable time frame processing. The approaches used to parallelize `HITEC` are fault parallelism and decision parallelism (see Figure 10.3).

Implementation of fault parallelism is relatively straightforward, since test generation for different faults is by-and-large independent. The use of decision parallelism was deemed necessary to achieve high efficiency on many processors while maintaining quality of results. Quality is higher for decision-parallel execution because the execution trace more closely matches the serial version when decision and fault parallelism are combined. In strictly fault parallel execution, all but one processor are working on a different fault than the serial algorithm; if additional faults are covered by patterns generated by a previous fault, all work done in generating tests for those faults is wasted. Moreover, since test generators generally spend most of their time generating tests for a relatively small number of hard faults, even with fault parallelism, execution time is bounded on the low end by the time required to test the hardest fault. Decision parallelism explores different areas of the search space in parallel and thus, for cases where a large portion of the search space must be explored, can provide significant speedup. Note that by casting the ATPG search in such a general framework, it is easy to enable purely fault parallel, purely assignment parallel, or assignment and D-Frontierparallel execution (`HITEC`), allowing extensive experimentation.

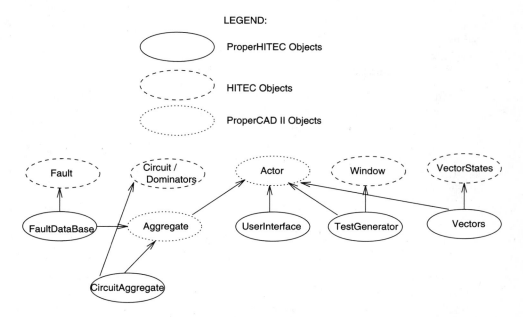

Figure 10.4 `ProperHITEC` organization

`ProperHITEC` uses lexicographically ordered bit-string priorities to guide the execution of `ProperHITEC` as closely as possible to the order used in the sequential algorithm. This technique is essentially the same as described in [37]. We note that in the ProperCAD II library the use of bit-string priorities for the test generator objects has no effect on the priority system used by the other objects in `ProperHITEC` or in the library in general.

Figure 10.4 shows the most significant objects in the `ProperHITEC` implementation along with the `HITEC` and ProperCAD II objects from which they are derived.

TestGenerator   The `TestGenerator` object is an actor that represents a test generator machine. The implementation is relatively straightforward; `TestGenerator` instances can be created for a specified fault to implement fault-parallelism or can be cloned from an existing instance and an alternate assignment to implement decision parallelism. To implement an efficient algorithm, fault parallelism is bounded by a user-specified limit, past which decisions are made in a depth-first manner.

Each `TestGenerator` new actor continuation is assigned a priority that the underlying runtime system uses to execute the `TestGenerator` objects in an order as close as possible to the serial algorithm. When run on a uniprocessor, the `TestGenerator` objects are executed in exactly the same order as the serial algorithm; on one processor, `HITEC` and `ProperHITEC` produce virtually identical results.

CircuitAggregate   The circuit is implemented as an aggregate with one representative on each processor. A limited form of sharing for shared memory machines (supported completely by the library) was considered but discarded, because the `HITEC`/`PROOFS` implication procedures are based on fault injection through circuit modification. Since only one `TestGenerator` object is active at a time on a processor, it is granted write access to the local `CircuitAggregate` representative. When the `TestGenerator` instance completes its work, it restores the circuit to its original state.

FaultDataBase   The fault database is implemented as an aggregate with a representative on each processor. Each representative stores the most recent state of the test generation process for each fault and provides the same interface to the test generator objects as the serial `Fault` object. When an update is received from a `TestGenerator` object or from the vector/states database in the form of a change of status, notification of resource usage, or detection of a new failed state, the `FaultDataBase` representative records the information locally and if, this results in a change of the local state, broadcasts that information to all other representatives. The broadcast operation is implemented completely via ProperCAD II intraaggregate addressing.

Vector   The `Vectors` object is essentially the same as the serial object but uses `ActorMethods` to record new vectors and to send results to the `FaultDataBase`. Currently, the fault simulator is the `FaultSimulator` object used in HITEC using the actor methods provided by the `Vectors` actor. This implies that fault simulation occurs sequentially on a single processor. This was done both for reasons of expediency and because test generators have been observed to spend little time in fault simulation relative to time spent in test generation. Parallel fault simulation in the ProperCAD II library is a topic of future interest.

UserInterface   The `UserInterface` object is used to interact with the user during the running of the test application. It creates the system objects and then creates test generator objects for each undetected fault in the circuit. If the progressive time limit feature of HITEC is used, the process of creating test generator objects is iterated using progressively larger time limits.

Performance   ProperHITEC runs on all platforms supported by the library. Results are presented on the Sun 4/670MP™ shared memory multiprocessor, the Intel iPSC/860 hypercube message passing multicomputer, and the Encore Multimax™ shared memory multiprocessor; the memory on the nodes of the Intel iPSC/2™ hypercube was too small to run all but the smallest circuits.

Tables 10.2, 10.3, and 10.4 show the results of `ProperHITEC` for a number of circuits drawn from the ISCAS-89 benchmark set. All times, T, are reported in seconds and represent the elapsed wall clock time. Fault efficiency, E, is computed as efficiency $= \frac{(\text{no. faults} - \text{no. aborted})}{\text{no. faults}}$. V is the number of test vectors generated. Higher fault efficiencies and lower numbers of generated vectors represent better solutions.

For each circuit, the results of the sequential HITEC algorithm and the `ProperHITEC` algorithms on various machine configurations are reported. The HITEC numbers presented are for the version of HITEC that shares code with `ProperHITEC`. Although the current version of HITEC takes more advantage of dynamic memory allocation, the amount of time spent doing memory management has been carefully analyzed and shown to be less than a fraction of a percent.

TABLE 10.2 Performance of the Portable Parallel Test Generator `ProperHITEC` on the Sun 4/670 MP™ Multiprocessor

Circuit/	HITEC			ProperHITEC					
Seconds				Processors					
Per				1			4		
Fault	T	E	V	T	E	V	T	E	V
s344/20	369.4	95.9	121	374.3	95.9	121	156.2	96.2	112
s820/20	435.9	99.3	956	396.8	99.3	956	140.3	99.1	1013
s953/20	125.8	100	20	134.2	100	20	47.24	100	12
s1238/2	13.13	100	386	21.64	100	386	16.18	100	385
s1494/20	722.0	99.1	1058	663.4	98.9	1058	240.1	99.1	1093

TABLE 10.3 Performance of the Portable Parallel Test Generator `ProperHITEC` on the Intel iPSC/860™ Hypercube

Circuit/	HITEC			ProperHITEC					
Seconds				Processors					
Per				1			8		
Fault	T	E	V	T	E	V	T	E	V
s344/20	481.4	94.2	89	485.8	94.2	89	142.1	96.5	102
s820/20	438.3	99.3	959	440.8	99.3	959	108.0	98.9	1034
s953/20	140.2	100	14	147.7	100	14	28.66	100	14
s1238/1	14.15	100	374	23.29	100	374	11.12	100	402
s1494/20	819.8	99.0	1079	821.3	98.7	1079	192.2	98.8	1151

The results show that `ProperHITEC` achieves consistent speedup with only marginal effect on quality across a range of moderately difficult test problems. The major effect on quality is the addition of a small amount of noise in the results; while `ProperHITEC` does not always achieve results identical to `HITEC`, the number of cases for which it does worse are on a par with the number of cases for which it does better.

The results show that `ProperHITEC` does not achieve particularly good results on the easy benchmarks, those for which 100% efficiency is achived by the serial algorithm in a few tens of seconds on current microprocessors. The reason for this is known; if the very first attempt at generating a test virtually always succeeds, the decision parallelism in `ProperHITEC` is not useful. Techniques are currently being developed for improving the response of `ProperHITEC` for these cases.

TABLE 10.4 Performance of the Portable Parallel Test Generator `ProperHITEC` on the Encore Multimax™ Multiprocessor

Circuit/ Seconds Per Fault	HITEC			ProperHITEC Processors					
				1			8		
	T	E	V	T	E	V	T	E	V
s344/20	484.2	93.9	105	493.2	93.9	105	131.2	94.7	108
s820/20	1200	97.8	891	1206	98.1	891	255.6	96.9	955
s953/100	572.4	100	20	597.1	100	20	166.7	100	10
s1238/10	65.41	100	386	97.49	100	386	55.35	100	406
s1494/10	2615	87.0	492	2920	84.2	402	540.2	85.5	510

10.3.2 Standard Cell Placement

The second application that we have implemented on the ProperCAD environment is standard cell placement using simulated annealing. The algorithm is based on parallel move generation and acceptance as discussed in Chapter 3.

   `ProperPLACE` is based on an existing uniprocessor simulated annealing placement tool, `TimberWolf`.[6] This application is parallelized using the parallel interacting moves strategy described previously.

   To allow for these parallel moves, the circuit must be divided among the available threads. Ownership of specific cells is determined for each layout row by partitioning consecutive standard cell rows as shown in Figure 10.5.

   An `Anneal` actor is then created to process each partition or processor grouping, and concurrency is achieved as each actor independently proposes moves for evaluation. Typically, for maximum performance, one actor is created for each processor available in the target machine.

   Each actor is responsible for moving cells that it owns, by completing the sequential simulated annealing schedule on its own partition. In `ProperPLACE` four different types of moves are possible (see also Figure 10.6):

M1	Intra-actor cell displacement
M2	Intra-actor cell exchange
M3	Inter-actor cell displacement
M4	Inter-actor cell exchange

   An example of each type of move is shown in Figure 10.6. In the figure, assume that the upper row is owned by PE0 and the lower row by PE1. Notice that the three moves (M1, M2, and M3) can be done alone by PE0, the owner of cell A. For move type M4, however, PE0 needs permission from PE1 which owns cell B. This is because it is possible that cell B may have already been moved to another location or is frozen due to some pending move. Consider an example interprocessor exchange move in which the exchange of cell A and

---

   [6] The work described here is based on an earlier version of `ProperPLACE` [27] which was implemented using the Charm language, but has since been modified to take advantage of the ProperCAD II library.

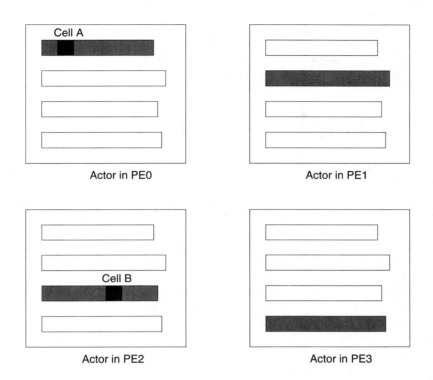

Figure 10.5 Row ownership in `ProperPLACE`. Example shows one row per partition

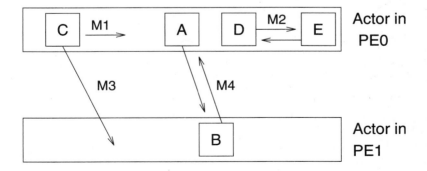

Figure 10.6 Moves in `ProperPLACE`

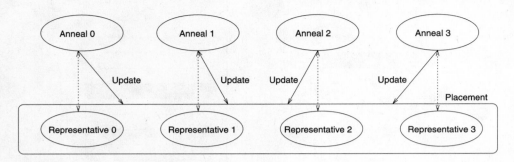

Figure 10.7 `Anneal` and `Placement` relationship in `ProperPLACE`

cell B is proposed by PE0. Because the information about cell B may be out of date in the database of PE0, PE0 locks (or freezes) cell A and cell B locally and sends a request message to PE2, the owner of cell B. Upon receiving the request message, PE2 examines the state of cell B and determines whether to allow the exchange. Upon making a decision, PE2 sends its decision back to PE0 by sending the `return-answer` message. When the `return-answer` message is picked up by PE0 from its message queue, PE0 unlocks cells A and B, and it makes the move if the returned answer is yes. It is important to note that PE0 does not wait until the `return-answer` message is received. Instead, it continues annealing by making other moves with unfrozen cells that it owns. This is another instance of why we call our method asynchronous. Because the interprocessor exchange move (M4) takes the most time due to extra message passing, we introduce a prioritized message scheme to reduce the time taken by M4 in the next section.

If a cell moves to a region owned by another actor (M3 or M4), the ownership of the cell goes to the new actor. To evaluate the cost function accurately, each processor must have complete cell location information in its local database. Therefore, after an actor accepts a move, it has to propagate the accepted move to other actors so that each actor uses more or less the same information about cell locations.

This task of maintaining a coherent state of the current placement is the responsibility of the `Placement` aggregate which has a representative associated with each actor, as illustrated in Figure 10.7.

Cell database management is the responsibility of the `Placement` aggregate. The relationships between the `Anneal` actors and the `Placement` aggregate are shown in the figure. The solid lines show the update messages that an actor will send to the aggregate every time it makes an accepted move. The dashed lines indicate a relationship between an `Anneal` actor and the corresponding `Placement` representative on its thread. It is through this latter association that an actor is able to access the cell location information. This ability to allow an actor access to internal representatives of an aggregate is a powerful feature of the ProperCAD II library.

Performance The ProperCAD II implementation of `ProperPLACE` has been run on all platforms supported by the library. Results are shown in Tables 10.5, 10.6, and 10.7 for a sampling of circuits from a standard benchmark set. All times, reported in seconds, represent

TABLE 10.5 `ProperPLACE` Results on the Sun 4/670MP™ Multiprocessor

Circuit	Original W	TimberWolf		ProperPLACE			
				1 processor		4 processors	
		T	W	T	W	T	W
fract	111779	398.7	20771	433.1	21184	265.1	22245
primary1	1202241	954.9	252777	1048	249982	607.2	276241
struct	2668124	2660	182930	2701	173730	1166	184613
primary2	7292946	3205	1417035	3201	1410450	1945	1678079

TABLE 10.6 `ProperPLACE` Results on the Intel iPSC/860™ Hypercube

Circuit	Original W	TimberWolf		ProperPLACE			
				1 processor		8 processors	
		T	W	T	W	T	W
fract	111779	506	20771	527	21184	179	22712
primary1	1202241	1435	252777	1442	249982	474	297821
struct	2668124	3592	182930	3795	173730	1301	225242
primary2	7292946	4298	1417035	4347	1410450	1352	1727345

the elapsed wall clock time. The wire-length measure, W, is a cost factor generated by `TimberWolf` that estimates the total wire length of the layout.

The results show that `ProperPLACE` achieves reasonable speedup with moderate impact on resultant quality. As circuit size and number of processors grow, the speedups become smaller because the amount of interactor communication grows. Notice, also, on circuits such as `struct`, where the wire length has been reduced by over a factor of 10, the speedups are small. This behavior is caused by the poor initial layout quality, which results in a dramatic increase in the number of accepted moves. This causes an increase in the number of update messages, and thus a drop in speedup. Layout quality declines due to algorithmic issues that do not allow interactor cell exchanges. Algorithm modifications are a subject of future work.

10.4 FUTURE OF PARALLEL CAD

As parallel machines continue to proliferate in the marketplace, we will see more and more multiprocessors appearing on desktop workstations. It is clear that the VLSI CAD community has to pay attention to how to use the computational power of these fast machines to their advantage. So there is a tremendous future for parallel CAD. However, the field has some difficulties ahead.

TABLE 10.7 ProperPLACE Results on the Encore Multimax™ Multiprocessor

Circuit	Original	TimberWolf		ProperPLACE			
				1 processor		8 processors	
		T	W	T	W	T	W
fract	111779	1406	20771	1491	21184	540.7	25523
primary1	1202241	4887	285000	4571	249982	1682	314727
struct	2668124	12098	182930	12477	173730	5252	228227
primary2	7292946	15266	1687487	15427	1410450	5403	1908339

A problem that is commonly faced in the design of efficient parallel algorithms for VLSI CAD placement is that every year better and better sequential heuristics are being discovered for solving various CAD problems, (for example, placement, routing, test generation), that improve on previous methods in terms of quality of layouts produced, in terms of better objective functions, and of runtimes. Unless the parallel algorithms can be designed such that these newer efficient techniques can be rapidly incorporated into the parallel implementations, the latter will become rapidly obsolete practical use.

Another problem with many parallel algorithms is that often they are targeted to execute on a specific parallel architecture for maximum performance, for example a shared memory multiprocessor or a hypercube based distributed memory multiprocessor. As newer parallel machines are introduced with different interconnect topologies and parallel programming models, again there is a danger of the parallel algorithms becoming outdated.

Future work in the area of parallel CAD algorithms therefore needs to address both the previously mentioned problems. One solution to the first problem is to develop a framework for parallel CAD algorithms in which the basic research that needs to be performed is how to partition a given CAD problem into subproblems. For example, individual placement subproblems can be solved by the best possible sequential methods as they become available. The interactions among the subproblems for various sequential heuristics is the important part of the parallel CAD algorithmic research.

A solution to the second problem is to develop parallel algorithms for an abstract parallel programming model that can be ported to a variety of parallel machines rapidly. Various efforts are underway in the parallel programming methodologies community to develop such abstract models. Some of them have been mentioned in this chapter.

Finally, and most importantly, all the parallel CAD algorithms that have been developed so far are mainly academic tools solving simple versions of complex real-world problems, and do not have the industrial strength required of the corresponding conventional tools running on uniprocessor computers. For example, the parallel placement and routing programs only work for regular-sized cells, and can handle two layers of interconnect, whereas in the real world, we have to deal with up to seven layers of interconnect, with complex interactions between the layers.

We believe that for the application of parallel processing to CAD to be successful all these objectives need to be met. It is important for industry to work together with academia to develop such industrial quality tools.

10.5 REFERENCES

[1]   G. A. Agha. *Actors: A Model of Concurrent Computation in Distributed Systems*. MIT press, Cambridge, MA, 1986.

[2]   G. A. Agha. *Foundations of Object-oriented Languages*, chapter The Structure and Semantics of Actor Languages, pages 1–59. Springer-Verlag, New York, NY, 1991.

[3]   W. C. Athas and C. L. Seitz. Multicomputers: Message-passing Concurrent Computers. *IEEE Computer*, 21(8):9–24, Aug. 1988.

[4]   H. Baker and Carl Hewitt. The Incremental Garbage Collection of Objects. *Conf. Record AI and Prog. Languages*, pages 55–59, August 1977.

[5]   B. N. Bershad, E. D. Lazowska, and H. M. Levy. Presto: A System for Object-Oriented Parallel Programming. *Software — Practice and Experience*, 18(8), August 1988.

[6]   A. D. Birrell and B. J. Nelson. Implementing Remote Procedure Calls. *ACM Trans. Computer Systems*, 2(1):39–59, February 1984.

[7]   Boyce, J., Butler, R. *Portable Programs for Parallel Processors*. Holt, Rinehart & Winston, New York, 1987.

[8]   R. Butler and E. Lusk. User's Guide to the p4 Parallel Programming System. Technical Report ANL-92/17, Argonne National Laboratory, Argonne, IL, June 1992.

[9]   R. Chandra, A. Gupta, and J. L. Hennessy. Integrating Concurrency and Data Abstraction in a Parallel Programming Language. Technical Report CSL-TR-92-511, Computer Science Laboratory, Departments of Electrical Engineering and Computer Science, Stanford University, February 1992.

[10]   K. M. Chandy and C. Kesselman. Compositional C++: Compositional Parallel Programming. *Proc. Fifth Workshop on Compilers and Languages for Parallel Computing*, pages 79–93, 1992.

[11]   C. M. Chase, A. L. Cheung, A. P. Reeves, and M. R. Smith. Paragon: A Parallel Programming Environment for Scientific Applications Using Communications Structures. *Proc. Int. Conf. Parallel Processing*, II:211–218, 1991.

[12]   J. S. Chase, F. G. Amador, E. D. Lazowska, H. M. Levy, and R. J. Littlefield. The Amber System: Parallel Programming on a Network of Multiprocessors. Technical Report 89-04-01, Department of Computer Science and Engineering, University of Washington, September 1989.

[13]   A. A. Chien. *Concurrent Aggregates: Supporting Modularity in Massively Parallel Programs*. The MIT Press, Cambridge, MA, 1993.

[14]   A. A. Chien, V. Karamcheti, and J. Plevyak. The Concert System — Compiler and Runtime Support for Efficient, Fine-Grained Concurrent Object-Oriented Programs. Technical Report UIUCDCS-R-93-1815, Department of Computer Science, University of Illinois, June 1993.

[15]   E. Gabber. VMMP: A Practical Tool for the Development for Portable and Efficient Programs for Multiprocessors. *IEEE Transactions on Parallel and Distributed Systems*, pages 304–317, July 1990.

[16]   W. Fenton, B. Ramkumar, V. A. Saletore, A. B. Sinha, and L. V. Kalé. Supporting Machine Independent Programming on Diverse Parallel Architecturs. *Proc. Int. Conf. Parallel Processing*, August 1991.

[17]   J. Ferber and P. Carle. Actors and agents as reflective concurrent objects: A MERING IV perspective. *IEEE Trans. Systems, Man, and Cybernetics*, 21(6):1420–1436, December 1991.

[18]   D. Gannon and J. K. Lee. Object-Oriented Parallelism: pC++ Ideas and Experiments. *Proc. Japan Society for Parallel Processing*, pages 13–23, 1993.

[19]   C. Hewitt. Viewing Control Structures as Patterns of Passing Messages. *Journal of Artificial Intelligence*, 8:323–364, June 1977.

[20]   C. Houck and G. Agha. HAL: A high-level actor language and its distributed implementation. *Proc. Int. Conf. Parallel Processing*, pages 158–165, August 1992.

[21]   I. Foster and S. Taylor. *Strand: New Concepts in Parallel Programming*. Prentice Hall, 1990.

[22]   D. Kafura and K. H. Lee. ACT++: Building a concurrent C++ with actors. *J. Object-Oriented Programming*, pages 25–37, May/June 1990.

[23]   L. V. Kalé. The Chare Kernel parallel progrmaming language and system. *Proc. Int. Conf. Parallel Processing*, II, August 1990.

[24]   L. V. Kalé and S. Krishnan. CHARM++: A Portable Concurrent Object Oriented System Based on C++. Technical Report UIUCDCS-R-93-1796/UILU-ENG-93-1711, Department of Computer Science, University of Illinois, March 1993.

[25]   L. V. Kalé, B. Ramkumar, V. Saletore, and A. Sinha. Prioritization in parallel symbolic computing. *Library Notes of Computer Science*, 1993.

[26]   V. Karamcheti and A. Chien. Concert — Efficient Runtime Support for Concurrent Object-Oriented Programming Languages on Stock Hardware. *Proceedings of Supercomputing '93*, pages 33–36, 1993.

[27]   S. Kim. Improved Algorithms for Cell Placement and their Parallel Implementations. Technical Report CRHC–93–18, UILU–ENG–93–2231, University of Illinois, Urbana, IL, July 1993.

[28]   W. J. Leddy and K. S. Smith. The Design of the Experimental Systems Kernel. *Proc. Fourth Conf. Hypercubes, Concurrent Computers and Applications*, pages 10–17, March 1989.

[29]   H. Lieberman. Concurrent Object-Oriented Programming in Act1. In A. Yonezawa and M. Tokoro, editors, *Object-Oriented Concurrent Programming*, pages 9–36. MIT Press, 1987.

[30]   N. Carriero and D. Gelernter. How to Write Parallel Programs: A Guide to the Perplexed. *ACM Computing Surveys*, pages 323–357, Sept. 1989.

[31]   T. Niermann and J. H. Patel. HITEC: A Test Generation Package for Sequential Circuits. *Proc. European Design Automation Conf.*, pages 214–218, February 1991.

[32]   T. M. Niermann. Techniques for Sequential Circuit Automatic Test Generation. Technical report, Coordinated Science Lab, University of Illinois, Urbana, IL, Mar. 1991.

[33]   S. Parkes, P. Banerjee, and J. Patel. ProperHITEC: A Portable, Parallel, Object-Oriented Approach to Sequential Test Generation. *Proc. 31st Design Automation Conf.*, June 1994.

[34]   S. Parkes, J. Chandy, and P. Banerjee. ProperCAD II: A Run-time Library for Portable, Parallel, Object-Oriented Programming with Applications to VLSI CAD. Technical Report CRHC-93-22/UILU-ENG-93-2250, University of Illinois, Coordinated Science Lab, Urbana, IL, Dec. 1993.

[35]   S. Patil, P. Banerjee, and J. Patel. Parallel Test Generation for Sequential Circuits on General Purpose Multiprocessors. *Proc. 28th Design Automation Conf. (DAC-91)*, June 1991.

[36]   B. Ramkumar and P. Banerjee. ProperCAD: A Portable Object-Oriented Parallel Environment for VLSI CAD. Technical Report CRHC-93-04/UILU-ENG-93-2205, University of Illinois, Coordinated Science Lab, January 1993. A shorter version of this report appears in the Proceedings of the International Conf. on Computer Design, 1992.

[37]   B. Ramkumar and P. Banerjee. A Portable Parallel Algorithm for Test Generation. *Proc. Int. Conf. Computer-aided Design (ICCAD-92)*, Nov. 1992.

[38]   B. Ramkumar and P. Banerjee. ProperCAD: A Portable Object-Oriented Parallel Environment for VLSI CAD. *Proc. Int. Conf. on Computer Design (ICCD-92)*, Oct. 1992.

[39]   C. Sechen and A. Sangiovanni-Vincentelli. The TimberWolf Placement and Routing Package. *J. Solid-State Circuits*, 20(2):510–522, 1985.

[40]   E. Shibayama and A. Yonezawa. Distributed Computing in ABCL/1. In A. Yonezawa and M. Tokoro, editors, *Object-Oriented Concurrent Programming*, pages 129–158. MIT Press, 1987.

[41]   B. Stroustrup. *The C++ Programming Language*. Addison Wesley, Reading, MA, second edition, 1991.

[42]   P. Suaris and G. Kedem. A Quadrisection-Based Combined Place and Route Scheme for Standard Cells. *IEEE Trans. Computer-aided Design Integrated Circuits Systems*, 8(3):234–244, Mar. 1989.

[43]   V. S. Sunderam. PVM: A Framework for Parallel Distributed Computing. *Concurrency: Practice Experience*, 2:315–339, 1990.

[44]   D. Theriault. Issues in the Design and Implementation of Act2. Technical Report 728, MIT Artificial Intelligence Laboratory, June 1983.

Index